T0306149

Defence Procurement and Industry Policy

Arms purchases are among the most expensive, technologically challenging and politically controversial decisions made by modern-day governments. Superpower spending on weapons systems is widely analysed and discussed but defence procurement in smaller industrial countries involves different issues which receive less attention. This volume presents a general framework for understanding smaller country defence procurement supported by country, industry and project studies.

Part I provides a general framework for analysing smaller country defence procurement, focusing on the formation of national defence capabilities. The framework is then used to analyse issues around the development of procurement demand, the characteristics of defence industry supply, contracts and relationships between buyers and sellers, and government policy for defence procurement and industry development. Part II focuses on defence procurement in seven smaller industrial nations with widely varying historical and political settings (Australia, Canada, Israel, Singapore, Spain, Sweden and The Netherlands). Part III consists of two Australian case studies of the procurement issues raised in, respectively, the naval shipbuilding industry and a major, complex defence project.

The book addresses the needs of public and private sector managers, military planners, procurement specialists, industry policy-makers, and defence procurement and industry educators. It presents general principles in an accessible manner and points to real-world experience to illustrate the principles at work. Therefore, it will be of interest to scholars and practitioners in defence economics, strategic procurement, public sector procurement, and defence industry policy.

Stefan Markowski is an Associate Professor in the School of Business at the University of New South Wales at the Australian Defence Force Academy, Canberra, Australia.

Peter Hall is an Emeritus Professor at the University of New South Wales at the Australian Defence Force Academy.

Robert Wylie is a Lecturer in the School of Business at the University of New South Wales at the Australian Defence Force Academy.

Routledge studies in defence and peace economics

Edited by Keith Hartley, *University of York, UK*, and Jürgen Brauer, *Augusta State University, USA*

Volume 1
European Armaments Collaboration
Policy, problems and prospects
R. Matthews

Volume 2
Military Production and Innovation in Spain
J. Molas-Gallart

Volume 3
Defence Science and Technology
Adjusting to change
R. Coopey, M. Uttley and G. Spiniardi

Volume 4
The Economics of Offsets
Defence procurement and countertrade
S. Martin

Volume 5
The Arms Trade, Security and Conflict
Edited by P. Levine and R. Smith

Volume 6
Economic Theories of Peace and War
F. Coulomb

Volume 7
From Defense to Development?
International perspectives on realizing the peace dividend
A. Markusen, S. DiGiovanna and M. Leary

Volume 8
Arms Trade and Economic Development
Theory, policy, and cases in arms trade offsets
Edited by Jürgen Brauer and J. Paul Dunne

Volume 9
Exploding the Myth?
The peace dividend, regions and market adjustment
Derek Braddon

Volume 10
The Economic Analysis of Terrorism
Tilman Brück

Volume 11
Defence Procurement and Industry Policy
A small country perspective
Edited by Stefan Markowski, Peter Hall and Robert Wylie

Other titles in the series include:

The Economics of Regional Security
NATO, the Mediterranean, and Southern Africa
Jürgen Brauer and Keith Hartley

Defence Procurement and Industry Policy

A small country perspective

**Edited by
Stefan Markowski, Peter Hall and
Robert Wylie**

Routledge
Taylor & Francis Group

LONDON AND NEW YORK

First published 2010 by Routledge
4 Park Square, Milton Park, Abingdon, Oxon OX14 4RN

Simultaneously published in the USA and Canada
by Routledge
605 Third Avenue, New York, NY 10017
Firstissuedinpaperback2014

Routledge is an imprint of the Taylor and Francis Group, an informa business

Typeset in Times New Roman by
Taylor & Francis Books

British Library Cataloguing in Publication Data
A catalogue record for this book is available from the British Library

Library of Congress Cataloging in Publication Data
Defence procurement and industry policy / edited by Stefan Markowski,
Peter Hall, and Robert Wylie.
    p. cm.
    Includes bibliographical references and index.
    1. Armed Forces–Procurement. 2. Defense contracts–Government policy.
3. Defense industries–Government policy. 4. Armed Forces–Procurement–
Case studies. 5. Defense contracts–Government policy–Case studies. 6.
Defense industries–Government policy–Case studies. I. Markowski, Stefan.
II. Hall, Peter, 1948– III. Wylie, Robert, 1947– IV. Title: Defense
procurement and industry policy.
    UC260.D44 2009
    355.6'212–dc22

                                                            2008046665

ISBN 978-0-415-36288-7 (hbk)
ISBN 978-1-138-80544-6 (pbk)
ISBN 978-0-203-01369-4 (ebk)

Contents

List of figures   vii
List of tables   viii
List of boxes   ix
Notes on contributors   x
Preface   xiii
Acknowledgements   xiv
List of abbreviations   xv

Introduction   1
STEFAN MARKOWSKI, PETER HALL AND ROBERT WYLIE

PART I
Conceptual foundations   9

1 Procurement and the chain of supply: a general framework   11
   STEFAN MARKOWSKI, PETER HALL AND ROBERT WYLIE

2 Demand: military products, user requirements, and the organisation
   of procurement   45
   STEFAN MARKOWSKI, PETER HALL AND ROBERT WYLIE

3 Supply: defence industry   82
   PETER HALL, STEFAN MARKOWSKI AND ROBERT WYLIE

4 Buyer–seller interaction in defence procurement   115
   STEFAN MARKOWSKI, PETER HALL AND ROBERT WYLIE

5 Government policy: defence procurement and defence industry   153
   PETER HALL, STEFAN MARKOWSKI AND ROBERT WYLIE

PART II
National perspectives 185

6 The Australian defence value-adding chain: evolution and
experimentation 187
ROBERT WYLIE AND STEFAN MARKOWSKI

7 Canadian defence procurement 209
UGURHAN BERKOK

8 Defence structure, procurement and industry: the case of Israel 228
KOBI KAGAN, OREN SETTER, YOAD SHEFI AND ASHER TISHLER

9 Small country 'total defence': a case study of Singapore 255
RON MATTHEWS AND NELLIE ZHANG YAN

10 Importing defence technologies: why have Spanish policies changed? 272
JORDI MOLAS-GALLART

11 From certainty to uncertainty: Sweden's armament policy in
transition 286
BJÖRN HAGELIN

12 National Defence Organisation and defence procurement in The
Netherlands 303
ERIK DIRKSEN

PART III
Industry case studies 321

13 Industry case study: Australian naval shipbuilding 323
STEFAN MARKOWSKI AND ROBERT WYLIE

14 Managing the defence value-adding chain: Australian procurement
of over-the-horizon radar 354
ROBERT WYLIE AND STEFAN MARKOWSKI

15 Conclusion 371
STEFAN MARKOWSKI, PETER HALL AND ROBERT WYLIE

Index of authors 375
Index of subjects 378

Figures

1.1 A stylised defence production/value chain 14
1.2 Decision-makers in national security production and defence
supply chain 25
2.1 Economies of scale in procurement 58
2.2 Quantity discounts in procurement 58
2.3 Economies of scope in procurement 60
2.4 Stylised weapons system lifecycle 64
3.1 Economies of scale 92
3.2 Economies of scope and agglomeration 95
4.1 Total agency cost 123
4.2 Stylised contract types 127
8.1 Structure of the Israeli Defence Force 234
8.2 Israel's defence expenditure as a percentage of GDP, 1950–2003 235
8.3 Israel's defence budget in US$billion 235
8.4 Israel's 2004 defence budget by type of expenditure 236
8.5 US assistance to Israel, 1948–2004 241
8.6 Military procurements of the USA, Western Europe and Israel,
1990–2002 243
8.7 Military exports of the USA, Western Europe and Israel,
1990–2002 243
8.8 Military procurement of the Israeli government and Israeli
defence exports, 1990–2002 244
11.1 The share of Sweden's military exports in total military
production and in war-fighting equipment, 1980–2004 295
13.1 Conventional value chains for support ship and weapons
upgrade: total project cost breakdown by supplier category 342
13.2 Complex supply chain for a naval combatant: total project cost
breakdown by supplier category 343

Tables

4.1	Advantages and disadvantages of competitive and sole source procurement	124
8.1	Military balance in the Middle East, 2003	230
8.2	The IDF's order of battle, 1982–2003	232
8.3	Israel's defence budget, total government budget and GDP in 2004	234
8.4	Sales, workforce numbers and production capabilities of Israel's six largest defence firms in 2001	246
9.1	Chinese diaspora: shares of private assets and population in selected South-East Asian countries	256
9.2	Defence and economic data for selected countries	259
11.1	Swedish defence characteristics	290
11.2	Foreign shareholders in military companies in Sweden	291
11.3	Swedish bi- and multi-lateral military-industrial cooperation agreements, 1995–2004	293
12.1	Sectoral distribution of defence-related firms in 2004	308
12.2	Employment by firm size in 2004	310
12.3	Distribution of defence contractors by their defence-related sales in 2004	310
13.1	Percentage cost breakdown in warship production	340

Boxes

2.1	The Joint Strike Fighter (JSF)	62
3.1	Economies of scale	91
3.2	Economies of scope and agglomeration	93
6.1	The JORN acquisition	205
6.2	The Collins Class acquisition	206
7.1	Trade-offs in procurement and defence industry policy	219
8.1	Innovative capability development programmes	240
8.2	The model	248
12.1	The TNO National Defence Group	309
13.1	*HMAS Success*: a triumph of hope over experience	327

Contributors

Ugurhan Berkok is an Associate Professor, Economics, at the Royal Military College, Kingston, Ontario, and adjunct at Queen's University, Ontario. He took his BA (Econ) at the Bosphorus University, Turkey, and has an MA (Quantitative Economics) from the University of East Anglia, UK, and a PhD in Economics from Queen's University. He has taught at Laval, McGill, Montreal, UQAM, Concordia, and Sussex in the UK and his interests are in public economics, and the economics of health and defence.

Erik Dirksen, MSc, lectures in strategic management at the Amsterdam Business School, University of Amsterdam, The Netherlands.

Björn Hagelin is an Associate Professor in the Department for Peace and Conflict Research, Uppsala University. He has a PhD in peace and conflict research and has led the Arms Transfers project at the Stockholm International Peace Research Institute (SIPRI) since 1998. He was a security analyst at the National Defence Research Institute, Stockholm, 1970–87.

Peter Hall is an Emeritus Professor of the University of New South Wales in the School of Business at the Australian Defence Force Academy, Canberra. From 1997–2006, he was Head of the School of Economics and Management and foundation Head of the School of Business at UNSW@ADFA. Peter has undergraduate and postgraduate degrees from Oxford University, has undertaken wide-ranging research into the economics of innovation, and has published numerous papers, many with Stefan Markowski, on defence industry and procurement, defence industry policy, and small arms production and trade.

Kobi Kagan has a PhD (Economics) from Bar Ilan University, Israel. He specialises in defence economics with a research focus on models of optimal resource allocation in asymmetric arms races. Kobi's main interest is in the security aspects of state-sponsored terror and on the monetary evaluation of international strategic terror weapons limitation agreements.

Stefan Markowski is an Associate Professor in the School of Business UNSW@ADFA, Canberra. He has a PhD from the London School of

Economics. Following an earlier academic career in the United Kingdom, Stefan was an economic and management consultant and professional researcher in Australia and the United Kingdom. He joined UNSW@ADFA from the (Australian) Bureau of Industry Economics where he was Principal Economist. He has published widely in defence, industry and urban economics and, over the past 15 years, has collaborated with Peter Hall on defence industry and trade, defence procurement and small arms proliferation.

Ron Matthews is Deputy Director, Institute of Defence and Strategic Studies (IDSS) at the S. Rajaratnam School of International Studies, Nanyang Technological University, Singapore. He holds the Chair in Defence Economics at IDSS and also at Cranfield University at the UK Defence Academy. Ron has a BSc (Aston), MSc Financial Economics (University College of Wales, Bangor), MBA (Warwick) and a PhD (Glasgow). He has gained research scholarships from Nuffield (Oxford), NATO and the World Bank, and has conducted research and lectured at numerous international defence-related institutions and universities.

Jordi Molas-Gallart has a PhD in Economics and is a Research Professor at the Spanish Council for Scientific Research (CSIC). He works at INGENIO, a joint research centre of CSIC and the Universitat Politècnica de València. Jordi is also Honorary Professor at the Science Policy Research Unit, Sussex. His research focuses on the study of innovation in the defence and aerospace industries and the evaluation of science, technology and innovation policies.

Oren Setter is an Adjunct Lecturer, Faculty of Management, Tel Aviv University. He received his BSc in Physics and Mathematics from the Hebrew University, Jerusalem, and his PhD in Operations Research from Tel-Aviv University. Oren worked for over ten years at the Israeli Ministry of Defence. He has published several scholarly articles and book chapters.

Yoad Shefi received his BA in Accounting and Economics from Bar-Ilan University, an MSc in Decisions and Operations Research from Tel-Aviv University, Israel, and is a PhD candidate in economics at the Graduate School of Business, the University of Chicago. His doctoral dissertation is an analysis of non-monetary returns to human capital and the relationship between education and health. His areas of expertise include industrial organisation and defence economics.

Asher Tishler is a Professor and the Dean of the Faculty of Management, Tel Aviv University, where he is also Director of the BRM Institute of Technology and Society and the Eli Hurvitz Institute of Strategic Management. His main research interests are applied microeconomics, models of research and development, energy economics, and defence-related issues. He has published in leading academic journals, and been consultant to

Israel's Ministry of Defence, the Israel Defence Forces, the Israel Electric Corporation, and Israel's Ministry of National Infrastructures, and firms in Israel and abroad. Asher received his BA in Economics and Statistics from The Hebrew University of Jerusalem, and his PhD in Economics from the University of Pennsylvania.

Robert Wylie teaches public sector management at the School of Business, the University of New South Wales at the Australian Defence Force Academy. Defence issues feature prominently in Robert's teaching, research and publications. He co-edits a scholarly journal and researches technological innovation in small open economies. Before entering academic life in 2004, Robert had a long professional career providing defence policy advice to Australian governments, as a senior Australian public servant and as a consultant.

Nellie Zhang Yan is a PhD candidate with the Defence Management Group at Cranfield University at the UK Defence Academy, where she is researching the development of China's aerospace industry. Nellie holds a BA in International Economics from Jinan University, China and a MBA from Birmingham University, UK.

Preface

The concept of this book has evolved with our interest in defence procurement and industry policy going back to the mid-1990s. What has emerged is a volume that aims to introduce defence practitioners to concepts and tools used by defence economists and expose academic economists to the challenges faced by contemporary defence procurement and industry practitioners. Although the book focuses specifically on defence issues, much of it has a broader applicability and should be of interest to anyone involved in procurement in large organisations, particularly in government departments. While most of the countries in the world can be regarded as small or at most mid-sized in terms of defence procurement, there is a paucity of literature in this area that adopts the small country perspective. Being based in Australia, we have come to believe that decision-makers in small countries face more acute economic choices than those in the larger powers and have less room for mistakes. The issues in such countries deserve, we feel, special treatment.

The book is divided into three parts. Part I provides a general overview of issues involved in defence procurement and industry policy making by smaller military powers. Part II contains a selection of national case studies mostly written by external contributors. Part III comprises two industry studies to highlight particular aspects of the procurement of complex military systems by small countries.

External contributions to this book comprise invited chapters on the experience of small, advanced industrial economies. Nearly all were written especially for this volume. Seven countries were selected for inclusion using a three-step procedure described in the Introduction. We are most grateful to the expert country specialists who accepted our invitation to write relevant chapters. Their contributions were peer-reviewed and revised before final submission to the publisher and highlight particular aspects of defence procurement or industry that their authors regarded as important. They were not structured around an editor's template. This approach, we hope, will give the contributions relevance well into the future while, at the same time, all the latest data can best be obtained from reliable internet sources and annual publications such as the *SIPRI Yearbook*.

Acknowledgements

The book took longer to produce than originally anticipated. We are most grateful to our external contributors and our publishers at Routledge for putting up with this protracted gestation period. We also wish to express our gratitude to Routledge (Taylor & Francis Group) for allowing us to include a refined version of a paper by Ron Matthews and Nellie Zhang, 'Small Country "Total Defence": A Case Study of Singapore', which was previously published in *Defence and Peace Economics*, 7(3) (2007): 376–95, and to use parts of a chapter by Markowski and Hall, 'Mandatory defence offsets – conceptual foundations', which was first published in Jürgen Brauer and J. Paul Dunne (eds) (2004) *Arms Trade and Economic Development, Theory, Policy and Cases in Arms Trade Offsets*, London: Routledge, pp. 44–53. We are grateful to the Editors of *Defence and Peace Economics* and Professors Brauer and Dunne for their kind permission to use the aforementioned work.

Stefan Markowski, Peter Hall and Robert Wylie
School of Business, the University of New South Wales at the
Australian Defence Force Academy, Canberra

Abbreviations

ACOA	Atlantic Canada Opportunities Agency
ADAS	amphibious deployment and sustainment
ADF	Australian Defence Force
ADI	Australian Defence Industries
ADM (Mat)	Assistant Deputy Minister (Materiel) (Canada)
AECMA	European Association of Aerospace Industries
AFP	Australian frigate project
AGP	agreements on government procurement
AII	Australian Industry Involvement
AIP	Australian Industry Participation
AIT	Agreement on Internal Trade
AMC	Australian Marine Complex
AMEC	Australian Marine Engineering Corporation
ANAO	Australian National Audit Office
ANZAC	Australian and New Zealand Army Corps in World War I
ANZUS	the Australia, New Zealand and the United States security alliance
ASC	Australian Submarine Corporation
ASD	AeroSpace and Defence Industries Association of Europe
ASPI	Australian Strategic Policy Institute
ASW	anti-submarine warfare
AWA	Amalgamated Wireless Australasia Ltd
AWACS	airborne warning and control system
AWD	air warfare destroyers
BHP	Broken Hill Propriety Ltd
CBRN	chemical, biological, radiological, and nuclear
CBW	chemical and biological weapon systems
CDC	Computing Devices Canada
CDF	Chief of the Defence Force (Australia)
CDIB	Canadian defence industry base
CEDQR	Canada Economic Development for Quebec Regions
CEO DMO	Chief Executive Officer Defence Materiel Organisation (Australia)

CF	Canadian Forces
CoA	Commonwealth of Australia
CoBPSC	Code of Best Practice in the Supply Chain
CoPS	complex product systems
COTS	commercial-off-the-shelf
CPFs	Canadian patrol frigates
CRS	Congressional Research Service (USA)
CSIC	Spanish Council for Scientific Research
CSP	Commercial Support Program (Australia)
CTC	competitive tendering and contracting
CTOL	conventional-take-off-and-landing
CUF	common user facility
CV	carrier version
DAO	Defence Acquisition Organisation (Australia)
DCP	Defence Capability Plan (Australia)
DDR&D	Directorate of Defence R&D in the MoD (Israel)
DER	Defence Efficiency Review (Australia)
DFAIT	Department of Foreign Affairs and International Trade (Canada)
DFO	Department of Fisheries and Oceans (Canada)
DIB	Defence industry base
DMO	Defence Materiel Organisation (Australia)
DMP	Defence materiel process
DMS	Defence Maritime Services Pty
DND	Department of National Defence (Canada)
DoD	Department of Defence (Australia)
DOD	Department of Defense (USA)
DPA	Defence Procurement Agency
DPDSA	Defence Production and Development Sharing Arrangements (Singapore)
D&S	defence and (national) security
DSO	Defence Science Organisation (Singapore)
DSTA	Defence Science and Technology Agency (Singapore)
DSTO	Defence Science and Technology Organisation (Australia)
EADS	European aerospace conglomerate
EC	Environment Canada
EDA	European Defence Agency
EDIG	European Defence Industry Group
EFA	European fighter aircraft
EREA	European Research Establishments Association
ESF	Economic Support Fund
ESDP	Europe's security and defence policy
EU BAM	EU Border Assistance Mission
EUFOR	European Military Force
EUMM	EU Monitoring Mission

EUPOL	EU Police Mission
EUROPA	European Understandings for Research Organisation, Programmes and Activities
EUSEC	EU Security Sector Reform Mission
FC	Finance Canada
FDA	Force Development and Analysis Division (Australia)
FDI	foreign direct investment
FFA	Aeronautical Research Institute (Sweden)
FFG	guided missile frigate
FMF	US Foreign Military Funded Program
FMS	US Foreign Military Sales program
FMV	Defence Procurement Agency (Sweden)
FOA	National Defence Research Institute (Sweden)
FOI	Defence Research Establishment (Sweden)
FTA	free trade agreement
GD	General Dynamics
GDP	gross domestic product
GMDD	General Motors Diesel Division
GNI	gross national income
GPA	Agreement on Government Procurement
GPFs	general purpose frigates
HRC	Human Resources Canada
HRSDC	Human Resources and Social Development (Canada)
IAI	Israeli Aircraft Industries
IC	Industry Canada
ICPs	industrial cooperation programs
ICT	information communications technology
IDF	Israeli Defence Force
IDSS	Institute of Defence and Strategic Studies
IED	improvised explosive device
IFOR	Peace Implementation Force
IMAT	International Military Advisory Team
IMI	Israeli Military Industries
IMOD	Israeli Ministry of Defence
INAC	Indian and Northern Affairs Canada
IP	intellectual property
IRB	Industrial and Regional Benefits (Canada)
ISAF	International Security Assistance Force
ISO	Industrial Supplies Office (Australia)
ITAR	International Traffic in Arms Regulations
JORN	Jindalee Operational Radar Network
JSF	Joint Strike Fighter
KFOR	Serbia-Kosovo-Albania and Kosovo Force
LAV	light armoured vehicle
LBD	learning-by-doing

LCH	heavy landing craft
LCS	littoral combat ships
LEO	low earth orbiting
LHD	landing helicopter dock
LoI	Letter of Intent
M&A	merger and acquisitions
MCP	major crown project
MDD	McDonnell Douglas
MEA	Ministry of Economic Affairs (The Netherlands)
MHP	maritime helicopter project
MINDEF	Ministry of Defence (Singapore)
MLRS	multiple launch rocket systems
MoD	Ministry of Defence (UK, The Netherlands)
MOTS	military-off-the-shelf
NAFTA	North American Free Trade Agreement
NDC	National Defence College
NDHQ	National Defence Headquarters (Canada)
NDIB	national defence industry base
NDO	National Defence Organisation
NFFP	National Aeronautical Research Programme
NRCan	Natural Resources Canada
NS	national security
NSA	new shipboard aircraft
OCCAR	Organisation Conjoint pour la Coopération en matière d'Armement
OEF	Operation Enduring Freedom
OEM	original equipment manufacturer
OTHR	over-the-horizon radar
PBS	portfolio budget statements
PCO	Privy Council Office (UK)
PFI	private finance initiative
PfP	Partnership for Peace
PLO	Palestinian Liberation Organization
PMC	private military company/contractor
PMO	project management office
PP	production package
PSOs	peace support operations
PWGSC	Public Works and Government Services Canada
RAN	Royal Australian Navy
R&D	research and development
RFI	request for information
RFP	request for proposal
RFT	request for tender
RIR	Riksrevisionen, Sweden's Audit Organisation
RLM	Lockheed Martin–Tenix joint venture

RMA	Revolution in Military Affairs
RSN	Republic of Singapore Navy
R&T	research and technology
SAF	Singapore Armed Forces
SAR	search and rescue
SCP	security cooperation participant
SEMA	Swedish Emergency Management Agency
SFOR	Peace Stabilisation Force
SIPRI	Stockholm International Peace Research Institute
SME	small and medium-sized enterprise
SPAC	Senior Project Advisory Committee (Canada)
SSMs	surface-to-surface missiles
ST	Singapore Technologies
S&T	science and technology
STOVL	short-takeoff/vertical landing
TB	Treasury Board (Canada)
TBS	Treasury Board Secretariat (Canada)
TNO	Dutch National Defence Group
TPC	Technology Partnerships Canada
TTCP	Technical Cooperation Program
TWP	terror weapons
UAV	unmanned airborne/aerial vehicle
UN	United Nations
UNMEE	UN Mission in Ethiopia and Eritrea
UNMIS	United Nations Mission in Sudan
UNPROFOR	United Nations Protection Force Bosnia
UNTAC	United Nations Transitional Authority – Cambodia
UNTSO	United Nations Truce Supervision Organisation
US DIB	US defence industry base
USN	US Navy
VTOL	vertical take-off and landing
WEAG	Western European Armaments Group
WED	Western Economic Diversification (Canada)
WEP	weapons effect and protection
WMDs	weapons of mass destruction
WTO	World Trade Organisation
WTO-AGP	WTO Agreement on Government Procurement

Introduction

Stefan Markowski, Peter Hall and Robert Wylie

This book is about defence procurement and industry policy in small, advanced industrial economies. It is largely an exercise in applied economics but the contributions of legal and management scholars and defence procurement and industry policy practitioners will also be apparent throughout. The book inevitably draws on themes and analysis treated in the defence economics literature and reviewed, for example, in publications such as Hartley and Sandler (1995) and Sandler and Hartley (2007). Our aim, however, is not to focus exclusively on issues in economic theory but rather to introduce a wider range of questions faced by defence procurement practitioners and policy-makers. We also aim to introduce practitioners to concepts and tools used in economics to show how the approach of the discipline might support policy making and the development of practical procurement guidelines.

Defence procurement

Procurement is simply another word for the process by which an economic entity, such as a business enterprise or a government agency, acquires the goods, services or assets which it needs to carry out its economic activities. The procurement process involves several dimensions of choice: the nature of what is to be acquired; the identity of suppliers; the legal mechanism to be used to effect the acquisition; and side-deals and wider economic and social effects that might accompany the purchase (Arrowsmith and Hartley, 2002: ix). Economics recognises the significance of these issues in analysis of product quality and characteristics, inter-firm performance differences, deficiencies and asymmetries in information in relationships between the buyer and the seller, transaction costs, and externalities and spillovers. This book illustrates the importance attributed by economics to how purchases and acquisitions are arranged and take place, even though the word 'procurement' itself rarely appears in the economic literature. For legal scholars and practitioners, the interest of the procurement process lies particularly in contracting relationships between parties and enforcement aspects. In management research, the focus is on the organisation and its relationship to suppliers in the supply chain or network. And for defence policy practitioners, the interest lies in how the procurement of goods and services by the National Defence Organisation (NDO) contributes to the formation and sustaining of national military capabilities and in how it could be conducted in the most efficient and timely manner.

For economic units producing any output at all, inputs must be acquired to enable production to take place; procurement is the process of implementing their demand for factors of production. In the case of *defence procurement*, inputs are acquired to enable the NDO, a publicly owned and government-controlled economic entity, to produce the output *defence*. By 'defence' we mean protecting, if need be by application of lethal force, the nation (its people and physical assets) from military threats posed by other nations, groups or individuals. Increasingly, these threats are posed by 'quasi-military' organisations and groups that aim to perpetuate armed violence and acts of terrorism and which may or may not be controlled by other governments. However, in the sort of mature democracies of primary interest to us in this volume, only governments organise the supply of national security, including 'defence', because in democracies only the state is empowered to use lethal force.

Value chain perspective

We shall focus below on the process of national security provision in its entirety – which occurs through what we refer to as the *defence value-adding* or *supply chain*. We need to consider this value-adding context since the nature of the end product determines the specific production *capabilities* that the NDO must possess and, thus, the inputs required to create them (e.g., military skills, equipment, and technical know-how). If essential inputs are unavailable domestically or if it is strategically or economically efficient to do so, the government may decide to substitute security 'imported' from allies for that produced at home. By determining the required volume and content of national security to be produced in-country, the government determines the volume of resources required by the NDO from domestic suppliers of inputs. Many inputs, however, are imported. Governments must therefore decide which source for the required inputs offers the best value for money, regardless of where suppliers are located, and whether value for money or other factors should determine the location of supply.

In principle, the NDO's demand for goods and services, such as military equipment, consumables, through-life support services and training, is a *derived* or *dependent demand* determined by the nature of military capabilities to be formed and sustained in-country. In practice, though, military products are sometimes sourced from legacy industries that governments wish to protect. To this end, governments may direct the NDO to buy goods and services from suppliers the government wishes to keep in business rather than those who offer the best value for money.

Defence procurement policy

Defence procurement policy is a key aspect of this book. As we argue in Chapter 5 of this volume, such policy has two general objectives: (1) to access and/or form dependable supply chains to form and maintain defence capabilities in the required state of operational readiness; and (2) to buy what is needed cost effectively and in accordance with Defence's quality and schedule requirements. These two objectives are not necessarily compatible and policy trade-offs are inevitable. For example, increased supply dependability may come at a price as more reliable sources of supply may also be more costly.

In functional terms, defence procurement policy should guide the NDO in determining:

- which of the required capability inputs should be made in-country and which is best sourced from either local or overseas suppliers on a best-value-for-money basis (*local content requirements*);
- which of the materiel required to be made in-country would best be made in-house, in government-owned and government-operated factories and shipyards, and which would best be sourced from external suppliers (*make-or-buy considerations*);
- how to go about selecting sources of supply, e.g., whether to rely on market competition or designate preferred suppliers (*source selection requirements*);
- which type of contract to use to engage the chosen supplier (*contracting arrangements*); and
- how to manage the delivery process and associated relationships with suppliers (*supplier relations management*)

We shall discuss challenges facing defence procurement policy-makers in Chapter 5.

Defence industry policy

Defence industry policy is another key aspect of this book. The most general definition of *industry policy* encompasses all the actions taken by governments to influence directly the production decisions of commercial and public production entities operating within national boundaries. The operation of industry policy reflects government perceptions that these entities could serve the national interest better by making different decisions than they would make in the absence of policy. Such policy might set out to influence industry *structure* directly (e.g., by restrictions and controls on mergers and takeovers) or the *conduct* of firms (e.g., by outlawing predatory pricing or encouraging business R&D). Or it might seek to influence conduct by exposing firms to more intense competition (e.g., by reducing levels of tariff protection). Ultimately, the objective of industry policy is to influence the *performance* of production entities by changing the settings within which these producers make their output, pricing, investment, operational and marketing decisions.

In Chapter 5, we argue that defence industry policy may be viewed as a sub-set of defence procurement policy. Defence industry policies become relevant if the government decides to rely to a greater or lesser extent on domestic suppliers to form and sustain the required military capabilities and assuming policy-makers believe domestic supply would be unavailable or impeded in the absence of active intervention. The policy takes the form of local content requirements in that either all or some of the capability inputs must be sourced from domestic suppliers in designated industry sectors. Defence industry policy complements defence procurement in the sense that it is designed to encourage or bring about the investments in domestic industry capabilities necessary if procurement is to be able to draw on local supply. That is, if the government deems it necessary for industry capability to be located in-country, defence industry policy is primarily concerned with establishing and maintaining indigenous supply and support options. We shall return to the concept of defence industry policy in Chapter 5.

Small country perspective

Much of the theoretical and empirical analysis of defence procurement has tended to focus, implicitly or explicitly, on the way the process has evolved and operated in the defence industry of a superpower, the USA, and to a lesser extent, the larger European countries, such as the United Kingdom. Rather less has been said about the experience of NDOs and their entanglements with defence industry policy in 'small' countries. Of particular interest to us in this volume are those '*small', advanced industrial economies* that are significant spenders on defence for their size. To differentiate 'small, advanced, industrial' economies from large and other small but less-advanced countries we use a three-step procedure. First, we use gross national income (GNI), to distinguish between large and small countries. Second, we use GNI per person to distinguish between advanced and less advanced economies. Third, we use a measure of military expenditure to draw up a list of small, advanced countries which spend enough on defence to face interesting make-or-buy choices and trade-offs in their procurement practices.[1] The final list of countries discussed in Part II of this volume includes: Australia, Canada, Israel, Singapore, Spain, Sweden, and The Netherlands. These national studies provide more detailed and country-specific perspective on defence procurement and industry policy challenges faced by small, highly industrialised countries.

From an analytical perspective, 'smallness' implies expected differences in the way defence procurement takes place relative to other countries. Small countries are hypothesised to procure defence-related goods and services (*military materiel*) differently from larger countries and we will be seeking evidence in support of this position. Economic theory might lead us to expect that small buyers have little *market* (bargaining) *power* and, thus, relatively little influence on the price and specifications of volume-produced products. In the case of defence procurement, we would expect small countries to have, individually, less, if any, influence on prices and the specifications of weapons systems and military consumables developed by large arms producers. That is, relative to large countries we would anticipate they are more likely to be *price (and specification) takers* in markets for volume-produced military materiel. We would also expect small countries to be restricted in their access to large weapons systems embodying the latest military technology. This is because they lack the resources or are reluctant to invest in the development of such systems while large countries that have the capacity to develop state of the art technologies will tend not to release them to other countries, even their closest allies.[2] We would also expect small countries to face scale-related production diseconomies because their own armed forces can only buy limited quantities of military equipment and consumables and, in the absence of export opportunities, their home production facilities are either small (below a minimum efficient scale of production) or, if large, underutilised. In either case we expect them to incur cost penalties associated with small-batch production.

Small countries may also find it difficult to attract and/or retain *internationally competitive* producers of defence materiel. As we see later, national security provision tends to be exempt from the competition-related provisions of international free trade agreements (see Chapters 4 and 5) thereby allowing governments extra freedom to pursue local content objectives that impede direct imports of military materiel and favour local production. In this environment, producers in small countries face relatively small domestic markets and barriers to entering foreign markets. As a result, there is a tendency to fragment and duplicate production capabilities (see Chapter 3).

But, even in the absence of such barriers to specialisation and trade, to be able to sell weapons systems and consumables to a third party, the prospective exporter may need to demonstrate the product's attractiveness by selling it to the exporter's home armed forces. It is also normal for buyers of expensive and durable products to seek assurances that supplies will continue and after-sale product support will be forthcoming. Thus, we expect it to be more difficult, although not impossible,[3] for firms in small countries to be internationally competitive. Other things being equal, the combination of larger domestic sales and better export prospects built upon them should make a larger economy more attractive as a location for an internationally mobile defence supplier. By the same token, defence suppliers based in large industrial countries (e.g., US, UK or French firms) find it relatively easy to establish a successful 'footprint' (e.g., subsidiaries, joint ventures) in small countries that procure reasonable quantities of military materiel (see, for example, the two industry case studies in Part III – Chapters 13 and 14).

Smallness also has significant *strategic* implications. Under various international conventions and understandings, such as the United Nations Charter, all national entities recognised as sovereign countries are deemed to be equally sovereign. But the formal acknowledgement of sovereignty is often at variance with the real ability of small nations to enforce their sovereign rights, i.e., to protect their interests, if need be by the use of force. History tends to show that large countries are often more 'sovereign' than the small, whose strategic options include:

- accepting the vulnerability of smallness, spend little or nothing on defence and take all risks that go with that decision; or
- declaring active neutrality, spending as much as is perceived necessary for unilateral self-defence (e.g., Sweden during the Cold War – Chapter 11); or
- seeking large and powerful protectors (e.g., Australia – Chapter 6, Canada – Chapter 7); or
- forming alliances of like-minded nations (e.g., The Netherlands – Chapter 12, Spain – Chapter 10).

(These strategies are not necessarily mutually exclusive.) However, countries such as Israel (Chapter 8) and Singapore (Chapter 9), are highly security-conscious and insist on a high degree of self-reliance to maintain the operational sovereignty of their armed forces and to use their dependence on allied support as a measure of last resort.

The neutrals are entirely self-reliant and must fend for themselves in the event of military threats materialising. Nevertheless, for a small country, neutrality may be an effective strategic posture if military threats are highly unlikely, or country geography provides an element of natural protection. Those entering international alliances can share the burden of defence by becoming direct importers and exporters of national security within the alliance, given the expectation that allies assist each other in military contingencies. (The credibility of such promises needs to be examined, however – see below.) What is important here is that small countries are obliged by their smallness to choose among strategic options and their choice shapes subsequent defence procurement decisions.

We expect small, advanced economies not only to face different choices and constraints in their defence procurement than large countries but also we expect *different* small countries to respond *differently* to challenges posed by the smallness of their demands for military equipment, services and consumables. In this volume we are interested in the different ways in which the defence procurement process is organised: the structure and conduct of defence procurement entities, their procedures for choosing suppliers and the nature of the relationships they form with suppliers. A mark of being small is that, on average, those involved in defence procurement have to be 'smarter' to achieve the same results as their counterparts in larger countries where order size and scale economies are more relevant. But because they are advanced economies, we expect them to be well positioned to generate imaginative policy experiments that enable them to be 'smart'. Thus, we have been particularly interested in exploring differences in the way small countries respond to the challenges of 'smart' defence procurement. Contributors were invited to focus on issues of particular significance to a country under consideration and, as a result, Part II of this volume covers a wide range of issues that complements the general conceptual framework in Part I.

Industry studies

In addition to case studies of defence procurement in a number of small, advanced industrialised countries, we also include in this volume a defence industry case study, naval shipbuilding in Australia (Chapter 13) and a case study of indigenous development of a leading-edge solution to a military capability requirement (Chapter 14 – the procurement of over-the-horizon radar by the Australia NDO). Australia is a particularly interesting case of a country that has been trying to strike a balance between membership of a military alliance and self-reliance – in the sense of having some independent capabilities to defend itself and committing to in-country industry capabilities to sustain these military capabilities in wartime. Thus, policy-makers in Australia have experimented with various instruments of defence procurement and industry policies to develop in-country, defence-related industry capabilities. Governments have also used defence procurement dollars to achieve broader economic and political objectives. In some areas, these attempts to set up viable industrial capabilities have backfired and presented policy-makers with industrial legacy issues that one normally expects to find in 'older' economies forced to adapt to new forms of international division of labour (see the case study of naval shipbuilding in Chapter 13). In other areas, policy-makers have been more successful in 'picking winners' but have been rather inefficient in their choice of policy instruments. Thus, there are both positive and negative lessons from Australian attempts to develop defence-related industry capabilities and implications for small-country defence procurement and industry policies are discussed in Part III.

As we prepared this volume, we tried to focus on issues we believed had enduring significance. We hope that the resulting discussion will thus remain relevant even as statistical details and institutional arrangements change. Current data are readily available from websites and annual publications such as the *Yearbook* published by the Stockholm International Peace Research Institute (SIPRI).

Notes

1 In identifying 'smallness', we began by excluding economies that were unambiguously large. Thus, we excluded countries whose gross national incomes (GNIs, in current prices) were larger than a certain threshold which we set at US$1000 billion in 2003 (World Bank, 2004, Table 1: 256–7). At the first step, we therefore eliminated from further consideration the then seven largest economies: the USA, Japan, Germany, the UK, France, China and Italy. To narrow down the choice of small countries to those which we, also arbitrarily define as 'advanced', we used the

same data source to select all those small countries that had GNI per capita of more than US$15,000 in 2003 (also in current prices). This income threshold was nearly three times larger than the then world average 'upper middle income' level of US$5,340 per head (ibid.). This second step elimination reduced the pool of 'advanced' small countries to 17. These countries were considered to be advanced in that they had small but relatively sophisticated economies capable of considerable import substitution. Finally, as we were interested in countries that were involved in defence procurement of some significance, we had to eliminate small-scale defence spenders such as Ireland or Austria. At the third step, we set the minimum 2004 defence expenditure level of US$5 billion in current prices (IISS, 2006, Table 44: 398–401) for our final list of small, advanced defence spenders. Since the largest defence spenders are also the largest economies that were excluded at step one and a number of other countries were excluded at step two as falling below the GDP per person threshold, we are left with a shortlist of Australia, Canada, Israel, Singapore, Spain, Sweden and The Netherlands, which are used in this volume to provide country-specific perspectives on defence procurement. In 2004, 26 countries spent more than US$5 billion on defence (ibid.). The USA was in a league of its own with an expenditure of US$455.6 billion. The 'second division' of military spenders comprised nine countries including China (the largest spender: US$84.3 billion) and India (the smallest: US$19.8 billion). The 'third division' comprised 16 countries and was led by South Korea (US$16.4 billion). The smallest spender in this group was Singapore (US$5.1 billion). All seven countries in our sample belong to the third division and a highly representative of the entire group. Australia (US$14.3 billion), Spain (US$12.6 billion) and Canada (US$11.5 billion) represented the top end of the 'third division', Israel (US$9.7 billion) and The Netherlands (US$9.6 billion) the middle, and Sweden (US$5.4 billion) and Singapore the bottom end of the 'division'.

2 For example, the USA, the leading developer and user of advanced military systems, prohibits exports of its most advanced technologies (e.g., at the time of writing, the F22 aircraft) even to its closest allies. (For further details, see Chapter 4.)

3 In our sample of small, advanced economies, Israel (Chapter 8) provides an example of a relatively export-oriented defence industry.

References

Arrowsmith, S. and Hartley, K. (eds) (2002) *Public Procurement*, Vol. 1, The International Library of Critical Writings in Economics, Cheltenham: Elgar.

Hartley, K. and Sandler, T. (eds) (1995) *Handbook of Defense Economics*, Vol. 1, Amsterdam: North-Holland.

IISS (2006) *The Military Balance 2006*, The International Institute for Strategic Studies, London: Routledge for IISS.

Sandler, T. and Hartley, K. (eds) (2007) *Handbook of Defense Economics: Defense in a Globalised World*, Vol. 2, Amsterdam: North-Holland.

World Bank (2004) *World Development Report 2005: A Better Investment Climate for Everyone*, Washington, DC, a co-publication of the World Bank and Oxford University Press, New York: Oxford University Press.

Part I
Conceptual foundations

1 Procurement and the chain of supply

A general framework

*Stefan Markowski, Peter Hall and
Robert Wylie*

As noted in the Introduction, procurement is another word for describing the activity of purchasing or acquisition, and defence procurement refers to these activities in relation to providing a country's national security. Defence procurement and the defence industry policy associated with it thus operate in the broad context of defence production and this chapter offers a framework for considering the relationships involved. In the next section, 'Defence products and capabilities', we present a bedrock model of the production of national security (defence) that focuses on the process that progressively converts intermediate inputs into final products. This section is primarily concerned with *what* is produced as a basis for understanding what is procured and with what implications for industry suppliers. The production of national security occurs within what we call the *defence production chain* which describes the physical process of national security production. To stylise the production process, we assume 'Defence' (the National Defence Organisation, NDO) to be the 'producer' of national security. In most countries, the NDO combines military and civilian elements as administrative and logistic capability involves the employment of civilian public servants as opposed to the military (in-uniform) public servants who are either drafted as conscripts or employed under military-specific contractual arrangements.

The NDO is a component of Government; the latter is ultimately responsible for the provision of national security and the allocation of resources to the NDO to carry out its tasks. However, the NDO may not produce all national security, some of which may be 'imported' from allies (see below) or produced by other government agencies (e.g., homeland security) and, increasingly, by private security firms.[1] The distinctions between the publicly and privately produced activities and combat-related and other support operations have, however, become increasingly blurred. Such complications are initially ignored in our stylised representation, or model, of the defence production chain but will be considered later in the book.

In the stylised model, the capital inputs and consumables needed to produce national security are sourced from Industry, which in some cases may be located partly or wholly within the organisational boundaries of Defence itself (see below). Similarly, some (or all) capital inputs and consumables may be imported from other nations. Human resources are obtained from domestic Households (either by conscription or through labour markets). They can also be imported in the sense that members of the defence force may be hired through international labour markets (e.g., the French Foreign Legion). This admittedly stylised setting is useful for considering a number of concepts fundamental for the discussion of defence procurement.

To respond to military contingencies, Defence must develop and draw on its *military capabilities*, that is, acquire the assets and know-how needed to undertake the activities required by Government under various military and civilian contingencies. Military capability calls for human and non-human (materiel) inputs, technical war-fighting knowledge and organisational structures. Defence procurement is about acquiring the non-human, physical elements of capability, the inputs needed to form new or to modify/sustain existing elements of military capability. These products may include simple civilian consumables and durable goods (e.g., photocopying paper and office furniture) and complex civilian capital goods (such as airliners and super-fast computers); simple military equipment (such as handguns) and complex military systems (e.g., fighter planes and command and control networks); and civil and military equipment services (for example, services provided by leased military aircraft or equipment maintenance provided by contractors).

The following section, 'Value creation', introduces the notion of value into the analysis and discusses how the defence production chain may also be interpreted as a chain of value creation and value adding.

Next, in 'Actors and decision-makers', we revisit the defence value-adding chain to examine the organisational decision-takers driving the production process. Given our focus on defence procurement and industry, we are mostly interested in the upstream suppliers of military materiel and those elements of Defence involved in forming military capabilities. In this context, the defence value-adding chain can be represented as the *defence supply chain* – the emphasis shifts from *what* is produced to *who* is doing it.

The NDO may take different organisational forms depending, for example, on whether its combat arm is structured as a single organisational entity or fragmented into Services and on how military and civil elements work together. The relationship with Government is particularly important as the NDO is a government agency dedicated to the production of national security. In this book, we are primarily concerned with the procurement-related tasks of the organisation. There may be a single, specialised unit within Defence responsible for all defence procurement – the Defence Procurement Agency (DPA). Or, procurement activities may be dispersed between operational elements such as the Services, or centralised within a specialised but organisationally detached agency. In the latter case, the detached agency may be Defence-specific (as in Australia) or it may act as a procurement agent for a number of government departments, including Defence as, for example, in Canada.

The procurement agency places orders with industry suppliers at home and abroad. The success (or otherwise) of the DPA in meeting the requirements of the Services depends on the efficiency and effectiveness of Industry and the relationships between industry suppliers and procurement personnel. Capital equipment and consumables may be produced in-house (e.g., in shipyards and arsenals owned and operated by Defence) or sourced from outside Defence. Thus, Industry, an upstream producer of intermediate inputs into the formation of military capabilities, may take many organisational forms: from complete integration of upstream industrial support into the NDO's organisational structure, to defence-focused private contractors (domestic and foreign), to private and public firms for whom Defence is one of many customers.

In the final section, 'Supply chain links and relationships', we focus on how entities involved in the production of defence are *linked* and *interact* with each other. We note first that when the interface between the DPA and Industry is market-mediated, the relationship between buyer and supplier is influenced by *industry structure*. A supplier of a product for which no close substitutes are available, and facing no threat from potential industry rivals, is potentially in a strong position to use its market (monopoly) power to demand higher prices, determine quality standards, or allow delivery schedules to slip. However, when the DPA deals with many sellers of close substitutes, it may rely on competition between sellers to ensure that prices charged are reasonable and product quality and the timeliness of deliveries are not compromised. Also, when the DPA is a very large or the only (monopsony) buyer of a product, it is potentially in a strong position to impose its terms on the supplier(s).

In this section we also outline the nature of *transactions* associated with the acquisition of goods and services by the NDO from Industry, that is, *how* procurements are arranged and executed:

- the nature of the *business deal* involved in the transaction, its scope, scale and timeframe, the nature of exchange involved (e.g., goods-for-money or barter), and the associated consideration (price);
- the *contract* determining rights and obligations of the parties in the context of the transaction;
- the *relationship* between the parties following the signing of the contract.

These issues are examined in greater depth in later chapters.

The present chapter is only intended to provide a framework for the subsequent discussion of defence procurement and the relationship between Defence and Industry, and many specific aspects of the defence production chain will be examined in greater detail in other parts of this volume.

Defence products and capabilities

Figure 1.1 is a stylised representation of the *defence production chain*. In Figure 1.1, domestic production runs from left to right, from upstream industry capabilities and the production of outputs that serve as intermediate inputs into downstream military capabilities and the production of the final output, national security. Arrows indicate flows of goods and services. Production capabilities, inputs and outputs are represented as boxes. The logic implicit here is that the requirement for the end product (i.e., military responses to threats to national security) determines inputs required by downstream defence activities and, thus, the outputs, activities and capabilities of upstream producers. If the final product was well defined and had a clear and observable market value, it would be relatively straightforward, in principle, to work out the derived demand for defence intermediate inputs and their associated industry capabilities. But the contingent nature of national security and its 'public good' characteristics complicate matters considerably.

National security as a contingent good

The end product, national security, may be viewed as a set or vector of final outputs (military responses) produced to counter threats to or violations of national sovereignty. Broadly, this set of final outputs comprises two sub-sets, one related to deterrence and the other to wartime deployment of military capabilities. Deterrence-related outputs comprise the (usually unobservable) instances of prevention of hostile acts against the country and its interests, which would have occurred if relevant military capabilities had not been in place. Deployment-related outputs comprise the actions Defence *takes* to counter threats to, or violations of national sovereignty, and provide other forms of service at the direction of Government (e.g., peacekeeping). The specific services comprising the deployment-related end products are

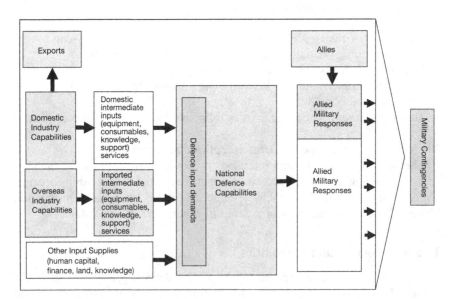

Figure 1.1 A stylised defence production/value chain

contingent on the state of the world – *military contingencies.* These end products are only produced if particular military contingencies actually materialise.

Ex ante, it is impossible to specify every relevant military contingency or, as we shall also call it, *scenario*. The latter may include global nuclear war, 'conventional' local wars, terrorist activities, and minor military emergencies during peacetime (e.g., intrusions into national waters or airspace, military espionage). In practice, only a limited number of scenarios can be envisaged in detail and some are better understood and thus easier to describe than others. Similarly, perceptions of the likelihood of different military contingencies can usually only be described in terms such as 'very likely', 'rather unlikely', or 'credible' rather than in precise, probabilistic terms. The development of 'credible' military scenarios is an art rather than a science, highly subjective and usually involves small groups of experts with access to classified data. Judgements about the likelihood of alternative states of the world also tend to be rather short-lived, and new scenarios and strategic outlooks are often required to reflect the impact of recent events.[2]

However, to determine what military capabilities are required, strategic planners seeking to act rationally have little choice but to develop a set of military scenarios to shape and frame their recommendations to Government. For each identified contingency they must also consider a range of *military response options*. For example, to deal with a scenario of peace enforcement in a neighbouring state, a broad response may involve the dispatch of a small expeditionary force. However, there are specific options within this broad response that may differ considerably in their particulars. For example, a peacekeeping operation may either be highly labour-intensive, with a relatively large number of peace-keepers on the ground to win the hearts and minds of the locals, or highly capital-intensive (aircraft, armour, etc.) to show the force needed to intimidate troublemakers.

To make decisions about acquiring various elements of military capability, such as weapons systems and consumables, personnel and operating skills, Defence and its political masters must determine which military contingencies are most likely to occur; what they involve; what needs to be done to handle them; and, given the budget constraint set by Government, what investments in new capabilities have to be made to produce the required military responses. Thus, most end products of Defence are *contingent outputs* in the sense that they are only produced if certain military contingencies occur. To the extent that the production of defence end products is conditional on the occurrence of certain military contingencies, their value can be judged and assessed only *ex post*, once the outputs are actually produced.[3] In the case of deterrence, success results in an absence of conflict and although peace may be taken as an outcome of deterrence-related national security production, it is not possible to determine the extent to which the absence of hostilities results from defence spending on particular capabilities or other factors. In peacetime, the capabilities of the NDO are not fully deployed or operational. At such times, the NDO concentrates on producing *intermediate services* such as training personnel, maintaining equipment, developing military response options, and so on.

National security as a public good

Many final outputs produced by Defence (e.g., deterrence, combat activities) are what economists call *public goods*. Such goods are characterised by *non-excludability* (of non-payers from consumption/use) and *non-rivalry* (among users – so that one user's consumption does not reduce the availability of the good for other users). These conditions discourage the commercial, private market provision of such goods, so that government may have to arrange to supply them if they are to be provided at all (Spulber, 2002).

Publicness poses the challenge of finding a workable and reliable way of placing a value – a social value – on such goods. There are no market-generated price signals to indicate preferences for one type of public good rather than another or one type of defence output rather than another. Such choices are usually made by Government as part of a broad 'package' of goods and services (some highly 'public' in content and some not) that it promises to deliver or have delivered. When political parties contesting an election promise alternative packages of public goods, the electorate influences the mix of what is to be provided, including defence. However, the electorate is not normally involved in deciding the specific composition of defence expenditure, which it leaves to 'experts' in Defence and other government agencies to determine.

Despite that, governments sometimes *frame* their relationship with Defence as a transaction-like exchange between a buyer and a seller. In Australia, for example, the government has described itself as buying 'outputs' from the Australian Defence Force (ADF) to achieve desired 'outcomes'.[4] The purpose of applying this quasi-transactional framework is to provide a basis for setting targets and measuring the performance of the ADF to make it more efficient and accountable to the government (ASPI, 2006b).[5] But this quasi-market exchange should not obscure the fundamental nature of national security as a public good and the attendant valuation problems.[6]

Contingent outputs and military capabilities

There is also an intermediate step between a NDO acquiring resources such as personnel, physical weapons and defence-related knowledge, on the one hand, and producing national security outputs, on the other. For the NDO to respond to military contingencies, it must acquire the *capability* or *capabilities* to produce military end products. The notion of capability generally refers to an organisation's ability to undertake an activity it wishes or may be called upon to perform.[7] Thus, to respond to military contingencies, Defence must generate appropriate *military capabilities* – it must be able to acquire and combine factors of production to form production units capable of delivering specific military effects or responses that may be required under various threat scenarios. Each of these capabilities can be viewed as a component of the nation's overall military capability and may take the form of production (operational) units (e.g., a tank regiment or an intelligence network). National military capabilities are shown in Figure 1.1 as (domestic) capabilities that could be deployed to produce the effects needed to address particular military contingencies. At the aggregate level, the key or 'core' capability to produce national security is the potential to deter hostile acts and/or engage effectively in military operations. In this volume, we are primarily concerned with capability *increments* in the sense that we focus on goods and services acquired to extend or enhance existing capability or procured to maintain elements of capability.

To know what specific military capabilities are required calls for knowledge of a wide range of different threat scenarios and how they might be dealt with. Since few, and possibly none of these threat scenarios will ever actually materialise, what the Government most of the time provides through its investment in military assets constitutes a *contingent* capability – a capability that has the potential to be used if certain contingencies occur but which will otherwise only ever be visible under the inevitably artificial circumstances of exercises or simulations.[8] To have this potential, Defence must acquire inputs, assets or resources such as weapons systems, facilities and other supportive physical assets, consumables and skills (for example, in Australia these inputs are referred to as 'fundamental inputs to capability' while in the United Kingdom they are described as 'defence lines of development'). It might also have to arrange for the production of new military knowledge (e.g., military intelligence, doctrine, operating instructions) The Defence resources of physical, human and knowledge inputs must be organised into operating systems capable of responding to challenges posed by different military contingencies. These operating systems may span the entire NDO (as with secure communications) but often appear in the form of organisational elements of capability such as combat units.[9] Defence may also have to ensure that certain upstream civil capabilities are available in-country (e.g., industry capabilities; see below).

For a capability to have the potential to be used if certain contingencies occur, it is likely to be hypothecated, that is, designated to be deployed under particular military response options. For example, a 'killer submarine' is needed to hunt other submarines. However, once these capabilities are formed, they may also be deployed 'flexibly' in circumstances that have not been anticipated. There is always an element of surprise, innovation and learning-by-doing when military capabilities are deployed. That is, new capacities, or capability boundaries, are discovered as capabilities are tested and their limits explored. The same discovery process may also reveal unanticipated limitations of various capability elements. In the above example, the capacity to track and kill other submarines may turn out to be limited or obsolete but the submarine may be usefully adapted to transport and land special force units and/or perform a wide range of intelligence-gathering tasks.

This process of discovery is common to production of many civilian and military goods and services. What distinguishes military from civilian activities, however, is the contingent nature of military deployments and the way the operational experience is acquired. Most civil, and in particular commercial, producers of goods and services tend to produce their end products on a day-to-day basis. There is opportunity to validate and fine-tune product specifications and refine production processes to accommodate changes demanded by customers. In contrast, there are limited opportunities to obtain real combat and operational experience in peacetime. Simulations and exercises may enhance learning about how military assets perform in controlled experiments but they lack the true dynamics of the real battlefield with their informational asymmetries and rapid product and process innovation by the combatants. Thus, like defence outputs, contingent military capabilities cannot be directly observed or measured in peacetime. It is only when particular contingencies materialise that their true performance characteristics and boundaries are discovered.

Products procured

Once desired capability is determined, NDOs must acquire the inputs with which to build their capability elements. Such inputs may be human (the business of recruiting), or non-human (the business of procurement). Knowledge inputs may be acquired through training and education (for which procurement agencies may acquire physical infrastructure), or through dedicated R&D (the business of procurement, if contracted out), or through intellectual property (IP) agreements with suppliers forming part of larger procurement contracts.

The non-human inputs can, in principle, be classified in terms of their technical complexity, the volumes in which they are procured, durability, and their value per unit. *Technical complexity* in our usage here refers to the number of separate components that are combined in generating a working system. *Complexity in acquisition*, however, may also reflect policy requirements to combine purchases of a physical system (be it simple or complex) with additional demands for related or unrelated products or activities – such as technological know-how or local production. *Volume* refers to the number of units of a product purchased with the scale of a transaction relating either to the volume or, in some cases, the value of the purchase. *Durability* concerns the life-span of a military system. Given the pace of innovation in much military technology, technological obsolescence can often precede the physical ageing of the equipment. Platforms such as ships or aircraft will often have long life-cycles punctuated by periodic modifications and upgrades while knowledge-intensive systems (like most software) will reach the end of their lives relatively quickly.

Consumables, like photocopying paper and catering supplies, are typically at the 'simple' end of the scale of technical complexity, perishable or readily disposed of, procured in consignments of many units and at unit prices that are relatively low across the spectrum of goods. Such products are not of great interest to us in this book. They are usually bought through straightforward, arm's length, off-the-shelf transactions in markets where suppliers are numerous and where the main issues surround timely delivery of products of known quality at a settled price.

Our focus, rather, is on technically complex products, or products procured in the context of complex acquisitions; products with long lives, sometimes comprising systems that are, per unit, among the most expensive traded in modern economies. Batch sizes in production may be as small as one; in many cases (especially in small countries) orders call for the supply of a dozen units or less; but in some cases involve purchases made by the fleet (e.g., of vehicles), or large consignments (e.g., of small arms). A further dimension relates to the regularity and potential repeatability of such purchases.

Knowledge inputs may be relatively simple if they require nothing beyond the recovery of existing information from public sources; they become complex once research, by definition with uncertain outcomes, is required. Knowledge once acquired through research or learning by doing can be stored, retrieved and transmitted relatively easily. However, knowledge transfers may be deliberately impeded and elements of knowledge may rapidly become obsolete when new knowledge is produced. Also, if its tacit components are known only by certain people, this tacit knowledge may disappear with the individuals involved. Thus, the price for acquiring new knowledge may be anything from trivial to stupendous; the quantity acquired to some extent non-measurable. How knowledge inputs are handled in procurement has an important bearing on organisational design, how contracts are written with suppliers, relations with foreign military organisations and governments, and the structure of incentives.

Industry production capabilities

To supply Defence with equipment and consumables and provide logistic support services, upstream Industry, whether located in-country or overseas, must have the appropriate production capabilities. These production capabilities upstream in the defence production chain are shown in Figure 1.1 as 'Domestic Industry Capabilities' and 'Overseas Industry Capabilities'. The military equipment used by Defence is analogous to the intermediate inputs into civil industry production and military consumables equivalent to civil industry materials inputs. In Figure 1.1, the defence intermediate inputs are shown to include goods such as equipment and consumables, and services such as research and development and through-life logistic support.

Most economies, and particularly smaller economies, can only produce domestically a few of the weapons systems and military consumables their defence forces require. The propensity to import intermediate products is partly explained by comparative advantage in international trade. However, since some industry production capabilities may be regarded as strictly complementary to domestic military capabilities, Defence or Government may require their location in country for strictly national security reasons. Government may also insist on additional local capability content for broad economic or political reasons. Thus, international specialisation is likely to be limited, with governments insisting on what economists describe as trade diversion to form and sustain local, defence-oriented industry capabilities. As many governments apply local content (trade diversion) policies, export opportunities for the producers of defence materiel in all countries – and especially small ones – are also likely to be impeded.

Derived demands and direction of causality

In describing the production chain in this section, our working assumption is that causality runs from the final demand for national security to demands for the intermediate products needed to form military capabilities. In that sense input demands are *derived* or *dependent demands*. This applies to all elements of the production chain. Demands for components and 'original equipment' (sub-systems) produced by upstream elements of Industry depend on the production activities of mid-stream system integrators and other assemblers of (intermediate) products required by Defence. The fundamental logic behind this production chain is that the end product, including deterrence, should drive the requirements for inputs into final activities and, thus, determine the outputs, activities and capabilities of upstream Industry. Benefit to the nation is only created downstream when the NDO's capabilities have been formed and sustained. In this context, a further distinction can be made between the *ex ante* valuation of defence capabilities, based on their expected performance under various military response scenarios, and the *ex post* valuation of these capabilities when they are actually deployed 'in anger'. The *ex post* and *ex ante* valuations are likely to diverge as unexpected surprises always arise when military capabilities are deployed in combat conditions, however intensive prior preparations may have been. (See discussion below in section 'Value creation'.) Costs to the national defence budget are incurred, however, before it is possible to fully judge operational performance.

Defence imports and exports

As Figure 1.1 shows, Defence produces some but not all national security: some of it is imported directly through international alliances such as the North Atlantic Treaty Organisation or the 1952 ANZUS Alliance between Australia, New Zealand and the USA. Similarly, some of the services produced by Defence may be exported in the form of a country's contribution to alliance-based military operations (e.g., allied contributions to the US-led coalition forces in the two Gulf Wars) or to other international military operations (e.g., Australia's contribution to the UN-led peace-keeping and-enforcement operations in East Timor in 1999–2000). In some cases, there are 'export markets' for defence services, for example, for contributing to peace-keeping operations or for commercial mercenary services. But most military alliances involve non-market exchange arrangements, where promises of mutual assistance are bartered between alliance members on the basis of 'equitable sacrifice'.

A key aspect of national sovereignty relates to the extent to which national security is produced in country rather than imported from allies. Alliance members determine how much in-country capability they require and decide the extent to which their requirements must reflect the demands of interoperability between allied forces. The ratio of imported security relative to domestic security production derives from high-level strategic decisions. That is, which military response options are available to governments depends critically on prior choices concerning the balance between domestic defence capabilities and outputs supplied by allies. In practice, how much national security is actually imported varies widely – for reasons that are political and technological as well as economic. The more a government decides to depend on imports from allies, the smaller will be its NDO and, thus, the smaller the requirement for upstream inputs necessary to form domestic defence capabilities.[10]

Most nations import at least some national security and 'self-reliance' is a phrase often used to describe a degree of self-sufficiency in national security provision. In Australia, for example, 'self-reliance' is about 'the defence of Australia without relying on the combat forces of other countries' (DoD, 2000). In practice, however, desired and actual levels of self-reliance may diverge widely. For example, when key enabling aspects of military capability (e.g., military intelligence, communications, and consumables) are not produced or available domestically and, like it or not, must be imported from allies, the real degree of self-reliance may be quite low even though a large proportion of inputs required for capability formation and to sustain it is locally sourced. That is, the criticality of various inputs to capability formation determines the real, as opposed to the apparent, degree of military self-sufficiency (for a more detailed discussion, see Chapter 8, which focuses on Israel, and Chapter 14, which is a case study of Australia's acquisition of the over-the-horizon radar network, JORN). Insofar as the formation of upstream defence capabilities is deemed necessary for national security provision, 'self-reliance' may also involve a degree of domestic self-sufficiency in the supply of capital goods and consumables for the armed forces.

Value creation

In a market economy, value is created when something is produced for which someone is prepared to pay. The 'someone' may be a group of people, or an entire community in the case of public goods.[11] As noted earlier, costs are incurred when resources are taken up to produce intermediate and final goods and services, regardless of whether the final product is sold or paid for at the end of the day. To avoid waste, it is important to demonstrate that the social benefit (value) attributed to an increment in in-country defence capability – say, an additional armoured battalion or a defence-specific industry capability – is equal to or greater than the cost to society of all the resources used to form and sustain that capability element. Thus, as national defence capability is formed, each new increment of it should be assessed to determine whether it delivers net social benefit (the difference between the total benefit and total cost to society) to the 'taxpayer' or 'society at large'.[12]

The term 'social' indicates that *all relevant costs and benefits* borne/derived by the taxpayer have been included in the assessment as opposed to only those costs and benefits which were incurred/derived directly by the owner/operator of a particular capability element.[13] For example, the total cost of acquiring, operating and decommissioning a firing range should include costs borne by adjacent land users in relation to noise or access restrictions and the cost of site clearance when the land is returned to civilian use. All such costs may be additional to what it cost Defence to acquire the site, build and maintain the necessary facilities, and operate and decommission the range.

The stylised defence production chain illustrated in Figure 1.1 can also be represented as the *defence value* or *value-adding chain*. In this representation, value is created downstream when military capabilities are formed. In line with earlier discussion, the formation of downstream military capabilities may be viewed as *driving* the defence value-adding chain and ultimately provides a justification for one resource allocation rather than another higher up the chain. This logic applies to the valuation of a military capability, say, a parachute battalion, and an industry capability for, say, making and maintaining the battalion's parachutes. By assigning value to the downstream military capabilities, the government imputes value to upstream intermediate products. If a particular downstream capability is deemed to be more valuable, Defence may be willing to pay higher prices for intermediate products that are inputs into this capability.[14]

The contingent nature of many defence outputs makes it very difficult to assess the true social worth of defence capabilities, both those that are deterrence- or combat-related and those that are formed upstream to provide war fighters with equipment, consumables and training. Capabilities to produce combat-related defence outputs have to be formed 'just in case', often on the understanding that it is most unlikely these capabilities will ever be deployed in anger. The true combat-related performance characteristics of defence capabilities are not observable in peacetime, nor can their true social value be determined until they are actually deployed. The availability of an incremental main battle tank may be both necessary and sufficient to achieve a victory of inconsequential nature for the nation's sovereignty or it may tilt the scales in a battle that changes the course of national history. In dollar terms, the value of the incremental tank could be anywhere in the range between zero and infinity (the Shakespearian horse that under right conditions would be worth a kingdom), with the expected average weighted value depending on a particular combination of most credible scenarios. And this could be true of every capability element. Also, if the formation of national defence capabilities deters potential adversaries, it is difficult to determine the precise extent to which they have provided value for money. As noted earlier, successful deterrence results in no observable conflict and if peace results from deterrence-providing military capabilities, it is usually not possible to determine the extent to which the absence of hostilities has resulted from defence spending on one type of military capability as compared with another.

Defence organisations are designed to fight wars, respond to other threats to national sovereignty, and signal their ability to do so to deter potential attack or intimidate foes. Stealth, deception and signalling skills, i.e., the creation of *informational asymmetries*, are thus critical attributes of military activity. Often, those keen on deterring aggression project an exaggerated picture of their military capability while prospective aggressors conceal their true potential.[15] But stealth and deception, combined with operational innovation, mean that military organisations do not know what they themselves or their enemies are actually capable of. In that sense, many military response options are simply *unknowable* at the time capability investment decisions are made, and this, in turn, renders the value of these capabilities equally unknowable. The proverbial 'fog of war' is a peculiarly acute form of this problem.

The ambiguity surrounding value-adding in producing defence outputs exacerbates the difficulty of knowing whether scarce resources are being optimally allocated to Defence generally and among competing uses within national security provision. Subjectivity is impossible to eliminate. Proponents of an asset will stress the likelihood of contingencies that imply the strongest support for their preference, while those against will argue the opposite case by emphasising the likelihood of alternative scenarios (for an illustration, see the initial responses of service chiefs to the proposed acquisition of the JORN over-the-horizon radar in Australia in Chapter 14). In such an environment we would expect to find a wide range of valuations placed on alternative capability options and correspondingly wide range of variation in offer prices (e.g., Throsby and Withers, 1999).

The production chain framework shown in Figure 1.1 implies a strong *complementarity* between investments in military capability and the capability of upstream defence suppliers. If government decides to acquire a particular force element to enhance national defence capability, and if it wants that force element to be available over time, it must also consider the security of upstream supply. However, the value chain framework obscures intrinsic ambiguities associated with determining the need for and value of domestic defence-related industry capabilities. In some cases, there may be irrefutable logic behind establishing and maintaining industry capability in country, dedicated to defence need of uncontested military importance. However, subjective judgements and political pressures both come into play in determining which Defence capabilities are actually essential and whether, and if so which, local Industry capabilities are genuinely required to support them in country. It follows that arguments proposing almost any investment in defence-related industrial capability may be pursued on a just-in-case basis as one can always think of a threat scenario calling for a particular military response option supported by a related industry capability. If budgetary considerations can be ignored, it is always prudent to have as many response options as possible and a wide range of associated military and industrial capabilities – just in case. It is only with the benefit of hindsight that we learn which particular military and industrial capabilities were actually useful. When budgets constrain choices, capability investments must be prioritised. This is a highly politicised process in which logic and cold-blooded assessment may easily give way to expediency.

Actors and decision-makers

Supply chain framework

This section focuses on the actors who make the decisions to buy, produce and sell, i.e., the emphasis shifts from *how* value is added along the production chain to *who* adds it. Figure 1.2 shows the stylised chain of supply-demand relationships – the *defence supply chain*. In Figure 1.2, Defence is the domestic producer of the end product of the defence value chain and an agency responsible for the formation of military capabilities that allow the government to select an appropriate military response option when a particular threat to national security (a military contingency) materialises. The Defence Procurement Agency (DPA) is shown in Figure 1.2 as a distinct organisational element within the NDO. As in Figure 1.1, some national security outputs are imported from Allies. The focus in Figure 1.2 is on the part of defence production/value chain that links upstream Industry capabilities with downstream military capabilities. To form these capabilities, the DPA sources inputs, such as defence materiel, from domestic and foreign Industry suppliers. Thus, a supply chain is formed in which upstream suppliers provide the downstream DPA with goods and services that are used in the formation of military capabilities by Defence. The supply chain runs from left to right in Figure 1.2 but the social value of national security provision is realised downstream. Defence demands for industrial supplies drive Industry sales and determine the value of upstream Industry capabilities. Figure 1.2 also shows exports providing upstream suppliers with an alternative source of demand. Finally, it highlights the opportunity for de-coupling supplies and demands for Industry products as Defence may create stocks of military materiel, which allow it to source its supplies from Industry at rate different from the rate at which it uses these products. Below, we briefly discuss each of the actors represented in Figure 1.2: Government, Defence, the Defence Procurement Agency and Industry Suppliers.

Government and the provision of national security

In democracies, Government derives authority from the will of the people to allocate resources to the defence of the community. It determines the range of outputs which Defence is required to produce and provides it with resources and the institutional support to form the necessary capabilities. This involves what might be called a cascading *principal–agent framework*, where Government is responsible to the public at large (the ultimate principal) for the *provision* of national security. In turn, Government acts as the principal vis-à-vis Defence which is tasked with the formation and sustainment of capabilities needed to provide government with the required military response options.

The provision of national security is a state (government) monopoly.[16] A high-level task for Government is to determine its national security strategy for which, ultimately, in a democracy, it is answerable to the electorate. Will a democratic state strive only to defend itself against potential attacks on or within its borders, or will it take a more aggressive stance beyond its borders? Will it seek alliances and, if so, with whom? Does it see the principal threat to its security in the asymmetric warfare waged by terrorists or the development of high-technology weaponry among traditional foes? The position taken by governments on such issues may be announced in carefully crafted White Papers of lengthy gestation (aimed at the general public) or regularly produced but classified strategic outlook documents and will imply in general

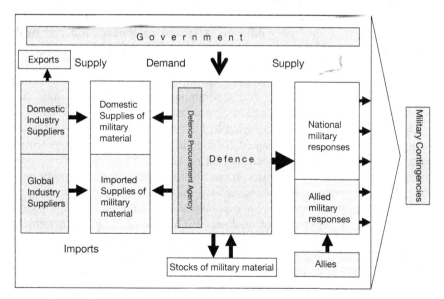

Figure 1.2 Decision-makers in national security production and defence supply chain

terms that certain military capabilities are required to meet the future. The problem is what military capabilities, precisely, and what inputs are required to form these capabilities?

Newsome (2003) has argued that high-level resource-related trade-offs must be addressed when governments consider their military strategies. Some contingencies, as we have described them, are best met with a capital-intensive military. Others may require a labour-intensive military. In choosing the degree of capital-intensity characterising their military, nations 'must make a trade-off between probability and consequentiality' (ibid.: 139).[17]

Governments are elected partly to organise national security and the use of defence capabilities for other purposes. Their difficulty in being answerable to the people lies not only in justifying what they do – as the governments of the USA and its allies discovered in 2003 when they tried to justify their decision to invade Iraq – but also in having to explain how they do it, given that the general public is poorly placed to evaluate alternative defence capability options (Throsby and Withers, 1999).

Defence: its mission, organisation and structure

Military organisations exist to implement the strategic security policy of Government. Generally, this task is entrusted to a dedicated government agency, the NDO, which specialises in the activities that surround state-sanctioned use of lethal force. This specialised activity calls for its own organisational culture supported by purpose-designed training and education and the acquisition of enabling combat systems. Historically, military technologies encouraged the fragmentation of Defence organisational structure into 'Services' with distinct environmental foci (land, air and sea) and traditions of independent operations using different skills and equipment. But even with the fragmentation of Defence capabilities into Service-specific capability elements, most nations favour the structuring of the NDO as a single, *national* military organisation capable of taking advantage of scale- and scope-related efficiencies[18] and, in particular, of the commonality of doctrine, training and technological standards in equipment and consumables.[19]

Defence organisations are designed to fight wars, respond to other threats to national sovereignty, and signal their ability to do so to deter potential attack or intimidate foes. In our stylised representation of the defence production chain, the NDO operates in two distinct operational modes. In *wartime*, Defence engages its combat-related capabilities but in *peacetime*, it focuses primarily on forming new capabilities and maintaining existing capabilities in the required state of readiness.[20] This diverse range of investment and operational activities presents challenges for the organisational design of Defence. Combat-related, lethal capabilities normally necessitate – by international war fighting convention – the use of military personnel, i.e., public employees or conscripts in uniform. Non-lethal capabilities, such as logistic support or the procurement of equipment, need not involve the use of uniformed personnel. Traditionally, operational logistics in an area (theatre) of military activity has involved the use of military personnel. But, increasingly, such activities are outsourced to commercial companies (e.g., coalition operations in Afghanistan and Iraq in the 2000s – we shall revisit outsourcing in Chapter 3). When non-combat capabilities are retained in-house, they are often delegated to a civil organisational element such as a defence department/ministry. This two-track (military-civil) organisational structure presents many managerial challenges that do not affect other public sector agencies (Bland, 1998; Markowski and Hall, 2007).

The defence procurement agency

The procurement of military materiel needed by Defence may be undertaken by a single, specialised organisational unit, or dispersed between larger organisational elements such as the Services, or delegated to a detached specialised procurement agency such as the British Defence Procurement Agency[21] or the Australian Defence Materiel Organisation, or, as in Canada, an all-of-government procurement agency.[22] Which approach is taken is a matter for Defence and/ or Government.

A further option is to cooperate with allies to set up a larger multinational defence procurement agency.[23] This is particularly relevant to small countries whose bargaining power as a buyer will, by definition, be limited by the level of its expenditures. Figure 1.2 abstracts from these details and shows all defence procurement as the responsibility of a single organisational element which we call the Defence Procurement Agency (DPA), located within the national defence organisation and acting as Defence's buyer of the goods and services forming inputs into military capability. DPA operates on the demand side of the market for military equipment and consumables (defence materiel) and seeks through its purchases to provide capability elements within a budget constraint set for it by Defence or Government.[24] Its purchasing decisions must also conform to any policy prescriptions applied to government procurement generally or flowing from defence industry policy, generic industry policy, and other economic, social and strategic policy.

While it is clearly not the job of the DPA to determine a national security strategy, it cannot do the job of purchasing inputs to enable the strategy unless it knows what sorts of inputs are required to achieve the objectives of the strategy. This, in turn, calls for a capability requirements analysis to bridge the logical gap. But is the DPA the place to carry out that analysis and how should it be done? This is a key institutional issue. If done within the DPA, such analysis gives the agency advanced technical expertise and intimate knowledge of what it should look for in seeking inputs into military capabilities. On the other hand, most countries have expertise on issues such as this outside the DPA in the Services and/or Intelligence and Force Structure elements of the NDO. In Australia, for example, the task of developing new capability options for consideration by Government and managing the (major) capital investment program is assigned to a separate Capability Development Group in Defence (DoD, 2006, and see Chapter 6). And it could often be beneficial to draw on a wider pool of knowledge in government research agencies, universities and corporate R&D labs.

The economic theory of bureaucracy suggests Defence itself will have a bias to undertake capability requirements analysis in house (Niskanen, 1971). In terms of agency theory, it will be undertaking many tasks hidden from the view of other government agencies and the parliament. In setting up the required structure and responsibilities in-house, governments may counter that bias by taking a broader view (e.g., by setting up alternative sources of strategic and capability advice outside Defence). In Australia, for example, the government has set up the Australian Strategic Policy Institute to provide alternative, well-informed (albeit it not always comfortable) advice (ASPI, 2006a).

Industry suppliers

Industry suppliers possess the industry capabilities underpinning the production chain discussed in the preceding section. Domestic defence suppliers are often viewed as the support (fourth) arm of Defence. But the meaning of 'defence industry' is rather ambiguous. The literature abounds with definitions covering firms, sectors, output and its criticality for national security (for a discussion, see Sandler and Hartley, 1995: 182–5). In principle, domestic defence industry comprises all those elements of in-country industry capable of undertaking work for the armed forces or export defence-related products to other countries. It includes business entities located in country and fully owned by residents as well as local subsidiaries of foreign companies. Some suppliers may be dedicated to defence in that most or all of their activity is defence-oriented. Others may supply military materiel occasionally and are essentially civil producers. Ambiguity stems importantly from the fact that almost any producer of goods and services could, potentially, be drawn into the service of national defence – not just shipbuilders and aircraft manufacturers, but also boot makers, cattle farmers and the providers of educational services. Hence determination of which suppliers form part of 'defence industry' and which do not is somewhat arbitrary.

Two sorts of factors determine the range and diversity of Defence's demands on industry suppliers: first, the *scale* of potential conflict or engagement; second, the particular demands of *specific types* of military activity. In relation to scale, a government involved in 'total' war may declare every asset and resource in the economy to be at the disposal of the 'war economy'. The national defence industry in this case coincides exactly with the country's entire domestic industry structure. On the other hand, if a country is, has been and expects to be involved only in border protection and occasional peace-keeping missions, the extent to which it may wish to engage the support of local industry will be rather limited. The second determinant is more subtle in its effects. The nature of actual and potential warfare changes continuously as the result of technological change and new developments in strategic thinking. Parts of the economy that would have supported defence in the past may no longer be relevant (think of arboriculture and timber ship-building); other parts may suddenly acquire new strategic significance (e.g., pharmaceuticals to prosecute or counter chemical and biological warfare).

On the input supply side, three points are worth noting. First, most countries, and in particular small economies, import a significant proportion of their defence equipment and intellectual property (designs, software source codes, etc.) and attract foreign direct investment (FDI) through the formation of wholly owned subsidiaries of multinational companies, the purchase of equity in local firms, joint ventures with foreign equity holders, or setting up new, green-field site operations. Second, many defence industry suppliers today see themselves more as system integrators than manufacturers. They are involved in the design of weapons systems and the business of integrating the components of complex systems and setting them to work. But they may do rather little manufacturing themselves, buying in component parts sourced domestically or overseas from companies which may or may not have a defence and security focus in their product lines. Third, movements of labour bring skills and expertise from abroad. Given this mobility of resources, especially human, financial and intellectual capital, it becomes difficult to be sure what domestic industry capabilities actually exist at any one moment and might be available in future.

Industry suppliers may also lie within the defence organisation – in the form of arsenals, factories and shipyards operated by the Services and employing public servants and, in some cases, using conscripted or hired military personnel. Alternatively, they can be outside contractors, public or private. Usually, Government determines whether defence supplies are to be produced in-house or purchased from external suppliers. In other words, government must take decisions that, in the commercial corporate world, would be described as 'make or buy?' And if it buys, the ownership characteristics of its suppliers may be a consideration. Both dimensions of the decision will be influenced by security requirements and judgements about production efficiency (see Chapter 3).

The 'publicness' of defence-related products normally decreases as we move back up the production chain, from final national security output to inter-mediate products. Incentives therefore exist for the private production of such goods (e.g., capital equipment, consumables, and logistic support services) and it is feasible to procure them through the market. Markets also exist for human capital services. Nevertheless, some intermediate outputs are produced by the NDO because they involve a high degree of 'publicness' (e.g., defence research and development, military intelligence, strategic planning).

Since the early 1980s, private ownership, or at the very least 'corporatised' state ownership, has been the dominant political model framing industry development in most English-speaking countries and, to a lesser extent, in other countries. It has led to the large scale privatisation of government enterprises and to contracting out to commercial suppliers civilian-type services previously produced in-house by Defence. While the driver for applying this model is the prospect of enhanced efficiency, important questions surround the potential of ownership transfers to achieve efficiency gains. It is often argued that exposure to competition is at least as important as ownership for increasing efficiency but debate continues about the relative importance of each factor and whether the focus should be on static cost-efficiency and allocative efficiency or on dynamic gains related to innovation. In the case of defence-related industry, the trade-offs are also constrained by political influences and economic realities. Exposure to international competition is often precluded by local content policies justified by the imperatives of national security provision. On the other hand, domestic demands are usually too small to sustain multiple sources of local supply. We revisit these issues in later chapters.

Supply chain links and relationships

Transactions and relationships

Earlier, we described the characteristics and dimensions of the products that change hands in the procurement process. The products travel along the supply chain as the result of transactions among the agents comprising the chain, including the DPA. Each *procurement transaction* between the DPA and its suppliers comprises three components:

1   the *deal* defining the content of deliverable, in particular its scope (the description of what is being acquired, including product performance/ quality), scale (how many units) and schedule (delivery date or dates), the nature of exchange involved (e.g., goods-for-money or barter), and the associated consideration (the price which the buyer agrees to pay the seller for the deliverable);
2   the *contract*, a formal agreement between the buyer and the seller that is normally legally enforceable, provides the formal description of the deal and the assignment of associated property and decision-making rights between the parties to frame the deal under the relevant legal system. The contract may also specify the nature of the relationship to be forged by the parties, the assignment of adjudication and enforcement rights, and other rules, vetoes and restraints.
3   the *relationship* between the buyer and the seller, i.e., the nature of interaction between them during the procurement process and, often, after the product is delivered.

Contract-governed relationships along the supply chain may take a variety of forms ranging from closely collaborative to arm's length and potentially adversarial. Contracts for the supply of products that can be specified clearly and in sufficient detail at the outset of the transaction can be followed by an arm's-length relationship between the parties in which legal redress is the principal mechanism foreseen to deal with contractual default or non-compliance. On the other hand, contracts for the supply of innovative products, which cannot be well specified in advance, may, and normally should, allow for innovation and/or adaptation to occur flexibly throughout the delivery process. These contracts should pave the way to collaboration and consultation between the parties to refine concepts and address problems as they emerge. Such contracts carry the risk, however, of *both* the buyer and the seller becoming 'parents' for the deliverable so that disputes regarding the precise nature of the deal may not be easily settled.

While explicit legal contracts for the supply of defence products frame many of the important relationships in the procurement process, we shall also be interested in other forms of relationship that influence the system. Such relationships include those between different types of agent (e.g., the DPA and Industry); those among the same type of agent (e.g., firms within Industry); and those within organisations themselves (e.g., between the DPA and its Service 'customers').[25] Not all such relationships are governed by formal and enforceable legal contracts. And, it is sometimes said that the procurement process operates to some extent as it does because of the personal relationships between individuals in DPAs and Industry representatives who once worked for the NDO.

An important body of economic literature builds on the insight that it is costly to perform business transactions (Williamson, 1975). Buyers and sellers must incur *search* costs to identify each other before a sale can be set up; the sale itself requires costly *negotiation* over the deal and, in many cases, the preparation of a formal contract; and costs are also incurred when contract *variations* are agreed by the parties and if *enforcement* is required. All these dimensions of transaction costs feature prominently in defence procurement (Bower and Dertouzos, 1994; Hartley, 2007). Competitive tendering, post-bid negotiations and legal wrangles during the project are common features, regularly reported in the media. Transaction costs may also include commitments associated with relationship-building – some, like lobbying political decision-makers, regarded as legitimate; others, like bribery, as illegal. Another approach to such expenditures sees deliberate short-term investments in relationships as a means of cultivating *trust* so that, in the longer run, at least some transaction costs may be avoided. Trust-based relationships acquire additional significance when information is asymmetric – as in cases where sellers know more about their own performance potential than buyers, or where purchasers are unable to observe the production performance of their suppliers (Parker and Hartley, 1997). The principal–agent literature on which we shall draw later offers a range of potential contractual and organisational solutions to the problems posed by such asymmetries.[26] In subsequent chapters, we adopt a broader perspective on contracting than that usually found in conventional defence economics literature. (Our approach is similar to that developed by Furlotti, 2007.)

How these factors influence the procurement process is in turn heavily influenced by the market conditions in which Defence operates. Its relationship with its suppliers is shaped by the relative bargaining power of each side and this, in turn, derives from the market structure. The more DPAs can deal with suppliers in a contestable environment (i.e., one in which the DPA can credibly threaten to use alternative sources of supply), the less the DPA will worry that Industry undertakes production hidden from their view. One of the main forces behind the outsourcing of much defence production has, after all, been the hope of efficiency gains gleaned from the opportunity to move custom from one source to another in the event of underperformance (Richardson and Roumasset, 1995). We shall see later, however, that the nature of defence contracting has somewhat blighted these prospects and the extent to which market conditions actually permit contestability may vary considerably.

Market structure, contestability and Defence–Industry relationships

The organisations that operate defence production capabilities may be exposed to actual or potential alternative sources of supply and the resulting *contestability of supply chains* is critical for Defence to derive value for money in procurement. This is particularly important when government insists on high 'local content' in defence projects. For larger defence spending nations, there may be more than one domestic source of supply; for smaller defence spenders, there is often only one such source – or none, unless government/ Defence is prepared to pay large cost premia for local production, subsidised duplication and underutilised production facilities.

Defence may increase contestability if it seeks to source supplies from overseas providers as well as domestic. For modest defence spenders, there is normally a choice between (mainly overseas) suppliers for most types of equipment and consumables. For reasonably standard types of equipment and consumables, where scale- and scope-related efficiencies result in declining average cost (see Chapter 3), direct imports of equipment produced on a large scale are likely to be the least-cost solution, with international co-production and collaboration being costlier, and independent local production being the costliest option (Hartley and Sandler, 2003). Small-country NDOs must therefore recognise that investments in local industry capability will often imply sacrificing opportunities to buy at lower cost in the international market.

When the interface between the DPA and Industry is market-mediated, the relationship between buyer and sellers will be shaped importantly by *market structure*. Conditions that have been observed and analysed in the literature include:

- *monopsony* – when the DPA is the only customer for goods and services produced by local defence-dependent suppliers and, thus, may have market

power to *impose* on these suppliers price limits, product specifications, and delivery schedules;
- *monopoly* – when there is only one source of supply and no close substitutes so that the supplier has market power over prices, product specifications and delivery schedules;
- *bilateral monopoly* – when monopoly (or market power) on the supply side confronts the demand side monopsony. This creates conditions for an essentially 'strategic' bargaining relationship between supplier and defence customer;
- *oligopoly* – when there is a small number of rival sources of supply, which are well aware of each other's market power over prices, product specifications and delivery schedules, and where suppliers act 'strategically' in anticipation of rival responses;
- *monopolistic competition* – when there is a number of specialised suppliers of partially differentiated but largely generic products who each compete for a market niche for their particular product variant but, given the presence of reasonably close substitutes, have relatively little market power to fix prices; and
- *atomistic competition* – when there are many suppliers, who produce highly substitutable products and act as price-takers.

The actual prices paid by Defence for military materiel depend on competition among producers for Defence business, and the skill with which Defence procures its inputs. If Defence is the only domestic buyer of a product which has no export potential, its bargaining power is relatively strong, especially when it can source the product from a number of keen-to-sell suppliers. If there is only one domestic supplier (sole source) and imports are restricted, the monopoly market power of the seller could counter the monopsony power of Defence. Under such conditions of *bilateral monopoly* the outcome of the bargaining process between the two parties is difficult to predict. Further, even if there is keen competition between potential sellers early on in the procurement process (*competition for the market*), the presence of *sunk* (irretrievable) *costs* in supplying the requirement may leave buyer and seller in a position of mutual dependence once the contract is signed, i.e., there is not much *competition in the market*. This could encourage opportunistic behaviour by either or both parties.

If small countries wish to create a competitive environment in downstream segments of defence supply chains, they will need to open their domestic market to overseas participants. This permits the entry of competing designs and combat systems as overseas consortia of platform builders, system integrators and original equipment manufacturers (OEMs) (usually combining with local firms) come to contest the market. Once a preferred product has been selected, move competition for the market follows with sub-contractors competing for various components of supply. However, once all contracts are signed, there is no competition for the market until a new set of requirements is competed and little competition in the market if switching of sub-contractors is technically non-feasible or too costly.

With their small procurement budgets, the DPAs of smaller nations lack the market power of a monopsonist in the world arms market, although a small buyer may still be able to strike a bargain when the seller of equipment is keen to obtain additional business. They may also be able to source their supplies from a range of producers thereby denying individual suppliers significant monopoly power. If, however, the government of a small country decides, for strategic or economic reasons, to promote *import substitution*, local producers of import substitutes may acquire market power if, as a result of trade diversion, the market becomes less exposed to competition. This may lead to some or all of higher costs, product performance degradation and schedule slippages. Governments often pay price premia (i.e., a price for local production in excess of the world low price) for locally sourced defence goods.[27]

Another structural dimension of the supply chain that influences relationships among the players is the degree of *vertical integration* between suppliers and users of inputs into defence capability, i.e., the extent to which a single agent in the supply chain owns and operates the assets at successive stages in production and use. On the one hand, full integration would involve Defence (government) ownership of all the production assets of domestic defence industry. Defence 'procurement' would then be limited to transmitting orders from military users of supplies to their in-house producers and the relevant set of relationships would be entirely encompassed within the NDO. On the other hand, Defence and its suppliers might be wholly independent of each other and the assets of suppliers at various stages of production separately owned. Relationships here would be largely market-mediated and governed by market contracts. The structures often observed in practice, however, fall into neither of these categories. Defence in some cases owns a limited range of 'production units', as in the case of defence research laboratories such as Australia's DSTO or the Dutch TNO. To meet the bulk of its requirements, it must deal with suppliers that are independently owned but often form consortia (business relationships) to meet the complexities and particular demands of the Defence client.

With private ownership of Industry, production and the through-life support of defence materiel tend to be separated from their use as the buyer and the seller are economically and legally different entities. As noted earlier, many countries in recent years have privatised their in-house production facilities and elected to purchase equipment and consumables through the market. The production of national security has fallen within a broader trend to outsourcing the production (as opposed to provision) of public goods to the private sector. Increasingly, the provision of intermediate capital goods inputs, consumables and human capital services has become market-mediated: it has been the subject of competitive tendering and contracting (CTC) reforms since the early 1980s, involving market testing and private finance

initiatives in countries such as the United Kingdom and Australia (Domberger, 1998; Hartley, 2007). Leasing of 'civilian-line' equipment is now commonplace and civilian contractors have been deployed in areas of operations
such as (at the time of writing) Iraq. Initiatives still regarded as controversial
involve the use of privately-owned and logistically fully supported combat
assets. But many privatised government factories continue to operate as
designated sole source suppliers and the change of ownership has not changed
their essentially 'quasi-vertical' relationship with Defence.

Defence demands

As we noted above, the nature of the relationship between the NDO and its
suppliers depends to a significant extent on the sort of transaction taking
place. If Defence cannot specify in detail, in advance, what it wants, it may
have to depend on its suppliers to help it learn what will serve its needs best
and what can be feasibly made available within budget and time horizons. This
learning process necessarily involves a closer relationship than that associated
with buying a ready-made product 'off the shelf'. In this section we draw
attention to how that process may structure Defence–Industry relationships
and why it may also pose problems for such relationships.

When it procures assets and consumables to form new capabilities, it is
often argued that Defence should, logically, first define its requirements in
broad *functional terms*, that is, with reference to the nature of a particular
threat scenario and *what* needs to be done to respond to it. *Functional specifications* describe the functions capabilities are expected to perform (e.g. the
ability to destroy specified, land-based targets up to a given distance behind
enemy lines, or the ability to prevent supplies reaching enemy forces). Such
specifications also describe lead times required to develop a capability to the
point of operational readiness, and the profile of its subsequent engagement
when a particular contingency occurs. Even at this early phase in new capability formation, the NDO may 'go shopping for ideas' (procure information) by seeking expressions of interest from suppliers capable of offering
technical solutions to the stated functional requirement.

Functional specifications are different from *technical specifications* which
relate to *how* the requirements might actually be met. There may be one or
many different technological approaches to and solutions for meeting the
stated functional requirement. For example, distant targets may be destroyed
by missiles, unmanned airborne vehicles (UAVs), or ground-based special
forces. Supplies might be disrupted by sea-borne blockade, bombing by aircraft, or land-based military action. Very detailed engineering design specifications may then be produced in relation to each technological approach. The
funnelling – or conversion and refinement – of functional into technical specifications is a non-trivial task that largely determines the NDO's relationship
with upstream Industry suppliers. Seeking Industry responses to functional
requirements may stimulate competition when alternative solutions/products

are offered by different suppliers. On the other hand, seeking supply responses to tightly defined technical specifications may have the opposite effect as supply responses are restricted to those who can comply with DPA's technical requirement. Tight specification of technical requirements is sometimes used deliberately and strategically to narrow down the field to a particular supplier while the semblance of competition is maintained by the open tendering of requirements.

Also, a major issue for procurement occurs when technical requirements are defined before functional specifications are considered, that is, the 'solution' to a 'problem' is offered before the problem itself is specified. This may happen because of a Defence focus on the technical aspects of equipment interoperability or 'fit' with existing systems rather than function *per se*. Similarly, Service users may have specific preferences for particular technical specifications (e.g., a simple replacement of legacy equipment with more recent vintage of otherwise similar equipment) and, sometimes, functional specifications and 'mission profiles' (use scenarios) are 'retrofitted' to justify the adopted technical solutions. NDOs may also seek to 'keep up with the (military) Jones' by replicating other nations' military investments, creating the danger of procurements that are inefficient and sometimes inappropriate for their particular military environments. Governments, perhaps under pressure from Industry, may also require that materiel is purchased in-country, even though imported products would have offered a better or more cost-effective solution. Ultimate, therefore, the funnelling of functional into technical specifications can become messy and fragmented.

That said, it is only when technical specifications are determined that the assets and inputs (in more general terms, goods and services) required to form new capability elements are sufficiently well defined to form the basis for placing orders. It is also possible for demands for military materiel to be progressively determined through interaction with Industry suppliers. For example, the functional specifications for capability elements may be determined by Defence and communicated to Industry to solicit alternative technical specifications (using differing approaches and solutions) from equipment suppliers. Defence will then choose a particular set of generic technical specifications, determine product quantities and delivery schedules to solicit offers of specific deliverables and price quotations. In such a case, input demands for defence capability elements are derived through the interaction between input users and producers.

Thus, Defence/DPA may initiate procurement processes for technologies and products still under development. Requirement specifications needed to initiate the processes may be fuzzy as the nature of the end deliverable, price and schedule cannot be specified up front with sufficient precisions. As the development of technology or product progresses, both the supplier and the buyer improve their understanding of what can actually be delivered, when and at what cost. The resulting incremental or 'spiral' acquisition model is discussed in more detail in Chapter 4. However, the initial gaps and asymmetries in knowledge about the product and the associated production process also encourage opportunistic supply responses. Industry suppliers may bid for work to get their foot in the door, as it were, without fully appreciating the complexity of the deliverable and the challenges posed by its production. A classic example of this 'foot-in-the-door' approach to user requirements was the development and production of over-the-horizon radar in Australia (see Chapter 14).

Earlier, we described the direction of causality in the defence supply chain as running from the final demand for national security to demands for intermediate and upstream products so that inputs demands were dependent or derived demands. This representation of national security production is sometimes at variance with reality of military capability formation. This is because:

- Sourcing decisions may be driven by upstream industry considerations independently of their downstream implications for national security provision. This is often the case when current equipment sourcing decisions are constrained and shaped by 'legacy' Industry capabilities which were developed in response to earlier demands from the NDO. For example, governments may direct NDOs to buy 'local' to keep a particular supplier in business rather than buy equipment that is most appropriate and/or affordable. The 'buy local' directive may nevertheless be presented politically as an important aspect of national defence 'self-reliance'.
- Defence equipment buyers are unlikely always to be immune to salesmanship and their governments may sometimes be persuaded to make opportunistic purchases of equipment before capability development plans have fully matured.
- Allied governments may negotiate deals with a view to providing business for their own industry.
- The NDO is not, in actuality, a monolithic decision-maker and views within it may vary widely in relation to what the end product should be. Rather than careful analysis shaping demand, decisions may instead follow institutional conventions. The 'Buggins turn' principle has often been used to allow different organisational elements, particularly the Services, to take turns at acquiring new equipment, i.e., if the Air Force gets helicopter gunships this year, it is the Army's turn to buy main battle tanks the next. Demand upstream then follows application of the institutional 'rules of the game' governing Defence acquisition.

In sum, the simple logic of derived demand implicit in our framework needs to be supplemented by the recognition that NDO decision-makers can sometimes be influenced by suppliers and that institutional conventions can override dispassionate analysis of need. The textbook logic of derived demand is often reversed with Defence acquiring its intermediate inputs only to discover later what can and cannot be done with them and at what cost in terms of lost opportunities for more and better national security.

Government policy and relationships

The provision of national security is only one of the functions of Government and the NDO only one organisational component of the machinery of government. What the DPA procures and how it goes about its business therefore depends on strategic policy for security, the funding of Defence relative to other claims on government resources, how vital local production is thought to be for strategic reasons, and the extent to which domestic defence industry is viewed as a means for achieving broader government objectives such as employment and technological innovation. Policy does not emerge or operate in a vacuum: it is the product of a political process that involves a multiplicity of relationships as described in this chapter. In later chapters we analyse arguments around support for domestic defence industry. Here we make a number of observations as a bridge to the rest of the book:

1   Defence and national security are key functions of Government and, given their public good characteristics, would not be provided to a sufficient extent (or at all) if left to market mechanisms alone. The right amount to spend on defence in total, and relative to other government functions, cannot be determined through a simple economic calculation, however. It is ultimately the result of political decisions.

2   Decisions about overall defence spending, of which the procurement budget is an important part, are made on the basis of inputs, interactions and debates among politicians accountable to the electorate, Government officials inside and outside of the NDO, Industry lobby groups and non-government organisations, and the media. Given that, as a broad generalisation, the specialist expertise and influence of Defence lie in how military operations are conducted rather than whether to conduct them, its impact at this level depends on the political skills of its political master in making the case for resources. Defence may argue that the cost of doing its job is increasing by the year but this alone will not secure it more resources in the face of competing claims from, for example, public health and education where costs are also rising.

3   The outcome of the debate is also importantly influenced by the information and quality of argument assembled by public servants in the NDO and other government departments. The more the debate hinges on the technicalities of warfare or keeping the peace, the more helpful it is likely to be for Defence in getting what it wants since NDOs usually enjoy an asymmetric advantage in terms of information about military technology.

4   Non-Defence departments such Treasury and Finance may be interested in containing Defence expenditure generally; those with a focus on industry and employment may be more interested in using Defence expenditure for their own policy purposes – and for that reason more inclined to support defence spending, as long as it supports domestic,

often regional economic objectives (for an interesting illustration of these processes in Canada, see Chapter 7).

5 Creating and maintaining domestic defence-related production cap- abilities is largely an issue for nations that believe they should maintain a degree of defence self-sufficiency.[28] As noted earlier, such decisions reflect political judgements: it is always possible to argue that depen- dence on overseas sourcing of a significant input into national security could result in catastrophic failure if the supplier refused to honour its contractual commitment or was forced to default by its home govern- ment. Accepting such a risk may be seen as tantamount to a government abrogating its stewardship of national sovereignty. But since only super- powers can afford high levels of autarchy in defence supply chains, smaller countries must recognise and respond as best they can to the inevitable risks surrounding dependence on imports.

6 Arguments apparently founded on the merits of self-sufficiency can easily be turned to other uses, both by Government itself and by the defence industry. In particular, defence materiel is exempt from restrictions on protectionist measures imposed by international free trade agreements. Such exemptions are intended to allow nations freedom to develop more self-sufficient defence value chains. However, governments may also use the defence industry exemptions for non-defence purposes perhaps with a view of creating jobs or protecting local industries against imports and foreign direct investment competition for reasons unrelated to national security provision.

7 Once defence industry capabilities are formed in country, lobbies often form to sustain them as legacy industries. The relationships between lobbyists and politicians may reverse the logic of defence value chains from demand-supply to supply-demand.

8 Policy-generated relationships with the rest of the world may include offsets schemes designed to create local employment or technology transfer from overseas suppliers, and export-oriented programmes aimed at using domestic defence industry capabilities to enter international markets. We shall have much more to say in later chapters about the need for care in assessing the real costs, as well as the perceived benefits, of such policies.

Conclusion

This chapter has outlined a framework for considering the procurement of industry inputs needed to produce national security. The social value – or benefit – of in-country defence capabilities, including upstream industrial capabilities, is subjective to the extent that it reflects judgements about the value of national defence in general, the most promising ways of achieving national security objectives, and the potential of domestic suppliers to deliver sought-for levels and quality of industrial support. The most appropriate, effective and efficient ways of pursuing defence procurement likewise remain controversial, not least because of the public scrutiny and attention they receive. The way these issues play out for small to medium-sized defence spenders has, however, not received the attention given to them in superpower and big-spending nations. That will be the focus for the rest of the book.

Notes

1 Over the past decade, and especially since the events of 9/11, the provision of broadly defined 'homeland security' has become an all-of-government responsibility with several government agencies jointly responsible for its production. Also, as demonstrated by recent conflicts in Iraq and Afghanistan, civilian contractors have been used in a wide variety of support roles in areas of military operations.
2 In Australia, for example, *National Security Strategic Updates* are published bi-annually (ASPI, 2006a: 10–11).
3 But some military activities are observable and measurable. For example, Defence is often involved in various 'functions of state', which may range from entertaining the public on festive occasions or welcoming visiting dignitaries, to assistance in civil emergencies such as floods, to second line of support for the police in counter-terrorist activities. Such activities can be monitored and measured (e.g., number of successful rescue missions completed).
4 Accordingly, the Australian Government (and the Australian Parliament) will measure Defence's performance in generating the following outcomes:

- Outcome 1: Australia's national interests are protected and advanced through the provision of military capabilities and the promotion of security and stability.
- Outcome 2: military operations and other tasks directed by government achieve the desired results.
- Outcome 3: Defence's support to the Australian community and civilian authorities achieves the desired results.

To achieve these outcomes, the Australian Defence Organisation generates a series of military outputs including, for example, a capability for major surface combatant operations, a capability for special operations, and a capability for strategic surveillance and maritime attack operations (CoA, 2008: 69–94).
5 In this accounting framework, however, inputs into national security provision are represented as outputs and input costs as the value of output. Also, this type of arrangement obscures the contingent nature of defence outputs, i.e., what government refers to as 'outputs' are Service capabilities to engage in particular types of operation. Indeed, the vocabulary of this transactional framework is rather misleading. '*Outcomes* are the results or benefits that the government aims to deliver to the community through work of its agencies' … while … *outputs* are the goods and services that each agency produces to achieve its outcomes' (ibid.: 13). But then outputs are described as Service *capabilities for particular type of operations* (ibid., Table 1) as opposed to the actual operations in which Services are engaged.
6 In this accounting framework, the value of 'defence' is measured as the cost of inputs (or government outlays on defence) and not as the value that the public, the ultimate beneficiary of defence services, attaches to Defence activities.
7 Such activities might be low-level operational routines such as completing a simple task on time, to specification, and at minimum cost (e.g., routine border surveillance tasks). Or they may be higher level organisational and strategic activities

such as a major combat operation. Clearly, a production activity can only occur if someone develops a capability to produce what is needed. Product-specific production *capacities* have often been used to describe the *scale* of production facilities, i.e., the maximum volume of output that a facility could produce per unit of time. The concept of 'production capability' focuses on the potential to produce different product lines by a multi-product production facility. It is only through use of the facility in different circumstances that its capacity to provide a range of services may be fully revealed and measured.

8 This is fundamentally different from the production of private goods and services, which are normally invented, developed, produced and delivered in the anticipation of adequate revenues being generated to recover the full (private) cost of production and achieve the required profitability. No commercial enterprise can invest in capabilities that are best never deployed and are not expected to produce any revenue.

9 For example, a navy might wish to acquire the capacity to strike surface, air and seaborne targets at long range, if the need arose. Acquisition of a guided missile frigate might be viewed as giving a navy, as an organisation element of the NDO, these capabilities. (And this is the way it is often stated.) But for Defence to say that it *possesses* such military capabilities in the full sense of the word, the resources or inputs on which the capability draws and is built of must include not just the frigate itself but all the knowledge and know-how the crew bring to operating it successfully, their equipment and their logistic support. It also includes relevant network capabilities to navigate the frigate, provide it with relevant intelligence, and endorse the choice of targets and the appropriateness of response at the higher level of command. There will then exist a 'production unit' capable of delivering specific services when required.

10 Only a superpower such as the USA may achieve high levels of military self-sufficiency since it cannot rely on a more powerful nation for support and must also protect its smaller allies and military dependants. But even the USA is not totally self-sufficient in all its military inputs and benefits by importing some defence materiel. It also imports national security directly as it often prefers to conduct its military business leading coalitions of smaller nations to increase the international legitimacy of its actions and to share its cost with allies.

11 In the case of defence spending, it is easily observable that community views differ as to whether a nation should have a defence force at all and, if so, what it should do and how it should be equipped. These views shift over time. Some eminent economists have also argued that defence should be given a negative value in the national accounts (e.g., Nordhaus and Tobin, 1972). We follow existing conventions here but, as the text indicates, recognise the immense difficulties that surround putting a value on defence outputs.

12 Also, the existing elements of capability should be assessed to ascertain whether they are obsolete or not, i.e., to determine whether they continue to add more value to national defence than it costs to retain them in service. Thus, to ensure the national defence as a whole provides value for money, the *total social benefit* of national defence should equal or exceed the *total social cost* of creating and sustaining the in-country defence capability. In other words, the social benefit must be equal or greater than the social cost both at the margin, for a new increment in defence capability, and on average, across all of its elements.

13 From a private perspective, an element of upstream capability may be of considerable value to its commercial owner if it generates profitable sales to a downstream buyer, regardless whether these products are subsequently used productively or wasted. It is possible to derive private benefit mid- or up-stream even if there is no end product or when it fails to attract a price high enough to cover the full social cost of resources used in production.

14 If an analogy were to be drawn with the derivation of input demands in a commercial production environment, the price that the input user might be willing to pay for an additional quantity of the input would reflect the contribution of the incremental unit of the input to revenue from sales of the end product.

15 In this respect, the often drawn parallels with civil insurance activities are misleading. Insurance industries offer loss compensation in exchange for premia if certain random events occur, where the randomness and the magnitude of potential losses can be ascertained through actuarial studies of past events or by using some *a priori* models of events to be insured against. Insurance premia can therefore be calculated. When the provision of insurance changes the nature of randomness of the event under consideration – the so-called moral hazard of insurance (e.g., careless behaviour by the insured when insurance policy is taken) – the insurance premium may have to be increased, or some incentive systems put in place to deter moral hazards, or it may not be possible to provide insurance on a commercial basis at all. Similarly, some moral hazards may be associated with in-kind provisions made against natural disasters and epidemics but, in essence, the statistical characteristics of such events do not change much because prudent counter-measures have been put in place to mitigate their impact. (Some changes may occur, however, e.g., the development of vaccines may induce or accelerate the mutation of viruses.)

16 Government provision is related directly to the public good nature of national security. The cost structure of defence provision might or might not provide the grounds for a natural monopoly argument for government provision – depending on the capabilities deemed necessary. Competitive provision, however, poses obvious problems for command, control and coordination in war-fighting situations.

17 A counter-terrorist capability, for example, may be thought crucial by the military strategists but no inputs can be procured for it before significant work has been done on what the capability actually might be in terms of the technology, skills and knowledge it called for. Trajtenberg (2006: 181–2), for example, argues that intelligence is the key requirement for fighting terrorism and that the technological means for providing it involve 'developing computerized sensory interfaces and increasing the ability to analyse vast amounts of data'. Should Defence be set up in a way that allows its own experts to compare propositions like this with competing ideas of how to address terrorism? Should it alternatively be required to outsource such analysis to a research agency within or outside Government? And when the research findings and recommendations are in, should it be Government and/or Defence that decides which capability option to take?

18 For a discussion of these concepts, see Chapter 2.

19 While the organisational fragmentation of Defence into Services continues in most countries, the nature of modern warfare increasingly favours the formation of military units capable of operating on land, at sea and in the air and supported by network-enabled and network-centric intelligence, command and control systems. In recent years warfare has become increasingly knowledge-intensive. Partly because of this, and because of the indivisibilities and interdependencies inherent in military networks, battlefield management and information systems have come to require a highly centralised approach to the formation and deployment of combat-related capabilities. Combat-related (lethal) technologies are highly dedicated and capital intensive and require massive investments with uncertain outcomes. Such investments have long-term maintenance and modernisation implications, and require the full integration of human and non-human elements throughout the entire life of a capability. Putting these technological factors together, a centralised, single organisation providing national security seems easy to explain.

20 As resources are limited, there is inevitable trade-off between the formation of new (future) capabilities and the sustainment of existing capabilities (e.g., people and equipment) at high levels of readiness over a long period of time.

21 Before its merger with the Defence Logistics Organisation in 2007.
22 The evolving organisational structure of the Australian defence procurement is discussed in Chapter 6 and the Canadian all-of-government procurement system in Chapter 7.
23 Under the European Defence Agency's Charter, collaborative armaments procurement projects can be set up by groups of member countries. Alternatively, the EDA can act as a collective procurement agency serving consortia of project sponsoring and funding national defence organisations (see Chapter 2).
24 Given the heterogeneity of the goods and services involved, strict accuracy would require us to say that it operates on the demand side of a *set* of markets.
25 The Australian DPA, the Defence Materiel Organisation (DMO), is an *agency* that has been partially detached from the Defence Organisation to handle procurement projects (see Chapter 6). The DMO enters into *Materiel Acquisition Agreements* with the Department of Defence to provide the Services with capital equipment it has been authorised by government to buy from Industry, and *Materiel Sustainment Agreements* to support equipment in use. However, it has no significant resources of its own to compensate Defence if it fails to manage its procurement business as agreed. Ultimately, regardless of the semi-autonomous status of the Organisation, it is the taxpayer who would have to absorb the cost of contractual failure to deliver goods and services as contracted/agreed.
26 The literature of principal and agent builds on the observation that due to *informational asymmetries*, principals cannot observe all that agents do nor know all the characteristics they have (Hendrikse, 2003).
27 Premia may be defended on the grounds of national security but are often also justified on general economic grounds, i.e., in terms of job creation, support for regional economic development, or preserving and stimulating 'leading' economic sectors. Another economic rationale for paying price premia might be to use them, for example, to make local defence producers undertake development and production work in-country, generating technology (knowledge) spillovers of benefit to the rest of the economy. How much and what industry capability is built are thus as often determined by political considerations as strategic or economic ones.
28 Strictly speaking, a country which has no interest in defence self-sufficiency could undertake defence goods production for export only. But a defence firm exporting all its products would have to be particularly competitive to remain in country and continue to export. Also, domestic sales are usually a pre-condition for successful exports as the willingness of the NDO to buy the product signals the endorsement of its quality and a commitment to future through-life support.

References

ASPI (2006a) *Australian Defence Almanac, 2006–2007*, Canberra: Australian Strategic Policy Institute.
—— (2006b) *Your Defence Dollar: The 2006–07 Defence Budget*, August, Canberra: Australian Strategic Policy Institute.
Bland, D. L. (ed.) (1998) *Issues in Defence Management*, Kingston, ONT: School of Policy Studies, Queen's University.
Bower, A. G. and Dertouzos, J. N. (eds) (1994) *Essays in the Economics of Procurement*, Santa Monica, CA: RAND, National Defense Research Institute.
CoA (2008) *Defence Portfolio Budget Statements 2008–09*, Canberra: Commonwealth of Australia.
DoD (2000) *Defence 2000: Our Future Defence Force*, Canberra: Department of Defence, Commonwealth of Australia.

—— (2006) *Defence Capability Development Manual*, Canberra: Defence Publishing Service, Department of Defence.

Domberger, S. (1998) *The Contracting Organization, A Strategic Guide to Outsourcing*, Oxford: Oxford University Press.

Furlotti, M. (2007) 'There is more to contracts than incompleteness: a review and assessment of empirical research on inter-firm contract design', *Journal of Management and Governance*, 11: 61–99.

Hartley, K. (2007) 'The arms industry, procurement and industrial policies', in T. Sandler and K. Hartley (eds) *The Economics of Defense*, Cambridge: Cambridge University Press, pp. 1139–76.

Hartley, K. and Sandler, T. (2003) 'The future of the defence firm', *Kyklos*, 56: 361–80.

Hendrikse, G. (2003) *Economics and Management of Organisations*, Maidenhead: McGraw-Hill.

Markowski, S. and Hall, P. (2007) 'Public sector entrepreneurialism and the production of defence', *Public Finance and Management*, 7(3): 260–94.

Newsome, B. (2003) 'Don't get your mass kicked: a management theory of military capability', *Defense and Security Analysis*, 19(2): 131–48.

Niskanen, W. A. (1971) *Bureaucracy and Representative Government*, Chicago: Aldine-Atherton.

Nordhaus, W. and Tobin, J. (1972) 'Is growth obsolete?', in R. A. Gordon (ed.) *Economic Research: Retrospect and Prospect, Economic Growth*, New York: National Bureau for Economic Research.

Parker, D. and Hartley, K. (1997) 'The economics of partnership sourcing versus adversarial competition: a critique', *European Journal of Purchasing and Supply Management*, 3(2): 115–25.

Richardson, J. and Roumasset, J. (1995) 'Sole sourcing, competitive sourcing, parallel sourcing: mechanisms for supplier performance', *Managerial and Decision Economics*, 16(1): 71–84.

Sandler, T. and Hartley, K. (1995) *The Economics of Defense*, Cambridge Surveys of Economic Literature, Cambridge: Cambridge University Press.

—— (2007) *Handbook of Defence Economics: Defence in a Globalized World*, Amsterdam: Elsevier.

Spulber, D. F. (ed.) (2002) *Famous Fables of Economics: Myths of Market Failures*, Oxford: Blackwell.

Throsby, D. and Withers, G. A. (1999) 'Individual preferences and the demand for military expenditure', *Defence and Peace Economics*, 11: 1–16.

Trajtenberg, M. (2006) 'Defence R&D in the anti-terrorist era', *Defence and Peace Economics*, 17(3): 177–200.

Williamson, O. E. (1975) *Markets and Hierarchies: Analysis and Antitrust Implications*, New York: Free Press.

2 Demand

Military products, user requirements, and the organisation of procurement

Stefan Markowski, Peter Hall and Robert Wylie

Introduction

To restate our definition at the outset of the book, procurement is another word for 'acquisition' or 'purchasing'. In this volume, procurement refers to the *activity* of purchasing defence materiel and other goods and services, including the associated ownership and use rights, needed by the National Defence Organisation (NDO) as the producer of national security.[1] In this chapter, we focus on the demand side of the market for defence materiel needed by the NDO. However, while 'procurement' normally includes the purchase of labour services performed by contractors, it does not relate to recruiting and employing (NDO) employees. Thus, we are only concerned with those inputs to Defence capability formation that are sourced from Industry, in country and abroad.

In most countries, defence procurement accounts for a significant proportion of all defence spending. In 2005, the 24 member states of the European Defence Agency (the European Union-at-25 less Denmark) spent on defence Euro193 billion (in current prices and at current exchange rates) while the USA spent €406 billion.[2] The burden of defence for the EDA member states was 1.8 per cent of their combined GDP and in the US it was 4 per cent (EDA, 2006). In 2005, EDA-EU members spent about 14 per cent of their combined defence budgets on weapons procurement with smaller arms producing nations spending proportionately larger shares of their defence budgets on arms acquisition (Sweden 27 per cent, Spain 21 per cent, The Netherlands 16 per cent) than the largest (arms producing) EDA members: the UK 15 per cent, France 13 per cent, Germany 11 per cent and Italy eight per cent (ibid.). Nearly half of the EU spending on the procurement of defence equipment was accounted for by the UK and France, the two largest European arms producers: France procured equipment to the value of €5.6 billion (at current prices and exchange rates), or 21 per cent of the EDA total procurement spending, and the UK spent €6.7 billion (25 per cent). But the defence procurement budgets of several other EDA member states were also quite large: Germany €3.4 billion, Italy 2.1 billion, Spain 2.2 billion, Greece 1.4 billion, Sweden 1.2 billion, and The Netherlands 1.2 billion (ibid.). Even a smallish country such as Finland spent over half a billion Euro on equipment acquisition and a larger but relatively impoverished ex-Communist Poland over €0.6 billion. This spending on defence equipment excludes the cost of equipment use and sustainment.[3] In 2005, EDA member countries spent an additional €40 billion on operations and maintenance (nearly 21 per cent of total defence expenditure), including the procurement of spare parts and consumables. In addition, in 2005, EDA members spent €9 billion on research and development (R&D). Non-European countries in our sample of smaller military powers (i.e., Australia, Canada, Israel and Singapore) are also spending a significant proportion of their defence budgets on equipment procurement, sustainment and defence-related research and development (see Chapters 6–9).

In comparison, the USA – at the very top of the defence expenditure scale – spent €77.6 billion on equipment procurement in 2005 (19 per cent of US total defence expenditure and nearly three times the amount spent by EDA member countries). The USA spent a further €53.2 billion on defence R&D (13 per cent of the US total defence spending and nearly six times the amount spent by EDA members) (ibid.). Also, in 2005, the US average capital/soldier ratio (spending on equipment procurement and R&D investment per soldier) was five times that of the EDA nations' average. The US spending on operations and maintenance was an additional €159 billion, nearly 39 per cent of its total defence expenditure and nearly four times the combined EDA members' spending under this heading (ibid.).

For the foreseeable future the USA is likely to lead the trend for advanced countries to invest in ever more capital- and technology-intensive military capabilities. Other advanced countries which share the US preference for labour-saving (and casualty limiting) warfighting technologies will follow with a lag, noting that no other country can at present match US total military spending, and only a handful can afford to keep up with its spending per soldier.[4]

As the above EDA statistics indicate, equipment procurement consumes significant resources in most developed economies but absorbs a larger proportion of resources allocated to defence by the smaller military powers considered in this volume. To analyse the procurement function in Defence, we first consider a number of concepts that are frequently referred to in the literature, and in Parts II and III of this volume, but which often lack clarity and precision. We begin by investigating what differentiates NDO acquisitions from those of other organisations; particularly in terms of specificity, scope, volumes (scale) and timeliness of Defence materiel requirements. We then consider the nature of ownership and use rights, such as intellectual property (IP), that Defence must acquire to be able to generate in-country military capabilities and deploy them when and as needed.

In our stylised representation of defence production (see Figure 1.1 in Chapter 1), only the NDO is designated by the government to form, sustain and, if need be, deploy military capabilities and, as such, has a national monopoly of military capability. To form these capabilities, Defence must acquire many defence-specific goods and services which we describe broadly as *defence materiel*. Military materiel is unique to the production of defence. A key task of this chapter is to ascertain the extent to which the specific characteristics of defence materiel – for example, lethality or technological complexity – result in defence procurement deals that are different from their civilian counterparts.

To this end, the analysis in the section 'Military goods and services' shows in terms of *what* is procured as opposed to *why* it is needed, *how* it is to be transacted, and *who* is to manage the acquisition process. (The 'why' of defence procurement was addressed in the previous chapter, the 'how' is considered in Chapter 4 and the 'who' is discussed later in this chapter.)

In addition to deciding what to procure, the NDO must also determine *how much* to acquire. This is important because even small buyers can increase their market leverage by widening the scope of the deal, i.e., by combining, where possible, what otherwise would have been separate acquisitions into a single larger purchase to increase the size of the deal and, thus, their bargaining power vis-à-vis suppliers. Buyers can take advantage of *quantity discounts* offered by sellers when they consolidate their requirements into larger deals. Also, it is costly to arrange transactions (i.e., deals, contracts and relationships with suppliers) and many of these *transaction costs* are 'lumpy', that is, they must be incurred irrespective of the size of the deal. Thus, the transaction cost per item purchased may decline with the increased scale and scope of the deal. It pays to consolidate requirements to reduce the transaction cost per item purchased. The NDO must therefore decide whether it is desirable to arrange separate deals/transactions for each product it wishes to purchase, or whether it is preferable to combine two or more products into a single deal, i.e., to take advantage of agglomeration economies in procurement (bulk buying efficiencies), which may combine quantity discounts and reduced transaction cost per item bought. For smaller countries in particular this is a non-trivial issue as the fragmentation-consolidation of demand is usually a matter of (policy) choice. This is discussed in the section 'Scale and scope of requirements'.

Some defence materiel, such as platforms, stay in service for decades, being modified and adapted to meet new user demands. Other materiel, e.g., software or the perishable components of munitions may have relatively short life spans. The expected life span of a new capability and provisions made for its support and modification over time will shape the content of the deal and the nature of the procurement contract: as the system becomes more durable, the acquisition deal gets more complex and this poses many problems for contract design, implementation and the relationship between the parties.[5] The durability of military equipment presents small military powers with many dilemmas which we explore in the section 'Timeframe'.

In the next section, 'Property rights', we consider ownership and use rights as key components of the procurement deal. While this aspect of the deal is often overlooked in the procurement literature, it is particularly important for small countries buying technologically complex military systems from larger powers while simultaneously wishing to retain the ability to make sovereign decisions about the use of their military capabilities so acquired. In addition, *uncertainty* about the nature of the deal and the subsequent behaviour of the parties often render procurement contracts incomplete. The degree of contractual incompleteness varies depending on the nature of the deal, the characteristics and attitudes of the parties, the verifiability of the terms of the deal, the parties' behaviour during the procurement process, and the legal system that is used to frame and enforce the contract.

These contractual challenges tend to be associated with the development of state-of-the-art weapons systems by superpowers where *ex ante* commitments to specific deliverables (outputs), delivery tasks, schedules and costs are unrealistic. But they are equally important when small countries seek to acquire commercial-off-the-shelf (COTS) and military-off-the-shelf (MOTS) products but also seek in-country adaptations and modifications to meet idiosyncratic local specifications, particularly when local suppliers have little experience in producing such 'tailored' systems.

This analysis of the differentiating characteristics of products procured by NDOs prepares the way for the section entitled 'Procurement function', in which we analyse how the NDO goes about buying all the goods and services needed for the formation of national defence capabilities, their maintenance at the required level of readiness and sustainment when deployed to produce military responses required by government. The efficient management of the procurement function also includes decisions about the scale and scope of transactions to take advantage of bulk buying advantages in purchasing.

The procurement function requires an organisational framework. In the previous chapter we referred to the Defence Procurement Agency (DPA) as an organisational element of Defence that orchestrated and undertook all procurement activities of the NDO. For example, the centralisation of procurement activities within a single organisational element allows Defence to take advantage of bulk buying opportunities and to reduce the overall transaction cost (and the cost of arranging acquisitions per item bought). In the final part of this chapter, 'Procurement organisation', we examine the organisational structure of procurement, including deciding whether to fragment the procurement activity by devolving it to Service operators (customers), or whether to centralise all procurement activities in a specialised, all-Defence Procurement Agency (e.g., as in Australia or The Netherlands). And, if a single DPA-style agency is to be used, should it be a part of the organisational structure of the NDO, or an organisationally-related but detached agency, such as the Australian Defence Materiel Organisation? Or, as in Canada, an all-of-government agency responsible for all government procurement, including Defence, at federal and provincial levels? Finally, this section explores the choices associated with organisational integration or separation of capital acquisitions and through-life sustaining of defence systems.

Military goods and services

In this section we discuss how the lethality and technical complexity of weapon systems affect procurement. We distinguish between the procurement of such systems and of the platforms enabling their operation, noting that for small countries procurement options include MOTS and COTS solutions to requirements. Finally, we distinguish between acquisition and sustaining elements of the procurement function.

Lethality

To differentiate defence materiel from civilian good and services, these products are often referred to as 'weapons systems'. This emphasises the *lethality* of military materiel as, ultimately, they are acquired to form combat-related capabilities. The demand by contemporary states for an ever increasing spectrum of military options, including for the non-lethal application of force, has, however, broadened the concept of 'weapons system' to include, at the one extreme, the highly lethal weapons of mass destruction (WMDs) and, at the other, less-than-lethal equipment (such as stun grenades or rubber bullets). In between these two extremes, there are small arms, such as assault rifles, handguns and grenades, and complex military equipment, e.g., knowledge-intensive fighter aircraft and command and control networks.

The NDO may also seek to purchase civil and military *services*, such as those provided by leased military aircraft and equipment maintenance sourced from contractors. It also draws on a wide range of 'dual technology' products, which can be used by either civil or military operators (e.g., telecommunications equipment, computers, 'civil-line' transport equipment), as well as simple and elaborate civilian products (e.g., consumables, such as pencils and paper, and capital goods, such as airliners and super-fast computers). However, while defence materiel are all those products that are acquired by NDOs to form and sustain military capabilities, it is the lethality (or near-lethality) of weapons systems that makes them distinct from goods and services purchased by most civilian government agencies and commercial enterprise. This is still the case when some of the NDO's combat-specific functions are contracted out to the commercial enterprise.

In procurement terms, the association of weapon systems with state-sanctioned violence, up to and including the application of lethal force means that the nature and scale of public sector involvement in the market for such items have no parallel in the normal commercial world.

Technical complexity

Other attributes of military materiel (or weapons systems) that have been noted in the literature are their *technical complexity* and *durability*. For example, Ergas and Menezes describe a weapons system as:

a composite of equipment employed as an entity to accomplish a military mission (such as destroying enemy installations, identifying hostile aircraft, protecting advancing infantry or surveilling territory) ... Complex weapons system are characterised by the substantial technical difficulties that are involved in their conception, development and production. These difficulties arise mainly from three sources ... Firstly, bringing each system into operation involves a large number of distinct technical problems, associated with the large number of subsystems each such system involves. Simply because of the sheer number of separate technical issues involved, the probability of encountering substantial problems in at least some aspects of the system must be high. Secondly, the difficulties involved in solving each such problem are greatly complicated by the inter-dependence between technical issues, as the subsystems need to interwork. Finally, further constraints on system design and redesign arise from the need for reliability under highly challenging conditions.

(Ergas and Menezes, 2004: 247–8)

Prominent examples of technically complex weapons systems include nuclear-powered aircraft carriers and submarines, intercontinental missiles armed with nuclear warheads, supersonic fighter and strike aircraft, stealth bombers, AWACS and global communications networks. Typically, they are highly automated systems using advanced IT, computer-enabled technologies and secure telecommunications. They tend to be labour-saving, to reduce the human footprint in the battlefield, and highly capital- and knowledge-intensive. And, increasingly, they are combined into complex networks of *inter-operative* weapons systems coordinated by equally complex network-enabled command and control systems. This presents further technological challenges when these already highly complex systems are further integrated into the even more complex *systems of systems* (US DoD, 2003; UK MoD, 2006). The competition for military advantage often results in a level of technical complexity that stretches the design and manufacturing capabilities of producers and the absorptive capacity of users.

At the extreme of technological sophistication stand the US network-enabled battlespace technologies, which allow the USA to project power anywhere in the world using rapid deployment platforms and lethal and precise engagement technologies integrated by highly centralised (network-centric) battlespace management systems. In future, these technologies will grow even more complex to:

- further reduce the human footprint in the battlefield through the use of robotics and unmanned equipment;
- improve surveillance capability through better sensors and data processing facilities;
- make use of space-based communications relays;
- provide shields against incoming missiles;

- enhance the precision and lethality of weapons systems;
- improve the coordination between different component of battlespace networks to increase their effectiveness;
- reduce the size of equipment through miniaturisation.

(US DoD, 2003; UK MoD, 2006)

But neither technical complexity nor system longevity are unique to weapons systems. Many civilian goods have similar characteristics. Large urban developments, from medieval cathedrals to twentieth-century new towns, and large civil infrastructure projects may take decades to plan and build and remain in use for centuries. Nuclear power stations and large telecommunications networks are technically complex and their life spans are similar to those of major weapons systems. Similarly, large cruise liners and civil space projects match their military counterparts in complexity and durability. Increasingly, civil industries are seen as producers or buyers of complex product systems (CoPS), which are:

> high-value, engineering- and software-intensive products, systems, networks and constructs, which are produced either as one-offs or in small batches, by a network of firms typically operating with some form of project organisation. CoPS typically comprise a large number of components and subsystems, which may be complex in their own right, and are often interrelated. Examples of CoPS include jet aircraft, air traffic control systems, telecommunications networks, intelligent buildings and flight simulators.
>
> (Hardstone, 2004: 173)

As in military applications, CoPS are increasingly important as 'carriers' of generic technological innovation as the latter involves digitisation, computerisation and automation of productive activities and has

> the capacity to transform the economic, social and technical landscape of producers, operators and users alike, across a range of mature industries. Taken singly, such developments can and do produce a steady flow of incremental innovations resulting in products that deliver to users lower input costs and higher, more varied outputs of better quality at greater speed. However, once a particular constraint such as interfacing problems begin to appear soluble, and initial integration issues have been addressed, a critical mass may be achieved, which opens the door to innovations that are 'radical' in many senses – technology-changing, product architecture-changing and market-changing.
>
> (ibid.: 274)

What gives the weapons systems their reputation for complexity and longevity is the strong military preference for capital- and knowledge-intensive combat technologies. As military budgets increase, NDOs show stronger preference for capital- and technology-intensive weapons systems to seek battlefield advantage through superior intelligence (knowledge edge) and the application of technology-based force multipliers. Such comments have often been made in the arms race literature (e.g., Brito and Intriligator, 1995) but they appear to have a broader significance. Technological rivalry between potential adversaries appears to permeate the process of weapons systems acquisitions and both rich and poor nations tend to invest in technologies that stretch their budgets and their absorptive capacity. For many nation-states, strategic ambiguity – particularly post-Cold War – has rendered simple force-on-force comparisons increasingly anachronistic. In these circumstances, military procurers are likely to face increasing pressure from military and political interests arguing that 'Our war fighters must have the best.'[6] Designing institutions – organisations and processes – to manage such pressures, particularly in the face of other socio-economic constraints, has thus been a major challenge for the small countries discussed in this volume.

Technical complexity is in one sense also a relative concept. Depending on a country's capacity to develop, produce and absorb a particular technology, a system 'complex' in the eyes of one nation may not be complex to another. Poor and technologically underdeveloped countries often insist on the local production (and sometimes design) of weapons systems. What appears to be a simple product from the perspective of a highly industrialised economy (e.g., an assault rifle) may stretch to the limit the technical capabilities of a nation with limited industrial experience. At the other end of the spectrum, the USA strives to maintain its global military superiority by developing the world's most complex and technologically sophisticated weapons systems, from nuclear submarines and aircraft carriers, to global battlefield management systems, to space-based weapons and other 'star-war' technologies (US DoD, 2003). Similar preferences for technical complexity and sophistication appear to be shared by the military in the sample of countries of interest to us in this volume.[7] In particular, Australia, Canada, Israel, Sweden and Singapore have sought to acquire the 'very best' they can afford and, often, produce in-country (see Part II of this volume). Among this group of countries, Israel regards the technology-based force multiplier as strictly necessary for its national survival (see Chapter 8). And Singapore, given its small population and territory, also views the technology-based force multiplier as very important (see Chapter 9). Other countries in our sample appear to feel less directly threatened and permit themselves a wider choice of options to balance the capital–labour–technology mix in the formation of national defence capabilities. Most countries in our sample of small countries have also tried to justify the technical complexity of their military acquisitions as a potential source of technological spill-ins into the civilian sector.

As the technological sophistication of weapons systems increases, their unit costs also increase, usually at a faster rate than military budgets. This 'capability/performance pull' or 'technology imperative' (Gansler, 1989: 145) has been a major factor contributing to the observed fast increase in equipment prices. For example, unit prices (per aircraft type) for a sample of 52 US tactical aircraft (types) introduced into service between 1950 and 1982, rose at a compound (annual) rate of 7.6 per cent per year, of which 6.1 per cent was attributed to increased technological sophistication and capability of successful aircraft (Hildebrandt and Sze, 1986: 35). The 'technology imperative' draws a large proportion of defence budgets into publicly-funded (high end) R&D and induces industry to respond by investing its own complementary resources in technology development and adaptation. This in turn increases the unit cost of production as, *ceteris paribus*, equipment makers find it harder to capture volume-related cost efficiencies (see Chapter 3). However, as unit costs of equipment increase faster than procurement budgets, states have typically responded to these pressures by buying less.[8] For example,

> in the 1950s Australia operated more than 500 fighter and bomber aircraft, by the sixties this had dropped to around 300, and by the seventies to around 150. By the eighties and nineties, the force had shrunk to a little over 100 aircraft.
>
> (ASPI, 2004: 20)

Import substitution (local content requirements) compounds the problem of rising production costs as many small countries source a large proportion of their materiel requirements locally rather than from world lowest-cost suppliers. This leads to a fragmentation of demand and, as we argue in the following chapter, the fragmentation of global industry structure. This fragmentation of national demands is exacerbated by a tendency to 'customise' and tailor acquisitions to 'unique' national requirements. As a result, the potential benefits of buying MOTS and COTS products are sacrificed and, in addition, ambitious local content targets and customisation demands increase the *relative complexity* of military requirements. This is because orders are now directed to less competitive, and occasionally technologically challenged, local suppliers and, as orders are small and infrequent, there are limited opportunities for retaining hard-learned technological know-how over time to maintain the competitiveness of local suppliers. (For an in-depth discussion of technological challenges posed by import substitution, see the case study of the over-the-horizon-radar network in Australia in Chapter 14.)

The observed preference for technologically complex products should not be confused with their battlefield effectiveness. Often technically simple products are successful against the state-the-art technologies when those who use them have a good understanding of relative strengths and weaknesses of each technology.[9] As we noted in the previous chapter, the value (or effectiveness) of an increment of military capability only becomes apparent when it is used in anger against a real adversary. As the NDO lacks the complete foreknowledge of true strategies and tactics which could be applied by its potential adversaries, it can only acquire all relevant experience when a military engagement actually occurs. In this respect, many technically complex weapons systems acquired in peacetime in anticipation of particular battlefield engagements can best be described as 'inexperience products' – it is not possible to test their true battlefield effectiveness in peacetime. Thus, when states procure weapons with a view to prevailing in future military contests with adversaries who consciously seek to thwart their intent, the use of the weapons so procured is characterised by informational asymmetries and moral hazards which have no counterpart in civilian production for commercial purposes.[10]

Platforms

Traditionally, weapons systems have been *platform-enabled* with munitions and target acquisition equipment mounted on vehicles, ships and aircraft. The 'platform' is usually envisaged as the long-lived 'integrating' component of a weapons system, that is, as a durable vehicle on which all other sub-systems are mounted and on which they depend for their effective functioning. Thus, for example, the hull and associated machinery of a warship or the airframe and associated propulsion system of a fighter aircraft tend to be referred to as platforms that can be modernised and adapted over time to carry more technologically dynamic weapons and other sub-systems which may have much shorter service lives but which determine the military competitiveness of the overall capability. Similarly, telecommunications network hardware and computers are seen as platforms that enable various software applications to be used. Thus, we have come to think of weapons systems as *platform-related product groups* such as missiles, bomber and fighter aircraft, helicopters, surface ships and submarines, and land vehicles. Further, industry capabilities have been built around product groups so their producers have usually been categorised as shipbuilders, aircraft makers, or heavy armour manufacturers (see the following chapter). However, we can also generalise and refer to 'platform systems', that is, systems that may be progressively adapted and modified over time to facilitate the use of specific lower-level 'applications' of particular value to a specific customer.

Unlike the long-lived platforms, many of these platform-enabled sub-systems or applications are relatively short-lived capability elements that require continuous modification, enhancement or replacement to keep them militarily competitive and technologically compatible with related systems in the inventory. Thus, the technical complexity of platform-enabled weapons systems is determined in part by the complexity of the platform and all the sub-systems that are mounted on or enabled by it and, in part, by the complexity of the overall system integration task. Increasingly, system integration is seen as the driver of technical complexity of weapons systems: they become network-centric rather than platform-enabled (US DoD, 2003; UK MoD, 2006). The shift in the focus of military competition in advanced countries away from platforms toward network-enabled capabilities has important implications for procurement options and for the management of the associated supply chains.

Developmental systems, MOTS and COTS

The competition for military advantage leads nations to procure complex materiel which is at the limits of both their capacity to absorb and the capacity of suppliers (either domestic or foreign) to produce at the prevailing state of knowledge. Such demanding acquisition is often associated with the USA and, increasingly, with smaller but technologically ambitious powers, such as the Russian Federation, France, the United Kingdom and increasingly China and India. In the sample of smaller countries represented in this volume, this may also be said about Sweden (see Chapter 11), and Israel (Chapter 8), both of which have relied on the in-country development of complex military technologies.

Most small countries, however, can choose between the in-country development of complex military technologies and importing technologically sophisticated but already mature products as MOTS or COTS products. This enables smaller countries to avoid much of the technical risk encountered by the leading technology innovators. Mature MOTS and COTS system can be imported from larger powers, often at marginal cost, and if need be adapted to local requirements. Similarly, when a weapons system requires significant R&D and technology innovation, it may be preferable to enter into international collaborative arrangements with other countries to share the large overhead costs associated with further development.

System sustainment

The *preparedness* of any given weapon system is a function of its readiness for operational deployment and of the time for which it can sustain such operations. Given the technical complexity, knowledge-intensity and durability of weapons systems, their preparedness depends on the availability of consumables and spare parts, software upgrades, training, regular maintenance, and periodic modification. Support services are often included in the specification of weapons systems, so that the 'system' is defined broadly to include the primary equipment, spare parts and consumables and the associated support services. The procurement of goods and services needed for the preparedness of military capabilities may occur together with or separately from the procurement of capital items. As we showed earlier, expenditure on 'operations and preparedness' – what we have called *sustainment* – is much larger than expenditure on 'procurement' (capital acquisitions). However, the 'preparedness' expenditure *per se*, should be distinguished from the cost of 'operations'. In Australia, for example, Defence expenditure on 'preparedness' (e.g., logistic support services, spares and consumables) provided by external suppliers in 2007–08 was about the same as the cost of (capital) 'acquisitions', each accounting for about Aus$4 billion at 2008–09 prices and exchange rates. However, while nearly 80 per cent of 'preparedness' was sourced from in-country suppliers, the local content of 'acquisitions' was about 40 per cent.[11]

The Australian figures are indicative of broader procurement expenditure on preparedness. There is clearly more scope for in-country sourcing of preparedness services as they tend to be provided locally usually in close proximity to the location of physical military assets. Examples include services associated with ship docking (maintenance) cycles, aircraft and vehicle maintenance services and battle damage repair. Small countries often insist on in-country production of some spare parts and consumables to maintain their operational sovereignty; the local production of munitions is classic example of investment in such 'strategic' preparedness capability. Also, as many components of complex weapons systems are standard civilian products (e.g., electronic components, vehicle parts), they can also be sourced from in-country commercial suppliers.

The case for in-country production of military equipment has often been made on the grounds that the learning experience acquired during the production phase could subsequently be used to support through-life support of equipment. Thus, cost premia incurred during the in-country production phase are partially or wholly offset by increased cost-effectiveness of subsequent sustainment support. As the case study of Australian shipbuilding (Chapter 13) demonstrates, this synergy between construction and sustainment phases is often overestimated in the case of platforms, where builders tend to be different business entities from maintenance contractors and there are limited opportunities for building skills to migrate to through-life support activities. However, as systems become more network-centric and knowledge-intensive, there are increased opportunities for system integration and adaptation skills acquired during the construction phase to migrate to provide through life support (see Chapter 13). The need to exploit these opportunities and to harvest the learning involved is becoming an increasingly important consideration in the design of procurement institutions, particularly in small countries.

Scale and scope of requirements

There are two dimensions of acquisition size: *scale* and *scope*. How the NDO manages the scale and scope of requirements can significantly affect the achievement of wider NDO/government policy objectives. As this chapter is focused on the demand side of the procurement deal, in what follows we consider the scale and scope of the procurement deal and the associated procurement efficiencies from the NDO/customer perspective. Chapter 3 explores economies of scale and scope in production.

Scope comprehends the acquisition, the *product range of the deal*, and the associated bundles of property rights that determine what can be done with each of these products once they are acquired. The *scale* of deal refers to the volume of the product that comprises the deal. But as most deals involve the acquisition of more than one product, how is the scale of the deal to be measured? We begin with the discussion of scale in the context of a simple acquisition that involves the purchase of single homogeneous product only. This is the conventional representation of 'scale' and we are particularly interested in scale-related benefits for the buyer, e.g., economies of bulk buying. As we noted earlier, two types of benefits are associated with bulk buying. First, the transaction cost per item purchased may decline as smaller deals are consolidated into larger ones. That is, it may cost the buyer just as much to arrange a large transaction as a small one. This is particularly important in defence procurement where the complexity of products requires large pre-acquisition investments in requirements scoping and specification. The acquisition approval process is also costly as larger procurements tend to be approved at very high levels of Defence and/or Government. These pre-procurement (overhead) costs often run into million of dollars. Second, sellers often offer quantity discounts as their unit production costs decline with the volume of items produced (see Chapter 3). However, to take advantage of quantity discounts, the buyer must consolidate its requirements into larger deals. It may be advantageous to buy larger quantities less frequently than small quantities often (but there are other offsetting costs that must also be taken into account as holding large inventories is also costly).

Next, we consider the scope of more complex transactions where two or more products are acquired under a single deal, creating potential for scope-related efficiencies. That is, it may be advantageous to 'package' into a single deal a number of different products as well as a number of identical items. Finally, we combine the considerations of scope and scale to focus on how a small nation can increase the size of the procurement deal to take advantage of scale-related efficiencies by widening the scope of the acquisition (agglomeration economies).

Scale

Consider Figure 2.1, where the volume/quantity of product X, the *scale of the acquisition* (deal), is represented by the horizontal axis and the unit cost of the product to the buyer is represented by the vertical axis. We define 'scale' simply as the number of items that make up the deal. In Figure 2.1, the unit cost is shown to decline (monotonically) with scale so that there are cost-related efficiencies as the scale of the deal increases: economies of bulk buying. This declining unit cost may be explained by the 'lumpiness' of acquisition costs, i.e., there may be some overhead (transaction) costs that must be incurred regardless of how many items are purchased and, thus, the transaction cost per item purchased declines.

Another source of bulk buying efficiencies is associated with quantity discounts offered by sellers: the unit price of an item decreases as the volume purchased increases. However, when quantity discounts are offered by sellers, the unit price does not decrease smoothly along a negative exponential curve shown in Figure 2.1 but, instead, it decreases stepwise with 'price breaks' offered when increased quantities of products are purchased. This is shown in Figure 2.2. For quantities up to and including X_1 the relevant price is P_3, for quantities greater than and including X_2 the price declines to P_2, and so on. X_1, X_2 and X_3 represent price breaks at which a particular price/quantity discount, P_1, P_2 or P_3, applies.

Why is scale important? Small-scale buyers lack bargaining power and are unlikely to benefit from volume-related efficiencies, such as price discounts associated with bulk buying. There is often a minimum volume that must be acquired to achieve scale-related cost efficiencies. We refer to this threshold scale as the *minimum efficient scale of the deal*. Small countries may not be able to achieve minimum efficient scale of acquisition when they try to source their defence materiel in-country, and they may also lack the market leverage

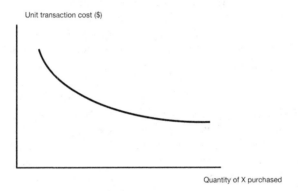

Figure 2.1 Economies of scale in procurement

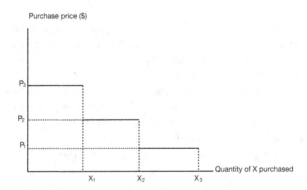

Figure 2.2 Quantity discounts in procurement

associated with large-scale acquisitions when they import such products from overseas.

However, a country may avail itself of quantity discounts associated with larger-scale deals even if the scale of its requirements is quite modest. Fortuitous market circumstances may allow a small buyer to strike a deal at the marginal cost of production. For example, when a producer is nearing the completion of a large order for another buyer and keen on further business to keep its production line busy, it may be possible for a buyer to negotiate a small deal at the marginal cost of production, that is, the producer may sell the product at a relatively low price to keep the production line open.

Another opportunity to buy at prices offered to larger purchasers of defence materiel is provided by the US programme of foreign military sales (FMS). In this case, US military equipment is sold to allies under government-to-government arrangements at prices normally paid by the US Service customers (Kausal and Markowski, 2000, Chap. 10). Here, a small country can benefit from the bulk-buying power of the US military even though its own requirement is too small to allow it to secure price discounts from the equipment manufacturer.

Similarly, there may be an incentive for small countries to club together to increase their market leverage through joint purchase of the product. If the size of the consolidated acquisition is large enough to secure bulk-buying efficiencies, it is advantageous for small countries to seek partners and form joint (procurement) ventures to increase their market power vis-à-vis suppliers. Examples of such joint acquisitions are European-style work-share contracts (see Chapters 4 and 10–12) or the Australia–New Zealand joint acquisition of ANZAC frigates (Chapter 13).

Scope

Consider now the *scope* of the acquisition. A simple measure of scope is the number of distinct products comprising the deal: its *product range*. We expect the scope of the deal to increase, when there are synergies associated with buying things jointly rather than separately. This is illustrated by Figure 2.3 where there are two products, X and Y, with the horizontal axes showing volumes of each product. The product range in this case is {X,Y}. The vertical axis shows the unit transaction cost associated with different quantities of X and Y acquired jointly or separately: the cost surface CXY. If X and Y are acquired separately, under two separate deals, we select the volume of each deal along the relevant horizontal axis and find the corresponding unit transaction cost as a point on the convex cost surface, CXY, shown in Figure 2.3. For example, if only product Y is considered, a smaller quantity of Y, say, Y_1, is associated with a unit cost, CY_1. When a larger quantity of Y is purchased, say, Y_2, the unit cost decreases slightly to CY_2. Similarly, if only product X is purchased under another deal, the X_1 quantity of X results in the unit cost of CX_1. However, when both products are purchased jointly rather than separately, say X_1 of X and Y_2 of Y, the unit transaction cost of each product purchased decreases to CX_1Y_2. In this particular case, there are scope-related cost efficiencies in procurement transactions: *economies of scope*. This is because the unit cost surface, CXY, slopes down with larger volumes of X and Y and becomes convex when the two products are acquired jointly rather than separately. If the unit cost surface CXY were drawn as a concave surface there would be diseconomies of scope and it would be pre-ferable to buy the two products separately, under two separate deals, rather than jointly (i.e., it would cost less to arrange two separate deals than a single complex deal).

In practical terms, separate transactions often incur lumpy transactions cost that do not vary either with the number of items purchased or their variety. For example, a number of different items may be tendered as a single package rather than acquired through a number of separate tenders. The tendering cost per item may be significantly lower when buyers agglomerate their diverse purchasing requirements into larger, heterogonous packages to be sourced from diversified producers or vendors. Similarly though, there are items that are too diverse to be bundled into such heterogonous packages, it may cost more to combine a requirement for a squadron of fighter aircraft and a submarine into a single deal than to arrange their purchase as two separate deals.

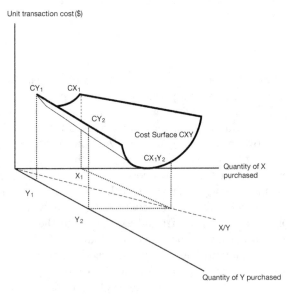

Figure 2.3 Economies of scope in procurement

Bundling of requirements

Figure 2.3 carries a profound message for small (country) buyers. If there are synergies in the acquisitions of different products, as illustrated by the convex cost surface in that figure, these products should best be *bundled* into a single acquisition.[12] In that sense, a larger deal is achieved and some cost efficiencies realised so that diseconomies of small scale acquisition of individual products are partially offset by economies of scope and the larger size of the overall deal. By widening the scope of the deal, separate requirements can be agglomerated to increase its size and this may result in agglomeration economies: the unit transaction cost declining with the overall size of the deal. In some circumstances, the buyer may also be able to increase its bargaining power and market leverage by agglomerating separate smaller demands into a single consolidated requirement. For example, when different products are supplied by the same seller, the latter may offer quantity discounts related to the size (money value) of the overall transaction.

As different items are combined into a single requirement, it is no longer possible to measure the size of the deal/acquisition in terms of a particular (homogenous) product. If a physical measure of size is to be used, then a particular combination of products comprising the deal will have to be selected. This will enable changing quantities of all products to be assigned particular unit cost values while preserving their proportions. (For a discussion of economies of scale and scopem, see Markowski and Jubb, 1989; and Jubb and Markowski, 1991.) (In Figure 2.3, this ratio measure of size is shown as a ray from the origin drawn on the horizontal product surface, X/Y, and the associated unit costs are represented by points such as CX_1Y_2 on the cost surface CXY.) However, measuring the size of acquisition in money terms may also be helpful.

The presence of scope and agglomeration economies allows small country NDOs to bundle their modest single-product requirements into larger, multi-product orders to increase their market leverage. The latter may entail enhancing their bargaining power so as to extract price concessions from producers/vendors or it may involve exploiting technological complementarities so as to create a sufficient incentive for suppliers to establish local industrial capacity. Similarly, there is scope for small countries to club together to combine their synergistic, albeit heterogeneous, requirements into larger deals to increase their market leverage. By insisting on local content and customisation of the product in an effort to advance other non-procurement policy objectives, small buyers fragment their demands and, to that extent, erode their capacity to extract price or other concessions from international vendors. More generally, small countries face important policy choices in trading off, on one hand, the advantage of scope-based demand consolidation for, on the other hand, the operational or political advantage of higher levels of local content – an issue we shall revisit in Chapters 3 and 5.

At the other extreme, the development of the Joint Strike Fighter (JSF) by the US-led consortium of military buyers illustrates how economies of bulk buying can be achieved through the standardisation and bundling of different Service and national requirements. That is, the project aims to maximise the commonality of requirements while allowing some product differentiation to suit particular customer needs. This complex bundling arrangement combined with limited product customisation is outlined in Box 2.1.

As we observed earlier, whether a small country takes advantage of scope-based demand consolidation is a matter of choice. There are potential advantages in opportunistic sourcing of requirements and/or in clubbing together to achieve economies of scale and scope. In practice though, the opposite is most likely the case. Small industrialised nations have a tendency to fragment their demands as they insist on extensive import substitution (local content) in procurement and product customisation. As a result, they divert production to inefficient local suppliers and pay price premia for small and highly idiosyncratic requirements. We shall revisit this issue in the following chapter.

Box 2.1 The Joint Strike Fighter (JSF)

The Joint Strike Fighter (JSF or F-35) is the next generation, multi-role strike fighter which combines high lethality, supportability (autonomic logistics), survivability/stealth with affordability. The single-engine, single-seat F-35 will be produced in three versions: a conventional-take-off-and-landing (CTOL) variant for the US Air Force; an aircraft-carrier version (CV) for the US Navy; and a short-take-off/vertical landing (STOVL) version for the US Marine Corps and the UK Royal Air Force and Royal Navy. The JSF is a multi-service and a multi-nation aircraft. In addition to the USA and the UK, seven other countries are also involved as partners in the F-35's system development and demonstration phase: Italy, The Netherlands, Turkey, Canada, Denmark, Norway and Australia. Israel and Singapore have also joined the JSF programme as Security Cooperation Participants. The partnership status allows each country to bid for work on a value-for-money basis and participate in the aircraft's development. To facilitate international collaboration, several agreements between the USA and foreign governments are already in place for the development phase of the programme. Lockheed Martin is the F-35 prime contractor with Northrop Grumman and BAE Systems as its principal partners in the project.

The single F-35 programme will replace different legacy aircraft. The US Navy will use the JSF in a 'first day of war', as a survivable strike fighter aircraft to complement F/A-18. The US Air Force will employ it as a multi-role aircraft, primary-air-to-ground, which will replace the F-16 and A-10 and to complement the F-22. The Marine Corps will use the STOVL variant of the aircraft to replace the AV-8B and F/A-18. In the UK, the JSF will be used as a multi-role aircraft and will replace the Sea Harrier and GR7.

To make the aircraft both highly advanced and affordable, the duplication of development and manufacturing effort is to be minimised and technology effectively leveraged. Economies of scope and scale are to be achieved through the joint acquisition of the F-35 by different Services and by several countries. The aircraft will have a 70–90 per cent commonality factor for all the variants, to reduce manufacturing, support and training costs. The overall commonality is to be achieved on the assembly line, through shared-wing platforms and a very high commonality of the avionics suite, and through common systems that enhance maintainability, supportability and interoperability of the aircraft. Component commonality across all three variants will reduce spare parts requirements and the logistics footprint. It is intended that support costs will be about half that of present-day fighters, and streamlined assembly methods will cut production time significantly. In addition to the lower capital (flyaway) cost, the F-35 is also designed to periodically integrate new technology during its entire life cycle at an affordable cost.

Source: http://www.jsf.mil./index.htm (accessed 22 November 2006)

Timeframe

Weapons systems tend to be technically complex not only because of their often highly advanced technology but also due to the durability of the military platforms and the time taken to design and produce such systems. For example, the average retirement age for US surface combat ships varies between 17 years (e.g., CGN 38 Class) and 30 years (DDG-37 Class) (Labs, 2008: Table 5). On the other hand, the effectiveness of each weapons system design tends to decline over time, often quite rapidly, as countermeasures are developed and new war-fighting technologies are advanced and diffused. Thus, a balance must be struck between those components of a weapons system that retain their technical effectiveness over time (e.g., platforms such as ships and aircraft) and those that age rapidly (e.g., software and electronics). As systems become technically obsolete relative to the new equipment fielded by potential adversaries, they must be either upgraded or replaced. Yesterday's state-of-the-art investment becomes today's 'legacy' system and, when the rate of technical change is high, new investments become legacy systems almost as soon as they enter service.

To slow down the aging of weapons systems, platforms may be designed for ease of upgrade (upgradeability) as opposed to high reliability and resistance to wear. That is, platforms need not be designed to remain unchanged and wear-resistant over time but rather for ease of radical re-building and upgrading to keep up with the rapid pace of technical change. An example of such a platform is the Joint Strike Fighter system, which is designed for inherent upgradeability (see Box 2.1).

Generally, the performance level of a particular capability tends to follow the pattern shown in Figure 2.4. Capability performance, relative to that of potential adversaries (and/or allies), increases rapidly during the early stages of system's development (development phase) and is enhanced periodically by means of upgrades and modifications during its in-service life (mature phase). A 15-year-old aircraft may not be a match for the latest design but, after several upgrades and modifications, it is likely to offer better performance than earlier versions. However, at some point in time the performance of the system begins to decline rapidly relative to that of potential adversaries (and/or allies) and further upgrades are unwarranted. We refer to this as the aging phase. The length of each phase is determined by the rate of technical change specific to this particular type of technology and the strategic context in which systems are developed and fielded. In the absence of an arms race, a new system may take a long time to be developed as technology changes and there is a reluctance to freeze the design prematurely. The acquisition becomes ever more complex when the buyer wishes the latest technological developments to be incorporated in the design. This is often referred to as *requirements creep* (Figure 2.4).

It has often been argued that, given the complexity of what is being acquired, the acquisition process itself is likely to be relatively long (see Ergas and Menezes, 2004). This too increases the complexity of the deal. But the impact of such complexity depends on national circumstances. Strategic

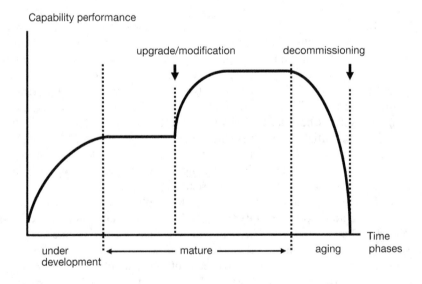

Figure 2.4 Stylised weapons system lifecycle

rivalry often takes the form of technological competition among major powers. In contrast, while strategic rivalry among smaller military powers may still generate technological competition, such powers typically have less need to develop new, technologically ambitious and risky systems. Generally, they can meet their strategic requirements at more acceptable cost by importing mature technologies from their superpower allies who have already absorbed much of the development time and cost. Many of these systems are MOTS and COTS designs that do not require radical adaptation or re-development to meet the buyer's requirements.

Procurement managers must also consider the trade-offs between, on one hand, bundling requirements at a point in time to capture scale- and scope-related efficiencies and, on the other hand, spreading them more evenly over time to incorporate the latest advances in technology or to smooth the work-load for Industry. On the demand side, it may be cost-effective in the short run to bundle small orders into larger but less frequent ones (i.e., to purchase six submarines as a single batch and replace them some 30 years later rather than split the requirement into three batches of two and order a couple of vessels every ten years). The bundling of requirements may reduce the unit cost per item providing the product design is stable over time. This often applies to platform design. However, when the pace of technological change forces frequent upgrades and adaptations, requirements bundling may no longer be advantageous. That is, scale- and scope-related cost efficiencies in system production may be more than offset by subsequent costly rebuilds and adaptations. Thus, as the tempo of technological change increases, it may be preferable to 'unbundle' lumpy demands and buy smaller quantities of increasingly more sophisticated items more frequently. Another cost trade-off to consider in this case, however, is the interoperability between different vintages of equipment. As new equipment is brought into service in small batches more frequently, operational efficiency may suffer. Costly interfaces between the 'old' and the 'new' capability increments may have to be formed and sustained over long periods of time.

There may also be supply side arguments for the 'unbundling' of lumpy demands. When orders for new materiel are large but placed rather infrequently, Industry producers may find it difficult to remain viable between successive acquisition cycles. They are also less likely to invest in new plant and machinery unless the existing production facilities are reasonably well utilised. This applies in particular to highly specialised, in-country producers who can only stay in business if the NDO is prepared to smooth its demand by spreading orders more evenly over time. But this smoothing of demand incurs costs. In the first instance, sustaining small batch production entails additional cost. Second, and more importantly, such demand smoothing entails subordinating strategic and operational priorities to the need to sustain in-country Industry capabilities. Particularly in small countries, governments must steer their way between conflicting pressures from, on the one hand, Industry lobby groups advocating ambitious local content targets and more spread-out distribution of orders and, on the other hand, military equipment users impatient with fragmented investment processes and long delivery cycles. The impact of this tension on the procurement process is a prominent feature of the country studies in Part II.

Property rights

As already indicated, a critical element of the defence procurement 'deal' is the bundle of ownership and use rights that determine what the buyer can do with the purchase. We now explore how such rights influence the relationship between the NDO and Industry and what implications they have for the design of procurement institutions.

Ownership rights and obligations

To allow the NDO to gain legal possession and make beneficial use of military materiel, the acquisition deal must also include relevant *property* or *ownership rights and obligations*. For a deal to be completed, these rights must be defined, agreed between the parties to the deal, and transferred from the seller to the buyer.[13] The same physical item becomes a different deliverable when a different bundle of property rights is attached to it. An aircraft that can be flown and maintained by the buyer NDO but with the condition that some maintenance tasks must be performed by the supplier is a different product from a physically similar aircraft which is not encumbered by such restrictions.

Property rights and obligations determine, *inter alia*, what can be done with the product after it changes hands: the duration of use/possession, mutual obligations of the parties to the deal, third party access to the product and to knowledge of how it was produced, freedom to modify and support the product over time, and the right to terminate the use/possession and destroy, sell or give away the product. Property rights include 'use rights' and 'intellectual property' (IP rights), which focus, respectively, on particular aspects of the system's use or the handling/accessibility of system-specific knowledge. There are also third party rights that impact on the bundle of rights specific to a particular procurement deal. These rights may be superior in that they may restrict what the parties to the deal can do or prescribe some form of action that the buyer and/or seller must take (e.g., US international traffic in arms regulations, discussed in Chapter 4). Two examples illustrate the point.

First, suppose that a firm in country A manufactures and supplies a weapons system to country B. Suppose that country A has also signed an international agreement restricting the availability of arms to country C. The government of country A may then impose on its domestic arms producers a requirement that any export deal they conclude is subject to a restriction prohibiting the subsequent re-export of the weapons to the embargoed nation C. Importers in country B may also be required to comply with this restriction, irrespective of the position taken by the government of B, backed by the threat that failure to comply with the requirement may jeopardise B's future prospects of importing from A. Effectively, by acquiring a weapons system produced in country A, the importer acquires an attenuated set of property rights that deprive it of the full and unencumbered ownership of the product. In our example, this restriction deprives importers in B of an opportunity to re-export the product to country C.

Second, in the early days of the semi-conductor industry, the US Department of Defense obtained a comprehensive 'license of free use' when it procured from contractors a patented product or process developed with Defence funds. This obliged suppliers to share information about their innovations with any firm that subsequently worked on a government contract or a private project supported by government funds (Stowsky, 1993). In this case, the supplier's IP rights were attenuated as it could not restrict access to its IP by third parties, although we would expect the price paid for the product to compensate the supplier for the loss of its intellectual capital.

Contractual incompleteness

Traditionally, economists had limited interest in the contracting process *per se*, as they often assumed it was possible to design and use complete (contingent claim) contracts. Thus,

> Economists' contractual benchmark is the complete contingent claim contract. 'Complete' means that it leaves no possibility to improve efficiency by an ex-post adjustment of actions. Ex-ante this is achieved by figuring out contingencies and prescribing a joint-surplus maximising action in correspondence to each of them ... but ... it is no wonder that it is a highly unrealistic depiction of real-world contracts. Sooner or later the assumption of 'completeness' had to be relaxed. Recalling this genealogy helps in understanding that 'incompleteness' is to be understood simply as 'possibility to improve efficiency ex-post' and that its main corollary is the need for governance devices in addition to the prescription of behaviour.
>
> (Furlotti, 2007: 78–9)

In reality, contracts are incomplete because the cognitive capabilities of the parties are limited, and because of differences in motivation and associated conflicts of interests, and differences in commitment to the procurement process. Negotiation and set-up costs also increase with every attempt to write a more complete contract. For many defence acquisitions this lack of contractual completeness has been of little practical importance. This is the case in, for example, the procurement of simple, mature products from well-known suppliers (e.g., simple munitions, small arms, civilian-line vehicles). In such cases both the deliverable and the delivery process are sufficiently well understood by all those concerned, all critical contingencies are foreseeable and can be delineated in a contract, and detailed performance obligations of the parties can be specified. Thus, for all practical purposes, the terms of the deal are sufficiently transparent to be articulated unambiguously in the contract, complied with and, if need be, enforced.

In other cases, however, military competition may lead NDOs to commit to the acquisition of defence materiel yet to be designed or incorporating technology yet to be fully developed and demonstrated. In such cases, the specific rights and obligations of the parties to the procurement process cannot confidently be established *ex ante* as aspects of the deliverable are, as yet, undetermined and transaction-related behavioural hazards cannot be addressed by making contracts more detailed and prescriptive. We refer to this case as the *limited contractibility of the procurement deal*.[14] This condition is often combined with informational asymmetry between the parties and imbalances in the distribution of bargaining powers between buyers and sellers. For example, the supplier is usually better positioned than the buyer to assess the likely technical challenges of new product development (see Chapter 4). In principle, this superior knowledge could be shared with the buyer for the parties to co-determine the best way of handling these challenges. However, if the supplier is keen to secure the contract, it may prefer to keep the buyer under-informed about the hazards of product development rather than risk the better-informed buyer changing its mind and drawing back from the deal.

Procurement function

The term 'procurement function' denotes processes for:

- determining and evaluating user requirements;
- identifying potential suppliers;
- developing and implementing sourcing policies;
- soliciting supply responses and selecting deliverers;
- developing appropriate arrangements for contracting suppliers and supplies;
- forging relationships with suppliers and managing the supplier base;
- taking delivery of the contracted product, assessing its quality and executing payments;
- evaluating the procurement process to ensure its continuous improvement.

As we observed in Chapter 1, the value-adding logic of the defence supply chain defines the key strategic goal of the procurement function in Defence. This is to source materiel inputs from Industry to form defence capabilities that closely align with national security objectives and organisational goals assigned to Defence by government. For major capital acquisitions, the procurement function in Defence takes the form of purchasing or materiel cycles that routinely involve of the following steps:

- reviewing the specifications of inputs required by Service 'customers' (particularly with a view to containing costs) and translating them into contractable requirements;
- market research to identify supply options;
- acting as the point of contact for suppliers;
- solicitation of supply offers, negotiation, evaluation and selection of suppliers;
- contracting;
- receipt and quality assurance of supplies;
- supply base management;
- supplier performance evaluation.

Challenges for the procurement function

The procurement function in Defence is particularly challenging, partly because of the nature of products acquired and partly because of the unique nature of new capability formation by NDOs. A fundamental challenge – particularly in the Anglophone democracies – stems from the inherently political nature of the choices involved in procurement. Procurement of major platforms and systems is highly visible and involves large opportunity costs for society in general and for competing interests within NDOs (where, say, procurement of surface combatants may require the deferral of air-borne early warning aircraft). Nor – to date – have electorates in Anglophone democracies demonstrated significant tolerance for the failure inherent in high risk/high payoff developmental projects. All this combines to make defence procurement one of the most intensely scrutinised activities that governments undertake.

Technologically ambitious defence acquisitions stretch the buyer's ability to understand the technology at the time the deal is arranged. This undermines the capacity of the buyer to negotiate ownership and use rights at the outset which it only later discovers it would have been justifiable, or useful, to put in place. Similarly, if the product is technologically innovative *per se*, or technologically challenging relative to its maker's technological capability, the seller/ producer may have a poor understanding of the deliverable at the time the deal is arranged. This undermines the capacity of the contractor to put in place protections against buyer claims that it later discovers it could justifiably have sought. That said, the seller/producer usually knows more about the product than the buyer.

The buyer may find it difficult to resist 'requirements creep', which in turn makes it difficult to freeze product specifications. Similarly, the seller may knowingly 'under-specify' the product to secure the deal. While the parties may be reluctant or unable to co-determine product specifications, they may nevertheless be keen to make binding commitments on procurement tasks, resources and outputs. That is, there is a tendency for the parties to accept ambiguous product/performance specifications and to 'mitigate' this ambiguity with over-specified delivery processes. This asymmetry undermines the process of establishing the most helpful balance of specific and residual rights in defence procurement contracts.

NDOs are typically responsible for the formation of military capabilities required by governments and are constrained in their ability to switch suppliers or terminate procurement contracts. Hence they tend to bear most of the risks inherent in the procurement of complex developmental and customised products. Given the governments' ability to pool such risks and to spread their costs over the entire population of taxpayers, governments (NDOs as their agents) are best placed to absorb these risks (Arrow and Lind, 1970). However, there is tendency for NDOs to shift residual rights to prime contractors or to share them with these suppliers under some rather ambiguous arrangements (e.g., partnering). Thus, there is a tendency to assign residual rights in acquisitions to parties that are not best suited to handle them.

A third party may impose restrictions on the transferability of property rights even when they can be effectively specified. For example, at the time of writing, countries such as Australia and the UK are concerned about restrictions imposed by the US government on access to US technology under US defence trade controls ITAR (Trope and Witt, 2007). In this case, even those rights that could have been made specific in the contract could not be assigned by the seller to the buyer when the selling country's government (a superior third party) restricts their transferability.

In many cases, especially those involving imports, non-compliant actions under the deal may be difficult to verify. Domestic sourcing of supplies allows the NDO to seek legal redress in the event of contractual failure by the supplier, but is often difficult to pursue when technical performance specifications are vaguely defined under the deal and poorly described in the contract. Importing adds a further complication as it may require the use of third party legal jurisdiction (e.g., claims for damages must be sought in a court of law of a previously specified country and at a designated location). More generally, the retention of residual rights by the buyer may be of little help if the buyer (small country NDO) has no means of influencing the behaviour of the seller (a large multinational supplier). On the other hand, by vesting all residual rights in the seller, the buyer may become a passive payer for whatever product the seller chooses to deliver.

In Defence and other public agencies, the procurement function has a further dimension of complexity compared with that in commercial organisations since governments tend to use public sector procurement to pursue broader socio-economic objectives. Thus, defence materiel may be purchased to create jobs in designated Industry sectors or to divert defence expenditure to particular regions. As we noted in the previous chapter, in democracies, governments are elected to pursue a wide range of objectives and the interests of national security provision may be combined with sectoral or regional objectives (for an illustration, see the discussion of Australian naval shipbuilding in Chapter 13 and the Canadian system of all-government procurement in Chapter 7).

A further challenge concerns the alignment of the domestic defence procurement function with those of other countries. That is, governments may negotiate international, collaborative procurement deals involving two or more participating nations. For example, to increase the scale of production and reduce costs, Western European countries have long been involved in such bi- and multi-lateral collaborative *juste retour* (work-share) arrangements (see Chapter 4 in this volume, and Markowski and Wylie, 2007: 44–5). These are normally set up on a government-to-government basis, with costs and workload distributed pro rata between project participants. Examples of such projects include: the Tornado combat aircraft (the UK, Germany, and Italy) and the Eurofighter Typhoon (the UK, Germany, Italy, and Spain). These forms of acquisition have been particularly attractive for governments that could secure a leading role in a project for their national champion and, not surprisingly, 'many of these programmes have been notoriously inefficient, with countries protecting their national economic interests and compromises resulting in high cost solutions' (ibid.: 45). Non-European examples of collaborative procurement project include the Australian-New Zealand ANZAC frigate project (see Chapter 13) and the US-led Joint Strike Fighter project (see Box 2.1). Negotiating a complex defence acquisition between a single buyer and a single seller is difficult at best of times. Such negotiations become much more complex when several buyers and sellers have to be coordinated to orchestrate a single acquisition deal. The assignment of specific and residual rights in such multifaceted procurement deals is particularly challenging and work-share programmes have been notoriously complex and inefficient.[15] We shall return to these issues in Chapter 4.

Procurement organisation

The theory of organisational design[16] suggests that specialisation in procurement can enhance efficiency through:

- agglomerating purchasing activities into cohesive and synergistic activity groupings to harness economies of scale and scope;
- matching people to tasks for which they are best fitted to maximise their operational effectiveness;
- giving staff opportunities to learn formally and on the job (learning by doing) about the tasks to which they have been allocated;
- retaining of procurement-specific know-how over time to facilitate continuous improvement in new product acquisition.

At a more specific level, specialised procurement activities are often grouped into:

- acquisition-focused research and intelligence;
- acquisition of new major and minor capital items;

- operational and through-life support for existing/legacy system, including spare parts provisioning, acquisition of consumables, and sourcing of services;
- management and administrative support.

Organisational design theory also sheds light on how procurement might best be organised to support the main goals of the organisation (Monczka *et al.*, 2005: 137). The procurement function plays a key role in Defence as the acquisition of military materiel provides a fundamental input to new capability formation and its sustainment over time. And, when the tempo of military activities accelerates, the procurement function may have to support a surge in organisational activity by fast tracking new equipment acquisitions, providing spare parts and consumables, and engaging and managing suppliers of services, including those engaged in areas of operation. Given the importance of the procurement function within the NDO, organisation elements involved in defence procurement tend to have a relatively high status and influence. In Australia, for example, the head of the Australian DPA (CEO DMO – see Chapter 6) is the highest paid public servant in country.

Centralisation of procurement function

The organisation of procurement within the broader organisational structure of Defence varies from country to country, depending on:

- the nature of defence materiel purchased (e.g., MOTS/COTS or customised products);
- where this materiel is sourced (e.g., global suppliers, local contractors, government armouries and shipyards);
- how it is sourced (e.g., through competitive tenders or sole source arrangements);
- the importance and maturity of local Industry as a source of supplies;
- the pace of technological change;
- the scope of the procurement function (i.e., the extent to which defence procurement is used by government to achieve broader economic objectives).

In most countries discussed in this volume, the procurement function is largely consolidated within a specialised defence procurement organisational element located within the NDO. We referred earlier to this organisational structure as the Defence Procurement Agency (DPA). In this centralised framework, the DPA acts as a go-between in-house 'customers' and 'owners' of military capabilities, mostly Services, and Industry suppliers. The agency is normally responsible for mediating all major capital acquisitions and bulk buying minor items and support services. As such, it is also accountable for the provision of expert advice to Government which is ultimately responsible to taxpayers. Other organisational elements of the NDO may be allowed to buy minor items directly, usually by following central procurement guidelines and subject to verifiable evidence that they sought 'value for money' source selection and contracting.

The defence procurement function has not always been highly centralised. In the USA, for example, individual Services are large enough to make their own, Service-specific arrangements. In other countries, the procurement function used to be more decentralised within the NDO. In the past, many NDOs included departments of supply that were responsible for provisioning capital items from government armouries and shipyards. But the past three decades have seen progressive consolidation of the procurement function within the NDO and the centralisation of procurement organisation within the DPA. (For an example of this progressive consolidation and centralisation of the procurement function in Defence, see the discussion of defence procurement in Australia in Chapter 6.)

General considerations driving the centralisation of procurement in Defence have included:

- scale and scope economies derived from consolidating the procurement function (e.g., the pooling of overhead costs and the elimination of functional duplication);
- further scope economies derived from consolidating of capital acquisition (new capability investment) and through-life support (logistic support to capability) within a single, organisational structure;
- increased market leverage associated with larger purchases;
- quantity discounts offered by suppliers to bulk buyers;
- the growing technological complexity of weapons systems, calling for the consolidation of scarce technical and project (acquisition) management expertise within the NDO;
- knowledge-intensive and network-based weapons systems that requiring through-life adaptation and modification benefit from highly centralised configuration management;
- network economies from standardisation of interoperable weapons systems and elimination of technological incompatibilities.

In many countries, the DPA leads and coordinates the procurement function for all major items acquired by the NDO. Apart from the provision of advice to political decision makers (see below), the DPA is responsible for:

- defining the general *criteria* for evaluating and selecting suppliers (some relating to the product, some to the supplier), the *process* by which selection should proceed (e.g., competitive bidding or negotiation with a sole source), and the principles that should guide the maintenance of *relationships* with suppliers;
- the *development of procurement procedures* and operating instructions describing the accepted procurement practice in the NDO and detailing functional duties or tasks;

- the *procurement process* that includes a number of steps to: identify internal user requirements, solicit and evaluate supplier offers, negotiate supplies and select suppliers, manage the delivery process and evaluate deliverables, and assess supplier performance;
- *conduct of procurement staff* to enable staff to behave appropriately in ambiguous circumstances, particularly if the buyer organisation has objectives couched in terms of forming synergistic relationships with suppliers;
- day-to-day *operational issues.*

There is much in common here with modern practice in large business organisations generally (for an extended treatment, see Monczka *et al.*, 2005). The increased centralisation of the defence procurement function makes procurement activities more transparent and open to high level scrutiny by governments. In most democracies broad procurement programmes and key acquisitions are subject to high levels of political scrutiny and parliamentary approval. In some countries, parliamentary approval is required for all major acquisitions while in others it is a matter of Cabinet decision (see Part II). The approval process is normally iterative and takes the form of a series of decision steps. For example, under the Australian 'two-pass' approval process, derived from the British 'smart procurement' model, the Australian Cabinet considers capability development options at 'first pass' and selects those it wishes to proceed to more detailed analysis and costing with a view to subsequent approval of a specific capability. At 'second pass', it determines whether to fund the acquisition of a specific capability increment with a well-defined budget and schedule. In addition to the Department of Defence, the Australian two-pass decision process also involves two key coordinating departments in the Australian government machinery: the Prime Minister and Cabinet, and Finance. Although this results in a significant dilution of Defence's policy autonomy, it provides the Cabinet with more information and alternative judgements on investment and procurement processes in Defence (for details see Chapter 6).

Centralised procurement arrangements are also better suited to use by governments to channel defence capital spending to designated sectors or regions and to extract offset-based transfers of technology and activity from overseas suppliers to local Industry. In our sample of countries, Canada has taken this model the furthest. The Canadian Department of National Defence (DND) is not an autonomous purchaser of military materiel even after receiving fiscal authority for acquisition from the government and the Department of Finance, and managerial authority from the Treasury Board (Williams, 2006). As shown in Chapter 7, all Canadian government procurement contracting, military and civil, is delegated to the Department of Public Works and Government Services Canada (PWGSC): the whole-of-government purchasing agent. PWGSC balances DND's objective of obtaining the best military hardware its budget can buy against other federal government industrial and regional objectives. These non-defence objectives are pursued by Industry Canada (IC) and the regional economic development agencies that represent regional interests as well as those of regionally-based industries. Special interest groups can also access the process through these agencies. While, in the principal–agent framework, DND is one of PWGSC's many principals, it is somewhat 'more equal than other equal principals', in that it has a large capital budget and ability to initiate new projects. National security is also accorded priority over the socio-political objectives of other principals. Thus, as Ugurhan Berkok notes in Chapter 7, in the complex agency model of Canadian all-of-government procurement, government departments 'behave like Niskanen bureaux maximizing their overall activity while it might be anticipated that regional principals would seek to maximize their share of the activity by trying to attract contracts or subcontracts'.

Effectiveness and accountability

Early advocates of consolidation emphasised the increased market leverage and monopsony power of the DPA vis-à-vis prime contractors. By combining increased purchasing power with fixed price contracts, the centralised DPA was expected to be able to shift a large part of procurement risk to the prime contractor. A centralised DPA was also expected to achieve better control of procurement projects to improve product performance, timeliness of delivery and cost discipline. Of the countries reviewed in this volume, Australia has gone furthest in making its Defence Materiel Organisation (DMO) adopt a back-to-back transactional framework involving, on one hand, buyer–seller contracts with prime contractors and other Industry suppliers and, on the other hand, purchaser–provider agreements with other organisational elements in Defence. In the Australian model, the DMO is responsible for both the initial acquisition of capital equipment from Industry and for arranging subsequent through-life support by Industry of that equipment. Thus, within the Australian NDO, the DMO concludes *Materiel Acquisition Agreements* with the Chief of the Capability Development Group in Defence to cover the acquisition of major capital equipment and *Materiel Sustainment Agreements*, under which the DMO provides services to Defence for the repair, maintenance and adaptation of platforms and systems and for the supply of consumable items and spare parts required to maintain the force in being at agreed levels of preparedness (see Chapter 6).

To give DMO management more commercial-style flexibility in recruiting and rewarding high quality staff and to clarify accountabilities, responsibilities and authority between DMO and the rest of Defence, it has been established as a prescribed agency within the Defence portfolio. Under this arrangement, the DMO's Chief Executive Officer is directly accountable to the Minister for Defence for the agency's performance while also remaining accountable to the Secretary of Defence and the Chief of Defence Force (for more details, see Chapter 6). This structure of internal and external governance reflects wider reforms initiated by the Australian government in the late

1990s aimed at improving the performance of government agencies. In relation to the Defence procurement function, the prescribed status of the DMO seeks to ensure that procurement processes in Defence comply with the legal requirements, general standards and community expectations of probity, accountability and openness (external governance) and intra-departmental arrangements for holding individual defence officials accountable for a responsibility conferred upon them (internal governance).

Yet the Australian defence procurement system remains a 'work in progress' with a newly elected government commissioning yet another review of defence procurement (Ferguson, 2008). But the review does seem to be based on better understanding of the actual problem than hitherto:

> The real power of ... [an earlier wave of reforms lies in] ... making the customer write down the specification and saying 'you deliver against it' ... Once you understand your risks, once you mitigate them, you are in a position to price those risks and once you price [them] you have the basis for a good contract.
>
> (DMO Chief Executive Officer, cited in ibid.: 11)

There appears to be a growing recognition that complex defence acquisitions should be costed (priced) to reflect, for example, the establishment of contingency funds in project budgets large enough to address potential risk at a realistic level. ('Large enough' in this case might be very substantial in dollar terms.) The use of fixed price or incentive contracts (discussed at length in Chapter 4) often creates a false sense of security for the DPA, i.e., there is an illusion that risks have been transferred wholly or partially to the contractor. But the supplier's willingness to absorb all or most project risks is often meaningless unless the firm has 'deep-enough pockets' to bear all costs of its miscalculations and has made adequate provision for handling their implications. In the past, the cost of such miscalculations (under-pricing of risks by suppliers) has often been sheeted back to the DPA, which has little choice but to vary the agreed terms of the contract and, faced with a 'hold up' situation, convert a *de jure* fixed price or incentive contract into a *de facto* cost reimbursement arrangement.

This tendency for DPAs to absorb risks of overoptimistic cost estimates by contractors raises the more fundamental issue as to *who* should best be assigned residual (decision-making) rights in defence acquisitions. If the armed forces demand new product technologies or extensive modifications of MOTS and COTS systems and/or if Government seeks ambitious local content targets, neither side to the deal may be able to foresee all the challenges involved, determine whether they can be met or judge the costs involved in trying to address them. This is because both sides (especially in smaller countries) will be relatively inexperienced in handling complex projects and even experienced players make mistakes when seeking to put new technology in place. As we noted earlier, fixed price or incentive contracting may not capture how risk is or should be shared by the various parties to a complex defence procurement deal. And ultimately, it is Defence (as Government's agent) that is responsible for the formation of the required capability increment and, thus, for arranging to make available all the materiel needed as inputs into that capability.[17]

Rather than relying purely on the contracting mechanism, an alternative way of handling the risks of complex procurements under conditions of considerable uncertainty is to recognise that the residual (decision-making) authority and responsibility for outcomes should be well aligned and vested in the party best able to mitigate the attendant procurement risks. In this approach, if the buyer is largely responsible for determining product specifications, delivery schedule and budget, then the buyer should also be allocated the overarching authority to manage the procurement process. This principle is recognised under cost reimbursement and cost-plus-contractual arrangements since the buyer must authorise delivery milestones and verify which cost items are to be reimbursed. But the disadvantage of all such arrangements is that they leave the buyer as a passive payer: since the buyer is not directly involved in the production process, information relating to product quality and cost is distributed asymmetrically between the parties. The buyer can assess the observable outcomes but cannot determine the true potential of the supplier to make products more efficiently (cheaply) and/or to make better products.

To remedy this situation, the buyer may insist on greater visibility in the delivery process and the shared authority to determine the specifics of the deliverable and the details of the delivery process. One way to achieve that is to integrate upstream production processes vertically into the NDO in the form of government factories and shipyards. Another vehicle to extend the residual decision-making authority over the delivery process is to enter into a *relational contract* with the supplier, e.g., to forge a partnering or alliance-style relationship with the contractor in which both parties jointly decide what is to be done as the project gets under way and the buyer has considerable visibility in the supplier's production processes. However, this requires the acceptance of shared responsibility for positive and negative outcomes. We shall return to these issues in Chapter 4.

The current organisational culture in defence procurement remains largely risk-averse and, thus, inimical to the use of business models that facilitate risk mitigation through effective sharing of the residual (decision-making) authority between the parties. That said, business models recently adopted by the Australian DPA to acquire new air warfare destroyers and to sustain fleets of submarines and frigates in service have started to evolve in the direction of shared decision-making authority within a multi-party governance structure (see Chapter 13).

Conclusion

In this chapter, we have highlighted the multi-dimensionality of the procurement deal. To source goods and services efficiently, it is critical to understand the physical content of the deal: goods and services to be procured, the time-frame, and the associated specific and residual rights created under the deal.

Much has been written about the technical complexity of weapons systems and the problems it poses for determining the terms of the procurement deal and, eventually, the nature of the procurement transaction. For small countries, technical complexity is often a matter of choice in that mature products are usually available as MOTS or COTS imports. But because governments of exporting countries control the diffusion of advanced technology closely, users of imported systems may not have full operational sovereignty over those systems and/or may be denied under some circumstances spare parts and consumables required for in-service support. When countries insist on import substitution for strategic or broader economic reasons, technical complexity may become a problem when orders are directed to inexperienced domestic producers. In such circumstances, it is difficult to determine the specific terms of the procurement deal and, thus, the specific rights and obligations of the parties to the deal. The assignment of residual rights then becomes critical and it is the poor understanding of the importance of residual rights that results in subsequent contracting problems between the parties.

The nature of the product procured and its associated property rights determine how the procurement transaction should best be framed, striking a balance between the specificity of the contract and the nature of the subsequent relationship between the parties – the business model to be applied in each transaction. We shall return to this issue in later chapters.

Notes

1 In this volume, we do not use the term 'procurement' to describe those organisational elements within the NDO that arrange these purchases.
2 The average Euro–US dollar exchange rate was 1.244 in 2005.
3 The capital expenditure may sometimes include the cost of support services, spare parts and consumables that are purchased with the primary equipment and included in the (capital) cost of equipment acquisition.
4 However, this growing technological intensity of weapons systems presents governments with a dilemma: should the burden of defence (the share of defence expenditure in GDP) be allowed to increase to fund this fast rate of technological change, or, should it be funded by allowing the expenditure on equipment procurement and R&D to crowd out other components of defence budgets, in particular personnel? And, if the crowding out (short-term) option is chosen, how far should this substitution of technology and capital for labour be allowed to go before it becomes non-sustainable?
5 This complexity is not only a reflection of the complex architecture of a modern weapons system when it is first acquired but also due to its ever changing configuration when in use as it is upgraded and modified.
6 For example, the acquisition of a fleet of 59 'combat-survivable' main battle tanks M1A1 Abrams by Australia (Gubler, 2007) begs an obvious question as to the nature of potential combat scenarios for which this enhanced survivability is so critical. Clearly a fleet of 59 tanks is unlikely to tilt the combat scales against a potential invader serious enough and capable of invading this enormous island-

continent. One can think of many cataclysmic global events or Cold War-like scenarios that could involve the use of this highly combat-survivable equipment. But these scenarios have not been very prominent in Australia's recent strategic outlook documents (see Chapter 6 for references).

7 For example, the construction of 'conventional' Collins class submarines in-country in the 1990s presented Australia with technological and organisational challenges that raised doubts about the capacity of the then Australian DPA to handle such complex acquisitions (see Chapters 6 and 13).

8 For a discussion, see Pugh (1993), Kirkpatrick (1995), Kirkpatrick and Pugh (1993) and Kirkpatrick (2004). This trade-off between the decreasing size of fleets and the ever more capable and costly equipment prompted Norman Augustine, the former CEO of Lockheed Martin, to observe that by the mid-twenty-first century the entire US defence budget would be required to pay for a single tactical aircraft with the US Air Force and Navy each having the use of the aircraft for 3½ days each week and the US Marine Corps would have it every 29 February (cited in Davies, 2008: 8; but also see Augustine, 1997).

9 At the time of writing, the use of simple technologies such as improvised explosive devices (IEDs) in Iraq has successfully challenged the technological superiority of the US-led coalition of forces.

10 In most civil applications, the true demand reveals itself when the end product is delivered to the customer/user. In some cases, it may take time for the customer to warm to a radically new product but, generally, a commercial enterprise has limited capacity to sustain loss leaders over long periods of time and it expects to produce good returns on its investments within a relatively short timeframe. Public good providers are often less responsive to market demands when governments insist that their products are provided 'on merit' irrespective of the strength of demand.

11 Informal communication from Director General Industry Capacity, the (Australian) Defence Materiel Organisation.

12 A different body of literature has focussed on the 'bundling of transactions' in domestic and export markets. These 'bundling' deals refer to 'counter-purchase', 'compensation trade' and 'buyback' arrangements that involve good-for-goods rather than goods-for-money exchanges (Mirus and Yeung, 2000). This is a different use of the term from the bundling of requirements to widen the procurement deal.

13 In some countries, the military may use force to confiscate other people's assets and, historically, military organisations have often acquired many of their assets (small weapons, means of transport), supplies and soldiers at gun point.

14 This is similar to the concept of 'the *uncontractibility* of the output expected from the relation' used by Furlotti (2007: 89).

15 In all such cases, the scope of the deal is broadened but its terms become more opaque in the process and may not be subsequently verifiable by a third party. This shifts the emphasis to the designation of residual rights.

16 According to Monczka: 'Organisational design refers to the process of assessing and selecting the structure and formal system of communication, division of labour, coordination, control, authority and responsibility required to achieve the goals and objectives of the organisation' (Monczka *et al.*, 2005: 136).

17 For example, the much publicised technical problems experienced by the Australian Collins class submarines in the 1990s forced the Australian government to intervene in the procurement process by assuming full ownership of the prime contractor: the Australian Submarine Corporation (see Chapter 13). Given the strategic significance of the submarine fleet, the government had no choice but to acquire the prime contractor to pave the way for remedial action rather than engage in acrimonious and time-consuming litigation with the Corporation.

References

Arrow, K. J. and Lind, R. C. (1970) 'Uncertainty and the evaluation of public investment decisions', *American Economic Review*, 60: 364–78.

ASPI (2004) *A Trillion Dollars and Counting: Paying for Defence to 2050*, Canberra: Australian Strategic Policy Institute.

Augustine, N. R. (1997) *Augustine's Laws*, 6th edn, Virginia: American Institute of Aeronautics and Astronautics.

Brito, D. L. and Intriligator, M. D (1995) 'Arms races and proliferation', in K. Hartley and T. Sandler (eds) *Handbook of Defense* Economics, Vol. 1, Amsterdam: North-Holland, pp. 109–64.

Davies, A. (2008) *How Much Will the Joint Strike Fighter Cost Australia?*, Policy Analysis Report No. 27, Canberra: Australian Strategic Policy Institute.

EDA (2006) 'European defence expenditure in 2005' and 'European – United States defence expenditure in 2005', Brussels, European Defence Agency, 20 November. Online. Available at: http://www.eda.europa.eu/facts.aspx (accessed 5 May 2007).

Ergas, H. and Menezes, F. (2004) 'The economics of buying complex weapons', *Agenda*, 11(3): 247–64.

Ferguson, G. (2008) 'Tighter management aims to cut waste', Defence Special Report, *The Australian*, 11.

Furlotti, M. (2007) 'There is more to contracts than incompleteness: a review and assessment of empirical research on inter-firm contract design', *Journal of Management and Governance*, 11: 61–99.

Gansler, J. S. (1989) *Affording Defense*, Cambridge, MA: MIT Press.

Grossman, S. J. and Hart, O. D. (1986) 'The costs and benefits of ownership: a theory of vertical and lateral integration', *Journal of Political Economy*, 94(4): 691–719.

Gubler, A. S. (2007) 'Simulation to relieve Abrams' high costs', *Australian Defence Business Review*, June–July: 27–38.

Hall, P. and Markowski, S. (1996) 'Some lessons from the Australian defense offsets experience', *Defense Analysis*, 12(3): 289–314.

Hardstone, G. A. P. (2004) 'Capabilities, structures and strategies re-examined: incumbent firms and the emergence of complex product systems (CoPS) in mature industries', *Technology Analysis & Strategic Management*, 16(2): 173–96.

Hartley, K. (2007) The arms industry, procurement and industrial policies, in T. Sandler and K. Hartley (eds) *Handbook of Defense Economics: Defense in a Globalised World*, Vol. 2, Amsterdam: North-Holland, pp. 1139–76.

Hartley, K. and Sandler, T. (eds) (1995) *Handbook of Defense Economics*, Vol. 1, Amsterdam: North-Holland.

Hendrikse, G. (2003) *Economics and Management of Organisations, Co-ordination, Motivation and Strategy*, New York: McGraw-Hill.

Hildebrandt, G. G. and Sze, Man-bing (1986) *Accounting for the Cost of Tactical Aircraft; A RAND Note*, N-2420-PA&E, Santa Monica, CA: RAND Corporation.

Jubb, C. D. and Markowski, S. (1991), 'Scale, scope and flexibility in Australian manufacturing', in C. Hamilton (ed.), *The Economic Dynamics of Australian Industry*, Sydney: Allen & Unwin, pp. 100–17.

Kausal, B. A. and Markowski, S. (2000) *A Comparison of the Defense Acquisition Systems of Australia, Japan, South Korea, Singapore and the United States*, Fort Belvoir: Defense Systems Management College Press.

Kirkpatrick, D. L. I. (1995) 'The rising unit cost of defence equipment – the reasons and the results', in K. Hartley and T. Sandler (eds) *Handbook of Defense Economics*, Vol. 1, Amsterdam: North-Holland, pp. 263–86.

—— (2004) 'Trends in the costs of weapons systems and the consequences', *Defence and Peace Economics*, 15(3): 259–73.

Kirkpatrick, D. L. I. and Pugh, P. G. (1993) 'Towards the *Starship Enterprise* – are the current trends in defence unit costs inexorable?', *Aerospace*, May: 18–19.

Labs, E. J. (2008) 'Current and Projected Navy Shipbuilding Programs', CBO Testimony before Subcommittee on Seapower and Expeditionary Forces, Committee on Armed Services, U.S. House of Representatives, 14 March. Online. Available at: http://www.cbo.gov/ftdocs/90xx/doc9045/Shipbuilding_Mainext.1.1.shtml (accessed April 2008).

Markowski, S. and Hall, P. (2006) 'The economic benefits of defence industries: a framework for cold-blooded assessment' in *The Business of Defence*, Melbourne: Committee for Economic Development of Australia.

Markowski, S. and Jubb, C.D. (1989) 'The impact of microelectronics on scale in manufacturing industries', *Australian Journal of Management*, 14(2): 12–55.

Markowski, S. and Wylie, R. (2007) 'The emergence of European defence and defence industry policies', Kokoda Foundation, *Security Challenges*, 3(2): 31–51.

Mirus, R. and Yeung, B. (2000) *The Economics of Barter and Countertrade*, Cheltenham: Elgar.

Monczka, R., Trent, R. and Handfield, R. (2005) *Purchasing and Supply Management*, 3rd edn, Thomson South Western: Thomson Learning.

Parker, D. and Hartley, K. (1997) 'The economics of partnership sourcing versus adversarial competition: a critique', *European Journal of Purchasing and Supply Management*, 3(2): 115–25.

Pugh, P. G. (1993) 'The procurement nexus', *Defence Economics*, 4: 179–94.

Sandler, T. and Hartley, K. (eds) (2007) *Handbook of Defense Economics: Defense in a Globalised World*, Vol. 2, Amsterdam: North-Holland.

Stowsky, J. (1993) 'From spin-off to spin-on: redefining the military's role in American technology development', in W. Sandholtz, M. Borros, J. Zysman, K. Conca, J. Stowsky, J. Vogel and S. Weber (eds) *The Highest Stakes*, New York: Oxford University Press.

Trope, R. L. and Witt, M. (2007) 'Allies at sixes and sevens: sticky issues in Australian-US defence trade controls', Kokoda Foundation, *Security Challenges*, 3(2): 73–92.

UK MoD (2006) *Defence Technology Strategy for the Demands of the 21st Century*, London: Ministry of Defence.

US DoD (2003) *Transforming the Defense Industrial Base: A Roadmap*, Washington, DC: Department of Defense.

Williams, A. S. (2006) *Reinventing Canadian Defence Procurement: A View from the Inside*, Montreal and Kingston: Breakout Educational Network, School of Policy Studies, Queen's University and McGill-Queen's University Press.

3 Supply

Defence industry

Peter Hall, Stefan Markowski and Robert Wylie

Introduction

In the value-adding framework introduced in Chapter 1 (see Figure 1.1), Defence Industry supplies the National Defence Organisation (NDO) with the non-human physical inputs into military capability and many of the services that support it. The focus of this chapter is on Defence Industry, but it is impossible to understand the industry and the firms comprising it without also acknowledging the key role of governments around the world in providing a market and in many ways determining how that market operates.

To understand how Defence Industry both enables and constrains NDOs, this chapter begins by discussing the concept of 'defence industry', surveys the sector from global and national perspectives, including what determines its structure and dynamics. It then examines the nature of the 'defence firm', how the conduct and performance of defence firms are affected by the market in which they operate, and how they may themselves seek to influence the competitive environment. The chapter concludes with a discussion of the inter-relationship between ownership of the productive assets at the enterprise level and how Defence Industry is organised and how efficiently it operates. In this chapter, we also make references to the two in-depth case studies in Part III of this volume: Chapter 13, which examines the Australian naval shipbuilding sector, and Chapter 14, which focuses on the acquisition of over-the-horizon radar by Australia.

Defence industry and the defence industry base

Definitions

As we noted in Chapter 1, there is no self-evident or natural definition of 'defence industry'. This is primarily because what is 'defence industry' depends on the relevant circumstances and context. As World War II attests, the ambit of 'defence industry' for a nation mobilising for total war is vastly more inclusive than what might be considered defence industry in peacetime. Second, the group of firms comprising 'defence industry' is importantly a function of opportunity and appetite for risk. As the conflict in Iraq demonstrates, profit-making opportunities created by military conflicts encourage some civil firms to re-direct their production to those goods and services that are in demand by the combatants.

Third, firms producing directly for Defence draw in a wide variety of intermediate inputs from firms in other industries. If firms supplying Defence directly absorbed a large proportion of the output of firms in an intermediate input industry, we might be inclined to say firms in the latter should be included in 'defence industry'. But how large would the defence-directed proportion of its output have to be before we could say the firms were in the defence sector? Would the proportion be measured in volume or value? And what would happen if that proportion fluctuated from year to year? Fourth, firms supplying goods both directly to Defence and indirectly as intermediate inputs may produce the same products for military and non-military markets or the same production facilities can make similar products for military and civil markets (e.g., firms producing 'ruggedised' laptop computers for civil and military customers). But when do these firms become parts of defence industry?[1]

Answers to these questions will always be arbitrary. Sandler and Hartley (1995: 182–3) give no fewer than six definitions of a country's Defence Industry Base (DIB). Todd (1988: 14–15) defines the DIB as all those industrial sectors that unambiguously manufacture military-specific goods (such as missiles, naval ships and artillery) and also sectors that produce civil goods if the majority of their output has the defence market as its destination. But this is almost certainly too narrow. It does not automatically embrace defence-related industry R&D that may not be carried out by defence-industry manufacturers; and it should perhaps include service activities that support NDOs in their work. An immediate implication of this discussion is that, whatever definition we use, defence industry is highly *heterogeneous* in terms of the actual goods and services it produces.

We have probed the subtleties of DIB definitions partly to show how they complicate comparisons between defence industries of different countries. It is not only that different concepts are used by different people and that these concepts often change over time; nations also use different concepts to define their defence industries and describe their activities. Thus, various definitions of national defence industries implicit in country-specific chapters of this volume are likely to differ. While any attempt to reconcile these differences is beyond the scope of this book, it is important that the reader bear them in mind, particularly in comparing national experiences.

Global defence industry: overview

Military spending worldwide runs at well over US$1 trillion each year. According to annual reports prepared by the authoritative Stockholm

International Peace Research Institute (SIPRI), totals at then-current prices and exchange rates were US$1.1 trillion in 2005 and US$1.2 trillion in 2006 (SIPRI, 2006, 2007: Chap. 8 in each case). While only approximations can be made for what was spent on the output of global industry, reported estimates suggest that equipment accounted for about 22 per cent of all NATO military spending in 2006 and 18 per cent of NATO Europe outlays (SIPRI, 2007: Tables 8A.1 and 8B.1). Focusing on equipment alone, such figures imply that the value of global industry production well exceeds US$200 billion per annum at 2003 prices.

About three-quarters of the value of total weapons output globally (excluding China) is accounted for by 100 arms-producing companies listed each year in the *SIPRI Yearbook* (SIPRI, 2006, 2007). We refer to these companies as SIPRI's Top 100. In 2005 (at then-prevailing prices and exchange rates), the Top 100 group of companies generated sales of US$290 billion (Sköns and Surry, 2007: 347). Small country NDOs face very large companies across the negotiating table if they buy from the industry's largest producers: annual arms sales in 2005 were running at US$28 billion in the largest, Boeing, and US$19.8 billion in even the fifth biggest, Raytheon (Surry and the SIPRI Arms Industry Network, 2007: 376). Post-Cold War, some big companies became even bigger through mergers and acquisitions. (For a detailed account of this history, see Pages, 1999, and Oden, 1999).[2]

Recorded world arms production is dominated by that of the USA and Europe. In the early twenty-first century, four of the largest five global defence firms – Boeing, Lockheed Martin, Northrop Grumman and Raytheon – were US companies; BAE Systems, the fourth largest, was a UK business. Of the Top 100, 40 companies were located in the USA and 32 in Western Europe. A number of smaller countries also host one or more companies in the SIPRI Top 100 list: for example, Israel, Sweden, Spain, South Korea, Switzerland, Canada, Norway, Finland, Australia, Singapore, South Africa and Brazil. The largest defence companies hosted by small countries, however, are nowhere near as big as those ranked near the top of the list. For example, the Swedish-based Saab was ranked 25th in the Top 100 for 2005 with arms sales of US$2.1 billion; Israel Aircraft Industries 35th, selling US$1.5 billion, and Spain's Navantia 53rd with revenues from defence sales of US$0.97 billion (Surry and the SIPRI Arms Industry Network 2007: 376–82).

The arms industry operates globally: while most major arms producers are headquartered in the USA or Europe, they source components throughout the world, seek new export markets where they can, and maintain production footprints in many countries. However, while globalisation of civil industry is largely driven by commercial imperatives (e.g., the continuous shift of production to reliable but low-cost suppliers), globalisation of the arms industry has largely been influenced by governments. In part, governments have favoured in-country sourcing of military supplies in peacetime to secure supply lines in wartime. In part, however, globalisation has been caused by strong mercantilist pressures (in particular, by a strong preference for import substitution that increases fragmentation of production capacities, exports and protection of domestic producers) that do not apply to civil commerce. These are usually justified by governments on security grounds, but, as trade in defence-specific goods and services is exempt from international trade agreements, governments support and protect in-country defence industries for a variety of non-defence reasons. And technology exports are often impeded, partly for strategic reasons and partly because where new defence technology has been publicly funded (developed with their taxpayers' money), governments may be reluctant to share the benefits with overseas users. Second, the organisation of global defence industry is partly the result of formal corporate ownership arrangements (that in many cases reflect the outcome of earlier merger and acquisition activity and foreign direct investment) and partly the result of government-arranged formal and less formal collaborative agreements and strategic alliances that bring firms together in programme- or project-specific consortia.

National defence industry base

Countries vary widely in the size of the defence industry base they maintain locally. Taking numbers employed as a measure of size in the world's ten largest national arms industries, totals varied in 2003 from 2.7 million in the first-ranked USA to 80,000 in Germany and Japan, ranked joint ninth (Hartley, 2007: 1145). Workforce numbers are considerably smaller in smaller industrialised countries and their particular experience is described and analysed in Part II of this volume. For smaller countries, the existence of a national defence industry base (NDIB) is likely to rest very heavily on the willingness of the national government to buy locally since, in most cases, limitations on scale, scope and innovation capability often prevent domestic firms from penetrating export markets. There are exceptions, however: Israel and Singapore are successful exporters (see Chapters 8 and 9).

Traditionally, many smaller economies have viewed the establishment of a local defence industry as a stepping stone to industrialisation. For example, a large number of countries manufacture small arms and ammunition.[3] This is because simple small arms are relatively easy to manufacture and many developing countries are prepared to absorb cost penalties for small-scale production. The local industry has often been established via a licensing agreement or an offsets arrangement under which major arms companies from the USA or Europe provide plant, equipment, training and employment (see, for example, Brauer and Dunne, 2004). An associated trend is the globalisation of component production (Control Arms, 2006). Small countries that may lack the breadth of expertise to operate a full weapons system plant may nonetheless have the skills and facilities to attract investors in the manufacturing of a single component or narrow range of parts which may then be exported for assembly elsewhere. An increasingly important issue for smaller countries has thus become the extent to which they can break into and participate in international supply chains.

Buyers

On the demand side of the defence goods market, every national government or coalition of governments that seeks to purchase arms and weapons is a potential buyer. (Strictly, this is the final defence goods market: the many firms that purchase intermediate inputs into producing arms and capability for NDOs also exercise demand further up the supply chain.) However, the defence goods market is segmented by the purchasing power and policy of national governments (see the previous chapter). Governments with large defence budgets seeking the perceived strategic benefits of cutting-edge defence capabilities have often used their procurement expenditure to foster domestic industry capacity across a wide range of technologies. Smaller countries with more modest defence budgets usually lack the capacity to develop the most advanced, complex modern weapons systems and must decide which weapons, if any, to produce in country and what to import. When smaller countries import from overseas suppliers, their market power will usually be relatively limited. To benefit from the most competitive prices, they must often wait until producers, having previously met the large-scale requirements of major powers, are then willing to sell additional units at prices reflecting prevailing marginal costs. Major powers have the market power to delay sales to smaller nations until the technology involved has become less strategically sensitive. For smaller or less wealthy countries, any monopsony power is usually confined to domestic production mandated by the government. This may include provisioning, repair and maintenance and the production of capability assets tailored to country-specific strategic needs. Small countries that aspire to develop more advanced systems locally may have to depend on a larger ally for technological assistance and incur significantly higher costs than they would for an imported substitute. (These costs are higher as they include cost premia that are incurred as a consequence of import substitution/local content preferences.)

The apparent market power of governments operating as monopsonists vis-à-vis local defence firms is not unqualified. Obviously, a supplier of products with no alternative market may well be ruined if the government withdraws its business. But a cautious firm is likely to be wary about investing in a productive asset, if the return on which is entirely dependent on future sales to a single customer that could, without warning, terminate its business. When firms have to invest in assets specific to the needs of a given customer, they are said to expose themselves to the threat of 'hold-up', i.e., carrying the entire risk of investing in capital without any power over the return it will generate. Assets specific to the needs of the Defence client may include equipment, new technological knowledge derived from R&D, and production skills. If firms invest heavily in defence-specific knowledge and related assets, they may fail to earn a return when Defence rejects their ideas or applications. However, knowing this risk in advance, firms may then not wish to commit in the first place, thereby frustrating the aims of policy-makers wishing to foster local industry capacity.

The willingness of industry to participate in defence business will then reflect, first, the extent (if at all) to which firms are prepared to bear the risk of hold-up and, second, the way governments respond to firms' perception of that risk. In this sense, the demand and supply sides of the defence market are interdependent. On the supply side, firms may seek to reduce the risk of doing business with Defence by investing in assets which have dual use, i.e., may be used for producing goods for the civil as well as military markets. But some products (e.g., aircraft carriers, submarines, and tanks) are intrinsically military in their nature and have no dual use. And some civil products would fail to meet military requirements (e.g., safety-critical software) or require expensive adaptations (e.g., the 'ruggedisation' of personal computers). On the demand side, governments may decide to own the means of production themselves, thereby obviating the need to induce private industry to bear the risk of defence-specific investments and enabling Defence to shape requirements without interacting with private industry. Governments might also offer subsidies on acquiring equipment specific to defence needs or offer to supply the assets directly at public expense (e.g., government-furnished production equipment). Economists describe this arrangement as quasi-vertical integration. Different contractual arrangements are also used to shift the risk of Defence-specific investments to the buyer (e.g., cost reimbursement contracts). We shall revisit these issues in Chapter 4.

Defence industry: structure and operations

Structure

Industry structure is of interest to us partly because it constitutes a key element of the economic context in which procurement occurs. Particularly in recent decades, governments generally and defence procurement agencies in particular have been keen to exploit competitive market mechanisms to achieve budget economies without loss of quality, i.e., greater 'value for money'. It has traditionally been argued that an industry's structure provides foundations for understanding how competitive it might be in terms of price, product quality, delivery schedule and innovation, providing insights into how firms within the industry (incumbents) compete and cooperate with each other, and how they are influenced by the threat of entry by firms outside it (potential entrants). This, in turn, leads to predictions about performance – industry-level profitability and other economic implications for society. According to standard text-book treatments of the structure-conduct-performance framework (for example, Scherer, 1980; Hay and Morris, 1991) key structural variables include the number and relative sizes of sellers, captured empirically through measures of industry concentration; the extent to which the products of the industry are differentiated from or substitutable for each other and from/for the products of other industries; and the technology characterising production in the industry which, in turn, is reflected in cost conditions. Research and development (R&D) can generate both product and process innovations which underpin and maintain product differences and production cost efficiency. Other structural variables of potential interest include the number and relative sizes of buyers, the degree to which firms in the industry are vertically integrated, and the extent to which they are diversified across product lines.

The degree of competitiveness present in an industry can be gauged in terms of the intensity of competition among incumbents and the extent the latter are protected from potential entrants. The theory suggests that competition among incumbents is most intense when they make similar products that are good substitutes for each other (i.e., product differentiation is low) and when there are many competing firms, implying ease of entry and low levels of industry concentration. When the industry product is relatively undifferentiated, price is the main or only competitive conduct variable and price-cutting wars among incumbents may be fierce, even if there are few competitors and industry concentration is thus high. On the other hand, high levels of concentration may also reduce the costs to incumbents of negotiating, monitoring and enforcing anti-competitive agreements and may encourage collusion to fix prices. The more product differentiation is possible within an industry, the less pressure there is for firms to collude on price since they can charge higher prices to segments of the market with marked preferences for particular brands or product variants. In the highly variegated world of defence industry, some products (such as provisions and fuel) are in the nature of undifferentiated commodities while others (such as submarines) are highly differentiated and sometimes almost unique.[4]

When the danger of collusion among incumbents is high, or when concentration reaches 100 per cent and all industry output is produced by a single, monopoly firm, competitive pressure is most likely to be found in the threat of potential entry by outsiders. This case is potentially relevant to smaller-nation domestic markets in which at least the essential elements of defence production may be undertaken by a single 'national champion'. The extent to which incumbents are protected from entry depends on barriers to entry – essentially any feature of the industry that inhibits new entry. National governments may use legislative and regulatory means, for example, to restrict foreign entry into their local industry. But even when governments are more open to international competition, new entrants may have to bear costs that incumbents have already incurred or do not need to incur to continue their operations. Here incumbents are protected to the extent to which they have already incurred sunk costs which a new entrant would face before being able to compete. Sunk costs relate to expenditures that cannot be recouped through future re-sale of the assets on which they have been spent. For incumbents such costs are bygones but for potential new entrants the prospect of incurring them may constitute a significant disincentive to enter (Spence, 1977; Dixit, 1980). If barriers to entry are low or non-existent, entry is easy or costless and incumbents are potentially vulnerable. To survive, they must be competitive with potential entrants.

A form of sunk cost with potentially important implications for competition in defence industry is R&D. As we noted above, R&D can sustain product innovation and differentiation as well as process innovation and cost competitiveness. R&D leading to successful innovation may thus enable firms within the industry to establish a competitive edge over rivals by enabling them to offer better 'value for money' to their customers. It also has the potential, however, to create and maintain barriers to entry. R&D costs usually include a sunk component which a new entrant would have to bear to become competitive.

In the defence market, as elsewhere, it is important to distinguish between barriers to entry arising from production conditions and those connected to how transactions are made, i.e., transaction costs. Defence industry customers, usually governments, use relatively costly tendering procedures to purchase, requiring suppliers to have extensive knowledge of specific administrative processes. Governments may also impose conditions on suppliers relating to location, nationality and security status of employees, commercial use of intellectual property, technology licensing, export restrictions, and so on. Firms already in the industry will have acquired specialist knowledge of dealing with national procurement agencies and may have incurred some or all of the costs relating to other aspects of government requirements. But firms outside the industry will lack familiarity with defence procurement procedures and may lack local production facilities or access to the pool of national labour.

In the following sections, we discuss how a number of these factors play out in global and national defence industry. We distinguish where relevant between industry at the global and national levels.

The key role of governments

Within any country, governments exert a key influence on defence industry structure. Only government can decide on how much to spend on defence capabilities and thus how much of the nation's spending power should be allocated to the goods and services supporting it. Government can decide whether to own and operate defence industry or not and, thus, what opportunities are potentially available to private sector suppliers. It determines who can compete for those opportunities, who wins and whether or not alternative sources of supply should be used, and it chooses whether to buy defence products at home or abroad (constrained by what is technically possible given the capability requirements it has determined) with implications for the distribution of employment, and investments in new capital and knowledge.

Beyond this, governments are often obliged by the requirements of public accountability to operate procurement processes and procedures that give advantage to firms with a track record of success (or those skilled in government lobbying and networking).

In the past, a focus on the national contribution of defence industry was pursued at the expense of keeping costs down. But increased emphasis on securing 'value for money' has led to a higher priority for cost efficiency, quality and innovation. These imperatives, in turn raise questions about what industry structure best suits these requirements and the appropriate nature and scale of defence industry to keep within national boundaries. The political advantages of local defence production encourage governments to trade off efficiency considerations against electoral consequences and restrict competition.

Industry concentration

The ever-increasing costs of maintaining a national DIB has encouraged governments, even in the largest countries to look overseas for sources of low-cost supply and for competitive sourcing. But local content schemes, defence offsets programmes and restrictions on defence trade continue to operate and to constrain global industry concentration which, nevertheless, has risen appreciably since 1990.

In 2003, the five largest arms-producing firms listed by SIPRI accounted for 44 per cent of the value of all global arms sales made by the SIPRI Top 100 compared with 22 per cent in 1990 (Dunne and Surry, 2006, Table 9.3). The largest ten companies accounted for 61 per cent of Top 100 arms sales (37 per cent in 1990), and the top twenty for 74 per cent (57 per cent) (ibid.). Dunne and Surry describe this as 'a very low degree of concentration compared to other high-technology markets' such as civil airliners and pharmaceuticals (ibid.: 404), and argue that this reflects the continuing influence of domestic policies to restrict purchases from multinational companies. This suggests that national governments continue to encourage local content policies in defence industry more than in other areas. As we noted earlier, national industry statistics do not usually identify firms as belonging to 'defence industry' so the levels of concentration at the national level are harder to compute than those for better defined sectors. That said, a focus on buying defence goods locally often appears to go with purchasing from one or a very few nationally located firms synonymous with military production. This, in turn, implies a relatively high level of concentration within national borders.

Defence industry may also be more concentrated than it initially appears for another reason. Because of the heterogeneity of defence industry, many sub-industries or sectors comprise the aggregate and it is therefore possible that a relatively large producer by the standards of a particular sub-sector may not appear in the SIPRI Top 100 list. For example, concentration of upstream suppliers to the manufacturers of major weapons systems can be quite marked – but invisible at the aggregate level. In the early 1990s, just six out of 200 first tier suppliers supplied 60 per cent of the total GKN purchases for the UK Warrior Armoured Fighting Vehicle programme, and only two out of 200 in another programme. In turn, first tier suppliers used an average of 18 suppliers each and second tier firms seven (Hartley *et al.*, 1997, cited in Dowdall, 2004).

Economies of scale and scope

A key determinant of industry structure – and, by extension, industry com-petitiveness – is the technology of production underlying production cost conditions. Particularly important for defence industry is the extent to which higher volumes of output may be produced without proportionately increas-ing all inputs, in turn allowing unit production costs to fall with increasing levels of output generated. In Box 3.1, we show how unit production costs fall with rising output when *scale economies* are present until a *minimum efficient scale of production* is reached.[5] If demand is limited to the range of output over which unit costs decline, preconditions exist for high-level concentration to occur within the industry since a single firm producing at a higher level of output will be able to produce at lower unit cost than two or more firms dividing the output level between them. At any given profit rate, larger firms will be able to offer their product to the market at lower prices than smaller firms. On the other hand, if scale economies permit a single firm to dominate the industry, it may use its market power as a monopolist to charge prices well above their unit and marginal costs. In an industry characterised by scale economies, then, price is not only a key competitive weapon but also a function of industry structure.

Scale economies have interested defence economists because traditional military products are manufactured using a technology requiring large initial

---

Box 3.1 Economies of scale

Figure 3.1 shows the volume (scale) of a representative defence product X, say, a machine gun, on the horizontal axis, and the unit cost of its pro-duction on the vertical axis. The product is initially produced by a pro-duction facility A. As shown, large-scale producers benefit from volume-related cost efficiencies (the unit cost of output declines as the scale of production increases). Small-scale producers are restricted to the upper end of the cost curve. Once a certain scale of production activity is reached, further reductions in unit cost are relatively small, i.e., at XAmin the cost curve becomes relatively flat and further efficiencies associated with volume production are rather insignificant. We refer to this threshold scale as the *minimum efficient scale* (MES) *of production*.

Figure 3.1 also shows the maximum level of output that can be produced by a single facility, A, or production unit, X_{Amax}. This is where the
maximum capacity (in output terms) of the facility or the unit is reached.
To increase output beyond this point, another facility, B, must be added
and the (possibly large) upfront cost of another production line incurred.
This is shown as the second unit cost curve to the right of X_{Amax}. Thus, to
produce an incremental unit of X beyond the initial capacity limit, X_{Amax},
a large increase in unit cost must be absorbed. Thereafter the unit cost
declines, rather rapidly, with the scale of the facility and, if the second
production line is very large and much more efficient than the first one, the
unit cost associated with large volumes of X produced by both production
lines may be lower than the lowest cost achieved by the first facility.

investments in fixed capital (e.g., shipyards, arsenals, tank assembly lines). As
production volumes increased, these characteristics enabled the fixed element
of total costs to be spread over increasingly numerous units of output, resulting
in lower unit costs. Other sources of scale economies include: (1) volume
and capacity increases in pipes, tanks and containment vessels which occur at
a rate proportionally greater than the quantity of materials used to construct
them – likely to be important in platform construction; and (2) a division
of labour, in which increasing output allows members of the workforce to

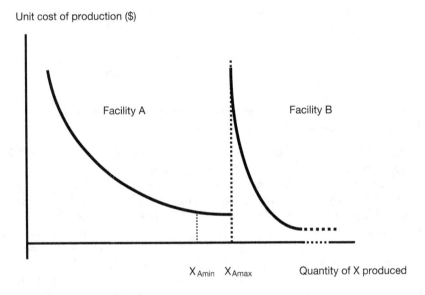

Figure 3.1 Economies of scale

specialise in tasks where they are relatively more skilful and expert than others.

Unit production costs may also fall *over time* as a result of learning-by-doing derived from growing *cumulative* output generating increasing experience among the workforce and its management. This effect should be distinguished from the benefits of division of labour where, at any given moment, the production of larger volumes alone permits workforce specialisation and thus enhanced efficiency. The *learning curve* associated with cumulative labour force experience may be characterised by its slope. A so-called 75 per cent learning curve, for example, suggests that direct labour used would fall by a quarter (25 per cent), every time cumulative output doubled. The extent to which such reductions are reflected in unit costs depends on the share of labour costs in total production outlays, often less than 50 per cent in capital-intensive defence industry.

The median slope of learning curves found in empirical work on European defence industry manufacturing lies in the range 85–90 per cent (Sandler and Hartley, 1995: 125). A 2003 study of the UK defence electronics industry found evidence of falling unit production costs with higher output, apparently due to spreading large fixed costs over longer production runs (Dowdall *et al.*, 2004). Howeve, smaller countries have greater difficulty exploiting the presence of scale and learning economies. While there is evidence that learning curves ultimately flatten where the limit of falling unit labour costs is reached, production runs in smaller country defence industries are rarely likely to exhaust cost-cutting possibilities unless they can develop substantial export markets for particular products. Except for Israel, which exports a relatively large proportion of its defence-related industrial output (see Chapter 8), few small countries have met this challenge.

The diversity of defence industry outputs draws attention to the potential significance of *economies of scope*, reflecting cost savings associated with producing a multiplicity of product lines and arising from using the same plant to produce different types of output or allocating flexible management inputs to work with a range of production activities. The advent of computer-facilitated flexible manufacturing systems suggests the concept, discussed in Box 3.2, may have more relevance now than in the earlier manufacturing era (Markowski and Jubb, 1989; and Jubb and Markowski, 1991).

Box 3.2 Economies of scope and agglomeration

Figure 3.2 is similar to Figure 2.3 in Chapter 2. It shows two products, say, missiles X and Y, with the horizontal axes representing volumes of each product. The product range is {X, Y}. The vertical axis shows the unit cost associated with different quantities of X and Y that are *produced* either jointly or separately. The convex cost surface C(XY) in Figure 3.2 shows the unit cost of production for different combinations of X and Y.

As in Figure 2.3, different combinations of X and Y can be selected to determine the corresponding unit production cost of each product. If X and Y are *produced* separately, say using two different production facilities, we select the volume of output along the relevant horizontal axis and find the corresponding unit cost as a point on the cost surface $C(XY)$. For example, if only missile Y is made by a production facility dedicated to Y, a smaller quantity of Y, Y_1, is associated with a higher unit cost of production, $C(Y_1)$. When a larger quantity, Y_2, is made, the unit cost decreases to $C(Y_2)$. However, when both products are produced jointly by a flexible (multi-product) facility, say, X_1 of X and Y_2 of Y, the unit cost of each product decreases to $C(X_1Y_2)$. In this case, there are scope-related cost efficiencies in production: *economies of scope*. This is because the unit cost surface, $C(XY)$, is convex (from above) when the two products are produced jointly rather than separately. Thus, if there are synergies in the production of different products by a single production line or facility, as illustrated by the convex cost surface in Figure 3.2, these products should best be combined into a multi-product production process. (If the unit cost surface $C(XY)$ were drawn as a concave (from below) surface there would be *diseconomies of scope* and it would be preferable to make the two products separately, in two separate facilities, rather than jointly.)

Figure 3.2 also shows that the ability to *agglomerate* different product lines within a single production facility can benefit the producer by lowering the average unit cost of production. This is because the cost surface $C(X,Y)$ is shown to be both convex across the product range and declining with the volume of production. There are *agglomeration economies* in production in this case. (If $C(X,Y)$ were concave and upward sloping with volume, the opposite would be the case: it would be more advantageous to operate separate, smaller facilities dedicated to specific products as their joint production would result in *agglomeration diseconomies*).

Also, when the scope of the production facility increases, it is no longer possible to measure its scale unambiguously in terms of a single, homogenous product. Some index of scale must be used. The scale can be measured, for example, in terms of a 'representative product' selected from a range of products comprising the deal, X or Y in our example. Alternatively, a particular combination (ratio) of products may be chosen so that quantities may vary while the product proportions are fixed. In the figure, this 'ratio' measure of scale is shown as a ray from the origin drawn on the horizontal product surface, X/Y. Points such as $C(X_1Y_2)$ on the cost surface $C(XY)$ show how the unit cost changes as we move along the ray. As noted previously, measuring the scale of production in money terms may also be helpful as long as it is remembered that the larger *value* of (heterogeneous) output may be the outcome of changes in *both* its *volume* and *composition* (a combination of scale and scope effects).

The cost surface C(X,Y) illustrated in Figure 3.2 represents the most efficient 'cost envelope' which could be achieved under ideal operating conditions. In reality, the unit cost of output incurred in actual operations will inevitably be higher than what would have been achieved if production tasks are performed most efficiently under ideal conditions. For example, in Figure 3.2, the actual unit cost $C^*(X_1Y_2)$ lies above the minimum unit cost $C(X_1Y_2)$. However, as firms learn by doing and the production experience accumulates, the actual unit cost is likely to decline over time and unit costs get closer to the cost envelope C(X,Y). One of the reasons why actual operating costs are likely to be higher than the ideal operating costs, C(X,Y), is due to the scheduling of production in multi-product facilities. Each time a product run comes to an end, a certain amount of downtime is incurred and some other resources are needed (e.g., labour, consumables) to set up another product run.

Despite mixed evidence on the characteristics of defence production technology, the huge wave of US merger and acquisition (M&A) activity in the 1990s has been partly attributed to a search for scale and scope economies at a time of shrinking demand (Markusen, 1997: 28–32). The degree of cross-sector diversification among the largest defence firms also suggests they perceive and value such economies. We have previously argued that the ability of the largest defence firms to exploit these economies was constrained by

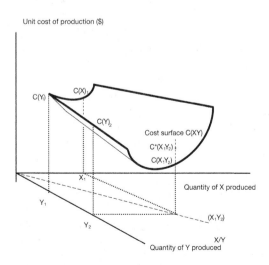

Figure 3.2 Economies of scope and agglomeration

national governments favouring the continued operation of locally based production units. The corollary is that national governments have been prepared to incur the consequences of the higher costs associated with lower-volume production and limited learning-by-doing, i.e., that they have been prepared to pay a premium compared to the lowest price for products made globally in larger volumes or longer runs. This may be changing. Governments now appear more sensitive to the extra costs incurred by small national production runs (and the high-technology nature of some manufacture) and more receptive to the argument that 'economies of scale need to be met through international collaboration and industrial restructuring' (Dunne and Surry, 2006: 411).

Overall, scale economies *per se* may have had only a modest influence on defence industry structure in the past, though the evidence for learning economies and their impact is more convincing (Sandler and Hartley, 1995: 194). But scale, scope and learning economies do appear to influence defence industry cost conditions, thereby helping prompt restructuring of the industry nationally and globally. We return to this issue when discussing barriers to entry.

Product differentiation and innovation

Scale economies help explain industry price competitiveness for a given type of product. Similarly, *product differentiation* explains how industries compensate for an apparent lack of price competitiveness with increased product variety, diversity and quality variation. Defence industry makes a relatively more diverse range of products than most other sectors[6] with the only unifying feature of its output being the intent of its customers to use its products in pursuit of national security and the other uses to which governments allocate defence resources. This unitary purpose makes it possible (and desirable) to investigate the relative merits of all available inputs into defence capability generally and to view the products of defence industry as substitutes for each other to the extent they deliver similar effects.

Defence industry will, in principle, be able to offer a range of solutions to any given capability requirement developed by the procurement agency. If the demand is for weapons systems, for example, defence industry can generate options that are differentiated in terms of lethality, speed to deployment, suitability for specified war-fighting or peace-keeping conditions (varied by climate, terrain, urban or rural environment), technical expertise required for operation, etc. If southern hemisphere countries, for example, develop a strategic requirement for submarines, the maritime conditions (ocean depth and temperature) will be different from those found in northern latitudes. In turn, that implies a possible opportunity for product differentiation in submarine design and manufacture (see Chapter 13). Similarly, ionospheric conditions vary around the globe and render it more or less beneficial for producers to think in terms of generating surveillance equipment that utilise the ionosphere to transmit, reflect and receive radar signals (see Chapter 14).

As the above examples indicate, the scope for product differentiation lies partly in the particulars of different countries' perceptions of their strategic needs and partly in the ingenuity with which defence industry can draw on science and technology to meet those needs within procurement agencies' budgets. Defence industry is thus characterised by highly differentiated products partly because countries' perceived strategic needs vary, partly because their budgets vary widely and partly because the breadth and depth of the military science and technology (S&T) base offers ample opportunity for meeting diverse requirements in a variety of ways. It is in the interests of industry players to pursue product differentiation to limit the pressure to cut price while allowing procurement agencies to achieve value for money. To the extent that industry players succeed in protecting themselves from the sharpest pressures of cost-cutting by offering products more tailored to specific nations' perceived strategic needs, they may survive longer than they would without differentiating their offerings. This is the obverse of our earlier point that when a national government seeks arms customised for its perceived needs, it denies itself access to the scale economies associated with standardised production and COTS and MOTS purchases. It also cedes to the seller bargaining power associated with producing an item for which the buyer perceives there are no good substitutes. This, in turn, allows producers the potential to make greater profit – essentially monopoly rent – and may also help explain why global defence industry has been less concentrated and producing more diverse outputs than other hi-tech sectors.

Product *innovation* sustains product differentiation in the long run and has often been associated with the production of defence and security goods and services. It is driven on the demand side by the aspirations of buyer governments to stay one step ahead of actual and potential adversaries and to cope with novel security challenges. Innovation is built on R&D within and outside industry, incremental learning-by-doing and the diffusion of new technology through labour mobility and purchases of new equipment and systems. It can affect industry structure in several ways.

First, the requirement to innovate-to-compete locks out firms lacking innovative capability or those without relevant (often arcane and specialised) expertise. It favours those possessing or having access to such capability. Traditionally, such firms were already well-established defence-industry suppliers, predominantly located in the USA and Europe, using their own and publicly funded R&D to entrench existing positions and shape technological developments in the sector for the next generation of government requirements. But military requirements are not the only driver of technological change. For example, organisations with little defence acquisition experience have developed technological responses to terrorist threats (Trajtenberg, 2006). Such technologies (including computer sensory interfaces for detection and intelligence, biological detection devices, and internet security applications) have not been developed with military uses primarily in mind and by organisations that focus largely on civilian markets. By exploiting such innovations, defence purchasers force the established defence industry to become more diverse and competitive than in the past. On the other hand, existing defence firms have been adept at acquiring innovative capabilities simply by acquiring the firms hosting them, thereby enabling established major suppliers to turn new technologies into new products.

Second, the impact of product innovation on product diversity in the industry depends on whether it displaces existing products or is a net addition to the list. Decreasing the number of different products but increasing scale of output through standardisation might offer enhanced opportunities to reap scale economies; but just increasing the number of product varieties could lead to cost efficiencies related to economies of scope (see Box 3.2).

Third, all innovation involves initial costs, some of which are sunk (i.e., not retrievable through subsequent sale: R&D costs, for example). Industries with relatively substantial product innovation might also be expected to have relatively high associated barriers to entry. This appears to have been true historically in the defence sector where membership of the industry was relatively stable and newcomers few. To the extent defence product innovations draw increasingly on technology developed outside the military (the use of commercially developed IT in the military command and control systems central to network-enabled operations is a prominent example), the industry's barriers will become more permeable.

Fourth, all product innovation necessitates process innovation. The new processes will offer new or enhanced opportunities for scale and scope economies, and may thus reduce the number of firms that can operate efficiently within a given market – perhaps to the point where costs can be minimised only if all production is undertaken by a single firm. This is a key concern for the defence industries of smaller countries.

Finally, the development of product innovations may be based on work done wholly within industry itself, by government agencies, or shared by government and industry. Recent analysis of innovation stresses how the process is distributed across the system of contributing organisations. Governments can use public research organisations, fiscal support for private sector R&D and innovation, and regulatory measures to shape the development, direction and use of new technological knowledge and, deliberately or otherwise, thereby influence the structure of defence industry. In smaller countries, public investment in defence science and technology can build opportunities for local industry and increase the prospects for its local industry to absorb new technology developed overseas (policy implications are discussed in Chapter 5).

Barriers to entry

Of the world's 100 top arms-producing companies identified by SIPRI in 1990, 53 were still operating in 2003, 25 had merged or been acquired and 18 had exited the industry (Dunne and Surry, 2006: 408). This suggests relatively little new entry to the industry (though there has been some at the lower end of the rankings) and thus the presence of barriers to entry.

Barriers to entry not only help explain why entry into an industry does not occur (Shy, 1995) but also how industry incumbents are shielded from competitive pressure exerted by firms outside the industry. Earlier in this chapter we explained why 'defence industry' is difficult to define precisely. There is an associated difficulty in identifying the extent to which entry barriers exist. Some parts of the defence supply chain may be harder to enter than others but the absence of a settled definition of 'defence industry' precludes any definitive assessment of barriers firms might encounter in entering the industry as such.

Setting these difficulties aside, however, it is useful to classify barriers to entry for defence industry in technological, market and procedural terms (Dunne, 1995). *Technological barriers* relate to the industrial capability required to support a weapons system through its life and include industry-specific knowledge, professional expertise and specialised equipment not usually found in civil sectors. *Market barriers* refer to the particular way in which defence industry products are sold. Given that their market is a government (and sometimes only one), lobbying and personal contact are often thought to offer more promise than general commercial marketing (for a discussion of 'marketing barriers' faced by small Israeli exporters, see Chapter 8). Time and effort are required to build and maintain the necessary networks. *Procedural barriers* reflect special knowledge and experience necessary to deal successfully with the complexities and legal and accounting demands of the procurement process (see Chapter 2).

Barriers to entry may derive from government requirements to obtain an approval or an operating/investment licence or arise from the fear that entry will involve incurring costs in excess of expected benefits. Economies of scale, learning effects, and product differentiation and innovation all have roles to play in generating barriers to entry. If incumbents are already reaping scale economies, newcomers must invest enough in new capital to produce at once at the high volumes necessary to be cost efficient. If incumbents have incurred learning costs in the past, their production costs will have fallen permanently as a result, while newcomers must not only enter but also produce output over time to accumulate a similar level of technical efficiency. If newcomers have to differentiate their product to displace existing entrenched products, this will also call for initial product development, pre-marketing and launch costs. Such barriers tend to deter newcomers unless they have large reserves to bear the risk of entering and failing, or unless governments are prepared to absorb a large part of the entry cost. Incumbent firms are thus protected even though there are no formal restrictions preventing firms from entering the industry.

Similarly, there may be barriers to exit that impose high cost of disengaging from an industry or a sector (e.g., the cost of litigation or redundancy payments). These barriers may restrict the sectoral mobility of incumbent firms and deter newcomers as the presence of exit barriers increases the cost of failure.

In the past, even smaller countries like Sweden could aspire to a national defence industry base which relied strongly on local production and into which entry was heavily regulated (see Chapter 11). It can be argued that barriers may have weakened because production and component sourcing are now transnational, if not global; new technology travels more from the civil to the defence sector than vice versa; and civil companies increasingly perform defence-related tasks, including support roles in combat areas (Singer, 2008). Dunne and Surry (2006: 414) argue that non-defence specialist firms still face substantial procedural and marketing barriers, and technological impediments in some areas. Long-term industry relationships with the NDO, knowledge about the commercial processes involved in doing business in the sector, and a good reputation in the eyes of the NDO are also still perceived to constitute barriers to outsiders (Dowdall *et al.*, 2004: 577). But according to the same study, UK defence electronics firms see trends such as commercial-off-the-shelf (COTS) design, manufacture and procurement, and innovations such as open systems architecture opening their market up to new competition (ibid.: 578).

Diversification

Defence industry produces a highly heterogeneous range of goods and services. But among the SIPRI Top 100, there is considerable variation in the extent to which individual firms are diversified, first, between arms and civil production and, second, among the various sectors of the arms industry.

In 2005, on average, arms accounted for three-quarters of the value of total sales for the largest five, ranging from just over a half (Boeing) to 90 per cent (Northrop Grumman). Over the full SIPRI 100 companies, arms sales average out at just over 60 per cent of total sales, with eight firms wholly arms-specialised and ten earning less than 10 per cent of total sales revenue from arms. Among firms in the smaller countries, there are firms with both a very heavy focus on arms (e.g., Sweden's Land Systems Hagglunds, 100 per cent; Israel's Elbit Systems, 100 per cent and Rafael, 95 per cent; South Korea's Korea Aerospace Industries, 89 per cent) and with rather limited involvement, relative to civil goods sales (e.g., South Korea's Samsung, 1 per cent; and Brazil's Embraer, 10 per cent).[7] The largest firms also span several arms sectors (BAE Systems supplying, for example, artillery, aircraft, electronics, missiles, small arms and ammunition, and ships) and although 60 per cent of the SIPRI Top 100 operate in only one sector, sectors like 'electronics' can themselves be quite diverse. (All figures are drawn from Surry and the SIPRI Arms Industry Network, 2007, Table 9A1.)

These are 'snapshots', however, taken in one year. In the post-Cold War period, the previous stability has given way to greater dynamism, with some firms specialising more in arms production and others diversifying away from it.

Of the 53 SIPRI Top 100 for 1990 still operating in 2003, seven had increased arms sales and reduced civil sales and 15 had reduced arms sales and increased civil sales. Arms represented an increased share of total sales for 23 companies, a constant share for two, and a smaller share for 28 (Dunne and Surry, 2006, Table 9.4).

Overall, defence industry tends to be dominated at the top end by firms specialising in the products required by a particular type of customer (Defence) but diversified across many sectors within that specialised niche. It reflects the outcome of competition shaped by buyers keen to exploit multi-dimensional capabilities, as in the provision of networked weapons systems, and dependent, by choice, on private providers to integrate systems for their government customers. As noted earlier, as the military technology require-ments of governments change, so defence firms have sought to diversify in the direction of acquiring capabilities new to them but essential for satisfying emerging customer needs.

Smaller countries simply cannot replicate within their own industries multi-dimensional diversification on this scale, though it is significant that a number of small country defence industries are characterised by highly diversified firms (e.g., in this volume, Sweden, see Chapter 11; Singapore, see Chapter 9; Israel, see Chapter 8; and Australia, see Chapter 6).

Vertical integration

Vertical integration describes the extent to which various stages of production take place within the boundaries of the same firm. To the extent that NDOs produce elements of capability (through the operation of historically common government-owned arsenals, shipyards and aircraft factories, for example), they themselves contribute to the vertical integration of defence industry. Discus-sion about the relative merits of public and private ownership, discussed later in this chapter, then become relevant (Markowski and Hall, 2007).

Within commercial defence industry, there is an observable trend away from vertical integration as firms trade higher transaction costs inherent in inter-firm dealings for lower input costs achieved by buying from firms specialising in a particular line of production. In the UK defence aerospace industry, for example, firms are outsourcing more manufacturing, maintaining only core competencies such as design and strategic elements like systems integration (Jackson, 2004). Of 17 US instances of defence industry restructuring in 1989–96 noted by Oden (1999), only one was described as a vertical merger.

The defence firm

NDOs buy defence materiel from *firms*, not from the defence industry. We turn now from the industry level to firms.[8] Firms are the economic units which decide how to assemble inputs (factors of production) and transform them through a production process into outputs for sale in the market. It is at the level of the firm that we observe decisions on how to compete for defence business – conduct relating to price, product and innovation which is shaped by the industry structure but can also help determine it. One distinguishing characteristic of a defence firm is that some or all of its output must form an input into defence capability or be an intermediate input into the production of other firms which sell directly to Defence.

Defence sector suppliers can be very large, sell a wide range of products that may not be dominated by sales of arms, and are sometimes highly profitable. On the other hand, some defence sector suppliers are small, specialise in defence-related sales and may or may not make profits all the time. In what follows we explore how individual firms compete with each other and what gives them competitive advantage. Firms are traditionally portrayed by economists as competing on the basis of price but the nature and quality of what they produce, the delivery schedule, and how they interact with their customers are equally important factors (see Dowdall *et al.*, 2004: 576, for a discussion of this aspect of the UK defence electronics industry behaviour). Competitive advantage is reflected in sustained, above-average profitability which implies there is something *different* (or unique) about the firm achieving it compared with its competitors. This difference may pertain, for example, to the nature of its technology, the knowledge that underpins it, how it organises itself, or how it interacts with its customers. We may expect the successful firm to possess, or have unique access to, resources, assets and capabilities that other firms cannot access. Such assets often have to do with specific knowledge of how to produce output and/or satisfy customers. A focus on the distinctive capabilities of firms also helps explain what firms make and what they buy in: where they will draw the boundaries of the organisation in order to make best use of their resources in competition.

The ways in which defence industry firms may achieve competitive advantage include:

- scale and scope economies;
- knowledge-base, innovation and learning;
- dynamic capabilities;
- supply chain management.

Scale and scope economies

A firm will derive competitive advantage from the scale economies inherent in a given technology to the extent it can access to those economies more readily than its rivals. This will most likely be the case if it has made past investments of a nature and on a scale capable of meeting the next and future rounds of demand, and if other firms in the industry operate on a smaller scale and cannot acquire new capital quickly enough to meet upcoming orders, or if they fear scaling up as they may not win defence contracts sufficient to yield a worthwhile return on the invested capital. The advantage could be undermined if competitors chose to merge and combine their capabilities: an example of how scale and scope economies can catalyse industry restructuring.

Firms enjoying an existing advantage of scale may have this position for historic reasons. Defence firms in the past have often invested in larger production facilities but carried spare capacity either because governments have required it (for example, to allow a wartime surge in production) or because government orders have been too widely spaced to allow continuous full-capacity employment. In the presence of scale economies not immediately available to its rivals, a firm can price lower than its competitors to win contracts and yet still make profit as the excess capacity is utilised. NDOs often lack enough information about the firm's cost curve to know, however, the price that would yield just enough profit to make the firm bid for defence contracts, i.e., the lowest price and best value for money the NDO could reasonably expect to achieve.

The configuration of a defence firm can be explained partly by the search for economies of scope as well as scale. For example, if the principal customer, Defence, seeks network-centric solutions, linking various platforms to form an integrated system of combat systems, firms may achieve competitive advantage by assembling within one organisation all the capabilities needed to meet that requirement and employing them in a way that reduces costs relative to more fragmented production and procurement alternatives (see the discussion of naval ship building in Australia in Chapter 13). Across the sector, firms that once specialised in producing weapons platforms for air, sea or land have engaged in horizontal integration (i.e., diversification), and as one commentator put it: 'Rationalisation ... across the entire defence industry (land, sea and air platforms and systems) [is] the mechanism by which economies of scale, scope and agglomeration are pursued' (Braddon, 2004: 503).

Knowledge-base, innovation and learning

A key source of difference among firms, and of the competitive advantage one firm can achieve over others, is the knowledge base that each possesses. Knowledge important to defence firms relates to the research, design and development behind new defence products and ways of producing them. It includes understanding how to bid for Defence contracts in a particular jurisdiction, which Defence decision-makers to interact with and how to do so. Defence firms also need to know how to produce defence-related goods and services themselves and how to forge relationships with other firms with complementary products. In each case, the firm exploits pre-existing knowledge in conducting these activities, and generates new knowledge in doing so. Some of this knowledge is documented (e.g., operations manuals, procurement procedures); some is known by individuals but not written down; some is reflected solely in the way the organisation works (its routines and culture). Knowledge that is documented is said to be codified; knowledge that is not written down is said to be uncodified. The more difficult it is to articulate and communicate uncodified knowledge, the more it is said to be 'tacit'. (For an extended discussion of these distinctions see Howells, 1996, and Cowan *et al.*, 2000.) The firm's *knowledge base* comprises all of its codified, uncodified, tacit and organisational knowledge.

Every firm has a different knowledge base. An important reason for this is that even if firms make the same type of product, their production processes must involve human inputs – and all humans are different from each other. For present purposes, the essential point is that the uncodified and tacit knowledge about, say, production, marketing, contracting and relationship-building maintained by each individual employee and manager varies both within and among firms and reflects into the performance of each firm, for better or worse. What individuals know also changes continuously: consciously or otherwise, performing their activities results in learning that alters their own and the firm's knowledge base.

In the case of defence firms, codified knowledge can play a particularly important role in defining competitive advantage. Engineering design knowledge codified in blueprints and patents is at the heart of the core capabilities of weapons manufacturers, and source codes underpin the competitive strengths of software producers. If the systems embodying this knowledge are sought by NDOs, then the knowledge itself is of great value to the companies possessing it and gives them a distinctive place in the industry. Rolls Royce, General Electric and Pratt and Whitney are all among the top 20 companies on the SIPRI 100 list: each one of them also possesses specialist engineering knowledge in the design of jet engines that no other company shares.

While defence firms are distinguished by the stock of particular, defence-relevant knowledge they possess at any particular moment, that stock is the outcome of formal and informal processes that have been going on in the past and will continue into the future. We consider two sources of new knowledge generation here: learning-by-doing and Research and Development (R&D). Both are associated with defence firms in the economic literature.

Learning-by-doing

Learning-by-doing (LBD) is the result of *cumulative* experience derived from repeating the same production process on multiple occasions. Such effects were observed long ago, for example, in naval shipbuilding (Searle and Goody, 1945) and aircraft production (Alchian, 1963). British defence electronics firms reported in the early 2000s that 'even though actual production "runs" were small, the cumulative output over time definitely resulted in cost savings' (Dowdall *et al.*, 2004: 580).

LBD offers the potential of allowing firms to *sustain* above-average profits (the indicator of competitive advantage). Increasing cumulative output will continuously reduce their unit production costs, possibly the more quickly if the same firm was involved in pre-production R&D and/or if it has earlier historic experience of similar production. This may help account for the persistence of some firms in the industry even in the midst of tumultuous change. A lesson for small country NDOs is to postpone placing orders until learning-by-doing is well underway. By then unit production costs should have fallen, taking prices down with them.

Research & Development

LBD leads to incremental changes in knowledge that might best be envisaged as movements towards maximising the efficiency of existing technology. Step-change improvements embodied in entirely new products and processes require formal investments in R&D. When the competition for military advantage causes NDOs to place a high premium on establishing and maintaining a 'technology edge' in defence capability inputs, they must induce the appropriate industry investments. And responding to changes in the security environment (for example, awareness of global terrorism post-9/11) may require NDOs to adapt existing capabilities or to introduce new capabilities, responses often requiring rapid innovation. However, the risk of hold-up may discourage firms from investing in the development of new defence-related knowledge. Since hold-up is related to the defence *specificity* of the knowledge, this may help explain why firms themselves have tended to draw on civil-oriented R&D that also has defence applications – so-called 'spin-in'. IT is a key example. (This has implications for how firms structure themselves and their relationships and is taken up again below.) For their part, governments have responded to the hold-up problem in a number of ways. Research work can be shared among universities and government laboratories, thus reducing the size of the industry commitment. In order to secure competitive advantage by accessing the new knowledge thus generated, individual firms must invest in relationships with other research organisations and to forge institutional arrangements that not only give access to important findings but, more importantly, confer the right to exclusive application.

The research itself, its exploitation, the relationship-building and effective participation in cross-organisational collaborative arrangements all require high levels of managerial, financial, legal and technical expertise. Since important elements of the expertise may be profoundly tacit and specific to particular individuals and organisations, they may give or deny a particular firm competitive advantage.

On the process side, new production knowledge can reduce production costs, shifting the unit cost curve downwards (see Box 3.1, also shifting down the cost surface in Box 3.2) and enabling defence firms to compete more effectively for contracts in a procurement environment focused on value for money and cost containment. A major incentive to undertake process-oriented R&D and design, especially if government-funded, is the prospect of taking forward lessons learned at the pre-production stage to the production phase. Implementing new technology is notoriously unpredictable and possession of knowledge from pre-production work can assist in building know-how (tacit knowledge) that will lead to success rather than failure and/or more rapid subsequent learning-by-doing. As such knowledge is often highly specific to the particular production processes of the firm, it is hard for competitors to acquire and technological imitation can often cost at least half the amount spent initially by the innovator. All this suggests that while the risks may be high, the potential benefits of process innovation can both be tempting and the basis for competitive advantage. Analysis of defence companies has often viewed large R&D expenditures as a key feature of their operations and strategy (see, for example, the important contribution of Rogerson, 1995), though evidence suggests that firms in civil industries have understood the same lessons and that defence companies are by no means unusual in the extent and intensity of their R&D spending.

Dynamic capabilities

Earlier in this chapter, we argued that the NDO customer's characteristics and requirements played a key role in shaping defence industry as suppliers sought to match their capabilities and behaviours to the needs and institutional peculiarities of their main client. This argument should not be overstated. Many firms that sell goods and services that finish up as inputs into Defence capability also have other markets. '[A] glance up and down the supply chain or value stream immediately reveals an extremely diverse range of markets or sectors that are associated with, or overlap, the defence industrial supply system' (Dowdall, 2004: 538). In many industrialised countries, the 'defence industrial supply system' includes firms that are also strongly export-oriented and serve global customers as 'original equipment manufacturers' (OEMs) or 'system integrators' (BAE Systems and Thales are examples of broad-based, multinational manufacturers and system integrators while Rolls Royce is an example of a global OEM). In our sample of small countries, companies such as Sweden's SAAB (see Chapter 11) or Israel's Rafael (Chapter 8) are examples of export-oriented system integrators.

A source of competitive advantage that builds on these observations is rooted in what Teece has termed *dynamic capabilities*: 'the capacity to sense opportunities and to reconfigure knowledge assets, competences and complementary assets and technologies to achieve sustainable competitive advantage' (Teece, 1998: 73). These capabilities amount to successfully identifying changes in market demand before they are well articulated and reorganising the resources and operations of the firm to address the changes more effectively than others can or do. Post-Cold War, changes in the nature of defence and security requirements have engendered considerable uncertainty in the defence industry investment environment. Strategies adopted by firms in the USA to manage these uncertainties are instructive. These include: (1) diversification – remaining in the defence sector but entering new non-defence product lines; (2) retrenchment – remaining in the defence sector but selling assets not thought likely to offer competitive returns in future; (3) spin-off – leaving the defence sector by selling off all defence-related businesses; and (4) consolidation (or market extension) – remaining in the defence sector and acquiring companies that served different defence-related markets (Susman and O'Keefe, 1998).

Consolidation appears to have been the favoured corporate strategy in the 1990s. At that time the US government was not expected to start new programmes needing substantial R&D for many years. Hence it seemed most profitable to acquire other defence businesses already generating good revenues and with limited R&D commitments (ibid.). Since then the threat of terrorism in particular has encouraged firms to develop technological capabilities in communication and surveillance that may be most readily obtained by acquiring non-defence businesses, a form of diversification not foreseen in the 1990s. The fact that strategies can change like this reflects dynamic capabilities at work – though only with the benefit of hindsight will we know which firms were able to claim competitive advantage from deploying them.

Supply chain management

As noted elsewhere in this chapter, the large defence industry prime contractors with which NDOs deal are supplied by several tiers of subcontractors – or, as some authors see it, an interdependent supply network or matrix (Dowdall, 2004: 539). The primes must be competitive on price, quality and schedule to win contracts. This leads them to demand equally high performance from their own suppliers and (1) to select efficient, flexible and innovative firms as their key partners; (2) to drop past suppliers who fail to meet current competitive requirements; (3) to manage the resulting network effectively. It has been argued that success in managing the whole process but, particularly, in addressing the demands of supply network management reflects a new form of competitive advantage (Braddon, 2004: 504). While this point is not new, it has acquired greater significance as firms have increasingly outsourced activities previously undertaken in-house and, as a result, become more dependent on the responsiveness and efficiency of their supply chains.

An extension of the same principle applies to the internationalisation of component sourcing. Civilian manufacturers increasingly source components worldwide from low-cost suppliers in order to maintain their own cost-competitiveness (Arndt and Kierzkowski, 2001). However, this outsourcing of military-specific components to least-cost overseas suppliers has been limited in defence industries. This is in part because governments, and especially the US government, apply export controls and restrict the diffusion of technology. In part, however, it is because governments in importing countries add import substitutions demands to their procurement requirements. To the extent that they succeed in diverting defence production to their domestic producers, global defence production becomes more fragmented than would otherwise be the case, with small batches of components produced in different countries under offset/import substitution arrangements. Thus, specialised defence manufacturers have not been as successful as their civilian counterparts in transferring manufacturing capability to lower-wage economies.

Ownership

Issues of ownership and control are of interest in the context of procurement for two reasons. Governments seek *security of supply* for inputs into their defence capabilities, and wish to achieve *efficiency* in the production of those inputs as a means of obtaining 'value for money' in what they purchase.

Ownership relates to who, within the nation's legal framework, owns the assets used to produce defence inputs. In the case of private ownership, the owners of the assets form a company, hold equity (stocks and shares) in it, and have a (residual) right to the revenue or income remaining once all legitimate claims have been settled with their workforce (wages); suppliers of materials, fuel and energy, and component inputs; and financiers (debt servicing). Some or all of the remaining income, i.e., profit, may be reinvested in the company rather than distributed to equity-holders, and shares may be traded during the life of the company or provide the basis for making a claim on the value of the assets of the company if sold or wound up. Companies may or may not choose to offer shares to the general public and see their share price quoted on the stock exchange. Publicly quoted companies are required to place information about their performance in the public domain on a regular basis (through, for example, annual reports).

In the case of public (or state, or nationalised) ownership, Government owns all non-human assets of production and employs the workforce that uses them. The production unit itself may be operated, in effect, as a government department with all costs covered at public expense and no profit generated; or it may be corporatised, i.e., required at least to break even financially, or to achieve a target rate of return on capital.

Between the polar extremes of pure private and pure public ownership lie hybrids that allow, for example, the state to own some shares or shares with special voting rights in otherwise privately owned companies, non-government-not-for-profit enterprises to operate as neither government agencies nor private enterprise, and so on.[9] Ownership arrangements may also vary from one part of a country's defence industry to another. For private companies, the owners are often most interested in the yield on their share of the equity – derived from a combination of dividends paid to them and gains in the value of their shares.

In order to secure supply, NDOs seek to ensure that, through an often-lengthy life cycle and changing technological and security conditions, the supply of inputs into capability is guaranteed. NDOs' objective of efficiency relates to the cost, delivery schedule, and the performance of the weapons systems they buy, again bearing in mind the overall life cycle and associated support services. Both security of supply and efficiency are difficult to achieve:

no nation (not even the USA) can any longer source all inputs from within its national borders while achieving efficiency is complicated by the difficulties in writing fully specified contracts with suppliers, and the costs of monitoring and enforcement (see Chapter 2). Further, the two objectives may not be compatible: a small increase in security of supply may require investments by suppliers that raise life-cycle costs substantially, for example.

Governments have experimented with all of the ownership alternatives outlined above. For the past 25 years, governments in many countries have tended to divest ownership of defence production assets into private hands and/or to seek supply from private rather than state-owned companies (outsourcing). The privatisation of defence services and support is drawing new kinds of supplier into combat zones and private military companies (PMCs) are now doing tasks such as guarding personnel and buildings that only armed forces would have undertaken in the past (Dunne and Surry, 2006: 413; Singer, 2008). In smaller countries particularly, it might be expected that service activities lend themselves to domestic supply rather more readily than manufacturing and that the future growth of commercial supply lies in that direction. It is estimated that the global revenue of military contractors was US$100 billion in 2004 (Holmqvist, 2005: 7). The contracting out of non-core military activities, primarily logistic support at bases and outside areas of operations, has long been a major feature of organisational restructuring of the militaries around the world.

Of the sample of small countries discussed in Part II, Australia has perhaps gone furthest in contracting out a broad range of non-combat-related services (see Chapter 6 and Wylie, 2006). These include, *inter alia*: the management of the storage, maintenance and distribution of explosive ordnance by Thales (formally ADI Ltd); the operation of the basic flying training school by BAE Systems; and garrison support to military units by The Spotless Group and Serco Sodexho Defence Services; the provision of Defence's national warehousing and distribution services by Tenix Toll under Aus$920 million, ten-year contract. But military outsourcing in Australia also includes government-owned but commercially operated and supported strategic-level information capabilities (e.g., Boeing Australia supports Defence satellite communication stations). Defence is also the largest buyer of non-military information and communications technology (ICT) in the Australian government. In 2004–05, it accounted for 22 per cent by value and 27 per cent by number of Australian government ICT contracts (Wylie, 2006: 53–6).

The practice of deploying contractors in areas of operations as a force multiplier and 'surge' capability is gaining momentum. During the 1991 Gulf War, the USA employed one contractor for every 100 soldiers to provide logistic and other support. In the early stages of the current Iraq War, the ratio was 1:10 (ASPI, 2005: 8). Since the early 1990s, the USA has been contracting out its logistics to large prime contractors and prime vendors. The UK has followed with similar, though much smaller, contracts. Contracting out in the USA and Western Europe has included military training and intelligence. Private Finance Initiatives (PFIs, pioneered in the UK) have involved the use of private capital to provide capital assets for the military (e.g., base facilities and training equipment) so that the outright purchase of capital assets has been replaced by the leasing of fully supported equipment with users contracting hours of service. Clearly, the private sector can respond to military demands in war and peacetime (Fredland, 2004) and is shortening the lead times for doing so. But the privatisation and contracting out of combat-related defence activities remain a contentious issue (Markusen, 2003).

Government ownership of the means of production is neither a sufficient nor necessary condition for achieving NDO efficiency objectives. It is not sufficient because incompetent or inefficient performance can exist as much under bureaucratic systems of control as they can in any other – but government organisations are not normally subjected to the market test and, thus, they are under less pressure to contain their costs. It is not necessary because mechanisms to monitor private companies' performance, above and beyond standard public accounting requirements, can be invoked. These include arrangements agreed in advance for government auditors to regularly inspect suppliers' books to check on their claims (see Chapter 4).

Such arguments tend to suggest that procurement from privately owned sources of supply might always be the better solution. The key difficulty with this is that there is also a security objective to consider. Privately owned companies may simply not have the capabilities to provide required supply and could never guarantee their survival into the distant future (see, for example, Chapter 13 for the discussion of publicly-owned common use facilities in Australian naval shipbuilding and repair). If Defence wants security of supply, it must make it worthwhile for the shareholders to wish to continue holding the shares: negotiating to eliminate profit may be good for efficiency but may imperil the company's future. In addition, governments may be unwilling to allow privately owned concerns to develop and acquire new technological knowledge which could be of benefit to enemy countries, non-state agents and terrorists. This suggests that countries will continue to have a case for maintaining in government ownership certain security-sensitive activities (e.g., defence laboratories).

Putting on one side the most security-sensitive acquisitions, governments might divest themselves of production assets and turn to the private sector with a view to maximising efficiency. However, as already indicated, private ownership alone will not necessarily lead to efficient performance. If internal industry conditions do not lead to efficiency-generating (active) competition, pressure for performance would have to be exerted by the threat of entry (contestability or latent competition). However, in world markets, competition is often limited to the activity of only very few firms in some parts of the industry, and if national governments also erect procedural entry barriers, the threat from potential entrants will appear weak. Second, private companies will be reluctant to make defence-specific investments if they believe they have only their national government to turn to for custom. Governments may then have to make arrangements to subsidise or underwrite those investments, or make them on behalf of the private sector. At that point, it becomes necessary to ask whether government might not have done at least as well to undertake production in public ownership in the first place.

The potentially ambiguous efficiency outcomes associated with ownership and control arrangements in defence industry mean that, over the decades, the policy pendulum has swung across the full spectrum, from full public ownership and operation to wide-ranging private ownership and operation. The only prediction that seems safe is that such change and experiment will continue.

Notes

1 Also, when civilian-line aircraft or vehicles are maintained by specialised defence contractors, they are described as 'defence industry' activities. If, however, similar services are produced in-house by logistics elements of the NDO, they are included in the NDO activity but not counted as defence industry support.
2 To keep things in perspective, however, the arms manufacturers remain small relative to the largest corporations in the world. In 2006, Exxon Mobil, ranked largest, had revenue of US$359 billion compared with Boeing's total (i.e., arms and non-arms) sales of US$55 billion (*Fortune 500*, 2006).
3 They are believed to be manufactured in at least 90 countries of the world (SAS, 2004) and ammunition for them in more than 75 (SAS, 2005).
4 Even commodities have dimensions that make differentiation possible and profitable for individual suppliers, however. These include location and timeliness of delivery.
5 Note that economies of scale and scope in *production*, and the related concept of the minimum efficient scale of production, are conceptually different from economies of scale and scope in purchasing (see Chapter 2). However, similar diagrams can be drawn to show how unit costs vary with changing scale and scope of production. In Chapter 2, we considered changes in unit costs as the scale and scope of acquisitions varied. However, as prices demanded by sellers are related to unit costs of production, scale- and scope-related efficiencies in production are normally associated with quantity discounts in purchasing.
6 This is if 'defence industry' is defined with reference to its main customer: Defence. But this broad approach is similar to defining all industrial firms that mainly produce consumer products: consumer industry.
7 Derived from Dunne and Surry (2006), Table 9A.1.
8 A useful analysis of the contemporary defence firm may be found in Hartley and Sandler (2003).
9 In our case study of the Australian naval shipbuilding (see Chapter 13), Tenix Defence, one of Australia's largest defence contractors, is an example of a privately owned but not publicly quoted company. ADI Ltd was formed in 1989 as a corporatised but government-owned defence company. In 1999, it was sold to the French company Thales and Australia's Transfield as a 50–50 venture and, in 2006, the Transfield share was purchased by Thales. Another major Australian naval shipbuilder, the Australian Submarine Corporation (ASC) was established as a joint venture between Sweden's Kockums, the Australian government-owned Australian Industry Development Corporation and Wormalds International and Chicago Bridge and Iron. In 2000, the Australian government bought Kockums' share of ASC equity.

References

Alchian, A. (1963) 'Reliability of progress curves in airframe production', *Econometrica*, 31(October): 679–93.

Arndt, S. W. and Kierzkowski, H. (2001) *Fragmentation, New Production Patterns in the World Economy*, Oxford: Oxford University Press.

ASPI (2005) *War and Profit: Doing Business on the Battlefield*, Canberra: Australian Strategic Policy Institute.

Braddon, D. (2004) 'The matrix reloaded – What future for the defence firm?', *Defence and Peace Economics*, 15(6): 499–507.

Brauer, J. and Dunne, J. P. (eds) (2004) *Arms Trade and Economic Development*, Abingdon: Routledge.

Control Arms (2006) *Arms Without Borders: Why a Globalised Trade Needs Global Controls*, Amnesty International, International Network on Small Arms, Oxfam. Online. Available at: www.controlarms.org.

Cowan, R., David, P. A. and Foray, D. (2000) 'The explicit economics of knowledge codification and tacitness', *Industrial and Corporate Change*, 9(2): 211–53.

Dixit, A. K. (1980) 'The role of investment in entry deterrence,' *Economic Journal*, 90 (357): 95–106.

Dowdall, P. (2004) 'Chains, networks and shifting paradigms: the UK defence industry supply system', *Defence and Peace Economics*, 15(6): 535–50.

Dowdall, P., Braddon, D. and Hartley, K. (2004) 'The UK defence electronics industry: adjusting to change', *Defence and Peace Economics*, 15(6): 565–86.

Dunne, J. P. (1995) 'The defense industrial base', in K. Hartley and T. Sandler (eds) *Handbook of Defense Economics*, Vol. 1, Amsterdam: North-Holland.

Fortune 500 (2006) 'Annual ranking of America's largest corporations'. Online. Available at: http://money.cnn.com/magazines/fortune/fortune500/2006/full_list/.

Dunne, J. P. and Surry, E. (2006) 'Arms production', in *SIPRI Yearbook 2006*, Oxford: Oxford University Press.

Fredland, J. E. (2004) 'Outsourcing military force: a transaction costs perspective on the role of military companies', *Defence and Peace Economics*, 15: 205–20.

Hartley, K. (2007) 'The arms industry, procurement and industrial policies', in T. Sandler and K. Hartley (eds) *Handbook of Defense Economics*, Vol. 2, *Defense in a Globalized World*, Amsterdam: North-Holland.

Hartley, K., Hooper, N., Sweeney, M., Matthews, R., Braddon, D., Dowdall, P. and Bradley, J. (1997) 'Armoured fighting vehicle supply chain analysis, study of the value of defence industry to the UK economy', unpublished report, Centre for Defence Economics, University of York.

Hartley, K. and Sandler, T. (2003) 'The future of the defence firm', *Kyklos*, 56(3): 361–80.

Hay, D. and Morris, D. (1991) *Industrial Economics and Organization: Theory and Evidence*, 2nd edn, Oxford: Oxford University Press.

Holmqvist, C. (2005) *Private Security Companies: The Case for Regulation*, SIPRI Policy Paper No. 9, Stockholm: Stockholm International Peace Research Institute.

Howells, J. (1996) 'Tacit knowledge, innovation and technology transfer', *Technology Analysis and Strategic Management*, 8(2): 91–106.

Jackson, I. (2004) 'The future of the defence firm: the case of the UK aerospace industry', *Defence and Peace Economics*, 15(6): 519–34.

James, A. (2004) 'US defence R&D spending: an analysis of the impacts', Report for EURAB Working Group.

Jubb, C. D. and Markowski, S. (1991) 'Scale, scope and flexibility in Australian manufacturing', in C. Hamilton (ed.) *The Economic Dynamics of Australian Industry*, Sydney: Allen & Unwin, pp. 100–17.

Markowski, S. and Hall, P. (2007) 'Public sector entrepreneurialism and the production of defence', *Public Finance and Management*, 7(3): 260–94.

Markowski, S. and Jubb, C. D. (1989) 'The impact of microelectronics on scale in manufacturing industries', *Australian Journal of Management*, 14(2): 12–55.

Markusen, A. (1997) 'The economics of defence industry mergers and divestiture', *Economic Affairs*, 17(4): 28–32.

—— (2003) 'The case against privatising national security', *Governance: An International Journal of Policy, Administration, and Institutions*, 14(4): 471–501.

Markusen, A. and Costigan, S. (eds) (1999) *Arming the Future: A Defense Industry for the 21st Century*, New York: Council on Foreign Relations.

Oden, M. (1999) 'Cashing in, cashing out, and converting: restructuring of the defense industrial base in the 1990s', in A. Markusen and S. Costigan (eds) *Arming the Future: A Defense Industry for the 21st Century*, New York: Council on Foreign Relations.

Pages, E. (1999) 'Defense mergers: weapons cost, innovation and international arms cooperation', in A. Markusen and S. Costigan (eds) *Arming the Future: A Defense Industry for the 21st Century*, New York: Council on Foreign Relations.

Rogerson, W. (1995) 'Incentive models of the defense procurement process', in K. Hartley and T. Sandler (eds) *Handbook of Defense Economics*, Vol. 1, Amsterdam: North-Holland.

Sandler, T. and Hartley, K. (1995) *The Economics of Defense*, Cambridge: Cambridge University Press.

SAS (2004) *Small Arms Survey, 2004: Rights at Risk*, Oxford: Oxford University Press.

—— (2005) *Small Arms Survey, 2005: Weapons at War*, Oxford: Oxford University Press.

Scherer, F. (1980) *Industrial Market Structure and Economic Performance*, 2nd edn, Chicago: Rand McNally.

Searle, A. D. and Goody, C. S. (1945) 'Productivity increases in selected wartime shipbuilding programs', *Monthly Labor Review*, 6: 1132–42.

Shy, O. (1995) *Industrial Organization: Theory and Applications*, Cambridge, MA: MIT Press.

Singer, P. W. (2008) *Corporate Warriors: The Rise of the Privatized Military Industry*, Ithaca, NY: Cornell University Press.

SIPRI (2006) *SIPRI Yearbook 2006: Armaments, Disarmament and National Security*, Oxford: Oxford University Press.

—— (2007) *SIPRI Yearbook 2007: Armaments, Disarmament and National Security*, Oxford: Oxford University Press.

Sköns, E. and Surry, E. (2007) 'Arms production', in *SIPRI Yearbook 2007*, Oxford: Oxford University Press.

Spence, M.A. (1977) 'Entry, capacity, investment and oligopoly pricing', *Bell Journal of Economics*, 8(2): 534–44.

Surry, E. and the SIPRI Arms Industry Network (2007) 'The 100 largest arms-producing companies, 2005', Appendix 9A, in *SIPRI Yearbook 2007*, Oxford: Oxford University Press.

Susman, G. and O'Keefe, S. (1998) 'Introduction: post-Cold War challenges for government and industry', in G. Susman and S. O'Keefe (eds) *The Defense Industry in the Post Cold War Era*, Amsterdam: Pergamon, pp. 3–21.

Teece, D. (1998) 'Capturing value from knowledge assets: the new economy markets for know-how and intangible assets', *California Management Review*, 40(3): 55–79.

Todd, D. (1988) *Defence Industries: A Global Perspective*, London: Routledge.

Trajtenberg, M. (2006) 'Defence R&D in the anti-terrorist era', *Defence and Peace Economics*, 17(3): 177–200.

Wylie, R. (2006) 'Supplying and supporting Australia's military capability', *Growth*, 57, Melbourne, Committee for the Economic Development of Australia.

4 Buyer–seller interaction in defence procurement

Stefan Markowski, Peter Hall and Robert Wylie

In Chapter 1, we referred to different forms of relationship in the procurement process, including those between different types of agent (e.g., the Defence Procurement Agency, DPA, and Industry), those between the same type (e.g., firms within Industry), and those within organisations themselves (e.g., the DPA and the Services). In this chapter, we focus on the interactions between the DPA and its Industry suppliers, taking the perspective of the DPA, which sets most such transaction in motion.

We also noted earlier that the 'publicness' of defence-related products usually diminishes as we move back up the production chain from final national security outputs to intermediate products. All small countries discussed in this volume are capitalist market economies in which defence-related goods and services are normally produced by private enterprise and, thus, a large proportion of the defence materiel purchased by the DPA (e.g., capital equipment, consumables, and logistic support services) is procured through the market from commercial suppliers. Some intermediate outputs are also sourced from 'corporatised' government-owned enterprises that operate in a manner similar to their private commercial counterparts.[1] However, Defence makes certain intermediate products (e.g., military intelligence reports, battle damage repair) in-house, because Government seeks, as result, to maintain the operational sovereignty of the NDO or because such products are characterised by high levels of 'publicness' and commercial enterprise has no incentive to supply them (e.g., defence-related 'blue sky' research). And, as noted in Chapter 3, government-owned shipyards and armouries are sometimes retained in-house by Defence as political legacy commitments even though they could be contracted out and privatised. In this chapter, we focus on the interaction between the NDO and those suppliers that are either privately-owned firms or corporatised publicly-owned enterprises. (We therefore exclude the DPA-mediated, intra-NDO supply arrangements between in-house production units, e.g., government-owned factories and Service 'customers'.)

When the relationship between the DPA and its suppliers is market-mediated, it is shaped by the relative bargaining power of each side which, in turn, derives from the market structure. As we noted in Chapter 1, the more a DPA can deal with suppliers in a contestable market environment (i.e., one in which it can credibly threaten to use alternative sources of supply without incurring great cost to itself), the greater its bargaining power vis-à-vis suppliers. And, if it is possible to move custom from one source of supply to another in the event of supplier underperformance, there is scope for efficiency gains to be realised by the NDO as it can credibly threaten inefficient or non-competitive suppliers with switching its business to those providers who offer better value for money. It is convenient to frame the relationship between the DPA and its suppliers as one between principal and its agents. This *principal–agent framework* is introduced in the following section.

However, the scope for switching suppliers depends on the number of potential sources of supply, the relative market power of each side, and the DPA's ability to use its market muscle, if any, to its best advantage. In the section entitled 'Source selection' we discuss the relative advantages and disadvantages of using sole or multiple sources of supply.

When the interaction between the DPA and its suppliers is market-mediated, it normally involves the use of formal legal contracts. These contract-governed supply relationships may take a variety of forms ranging from closely collaborative to arm's length and adversarial. In the section entitled 'Contracting and contract management', we use the principal–agent framework to discuss contracting arrangements between the parties.

Defence offsets taking the form of countertrade, buyback, local content requirements and other compensatory arrangements are widely used by DPAs around the world. The inclusion of offsets requirements broadens the scope of the procurement deal and makes it more complex. For this reason, we discuss offsets as a distinct type of procurement transaction. Offsets can be described as compensatory procurement requirements designed to offset the cost of purchasing defence equipment from overseas by means of a reciprocal commitment by suppliers in support of a purchaser's defence effort or domestic economy. They represent additional requirements stipulated by the buyer that may or may not be included in the procurement contract. Many of these compensatory arrangements are mandatory, i.e., they must be applied by the DPA as a result of government offsets policy. All forms of offsets arrangements involve reciprocity but there are distinctions in the nature of the transactions. In the section entitled 'Defence offsets', a distinction is drawn between three broad categories of offsets: countertrade, local content requirements and bundling. *Countertrade*, if applied to products that were previously only traded domestically, amounts to export creation. *Local content requirements* induce import substitution. *Bundling of requirements* influences the quantity and composition of a country's imports of goods and services. Many offset-type arrangements used by small countries involve a mixture of all three categories.

Next, we consider *international collaborative procurement*. This is the case when two or more DPAs join forces to consolidate their requirements and source them jointly rather than separately. These arrangements are common in Europe, where work-share and cost-share (*juste retour*) procurement projects have long been sponsored by governments, including small country governments. One-off collaborative arrangements have also been used by non-European small countries (e.g., Australia and New Zealand). And, if it succeeds, the development and acquisition of the Joint Strike Fighter by the US-led consortium of 'partner' nations (see Box 2.1 in Chapter 2) will take one-off international collaborative procurement to a new level. We conclude the chapter with a brief discussion of European attempts to move away from one-off work-share arrangements to form multinational procurement agencies.

Finally, in the section entitled 'Free trade facilitation and regulation', we focus on international attempts to enhance the cross-border trade in goods and services purchased by governments: the so-called agreements on government procurement (AGP). We also consider the US government's International Traffic in Arms Regulations (ITAR), which aim to restrict access to advanced US military technology.

Principal–agent theory framework

In this chapter, we analyse how Defence and Industry shape the procurement transaction in terms of *principal and agent* theory. The principal and agent framework focuses on the determination of price, schedule and other key elements of the procurement deal in transactions between two parties, one of whom, the principal, seeks to have work performed by the other, the agent. In our analysis of defence procurement, we shall refer to Defence or its procurement arm (the DPA) as the principal and any individual firm from which it purchases equipment as the agent. Defence may be viewed as having three sorts of interest: to have its product specifications met, to keep production costs down, and to minimise the extent to which firms derive 'rents' from the contract.[2] Firms are considered to be interested in making profit (or, more broadly, in meeting their key business objectives) but are also influenced in their behaviour by the 'effort' they must exert to achieve one cost level rather than another.[3] Generally, lowering production costs, a benefit to Defence, requires increased effort on the part of the firm that it would not exert without an incentive to do so.

Notice also, that the sort of one-to-one arrangements examined here imply that Defence is dealing (in relation to a given acquisition) with only one potential supplier at a time. However,from what we have said in Chapter 1, it is clear that principal–agent relationships occur between a range (and often a chain) of pairs of players: Defence is a single department of state and may be viewed as an agent in the context of wider and higher-level policy-making where the principal is Government; and principal–agent arrangements also exist between the prime contractors that sign contracts with Defence and their component suppliers and sub-contractors.

The principal–agent lens is particularly useful for analysing economic transactions which characterise defence procurement. We saw in Chapter 3 that there are relatively few major defence contractors even in large countries and, especially in smaller countries, there may often only be one. On the other side of the market, the country's NDO may be the only potential buyer of at least some of the firm's range of products. Since the market structure here may thus be bilateral monopoly, outcomes are indeterminate without the assistance of tools that permit analysis of one-to-one trade, a particular strength of principal–agent analysis.

Source selection

Competition for and in the market

As noted in Chapters 1 and 3, for larger defence spending nations, there may be more than one *domestic* source of supply. But for smaller defence spenders, which are the focus of this volume, there is often only one such source – or none, unless Government/Defence is prepared to pay large cost premia for local production. In small countries, the contestability of supply depends on the extent to which governments allow their DPAs to source supplies from overseas providers as well as domestic. As we observed earlier, for reasonably standard types of defence materiel, where scale- and scope-related efficiencies result in declining average unit costs (see Chapter 3), direct imports of equipment produced by large-scale suppliers are likely to offer the least-cost solution, with international co-production and collaboration being costlier, and small-scale local production being the costliest option (Hartley and Sandler, 2003).

It follows that if small countries wish to minimise their procurement costs, they will need to open their domestic market to overseas suppliers. This permits the entry of competing products as overseas platform builders, system integrators and OEMs (often combining with local firms) come to contest the market. Increased *competition for the market* should offer the NDO buyer more choice and, most likely, better terms of supply. Further, once a preferred product has been selected, *competition in the market* follows with sub-contractors competing for various components of supply. However, once all contracts are signed, there is no competition for the market until the next batch of materiel requirements is acquired by the NDO and little competition in the market if switching of sub-contractors is difficult or too costly. As we noted in Chapter 1, the presence of sunk (irretrievable) costs in supplying the requirement tends to leave buyer and seller in a position of mutual dependence once the contract is signed. However, the extent and criticality of the DPA's dependence on a particular source of supply are sometimes a matter of choice. By postponing commitment to a single source of supply until the late stage of the procurement process, the buyer may increase its bargaining power and secure a better deal. Alternatively, the buyer may be prepared to pay a cost premium in order to maintain parallel sources of supply. Such arrangements increase competition in the market and the increased cost of supply may be more than offset by the higher quality and improved dependability of supply. On the other hand, suppliers are often keen to secure an early commitment from the buyer and offer a variety of 'early bird' incentives to induce the buyer to pick a front runner (preferred supplier) early in the procurement process. Thus, the actual terms of procurement deals negotiated by the DPA (i.e., price, product quality and delivery schedule) depend not only on the extent of competition among suppliers but also on the skill with which the buyer takes advantage of rivalry among them.

As we noted in Chapter 1, the NDOs of smaller nations have limited purchasing power, thus, they lack the market power of a monopsonist in the world arms market. But a small country DPA may still be able to secure a good deal when the seller of equipment is keen to compete for the market to obtain additional business. They may also be able to use parallel sources of supply in the market thereby denying individual suppliers large monopoly power. Thus, by opening the domestic defence market to imports and through the increased competition for and in the market, the DPA is likely to source its requirements at a lower cost to the taxpayer.

If, however, the government of a small country regards high import-dependence as a threat to the operational sovereignty of its armed forces, or is committed to mercantilist trade policies *per se*, it may actively promote import substitution and, as business is diverted from more efficient international suppliers to less efficient indigenous firms, the market becomes less exposed to competition. This, as we said earlier, may lead to some or all of higher costs, product performance degradation or schedule slippages. By favouring in-country sources of supply the DPA may acquire a degree of monopsony power although this is not very likely when it deals with local subsidiaries of large international suppliers. However, if imports are effectively restricted, the monopoly market power of key domestic suppliers could more than counter the monopsony power of Defence. Under such conditions of *bilateral monopoly* the outcome of the bargaining process between the two parties is difficult to predict but as country-specific chapters in Part II show, defence industry suppliers appear to have more market (and government lobbying) power than civil firms of comparable size.

Alternative market structures

In Chapter 1, we noted that the market-based relationship between the DPA and Industry is shaped by market structure. In particular, we distinguished the following market structures:

- *monopsony* – when the DPA is the only customer for products made by local suppliers and, thus, may have market power to impose on these suppliers price limits, product specifications, and delivery schedules. As the sole source of demand, the DPA then becomes responsible for the continuing existence of such suppliers;
- *monopoly* – when there is only one source of supply and no close substitutes so that the supplier has market power over prices, product

specifications and delivery schedules. This case arises if a DPA chooses to buy only from domestic sources and only one home-based supplier exists. If a domestic monopolist also exports military products, however, it will normally face competition internationally where it will have less, if any, market power over prices and product characteristics;

- *bilateral monopoly* – when monopoly on the supply side confronts the demand side monopsony. This creates conditions for an essentially 'strategic' bargaining relationship between supplier and the DPA where the outcome depends upon the relative strengths of the bargaining positions of the parties;
- *oligopoly* – when there is a small number of rival sources of supply, all well aware of each other's prices, product specifications and delivery schedules, and where all suppliers make decisions (e.g., over price) taking into account the anticipated responses of their rivals. When oligopolistic suppliers operate in international defence markets, their clients are different DPAs most of which, individually, have little market power. In a national market, though, oligopolistic suppliers confront a single DPA and the market power of that DPA depends on the size of its procurement budget, its share of any or all suppliers' sales, and its expected future requirements relative to those of other DPAs. The market power of individual firms depends on country-specific 'sunk' capital commitments of each oligopolist, i.e., an established supplier with a significant production footprint in-country is well placed to fend off competition from newcomers who can only compete if they invest in new facilities and client-specific knowhow (see the discussion of barriers to entry and exit in Chapter 3);
- *monopolistic competition* – when there are many specialised suppliers of differentiated but largely generic products (e.g., small arms manufacturers) who each compete for a market niche for their particular product variant but, given the presence of reasonably close substitutes, have relatively little market power to fix prices; and
- *atomistic competition* – when there are many suppliers, who produce highly substitutable products and act as price-takers. In this case, the DPA has considerable market power and is well placed to benefit from active rivalry between sellers for and in the market.

If a DPA can choose the number of suppliers it wishes to deal with, it will need to understand the dynamics of each market structure in order to determine how best to use that structure to its advantage. It makes little sense for a small buyer with little or no market power to flex its muscles against large and powerful international suppliers. A small buyer would be better served by an opportunistic strategy that acknowledged the supply side's strengths and explored its weaknesses. For example, many large sellers quote different prices at different points in time and to different buyers as they try to segment the market to make those who value or need the product most to pay the most for it. There are bargains for those who 'shop around' and buy opportunistically by timing their purchases to take advantage of end-of-the-batch production deals and other special offers.

Market power allows buyers and sellers to shift a larger proportion of cost to other parties and appropriate a larger proportion of value for themselves. But market power does not have to be applied ruthlessly by either side. A monopsonist may find it prudent to offer suppliers better terms than the bare minimum needed to keep them in business. It is 'good business practice' to encourage supplier loyalty and long-term commitment to product and process innovation. And, for potential monopolists, the ruthless exercise of market power may yield large short-term profits but such profits invite competition from challengers and encourage buyers to seek other sources of supply and to search for substitute products.

The DPA's ability to use its market power, if any, to its best advantage depends on the size of its total spend, the number of potential sources of supply, the government's willingness to open the economy to import-led competition, and the relative bargaining power of suppliers. Also, as we noted in Chapter 3, governments of potential exporters often control/restrict exports for strategic reasons or because the taxpayers' money was used to develop the product. But even when imports are unimpeded, the size of the market is often limited to only a small number of firms able and willing to bid for work. There are only a handful of shipyards around the world that can build conventional submarines and an even smaller number of manufacturers who can supply heavy-lift aircraft. However, there are many producers of small arms and light weapons. Thus, in some cases, even a small country DPA may have a real choice of whether to deal with many potential suppliers; or a small group of preferred suppliers, or to designate one supplier as a sole source.

Source selection strategies

We may now consider an example of how the buyer faced with a number of alternative sources of supply can decide whether to rely on many suppliers, or a small number of preferred suppliers, or a sole source of supply. This discussion draws on Richardson and Roumasset (1995). In this stylised approach to source selection, the DPA can choose between three types of sourcing arrangements:

- *multiple sources of supply* with active competition in and for the market. This allows the buyer to switch (substitute) suppliers, relatively costlessly, before and after supply contracts are let; or
- *parallel sources of supply* with active competition *for* the market but limited competition *in* the market. That is, many suppliers are invited to tender for the status of preferred/designated supplier. Two (*dual sourcing*) or a handful (*parallel sourcing*) of suppliers are selected for each procured product or product group. Once the buyer has identified which two or more suppliers it prefers, it can switch orders between them at a relatively

low cost. Thus, parallel arrangements are highly contestable as the DPA may switch its requirements from one supplier to another;[4] or

- *sole source of supply* with limited competition for and no competition in the market. However, if the sole source supplier is selected by the DPA from a group of two or more potential contractors, there is scope for some contestability of existing arrangements if the sole source contract can be terminated and another source selection process initiated to replace the incumbent.

In principal–agent terms, the DPA (the principal) minimises its total costs of managing suppliers by balancing the cost of performance assurance against the cost of underperformance. *Performance assurance costs* arise from the tasks the DPA performs to ensure that supplier performance is satisfactory. These include *coordination costs* (investments in building and maintaining relationships with suppliers through, for example, search and communicating product specifications); *monitoring costs* (monitoring supplier performance); and *incentive costs* (applying good-performance incentives). *Under-performance costs* result from supplier under-performance relative to what could otherwise have been achieved or what was expected.

Application of more effort to performance assurance leaves less scope for supplier under-performance. Thus, the DPA (principal) must consider trade-offs between the cost of performance assurance and the cost of supplier under-performance. These two cost elements comprise the total agency (supplier management) cost. This is illustrated in Figure 4.1, where the performance assurance effort, E, is measured along the horizontal axis and the total cost, TC, and its two cost components (one decreasing with E and the other one increasing) are plotted on the vertical axis. TC is minimised at E*, which represents the optimal (TC-minimising) amount of effort devoted to performance assurance that balances the decreasing cost of supplier under-performance against the increasing cost of performance assurance.

The technicalities of the cost minimisation approach as applied to different sourcing options do not concern us here (for details, see Richardson and Roumasset, 1995). Some of the inferences that can be drawn from the agency model are summarised in Table 4.1 and its implications for source selection strategy are discussed below.

Inferences that may be drawn from the Richardson and Roumasset source selection model include:

- 'Without competitive pressure and the threat of losing business, suppliers have the opportunity to hold up the buyer with increased prices, lower quality and generally lower performance' (ibid.: 72).
- It thus follows that if it is not feasible or too costly to use multiple or parallel sources of supply, it will be difficult for the DPA to apply a credible threat of switching/replacing an under-performing supplier. Thus, other things being equal, in the absence of a credible threat to switch/

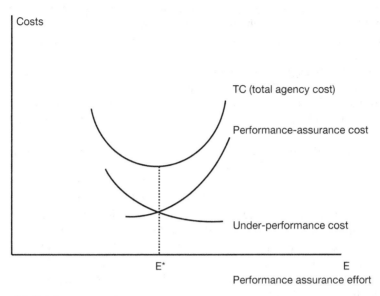

Costs

TC (total agency cost)

Performance-assurance cost

Under-performance cost

E*   E

Performance assurance effort

Figure 4.1 Total agency cost

replace under-performing suppliers, there is an incentive for suppliers to under-perform (e.g., to drop the quality of deliverables or allow the schedule to slip).

- 'Co-ordination combined with competition seems to be the most cost-effective mechanism for achieving high supplier performance' (ibid.: 72).
- The sourcing arrangement that achieves the highest level of coordination between the DPA and its suppliers is the sole-source relationship (as there is only one supplier to coordinate). Normally, however, sole sourcing produces neither the best supplier performance nor best value for money for the buyer. Despite lower supplier coordination costs under this arrangement, the cost-effectiveness of coordination is least for sole sourcing, especially when high performance targets are sought. This is because although 'sole source reduces the cost of co-ordination, it forgoes the highly effective instrument provided by credible threat to switch suppliers' (ibid.: 80).

Richardson and Roumasset (ibid.: 72, 80–1) conclude that:

- When supplier performance (e.g., product quality) is critical, parallel sourcing is superior to sole sourcing. And if (supplier) set-up/switching costs are also high, multiple sourcing is also superior to sole sourcing because higher coordination costs are offset by lower monitoring costs and superior supplier performance.

- Parallel sourcing is usually preferable to multiple sourcing because less coordination is required in the former case but the DPA can still credibly apply the threat to switch away from under-performing suppliers.
- High fixed set-up (relationship-specific) costs may shift relative advantage from parallel to sole sourcing because their repeated impact in the former case can outweigh lower monitoring and under-performance costs.
- Sole sourcing may offer superior performance under bilateral monopoly (the buyer's market power matching the seller's) or when reputational value is important and the supplier's survival and prosperity depend on the DPA.

Thus, we draw the following implications of the model for the development of a *source selection strategy* by the DPA:

- counter-intuitively, using a sole source may be inferior to other options when supplier performance is important since there is a greater risk of supplier under-performance and a larger disincentive to innovate by the sole source;
- sole sourcing offers advantages when high supplier-specific investment is needed (e.g., costly technological complementarity);
- this may be stronger when both the DPA and the supplier have to make long-term, relationship-specific investments;

Table 4.1 Advantages and disadvantages of competitive and sole source procurement

Sourcing arrangements	Advantages and disadvantages
Competitive • Multiple sourcing • Parallel sourcing	• The DPA can apply a credible threat to switch suppliers despite its relationship-specific investment (the costs of tendering and, when applicable, the cost of preferred supplier arrangements) • Relationship set-up costs are sunk (irretrievable) but may allow subsequent costless switching of suppliers (i.e., all 'parallel' and 'multiple' suppliers are 'identical' once they are set up by the DPA) • No failure to comply under the competitive arrangements but, in practice, increased post-contract coordination between the DPA and its suppliers may enhance supplier performance
Sole source	• The DPA can apply a credible threat to replace the supplier if there are alternative sources of supply and if switching costs are less than the cost of under-performance (non-compliance). • If switching costs are positive and exceed the cost of under-performance (non-compliance), the supplier may under-perform and harvest monopoly profit with impunity • If switching costs are relatively high, the supplier may choose performance outcomes different from those specified by the DPA

- when higher coordination costs are offset by higher performance (due to competition), competitive sourcing is preferred to sole source;
- parallel sourcing (open competition *for* the market but restricted *in* the market) may be preferred to multiple sourcing (open competition for and in the market).

Contracting and contract management

As noted in earlier chapters, contracting lies at the heart of the procurement process. The contract is the legal document in which the NDO stipulates what its supplier is to deliver, on what schedule, and at what price.[5] From the point of view of the NDO, the contract is the instrument by which the country realises the deal negotiated by the NDO with the supplier (see Chapters 1 and 2). From the point of view of Industry, the contract embodies a key element of the reward it receives for supplying the NDO. Price, when compared with the costs incurred by the supplier, yields profit which, in turn, determines how well the firm and its shareholders do out of defence contracting (see Chapter 3). The arrangements between the buyer and the seller may also take a variety of forms, allowing more or less flexibility in price relative to costs incurred.

Although the DPA, as a specialised procurement arm of the NDO, will often be well acquainted with the identities of potential suppliers, information surrounding the transaction will nonetheless be imperfect and incomplete. In particular, production costs may diverge from initially predicted levels because:

- of developments that neither side could foresee or control (e.g., an increase in the world price of a scarce materials input);
- the efficiency of any particular firm, while known to that firm, is not known to the DPA (i.e., firms are of an intrinsically high- or low-cost 'type' but, *ex ante*, the DPA may lack the ability to distinguish between different types of suppliers).[6]

The contracting environment varies with these dimensions of uncertainty and the DPA seeks to put in place contracts designed to achieve its ends in the knowledge that: (1) it cannot contract directly on the level of effort of firms as its agents exert to reduce costs; (2) many critical features of the contracting environment that affect costs are beyond its direct control (i.e., they are determined exogenously); and (3) other important features of the contracting environment cannot be observed from outside the firm, but may be known within it.

Depending on the design of the contract (see below), firms face different sorts of incentive to perform. Failure to comply with the contract, slippages of schedule and questions of quality may call for the DPA to apply legal or other forms of pressure to ensure its requirements are met. While legal contracts tend to imply the potential for an adversarial and arm's length relationship between the DPA and its suppliers, difficulties in specifying the contract fully at the outset and the costliness of litigation suggest there are advantages in forging relationships more akin to partnerships. Below, each of these issues is addressed in turn.

Contracting arrangements

In practice, DPAs tend use a particular range of contract types which can be represented in diagrammatic and algebraic form for the purposes of analysis. The contract type offers the supplier a total price comprising two elements: a fixed 'fee' and a variable sum reflecting the proportion of overall production costs which the DPA reimburses (or, alternatively, obliges the supplier to bear). Algebraically:

$$P = a + bC \tag{4.1}$$

where $a \geq 0$ is the fixed fee, C the supplier's production costs (measurable through normal accounting conventions), and $b \geq 0$ represents the fraction of production costs reimbursed by the DPA, the 'power' of contractual incentive.[7]

The most familiar contract types are:

- *firm or fixed price*, under which the DPA sets a price to be paid irrespective of the production costs incurred by the supplier. In this case, $P = a$ and $b = 0$.
- *cost-reimbursement*, under which the DPA pays all the supplier's audited production costs. Here $a = 0$, $b = 1$ and $P = C$.
- *cost-plus*, under which the DPA pays all the supplier's production costs plus an additional amount representing profit. As above, $b = 1$ but $a > 0$ if the profit is calculated as a fixed dollar amount or $b > 1$ if the profit is calculated as a percentage on top of each dollar amount required to reimburse successive additions to costs.
- *cost-sharing*, under which the DPA shares the burden of cost variations with the supplier at some level between 0 and 100 per cent (e.g., $a \geq 0$ and $b < 1$).

The choice of contract type reflects the strategy the DPA adopts to induce suppliers to make cost-saving effort and to prevent contractors earning 'excessive' profits (i.e., rent). As a preliminary to the analysis of the next section, Figure 4.2 presents the basis for making comparisons among alternative contract types.

First of all, note the 45 degree line, labelled P = C, starting at the origin. We call this the *break-even line* since it is the locus of all points at which the contract price exactly covers production costs: P_1 at C_1, P_2 at C_2 and P_3 at C_3.[8] All points above the break-even line yield profit for the supplier. This allows us to call the entire area above the break-even line the 'region of profit'.[9] By the same sort of argument, all points below the break-even line are associated with losses on the project for the supplier ('region of loss').

We next ask how the supplier may reach a point in the region of profit at various cost levels. It is clear that it can never do so with a *cost-reimbursement* contract, labelled CR, since the results of operation under such an arrangement, at any cost level, are shown *along* the break-even line and not by points above it. On the other hand, suppose the supplier is offered a fee or an additional margin to supplement cost reimbursement: a *cost-plus* contract. In Figure 4.2, a = OP_1 represents the fixed fee and the line labelled FFCR represents the fixed-fee-cost-reimbursement contract (the slope of FFCR line is the same as that of CR line). On the other hand, the line labelled CP represents the cost-plus contract achieved through a constant percentage margin (no fixed fee). Both schemes are forgiving in the sense that the supplier is guaranteed profit under either of them, irrespective of the production costs it incurs.[10]

The *fixed price* contract is represented in Figure 4.2 by the horizontal line labelled FP, where the price is fixed at P_2 level. Note that P_2 is the amount paid to the supplier whether its costs are high or low. This amount will yield profit for the supplier if its production costs are less than C_2. At C_1, for example, the project would generate profit of $(P_2 - C_1) = (P_2 - P_1)$. On the other hand, once production costs rise above C_2, they exceed the fixed

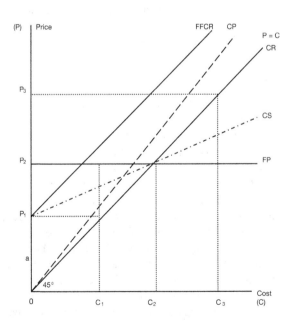

Figure 4.2 Stylised contract types

price for the contract and the supplier makes a loss on the project. In general, the more the supplier reduces its costs below the break-even level of C_2, the larger its profit will be; the more it allows costs to rise above C_2, the larger will be the loss it incurs.

To understand the working of *cost-sharing* contracts, one of which is represented in Figure 4.2 by the line labelled CS, consider first who is pena- lised when production costs increase. Under a cost-reimbursement contract, higher costs incurred by the supplier are reimbursed in their entirety by the DPA: the supplier bears none of the cost. Under a fixed-price contract, the DPA pays the same amount (P_2), whether costs are low or high, and the supplier bears all of the cost and, thus, experiences a dollar's decline in profit every time costs rise by a dollar.[11] In terms of Equation 4.1, the DPA bears the burden when $b \geq 1$ while the supplier carries all the costs when $b = 0$. Since b shows how P varies with changes in C (i.e., $dP/dC = b$), it appears in Figure 4.2 as the slope of the line representing the contract: FP is flat ($b = 0$); the break-even line has a 45 degree slope ($b = 1$). Now CS has been drawn with a slope less than that of the break-even line but greater than FP. Given our argument above about the incidence of burden-bearing when costs rise, it should be clear that, along CS, any increase (or reduction) in costs has an impact which is shared between the principal and the agent, not borne wholly by only one of them. If costs ran at C_3 rather than C_2, for example, the DPA would pay less under CS than it would have with a cost-reimbursement (or cost-plus) contract, though more than it would have under the fixed-price contract, FP. By the same token, the supplier will make a smaller loss than it would have under the fixed price contract, though cost-reimbursement would have allowed it to break even. Both sides thus share in the pain. They would also share in the gain if costs were reduced.

Incentives and contract design

Analysis of why the DPA might choose one contract type rather than another builds on work by Loeb and Magat (1979), Baron and Myerson (1982), Baron and Besanko (1987, 1988), Laffont and Tirole (1986, 1993), McAfee and McMillan (1987), and Rogerson (1994, 1995). This section draws particularly on the studies in Rogerson (1995) and de Fraja and Hartley (1996).

Whenever the DPA negotiates a contract, it does so in the knowledge that the future is uncertain. While this might not matter much for immediate purchases of simple consumables, it is a key feature in the procurement environment surrounding acquisition of complex and highly innovative equipment which may take years to produce and deliver. The type of contract the DPA should choose from the contract range outlined above depends on the nature of the uncertainties present in the contracting environment and what the DPA seeks to achieve within that environment. We assume the DPA will be interested in keeping production costs down, but since production costs reflect the effort suppliers put into containing them, the DPA has the problem of designing contracts that provide, where appropriate, incentives to suppliers to exert such effort. While costs may be higher or lower for reasons to do with unforeseen economic changes or because of variations among suppliers in intrinsic efficiency, the DPA should consider what incentives can be built into the contract to encourage effort, whatever the circumstances.

Following Rogerson (1995), we break the problem up into two parts. First, we imagine that the DPA and the supplier are equally well informed about the supplier's performance characteristics in production but both are uncertain about the external factors which might cause costs to be higher or lower during the course of the project.[12] We refer to this as the *symmetric uncertainty* case. Second, we allow for the possibility of a key asymmetry in information: the supplier knows its cost functions but the DPA does not. We refer to the latter possibility as the *asymmetric uncertainty* case. We believe the first case is of particular interest to small countries in which the DPA procurement staff may well be acquainted with domestic suppliers but production costs may also be subject to external influences generated in the global economy beyond the control of either party. The second case is also important, however, since the DPA procures from both domestic and overseas suppliers and may not be fully informed about the performance characteristics of all potential contractors.

To see the implications of symmetric uncertainty, we follow Rogerson in assuming that suppliers exert a given level of effort to control production costs. Actual production costs over the project may, however, turn out to take any one of a range of values – perhaps, in this symmetric uncertainty case, because exchange rates fluctuate and increase the domestic currency price of inputs or because unforeseen changes in world demand for material inputs change their supply price. In negotiating the contract, the DPA negotiators envisage a distribution of probabilities relating to future cost levels, based on their expectations of how world economic conditions may evolve.[13]

While each of these future cost-levels is associated with a particular state of the world over which it has no control, the DPA would nonetheless like to see production costs reduced. To do this, it must offer incentives to suppliers to exert greater effort so that all cost levels shift downwards. Neither a cost-reimbursement nor cost-plus contract will have that effect. If the supplier is guaranteed to break even or make a profit without exerting any more effort, then it has no reason to make a greater effort.

There is an implication here that the DPA should always seek to use fixed-price contracts when confronted with symmetric uncertainty (Rogerson, 1995: 322). But two caveats are in order. First, it is not necessary to reward the supplier at the rate of a dollar per dollar for reducing costs, the implication of a fixed-price contract. A cost-sharing or incentive contract will have the same qualitative effect, though less strongly. Second, while a fixed price contract is efficient in one dimension, it leads to other problems if suppliers are risk-averse. A risk-averse supplier will worry about the possibility that its actual cost may not fall below the contracted fixed-price level, even if it exerted a great deal more effort, because of unforeseen events beyond its control. It would in that case make a loss on the contract as well as suffering the dis-utility of exerting additional effort. If there is a significant probability of higher costs occurring despite higher rates of effort to reduce them, the sup-plier will naturally prefer a cost-reimbursement or cost-plus contract to a fixed-price contract. Indeed, this would be desirable from other points of view too if the DPA could afford to bear the risk of paying for higher costs more willingly than suppliers could afford to see higher costs leading them into loss-making situations. This would be the case, for example, if the acquisition under consideration required the supplier to engage in highly innovative activity where the cost outcomes largely depended on factors outside its con-trol. Under such circumstances, cost-sharing would be a good compromise solution. With reference to Equation 4.1, what remains to be determined, however, is the size of fixed fee, a, and the actual value of coefficient b, the 'power' of the cost-sharing incentive.[14]

It turns out there is no straightforward answer to that question since the best way of sharing costs or incentives, taking into account the perspectives of both parties and their objectives, will depend upon their perceptions of the uncertainty surrounding the contract and their reactions to it. It does appear, in practice, that governments tend to shoulder a larger share of the costs (higher b) the more the contract is affected by uncertainty (roughly speaking, the larger the variance of production costs around the mean of their dis-tribution). Intuitively, we would expect symmetric uncertainty to be largest for projects in earlier rather than later stages and for projects with a larger developmental content rather than more routine production. And, in general, it is usually the case that when Government lets research contracts, they take a cost-plus form while for standard production work, fixed-price contracts tend to be the norm (Rogerson, 1995: 324).

We turn now to asymmetric uncertainty. Here, the DPA must somehow progress the project but is uncertain about the type of supplier with which it is dealing. By 'type', in this case, we mean simply whether a particular firm is an inherently high-cost or low-cost supplier. That is, for any given level of effort, the supplier may operate at a relatively high or relatively low level of production costs. While each supplier knows its costs and, thus, has no uncertainty about its type, the DPA knows only that there is a distribution of supplier types and is uncertain whether any particular supplier is a high-cost or low-cost contractor.

If there are several potential suppliers, the DPA may invite them to tender competitively for the project. Under competitive tender, low-cost suppliers are likely to tender lower prices for the work under consideration than high-cost suppliers and the DPA will be able to differentiate between different types of suppliers. If contractors are risk-averse, and if *ex post* contract variations are not allowed, they are unlikely to tender prices that would leave them with little or no profit. But competitive tendering may be of little help to the DPA if suppliers are not risk-averse or when they anticipate *ex post* variations in contracted prices (a credible proposition once contracts are signed and it is costly or impossible for the DPA to switch suppliers: the classic hold-up scenario). In this case, the DPA does not know whether a low price bidder is an inherently low-cost supplier or a high-cost supplier keen to 'get its foot in the door', as it were.

To give itself the potential of contracting with any supplier, the DPA must set the price at a high enough level to ensure that contractors of any type could accept the contract. But what form should the contract take? If the DPA uses a fixed-price contract, the price must be set at a high enough level to ensure the work would be undertaken without loss by high-price suppliers. The difficulty for the DPA is that when it offers a high-price contract to a supplier, the latter might have a low-level cost structure. Then, even without increasing it effort, such a supplier could make a substantial profit. And if a low-cost supplier responded to the incentive created by a fixed-price contract offering a 'high' price (i.e. a price high enough to induce a high-cost firm to tender), it might exert more effort to reduce its costs and increase its profits further. This is a difficulty for the DPA not just because governments are often criticised when defence contractors make large profits out of funds raised from the taxpayer. Of greater concern is the supplier's capacity to profit from the ignorance of the DPA and to earn 'rent' from information that it possessed and the DPA lacked (Rogerson, 1995: 326).

To avoid this difficulty, the DPA could resort to a cost-reimbursement contract, awarding the contract on the lowest price bid and paying after the event the costs incurred by whatever supplier it employed. Given that cost-reimbursement contracts offer no incentive to increase effort, the DPA could finish up paying less to the low-price bidder if it were a low-cost firm than a high-cost type. No contractor would earn any profit or rent. However, if the low-price bidder turned out to be a high-cost supplier, the DPA would have to pay whatever price was associated with the cost-structure of the supplier it employed when the supplier was also operating without the exertion of extra effort to contain costs. This would expose it to the criticism that it had used a relatively inefficient contractor and allowed it to perform at a sub-optimal level.

As in the case of symmetric uncertainty, it is possible to show (and appears intuitive) that the compromise solution lies somewhere between fixed-price and cost-reimbursement contracts. As Rogerson shows, a cost-sharing contract could be offered that would induce all potential suppliers to accept the contract, offer incentives to all of them to increase cost containment effort, and would reduce the level of rent or 'excessive profit' earned by lower-cost suppliers. But if the low-cost supplier were selected, what should be the detail of the contract?

To answer this question, recall Equation 4.1. In the discussion of that equation, we saw that when the parameter *b* (the slope of the line) takes a value *between* 0 and 1, it implies that if costs change, the price paid to the supplier rises by only a fraction of the change itself. (Contrast this with the fixed-price case, $b = 0$, where the supplier receives a dollar-for-dollar profit reward for cutting costs, and the cost-reimbursement case, $b = 1$, where the supplier makes zero profit and its payments simply vary exactly with its production costs.) Rogerson shows that, under certain fairly general conditions, relatively low-cost suppliers will prefer to take higher-powered (lower b) contracts while relatively high-cost suppliers will prefer lower-powered (higher b) contracts.[15]

While the DPA cannot know which type of supplier it is dealing with directly, it can offer suppliers a range of alternative contracts of varying degrees of power where b could vary, in principle, from 0 to 1 and where, in addition, there could be a fixed fee. Ideally, low-cost suppliers will find it optimal to accept lower-price contracts than high-cost suppliers as long as they can still earn sufficient profit to compensate them for the effort they exert. It is therefore to the advantage of the DPA to offer cost-sharing contracts elicit offers from suppliers that may allow it ultimately to incur low levels of outlay. However, the actual contracting reality is likely to differ from the stylised contracting processes described above.

Qualifications and caveats

To keep the argument as clear as possible, we have avoided complications (some of them quite important) that only exacerbate the challenges of designing contracts. First, the DPA is not obliged to adhere rigidly to every detail of the initial contract. In practice, the issue of uncertainty that lay at the heart of the foregoing analysis is often addressed in a way that blurs the distinction between contract types. If, for example, a fixed price contract is agreed but input or component prices then rise, the DPA may agree to adjust the terms of the contract to reimburse the supplier for additional outlays not foreseen at the outset. A fixed price contract with explicit or implicit scope for adjustments and amendments of this kind starts to look increasingly like a cost-reimbursement contract. In terms of risk-bearing, the implication is that while governments may seek to shift the burden of risk to suppliers by negotiating fixed price contracts, the reality is that the burden of risk will move back to the government if they feel obliged to concede contract amendments. Such a shift becomes increasingly difficult to avoid as the contract moves towards completion. Given the high premium the DPA places on seeing the work complete, it may well be prepared (even if reluctantly) to concede successive increases in cost (and even cost-plus) reimbursements just to ensure delivery on or near to schedule. In such instances, the principal (the DPA) is increasingly subject to hold-up by its agent.

Second, while fixed price contracts have the apparent virtue of encouraging suppliers to save on costs, cost-saving will be unwelcome if it is achieved by reductions in the quality of work or delaying the date of delivery (Hart *et al.*, 1997). The same argument applies to any form of incentive contract, even if the risk is shared between principal and agent.

Third, the trade-offs between contract type considered in the above analysis do not address the issue of how to induce efficient quantities and types of innovation. In general, though, the share of performance risk borne by the supplier should increase with the maturity of product technology and the production experience of supplier. This share is normally the lowest for developmental products and R&D-intensive acquisitions and the highest for mature, well-specified products.

Contract management and enforcement

In Chapter 2, we referred to the limited contractibility of the procurement deal when specific rights and obligations of the parties to the procurement transaction could not be established *ex ante* as aspects of the deliverable were, as yet, undetermined and transaction-related behavioural hazards could not be mitigated by making contracts more detailed and prescriptive. We now relax the assumption that the buyer knows precisely what it requires and can therefore specify exactly the nature of the deliverable. In reality, a learning process is involved and uncertainty about the nature of requirements is only removed gradually as the procurement transaction unfolds and knowledge about what is needed and what can, in actuality, be delivered accumulates.

There is always a danger that the DPA will respond to the limited contractibility of the procurement deal by denying that the problem exists and proceeding as if all aspects of the deal were fully contractible using a conventional ('discrete') form of procurement contract. However, as the terms of contract can be varied by mutual consent, *contract variations* provide a vehicle for making *ex post* adjustments to the contract.[16] Another approach is to 'restore flexibility in a contract' by accepting its inherent 'ambiguity, that is, to state broad requirements without restricting the parties to specific actions' (Furlotti, 2007: 84). However, the acceptance of the inherent ambiguity of the procurement deal may not help the DPA to avoid subsequent costly disagreements about the specifics of the deliverable, details of the delivery process and, thus, the parties' mutual obligations under the procurement deal. While this form of acceptance of the inherent ambiguity of deal makes the parties aware of the limited usefulness of the conventional discrete contract, *per se*, this is not sufficient to provide an effective mechanism to deal with the vagaries of complex procurement processes.

To address contractual incompleteness, it is necessary to include provisions in the contract that reflect the limited contractibility of the procurement deal and designate management processes and decision-making structures to facilitate the progressive adaptation of the deal to previously unanticipated circumstances and the associated behavioural hazards. That is, the emphasis in the contracting process shifts from the design of a discrete contract that delineates all relevant contingencies to one that provides a vehicle for a relationship to be formed by the parties to allow them to adapt to changing circumstances while preserving the original intent of the deal.[17] As Furlotti

(2007) has argued, contracts comprise two elements: one transactional, the other procedural. Within the transactional dimension, one party commits itself to undertake specific performance in relation to tasks, resources and outputs in exchange for reciprocal undertakings by the other party covering remuneration. The procedural element 'designates rights and processes that are intended to serve purposes of dynamic adaptation, integration and pre-servation of a shared understanding' (ibid.: 64). Included among procedural elements are decision-making processes to determine the contractor's financial returns; rules and restraints to generate predictability within the relationship; rights to secure enforcement of contractual undertakings; and monitoring arrangements. Thus, Furlotti concludes: 'Contracts are not just collections of promises … They are also "constitutions" that establish procedures to govern the relationship over time' (ibid.: 87).

The relational contract may comprehend a variety of relationships between the parties. It may involve the assignment of decision-making authority to one of the parties (e.g., a labour contract where the firm's management retains to right to monitor workers' behaviour, direct their activities and, if necessary, terminate their employment). Alternatively, both parties could share decision-making authority (e.g., an alliance or a partnership contract). Finally decision-making authority could be assigned to third party (e.g., an agent hired by the parties to manage the deal on their behalf).

Specific and residual rights

In analysing procurement transactions it is also useful to distinguish between, on one hand, observable and verifiable behaviour of the parties to the deal and, on the other hand, observable but non-verifiable behaviour of those parties. Observable and verifiable behaviour pertains to actions that can be observed by both the buyer and the seller and, if required, verified by a third party; e.g., a court of law or a designated arbitration authority (Hendrikse, 2003). Observable but non-verifiable behaviour involves actions that are observed by the parties to the deal but which cannot be verified by a third party. All forms of adjudication and enforcement require both the visibility and verifiability of the parties' behaviour. Only actions that are observable by both the buyer and the seller *and* which are verifiable by a third party can form the basis of a *legally* enforceable procurement contract. However, the parties may waive rights to court access for disputes and may use other mechanisms to settle their disagreements (e.g., post-contractual negotiations) (Furlotti, 2007).

It is also useful to distinguish between specific and residual property rights included in the deal. Specific rights relate to those aspects of product delivery and subsequent possession and use that are observable and verifiable after the deal is agreed by the parties.[18] In many defence acquisitions though, the nature of the deal makes it impossible to identify all contingencies and assign all property rights unambiguously at the outset. Disputes between the buyer and the seller are bound to occur when unforeseen problems arise with the deliverable or the parties' behaviour during the procurement process. One way of forestalling such conflicts is to assign residual rights to one or both of the parties (or to a neutral third party) to facilitate *ex post* coordination. The party that retains residual rights determines what may be done in all such unforeseen situations. For example, this party could be the seller, if the buyer decides to transfer all the risks and rewards of product adaptation to the seller in exchange, say, for price certainty (e.g., under a fixed price contract). Or, it could be the buyer, when the supplier is instructed to develop or modify the product under a cost reimbursement contract with the buyer authorising each major step in the development/adaptation process (thus, which costs to reimburse). Or, both parties could share the decision-making process under some 'partnering-style' arrangement. The assignment of residual rights allows the parties to make procedural arrangements to address the unforeseen aspects of procurement deals and the associated behavioural hazards.

Logically, contracts are never complete in that, with hindsight, it is always possible to identify *ex post* improvements that could have been but were not taken into account beforehand. Practically though, the explicit inclusion of procedural arrangements in complex procurement contracts goes a long way to produce transactional outcomes that should satisfy the transacting parties. Thus, contractual arrangements can be envisaged as a continuum of contract designs along which different mixtures of specific and residual rights can be selected to best match the particular circumstances of a procurement deal. At the one end of this continuum there are purely 'transactional' contracts committing the parties to specific activities and delineating their mutual obligations but excluding procedural provisions to handle unforeseen developments (e.g., fixed-price or cost-plus contracts). At the other end, there are purely 'procedural' (relational) contracts designed to facilitate dynamic adaptation to unforeseen developments in procurement processes by allocating residual rights to the parties and including provision for decision-making processes to deal with these unforeseen circumstances (e.g., partnering or alliance contracts). In between these two extremes, there is a broad spectrum of contract designs that combine transactional and procedural elements in different proportions.[19]

All complex acquisitions require the specification and assignment of residual decision-making rights to either one or both of the parties or to a nominated third party. In principle, these rights should be assigned to a party best placed to use its residual decision-making authority to enhance the overall efficiency of the transaction (e.g., the party best able to absorb or mitigate the associated procurement risk).[20] Technology-related uncertainty, for example, is best dealt with by the party responsible for technology development. In principle, procurement managers can gauge residual authority in terms of its:

- *responsiveness* to changing circumstances of the procurement deal, i.e., the ability to recognise a need to adapt and authorise a response;

- *agility*, i.e., the speed of adaptation;
- *flexibility*, the ability to reassign priorities and adapt to new circumstances;
- *resilience*, the ability to absorb unanticipated external shocks (e.g., massive price increases) and deals with local failure (e.g., a subcontractor's failure to deliver a component).

In practice, though, the allocation of decision-making authority in procurement business models may be more influenced by the distribution of market power between the parties than by the underlying efficiency considerations.

Implications for defence procurement

The competition for military advantage often creates an incentive for NDOs to acquire technologically complex weapons systems – complex both technologically and in terms of the processes used to acquire them. In all such cases, the effectiveness of the procurement process largely depends on what procedural arrangements are built into contracts to deal with unforeseen developments and behavioural hazards, who is assigned decision-making authority (residual rights) under different procedural arrangements (business models), and how effectively the process adapts to changing circumstances and external shocks. The attendant uncertainty cannot be mitigated by relying on highly detailed and prescriptive contracts.

Particularly in English-speaking countries, the media report extensively on problems encountered by defence acquisition programmes, ranging from over-specified requirements to cost overruns and schedule slippages. In our view, such unsatisfactory outcomes can often be attributed to inappropriate contracting arrangements made by DPAs. There appears to be a persistent tendency to disregard the inherently limited contractibility of complex acquisition deals, that is, to underestimate the risks inherent in complex defence acquisitions.[21] This is exacerbated by a tendency in some countries (e.g., the use of fixed-price contracts in Australia in the 1990s) to use 'one-type-fits-all' contracting arrangements (and contract types) that fail to facilitate dynamic adaptation to unforeseen developments and behavioural hazards associated with complex defence acquisitions. And, when a particular contracting arrangement is found deficient, another 'one-type-fits-all' solution is put in its place as yet another universal solution to all procurement woes (e.g., in Australia, the fixed-price contract replaced the cost-plus contract that was used in the 1970s and the early 1980s).

To understand the above tendencies, we first review the evolution of procurement contracting arrangements since the Second World War. In this respect, the experience of industrialised English-speaking countries (e.g., Australia and Canada in this volume) is quite different from that of many other developed nations. Defence procurement in Anglophone countries has been heavily criticised in the media and by elected representatives of the community, causing governments in these countries (especially the USA, the

United Kingdom and Australia) to initiate extensive defence procurement reforms.

Between the 1950s and well into the 1970s, it was generally accepted, at least by procurement practitioners, that DPAs should be given the (residual) decision-making authority to handle limited contractibility of complex acquisition deals. This could be done by vertically integrating key production facilities (for example, armouries and shipyards) into the NDO to internalise the defence supply chain and avoid the sourcing of materiel from external suppliers. Another approach was to arrange external supplies of defence materiel under 'cost reimbursement' and 'cost-plus' contracts, where all key product development and production decisions by the supplier had to be *authorised* by the DPA. In both cases, the NDO was both the *de jure* and *de facto* party responsible for dealing with all unforeseen aspects of procurement processes and both business models enjoyed full government support.

Nevertheless, neither of these two sourcing arrangements turned out to be satisfactory in the long run. Government-owned armouries and naval ship-yards operated under weak incentives to develop new products and processes, contain production costs, produce to schedule, and maintain product quality (for an account of the Australian experience see Chapter 6). Cost reimburse-ment arrangements, on the other hand, tended to be abused by suppliers when informational asymmetries turned DPAs into 'passive payers' of over-stated costs. Further, cost reimbursement procedures came to be applied broadly to most materiel sourcing and, thus, extended to acquisitions that would normally be arranged using discrete (fixed price) contracts.

In the 1980s and 1990s, widespread disillusionment with cost reimbursement arrangements and dissatisfaction with the performance of government-owned factories and shipyards led to wide-ranging privatisation, the contracting out of materiel production and the increased use of fixed- and firm-price con-tracts. In English-speaking countries, this defence-focused efficiency drive was a part of broader public sector reform (often dubbed New Public Manage-ment) aimed at reducing the scale of government activity and increasing the engagement of private enterprise in the provision of public goods. It was now the supplier to whom the residual decision-making authority was assigned – at least notionally – as a reform aimed at making Industry rather than the NDO bear the risk of complex product development and production.

The political imperatives driving this shift of decision-making authority from the buyer to the seller swamped recognition of the inherently limited contractibility of complex procurement deals in defence supply chains. For complex developmental products and extensive COTS and MOTS modifica-tions, detailed specifications of deliverables continued to be determined by the NDO. Under fixed-price contracting arrangements, the supplier has a power-ful incentive to contain production costs but, in the case of complex devel-opmental and adaptive acquisitions, it has little control over product development and adaptation costs. There is a fundamental tension between the intent of fixed-price contracting, which is to make the supplier absorb all risks of product delivery, and the reality of its implementation where the customer, the NDO, and its procurement arm, the DPA, remain in control of product specifications *during* the procurement process.

In practice, this tension can be ameliorated in one of two ways. First, the NDO can fix prices at levels high enough to provide adequate, if implicit, premia for suppliers to absorb the risks thought to be associated with development and adaptation activities but lying outside their direct control. Prices may then remain fixed if they contain enough leeway to absorb unexpected costs. But as procurement projects are highly idiosyncratic, there may be little or no market-based evidence from comparable transactions to help the parties benchmark development risk premia under fixed price contracting arrangements. In addition, there is a tendency for these risks to be under-priced, given that suppliers have an incentive to tender at unrealistically low prices in order to win contracts. Second, if implicit risk premia are for such reasons pitched at too low a level to meet surprise costs, the supplier may in some cases avoid losses by shifting them back to the NDO. Such cases arise when the procurement is of a size or type to have the potential to create political embarrassment, leaving the NDO, effectively, as the hostage in a classic 'hold-up' situation. The importance and high political profile of major defence acquisitions and the lack of alternative sourcing arrangements undermine the buyer's ability to enforce contractual obligations under fixed-price arrangements and may force the buyer to adapt, *ex post*, to the reality of the procurement deal by authorising contract variations.[22] Nevertheless, fixed-price contracting arrangements continue to be used by many countries to source complex acquisitions as they are *believed* to provide high-powered incentives for suppliers to contain costs and prevent delivery slippages.

By the late 1990s, practitioners had increasingly recognised the limited contractibility of complex procurement deals and the disadvantages of using discrete contracts under the fixed-price business model. As a result, DPAs began a search for a 'third way'. This entailed a combination of partnering arrangements and alliances with suppliers and incentive contracting. Subsequently, the emphasis began to shift from arrangements based on the use of discrete, fixed-price contracts to those involving the use of relational contracts to forge relationships between the parties to share the residual decision-making authority. Incentive contracting, on the other hand, can be implemented so as to provide a means of re-determining, *ex post*, the variable component of the contract price to align it with the supplier's actual performance. These new developments are increasingly apparent in English-speaking countries such as Australia (e.g., in alliance contracting in naval ship-building and maintenance – see Chapters 6 and 13) that were at the forefront of 1980s-style procurement reform and were thus the first to learn the limitations of the arrangements under these reforms in the 1990s and the early 2000s.

As the search for an effective 'third way' continues, practitioners may find government reluctant to allow their NDOs to assume once again full residual authority under relational contracting. They may well also resist a return to old-style public ownership of key industrial facilities. But the new business model remains ambivalent on how the (residual) decision-making authority is *de facto* shared under the 'third way' alliances and partnering arrangements. At the time of writing, DPAs continue to struggle with limited contractibility of complex defence acquisitions and the inherent ambiguity of the relational contracts.

Defence offsets

Defence offsets taking the form of mandatory countertrade, local content requirements and other compensatory arrangements are widely used by DPAs around the world.[23] Hall and Markowski (1996: 289) define defence offsets as 'compensatory procurement arrangements designed to offset the cost of purchasing defence equipment from overseas by means of a reciprocal (countertrade) commitment by suppliers in support of a purchaser's domestic economy'. This form of transactional reciprocity is not peculiar to defence and other government imports. Offsets-type deals are often arranged by the parties to commercial transactions when a 'purchase or sale is contingent on tied purchase or sale of other products. In that sense, offsets are an aspect of the normal transactional reciprocity between willing buyers and sellers' (ibid.: 308). Package enhancements added to the purchase of another product (e.g., an offer of a 'free' cellular phone with a telephone subscription plan or car bargains with 'extras thrown in at no extra cost' by car dealers) are common everywhere. However, defence offsets differ from normal transactional reciprocity in commercial deals in that these compensatory procurement arrangements may be *mandated* by governments applying to either all government imports or, most commonly, to imports of defence equipment above certain value (main capital acquisitions) contracted by the DPA. Defence offsets schemes vary widely in their detail and not all of them mandate the provision of offsets in relation to any or all defence acquisitions. Various waivers and value 'multipliers' are used by DPAs to exempt certain imports or, as incentives, to attract particular types of offsets (e.g., access to proprietary technology, investment in in-country production facilities, countertrade). (For an in-depth discussion of offsets see Brauer and Dunne, 2004.)

Markowski and Hall (2004a) distinguish three basic categories of offsetting arrangements:

- *Countertrade*: the arms-importing country makes a purchase of required goods conditional on a reciprocal (offsetting) sale of local products worth an agreed fraction of the value of the imported equipment. In effect, the seller undertakes to arrange a reciprocal purchase of goods and services from the buyer, e.g., to buy from a list of exportable products prepared by the buyer.
- A special case of countertrade involves a *local content requirement:* the buyer makes its purchase conditional on the seller's commitment to source

an agreed proportion of the contract value in the buyer's territory (*buy-back*). Use may be made of existing local suppliers through subcontracting and licensed production, or new production facilities may be set up through foreign direct investment, joint ventures, and co-production arrangements.

- *The bundling of requirements*: the buyer ties its purchase decision to the supply of other, related or unrelated, products. Such products may be goods or services which the supplier would not otherwise be willing to offer to this particular purchaser, or products which the buyer seeks to have supplied for less than the current market price (or free of charge). Examples include technology transfers, technical training, through-life support, and marketing assistance.

As the term 'local content' suggests, offsets arrangements are normally applied to 'foreign' vendors while 'local' prime contractors are exempt from such offsetting requirements. However, the distinction between 'foreign' and 'local' may be difficult to apply in practice. The prime contractor may, for example, be a 'local' subsidiary of a multinational firm. The prime may also be a local system integrator that imports a significant proportion of its inputs.

All forms of offsets arrangements involve reciprocity but there are distinctions in the nature of the transactions. Countertrade, if applied to products that were previously only traded domestically, amounts to export creation. Local content requirements induce import substitution. The bundling of requirements influences the quantity and composition of a country's imports of goods and services. Many offset-type arrangements involve a mixture of all three categories. Offsets arrangements can be included in the primary (import) deal, in which case they are included in the procurement contract as a part of the deliverable. Or, they can be arranged as extra-transactional commitment by the seller to deliver some extra-contractual 'add-ons', often with their own delivery schedule independent of the primary deal. Thus, offset obligations are sometimes left to be discharged by the supplier well after the primary transaction is completed (see Hall and Markowski, 1996).

In essence, a distinguishing characteristic of offsets is this: they are *trade restrictions* (such as bundling requirements) *imposed on exporters by an importing country*. These restrictive trade practices are applied by importing countries for either strategic defence reasons or economic reasons. The public and political justifications for defence offsets requirements invoke a range of stated (and sometimes unstated) objectives and it is often difficult to discern which, if any, of them have been met. Policies that mandate defence offsets thus require public agencies to obtain offsets even when it is unclear what net benefits will accrue to them as a result. In logic, we would argue that if the DPA has the necessary market power to arrange a more advantageous procurement deal through a price cut or a package enhancement from an overseas prime contractor, it should be able to use its market power effectively with or without offsets obligations. If it lacks such power, the application of mandatory offsets are unlikely to provide the benefits it seeks since suppliers will be in a position to determine themselves how to discharge their offsets obligations and will choose to do so in a way most advantageous to them. They may comply with the letter of the law by, for example, providing offsets to a mandated dollar amount. But the offsets themselves may nonetheless be quite different from what the buyer had expected, and of much less benefit.

Why do governments, despite the doubts about the efficacy and social usefulness of such policies, persist with mandatory, broadly targeted offsets rather than leaving DPAs to negotiate specific offsets on a case-by-case basis when advantageous? If a government mandates offsets requirements, it suggests it may lack confidence in the negotiating and market scoping skills of its procurement agencies. Individual countries may argue that since everyone else insists on offsets and international suppliers thus price them in as a matter of course – they should demand offsets themselves as they are paying for them anyway. However, buyers with any market power at all can negotiate price discounts as easily as package enhancements. Thus, their preference for mandatory offsets remains to be explained.

Despite widely expressed doubts about the effectiveness and social usefulness of offsets policies, many countries impose mandatory offsets demands in their defence acquisitions. This applies in particular to some NATO members but also to a wide range of developed and developing countries (see Brauer and Dunne, 2004). Of countries discussed in this volume, different forms of offsets continue to be applied by: Canada, Singapore, Spain, Sweden and The Netherlands. In Canada (see Chapter 7), offsets take the form of Industrial and Regional Benefits (IRB) requirements which can be direct (defence-specific) or indirect (offering broader economic benefits). As Ugurhan Berkok reports, the push for mandatory offsets reached its peak in the 1970s but IRBs are still applied. Singapore has never issued a set of formal offsets guidelines (see Chapter 9). But offsets appear in the guise of Industrial Cooperation Programs (ICPs), particularly to diffuse the use of dual-use technology. ICPs are negotiated on a case-by-case basis. Jordi Molas-Gallart traces Spain's experience in Chapter 10 of this volume, evolving from a mandatory offsets programme in the 1980s through other variants subsequently. Björn Hagelin notes that Sweden has retained offsets as a *quid pro quo* measure in response to the actions of other countries but recognises the ambiguous merits of such requirements (Chapter 11). Erik Dirksen describes how The Netherlands applies mandatory offsets requirements to provide work for Dutch industry (Chapter 12). Interestingly, Australia, arguably one of the leading institutional innovators in defence procurement (see Chapter 6), abandoned its mandatory offset policies in the early 1990s (Markowski and Hall, 2004b). Following a 1992 review of defence industry policy, Australian Defence decided to reduce its reliance on less focused offsets-type mechanisms and *de facto*, the mandatory offsets scheme was abolished and replaced by more specific local content provisions implemented through 'normal' procurement contracts.

International collaborative procurement

To increase the scale of acquisition and reduce unit costs of equipment, small countries have often tried to consolidate their demands through bi- or multi-lateral collaborative projects. By and large, these are arranged as one-off joint procurements by two or more countries that find it advantageous to pool their requirements into a single multinational project with work shared equitably between industries of project participants. Often, under these arrangements, the efficient allocation of industry workload has been sacrificed to share the work more equitably among project-sponsoring nations. However, there have also been two attempts, both in Europe, to put in place a permanent multi-lateral structure to manage multinational projects jointly and to disperse industry work-share more efficiently over time. These developments are briefly discussed below.

Collaborative procurement and one-off work-share arrangements

European countries have led the way with collaborative projects arranged on a one-off, government-to-government basis and based on the principle of *juste retour* with costs and workload distributed pro rata between project partici-pants.[24] The emphasis here is on the demand side of the procurement process: the work-share projects involve the consolidation and coordination of buyer requirements and the formation of *ad hoc* consortia of buyer states. Examples of such projects include: the Tornado combat aircraft (the UK, Germany, and Italy) and the Eurofighter Typhoon (the UK, Germany, Italy, and Spain). But many of these programmes are reportedly inefficient, with countries protect-ing their national economic interests and compromises resulting in high-cost solutions. While collaboration offers savings through scale and scope econo-mies, work-share programmes are usually more expensive and slower than uni-national programs of comparable scale and complexity (NAO, 2001).[25] The case study of the German-Dutch Boxer programme discussed in Chapter 12 provides a good illustration of problems associated with the setting up and management of multi-national work-share programmes. In the sample of countries discussed in this book, Spain and The Netherlands have both used *juste retour* arrangements as a means of overcoming issues arising from offsets requirements.

Work-share projects have not been limited to European countries. The joint acquisition by Australia and New Zealand of ten ANZAC frigates in the 1990s is an example of a successful and relatively friction-free project (see Chapters 6 and 13). The industry workload was shared between the two countries. Neither navy was expected to cross-subsidise the shipbuilding costs of the other; sub-contractors were to be selected competitively; and the achieved work-share between the two countries was to reflect the overall cost shares. Although some small cost premia are likely to have been incurred for building the ships in Australia (eight ships) and New Zealand (two ships), as opposed to buying them at marginal cost from an overseas shipyard, there have been no reports of large cost penalties and schedule slippages similar to those reported to have been incurred by some European work-share projects.

As noted in Chapter 2, the main benefit of collaborative acquisition is scale- or agglomeration-related. As the requirements of different countries are standardised, a large scale of acquisition should result in some bulk-buying economies for the buyer countries. Alternatively, there are agglomeration economies as the bundling of national requirements results in the increased scope and scale of the combined acquisition. However, as the workload is fragmented and distributed between the countries, much of the scale- and agglomeration-related efficiencies tend to be lost through the duplication of effort and under-utilisation of capacity. Efforts have been made to avoid such fragmentation of effort under the international collaborative model that forms the basis of the Joint Strike Fighter (JSF) work-share arrangements (see Box 2.1 in Chapter 2). In principle, there are no offsets-style deals under the JSF model and work-share is determined *ex post*, as orders flow to the most competitive subcontractors, rather than *ex ante*, through *juste retour* agreements among governments.

Collaborative acquisitions have been particularly attractive for governments seeking a leading role in a project for their national champion, reductions in the unit cost of procured equipment and/or a wider spread of workload among defence industries internationally. In contrast, when a country develops a 'winner' product, that is easy to export and 'offsets-resistant', it is unlikely to seek 'equity' partners to share the profit with.[26] And international collaborative arrangements have often added a degree of stability to national procurement plans as the cost of terminating collaborative projects is economically and politically high.[27]

Multinational DPAs and inter-temporal work-share facilitation

To remedy acknowledged deficiencies in the *juste retour* model of international collaboration in defence procurement, European nations have sought to develop a model of a multinational DPA that would facilitate permanent procurement collaboration among member states and allow work-share entitlements to be settled over a long period rather than confined to project-by-project arrangements. In this section we look at two such European institutions, the Organisation Conjoint pour la Coopération en matière d'Armement (OCCAR) and the European Defence Agency (EDA).

Organisation Conjoint pour la Coopération en matière d'Armement (OCCAR)

The OCCAR Convention was ratified in 2000 and provides for membership of all European countries and for non-member participation in OCCAR-managed programmes. The foundation member countries were France, Germany, Italy and the United Kingdom. Belgium joined in 2003 and Spain in 2005. The Netherlands, Luxemburg and Turkey participate as non-members (OCCAR, 2005). The formation of OCCAR was an attempt to progress beyond cumbersome, project-by-project work-share arrangements. To this end OCCAR aimed to improve the harmonisation of requirements and encourage multinational collaboration in defence acquisitions by balancing work-share–cost–share arrangements over time rather than on a project-by-project basis. Key projects managed by OCCAR have included: A400M transport aircraft (sponsored by France, Germany, the UK, Belgium, Spain and Turkey); the Tiger attack helicopter (France, Germany and Spain); and the Boxer armoured vehicle (Germany and The Netherlands – see Chapter 12) (ibid.).

Towards the end of the first decade of the twenty-first century, OCCAR was still handling projects transferred to it by sponsoring nations on an apparently *ad hoc* basis with pre-defined work-share arrangements and pre-engaged prime contractors. Thus, there had been limited scope for achieving cross-project efficiency dividends and the inter-temporal, as opposed to one-off, 'clearance' of work-share allocations. While progress has been slow, OCCAR offers potential benefits to small countries that wish to enhance the efficiency of work-share arrangements and take advantage of its multinational project management capabilities.

The European Defence Agency (EDA)

To increase the scope for European collaboration in armaments production and procurement, the European Defence Agency (EDA) was established in Brussels in 2004, reporting to the Council of the European Union.[28] The EDA is open to all European Union (EU) member-states. One of its tasks is to promote and enhance European armaments cooperation, including project/ programme management, that is, to act as a multinational DPA. The EDA aims to work towards a Strategy for European Defence and Technological Industrial Base and identify practical opportunities for collaboration by exploiting the 'cooperative armaments process' (EDA, 2007b).

To improve collaborative procurement of military materiel, the EDA is to focus on early requirements phase with collaborative work-share-based initiatives redirected upstream to R&D rather than to downstream production. The EDA is to help align national requirements, budgets, timeframes, industrial capacities and technologies required to deliver collaborative programmes (ibid.). In this respect, the EDA is more likely to benefit smaller member countries that are particularly disadvantaged by small scale and limited scope of their defence procurement.

In looking for practical ways to strengthen the European defence technology and industrial base, the EDA has to date focused on aligning members' defence business practices through, for example, promulgating the *European Handbook for Defence Procurement* and developing the European Defence Standardisation Information System. The Agency has also secured ministerial approval of a Voluntary Code of Conduct on Defence Procurement which requires participating nations to publish their procurement requirements on the Agency's website (Electronic Bulletin Board).[29] Under the Voluntary Code, signatories undertake to open up to suppliers from subscribing member nations,

> all defence procurement opportunities of €1 million or more where the conditions for application of Art. 296 are met, except for procurement of research and technology; collaborative procurements; and procurements of nuclear weapons and nuclear propulsion systems, chemical, bacteriological and radiological goods and services, and cryptographic equipment.
>
> (ibid.)

The Code also seeks to ensure that 'fair competition and the benefits of the regime are driven down the supply-chain through a proposed voluntary Code of Best Practice in the Supply Chain (CoBPSC).

Free trade facilitation and regulation

In this section, we focus on international attempts to enhance the cross-border trade in goods and services purchased by governments: the so-called agreements on government procurement (AGPs), the best known of which is the World Trade Organisation (WTO) Agreement on Government Procurement. We also consider the US government's International Traffic in Arms Regulations (ITAR), which aim to restrict other countries' access to advanced US military technology, that is, they impede cross-border trade in advanced US military technologies and foreign direct investment activity that would use these technologies.

Agreements on government procurement

The WTO plurilateral Agreement on Government Procurement (GPA) represents an attempt to incorporate government procurement in the world's free trading rules.[30] The (revised) 1996 Agreement covers the procurement of supplies, works and services by public entities and provides for guaranteed market access in the areas which a reciprocally covered by signatories (WTO, 2006). It includes a number of provisions to ensure that bidding procedures in signatory countries are transparent, effective, fair and, if need be, open to challenge (for more in-depth discussion, see Mattoo, 1996; Martin and Hartley, 1997; Gordon *et al.*, 1998; Wang Ping, 2007). In 2007, 28 WTO member states were signatories to the GPA, including all small countries discussed in this volume with the exclusion of Australia. Like other bi- and multi-lateral free trade agreements (FTAs), the GPA excludes military-specific goods and services, which are considered essential for countries to maintain the operational sovereignty of their armed forces and other national security interests. However, the status of 'dual technology' goods and services is more ambiguous as many of predominantly civil products with military applications are covered by the GPA. Also, as NDOs are increasingly dependent on the use of civil technologies in military applications, the relevance of the Agreement for military buyers is likely to increase.

The US International Traffic in Arms Regulations (ITAR)

Export controls are aimed at restricting cross-border trade in controlled products. They are applied by countries that wish to protect their technological superiority in the controlled product area or try to prevent the proliferation of products that could be harmful to use (e.g., illegal drugs) or could benefit potential adversaries (e.g., weapons systems). A prominent example of this phenomenon is efforts by successive US governments to control the proliferation of US-made military equipment and the dissemination of US military technologies pursuant to the US Arms Export Control Act 1968 (Public Law 90–269) and the associated International Traffic in Arms Regulations (ITAR).

The USA is not only the world's largest arms producer and exporter: its massive investment in military R&D also enables it to dominate the global arms market. The resulting market power enables the USA to manage access by other countries, including the small countries discussed in this volume, to its military technology so as to protect and advance US national security interests.

The ITAR is the formal instrument by which US governments exercise this power. Under the ITAR, US exporters of military goods, services and technology (defined very broadly in the US Munitions List) are required to obtain a US government licence in a process administered – and vigorously enforced – by the US State Department. By granting or withholding export licences, by imposing conditions on licences granted (including restrictions on unauthorised access by third parties to exported materiel) and by imposing draconian sanctions on violators (both government and commercial) of ITAR licence conditions, US governments orchestrate access by non-US governments to US materiel in accordance with US political and strategic interests.

The US Government's Defense Trade Cooperation Treaties signed in 2007 with the UK and Australia, two close US allies, illustrate how this process of non-market discretionary policy-making works in practice. In essence, the Treaties, signed at presidential/prime ministerial level, provide a head of political authority for officials to negotiate a detailed framework within which agreed defence goods, services and technology can be traded among trusted recipients without the need for licences or other written authorisation. In each case, the Treaties are intended to facilitate:

- bilateral cooperation in specified military or counter-terrorism operations;
- bilateral cooperation in specified security and defence research, development, production and support programmes;
- specific security and defence procurement projects in which the UK or Australian governments, respectively, are the end-user (see DFAT, 2007).

At the time of writing, neither Treaty had been ratified by the US Congress and, respectively, the British and Australian parliaments. Assuming the Treaties are ratified, then the USA and its two close allies can be expected to initiate a period of administrative learning as practical implementing arrangements are sorted out. It seems likely that, as this process matures, the USA will extend the model to other similarly trusted allies.

Conclusion

Two issues have been emphasised in this chapter as being of major concern to small countries discussed in this volume. First, there is considerable uncertainty, given the competition for military advantage and the pace of technological change, as to what is actually required from suppliers and what the latter are capable of delivering. In the past, to address this issue, DPAs have tended to rely on detailed and highly prescriptive contracts aimed at shifting procurement risks to the supplier while also giving the latter an incentive to perform as required. Increasingly, though, it is apparent that detailed contracts cannot be designed given the uncertain and evolving nature of buyer requirements and the uncertainty about the supplier's capacity to deliver. It is therefore preferable to form relationships that allow the parties to continuously review and adapt to changing circumstances in collaborative framework provided by relational contracting.

Second, the paucity of small country requirements and the associated lack of bargaining power in the global marketplace for defence materiel have induced governments to enter into international collaborative arrangements to benefit from economies of scale and agglomeration or to protect their home industry base by arranging a share of a larger multinational requirement. In most cases, these multinational arrangements have been dominated by political and mercantilist interests. This has resulted in trading the efficiency of workshare arrangements for a more 'equitable' (or more evenly shared) distribution of industry workload. However, European countries have been increasingly determined to enhance the efficiency of these collaborative procurement efforts through the use of a multinational DPA. The formation of OCCAR has been the first step in this direction and the creation of the EDA has provided a fledgling multinational DPA. As the European defence industry consolidates, the EDA will increasingly be used to multilateralise European defence procurement deals to reap the benefits of scale and scope for member countries.

Notes

1 While their business objective is to make profits for the taxpayer, they differ from commercial firms in some important respects, for example, they cannot merge with other firms or take them over unless authorised by the government.
2 'Rent' is profit derived from payments above the level that would have been required to induce the firm to do the work in the first place, given the other opportunities available to it.

3 'Effort' is a term used generically in the principal–agent literature to capture the notion of actions undertaken by the firm to reduce costs. An increase in effort is also costly to the firm. A specific illustration of the variable may be managerial effort, but the term has wider application and could include the profit foregone on commercial contracts that the firm could have won had it not undertaken the defence contract (Rogerson, 1995: 320).

4 A similar arrangement is the so-called 'cross-sourcing' where the DPA uses one preferred supplier for one type of product and another supplier for another product but where the two suppliers have similar capabilities so contracts can be switched between them at a reasonable cost. The position of preferred suppliers can also be contested giving them an incentive to improve performance.

5 The three (legally) essential elements of a contract comprise: offer, acceptance, and consideration. That is, a contract must describe, as much as is practicable, the terms of the deal (Monczka *et al.*, 2005). In addition, two other conditions apply: (1) the parties to a legally enforceable contract must have full contractual capacity and indicate their willingness to enter into the agreement and be bound by its terms; and (2) the subject matter of the contract must be legal under the appropriate law.

6 Firms of a low-cost type may have achieved this status by investing in the past in skills and expertise, learning-by-doing, new equipment, or R&D on a scale unmatched by firms of a higher-cost type. Knowledge acquired on the job and managerial capabilities developed through long practice contain significant degrees of tacitness which cannot be observed by external parties, easily or at all.

7 Thus, b could take values in excess of 1 and would do so if the DPA reimbursed the supplier on a scale of more than a dollar for each dollar's expenditure. Equation 4.1 is a simple linear equation. But, either a or b could vary continuously or in discontinuous jumps, in which case the equation would become non-linear.

8 In this particular illustration, P_2 also is the price level used to represent the fixed price contract, i.e., the price is 'fixed' at P_2 level. But 'price' under the fixed price level can be set at any level that is mutually acceptable to the parties.

9 To see this look, for example, at the points vertically above C_1. On the break-even line $P = P_1$ and just covers production costs. Above the break-even line, prices associated with C_1 include P_2 that is greater than P_1 and thus more than covering production costs. Thus, at P_2 profit is $(P_2 - C_1) = (P_2 - P_1)$. The same exercise may be repeated for any cost level shown on the horizontal axis.

10 Note that at some point the two lines will cross. In the lower-cost ranges, the size of the fixed fee is so large relative to production costs that the rate of profit earned must exceed any that might be achieved through a simple margin. In the higher-cost ranges, applying the fixed margin to the high levels of cost reimbursement generates profit greater than the fixed fee.

11 For example, when costs increase from C_1 to C_2, profit declines by the same amount, falling from $(P_2 - C_1)$ to $(P_2 - C_2) = 0$.

12 The specifics of the uncertainty may be captured by a probability distribution. While the fine detail of the analysis will be sensitive to the form of the distribution, the qualitative results we wish to present here do not require us to be specific. For more detail of the formal analysis, readers are referred to references given in this chapter.

13 The qualitative results are not sensitive to the form of the distribution assumed (see previous note) though the specific detail of the contract the DPA would prefer may well vary with its perceptions of the future reflected in the shape of the distribution.

14 The larger is the value of b, the steeper is the contract line, the closer the contract is to the cost-reimbursement case and the less any reduction (or increase) in costs is thus reflected in the supplier's profit. The smaller is the value of b, the flatter is the contract line, the closer the contract is to the fixed-price case and

more any reduction (or increase) in costs is thus reflected in the supplier's profit. The parameter *b* is thus an indication of what is termed the *power* of the contract: the lower it is, the greater is the inducement and reward for cutting costs; the higher it is, the less is the inducement and reward. On the other hand, the lower is *b*, the more profit the supplier sacrifices for any given increase in costs (and the greater is the potential loss); the higher is *b*, the less profit is reduced and the less is potential loss.

15 First, compared to high-cost suppliers, low-cost contractors always earn more profit absolutely and as a fraction of the overall price when working at the same level of effort under the same fixed price contract rather than a cost-sharing contract. Second, if lower-cost suppliers suffer less than higher-cost suppliers for reducing costs at the margin, then low-cost suppliers can reduce costs by more, and increase profits by more, than high-cost suppliers for the same extra exertion of effort. This increases the attraction of accepting a high-powered contract.

16 Another version of this approach is to identify every conceivable contingency and include it in a contract. However, since the limited contractibility of the procurement deal is largely a product of insufficient cognitive capabilities of the parties, especially the buyer, this approach is unlikely to be of much practical use.

17 This is based on the recognition that success in complex defence procurement is conditioned on adaptation to changing circumstances of procurement deals.

18 For example, a particular performance indicator may be agreed by the parties to measure the performance of a deliverable. The buyer has a specific right to test the deliverable to verify its compliance with agreed performance requirements using the agreed measure of performance and to reject the delivery if the deliverable fails the performance test. This right is specific as long as the observed non-compliance of the deliverable can be verified by a third party (although not always easily and usually at a cost). If need be, the seller may also be directed by the same third party to replace or repair the non-compliant product.

19 This approach appears to be similar to that of Furlotti (2007: 88–9), who distinguishes between relational and discrete contracts but argues that most contracts combine elements of both.

20 The classic textbook example of a contract combining a mixture of specific and residual rights is the labour employment contract when the owner of a commercial firm hires workers using contracts that specify detailed duty statements but also assign to the firm's proprietor the residual right to monitor the workers' behaviour to deal with moral hazards of employment (e.g., shirking) and, if need be, to use the ultimate sanction of contract termination. Our approach in this chapter is similar in that we view every procurement contract as a mixture of specific and residual rights whereby the parties, where practicable, include a list of (specific) verifiable mutual obligations in the contract provisions and assign the residual decision-making authority to either the buyer or the seller, or both parties, or a third party, to deal with all transaction-related matters that cannot be specified *ex ante*.

21 Or, from the budgetary perspective, to under-price the attendant risk premia.

22 This problem is compounded when there is active competition *for* the market but little contestability *in* the market. The DPA can effectively be held to ransom when the cost of switching to an alternative source of supply is prohibitive and/or when the buyer in no position to cancel the contract. This is often the case when governments insist on ambitious local content targets, or divert business to protected national champions, or engage in various forms of pork-barrelling to assist businesses in politically sensitive locations.

23 This section is based on Markowski and Hall (2004a). We are grateful to Routledge, the publisher, and Professors Jürgen Brauer and Paul Dunne, the editors of the volume (Brauer and Dunne, 2004), for a permission to reproduce a part of the chapter.

24 This section draws on a paper by Markowski and Wylie (2007) published in the June 2007 issue of *Security Challenges*. The authors gratefully acknowledge the publisher's (Kokoda Foundation) and editors' permission to reproduce parts of the paper.
25 Overall, *juste retour* arrangements have perpetuated the fragmentation of European defence industries by creating legacy structures requiring support after collaborative projects ended. This outcome was often the very opposite of what the sponsoring governments intended to achieve.
26 In general, it is attractive for countries to 'collectivise' high-cost acquisitions through agreed international workshare arrangements but keep their most profitable activities and technological 'crown jewels' under uni-national control.
27 However, the joint development of an air-warfare destroyer as a part of Project Horizon (France, the UK and Italy), initiated in the early 1990s, was terminated in 2000. France and the UK also withdrew from the early phase of the OCCAR-managed Boxer project (see Chapter 12).
28 For a discussion of the European defence and armaments initiatives, see Markowski and Wylie (2007).
29 The Voluntary Code of Conduct provides for: *fair and equal treatment of suppliers* involved in the procurement process with regard to market access, selection criteria, product specifications and statements of requirements, evaluation criteria and debriefing; *transparency and accountability* in procurement processes; *reciprocity*, i.e., an opportunity to sell in other members' defence markets implies a reciprocal obligation to provide access to the seller's home market. This applies to governments as well as suppliers; and *mutual benefit*, i.e., all participants should find it beneficial to subscribe to the Code arrangements.
30 Public procurement typically accounts for between 12 and 19 per cent of the EU member state's GDP and it is estimated that by opening its public procurement to international competition, a country can save between 10 and 15 per cent of its procurement expenditure. See 'Procurement', UK Department for Business Enterprise and Regulatory Reform, available at: http//www.berr.gov.uk/europeandtrade/key-trade-issues/procurement/page23706.html (accessed 15 August 2008).

References

Baron, D. P. and Besanko, D. E. (1987) 'Monitoring, moral hazard, asymmetric information, and risk sharing in procurement contracting', *Rand Journal of Economics*, 18: 509–32.
—— (1988) 'Monitoring of performance in organizational contracting: the case of defense procurement', *Scandinavian Journal of Economics*, 90: 329–60.
Baron, D. P. and Myerson, R. B. (1982) 'Regulating a monopolist with unknown costs', *Econometrica*, 50: 911–30.
Brauer, J. and Dunne, J. P. (eds) (2004) *Arms Trade and Economic Development: Theory, Policy and Cases in Arms Trade Offsets*, London: Routledge.
De Fraja, G. and Hartley, K. (1996) 'Defence procurement: theory and UK policy', *Oxford Review of Economic Policy*, 12(4): 70–88.
DFAT (2007) *Treaty Between the Government of Australia and the Government of the United States of America Concerning Defense Trade Cooperation*, Sydney: Department of Foreign Affairs and Trade: 3. Online. Available at: http://www.defence.gov.au/publications/defencetradecooperation_treaty.pdf.
EDA (2007a) 'Solana, Verheugen, Svensson at EDA Conference – Radical change and true European market needed to secure future of European defence industry', Press Release 1 February, Brussels: European Defence Agency.

—— (2007b) 'EDA Work Programme 2007', European Defence Agency, Brussels. Online. Available at: http://www.eda.europa.eu (accessed 5 May 2007).

Furlotti, M. (2007) 'There is more to contracts than incompleteness: a review and assessment of empirical research on inter-firm contract design', *Journal of Management and Governance*, 11: 61–99.

Gordon, H., Rimmer, S. and Arrowsmith, S. (1998) 'The economic impact of European Union regime on public procurement: lessons for the WTO', *World Economy*, 21(2): 159–87.

Hall, P. and Markowski, S. (1996) 'Some lessons from the Australian defense offsets experience', *Defense Analysis*, 12(3): 289–314.

Hart, O., Shleifer, A. and Vishny, R. W. (1997) 'The proper scope of government: theory and application to prisons', *Quarterly Journal of Economics*, 112: 1127–61.

Hartley, K. (2004) 'Offsets and the Joint Strike Fighter in the UK and the Netherlands', in J. Brauer and J. P. Dunne (eds) *Arms Trade and Economic Development: Theory, Policy and Cases in Arms Trade Offsets*, London: Routledge, pp. 117–36.

Hartley, K. and Sandler, T. (2003) 'The future of the defence firm', *Kyklos*, 56(3): 361–80.

Hendrikse, G. (2003) *Economics and Management of Organisations, Co-ordination, Motivation and Strategy*, New York: McGraw-Hill.

Laffont, J-J. and Tirole, J. (1986) 'Using cost observation to regulate firms', *Journal of Political Economy*, 94: 614–41.

—— (1993) *A Theory of Incentives in Procurement and Regulation*, Cambridge, MA: MIT Press.

Loeb, M. and Magat, W. (1979) 'A decentralized method of utility deregulation', *Journal of Law and Economics*, 22: 399–404.

Markowski, S. and Hall, P. (2004a) 'Mandatory defense offsets – conceptual foundations', in J. Brauer and J. P. Dunne (eds) *Arms Trade and Economic Development: Theory, Policy and Cases in Arms Trade Offsets*, London: Routledge, pp. 44–53.

—— (2004b) 'Defense offsets in Australia and New Zealand', in J. Brauer and J. P. Dunne (eds) *Arms Trade and Economic Development: Theory, Policy and Cases in Arms Trade Offsets*, London: Routledge, Chapter 18.

Markowski, S. and Wylie, R. (2007) 'The emergence of European defence and defence industry policies', *Security Challenges*, 3(2): 31–52.

Martin, S. and Hartley, K. (1997) 'Public procurement in the European Union: issues and policies', *Public Procurement Law Review*, 6(2): 92–113.

Mattoo, A. (1996) 'The Government Procurement Agreement: implications of economic theory', *World Economy*, 19(6): 695–720.

McAfee, R. P. and McMillan, J. (1987) 'Competition for agency contracts', *Rand Journal of Economics*, 18: 296–307.

Monczka, R., Trent, R. and Handfield, R. (2005) *Purchasing and Supply Management*, 3rd edn, Thomson South Western: Thomson Learning.

NAO (2001) *Maximising the Benefits of Defence Equipment Co-operation*, London: The Stationery Office.

OCCAR (2005) *OCCAR: The Multinational Defence Acquisition Organisation*, Bonn: Organisation Conjointe pour la Coopération en Matière d'Armement.

Richardson, J. and Roumasset, J. (1995) 'Sole sourcing, competitive sourcing, parallel sourcing: mechanisms for supplier performance', *Managerial and Decision Economics*, 16(1): 71–84.

Rogerson, W. P. (1994) 'Economic incentives and the defense procurement process', *Journal of Economic Perspectives*, 8: 65–90.

—— (1995) 'Incentive models of the defense procurement process', in K. Hartley and T. Sandler, T. (eds) *Handbook of Defense Economics*, Vol. 1, Amsterdam: North-Holland, Chapter 12,

Wang Ping (2007) 'Coverage of the WTO's Agreement on Government Procurement: challenges of integrating China and other countries with a large state sector into global trading system', *Journal of International Law*, doi:10.1093/jiel/jgm034: 1–34.

WTO (2006) 'General overview of WTO work on government procurement', Geneva: World Trade Organisation. Online. Available at: http://www.wto.org/english/tratop_e/gproc_e/overview_e.htm (accessed 15 Aug 2008).

5 Government policy

Defence procurement and defence industry

*Peter Hall, Stefan Markowski and
Robert Wylie*

In Chapter 1, we introduced the idea of a defence value-adding chain. We argued that the value-adding chain is driven by meeting the requirements of providing national security in general and defence in particular, the focus of that chapter. We also noted that the true social value of national defence capabilities cannot be determined until they are tested in actual military engagements. In peacetime, it is hard to determine precisely the true social worth of defence capabilities. The resulting ambiguity exacerbates the difficulty of knowing whether scarce resources are being optimally allocated both among competing defence capabilities and between defence and other social priorities. In turn, this makes it difficult to determine the need for and, thus, the true social value of upstream defence-related industry capabilities.

And yet, as the country case studies in Part II of this volume show, governments *do make choices* among different defence capabilities and about the balance between local and imported supply of and support for required capability elements, including goods and services supplied by Industry. The country case studies suggest that, while the nature of these choices and how they are made vary widely among nations, those choices are neither adequately explained in terms of, say, the random outcome of blind bargaining among different elements of the societies concerned, nor in terms of capture of the defence capability formation process by one set of interests or another. In this chapter, we discuss the decision-making processes involved in the sourcing of defence materiel from Industry and Government's commitment to in-country industry capabilities, and the associated policy dilemmas and options.

We begin by analysing in more detail the role of Government in the defence value chain. This leads to a discussion of the different institutional arrangements which mature democracies use to determine the value of national defence and the nature of military capabilities needed to produce desired defence outcomes. Next, we focus on the procurement and industry policy framework as a sub-set of broader defence policies. This framework guides Defence in determining how to procure the required defence materiel and who should they be sourced from. It also helps Defence to establish and sustain local supply capabilities when the Government deems it necessary to source supplies from in-country producers. The following two sections explore procurement and industry policy challenges confronting small countries seeking to balance local and overseas sources of supply and support for military equipment. Finally, we consider Industry-focused procurement strategies as a means of achieving import substitution or increased local industry activity through international work-share arrangements.

In developing this approach, we start from the proposition that a key reason for Government to engage in national security provision is the public good nature of 'defence'. Since public goods are, by definition, non-rival and non-excludable, market incentives alone could not be expected to provide the level of national security that is *best* for the country. Also, while the term 'best' implies an optimal volume and structure of defence, it is difficult to determine, in principle and in practice, how much and what sort of defence is best for a nation to produce and who is best equipped to make such judgements (e.g., governments, parliaments, military experts). It is even harder to know for certain how to divide up the overall defence budget between different military capabilities to achieve the best overall defence potential. In practice, the choices involved are inevitably matters for political judgement as well as technical military expertise. Recognition of the inherently political nature of these choices is the starting point of the following analysis, which focuses on:

- *defence value creation*, that is, alternative uses of scarce social resources to produce public goods and services comprising defence;
- *public choice* issues involved in how societies design and operate institutions to make choices about alternative uses of social resources to produce public goods in general and defence in particular.

Defence value creation and public policy framework

Decision-making framework

In Chapter 1, we sketched out a generic process by which societies produce national security through the formation and, if need be, deployment of in-country defence capabilities and by forging military alliances with other nations to import defence directly from allies, if and when certain threats to national security actually materialise. This process can be represented as the chain of value-adding activities that progressively transform simple into more complex products (goods and services) to produce the end product – defence. This progressive value-adding has been described as *defence value creation*. Given the public good nature of defence, this is a sub-set of overall public value creation. At its broadest, *public value* is the value created by governments and public agencies through the provision of public goods and services such as defence and homeland security, public health, education, and laws and regulations.

This volume focuses on the creation of defence value in mature democratic societies in which the provision of public goods in general, and defence in particular, is determined by citizens' preferences. These preferences are communicated to governments, as the elected decision-makers, by a variety of channels – including the ballot box – and refracted through decisions by elected representatives and their administrative agents. As we argued in Chapters 2 and 4, this decision-making process can be thought of in terms of a *cascading principal–agent framework*, where citizens are the ultimate principal and elect governments as their agents and where government decisions are subsequently refracted by and implemented through the administrative machinery of non-elected 'public servants' who serve the government of the day as its agents but who, as the name suggests, are ultimately the agents of the paramount principal – the general public (citizens).

The concept of the 'state' is the starting point for analysing how citizens define public value and devise institutions for creating it. For present purposes, a 'state' is an integrated social unit comprising a formal collection of actors, institutions and processes which, together with the informal dynamics of social organisation, values, religion and ideology, empower a process for making and enforcing social decisions (Michael, 2006: 14). Within this framework, democratic states function on the basis that the authority of the state derives directly from its citizens who consent to its practices and so are deemed to authorise its actions. Those citizens periodically revisit their endorsement and renew or revise their consent through institutional mechanisms like elections.

In practice, democracies require executive leadership able to make decisions about the issues that confront them routinely and which the leadership will often lack a clear mandate to resolve. That is, in order to accommodate the realities of representation and the limitations of electoral systems, democracies mandate only a few individuals to act on behalf of the majority who have an opinion about some critical issue or issues and entrust those same elected individuals to act on all matters of public concern.

The state's decision-makers are, however, vulnerable to capture by particular interest groups. To mitigate this risk, all the mature democracies canvassed in this book institute accountability mechanisms through which decision-makers are held responsible for adherence to due process, which enable public scrutiny and ensure the transparency of any relationship between decision-makers and interest groups. The notion of transparency as a mechanism that augments laws and regulations in ensuring that governments adhere to due process as agreed over time is crucial for public decision-making, including the provision of national security. Transparency offers citizens the means: (a) 'to check and validate the actions of decision-makers and … public sector administrators'; and (b) 'to hold public officials accountable for breaches of responsibility or due process' (ibid.: 221). Citizens' trust in their system of governance then becomes contingent on the effective working of the mechanisms of transparency.

For example, Canadian arrangements for managing defence and other government procurement illustrate transparency at work (see Chapter 7). All Canadian government procurement, including that for defence, is managed by a centralised, whole-of-government agency (Public Works and Government Services Canada – PWGSC) responsible for ensuring that the economic benefits of procurement are distributed equitably among Canadian provinces. Contestable decisions involving inter-agency and inter-regional resource allocation are made overtly within an institutional framework that, although complex, is sufficiently transparent to produce outcomes accepted as legitimate by the Canadian electorate. In Australia, the defence procurement reforms discussed in Chapter 6 were driven by the need to ensure that elected government ministers had greater visibility of, and their supporting officials were more clearly accountable for, capital equipment procurement decisions.

That said, some aspects of public decision-making remain opaque. In the mature democracies discussed in this volume, it would be most unusual for citizens' representatives to seek a mandate to procure a particular item of capital equipment but those representatives will routinely ask citizens to reaffirm, say, the proportion of GDP or national budget allocated to that country's defence.

Defence value creation

The creation of defence value presents particular challenges owing to:

- the contingent nature of defence capabilities;
- the technological complexity of the capabilities;
- informational asymmetries inherent in defence activities;
- the long gestation periods associated with investment in complex defence assets.

These challenges suffuse five key characteristics of the defence value creation process which we now discuss.

First, the value of a good or service provided by Government can only be determined as and when it is apparent what citizens are required to give up for the additional good or service (Moore, 1995: 29). Governments raise the resources required to create goods of public value through their coercive power to tax. Resources directed to defence activities are lost to other potential uses. The idea of *opportunity cost*[1] – the most highly valued goods or services a society chooses to forego (say, education) in order to produce or obtain another product (say, defence) – is central to any analytically useful concept of public value and, thus, assessments of the *net* social benefits of public good provision (see below). The contingent nature of defence capabilities presents a particular challenge in judging the relative value of alternative uses of public resources.

Second, in assessing the public value generated by a given activity, it is important to distinguish between the value accorded by citizens to that activity and the value accorded to it by individuals who directly benefit from or who are otherwise directly affected by it (e.g., particular client groups). The public value of an activity is that collectively accorded to it by a nation's citizens. In practice though, technological complexity and informational asymmetry make it difficult for the electorate to make judgements about the value of alternative defence capabilities and military or public service 'experts' may identify alternative capability investments, normally leaving final decisions to be made by citizens' representatives in Government. (The Australian two-pass approval system (Chapter 6) and the work of the lower chamber of the Dutch parliament (Chapter 12), provide examples.)

Third, our interest is in the social value added through the provision of public goods, the difference between citizens' perceptions of social benefit generated by a public good or service and the value of resources taken up to produce it (see Chapter 1 for an earlier discussion). Normally, the budgetary cost incurred by Government in providing a given good or service with the taxpayer's money is only a proxy for the social cost of consumption and investment opportunities foregone as a result. The valuation of the social opportunity cost of defence activities, as opposed to their budgetary cost, is often as challenging as the valuation of defence social 'outcomes' (benefits). The calculation of social net benefits is challenged by all of the factors noted at the outset of this section – long gestation, for example, posing a difficulty for individuals (often assumed the majority) unable make good judgements about a distant future, uncertain or not.

In practice, the net social value of defence as perceived by citizens may differ from its valuation by Government and when citizens have little interest in defence issues, the process of defence value creation is open to 'capture' by politicians and 'military experts'. The ambiguities around calculating the social value of defence can make the process of capture easier than it might otherwise have been.

Fourth, while defence value depends on creating contingent capability, the deliberate creation of informational asymmetries (e.g., stealth and deception as important aspects of military activity) means that NDOs often do not know what they themselves or their enemies are actually capable of. In that sense, many military response options are simply unknowable at the time capability investment decisions are made, and this, in turn, renders the value of these capabilities equally unknowable. Subjectivity is thus impossible to eliminate in decision-making. In such an environment we would expect to find a wide range of valuations placed on alternative capability options but little or no means of distinguishing among them.

Fifth, the logic of public value creation transcends the more familiar but narrower 'market failure' rationale for Government action. The public value logic extends market failure logic by recognising that citizens and/or their representatives may want Government to engage in activities beyond those associated with the traditional market failure. Public value logic, then, recognises an inherently subjective rationale for Government action. In creating defence value, governments will not only want to improve their understanding of established/revealed community preferences to provide the nature and scale of defence desired by citizens, which the private sector could not or would not provide, but will also try to predict emerging attitudes and expectations and shape as well as accommodate public preferences.[2]

As the above discussion of defence value suggests, what the citizens deem of value varies widely among nations. An attack on Canada, for example, would practically constitute an attack on the United States (see Chapter 7). Hence, Canada's strategic outlook is influenced directly by the deterrence provided by the massive investment of the USA in military capability, enabling the Canadians to divert a relatively modest proportion of their GDP to achieving a level of security acceptable to Canadian citizens. This strategic outlook encourages Canadian citizens to accept the use of Canadian defence procurement to advance non-defence regional economic development objectives to a relatively great extent. In Israel, on the other hand, citizens allow their governments much less scope for using defence procurement to advance non-defence objectives and are highly responsive to what they regard as the value for money provided by defence (see Chapter 8).

Public policy process and institutions

In democracies, citizens and their representatives define public value via the *public policy process*. Public policy process is a dialogue between a state's citizens and their elected representatives about how the latter (supported by public sector managers) will generate public value by pursuing socially endorsed objectives by engaging in value-adding activities using public resources to fund them (Moore, 1995: 55).[3] In mature democracies, this public policy process provides a decision-making framework for the creation of defence value in that governments periodically initiate dialogues with citizens about means and ends of defence capability formation, including defence-related Industry capabilities. For example, this may take the form of periodic 'defence White Papers' and strategic update documents (see Chapter 6, for an example of the White Paper-based public dialogue tradition in Australia) or less frequent but more seminal defence policy documents (for example, see Chapter 11, for a discussion of the post-Cold War shift in Sweden's strategic stance).

To explain how the public policy process applies to defence procurement and defence industry policy, one possible approach is to use the organising principles of public choice theory (Buchanan, 1989) to orchestrate the following interdependent elements:

- the setting of public policy objectives;
- the choosing of ways to achieve these objectives;
- the marshalling of the human and financial resources required to realise objectives in the ways so chosen.(Wylie, 2007: 53–4)

Public choice theory assumes that individuals, whether citizens or their representatives, behave so as to maximise their utility subject to the constraints they face. A public choice perspective conceives the policy process 'as the means through which (individuals') possibly diverging preferences are somehow combined or amalgamated into a pattern or outcome' (Buchanan, 1989: 17) and views the challenge for governance as that of 'constructing and designing framework institutions or rules that will, to the maximum extent possible, limit the exercise of (self-) interest in exploitative ways and direct (it) to furtherance of the general interest' (ibid.: 22).

Public choice theory implies that, in mature democracies, the setting of defence policy objectives is a contested process that reflects the efforts of various defence policy stakeholders to maximise their individual utility within the constraints of the resources allocated to Defence. In public choice terms, defence planners might be expected to place greater weight on achieving defence-specific capability outcomes in allocating limited resources earmarked for defence. Conversely, in peacetime, elected politicians might be expected to give greater weight than military planners to the achievement of, say, broader economic objectives (e.g., job creation, regional assistance) in allocating those resources. Within a National Defence Organisation, the constituencies of specific military capabilities (say, the Navy, the Army and the Air Force) are expected to pursue their own interests in vigorous competition for their allocation of Defence resources. Finally, non-Defence stakeholders in defence value chains – for example, Industry suppliers – will seek to ensure that their particular interests are taken into account in setting Defence policy objectives (e.g., shipbuilders lobbying for the maintenance of naval shipbuilding programmes).

Each of the mature democracies canvassed in this book have evolved what Buchanan (ibid.: 18) calls the 'rules of the game': institutions (i.e., organisations and processes) for managing the contested process of defence policy-making to achieve defence outcomes accepted as legitimate by the citizens concerned. In Australia, for example, defence institutional reforms, that began in the early 1970s and continued for three decades, have entailed far-reaching organisational changes and process refinements to 'change the rules' in an effort to improve the transparency of and accountability for defence resource allocation decisions. Chapter 6 explores Australia's post-1970 experiments with different organisational structures. These include: consolidating defence functions in a single department to improve cost-effectiveness; introducing formal targets for Defence 'outcomes' and 'outputs' in the annual defence portfolio budget statements; and instituting formal departmental reports to parliament on the achievement of those targets to enhance the transparency and accountability of resource allocation processes.

Procedural transparency and associated arrangements for holding decision-makers accountable for defence procurement choices will not completely eliminate the wastage and inefficiency inherent in the contested defence policy-making that characterises all mature democracies. As indicated earlier, however, such transparency and accountability are crucial in retaining citizens' trust in the defence procurement system and their confidence that, on balance and despite its imperfections, the system operates *reasonably* efficiently and in the national interest. The relationship between the parliament (as the institution representing citizens) and the executive (as the institution entrusted by the citizens to exercise state authority on their behalf) is critical to the maintenance of such trust in all mature democracies. In Australia, for example, a key element of this relationship is the convention that officials (including those responsible for advising the elected minister for defence on defence procurement matters) appear before the relevant parliamentary committee to explain – often at a level of detail beyond what ministers might be expected to address – the rationale for a particular decision by the executive.

Each of the countries discussed in this book has developed specialised institutions dedicated to marshalling the human and financial resources required to give effect to policy choices in ways considered legitimate by the citizens – and taxpayers – concerned. In managing defence procurement, most mature democracies have developed arrangements by which the need for stable and predictable rules for investment are reconciled with demands from parliament and economic managers to adjust resources in response to changing circumstances. To continue the Australian example, the executive publishes a rolling ten-year plan for the development of Australian Defence Force capability but the parliament appropriates the requisite financial resources in the annual budget process (see Chapter 6).

We now turn to discussion of how the procurement process may be used to support and complement both Defence's own objectives and any other economic and social policy goals which Defence is obliged to satisfy.

Procurement and industry policy framework

Up to this point in the chapter, we have been mostly concerned with a conceptual schema within which to place the process of policy-making framing the allocation of scarce resources to form national defence capabilities. We now focus specifically on defence procurement policies as a distinct sub-set of broader defence policies and defence industry policy as an element of that sub-set. This hierarchical structure of policy-making is discussed in more detail below. In essence, though, defence policies determine, subject to budgetary constraints, *what* defence capabilities are needed in-country to meet national security objectives. Defence procurement policies focus more specifically on whether, in principle, it is more desirable to acquire defence capabilities locally or overseas, and what processes are best invoked to acquire the materiel inputs needed to form and sustain these capabilities. The latter policies relate to issues such as the extent to which competition might be used in seeking to source materiel inputs and the contractual framework within which deals are ultimately cast. Any policy-driven preference for acquiring defence inputs domestically is contingent, in practice, on the existing or prospective capability of local Industry. Defence industry policy complements defence procurement in the sense that it is designed to encourage or bring about investments in domestic Industry capabilities necessary if procurement is to be able to draw on local supply. Government may deem it necessary for Industry capability to be located in-country to maintain the operational sovereignty of the armed forces or for broader economic reasons. Thus, defence industry policies are primarily concerned with establishing and maintaining indigenous supply and support options.

The distinction between broader defence policies and more narrowly focused defence procurement policies is largely informed by the experience of countries discussed in this volume. Most of these countries have developed all-of-government procurement policies and guidelines that are aimed at making all public procurement, including defence acquisitions, efficient and open to parliamentary (and public) scrutiny. Canada, where defence procurements are effectively all-of-government acquisitions, provides an example of, arguably, the most complex all-of-government procurement policy frameworks (see Chapter 7). In other countries, specialised DPAs are usually embedded in or attached to their parent NDOs and, while subject to all-of-government procurement policies and guidelines, also tend to be guided by defence-specific procurement policies (see below). In particular, while all-of-government procurement polices may incorporate provisions derived from international agreements on government procurement (see Chapter 4) and bilateral free trade agreements (FTAs) between trading nations, defence procurement polices tend to evolve in parallel as a separate policy domain. This is, as we noted in earlier chapters, because defence procurement is normally exempt from the WTO or FTA requirements.

Similarly, most countries canvassed in this volume have adopted general industry policies designed to provide industry-wide support and/or protection or more narrowly targeted sectoral or regional assistance (e.g., to transform legacy industries in declining regions, or promote new high-tec sectors). Such general industry policies tend to be constrained by compliance with international agreements on industry protection and trade.[4] But defence-specific industrial activities are normally exempt from such agreements and defence industry policies may therefore be developed independently of, albeit in parallel with, general industry policies. The exempt status of defence-focused procurement and industry policies has allowed governments to use them to further broader protectionist or mercantilist objectives. In a number of countries discussed in this volume, governments use defence budgets to provide sectoral and regional industry support or to prop up particular suppliers (e.g., national champions). It is often difficult to be sure how far such policies are driven by purely strategic considerations of national security, as it is usually declared, and how much by non-defence considerations of broader industry assistance.

Defence procurement policies

Defence procurement policy has two general objectives:

- the *supply dependability objective* – to access and/or form dependable supply chains to secure reliable and sustainable deliveries of goods, services and know-how to form and maintain defence capabilities in the required state of operational readiness;
- the *value-for-money objective* – to buy what is needed cost effectively (which should not be taken to mean 'at the least cost' – see below) and to meet Defence's quality and schedule requirements.

These two objectives are not necessarily compatible and policy trade-offs are inevitable. That is, increased supply dependability comes at a price: more reliable sources of supply may also be more costly and buffer stocks of critical materiel may have to be put in place to insulate the armed forces from unreliable suppliers and capricious foreign governments.

In functional terms, the defence procurement policy should guide the NDO in determining:

- which of the required materiel should be made in-country and which should best be sourced from either local or overseas best-value-for-money suppliers (*local content requirements*);
- which of the materiel required to be made in-country should best be made in-house, in Defence-owned and-operated factories and shipyards, and which should best be sourced from external suppliers (*make-or-buy considerations*);
- how to go about selecting sources of supply, e.g., whether to rely on market competition or designate preferred suppliers, how to go about soliciting supplier offers and expressions of interest (*source selection requirements*);
- which type of contract to use to engage the chosen supplier (*contracting arrangements*);
- how to manage the delivery process and associated relationships with suppliers over the entire duration of the procurement cycle (*supplier relations management*).

The first two requirements (local content and make-or-buy) require higher level decisions by the Government as they determine the organisational and operational boundaries of Defence and the structure and conduct of domestic defence-related Industry. This is the strictly *strategic* dimension of the defence procurement policy. However, other broad aspects of the procurement function may also be determined at this strategic level (e.g., the commitment to market competition or the type of contract to be used by the DPA). These basic principles are often derived from all-of-government procurement policies so that Defence procurement activities are well aligned with broader all-of-government procurement practices.

Alternatively, once the two strictly strategic dimensions of the defence procurement process (local content requirements and make-or-buy) are determined, the DPA may be delegated the task of developing all other aspects of defence procurement policy, both at the strategic and operational levels. That is, it may be tasked to decide, in principle and on a case-by-case basis, how to select sources of supply, which types of contracts to use and how to manage its relationships with suppliers. Clearly, all such policy decisions are also constrained by broader government policies (e.g., government policies on public sector outsourcing practices and market competition) and the law of the land (e.g., laws prohibiting anti-competitive conduct by market players). We shall return to the challenges of defence procurement policy-making below.

Defence industry policies

We describe *defence industry policies* as a sub-set of defence procurement polices focusing specifically on the formation and sustainment of in-country Industry capabilities for defence purposes. Defence industry policies become relevant if there is a strategic level decision to rely to a greater or lesser extent, currently or prospectively, on in-country suppliers to build or support domestic defence capabilities – assuming policy-makers believe domestic supply would be unavailable or compromised in the absence of active intervention. In its implementation, such policy takes the form of local content requirements that either all or some of the capability inputs must be obtained from domestic suppliers in designated industry sectors. The policy may also target particular types of domestic suppliers (e.g., through the preferential treatment of small and medium-sized enterprises (SMEs), or 'national champions').

The overarching aims of defence industry policy are to secure the availability, dependability and cost-effectiveness of local sources of supply. In practice, though, these objectives are not necessarily compatible. The availability of local sources of supply may require a significant in-country investment in new facilities and skills. Small-scale production may be costly to sustain so that the dependability of in-country supply can only be achieved if premia are incurred relative to imports. In small countries, cost-effectiveness may often constitute a lower-order policy aim. It is usually more cost effective to import but if local content requirements are paramount, it will be important to limit, through incentives or regulation, the size of the cost premia incurred.

In functional terms, defence industry policy provides a framework to guide decision-making in relation to the following:

- forming, sustaining and protecting required domestic Industry capabilities;
- securing sufficiently dependable supply chains for required Industry capabilities;

- maintaining the viability of preferred domestic suppliers for the period relevant to meeting contract requirements – and/or devising back-up arrangements if existing suppliers collapse;
- limiting cost premia associated with local content preferences.

The availability of the decision-making framework does not *per se* ensure that industry policy objectives are achievable and achieved. Even highly industrialised small countries face formidable challenges when seeking to form and sustain in-country defence Industry capabilities. These challenges are discussed later in this chapter.

Procurement policy challenges

In this section, we review challenges facing procurement policy-making and implementation, considering in turn the key aspects of the defence procurement function detailed above.

Local content requirements

The availability of in-country Industry supplies has traditionally been regarded as necessary for increased supply *dependability*. This rather simplistic belief in the inherently greater dependability of local sources of supply relative to imports has biased procurement sourcing towards countries' national defence industry base (NDIB) even though most small countries recognise that high levels of supply self-sufficiency (high levels of local content) are an illusion for all but the most simple acquisitions. While there are many historic accounts of foreign suppliers and governments depriving combatants of essential supplies during conflicts, numerous other reports relate the destruction of in-country production facilities and the disabling of local sources of supply. Thus, the alleged poor dependability of foreign sources of supply needs to be examined.

First, there is no obvious reason to assume that imports are inherently less dependable than local production. As conflicts escalate, local industrial capabilities are just as (if not more) exposed to battle damage as are the nation's military capabilities. And, in contrast to mobile military assets, industrial facilities are static. Thus, in the event of major hostilities, sourcing supplies from the industries of allied nations could offer a more dependable flow of consumables, spare parts and replacement equipment.

Second, modern conflicts between states tend to be relatively quick affairs with combatants coming to war with whatever capabilities are to hand. There is often little or no time to 'surge' into wartime production or engage in time-consuming battle damage rectification. If urgent supplies are needed they draw on strategic in-country stockpiles or are provided by allies as just-in-time assistance (e.g., the US re-supplying of Israel during its periodic confrontations with Arab neighbours). Ultimately, this is what military alliances are all about. Thus, investments in national, just-in-case NDIB capabilities are hard to justify on the grounds of their greater dependability relative to imports.

Third, preferred local suppliers may be less competent and reliable than overseas sources of supply. Most international suppliers have strong commercial incentives to deliver. This is most apparent in the case of Private Military Contractors (PMCs) operating in Iraq and Afghanistan who have responded to changing customer requirements as flexibly and fast as circumstances on the ground demand (see Singer, 2008). Global defence industries and multinational firms may also have greater 'surge' capacity to meet escalating and changing demands than small national contractors set up and protected under the local content arrangements.

While, *a priori*, there is no obvious reason to assume imports to be inherently less dependable than local production, it is also quite apparent that no source of supply or supply chain is ever completely dependable. Imports are always vulnerable to foreign government interference. On the other hand, military alliances make it less likely for allied governments to prohibit or restrict supplies destined for friends in need. Furthermore, dependability of supply is an important aspect of the military supplier's competitive advantage. Future exports depend on a supplier's reputation earned in times of conflict and neither it nor its government may wish to jeopardise the firm's long-term future prospects by interrupting supply in the short run.

To maintain the operational sovereignty of their armed forces, governments and their NDOs must determine, on an item-by-item basis, whether imports offer a more dependable source of supply or whether national suppliers are more likely to deliver what is needed. The sample of small countries discussed in this volume provides a diverse range of attitudes to local content requirements. Israel (Chapter 8) stands out as the country most focused on maintaining a highly diverse local supply base, even though it benefits from US military assistance, most of which takes the form of US-made military materiel. Singapore (Chapter 9) has also shown a considerable degree of determination to maintain strong local industry capabilities. Australia, as an island-continent, has attached significance over the years to defence industry self-reliance (Chapters 6 and 14). Of other countries in our sample, Sweden was keen to maintain high levels of defence industrial self-sufficiency during the Cold War but has since increased its import dependence (see Chapter 11). The remaining three countries (Canada, Spain and The Netherlands) appear to have little strategic justification for high levels of NDIB self-sufficiency and their local content requirements are in part driven by legacy considerations and in part by broader economic objectives (e.g., technology diffusion, employment, exports) (Chapters 7, 10 and 12).

The obvious downside of focusing on security of supply based on domestic industry capability is cost. However, product quality and schedule requirements may also have to be sacrificed when high levels of local content are mandated by governments. Even in advanced industrial economies, local manufacturers and system integrators find it challenging to provide state-of-the-art products of which they have little prior experience and which are only produced in small quantities. And when high quality standards are insisted on, this can only be achieved at the cost of significant schedule slippages and budget overruns (see Chapter 14, for a discussion of the acquisition of the Jindalee over-the-horizon-radar-network by Australia).

The polar opposite to local content requirements is to allow the DPA to purchase whatever is needed from the best value source regardless of whether it is in-country or overseas based.[5] Acquiring best value-for-money requires a simultaneous comparison of price, performance and schedule as between competing offers though what gives best value for money may be moot (see Chapter 2).[6]

If best-value supply could only be achieved through imports, security of supply would become an issue if there were a significant risk of a supplier holding the buyer NDO to ransom or foreign government interfering in the delivery process. On the other hand, domestic sourcing does not guarantee security of supply either.[7] It is likely there will be at least some potential for a trade-off between price and perceived security of supply – which could go either way in terms of domestic or overseas sourcing. The DPA would thus invite bids from all potential suppliers and, without any regard for their location, choose the one that achieved the desired level of performance or quality at the most acceptable price – assuming no perceived asymmetry between domestic and overseas firms in offering secure supply. The local NDIB will win work, if it is internationally competitive; the work will go abroad if not.

If the case for imposing local content requirements on the grounds of higher dependability of local suppliers is weak, their inclusion in the Defence procurement function should be justified on other grounds, which could be defence-specific (e.g., military innovation) or broader-economic (e.g., jobs). The rationale for disposing with local content requirements would be that: (1) Defence is exposed to the widest possible range of potential suppliers (competition for the market) and, thus, alternative solutions to its sourcing requirements; (2) it has a mechanism for selecting, on behalf of the nation, the most competitive solution for the country's needs; and (3) the selected contractor performs efficiently both because of incentives implicit in the contract and because of the threat that it will lose the work if it fails to deliver (competition in the market).

As a concluding observation here, it is common to find countries providing repair and maintenance services for military equipment even when they concede they are at an international disadvantage in weapons production. On both cost and security grounds, it might appear that countries would nearly always have a better case for sourcing these services efficiently from local Industry than they do for making the equipment concerned. Whether this is true or not depends, however, on the local availability of the specialised skills, expertise, testing and diagnostic equipment and components required to provide high-quality support for specific weapons systems. Some repair and maintenance tasks are generic and routine and readily replicable in purchaser territory. And some overseas producers readily supply and support specialist repair and maintenance capabilities for local use, and offsets programmes may be employed to encourage them to do so. But repair and maintenance can be as technically demanding as production and involve continuous technological modification, implying much that is non-routine and possibly security-sensitive, commercially and militarily. Moreover, some suppliers may be unwilling to provide meaningful support to local Industry and, in any case, the domestic skill-base may lack the depth and breadth found in the supplier's own environment.

Make-or-buy

Traditionally, the advantage of in-house production over external suppliers was linked to the security and responsiveness of supply: Defence could rely on in-house production facilities and service providers (e.g., munitions factories and base workshops maintaining equipment) as it had the freedom to direct their production activities unencumbered by contractual limitations. As the owner of these upstream facilities, Defence could also direct rapid adjustments in production as Service demands changed. In practice, though, the integration of production facilities into the organisational structure of Defence presented problems for efficiency. (Chapter 13 discusses the history of government-owned Australian naval shipyards.) And for the past 20 years, many industrialised countries have been committed, as a matter of policy, to buying supplies from external contractors, domestic or foreign, rather than 'making' them in-house. The case for a general policy on public versus private ownership remains, however, ambiguous, and it can still be argued that case-by-case analysis of the socio-economic benefits is essential before privatising publicly-owned facilities (King and Pitchford, 2008).

However, when local content requirements also come into play, opportunities for commercial sourcing of supplies could be limited. This applies in particular to capital-intensive industries such as naval shipbuilders and air-craft manufacturers and knowledge-intensive suppliers of network-enabled complex weapons systems. Even when protected from overseas competition, there are barriers to entry and exit, as local commercial suppliers would not invest in capital-intensive facilities and knowledge-intensive capabilities unless they were offered adequate returns on their investment. This is unlikely to be the case when only small batches of equipment are subsequently purchased by Defence, often with gaps of several years between acquisitions. Thus, while governments continue to apply policies that commit their NDOs to external sourcing of supplies, the pendulum of privatisation and contracting out may have started to move in the opposite direction. For example, in Australia, 'common use facilities' have been built in two states to allow private ship-builders and repairers to use publicly-funded capital-intensive infrastructure on a time-share basis. This reduces the height of barriers to entry in naval

shipbuilding and repair (see Chapter 13). Similarly, small country governments continue to fund defence-oriented R&D organisations which assist
both their home NDOs and local Industry suppliers.

Source selection requirements

One reason that Government may want to dispense with local content
requirements is to gain access for a DPA to the widest possible range of
potential suppliers and, thus, alternative solutions to its sourcing requirements. Access to such increased competition in the market could also induce
contractors to perform more efficiently. However, to manage many sources of
supply increases transaction costs and DPAs are often tempted to replace
open competition with 'trusted' and 'dependable' parallel suppliers or sole
source contractors. In small countries in which governments mandate local
content requirements, DPAs have little opportunity to rely on competition as
a means of securing value for money in materiel procurement. Parallel or sole
source arrangements are often the only options available.

Even in the absence of local content requirements, the scope for using
competition in the market to secure efficient supplier performance under the
contract is likely to be limited. As procurement projects progress, there are
fewer opportunities to substitute for an existing contractor if it fails to deliver.
If a contractor falls behind on delivery or quality criteria, an alternative
supplier is unlikely to have all the tacit knowledge required to complete a
contract that is already well under way. Thus, incumbent suppliers are more
likely to be motivated by in-contract incentives and expectations of future
Defence work than the threat of contract termination.

The implications drawn in Chapter 4 for source selection included the
following:

- competitive sourcing is superior to sole source arrangements when the
  higher costs of managing competition are more than offset by enhanced
  contractor performance;
- parallel sourcing may be preferable to competitive sourcing if the cost of
  managing more wide-ranging competition outweighs the improvement in
  supplier performance relative to that achievable with fewer suppliers;
- when supplier performance is paramount, parallel sourcing is preferable to
  sole source arrangements. While parallel sourcing is likely to be more
  costly to set up, it allows the DPA to switch orders from non-performing
  suppliers to other active deliverers at a reasonable cost;
- sole sourcing is likely to be attractive if the DPA has to make large supplier-
  specific investments and when both the buyer and supplier have to make
  long-term relationship-specific investments.

In general, the most effective mechanism for value-creation in defence procurement is achieved through contestability of supply (among existing

suppliers and/or through the threat of entry) while the absence of competition encourages suppliers to reduce the quality of deliverables, and allows costs to rise and schedules to slip. As we observed in the previous chapter, competition also elicits information valuable for good decision-making that might not otherwise have been made available. The DPA is able to learn which firms are potentially able and willing to offer supply and on what terms.[8]

Further, it is often advantageous for small countries to enter international collaborative arrangements to benefit from economies of scale and agglomeration or to protect their home industry base by arranging a share of a larger multinational requirement. International work-share arrangements could potentially broaden source selection option by allowing more competition for the market and, if parallel arrangements are put in place, also in the market. However, traditional *juste retour* arrangements restrict competition both for and in the market as governments secure work shares for their preferred suppliers (see Chapter 12, for a discussion of the German-Dutch Boxer project). The Joint Strike Fighter (JSF) model (see Chapter 2, Box 2.1) provides a potentially radical departure from the non-contestable work-share arrangements by allowing competition both for and in the market.

Contracting arrangements

As we argued in the previous chapter, there appears to have been a persistent tendency for DPAs to disregard the inherently limited contractibility of complex acquisition deals, thus, to underestimate the risks inherent in complex defence acquisitions. This has been exacerbated by political imperatives forcing the shift of decision-making authority from the buyer to the seller and a tendency to use 'one-type-fits-all' contracting arrangements (and contract types) that fail to facilitate dynamic adaptation to unforeseen developments and behavioural hazards associated with complex defence acquisitions. In particular, since the late 1980s, several countries have made policy commitment to use fixed-price contracting arrangements to shift procurement risks from the DPA to the contractor.

We also argued that there exists a fundamental tension between the intent of this risk mitigation strategy, which seeks to make suppliers absorb all the risks of product delivery, and the reality of its implementation, where the customer retains control of product specifications during the procurement process. The operational importance and high political profile of major defence acquisitions and the lack of alternative sourcing arrangements together undermine the buyer's ability to enforce fixed-price contracts and oblige the DPA to adapt, *ex post*, by authorising variations. There is also a tendency for risks to be under-priced if suppliers anticipate invoking future contract variations. The resulting culture of overoptimistic bids and subsequent contract variations encourages adverse supplier selection with successful tenderers often lacking the capability to produce quality products, contain costs and stay on schedule.

170 Peter Hall, Stefan Markowski and Robert Wylie

Growing practitioner recognition of these has led to an emerging tendency to use a range of contract types to fit the spectrum of procurement deals, and contractual arrangements that implicitly reflect the limited scope for NDOs to shift risk in such acquisitions to the contractor. Instead, partnering arrangements are now increasingly considered to allow the parties to share the residual decision-making authority to improve project performance and adapt to changing circumstances. Of the sample of countries represented in this volume, Australia has been a leader in alliance contracting arrangements in naval ship-building and maintenance with the Australian DPA (the Defence Materiel Organisation) cast as an alliance partner co-responsible for project outcomes (see Chapters 6 and 13). The new business model remains ambiguous, however, as to how the residual decision-making authority will in actuality be shared between prime contractors and the DPA as most such arrangements remain ambiguous until unsatisfactory outcomes force the parties to contest the specifics of the underlying deals in courts.

Supplier relations management

Supplier relations management by the DPA is largely determined by the adopted contracting model. Under contracting arrangements intended to shift risks inherent in the procurement of complex products away from the NDO, relationships with contractors are essentially distant and sometimes adversarial. This applies to all forms of discrete contract types discussed in Chapter 4. By contrast, relational contract types switch the emphasis to shared decision-making and, thus, joint responsibility for outcomes.

As noted above, there is a growing acceptance of such relational contracts as a means of improving the efficiency of complex defence procurements. But for many policy-makers these are highly risky arrangements that are often at variance with the culture of risk-aversion and non-entrepreneurial decision-making (Markowski and Hall, 2007).

Industry policy challenges

Supply dependability

Defence procurement policies that include local content arrangements have been adopted widely by industrial economies. Such arrangements range from mandatory offsets policies and domestic preference margins (see below) to more subtle 'two-envelope' tenders that encourage suppliers to make one offer that complies with stated user requirements and another that includes, in addition, an offset type 'package enhancement', e.g., a promise to invest in the buyer's NDIB or an undertaking to source components from local suppliers. Once local content requirements or preferences are incorporated in defence procurement policies, the broader procurement policy framework must be viewed as incorporating a defence industry policy element.

Practically, all countries included in this volume apply one form of defence industry policy or another. Below, we first consider the scope of and challenges posed by defence industry policy. Later we focus on industry-focused defence procurement strategies.

Sustaining local industry capabilities

The ability of domestic Industry to meet national defence requirements at any given time depends on the investments they have made in the past. Firms' own investments in capability relate to plant and equipment, buildings, R&D and testing and evaluation infrastructure, human skills and technical know-how, and intellectual property. Converting these assets into industry capability, however, will call for learning-by-doing that comes only from putting them to use and developing organisational processes to support them.

The role of a DPA in seeking to draw on domestic sources must therefore involve taking steps that make it profitable to firms in the first place to invest in relevant assets and then subsequently to maintain the Industry capabilities to support defence acquisitions in the future. Steps associated with encouraging initial investments might include:

- the provision of early information and warning about emerging defence capability requirements so that firms know the particular types of asset they should acquire to meet Defence needs (an example of this approach is the publication of the rolling Defence Capability Plan in Australia – see Chapter 6);
- promising profitable production contracts contingent on firms/consortia winning design competitions;
- sustaining or smoothing out demand so that learning can take place and essential tacit knowledge (know-how) be built up.

On the other hand, promising too much too soon may remove incentives for efficient performance, encourage rent-seeking and could even lead to corruption.

Even if domestically located firms are already internationally competitive in producing the inputs required for national defence capability and would win current contracts with its national DPA, they may not be able to penetrate export markets (see below) and the longer-term future of the NDIB might be threatened. Firms also often face long intermissions between defence procurement peaks (see Chapter 13 for a description of Australian naval shipbuilding cycles) and even if they have profits to reinvest, they may be uncertain about the new capabilities they should develop to align with future NDO capability requirements and may therefore be reluctant, even resistant, to acquiring new assets for defence-oriented production. Government initiatives to maintain domestic industry capabilities into the future may include 'demand stretching' over time, placing 'precautionary orders' with or paying retainers to designated Industry suppliers. *Demand stretching* involves spreading out requirements and delivery dates over an extended future (for application in naval shipbuilding in Australia, see Chapter 13). *Precautionary orders* are procurements involving larger batches than might seem currently justified by strategic conditions. Similarly, firms may be paid retainers to maintain certain production capabilities and allow Defence priority access to them in the event of military contingencies.

Other responses might include making industry capability investments in the public sector domain (government factories and shipyards); sharing or bearing key costs with industry (government-furnished equipment, government-sponsored training schemes); arranging international joint procurements to enable domestic firms to work- and cost-share with other members of multinational projects.

For locally-based firms, the difficulty with penetrating export markets is that the industry capabilities that made them successful in meeting the specific and perhaps unique requirements of the NDO of their home country may be an impediment when tendering for work in other countries with their own particular demands. Moreover, whenever countries favour their own domestic firms, suppliers in other countries will encounter a barrier to entry. Thus, as we noted above, small countries often find it difficult to sustain their NDIB through exports. On the other hand, some smaller countries, like Israel, have been successful exporters and Government may in many cases have a role to play in helping to open the door to overseas sales. Export assistance may involve a national government negotiating with other governments to arrange joint procurements and industry work-share (see Chapter 4) or supply weapons as military aid; or the use of export subsidies as (government-provided) financial incentives that have the effect of reducing the price of domestically produced arms to foreign purchasers.

Broader economic objectives

Aside from arguments about security of supply, governments often seek to find work for their NDIB for reasons related to employment, innovation and the balance of payments. When they do so, conflicts may arise in the pursuit of goals other than those related to national security objectives. Legacy industries may be targeted, for example, to protect jobs when investment in new industries might be preferable to support the armed forces in future. As a possible illustration, large investments in ship consolidation facilities were made in Australia in the 1980s while, from a strictly military perspective, the real challenge was to develop capabilities for combat system integration (see Chapter 13). Below, we look briefly at the arguments for and against using defence procurement to address policy goals unrelated to national security *per se*.

Employment

Procurement sourcing in-country rather than abroad is often justified in terms of the employment it creates. We can also distinguish between the potential for creating new jobs and maintaining existing ones.

In general, if the aim of policy is to create jobs, it is hard to justify it if the economy is already operating at full employment. If there is less than full employment, awarding defence contracts to domestic firms should lead to a net increase in employment so long as the unemployed have the skills to take NDIB jobs, or to fill the gaps created if non-NDIB workers transfer to defence work, and are willing to do either sort of work at the wage rates offered. If unemployment is concentrated in specific regions rather than spread evenly throughout an economy, creating employment through new defence contracts may require setting up production lines in areas of high unemployment – or providing incentives for workers to relocate to existing factories (see Chapter 7,for a discussion of regional industry policy in Canada). On the other hand, the employment-creation argument, even under less than full employment, is weakened if defence industry is less labour-intensive in its production processes than other sectors – and, in general, defence manufacturing has appeared relatively more capital-intensive and less labour-intensive than, say, many service industries.

The employment argument appears in a different form if existing contracts support jobs in the NDIB and it is feared that sourcing new contracts abroad would create unemployment once current work runs out. This is unlikely to be an issue in a growing economy as NDIB workers might find work in other employments quite easily if their skills were in short supply, if they were prepared to re-train, and/or if they were prepared to accept a lower wage. The option of international mobility is also available. As an illustration of how the growing economy can absorb workforce released by stagnant or declining industry sectors, it should be recalled that US Defence procurement expenditure was cut heavily in the 1990s and that in the same period the US economy ran continuously at nearly full employment.

A variation on the job creation argument is that the NDIB offers skill-enhancing opportunities that would not be available if defence contracts were awarded to foreign suppliers. It is unclear, however, why this proposition should apply specifically to defence contracts since skill-enhancement can occur in sectors throughout the economy, many of which have little to do with defence. More importantly, if skill enhancement is really the policy objective, then it should be the target of training and education policy, not defence industry policy. The same remarks apply to the extension of this argument – that skills created in the NDIB have greater value than might initially appear because they can be and are used to raise productivity in civil-sector employments if employees move on. This *knowledge spillover* (or externality) argument provides additional support for awarding contracts to domestic suppliers only if it can be shown that the beneficial effects outside the NDIB exceed the levels of benefit that would have been reaped if the people involved had worked, learned and acquired skills in alternative, civil employments.[9] Clearly, if the employees who acquired the skills then take them abroad, there is no positive externality at all within the national economy.

Innovation

For several decades now, governments have been interested to encourage product and process innovation as a route to achieving sustained higher economic growth. Product innovation potentially offers higher quality, wider choice and greater value for money in consumer purchases. On the production side, technological advance raises productivity and with it real incomes. To the extent that innovation can be generated in defence industry, it offers the potential of economic benefits that might not otherwise have occurred. But if innovation is the target, then policy aimed directly at innovation enhancement is the relevant focus. Such policy might include, for example, subsidies, tax credits and tax concessions to support the innovating activity of all firms in an economy – including but not restricted to firms in the NDIB.

Innovation in military systems themselves is at the heart of meeting the threats posed by potential adversaries and meeting emerging new calls on the Defence Force. And in that connection, defence-related R&D and Industry investments in developing new systems contribute to upgrading Defence capabilities through innovation. Government support for such activities include public expenditure on defence laboratories, government-funded research contracts to Industry, in-contract development provisions, and the operation of offsets programmes designed to encourage overseas suppliers to transfer new technology to domestic production sites. It is possible to argue for support of this kind solely on the grounds that it extends and deepens the local defence-related technology base and enhances Industry capabilities, thereby increasing the potential of the local economy to support Defence (though, as we have seen, it is an open question whether support for a NDIB is in all cases justified). But this is a matter specific to the provision of a country's national security. If it is to be argued that Government support for NDIB innovation meets broader, innovation-related objectives, then it must be shown that additional benefits have accrued in the civil environment which would not otherwise have been reaped. And, for the case to be made fully, it must be shown that Government support for defence-related innovation has yielded greater benefits outside the military environment than would be generated by equivalent support for innovation in other parts of the economy.

On the first point, a number of examples suggest that defence-related innovation or innovation undertaken with defence applications in mind may have had valuable applications in the civil arena (Ruttan, 2006). Semiconductors, a key element of modern computers, were developed in response to military requirements using silicon rather than the cheaper germanium (Langlois and Steinmueller, 1999). Taken together with the procurement decisions of US Defense Department in the 1950s, this has led commentators to conclude that defence-directed, government-sponsored R&D can do much to account for the emergence of the modern computer (Flamm, 1988; Mowery and Nelson, 1999). Raytheon's development of the microwave oven from magnetron-based radar innovations is another proposed example

(Alic *et al.*, 1992). Boeing's civil airliner technology in the 707 and subsequent series sprang from a parent prototype designed to meet the requirements for a new military refuelling tanker (ibid.).

However, it is easy to overstate the strength of this argument, especially for smaller countries. First, a focus on high performance rather than price competitiveness can inhibit NDIB firms in their efforts to develop products for less demanding but more price-sensitive civil markets. Second, secrecy often surrounds production for the military and amplifies the problem that tacit knowledge essential for production in a civil environment is hard to transfer. Third, firms producing innovations for Defence can lack the marketing skills and distribution networks to penetrate civil markets new to them. For these and other reasons, it appears lastly that the relationships between defence-related innovation and civil benefits are less predictable than are represented in simple 'spin-off' accounts (Stowsky, 2004). There appear to be as many impediments to the civil application of military innovations as there are incentives. And in the absence of direct, strong and predictable relationships, it seems unwise to rely on them to transmit value from defence innovation to the broader economy. As for the special advantage of defence sector in generating innovation, military systems seem to have borrowed more from civil innovation since the end of the Cold War than their development has contributed to civil technological advance. The cutting edge of sector-specific innovation has been located less in defence than in civil industry developments in IT, biotechnology and new materials.

Finally in this area, it is now acknowledged that performing innovation domestically adds to a country's ability to absorb new technology successfully from overseas (Cohen and Levinthal, 1989, 1990). Innovation is generated in a huge variety of ways and locations throughout the world and any single relatively small country will perform no more than 1 or 2 per cent of the entire world's innovation activity. It stands, therefore, to benefit from the global pool of innovation (the remaining 98 per cent) if it makes appropriate investments locally to draw on and absorb ideas, equipment and products from the rest of the world. In that context, local investment in military-oriented innovation may make a useful contribution to supporting absorption and adaptation processes, particularly in relation to new defence technology. But it is unclear why it should be expected to have more promising implications for absorbing civil technology locally than innovation investments in other sectors.

Balance of payments

Arguments for local production sometimes also invoke balance of payments or exchange rate benefits. By making defence products in country, it is said, it will be possible to reduce imports and thus take the strain off the balance of trade and downward pressure on the exchange rate. In fact, adding value locally will always involve importing the intermediate inputs and raw materials which must then be transformed into defence products in domestic factories. The saving will be much less than the value of the final product. Second, local production of defence goods draws resources away from producing other goods and services in which, potentially, they might have been employed more productively and where they might have contributed to producing competitive exports. If this is the case, diverting resources to local defence production might have contributed negatively, not positively, to the balance of payments. Third, national benefits are unlikely to be substantial. Defence industry rarely contributes more than a very small fraction of value added to total GDP and while importing a military aircraft, for example, may make a noticeable impact on one month's balance of payment figures, its effect over the year may be very much less.

Industry-related procurement strategies

While recognising that questions can be raised about the efficiency implications of using defence procurement to pursue broader economic objectives, we simply accept in this section that governments are political institutions and subject to political pressures that are likely to drive them in the direction of having a NDIB, whether it is internationally competitive or not. Taking that stance, we now look at the *procurement strategies* they may adopt and the implications that follow.

From what we have already said in this chapter, a procurement approach that seeks aggressively to minimise the costs of purchasing any given system will provide support to the domestic NDIB only if it contains suppliers able to meet the requisite specifications at internationally competitive prices. For most small countries, such an approach implies a relatively small-scale NDIB, probably focused on maintenance and support.

By contrast, an approach that seeks to provide as much work as possible for the domestic NDIB will limit tenders to firms operating within the national boundaries, or will allocate work directly to them. (In many countries, there may often be no more than one firm to choose from. If, in addition, the government aims to prevent earnings from flowing overseas, it may restrict selection to firms that are owned by nationals as well as located within national boundaries.) For most small countries, this approach will support a larger and more varied NDIB than would be found under competitive international supply, but almost inevitably with the consequences of lower productivity and higher production costs.

Lying between the polar extremes are four other possibilities:

1   import substitution with domestic preference margins;
2   import substitution with local content requirements;
3   import substitution with offsets;
4   multinational purchases supported by work-share agreements.

These are now considered in turn.

Import substitution with domestic preference margins

This is the first of three strategy variations on the theme of import substitution (i.e., substitute locally-made products for imports). In common with the others considered below, it reflects policy-makers' understanding that the more aggressive forms of 'buy local' approach will almost inevitably lead to economic inefficiency and waste, and in extreme cases to corruption. To temper those tendencies, tendering under these strategies is open in all cases to local and overseas firms but source selection is at least partly determined by the potential implications for the domestic NDIB.

In the case of *domestic preference margins*, overseas firms are, in effect, given a handicap by permitting internationally uncompetitive local firms to win contracts so long as their price is not 'too high'. If a margin of 20 per cent were specified, a local firm would win the contract even if its price were 18 per cent higher than the most competitive overseas tender. One difficulty with this approach is comparing quality with quality as well as price with price. Open tendering should, at a minimum, encourage local firms to keep their costs within 20 per cent of the most competitive international supplier to have revealed its hand. But given that the handicap they face may have discouraged potential international suppliers from tendering at all, this may be further from world's best practice than the size of the preference margin suggests. Furthermore, by obliging foreign suppliers to tender with a handicap, it is less likely that they will offer to share innovations with the buyer than if they had more room for manoeuvre on price and profit.

Import substitution with local content requirements

Where *local content requirements* are invoked directly, the invitation to tender will either impose a mandatory requirement for a certain fraction of the value of the work to be performed within national boundaries, or seek undertakings that contractors use their 'best endeavours' to produce locally, or solicit proposals as to what contractors believe they can achieve. As noted earlier, however, even if work is performed locally, intermediate inputs will still be imported and, given that the final product lacks a market-determined price, the extent of local value added will necessarily be ambiguous and open to interpretation. Two other points should also be recalled. First, performing work locally is only economically efficient if the net benefits (total economic benefits less total economic costs) outweigh any alternative uses of the resources involved. Second, the work performed locally may offer relatively little opportunity for long-term capability building or the acquisition of lasting competitive advantage. For defence work to generate new skills and technological capability with long-lasting benefits requires training programmes and opportunities to undertake sustained projects into the future. The former may or may not form part of the local content deal; the latter are unlikely to eventuate if overseas contractors have to satisfy similar requirements in other countries for other work.

Import substitution with offsets

Where *offsets* are applied, suppliers will be asked to provide benefits to the country purchasing from them equal to some fraction of the value of the contract, or the imported component of it. Offsets arrangements are widely used but also widely recognised for the issues they raise (see Chapter 4). First, the later offsets are delivered, the more the real financial value declines. This is because, given the opportunity cost of not being able to invest at a compounding return, one dollar received in future is worth less than one dollar received today. Thus, an agreement to supply offsets worth 20 per cent of a contract running over ten years will yield less value if offsets are delivered in years nine and ten of the project rather than in years one and two.

Second, defence contractors have an incentive to minimise the cost of offsets to themselves while the governments of recipient nations have a political incentive to overvalue them. The result is that artificially inflated estimates of the value of offsets may occur. Particular examples of artificial inflation may involve, for example, valuing older-version software at current-version prices or supplying offsets products that could be bought more cheaply in the open market.

Third, the only fully satisfactory measure of the value of an offsets programme is its net benefit to the economy, the result of a full social benefit-cost analysis. Given that such an analysis would require estimating technology and other spillovers from the offsets, performing such a calculation will always be difficult and the results usually open to challenge.

Multinational purchases supported by work-share agreements

In seeking to benefit their NDIB through defence procurement, the final option Government may wish to consider involves participating in multinational arrangements to share work. Such multinational procurement agreements may take place within military alliances or between unallied nations. The economic principle of comparative advantage also offers potential at the level of industry supply. Compared with national procurement agencies purchasing from national defence industries, either national or alliance-level procurement from a cross-national defence industry base offers potential efficiencies arising from: (1) specialisation in production in locations where comparative advantage offers most benefit; and (2) larger-scale demand leading to scale economies in production.

Military alliances occur throughout the world and have been the subject of intensive scholarly analysis and the focus of policy interest. Of particular interest to this chapter are the implications of alliances for procurement and industry policy. (See Hartley, 2006, for an extended analysis on which we draw here.) Alliance members negotiate to determine group decisions on their joint defence strategy and, analogously with the single-country case we have considered through this book, the strategy may then be converted by an alliance procurement agency into demand for the capability inputs required to support alliance-level public goods. Defence industry policy in the case of an alliance addresses questions of openness to competition for its defence contracts, the prospects for achieving scale economies in production, and the costs and benefits of pursuing innovation for alliance capabilities. Increasing openness to competition should cut alliance Industry production costs and can be achieved by allowing firms in any member state to bid on a level playing field for work at national or alliance level. This calls for alliance-level policy under which member states abandon domestic preference at the national level. Firms or consortia that win competitions on these terms should also be able to reap scale economies unattainable when selling to only one government or when prevented by domestic preference arrangements from producing for all.[10] In relation to innovation, duplication costs may be avoided or reduced by operating alliance-level defence laboratories and incurring lower overall development expenses if fewer types of weapons system were required by an alliance than by its individual members.[11]

It is interesting, however, that relatively little procurement coordination and 'planned' industry consolidation have taken place within military alliances, particularly within NATO, the world's dominant military alliance.[12] Clearly, common military standards (e.g., NATO munitions standards) are helpful in facilitating joint procurement by member states. Yet, while the concept of a NATO-wide DPA has been canvassed over the years, and some coordination of requirements has taken place, strong uni-national sentiments prevail (Markowski and Wylie, 2007). The consolidation of defence industry that occurred in the 1990s was driven by the US government in the case of the US industry and was largely forced on European countries by the market (see Chapter 3). There has been no successful, NATO-led initiative to 'rationalise' NDIBs across all member states. To date, joint procurements by NATO members have taken the classic form of one-off *juste retour* arrangements described in Chapter 4.

An impediment to achieving the benefits of alliance-based defence procurement and industry policies lies in the reluctance of individual alliance members to sacrifice the sovereign power associated with an independent military capability and allow their NDIBs to shrink. 'Such behaviour reflects a lack of trust that other member-states will "honour their commitments" and also reflects divergent national interests within an alliance' (Hartley, 2006: 474). To extend Hartley's argument, governments are reluctant to be seen presiding over job losses in defence industries when contracts are awarded to firms in other countries. And, even if all alliance members succeeded in forming a 'procurement club', a commitment to fully competitive tendering in the search for value for money would imply non-member countries could also bid for work. This would be politically hard to accept for member states if it were perceived that employment or other economic objectives were being jeopardised as a result.

Paradoxically, efforts to establish a multinational DPA have been most vigorous in the context of the European Union, which is not a military alliance and where a fully-fledged common defence policy has yet to emerge (see Chapter 4 and Markowski and Wylie, 2007). The establishment of OCCAR in 1996 and the EDA in 2004 has led to other developments in common EU defence as the view took hold that European defence industry was having difficulty competing effectively with the US NDIB. The short-comings of *juste retour* procurement arrangements had also been becoming apparent since the early 1990s. As European countries were finding to their cost, playing under the old rules of the uni-national procurement game was becoming so unsatisfactory that a new multi-national procurement game was recognised to be necessary – built on rules (policies) that encouraged con-solidation of national requirements and their joint sourcing.

Conclusion

In the case of defence procurement, Government must, by construction, have an influence over how things are done. In mature democracies, only govern-ments buy military systems so in the very act of participating in the arms market as customers, governments explicitly or implicitly also determine and implement their policy. Open tendering and contract awards on the basis of best value, wherever sourced, reflect a policy emphasis on competition and a preference for local supply linked only to economic efficiency. Sole sourcing and local content provisions suggest a preference for self-sufficiency, perhaps related to perceptions about security of supply or wider economic objectives, even if price premia are incurred.

In this chapter, we have traced how any country's approach to defence procurement is shaped in a public policy process that yields institutions and procedures specific to each nation and reflecting a variety of governance responses to the problems of military capability acquisition common through-out the democratic world. The political forces at work in this process vary not only across countries, but also over time: the world of government factories and shipyards gave way to wide-ranging privatisation and outsourcing for political as well as economic reasons.

In the following chapters, we shall see how different countries have grap-pled with the economic and political tensions inherent in the defence pro-curement process. We do not take the view that there is any single, obviously best approach though we think it is clear that cost efficiency is likely to suffer whenever exposure to competition is limited, either by policy design or tech-nological and other factors shaping industry structure. A key lesson we draw from our work to this point in the book is that the prospective benefits of investments in defence capability will always be uncertain so it is more than usually important to achieve control over costs. It unnecessarily muddies the waters of decision-making to seek to justify escalating costs in terms of yet further alleged benefits whose credentials may themselves be open to debate.

One aspect of defence procurement that makes it unique in the world of public procurement generally is that international treaties which usually constrain restrictions on trade and industry support do not apply to defence products. It is therefore a temptation for governments to use defence expenditures to pursue more general goals such as employment creation or regional assistance. To the extent that higher costs stem from deliberate policy decisions involving such goals, then at least there is the basis for an honest debate about trade-offs. It is unusual, however, to see much publicly available analysis of the size of cost premia or debate on how large they should be. Ultimately, these are political choices. To the extent that higher costs reflect choices to use contractual means that invite slippages and 'rents', the implication is that other contract types should be tried. Significant technical analysis is required to determine what type of contract is likely to yield the best results but political trends can, as we saw in Chapter 4, have a substantial influence on contract design.

Our conclusion is that certain aspects of the defence procurement process and the policies that surround it unavoidably involve political judgements. In the following chapters, we see not just the acquisition of weapons systems but also how political forces shape decisions on what and how to procure. Given the adversarial nature of politics in democratic states, it is not surprising that successive national governments throughout the world have felt obliged to review and 'reform' the widely reported system 'shortcomings' of their predecessors. In many ways this is a good thing – but only if lessons are learned along the way. It guarantees, however, that change is likely to continue into an indefinite future.

Notes

1 Described by Buchanan (1987) as the basic relationship between scarcity and choice.
2 For example, US President Nixon's call in July 1969 for US allies to assume greater responsibility for their own defence prompted the Australian government of the day to publish a wide-ranging Defence White Paper setting out a doctrine of defence 'self-reliance' (see Chapter 6). In subsequent Defence White Papers and related strategic guidance published by succeeding Australian governments of different persuasions, the notion of 'self-reliance' was refined and amplified; public expectations of the practical significance of the Australia–United States Alliance calibrated; strategic tasks and capability development priorities for the Australian Defence Force defined and the rationale for – and limits to – local industry involvement in supply and support of military equipment explained. For over twenty years, during which public interest in national security provision was limited, successive Australian governments were more determined to influence and shape rather than accommodate public preferences (see Chapter 6).
3 Note, however, our earlier comments about the inherently limited measurability of outputs, outcomes and resource costs of public activities.
4 Particularly, those focused on the use of tariffs and non-tariff barriers to trade in goods and services and impediments to the flow of capital and human factors of production.
5 This form of unconstrained acquisition aligns well with broader policy objectives related to seeking the most efficient use and allocation of the nation's economic resources.

6 The water is further muddied by two other factors. First, in the absence of information to the contrary, buyers sometimes take price as a signal of quality. But this can be misleading and ignores the simple fact that some producers are more cost-efficient than others and can sell profitably at lower prices without reducing quality. An overseas low-price producer should therefore not be ruled out because of presumed quality issues, nor a local high-price producer employed on value-for-money grounds because higher quality is taken to be associated with the higher price. Second, prices quoted at the outset are, as we have seen in Chapter 4, subject to variation. A DPA that buys at lowest price from any supplier, domestic or foreign, should be alert to the possibility of demands for contract variation yielding a higher price as the contract proceeds, especially if alternative sources of supply (competition in the market) are hard to invoke.

7 Other alternatives are also possible, including overseas manufacture combined with post-delivery domestic support.

8 However, it is also costly to bid in competitive tenders and the larger the pool of potential bidders, the lower some or all firms will perceive their probability of winning. This may discourage firms from participating, or discourage them from giving much effort to bidding. The DPA may thus not be in a position to judge the identity of the most promising solution.

9 Strictly, we should compare the benefits *minus* all costs of skill acquisition in the NDIB, on the one hand, and in the next most productive civil employment, on the other. Thus, if the benefits were the same in each case but the costs of training and learning were higher in the DIB than elsewhere, it would be hard to argue that the externalities argument worked to favour awarding contracts locally.

10 The traditional argument in favour of consolidating the industry base within an alliance is to avoid 'wasteful duplication' arising from having parallel NDIB capabilities. But duplication ('wasteful' or otherwise) is also a precondition for parallel and competitive sourcing of supplies. If individual industrial sectors exhibit strong elements of 'natural monopoly' (a single supplier could best satisfy the combined demand for a particular product from all alliance members so each industry sector is dominated by a single producer), the only way to maintain contestability efficiently is to invite suppliers from outside the alliance to bid to win contracts on merit.

11 That said, duplication of innovation capability has the merit of facilitating competition among alternative technologies and encouraging experiment and diversity.

12 In the 1980s and early 1990s, Australia and New Zealand attempted to integrate their NDIBs into a single trans-Tasman defence industry with firms in both countries free to bid for defence work in Australia and New Zealand. This concept of the defence 'common market' was largely influenced by the successful ANZAC ship project (see Chapter 13) and the special economic relationship between the two countries. However, as the military expenditure of New Zealand declined in the 1990s and the country's commitment to the military alliance with Australia and the USA weakened, the concept of the integrated NDIB has received less attention.

References

Alic, J. A., Branscomb, L. M., Brooks, H., Carter, A. B. and Epstein, G. (1992) *Beyond Spin-Off: Military and Commercial Technologies in a Changing World*, Boston: Harvard Business School Press.

Buchanan, J. M. (1987) 'Opportunity cost', in J. Eatwell, M. Millgate and P. Newman (eds) *The New Palgrave: A Dictionary of Economics*, Vol. 3, London: The Macmillan Press, pp. 718–21.

—— (1989) *Essays on the Political Economy*, Honolulu: University of Hawaii Press.

Cohen, W. M. and Levinthal, D. A. (1989) 'Innovation and learning: the two faces of R&D', *Economic Journal*, 99(397): 569–96.

—— (1990) 'Absorptive capacity: a new perspective on learning and innovation', *Administrative Science Quartery*, 35(1): 128–52.

Flamm, K. (1988) *Creating the Computer: Government, Industry and High Technology*, Washington, DC: Brookings Institute.

Hartley, K. (2006) 'Defence industrial policy in a military alliance', *Journal of Peace Research*, 43(4): 473–89.

King, S. and Pitchford, R. 'Private or public? Towards a taxonomy of optimal ownership and management regimes', *Economic Record*, 84(266): 366–78.

Langlois, R. N. and Steinmueller, W. E. (1999) 'The evolution of competitive advantage in the worldwide semiconductor industry, 1947–96' in D. Mowery and R. Nelson *Sources of Industrial Leadership: Studies of Seven Industries*, Cambridge: Cambridge University Press.

Markowski, S. and Hall, P. (2007) 'Public sector entrepreneurialism and the production of defence', *Public Finance and Management*, 7(3): 260–94.

Markowski, S. and Wylie, R. (2007) 'The emergence of European defence and defence industry policies', *Security Challenges*, 3(2): 31–52.

Michael, E. J. (2006) *Public Policy: The Competitive Framework*, Melbourne: Oxford University Press.

Moore, M. H. (1995) *Creating Public Value: Strategic Management in Government*, Cambridge, MA: Harvard University Press.

Mowery, D. and Nelson, R. (1999) *Sources of Industrial Leadership: Studies of Seven Industries*, Cambridge: Cambridge University Press.

Ruttan, V. W. (2006) *Is War Necessary for Economic Growth? Military Procurement and Technology Development*, Oxford: Oxford University Press.

Singer, P. W. (2008) *Corporate Warriors: The Rise of the Privatized Military Industry*, Ithaca, NY: Cornell University Press.

Stowsky, J. (2004) 'Secrets to shield or share? New dilemmas for military R&D in the digital age', *Research Policy*, 33(2): 257–69.

Wylie, R. (2007) 'A defence policy for Australian industry: are we there yet?', *Security Challenges*, 3(2): 53–72.

Part II

National perspectives

6 The Australian defence value-adding chain

Evolution and experimentation

Robert Wylie and Stefan Markowski

Australia, like the other countries analysed in this volume, has developed specialised institutions – organisations and processes – in order to allocate the limited resources the Australian community makes available for national defence in a way considered legitimate by both the general community and those more directly involved in the defence value-adding chain. These institutions are designed to enable governments to make legitimate choices among competing priorities for investment in, say, platforms required for land, sea or air operations. The institutions must also enable governments to trade off investment in longer-term force development and expenditure on shorter-term preparedness in ways considered appropriate to the nation's strategic circumstances – noting that an existing force can only be maintained at high levels of preparedness for a limited period and then at the expense of longer-term force structure development (Betts, 1995: 43).

In this chapter, we analyse the structure and operation of selected defence institutions in terms of their involvement in the Australian defence value-adding chain. In doing so, we have adopted an historical perspective, recognising that these institutions have evolved through trial and error in response to Australia's particular circumstances.

The Australian defence value-adding chain

When we refer to 'military capability' in this chapter we mean the power to achieve a desired operational effect in a particular operational environment (land, sea or air) within a specified period and to sustain that effect for a designated period (DoD, 2006: 5). Australian governments orchestrate the force structure and preparedness elements of military capability to generate military capability 'outputs'. These include, for example, capabilities for command of operations, major surface combatant operations, motorised combined arms operations and airlift operations (CoA, 2006: 102).

Australia aggregates military capability outputs further into military capability 'outcomes', which include capabilities for joint operations and for operations in the maritime, land and air environments. In this representation, therefore, the Australian Defence Force is a portfolio of military capability outputs.[1] Over the longer term, governments can adjust the composition of this portfolio in response to changing strategic circumstances. In the shorter term, the composition of the military capability portfolio is relatively fixed but, depending on the flexibility of the assets involved, governments can generate a spectrum of military options by changing the preparedness of individual assets and by combining them in different ways.

In Chapter 1, we argued that governments should manage the defence value-adding chain so that, at least in principle, the expected national security outcomes provide a rationale for one resource allocation over another higher up the value chain. In the next section, we analyse, from a defence value-adding chain perspective, Australian experience with adjusting its portfolio of military capabilities in response to changing strategic circumstances.

Australian strategic and defence policy objectives

Three global security developments have marked the evolution of Australian strategic policy since conclusion of the ANZUS Treaty in 1951. The first was the call, made by the then US President Richard Nixon during a press conference in Guam in 1969, for America's allies and partners to accept primary responsibility for their own defence – the Guam Doctrine.[2] The end of the Cold War in 1991 is the second development. The third is the terrorist attacks on the USA in 2001 and on Western tourists visiting Bali in 2002. Australia's response to these three developments illustrates how changing strategic perceptions have affected management of the Australian defence value-adding chain.

Australia's response to the Guam Doctrine

Australia's policy response to the Guam Doctrine proposed by the United States is apparent in a review of Australian defence policy published by the Department of Defence in 1972. The review concluded:

> Australia would be prudent not to rest its security as directly or as heavily, as in its previous peacetime history, on the military power of a Western ally in Asia. As for other nations, self reliance in situations of less than global or major international concern will lay claim to being a central feature in the future development of Australia's defence policy.
>
> (DoD, 1972: 9)

The subsequent evolution of Australian strategic policy is largely a record of efforts by successive Australian governments to explain, and to give practical effect to, this notion of 'self-reliance' (Brabin-Smith, 2005).

For the next decade, efforts to translate 'self reliance' into decisions about defence force structure development and preparedness were impeded by disagreement between the Department of Defence and the Australian Defence Force (ADF) about the level of conflict for which the ADF should be structured. Civilians in the Defence Department tended to accord priority to Australia's capacity to respond effectively, and at short notice, to low-level harassment, particularly in northern Australia, designed to extract political concessions from the Australian government of the day. The ADF, on the other hand, was much more concerned about retaining its capacity to expand in response to more substantial threats (not then in prospect) within the warning time likely to be available. This debate focused on the value added by different capability outputs and, hence, their priority in terms of the allocation of scarce resources. The debate intensified as successive governments constrained defence funding.[3]

In 1985, this disagreement caused the Minister for Defence to engage an external advisor, Paul Dibb, to review present and future force capabilities, the feasibility of making strategic guidance more explicit for defence planning purposes and the role of local industry in supply and support of the ADF (Dibb, 1986: xv). Dibb argued that defence force planning could be soundly based on understanding of the physical characteristics of the sea and air gap to Australia's north, and of long-term trends in regional military capacity and potential (ibid.: 2). The government incorporated the broad thrust of Dibb's thinking into the *1987 Defence White Paper*. By this time the Australian defence policy community had generally accepted that:

> self reliance is a concept which focuses on our ability to defend Australia without assistance from the combat forces of other countries. While it does not mean that we should aspire to self sufficiency across all the areas that provide support to our combat forces, it does provide a framework within which to consider priorities for this support.
>
> (DoD, 1987: 48)

This bland formulation of Australian defence policy masked intense debate within the defence policy community about what military capabilities Australia needed to counter a credible regional adversary, how much to spend on the preparedness of those capabilities and the appropriate balance between local production and imports in supplying and supporting them. Nevertheless, the broad thrust of Dibb's thinking shaped investment in Australian defence force structure and the formulation of Australian defence industry policy for the next 15 years.

Australia's response to the end of the Cold War

In response to the easing of superpower competition in the late 1980s and to the collapse of the Soviet Union in December 1991, the Australian government noted that

> the end of the Cold War means the passing of the structures which have shaped the regional strategic environment. Previously our defence

planning has been able to assume a degree of predictability in our strategic circumstances. Now we need to take account of a more complex
and changeable strategic environment. Australia's ability to shape that
environment will become more important to our security, and our policies will need to encompass a wider range of possible outcomes than in
the more predictable decades of the Cold War.

(DoD, 1994:10)

The *1994 Defence White Paper* reaffirmed the doctrine of self-reliance as the
foundation of Australian defence policy, noting that 'Australia's security is not
so vital to other nations that we can assume others would commit substantial
resources to our defence. This will become increasingly so as our strategic
environment becomes more complex' (ibid.: 13).

Australia's sense of strategic uncertainty following the end of the Cold
War was sufficient to maintain support for prior investments in, for example,
the Jindalee operational radar network, ANZAC frigates and Collins Class
submarines, geared as they were to maintaining a *regional* capability edge
(ibid.: 34). But post-Cold War uncertainty was not sufficient to prompt
any radical increase in investment in future defence capability or in expenditure on current preparedness. The uncertainty also extended to the US
alliance:

The United States will retain important interests in our region and strong
forces to protect those interests. Yet the nature and perception of American interests and the capabilities of US forces will change. American
expectations of the alliance will change with them, as the previous
emphasis on alliance cohesion against the Soviet bloc is replaced by a
more complex and evolving US posture.

(ibid.: 95)

Australia's response to terrorist attacks

In contrast, the terrorist attacks on the United States on 11 September 2001
and the slaughter of Australian tourists in terrorist bombings in Bali on 12
October 2002 prompted an urgent defence policy debate. On one hand, the
'geographical determinists' continued to focus on the defence of Australia and
its vital regional interests (particularly those in the neighbourhood) as the
primary driver of the Australian defence force structure, arguing that this
would provide Australian governments with sufficient options for niche contributions to more distant coalition operations (Dupont, 2005: 27). On the
other hand, the 'expeditionary school' (Dibb, 2006: 27) discounted the relevance of state-on-state conflict or defence of the Australian continent and its
immediate neighbourhood and argued that 'the compression of time and
space that is the defining characteristic of a globalised world' meant

according priority to developing the ADF's capacity for distant operations with like-minded countries (Dupont, 2005: 6).

This post-9/11 debate gained edge from the underlying dispute over the relative value accorded various military capabilities. One strand of the debate was about the extent to which the Army should be hardened (to include procurement of Abrams main battle tanks for armoured protection and firepower) and networked (to enable it to deploy effective combined arms teams comprising infantry, armour, artillery, aviation and signals supported by a range of ground and air-based indirect fire and logistic support) (Leahy, 2005: 33). A second aspect of the debate was about the impact on naval and air force capabilities of the need to transport an expeditionary ground force (amphibious support ships and C12 aircraft), protect that force (air warfare destroyers) and support it. A third aspect of the debate involved what – if any – adjustment of other elements of the ADF structure was required to release funds for the hardening and networking of the Army already mentioned (Dibb, 2006: 1–5).

As of 2008, Australia's involvement in the so-called 'War on Terror' has not prompted any wholesale restructuring of the ADF. It has, however, prompted an accelerated tempo of operations by selected elements of the existing force (involving a concomitant increase in expenditure on the preparedness of those force elements) and a rapid increase in investment in the internal and external intelligence capabilities and police capacity required for defence of the Australian homeland.

Australian institutional experiments

This section explores Australia's post-1970 experiments with institutional arrangements and processes to define and capture the value added by different elements of the defence value-adding chain. It starts with an analysis of Australian experiments with different organisational structures in an attempt to improve the value generated by defence expenditure. This leads to discussion of Australian experiments with incentives to improve the performance of organisations and people within them. The section concludes with a survey of local industry's role in supply and support of the ADF, including Australian experiments with different defence business models.

Reforming the defence organisation

The Australian Minister for Defence is an elected member of Parliament and a member of the Cabinet of ministers drawn from the party with a parliamentary majority. The Minister for Defence heads the Defence Portfolio which comprises a number of legally distinct entities, of which the most significant are:

- the Department of Defence which, as a department of state, is headed by the civilian Secretary of Defence;

- the Australian Defence Force which is commanded by the Chief of the Defence Force (CDF) and which comprises the Navy, Army and Air Force, led by a Service Chief responsible for raising, training and sustaining their respective forces;
- the Defence Materiel Organisation, a prescribed agency headed by a civilian Chief Executive Officer (CEO DMO).

Together the Secretary and the Chief of the Defence Force (CDF) comprise a 'diarchy' in which the Minister looks to the Secretary, as principal civilian advisor, for guidance on, among other issues, defence policy and stewardship of the resources appropriated by the parliament for defence. As the commander of the ADF, the CDF is the Minister's principal military advisor, responsible for advice on matters that relate to military activity, including operations.[4] The origins of this division of labour illustrate how Australian Governments have experimented with different institutions in an attempt to extract greater value from the defence value-adding chain.

The diarchy dates from the election of a reformist government in 1972. As part of its response to the Guam Doctrine, the new government instructed Sir Arthur Tange, then Secretary of the Department of Defence, to report on how the government might consolidate the Australian defence functions then dispersed among five departments of state – Defence, Navy, Army, Air and Supply (Tange, 1973: 1). Tange's 1973 report focused on the question of 'how to provide effective ministerial supervision of the management of resources and of the exercise of command in the Services, and how to ensure that both conform to the policies for which the Minister is accountable to Parliament?' (ibid.: 13).

To this end, Tange recommended subsuming the five separate departments into a single Department of Defence, the management of which would be supported by:

- a series of major policy and management committees, including one for advising on Defence force structure and another for advising on the Defence five-year forward procurement programme and on the annual budget estimates;
- specialist organisations responsible for research, development, test and evaluation and for intelligence;
- a departmental organisation responsible for strategic policy and force development;
- a single supply and support organisation;
- a departmental resources and financial programs organisation.

Tange further recommended the creation of a Chief of Defence Force Staff as a statutory officer in the Department of Defence, directly responsible to the Minister for the command of the Navy, Army and Air Force. The Commonwealth legislation implementing Tange's Report took effect in February 1976.

But such far-reaching reforms, naturally, took years to bed down. Criticism of, among other matters, defence procurement, defence industry support for the ADF and the roles and responsibilities of, respectively, the Secretary and CDF prompted the Australian government to commission John Utz to review the Defence organisation in 1982. This led the government of the day to establish a separate Minister and associated Department of Defence Support to manage, within defence policies approved by the Minister for Defence, the government aircraft factories, the government munitions factories, naval dockyards, defence R&D and certain purchasing and defence industry development functions (Utz *et al.*, 1982: xxviii). However, these administrative changes did not address structural problems besetting the government factories and shipyards. Substantive response to criticism of defence procurement and management arrangements had to await the Kinnaird Review, some 15 years later.

Experimenting with defence capability development processes

During this period Defence management of, for example, the Collins Class submarine project, Sea Sprite helicopters for the ANZAC frigates, and the Jindalee Over-the-horizon Radar Network (JORN) was widely criticised. This criticism prompted the government to appoint, in 2002, a small team headed by Malcolm Kinnaird 'to assist with a range of issues associated with major Defence acquisitions to ensure we continue to spend taxpayers' money wisely and maintain public confidence in the procurement process'.[5]

Kinnaird reported in 2003. He attributed Defence's well-publicised difficulties in the downstream part of the defence value-adding chain to a lack of rigour and discipline in capability specification further upstream in that chain (Kinnaird *et al.*, 2003: 9). At issue here was unresolved tension between centralised adjudication of competing priorities for military capability development controlled by the Secretary and single Service-based advocacy of particular solutions to capability requirements.

Thirty years earlier, Tange had established a civilian organisation (modelled on the Program Analysis and Evaluation organisation created by US Defence Secretary McNamara) and called Force Development and Analysis Division – FDA. The latter was intended to forge the link between strategic guidance and military capability development and to adjudicate on competing Service capability development proposals. According to Utz, the role and style of the civilian FDA were the focal point of the administrative problems besetting the post-Tange Defence Organisation (Utz *et al.*, 1982: 42–7). By 2003, the responsibilities of the Service Chiefs for raising, training and sustaining their respective forces had been clarified and their relationship with the CDF had been settled clearing the way for a centralised military organisation responsible for preparation of capability development options for consideration by government.[6] Accordingly, Kinnaird recommended and the government agreed to appoint a three-star military officer as Chief, Capability

Development Group, responsible and accountable for managing capability definition and assessment.

Kinnaird also argued that it was for governments, not officials, to decide which contingencies were most critical; the type, number and mix of equipment to deal with them; and what trade-offs best suited the national interest (Kinnaird *et al.*, 2003: 4). To reinforce government control of this decision-making process he recommended that the government revamp the two-pass system for government approval of capability development and acquisition.

The two-pass approval process was an Australian adaptation of British practice. At first pass, government considered alternatives and approved those capability development options to proceed to more detailed analysis and costing with a view to subsequent approval of a specific capability. At second pass, government agreed to fund the acquisition of a specific capability system with a well-defined budget and schedule.

To reinvigorate the two-pass approval process the government embedded it in formal Cabinet procedures. To improve the information available to Cabinet, the government required officials from two key coordinating departments in the Australian government machinery (Prime Minister and Cabinet, and Finance) to participate in the defence capability development process. While this was a very substantial dilution of the policy autonomy Defence had previously enjoyed, it gave Cabinet ministers involved in the two-pass approval process access more diversified information and judgements.

Prior to the Kinnaird review, the government had sought to capture the synergies between materiel acquisition and in-service support by making a single organisation – called the Defence Materiel Organisation (DMO) – responsible for not only the initial acquisition of capital equipment from industry but also for arranging subsequent support by industry of that equipment once the Services concerned accepted it as fit for purpose. Kinnaird concluded that the DMO's organisational culture was inimical to development of the commercial skills required for this task. To remedy this cultural problem, to give DMO management more commercial-style flexibility in recruiting and rewarding high quality staff and to clarify accountabilities, responsibilities and authority between the DMO and the rest of Defence, Kinnaird recommended establishing the DMO as an executive agency, operating within the Defence portfolio but with a separtate financial identity and full autonomy in recruitment and management of staff (ibid.: 33–8).

The government declined to accord the DMO this degree of autonomy, opting instead for the more limited management autonomy and greater financial transparency of a prescribed agency. In doing so, the government avoided repeating the wasteful experiment with the Department of Defence Support 20 years earlier. The DMO achieved prescribed agency status on 1 July 2005. Under these arrangements, the DMO's Chief Executive Officer (CEO DMO) is directly accountable to the Minister for Defence for DMO's performance while remaining accountable to the Secretary and the CDF (DPBS, 2006: 15). The mutually reinforcing governance structures underpinning these arrangements are an important element of Australia's defence value-adding chain.

Defence governance reflects wider reforms initiated by the Australian government in 1997, to improve the performance of Commonwealth agencies.[7] The following governance arrangements determine how Defence contributes value to, and draws value from, the defence value-adding chain:

- extra-departmental arrangements for ensuring Defence complies with the legal requirements, published standards and community expectations of probity, accountability and openness (external governance);
- intra-departmental arrangements for holding individual defence officials accountable for a responsibility conferred upon them (internal governance).

(ibid.: 6–8)

External governance

Since its introduction in the early 1990s, the accrual-based outcomes/outputs framework has become increasingly important as a means by which the elected government ensures that Defence (and other Commonwealth departments) conform to the government's requirements for managing resources appropriated by parliament. This framework is intended to improve the value added by departments by measuring their performance in terms of what they produce, what they achieve and at what cost. In the Defence case, the framework complements the Tange organisational reforms introduced 20 years earlier.

In Australia, the long-term outcomes sought by government and the shorter-term outputs generated by government departments in pursuit of those outcomes are promulgated in the annual Portfolio Budget Statements (PBS). Each year, the PBS publish the performance targets for achieving outputs set for each department together with the resources allocated to them for this purpose. A year later the responsible minister tables in Parliament the department's annual report on its achievement of the performance targets and what it actually did with the resources appropriated by Parliament the previous financial year

This outcomes/outputs framework was first used in the 1999–2000 Defence PBS and then refined in subsequent budget cycles. The Defence PBS includes a qualitative explanation of planned performance and key risks to, and limitations on, achievement of that performance at *outcome* level. The PBS also promulgates quantitative performance targets for the assets responsible for generating each military output. For example, Military Output 4.3 (Capability for surveillance and response operations) is generated by, among other assets, 19 P-3 Orion aircraft operated by Air Force. The performance target for these aircraft was 8,200 flying hours in 2006–07.

The need for concordance between Defence PBS at the beginning of the performance management cycle and Defence annual reports at the end of the

cycle has prompted Defence to move away from simply reporting administrative detail to the provision of more information about actual programme
performance in its annual reports. At the defence outcome level, for example,
the 2004–05 Defence annual report refers back to the two key risks (personnel
and logistic support) the Army identified in the 2004–05 PBS.[8] At the military
capability output level, the report explains why, for example, the RAAF's
24 C-130 aircraft achieved only 84 per cent of their planned flying hours
(ibid.: 202).

The key instrument for determining the performance targets stipulated in
the PBS – C130 flying hours in the above example – is the Preparedness
Directive issued by the CDF. In principle, this directive reflects the balance
struck by Australian governments between investment in development of
future military capability outputs and expenditure on the preparedness of
existing outputs.

The degree to which individual military capability outputs achieve performance targets specified by the CDF Preparedness Directive is an important
measure of the capability value they generate for government. Conversely, the
degree to which individual military capability outputs fail to achieve performance targets specified in the CDF Preparedness Directive becomes a measure
of the resulting loss of capability value.

The same logic applies to investment in development of future military
capabilities. In Australia, the annual Defence PBS includes an estimate of the
amount of money the government expects to spend in adjusting a military
capability (output) once the equipment concerned has received second pass
approval. As resources are limited, this estimate of project cost becomes a
measure of the value government accords that military capability adjustment
relative to alternative uses of the resources involved.

Internal governance

The above external accountability arrangements operating at the institutional
level are complemented by internal accountability arrangements operating at
the individual official level. Defence arrangements for *internal* conformance
and accountability start with the Ministerial Directive to the Secretary and
the CDF. The Ministerial Directive renders them accountable for specified
results which are cascaded down the Defence organisational hierarchy via
subordinate performance charters between the Secretary, CDF, Defence
Group Heads and the Service Chiefs.

These personal directives are supplemented by a series of purchaser-provider
agreements instituted as part of the prescription of the DMO already described. Of these agreements, the following are of most relevance to the defence
value-adding chain:

- *Materiel Acquisition Agreements*, under which the DMO provides services
  to Defence for acquisition of capital equipment as approved by government;

- *Materiel Sustainment Agreements*, under which the DMO provides services to Defence for the repair, maintenance and adaptation of platforms and systems and for the supply of consumable items and spare parts required to maintain the force in being at agreed levels of preparedness.

The CEO DMO concludes Materiel Acquisition Agreements with the Chief of the Capability Development Group to cover the acquisition of major capital equipment. In 2006–07, for example, the DMO planned to spend nearly Aus$5 billion on the acquisition of capital equipment under a suite of Materiel Acquisition Agreements (one for each project).

Embedded in each Materiel Acquisition Agreement are key performance indicators: the project scope covers underlying customer specifications and key measures of capability effectiveness as selected by the Capability Manager. The project schedule sets out such key milestones as project start up, contract negotiations and acceptance into service. The project budget information includes, for example, estimates of percentage spent at each schedule milestone, the current expenditure programme, and assessments of the adequacy of provision for contingencies.

The CEO DMO concludes Materiel Sustainment Agreements with the Service Chiefs in their capacity as defence capability managers. In 2006–7, for example, the DMO planned to spend Aus$3.5 billion on sustainment of military equipment operated by the ADF. The level of services DMO provides to Capability Managers under Materiel Sustainment Agreements is linked to the level of capability preparedness those managers are directed to maintain under the CDF's Preparedness Directive already explained. The Materiel Sustainment Agreements between the CEO DMO and the respective Service Chiefs are structured around key platforms (for example, Collins Class submarines), fleets (for example, Army field vehicles and trailers) or systems (for example surveillance and control systems) supported by the DMO.

The performance of the Chief of the Capability Development Group depends on the effectiveness of the Materiel Acquisition Agreements with the CEO DMO. The performance of the Service Chiefs in meeting the CDF's standards of preparedness hinges on the efficacy of the Materiel Sustainment Agreements they have concluded with the CEO DMO. In both cases, the performance of the CEO DMO in meeting agreed targets for materiel acquisition and sustainment is hostage to industry performance, the subject of the next section.

The role of industry in the defence value-adding chain

The following analysis of industry's role in the defence value-adding chain begins with reform of the government factories and dockyards largely inherited from World War II and engaged in supply and support of ADF requirements ranging from ships, aircraft and weapons to ammunition and clothing. We then explore how far-reaching developments in the commercial sector of the Australian economy enabled the government to extricate itself from most of the actual production of the goods and services defence needs. The section concludes with a discussion of the resulting changes in Defence business practices.

Reforming the government factories and dockyards

The Australian government had experimented in the early 1980s with a Department of Defence Support to manage the government factories and dockyards then dominating defence industry. While the experiment was ultimately abandoned, it set in train a series of developments leading to privatisation of the Australian defence industry. These developments constituted a major adjustment of the Australian defence value-adding chain.

By the mid-1980s, the government had recognised the impracticability 'of attempting to make one minister and his department substantially subordinate to another within a legal and administrative framework which provide for the independence of both' (Coulthard-Clark, 1999: 70–2). To raise the productivity of the government-owned factories and dockyards by matching their workforce to current and projected workloads, the government began by returning them to the Defence portfolio and abolishing the Department of Defence Support. It then proceeded to establish the Government Aircraft Factory as a wholly government-owned but new and separate company, to sell Williamstown Naval Dockyard in Melbourne to private interests (who subsequently completely restructured the dockyard's), to introduce full cost recovery and associated reforms at Garden Island Dockyard in Sydney, and to close Cockatoo Island Dockyard, also in Sydney (see Chapter 13). In 1989, the government established the facilities remaining in the Defence portfolio as a government-owned company, Australian Defence Industries (ADI).

The government required ADI to compete for Defence contracts. At the same time, however, it provided the political support the company needed in rationalising and modernising ammunition production (much of the equipment and facilities for which dated from World War II). As a result, the value of annual production/sales per employee rose from some Aus$20,000 in 1984/85, under the Department of Defence Support, to just over Aus$40,000, when ADI was established in 1988/89, to Aus$148,000 five years later. The value of annual production/sales per employee stood at Aus$180,000 when the government announced the sale of ADI to a private consortium in 1997 (ibid.).

The above process of corporatisation and subsequent privatisation of the government factories and dockyards was complemented by equally far-reaching changes in the role of commercial suppliers more generally.

Export assistance

Unlike some other small, developed countries, Australia has not been a major exporter of defence materiel after World War II. This reflects Australia's limited competitive advantage in exports of military systems. In part, this is because of Australia's geographic isolation and the lack of physical market contiguity: smaller European countries have benefited from their membership of European Union and the intra-EU trade (see Chapters 10–12) while Canada has largely been involved in bilateral trade with the USA (see Chapter 7). Also, unlike Israel (Chapter 8), Australia has rarely engaged in hostilities that required it to supply and support Australia-unique eqipment which it could then market as 'operationally proven'. And, not being a member of NATO, Australia has not been a part of the intra-NATO division of labour (see Chapters 4 and 5). Finally, where Australia has developed world class solutions to niche capability requirements (for example, the NULKA anti-ship missile decoy system, Jindalee operational radar network or anechoic tiles for the Collins Class submarines), exports have been inhibited by overriding security constraints. Thus, defence exports only account for an estimated 2.7 per cent of total sales in the Australian defence sector.[9] Foreign direct investment has been strong in Australian defence industry with many US and European major defence companies setting up subsidiaries in Australia to establish and sustain their local presence. However, these activities have largely been focused on in-country demands rather than exports.

Australian policy has largely focused on import substitution, normally by relying on local content policies (initially mandatory offsets, later local content targets, and, more recently, commitment to in-country sourcing). Increased export opportunities have always been emphasised in the application of these policies as policy-makers have been keen to use their procurement leverage to create a sustainable base for exports. In practice, though, this optimistic reliance on local content policies as a means of pump priming exports has produced rather disappointing results. (As discussed elsewhere in this volume, mercantilist policies of many countries make it hard for small defence industries to export their products even if the application of local content policies results in the development of good quality products and efficient production processes.) The ANZAC frigate project has provided a limited opportunity to engage in a bilateral work-share arrangement with New Zealand (see Chapter 13). Similarly, projects such as NULKA have involved collaborative product development with US firms. Recently, the deployment of Australian-made Bushmaster armoured vehicles in Afghanistan has provided an opportunity to export a small number of these 'operationally-tested' vehicles for use by the Dutch forces in Afghanistan.

Australia's participation in the Joint Strike Fighter (JSF) Project has opportunities for the involvement of Australian firms in the intra-JSF division of labour and for exports of associated components and expertise. As this involvement is based on competitive tendering for work, rather than a pre-arranged work-share agreement, Australian industry participation in the JSF project is likely to be small.

Leveraging industry support

Thirty years after the event, Australia's experience with mobilisation of Australian industry for World War II still coloured views as to what constituted the appropriate balance among local industry, selective stockholding and reliable overseas sources of supply (DoD, 1976: 51–4). In order to foster local defence industry capacity, the *1976 Defence White Paper* envisaged:

- selectively directing defence procurement in whole or in part into Australian industry and accepting any higher costs and delays that might be legitimately incurred;
- separately funding feasibility and project definition studies and the establishment costs of local production and/or support facilities;
- including in defence overseas procurement contracts provision for offset work by Australian companies, on a competitive basis, in similar technologies; and
- local development of equipment and systems either in industry or in Defence establishments with subsequent production in industry or government factories.

(ibid.: 52)

The management of overseas procurement to create opportunities for local industry is particularly relevant. In 1981, Australia decided to replace its French-designed Mirage III-0 (built under licence at the Government Aircraft Factory) with the McDonnell Douglas F/A-18 Hornet. The F/A-18 project provided for extensive involvement by Australian industry aimed at establishing 'the capability to undertake the required engineering, maintenance, and spares provision support for the aircraft, its systems, equipment, and support facilities, during the service life of the aircraft' (IICD, 1994: 36). In the event, however, the RAAF supported the F/A-18 largely in-house and made little use of the capacity established in industry (ibid.: 38–9). The major loss of value inherent in the duplication of support capacity in industry and in the armed services dramatised the need for a further major adjustment of the Australian defence value-adding chain.

In 1989, the Minister for Defence commissioned an ex-Defence official, Alan Wrigley, to investigate unnecessary duplication of civil and military capacity to support the ADF and to identify opportunities for military use of civial capabilities that exist or might be developed in the Australian community. Wrigley argued that defence efficiency had been reduced by 'doctrines which emphasise military self sufficiency in a way that is no longer appropriate' (Wrigley, 1990: xiii). While the government subsequently rejected Wrigley's more ambitious proposals, it did pursue selected opportunities for competing in-house service provision with external sources and contracting out where this was more efficient and effective – the Commercial Support Program (CSP). The government permitted Defence to retain the savings generated by the CSP, thereby giving it an incentive to redirect resources from the support areas to the sharp end of the defence force.

The initial tranche of CSP began in 1991 and resulted in the contracting out of some 2,100 service and 1,100 civilian positions – a cautious 7 per cent of the service and civilian personnel then employed in logistic, support and training functions (DoD, 1991: 42). The *1997 Defence Efficiency Review* (DER) boosted the CSP substantially. It identified over Aus$500 million worth of one-off savings and Aus$770 million mature annual savings, to be achieved by reducing military staff by 4,700, transferring the military positions involved to the combat force and reducing civilian staff by 3,100. The DER identified a further 7,000 military and 5,900 civilian positions to be market tested (DoD, 1997). By the time the CSP initiative had run its course, Defence had tested nearly 16,000 positions, with 68 per cent of the contracts involved awarded to commercial suppliers, 27 per cent awarded to defence in-house options and the status quo retained for the balance.[10]

In parallel with the CSP initiative, Defence had begun requiring contractors to compete for defence capital equipment contracts on a through-life cost of ownership basis, rather than on the basis of the cost of acquisition alone. This initiative reflected a desire to avoid a repetition of the above F/A-18 experience, CSP-induced acceptance by Service operators of greater dependence on industry for support and – perhaps most important – pragmatic recognition of the difficulty the Services encountered in recruiting and retaining sufficient engineering and technical personnel.

In 1997, for example, Defence awarded BAE Systems a contract to supply and support 33 Hawk 127 aircraft used for the fast jet training of Air Force pilots. The in-service support contract requires BAE Systems to provide deeper maintenance support throughout the Hawk's 25-year life of type under arrangements renewed every five years. To this end BAE Systems has established the requisite capacity for engineering, logistics and whole of life supply chain management, delivered through the company's support facility located on the Air Force base concerned.[11]

Defence took this business model a step further in procuring Armidale Class patrol boats in 2004 (Wylie, 2006a: 58, and Chapter 13 in this volume). In this case, Defence eschewed its traditional procurement approach of specifying in detail, for example, the number of vessels it required, their dimensions and construction standards. Instead, Defence invited companies to tender for a patrol boat *system* able to generate 3,000 days of operational availability per year for 15 years, and to surge to 3,600 days per year. As part of this performance-based procurement model, Defence required tenderers to construct and provide through-life support of patrol boats able to conduct surveillance and response boarding operations at the top of Sea State 4 (wave heights of 2.5 metres) and to maintain surveillance to the top of Sea State 5 (wave heights of 4 metres).

These major changes in the way Australian industry has been engaged in support of the nation's defence capability both drove, and were enabled by, corresponding changes in Defence policy settings and associated business models.

Defence industry policy

Since at least the 1970s Australian governments and their defence advisors have sought a robust policy framework to guide the choice of local and overseas options for supply of ADF materiel. It was generally recognised that:

> Australia's ability to supply defence equipment at the requisite level of technology, with acceptable lead times, and at an acceptable cost is, and will remain, very limited. Pursuit of any substantial defence independence of overseas sources of supply is not feasible and would be counter to world-wide commercial trends. Nor does it have priority in our strategic circumstances. Australian industry should not plan on a repeat of its experience in the Second World War when a broad range of defence equipment was locally manufactured. Finally, and noting the limited effect that defence expenditure has on our overall economy, defence industry should be used to support defence, and not as a convenient prop for ailing industrial sectors.
>
> (Dibb, 1986: 114)

As successive Defence White Papers have acknowledged, Australia's privi-leged access to US technological innovation has been one of the more tangi-ble benefits of the ANZUS alliance and contributes fundamentally to Australia's knowledge edge. But the US government controls access by both allies and adversaries to its military technology, forcing countries like Aus-tralia to focus more policy attention on what technology they develop them-selves and what they import from the USA and elsewhere (Wylie, 2004). Since the *1994 Defence White Paper*, therefore, Defence has accorded priority to development of local industry capabilities for:

- combat and systems software and support;
- data management and signal processing, including for information gathering and surveillance;
- command, control and communication systems;
- systems integration;
- repair, maintenance and upgrades of major weapons and surveillance platforms;
- provision of services to support the peacetime and operational requirements of the ADF.

(DoD, 2000: 99)

To give practical effect to defence industry policy, successive Australian gov-ernments have provided for *Australian Industry Involvement* (AII) in the supply and support of defence capital equipment. In 2003, however, the Auditor General concluded that:

> In the absence of quantitative and/or qualitative performance measures for the AII Program as a whole, it was not practicable for Defence to demonstrate whether, over the many years of its existence, the AII program has been making real progress or is losing ground, in seeking to meet its objectives.
>
> (Auditor General, 2003: 14)

In 2006, pervasive dissatisfaction with the effectiveness of defence industry policy generally and of the AII programme in particular prompted a newly appointed Minister for Defence to make what was at least the eighth attempt, since the mid-1980s, to promulgate an effective policy. The resulting incremental improvement suggested that Australia had far to go before it resolved such perennial issues as how best to use defence procurement in developing strategically important industry capabilities, how to choose between indigenous development and imported platforms and systems and how to link defence industry performance to arrangements for defining and enforcing accountability for Defence capability management (Wylie, 2006b).

Business models in Australian defence procurement

In Australia, Defence is effectively the sole buyer of military goods and services. Hence local industry capabilities are shaped not only by what Defence buys but also by how it does so. The defence business model is therefore a key element of Australia's arrangements to capture capability value.

The defence business model has evolved considerably from that based on full and open competition inherited from the Department of Supply following the Tange reforms of 1973. That evolution has been influenced by a combination of indigenous experiments and diffusion of overseas experience which aimed at:

- determining the balance between competition and regulation in the quest for value for money;
- changing the distribution of project risk between customer and supplier;
- testing the limits of CSP, including the use of contractors in an operational theatre and the private financing of defence capability.

As in most countries – and particularly smaller ones – the local market for defence industry products is dominated on the demand side by a single buyer. On the supply side, there is also substantial concentration in a number of key industry sectors. Thus, the Australian defence market is highly imperfect and market power is distributed very unevenly between market players. Increasingly, therefore, the Australian defence business model combines different measures of competition and regulation. The latter includes the active structuring and management of acquisition and sustainment programmes with the goal of achieving the best outcomes for Defence, noting that the weaker the competitive pressures at work in a given programme, the more Defence needs to rely on regulatory instruments to achieve value for money. But Defence in general and the DMO in particular have been wary of regulatory-based business models, partially because of the transaction costs involved and also because of a chronic shortage of the policy and administrative skills required to achieve value for money on this basis.

In Australia, Defence has tended to eschew the kind of cost plus contracts that feature so prominently in, for example, US development projects. In the past, Australia has used competitive pressure to force the supplier to accept fixed price contracts and, hence, most of the technical risk. If, as was often the case, the supplier underestimated and/or under-priced the risk, the record suggests that Defence was prepared to relax the delivery schedule rather than adjust the price. In effect, this meant trading off preparedness for budget integrity.

Australia's defence managers increasingly acknowledge, however, that the uncertainties inherent in development projects render fixed price contracts vulnerable to costly and, all too often, contentious renegotiation. As the initial contract for acquisition of the Jindalee Over-the-horizon Radar Network (JORN) in 1986 shows (see Box 6.1 and Chapter 14), fixed price contracts and their derivatives rarely succeed in transferring the risk inherent in developmental projects from the Defence principal to the industry agent. More broadly, it demonstrates the fundamental importance to the success of high risk developmental projects of the non-contractual elements of the 'deal' discussed in Part I of this volume.

The acquisition of Collins Class submarines is another example of a complex acquisition that has profoundly affected the philosophy and mechanics of defence procurement in Australia. In this case, Defence sought to reduce project risk by accessing both overseas technological innovation and overseas management expertise in a 'deal' that went far beyond the relatively simple verities of a contract. (For a discussion of the Collins Class acquisition, see Box 6.2 and Chapter 13.)

Defence seems to have incorporated the lessons learnt from the Collins programme in the alliance-based model being used to procure the air warfare destroyers (see Chapter 13).

Conclusion

The Australian experience demonstrates the importance to a viable defence value-adding chain of robust links between strategic perceptions and procurement processes. It also indicates the importance of political processes in establishing that link in the kind of small democratic countries that are the subject of this volume.

The Australian experience tends to corroborate the proposition that the value to national security of the defence capability produced downstream in

---

Box 6.1 The JORN acquisition

JORN uses radio energy refracted through the ionosphere to detect and track aircraft and surface ships over the horizon at ranges of 1,000–3,000 kms. In awarding the contract for supply of JORN in 1991, Defence recognised the technical risk involved in development and production of JORN and adopted a price ceiling/incentive contract. In doing so, it recognised that if the contractor was required to bear all the risks, either none would bid for the business, or those that did so would charge a price based on a worst case outcome. Accordingly the JORN price ceiling/incentive contract provided for the Commonwealth and the contractor to share the financial risk by:

- negotiating a target price for development and production of JORN;
- setting maximum (ceiling) price payable by the Commonwealth equal to the target price plus 60 per cent of any cost overruns up to a maximum of 10 per cent above the target;
- a financial risk share in which Telstra was responsible for 40 per cent of any cost overruns up to the ceiling price, and 100 per cent of all costs that exceeded the ceiling price;
- a saving share that entitled Telstra to 40 per cent of the savings if it completed JORN for less than the target price.

(ANAO, 2006: 41–3)

In the event, both Defence and the contractor underestimated the development task and the resulting cost and schedule overruns swamped the above arrangements. In 1999, Defence changed the JORN contract to a joint venture between a US company (with experience in a comparable US programme) and an Australian company. This new team succeeded in delivering a fully compliant JORN system in 2003. (For further details, see Chapter 14.)

---

the defence value-adding chain should provide a rationale for one resource allocation over another further upstream in the value chain. But the Australian experience also suggests that, in democracies, judgements about relative 'value' in this context will often be contested. To reduce the cost of friction, it is important to apply clearly articulated and broadly accepted procurement principles in a transparent way.

Australia's extensive experiments with industry involvement in the defence value-adding chain range from almost complete government ownership of the means of production to almost total reliance on commercial suppliers for supply, repair and maintenance of platforms and systems. The shift across this spectrum of ownership has occurred within a relatively small market that

Box 6.2 The Collins Class acquisition

When it contracted to design and build the Collins Class submarines, the Australian Submarine Corporation (ASC) was owned by, among other interests, the Swedish submarine designer, Kockums (who had the controlling interest in ASC). This arrangement reflected two imperatives: first, the Commonwealth sought to maximise Kockum's incentive to design a submarine that met Defence's demanding requirements. Second, Kockums wanted to protect its intellectual property (which the Commonwealth had decided not to buy). At the same time, Kockums retained separate design authority for the Collins Class.

These arrangements placed Kockums in a debilitating conflict of interest when the Collins Class subsequently encountered widely publicised – and politically embarrassing – design and construction problems (McIntosh and Prescott, 1999). The problems were exacerbated when Defence decided to purchase a US-designed replacement for the troubled Collins Class submarine combat system, and (in 2001) to enter into a strategic alliance with the US Navy on submarine matters, including the future enhancement of the Collins Class submarines.

In late 2000, the Australian government assumed full direct ownership of ASC. In order to restore public confidence in the Collins Class submarine project and in ASC's ability to manage it, the government then directed ASC to engage Electric Boat Corporation (the major US submarine builder) as a capability partner. Accordingly, in 2002, ASC and Electric Boat concluded a three-year agreement (with provision for extensions) for the latter's provision of specialist management and technical advice on modernised life cycle support, strategic business planning, work packaging and scheduling, business processes and systems, management practices and on-going engineering support.

But Kockums was unenthusiastic about Australia's embrace of US Navy and US commercial expertise in submarine matters. After protracted negotiations with ASC over the latter's access to Kockums' Collins Class intellectual property needed for in-service support of the submarines, Kockums exited the Australian defence industry. (For further details, see Parliament of Australia, 2006 and Chapter 13.)

imposes stringent constraints on local suppliers' capacity to capture economies of scale and scope enjoyed by suppliers in larger defence markets.

In response, Defence has tended to modify its traditional emphasis on competition across the full spectrum of defence business. Australia's defence procurement history has tended to emulate trends set in the USA and the UK. After several decades of experiment, however, there were signs that Australia in the early twenty-first century was learning from its cumulative experience to develop a more Australian-specific model crafted to fit its particular circumstances.

Notes

1 This concept of 'defence output' differs from what we describe as 'output' in Chapter 1. Here, military 'capabilities', as we define them, are referred to as 'outputs' and 'outcomes'. In our nomenclature, these capabilities are intermediate outputs. Final outputs are generated when these capabilities are deployed in specific operational environments.
2 Public Papers of the Presidents of the United States: Richard Nixon, 1969: 901–9, quoted by Vassar College at: http://vietnam.vassar,edu/doc14.html.
3 DoD (1991: 8) and Australian Bureau of Statistics, *Year Book Australia 2005*, 'defence resourcing' (available at: http://www.abs.gov.au/Ausstats).
4 See http://www.defence.gov.au/secretary/diarchy_full.htm (accessed 5 March 2008).
5 Hill, R. 'Review team to assist with Defence procurements', Media release MIN749/02, 12 December 2002. Online. Available at: http://www.minister.defence. gov.au/Hilltpl.cfm (accessed 28 November 2006).
6 For a fuller explanation, see DoD (1997): 7–15 and Annex E: E1–E2.
7 As, for example, summarised in ANAO (2003): 14–15.
8 *Defence Annual Report 2004–05*, 'Outcome Performance: Outcome Three Army Capabilities', Chap. 4: 2. Online. Available at: www.defence.gov.au/budget/04–05/ dar/04–05 outcome3 (accessed 6 June 2006).
9 See http://www.austrade.gov.au/Defence-Homeland-Security-overview/default.aspx (accessed 9 May 2008).
10 See http://www.defence.gov.au/budget/02–03/dar/04_01_1csp.htm (accessed 27 November 2006).
11 See http://www.defence.gov.au/dmo/asd/air5367 (accessed 28 November 2006).

References

Auditor General (2003) *Australian Industry Involvement Program*, The Auditor General, Canberra: Commonwealth of Australia.
ANAO (2003) *Public Sector Governance, Better Practice Guide*, Vol. 1, Canberra: Australian National Audit Office.
—— (2006) *Jindalee Operational Radar Network*, Department of Defence Performance Audit No. 28, 1995–96, Canberra: Australian National Audit Office.
Betts, R.K. (1995) *Military Readiness: Concepts, Choices, Consequences*, Washington, DC: Brookings Institute.
Brabin-Smith, R. (2005) 'The heartland of Australia's defence policies', Strategic and Defence Studies Centre, Working Paper No. 396, Canberra: Australian National University.
CoA (2006) *Defence Portfolio Budget Statements 2006–07*, Canberra: Commonwealth of Australia.
Coulthard-Clark, C. (1999) *Breaking Free: Transforming Australia's Defence Industry*, Kew: Australian Scholarly Publishing.
Dibb, P. (1986) *Review of Australia's Defence Capabilities*, Canberra: Australian Government Publishing Service.
—— (2006) *Essays on Australian Defence*, Canberra Papers on Strategy and Defence, Paper No. 161, Strategic and Defence Studies Centre, Canberra: Australian National University.

DoD (1972) *Australian Defence Review*, Department of Defence, Canberra: Australian Government Publishing Service.

—— (1976) *Australian Defence*, Department of Defence, Canberra: Australian Government Publishing Service.

—— (1987) *Australia's Strategic Policy*, Department of Defence, Canberra: Commonwealth of Australia.

—— (1991) *Force Structure Review 1991*, Department of Defence, Canberra: Commonwealth of Australia.

—— (1994) *Defending Australia: Defence White Paper 1994*, Department of Defence, Canberra: Australian Government Publishing Service.

—— (1997) *Future Directions for the Management of Australia's Defence*, Report of the Defence Efficiency Review, Canberra: Commonwealth of Australia.

—— (2000) *Defence 2000: Our Future Defence Force*, Canberra: Defence Publishing Service.

—— (2006) *Defence Capability Development Manual*, Department of Defence, Canberra: Commonwealth of Australia.

DPBS (2006) *Defence Portfolio Budget Statements, 2006–07*, Canberra: Commonwealth of Australia.

Dupont, A. (2005) *Grand Strategy, National Security and the Australian Defence Force*, Sydney: Lowy Institute.

IICD (1994) *Review of the F/A-18 Industry Program*, Industry Involvement and Contracting Division, Canberra: Department of Defence.

Kinnaird, M., Early, L. and Schofield, B. (2003) *Report of the Defence Procurement Review*, Canberra: Department of Defence.

Leahy, P. (2005) 'Towards the hardened and networked army', *Australian Army Journal*, 11(1): 27–36.

McIntosh, M. K. and Prescott, J. B. (1999) *Report to the Minister for Defence on the Collins Class Submarine and Related Matters*, Canberra: Commonwealth of Australia. Online. Available at: http://www.minister.defence.gov.au/1999/Collins.html (accessed 3 January 2007).

Parliament of Australia (2006) *Blue Water Ships: Consolidating Past Achievements*, Senate Foreign Affairs Defence and Trade Committee, Commonwealth of Australia. Online. Available at: http://www.aph.gov.au/Senate/committee/fadt_cttee/shipbuilding/report (accessed 3 January 2007).

Tange, A. (1973) *Australian Defence: Report on the Reorganisation of the Defence Group of Departments*, Canberra: Department of Defence.

Utz, J. W., MacDonald, A. L., Neal, E. J. and Wheeler, F. H. (1982) *The Higher Defence Organisation in Australia: Final Report of the Defence Review Committee 1982*, Canberra: Australian Government Publishing Service.

Wylie, R. (2004) 'A profile of the Australian defence industry: helping align defence industry, defence industry policy and defence strategic planning', Canberra: ACIL Tasman Consultants.

—— (2006a) 'Supplying and supporting Australia's military capability', in CEDA *The Business of Defence – Sustaining Capability*, Melbourne: Committee for Economic Development of Australia.

—— (2006b) 'Defence industry policy and defence accountability', *Security Challenges*, 2(2): 70–1.

Wrigley, A.K. (1990) *The Defence Force and the Community: A Partnership in Australia's Defence*, Canberra: Australian Government Publishing Service.

7 Canadian defence procurement

Ugurhan Berkok

The framework in which Canada's defence policies are formulated and implemented reflects the unique features of its geo-strategic position and history. The most important component of this framework is Canada's proximity to the United States, its only real neighbour, a long-time ally and the sole superpower of the post-Cold War era. Thus, Canada's only land border, to the south, is heavily protected against military threat, whether Canada invests in its protection or not. Based on the level of perceived threat to the country, economic analysis would suggest only a modest demand for defence. No wonder, then, that Canada's defence expenditure, at 1.2 per cent of GDP, exceeds only that of Luxembourg among the OECD countries (CDIA, 2004). Nevertheless, Canadians reckon, a degree of self-reliance in the provision of national security is necessary. Also, there are at least three reasons why Canada should contribute to international security by participating in peace support operations (PSOs).[1] First, the Canadian economy is one of the most open in the world. Thus, the maintenance of international stability is vital. Second, since the 1956 Suez Canal crisis, Canada has been involved in international PSOs. This has become an enduring and cherished tradition of 'good international citizenship'. Third, rapid demographic change due to immigration has produced an ethnic and cultural mosaic that provides a powerful domestic constituency for Canada's continuing involvement in international PSOs.

The recent reorganization of Canada's defence command reflects these sentiments. To support international operations, Canada has been restructuring and equipping its defence force to generate a 'rapidly deployable, expeditionary force that is 'light-weight', highly mobile, and self-contained' (DeMille and Priestley, 2005). And, for homeland security that requires capacity for swift action, the new Canada Command envisages decentralization and enhanced cooperation with civilian authorities (DND, 2005a).

This chapter is divided into two parts: the first part outlines Canadian defence and defence procurement and the second comprises case studies of two distinctly Canadian acquisitions.

Canadian Defence and procurement

The Canadian defence organization

Canadian national security policy

Canada's national security policy is based on three national security imperatives (PCO, 2004). First, Canadians' safety and security must be protected.
This includes the protection of Canadians' personal security at home and
abroad, their values and institutions, and Canada's territorial integrity.
Potential threats include natural disasters and emergencies (e.g., the SARS
epidemic), organized crime, illegal immigration, and the violation of territorial waters. Direct terrorist threats, though taken seriously, are not as high on
the Canadian agenda as in the United States. Second, Canada's geographic
proximity makes it a potential base for threats against the United States. It is
thus recognized that Canada should not allow its territory to be used to perpetuate acts of aggression against other countries and, in particular, that it
should participate in the joint defence of North America. Third, as noted
above, Canada, as a member of the international community of nations, must
contribute to global security.

   With the appointment of a new Chief of Defence Staff in 2005, Canadian
Forces began reorganizing their command structure with the first and third
national security imperatives in mind, the second falling largely within the
jurisdiction of other security agencies. Since 1968, the three services of the
Canadian Forces (CF) have been unified under a central command at
National Defence Headquarters (NDHQ). The current reorganization
involves geographic decentralization of the command structure to form local
unified commands to better coordinate responses to natural disasters and
emergencies, enhance collaboration with civilian safety and security agencies.
As for the third national security imperative, Canada's ability to send expeditionary PSO forces abroad remains a matter of concern both in terms of
personnel and equipment.

The organization of national defence

The Canadian Forces and the Department of National Defence (DND) are
accountable to the Minister of Defence of the Government of Canada. The
minister is mandated to implement the government's national defence policy
by using the power and the resources with which the department is entrusted,
subject to parliamentary oversight. NDHQ integrates the civilian and military
components of DND. In addition to national defence, DND is responsible for
conducting the nation's search and rescue (SAR) operations. (For details of
the Canadian national defence organization, see CDIA, 2004.)

   CF consists of air, land and maritime forces, their reserves, and a unified
command at NDHQ. When the size of the regular forces was cut at the end

of the Cold War, the Canadian reserve forces increased in their relative numerical importance. They now have both an independent surge capacity and a role that complements the regular forces.

Accountable to the Deputy Minister of Defence is the Assistant Deputy Minister (Materiel), ADM (Mat), responsible for capital acquisition and procurement within the DND. The ADM (Mat) plays 'a major role in the planning and implementation of the Long-Term Capital Equipment Plan, [and] the National Procurement Plan to sustain in-service equipment' (DND, 2005a). In fact, ADM (Materiel) runs the Capital Acquisition and National Procurement corporate accounts, controls and administers approved equipment projects and maintains overall design authority of Forces' equipment and systems. The Chief of the Defence Staff is ADM (Mat)'s main client. ADM (Mat) also performs a significant bridging role between the DND and Public Works and Government Services Canada (PWGSC) (DND, 2005b). Since major acquisitions have to pass the Industrial and Regional Benefits (IRBs) test, ADM (Mat) has to extend its bridging role to Industry Canada that is mandated to implement the IRBs policy (see below). This multi-faceted role turns ADM (Mat) into the pivotal player in the defence procurement process.

Defence procurement: organizational framework

The Canadian procurement process is complicated and unusual by international standards. DND is not an autonomous purchaser of military hardware even after receiving fiscal authority for acquisition from the Government and the Department of Finance, and managerial authority from the Treasury Board (TB). All Canadian government procurement contracting, defence and civil, is delegated to the PWGSC: the whole-of-government purchasing agent (Martimort, 1996). In this process, PWGSC balances DND's goal of obtaining the best military hardware for given resources against other federal government industrial and regional objectives (Manson, 2005). These non-defence objectives are pursued by Industry Canada (IC) and the regional economic development agencies[2] that represent regional interests as well as those of regionally-based industries. Special interest groups can also access the process through these agencies. The PWGSC balancing role is not supposed to – and normally does not – compromise the integrity of military operational requirements. It has the implication, however, that equipment cannot be 'hard-wired', that is, while the intended acquisition has to satisfy stated operational requirements, it should not be limited to specific technical options designated by the military.

DND is one of PWGSC's many principals. However, there is 'substantial duplication of effort and functional overlap between DND and PWGSC' (SAG, 2004; Williams, 2006), implying that DND has more of a leading role than the other principals. Its leadership position in defence acquisitions derives from the significant size of DND's capital budget, its capacity to initiate projects, and the perception that national security should take priority over the socio-political objectives of other principals.

In this complicated agency, government departments could be expected to behave like Niskanen bureaus maximizing their overall activity while it might be anticipated that regional principals would seek to maximize their share of the activity by trying to attract contracts or subcontracts (Niskanen, 1971). Thus, relationships among principals may exhibit complementarity as well as substitutability (Salanié, 1997). For instance, both the DND and all regional agencies are likely to prefer larger projects (strategic complementarity), thereby reinforcing an above-optimal level of activity, in any case facilitated by the bureaucratic interests of PWGSC. However, DND and Treasury Board Secretariat (TBS) or Finance Canada (FC), insofar as they represent interests of other non-defence government departments, are likely to exhibit strategic substitutability in that larger projects are desirable to DND but not to other departments given that the citizen-taxpayer might not want to carry any further fiscal burden. Subject to this nexus of forces, the outcome with respect to the optimal project scale and scope will depend on the bargaining process.

DND's unique position among the federal departments is due to three factors. First, the importance of scope and scale economies in defence procurement means that acquisitions of major military hardware are quite unlike the purchases of other government departments. The sheer size and sophistication of DND major crown projects (MCPs), i.e., acquisitions of Can$100 million or more, as well as their specificity, require specialized knowledge and expertise beyond PWGSC's mandate. The defence-specific characteristics of DND projects restrict the potential for achieving economies of scope in government-wide procurement, thus, undermining or diluting the benefit of engaging the PWGSC. But some DND procurement, including certain MCPs, may benefit from the contracting expertise common to all departments, giving a basis for scope economies to be reaped from PWGSC's involvement. In some other countries (e.g., Britain and Australia), the existence of a dedicated defence purchasing agency is a sign that the potential scope economies from using a government-wide procurement agency are not perceived to be as large as in Canada (US-GAO, 1999). The current Canadian framework must certainly be revisited as duplication seems to outweigh potential scope economies. Following the British and Australian examples, a defence procurement organization encompassing PWGSC's defence-specific functions, whether such an organization is stand-alone or is within DND, may be a better option (Williams, 2006).

A second distinguishing mark of DND procurement is that MCPs are deemed high risk and typically become politicized due to the stringently applied procurement policy of Industrial and Regional Benefits (IRBs).[3] Within the federal structure, provincial governments intervene alongside non-governmental groups representing, for example, industry and labour as well as purely regional interests. Such multiple access to the procurement process has been one of the major factors that make it highly protracted (*The Economist*, 1999; and case studies below).

Third, Canada's federal governance structure complicates the trade-off between defence and socio-political objectives and lengthens the procurement cycle. Regional economic development agencies formally participate in the process during the IRBs evaluation and they are typically backed by provincial governments. This is one of the major access channels for interest groups like labour and industry.

Despite the unusual institutional structure in which it is embedded, an MCP process bears a strong family likeness to procurement processes elsewhere insofar as it encompasses successive phases of needs and requirements definition, requirements validation, procurement strategy selection, project approval, bid solicitation, source selection, negotiation and contract award, contract performance and administration (IC, 2002). For MCPs, two specific administrative bodies are formed for the duration of the procurement, an interdepartmental Project Management Office (PMO) and a Senior Project Advisory Committee (SPAC). DND assumes the lead role in overall project management but seeks the required project approvals and reports on progress to the Treasury Board (Fergusson, 1996; IC, 2002). PWGSC acts as contracting authority during the entire process by supplying their contracting expertise as well as actually carrying out the purchase. The delegated authority of the PWGSC can be partially repatriated to DND. IC may intervene in the validation of procurement strategy selection, project approval, source selection, negotiation and contract award phases in order to implement the industrial and regional benefits policy. The regional agencies ACOA, CEDQR and WED are represented in SPAC as well as the IC-led IRB Evaluation Team.[4]

SPAC can be portrayed as the focus in the common agency game with DND acting as the 'leading principal', as described above. Apart from the agent PWGSC, the IRB's 'enforcer' IC and the regional agencies ACOA, CEDQR and WED, Privy Council Office (PCO), Treasury Board Secretariat (TBS), Finance Canada (FC) and Human Resources Canada (HRC) sit in SPAC. This all-important committee makes the final bid recommendation to the government.

One notable difficulty in this organizational framework concerns the ADM (Mat)'s interfacing role when the military 'hard-wires' the process to acquire a specific, pre-designated product rather than acquiring the best of several products that satisfy the pre-established functional and technical requirements. Whereas normally ADM (Mat) would complete the acquisition in cooperation with PWGSC and IC, the 'hard-wiring' of requirements blurs the accountabilities (Williams, 2006). Similarly, the politicians' attempts to structure the system to favour their constituencies must be seen in the same light.

Defence industrial base and trade

Defence industry base

Canada's DIB is small, comprising about 1,500 firms and employing approximately 50,000 people. It is technologically advanced and internationally competitive in niche areas (CDIA, 2004). A sign of the industry's international competitiveness has been its export capability (CDIA, 2002). In 1998, the industry exported 37 per cent of its output and 57 per cent of employment in the DIB was defence-specific (Grover, 1999). (The employment attributed to defence production has to be treated carefully because many of the firms are diversified into non-defence sectors.) Canada's DIB is highly concentrated and a significant majority of the largest defence-related firms are subsidiaries of US manufacturers (Pepall and Shapiro, 1989). Over the period 1996–2000, Canada ranked as the world's 13th largest arms exporter (SIPRI, 2000). However, Canadian export figures produced by the (Canadian) Department of Foreign Affairs and International Trade (DFAIT) and the US Congressional Research Service (CRS) differ from SIPRI estimates (Regehr, 2007). For 2002, using data derived from mandatory reporting of exports shipped in accordance with export permits, DFAIT estimated exports to non-US customers to reach US$678 million (ibid.). Sales to the US are not included in this total since they do not require export permits. Regehr (ibid.: 6) estimates that, in 2002, Canadian non-recorded direct sales to the US Department of Defense, arranged through the Canadian Commercial Corporation, totalled US$650 million. Canadian firms, in addition, export goods and services as subcontractors to US defence producers. If non-recorded exports to the USA are included in the total, Canada's defence exports in 2002 stood at US$1.4 billion and if industry subcontracting is also added, could have reached US$2 billion (ibid.: 7). This would place Canada in the top ten of global exporters of defence materiel. In 2005, SIPRI estimated Canadian exports to be US$365 million and the CRS estimate for 2006 was US$600 million.

Thus, Canadian defence industry is an important producer and is a significant exporter of components and sub-systems. If the industry is narrowly defined to include industries specializing in military equipment production, then the DIB is concentrated on 'aerospace and defence electronics, shipbuilding, military vehicles and ammunition' (Solomon, 1999). Among these sectors, shipbuilding is excluded from international trade agreements (Alton, 2004). Although many countries use the national security (NS) exemption to exclude certain sectors from trade agreements, 'this heavily used and legal "non-tariff barrier" places all Canadian defence and aerospace firms at a distinct disadvantage as Canada itself conducts very little, if any, procurement under the NS exemption' (CDIA, 2002). It is precisely those sectors that are the most technologically advanced that find it difficult to export to countries pursuing import replacement policies. Nevertheless, 'During the past two years, Canadian defence firms have made substantial export sales. The three largest: General Motors Diesel Division (GMDD) sale of light armoured vehicles (LAV) to the US Army; Computing Devices Canada (CDC) sale of communications equipment to the British Army; and CAE sales of training packages in the UK, totaled over $10 billion' (ibid.). With the 1992–96 deliveries of Canadian Patrol Frigates (CPFs), the shipbuilding industry closed a chapter in its history and is yet to open the next. The impending procurement of joint supply ships reopened, in a piecemeal fashion, the defence industrial policy debate (see Williams, 2006).

Two questions should be addressed in this context. The first is whether domestic industry can supply defence goods and services competitively. The second is whether procurement – domestic or offshore – can be used to develop the DIB and, as a rider, whether it is desirable to do so. Domestic procurement policy would provide direct support to industry (through purchases, and tax and subsidy policies) whereas offshore procurement could be organized to seek similar effects through offsets. However, in the absence of a defence industry policy, defence procurement continues to cost DND with the imposition of IRBs without clear benefits due to lack of strategic thinking. The joint supply ships acquisition debate is a clear example where a domestic shipbuilding capability may be revived at a certain cost (premia) that must be transparently calculated, incorporated into an industrial policy 'and defence budgeting should compensate DND for any resulting cost increases' (Williams, 2006).

In the Canadian context, the answer to the first question is affirmative (Fergusson, 1996; Solomon, 1999). However, a 'qualified' yes is in order for the second. In the 1950s, Canada attempted the full indigenous development of the fighter aircraft AVRO Arrow CF-105. Cancellation of the project in 1959 exposed the difficulties that small and medium-sized countries face in supporting a large defence industrial base. The shrinkage and specialization of Canada's DIB have been forced further by the end of the Cold War as well as by international trade agreements (Alton, 2004). By exposing weaker domestic industries, international trade agreements will likely reinforce the current structure of the DIB. That is, as importing countries impose defence offset requirements, it is increasingly difficult to retain jobs in Canada in industry sectors that depend for their viability on exports to countries other than the USA. However, opportunities are expanding for subcontracting to US primes and taking advantage of US direct investment in Canada (see below).

Trade issues and the Canadian International Trade Tribunal

Both the North American Free Trade Agreement (NAFTA) and the WTO Agreement on Government Procurement (WTO-AGP) have a national security exemption clause. Canada's policy of limiting its use of the clause flows from the close relationship between Canada's DIB and US defence industry and the defence production agreements between the two countries. The Agreement on Internal Trade (AIT)[5] also has such a clause in the final provisions chapter rather than in the procurement chapter. In this respect, AIT is not aligned well with NAFTA and WTO-AGP (Alton, 2004).

Canada has not widely used this national security exemption clause[6] (except for munitions and shipbuilding) but in the one case where it was used, it imposed severe constraints on the Canadian procurement process. The case involved Rolls Royce. The DND requirement for repair and overhaul of its Rolls-Royce aircraft engines imposed the condition that the 'work must be performed in Canada for reason of military operational readiness and security' (CITT, 2000). Standard Aero Limited was eventually declared the winner in 1997 as the sole compliant contractor and was awarded the contract for a two-year period. Rolls-Royce Canada appealed to the Canadian International Trade Tribunal (CITT) and won. Rolls-Royce Canada argued, on the basis of AIT, that DND may not select a contractor on the basis of Canadian value-added beyond 10 per cent (the threshold under AIT) unless there exists a valid national security reason (NAFTA and WTO-AGP exclusions). Furthermore, even if one assumed an overriding national security concern to justify the performance of the work in Canada (i.e., to maintain an indigenous capability), DND had failed to demonstrate how a fair and legitimate competitive solicitation would necessarily result in the lessening or disappearance of that capability from Canada (i.e., Standard Aero's ability to perform such repair and overhaul work) as Standard Aero was actually performing the same type of work for other customers such as Honeywell, Pratt & Whitney, General Electric, and even Rolls Royce itself (CITT, 2000).

This incident broke new ground because it raised key issues at the interface between internal and international trade, and removed one of the significant discretionary policy tools of the government. In fact, the 10 per cent threshold is so low and the onus of demonstrating the national security concern is so strong that compliance requirements may, in practice, no longer include Canadian content. Although its original mandate was solely to rule on international trade disputes, CITT became, *de facto*, the federal government procurement tribunal. It now reviews all challenged federal procurement decisions. The deliberate sole sourcing of contracts to support an industry deemed essential under national security exemption clauses is now more open to challenge. The wider consequence of this ruling is that defence procurement has become a weaker policy tool in nurturing or sustaining DIB capabilities unless they are already competitive.

Links with the US defence industry

The cancellation of three full-development projects (AVRO-Arrow CF-105 in 1959, BOBCAT amphibious armoured personnel carrier in 1963 and BRAS D'OR hydrofoil in 1971) marks the period of transition from aspirations to CDIB self-sufficiency to increased trade dependence. In particular, the period saw the signing of Defence Production and Development Sharing Arrangements (DPDSA) with the US DOD (Department of Defense), which paved the way to an increased dependence of the CDIB on subcontracting to the US defence firms (Middlemiss, 1995).

Ironically, as US subcontractor, CDIB has continued its specialization in precisely those areas where it had received government support (aerospace and electronics, shipbuilding and munitions). That said, DPDSA agreements re-oriented CDIB to meet US rather than Canada's demand for military equipment and the US parent organizations and primes had never been interested in importing complete systems. Overall, these arrangements consolidated demand for CDIB and have enabled the evolution and consolidation of the narrow but competitive CDIB that we observe today (CDIA, 2004; Solomon, 1999).

Reduced defence requirements in the post-Cold War environment have placed pressure on both Canadian and US defence industries to rationalize. Moreover, the post-9/11 period has witnessed US initiatives to apply restrictive trade measures (especially on technology transfers) and to renegotiate the DPDSA because of US security concerns. The resulting changes could reduce the benefits currently derived by CDIB from its arrangements with the USA.

Government technology policy and CDIB

To compete for work, defence industries typically have to be technologically advanced. Since the inception of the Industrial and Regional Benefits (IRB) policy in the 1970s, successive Canadian governments have sought to use it to attract technology transfers from abroad. Their ambitions, however, have been thwarted by various impediments and, in particular, small and uncertain demands for final products (Baldwin and Lin, 2002). The attractiveness of technology transfer to the donor firm depends, in large part, on the profitability of new investment which, in turn, depends on potential markets. If an indigenous government's orders are small and exports uncertain, technology transfer may not be profitable.

Technology Partnerships Canada (TPC), an agency of Industry Canada, is a technology investment fund established in 1996 with an initial budget of Can$150 million. The objective of TPC is to invest strategically in research, development and innovation to encourage private sector investment. The ultimate aim is to enlarge the technology base and to enhance the technological capabilities of Canadian industry. Interestingly, TPC encourages the development of small and medium-sized enterprises (SMEs) in all regions of Canada. The TPC disbursement level in 2004 reached Can$312 million. The TPC programme was restructured in 1999 to be fully consistent with Canada's WTO obligations, resulting in a shift away from assisting specific product development activities to providing industry with more generic or non-product specific R&D assistance. In 2001, a new policy framework for the shipbuilding and industrial marine industry was announced with TPC providing access to finance to develop innovative technologies (OECD, 2002).

In 2003–04, defence, including aerospace, received TPC support of over 50 per cent of its total budget of Can$312 million. This was planned to decrease to about 40 per cent in 2007–08 (TPC, 2004). Beyond aerospace, the TPC defence category covered electronics and communications, and some manufacturing. TPC programme was discontinued at the end of 2006 and no new programme has replaced it.

Two observations relate to the interaction between DIB and defence procurement policies. First, off-the-shelf purchases are less conducive to technology transfers, merely due to the fact that the acquired platform is ready for use. Thus, if technology transfer is an overriding government procurement policy concern, platforms in development must be targeted for acquisition. Second, with the emergence of a transatlantic DIB (Becker, 2000), opportunities for technology acquisition or development by CDIB may increase due to lower non-tariff barriers.

Canadian procurement policy and its conflicting objectives

Defence procurement policy sets out the broad guidelines for filling capability gaps. It consists of: gap identification (*capability demand analysis*) on the basis of projected force requirements; definition of equipment requirements (*investment analysis*); and selection of the mode of acquisition for identified equipment (*public choice analysis*). Although the process is fairly integrated, we concentrate on the modes of acquisition which comprise indigenous production, joint ventures, licenced production and off-the-shelf acquisition (Byers, 1985), by and large in a descending order of Canadianization of procurement. Noting that these modes are intimately related to offsets policies (IRBs in Canada), Canada's procurement policies can historically be divided into a sequence of distinct phases.

Canadian procurement and IRB policies have gradually evolved in tandem since World War II (Fergusson, 1996). This evolution has been shaped by the belief that offshore procurement must do more than just inject military hardware into the Canadian economy. Assigning further objectives to seemingly simple military acquisitions might be seen as introducing distortions into the economy. However, in the light of second-best analysis, the value of IRBs should take into account their contribution to the DIB's technology absorption potential (Baldwin and Lin, 2002) and the spillover potential of new technologies (*The Economist*, 1995).

The phases of Canadian procurement policies

The first phase of Canadian procurement policy in the 1950s into the 1960s consisted of experimentation with indigenous production, from conception to production. Attempts to integrate with the US DIB were intertwined with aspirations to develop an autonomous DIB.

The second phase, a period of transition, started with the AVRO-Arrow cancellation in 1959 and ended in 1971 with the cancellation of the BRAS D'OR hydrofoil and the completion of the DDH280 destroyers. This second phase embraced the lead into and launch of IRBs.

The third phase is marked by three major acquisitions and the associated IRBs. The platforms acquired were Leopard C1 tanks in 1978, Aurora P-3 Long Range Patrol Aircraft (LRPAs) in 1980, and CF-18 Hornets that entered service in 1984. This phase of policy-driven competition among compliant manufacturers (see Box 7.1) ended shortly after a cost-benefit analysis of IRBs by the Auditor General in 1984 and Nielsen Task Force Report in 1985.

The current phase started with a fiscal crunch but has since been dominated by external factors such as the end of Cold War – implying a contraction of defence industries; the rising importance of failing states – requiring expeditionary forces; and the emerging phenomenon of transnational terrorism – driving a reallocation of security expenditures from defence proper to other security projects. This phase is yet to lend itself to full analysis but it appears that procurement policies have been responding by a more balanced approach to IRBs. This can be seen in the 2004 switch from EH-101s to Sikorsky helicopters. The 'replacement' of Leopard tanks by Mobile Gun Systems in 2003, early on seen as ditching the legacy mentality, has now been reversed in the light of operational requirements in Afghanistan.

The recent development in Canadian procurement has been the use of AIT article 506 to accelerate procurement to support Canadian combat requirements in Afghanistan. Canada acquired unmanned aerial vehicles (UAVs) and counter-bombardment radar systems in 2003 (Williams, 2006), mine-protected vehicles (Nyala) in 2006[7] (DND, 2006), and, at the time of writing, is in the process of acquiring route-clearing vehicles (Buffalo, Cougar and Husky) against improvised explosive devices (DND, 2007a). The large C-17

Box 7.1 Trade-offs in procurement and defence industry policy

The third phase of Canadian procurement policies constituted the culmination of IRBs. What was to be known as the New Fighter Aircraft project had started in 1977 and by 1978 two candidates (the F-16 Fighting Falcon of General Dynamics (GD) and the F/A-18 Hornet of McDonnell-Douglas (MDD)) were shortlisted. The contest boiled down to the IRBs packages offered by each contender, culminating in a win for MDD (Boyd, 1988). Although the overall functional comparison clearly favoured Hornet over Fighting Falcon, GD played the regional benefits card to associate with Québec interests and, with a referendum in sight, forced the selection debate to revolve around IRBs. This project demonstrated the extent to which IRBs came close to subverting the defence procurement objectives by relegating the military requirements to the secondary status behind IRBs. A different interpretation of this case is that the short-listing of the Fighting Falcon was ' ... an attempt to pressure MD into improving its offset package' (Boyd, 1988; Fergusson, 1996).

Globemaster strategic lift aircraft delivery started in August 2007 (DND, 2007b) and, at the time of writing, negotiations continue to acquire Chinook helicopters.

Offsets (IRBs)

The choice over procurement policy options noted above reflects trade-offs between defence and non-defence returns to government defence equipment expenditures. Driving a hard bargain for IRBs (especially direct offsets) is akin to extending the Ricardian 'intensive margin' of the DIB, with rising unit costs of production as a result. The Canadian push for offsets peaked in the 1970s and has since continued sporadically. As a Senate Committee was told in 2004:

> Unquestionably, we paid more for the frigates in the 1980s and 1990s by building them in Canada rather than purchasing them abroad ... It was right to pay $85,000 for Iltis jeeps built by Bombardier rather than $25,000 for jeeps purchased in Germany. But only if the capacity was sustained and if skilled jobs were created. In both cases, unfortunately, the capacity withered, the employment gains and skills learned were squandered. This does not make sense. Neither does it make sense to charge the DND budget the extra costs of made in Canada purchases; the Department of Industry ought to pick these up.
>
> (Granatstein, 2004)

The project cost will, in general, increase at an increasing pace the more off-sets are bargained for because the contractor will simply build the higher costs into the bid.

Defence objectives would be better served if platforms with lower offset requirements were chosen as the lower project price would help to achieve defence objectives at a lower cost. In fact, such a decision reversal requires that defence objectives outweigh IRBs. From a public choice perspective, a legitimate question is whether a unitary state is better suited than a federation to resist industrial and regional pressures on defence procurement decision-making (*The Economist*, 1999).

Case studies of frigate-destroyer and helicopter acquisitions

This part of the chapter addresses the two most-protracted procurements in Canadian history and illustrates the intricacies of the Canadian procurement process. The frigate-destroyer acquisition is a domestic acquisition with industrial and interregional benefit tradeoffs realised through public choice processes (this section draws heavily on Arseneault, 1988); the helicopter acquisition is a prime example of defence demand analysis and, to a much lesser degree, shows IRBs in action. In both cases requirements shifted and the delivered product was significantly different from what was intended at the outset.

DDH-280 frigates-destroyers

A brief history of the procurement

Debate over replacing existing ships began in Navy in the early 1960s and culminated in the government's approval in 1962 of eight general purpose frigates (GPFs) at an expected cost of Can$264 million. Following elections in 1963, a new defence minister favoured a navy specializing in anti-submarine warfare (ASW) within the NATO alliance and, thus, cancelled the GPF order. A 1964 White Paper reemphasized the value of ASW and, in the face of Navy dissent, the elected representatives prevailed (*The Economist*, 1999). The minister announced a new programme of four vessels at a cost of Can$142 million (excluding helicopters and missiles), the cheapest among the options although requiring the lengthening of an existing design and addition of a helicopter pad.

The new vessel required about 300 design changes for modernization and the addition of a helicopter. The Canadian tradition of keeping multiple shipyards alive, an IRB policy, dashed any prospect of reaping scale economies. The government shared the four-vessel order equally between two shipyards in Québec, a province always crucial in federal elections. Moreover, instead of setting up a fixed price contract for a proven design and nearly off-the-shelf acquisition, the government awarded contracts on a cost-plus basis inviting all the usual risks of cost escalation.

A Navy request for a 'minor' design change allowing the vessels to carry a second helicopter was approved by TB in 1965. The sponsor (the government) was less informed than the Navy (the bureaucracy) and went along with the request without fully realizing that it would increase the number of design changes tenfold to about 3,000. While it is still debatable whether Navy itself understood the eventual cost consequences of such an immense design modification, the government was apparently not fully aware of the cost burden of achieving what it saw as a desirable boost to the vessels' ASW capabilities.

The 'minor' design modification forced an upgrade of the vessels from frigates to destroyers and cost taxpayers in excess of Can$255 million instead of the original estimate of Can$142 million. The ships were eventually all launched by 1973.

A brief analysis of the process

Lessons from this case fall into three categories. First, major organisational-cum-administrative failure pertained to a lack of precise programme definition based on clear functional requirements and the absence of an authoritative programme office to monitor and enforce the programme. The procurement process has since been modified accordingly.

The second lesson lies in the seeing how information asymmetries can yield inefficient outcomes. Cost-plus contracts were used even though the vessel procurement took a complicated turn later which should have required at least an incentive contract to take account of changing the vessel design and construction to accommodate the second helicopter. Information asymmetries arose between PWGSC and TB as enforcers of the contract (administratively and financially, respectively) and the contractors themselves, creating a strong incentive to exploit cost-plus contracts through cost padding.

Another, and persistent, procurement problem is that the project financial sponsor (the government) is not technically as well informed as the buyer (the Navy). In this particular case, TB approved the 'minor' design change without being able to predict the 'major' consequences of the proposed redesign – the latter information was 'private' to naval designers and the Navy. The Navy's objective was to get better equipment and financial considerations were secondary as it was not facing a hard budget constraint. Fearing cancellation, Navy had an incentive to conceal from TB any cost increases it thought might flow from the redesign. With hindsight, TB should not have assumed that naval planners' assurances were credible. This lesson is cardinal because information asymmetries are pervasive and emerge in different forms. The organizational safeguards are expensive. For government (in particular TB) to maintain an in-house expert team of naval designers for such infrequent acquisitions would be prohibitively costly. That an external audit was not used is another shortfall in this particular project.

Finally, it is well known that a procurement process is vulnerable to uncertainties due to electoral cycles. Not only the change of defence minister[8] but, probably more importantly, the change in strategic priorities may increase acquisition delays. In fact, the frigate acquisition is a fitting example. The 1963 election brought with it a new defence minister committed to ASW rather than GPFs, and the new government's fiscal concerns led to scaling down the project. Thus in this particular case both changes were present.[9]

Maritime helicopters

A brief history of procurement

This is a case of EH-101 helicopter ('Cadillac') ordered, cancelled, and replaced by Sikorsky H-92 ('Volkswagen'). The maritime ASW helicopter project started in the 1970s, officially became the new shipboard aircraft (NSA) project in 1983 and, at the time of writing, is expected to be completed as the maritime helicopter project (MHP) with deliveries by 2010. It is the longest project in Canadian defence procurement history with at least '18 different Ministers of National Defence and nine changes of government' (Priestley, 2004) and two different helicopters, the first cancelled after the 1993 federal elections.

In the mid-1970s, Canada's Sea King maritime helicopters went through a mid-life modernization, including their ASW avionics. Flown from ASW warships' decks, they are an element of ASW capability. New maritime helicopters appeared on the defence procurement agenda with the GPF replacement project, but their procurement was put on ice until after the 1984 elections. Three off-the-shelf helicopters were on offer: Sikorsky's S-70, Aérospatiale's SA332 Super Puma and EH Industries' EH-101. (EH Industries comprised Italy's Agusta and Britain's Westland.) EH-101the largest and, with a third engine, offered greater lifting power and longer range. In 1987, DND opted for the EH-101, intending to purchase 35 shipboard aircraft and 15 search and rescue (SAR) versions known as Cormorants.

However, shipboard helicopters were not a priority for either Air Force or Navy and the project was put on the back burner (Jaggi, 2003). In 1992, the government firmed up the order and awarded the avionics to Paramax of Montréal. But fiscal pressures, the end of Cold War and the 1993 election results, spelled the end of EH-101. The incoming Liberal government honoured a pre-election commitment to cancel the NSA project, which cost the Canadian taxpayer just under half a billion Canadian dollars (Rossignol, 1998). The cancellation did not stop the purchase of 15 Cormorant search and rescue helicopters.

The NSA project reappeared in 2002, albeit in a different form and for littoral security purposes rather than anti-submarine warfare, when the cost of maintaining 40-year-old Sea King became unacceptable and the operational safety concerns became paramount. A government-wide spending freeze excluded only the MHP (NSA) project. Contenders included Agusta-Westland's EH-101 again, Sikorsky's H-92 (the Cyclone or Superhawk) and NH Industries' NH-90 (the Eurocopter). The government declared the NH-90 non-compliant (*Globe and Mail*, 2003). The least-cost-compliant principle counted against the EH-101 with its bigger airframe and three engines as opposed to the H-92's two. Finally, H-92 was declared winner in 2004 with the delivery of all 28 Cyclones expected before 2010, 33 years after the beginning of MHP.

In the critical area of IRBs, both compliant teams had submitted acceptable bids. Agusta-Westland would have provided Can$3.5 billion worth of offsets (Jaggi, 2003) and Sikorsky Can$4.5 billion (DND, 2004). Including the long-term maintenance cost for 20-years' in-service support, the purchase of the fully-integrated helicopters amounted to Can$5 billion.

A brief analysis of the process

The key period in the MHP procurement process was the early 1990s when the first project had, in effect, ended with a no-purchase decision and the second, to acquire the H-92s, had not yet been initiated.

The hiatus arose because: (1) the end of Cold War removed the perceived threat from Soviet submarines and forced a reassessment of the strategic primacy of ASW in Canadian maritime defence; and (2) an exceptionally high

Canadian government debt resulted in a fiscal squeeze throughout the government, including Defence. Playing against the no-purchase decision, however, was a legacy mentality.

The legacy mentality (or 'equipment replacement syndrome' of Middlemiss, 1995) derives from a failure to reassess strategic priorities as conditions change and is symptomatic of inertia in decision-making. In the case of the MHP, the legacy argument aligned with 'value-for-money' in project selection according to which EH-101 could have stood a chance against H-92 because it was indeed the faster, stronger aircraft with a longer range. However, according to the 2003 announcement of requirements, EH-101 was clearly 'over-specified'.

Conclusion – what lies ahead?

In the 2000s, procurement decisions have become less protracted and less controversial than many in the past. On the basis of this evidence, Canadian procurement is exhibiting greater maturity in striking the delicate balance between rejuvenated and apparently transparent defence objectives and the IRBs.

However, three propositions about the future of Canadian procurement policy remain undebated. First, it may be the case that, by reducing the duplication of functions and the associated effort between DND and PWGSC, both departments can better concentrate on their respective areas of specialization. In particular, DND may seek the delegation of contracting authority for militarily-specific requirements. DND's specialisation in such tasks may outweigh the scope economies generated by PWGSC's joint inter-governmental agency.

Second, it might be that the development and growth of transatlantic defence industries (Becker, 2000) and the post-Cold War irrelevance of full-scale national DIBs could make it worthwhile to set up a co-operative procurement policy (under the NATO umbrella or otherwise). This could take the form of co-operation with allies in the acquisition of materiel, which increases interoperability while reducing the time and cost of procurement, or the formation of multinational, collaborative procurement projects (Markowski and Hall, 1998; Williams, 2001).

Third, a break from the Cold War past in terms of military thinking could enhance the application of the 'commercial off-the-shelf' (COTS) procurement policy as small and medium-sized countries specialize in combat capability niches.

Acknowledgements

My sincere thanks go to Alan Williams and Sabrina Rizk. They read the chapter and corrected my mistakes. Moreover, their suggestions found their way into this final version. Any remaining errors and omissions are mine.

Notes

1 These comprise both peace-keeping and-enforcement operations.
2 Atlantic Canada Opportunities Agency (ACOA), Western Economic Diversifica-tion (WED) and Canada Economic Development for Quebec Regions (CEDQR) (IC, 2002).
3 IRBs constitute an implementation of federal government's industrial and regional policies by using major government purchases. Instituted in 1986, this 'local content' policy aims to obtain direct (supplier of the procured system commits to manufacture a large part of it in Canada) and indirect (supplier commits to provide industrial benefits in other sectors of the Canadian economy) industrial commitments while preserving a competitive and internationally open marketplace. Formally, IRBs are mandatory direct and indirect offset requirements for MCPs equivalent to the value of the project. Industry Canada evaluates the bidders' IRBs commitments.
4 Moreover, HRSDC (Human Resources and Social Development Canada) – Employment Equity, INAC (Indian and Northern Affairs Canada) – Procurement Strategy for Aboriginal Business, EC (Environment Canada) – Green Procure-ment, DFO (Department of Fisheries and Oceans), NRCan (Natural Resources Canada), and Transport Canada also sit in SPAC.
5 In force from 1995, AIT is an internal trade agreement binding on federal, pro-vincial and local governments, allowing all Canadian companies to bid for defence procurement contracts and, interestingly, with its own specific tribunal CITT should disputes arise and redress is needed (see the Rolls-Royce case below). Iro-nically, AIT effectively opened up defence procurement internationally, beyond NAFTA and WTO-AGP, by defining any domestically registered company as Canadian. However, the special clause 1804 on national security exemptions can be invoked in exceptional cases to sole source contracts. Another clause, 506, may allow bypassing the open-competition procurement when urgent need for equipment can be justified (Williams, 2006).
6 It has recently been used to accelerate procurement for the specific operational requirements in Afghanistan.
7 This acquisition was a truly accelerated but competitive procurement with three bids entered.
8 The change of defence minister may be accompanied by changes in other pro-curement-related ministries thus creating conditions for further delays due to new ministers' learning curves. For instance, ministers for IC and PWGSC are intimately involved in defence procurement.
9 Between 1993 and 2006, Canada had five successive Liberal governments (the first three under the same prime minister and the last two under another) yet six Cabi-net ministers held the defence portfolio. Given the changes to procurement-related ministries, the learning curve effect played a delaying role in many acquisition processes.

References

Alton, S. (2004) 'Understanding government procurement liberalization in Canada and its implications for the federal procurement process', Master's thesis, Institute of Political Economy, Carleton University.
Arseneault, J. W. (1988) 'The DDH 280 program: A case study of governmental expenditure decision-making', in D. G. Haglund (ed.) *Canada's Defence Industrial Base*, Ottawa: R. P. Frye.
Baldwin, J. and Z. Lin (2002) 'Impediments to advanced technology adoption for Canadian manufacturers', *Research Policy*, 31: 1–18.

Becker, J. (2000) 'The future of Atlantic defense procurement', *Defense Analysis*, 16(1): 9–32.

Boyd Jr., F. L. (1988) 'The politics of Canadian defence procurement: the new fighter aircraft decision', in D. G. Haglund (ed.) *Canada's Defence Industrial Base*, Ottawa: R. P. Frye.

Byers, R.B. (1985) 'Canadian defence and defence procurement: implications for economic policy', in G. R. Winham and D. Stairs (eds) *Selected Problems in Formulating Foreign Economic Policy*, Toronto: University of Toronto Press.

CDIA (2002) 'The future of Canada's defence industrial base', CDIA DP, Canadian Defence Industries Association, November.

—— (2004) *Canadian Defence Almanac*, Ottawa: Canadian Defence Industries Association.

CITT (2000) 'Determinations: Rolls-Royce Industries Canada Inc., File No.: PR-99-053', Canadian International Trade Tribunal. Online. Available at: http://www.citt-tcce.gc.ca/procure/determin/pr99053_e.asp#P97_6149

DeMille, D. and Priestley, S. (2005) 'Streamlined, integrated and effective: how will General Rick Hillier help hone the Canadian Forces?' Online. Available at: http://www.sfu.ca/casr/ft-column2.htm.

DND (2004) 'Backgrounder: The Maritime Helicopter Project', Department of National Defence, November. Online. Available at: http://www.forces.gc.ca/admmat/mhp/backgrounder_e.asp.

—— (2005a) 'Backgrounder: Canada Command', Department of National Defence, June. Online. Available at: http://www.forces.gc.ca/site/Newsroom/view_news_e.asp?id=1692.

—— (2005b) 'ADM (Mat) responsibilities'. Online. Available at: http://www.forces.gc.ca/admmat/site/index_e.asp.

—— (2006) 'RG-31 Nyala Armoured Patrol Vehicle'. Online. Available at: http://army.ca/wiki/index.php/RG-31_Nyala_Armoured_Patrol_Vehicle.

—— (2007a) 'DND/Canadian Forces news release: new vehicles to enhance protection against improvised explosive devices', NR-07.034, May, Ottawa.

—— (2007b) 'DND/Canadian Forces news release: on track for C-17 training is key to readiness', NR-07.038, May, Ottawa.

The Economist (1995) 'Of strategies, subsidies and spillovers', 18 March.

—— (1999) '*Ex uno, plures*', 21 August.

Fergusson, J. (1996) 'In search of strategy: the evolution of Canadian defence industrial and regional benefits policy', in S. Martin (ed.) *The Economics of Offsets: Defence Procurement and Countertrade*, Amsterdam: Harwood.

Globe and Mail (2003) 'Helicopter checklist cut back', 16 April.

Granatstein, J. L. (2004) 'Opening Statement to Senate Standing Committee on National Security and Defence'. Online. Available at: http://www.ccs21.org/articles/2004/apr04/OpeningStatement.pdf

Grover, B. (1999) *Canadian Defence Industry 1999: A Statistical Overview of the Canadian Defence Industry*, Canadian Defence Industries Association (CDIA), December.

IC (2002) 'The procurement process in Canada', Industry Canada, December. Online. Available at: http://strategis.ic.gc.ca/epic/internet/inad-ad.nsf/en/ad03666e.html.

Jaggi, U. (2003) 'Defence acquisition in Canada: a study of the decision to cancel the EH-101', Master's project, MA(DMP) Programme, Royal Military College of Canada.

Manson, P. (2005) 'Procurement cycle growth: the race between obsolescence and acquisition of military equipment in Canada 1960 to the present', Presentation to the Conference of Defence Associations Institute, Canadian Institute of Strategic Studies Seminar, 22 July.

Markowski, S. and Hall, P. (1998) 'Challenges of defence procurement', *Defence and Peace Economics,* 9: 3–37.

Martimort, D. (1996) 'The multiprincipal nature of government', *European Economic Review,* 40: 673–85.

Middlemiss, D. (1995) 'Defence procurement in Canada', in D. Dewitt and D. Leyton-Brown (eds) *Canada's International Security Policy,* Englewood Cliffs, NJ: Prentice-Hall.

Niskanen, W. A. (1971) *Bureaucracy and Representative Government,* Chicago: Aldine-Atherton.

OECD (2002) *STI Outlook 2002: Canada Response,* Paris: OECD.

PCO (2004) 'Securing an open society: Canada's national security policy', Privy Council Office. Online. Available at: http://www.pco.cp.gc.ca/docs/Publications/NatSecurnat/natsecurnat_e.pdf.

Pepall, L. M. and Shapiro, D. M. (1989) 'The military-industrial complex in Canada', *Canadian Public Policy,* 15(2): 265–84.

Priestley, S. (2004) 'Politics, procurement practices, and procrastination: the quarter-century *Sea King* helicopter replacement saga', July. Online. Available at: http://www.sfu.ca/casr/ft-mhp1.htm.

Regehr, E. (2007) *Behind the Headlines, Canada and the Arms Treaty,* The Centre for International Innovation, Canadian Institute of International Affairs, November, Vol. 64, No. 6.

Rossignol, M. (1998) 'Replacement of shipborne and rescue helicopters'. Online. Available at: http://dsp-psd.pwgsc.gc.ca/Collection-R/LoPBdP/CIR/943-e.htm#3.%20Final.

SAG (2004) 'Streamlining defence procurement: can NDHQ deliver?' Select Advisory Group on Administrative Efficiencies to the Minister of National Defence. Online. Available at: http://www.sfu.ca/casr/ft-advisory1–1.htm.

Salanié, B. (1997) *The Economics of Contracts,* Cambridge, MA: MIT Press.

SIPRI (2000) *SIPRI Yearbook 2000,* Oxford: Oxford University Press.

Solomon, B. (1999) 'The Canadian defence industrial base', unpublished manuscript, Strategic Finance and Economics, Department of National Defence.

TPC (2004) *Investing in Canadians with Great Ideas: 2003–2004 Year in Review,* Ottawa: Technology Partnerships Canada, Industry Canada.

US-GAO (1999) *Procurement Reform: How Selected Countries Perform Certain GSA Activities?,* July, Washington, DC: General Accounting Office.

Williams, A. (2001) 'The Canadian way of procurement', *NATO's Nations and Partners for Peace,* Military Module: 117.

—— (2006) 'Reinventing Canadian defence procurement: a view from the inside', Breakout Educational Network/School of Policy Studies at Queen's University, Montreal and Kingston: McGill-Queen's University Press.

8 Defence structure, procurement and industry

The case of Israel

Kobi Kagan, Oren Setter, Yoad Shefi and Asher Tishler

Introduction

This chapter describes the structure of the Israeli defence establishment, the development of its budget, the procurement process, and the defence R&D effort. It also emphasises the unique characteristics of the country's defence industry as an integral part of the global defence industry.

Israel is a small developed country with a geographic size of about 22,000 square km.[1] Since the country's establishment in 1948, Israel's sovereignty has been contested by most of its Arab neighbours and the Israeli Defence Force (IDF) has been engaged in conflicts that have varied from all-out wars with neighbouring states to counterinsurgency and peace-enforcement operations in areas under its control. Despite its small size and overwhelming strategic and political problems – or perhaps because of them – Israel has succeeded in developing the most powerful military establishment in the Middle East (see Gordon, 2003).

To provide a context for our discussion, we start by briefly outlining Israel's strategic position in the Middle East at the beginning of the present century. This is followed by a description of the structure of the Israeli defence establishment and a discussion of its budgetary, procurement and R&D processes. We analyse interactions between Israel's choice of national security level and the market structure of the world's defence industry and conclude that the country's military superiority in the Middle East may be attributed to Israel's huge advantage in skilled human resources and technology, and the military support that it receives from the USA.

Policy implications are twofold. First, Israel's net defence costs (its expenditure on defence minus the profits of its defence industry) could be minimised if defence industry comprised a single firm, that is, Israel would likely gain from a consolidation of its defence industry. Second, whatever the benefits of the US military aid in reducing Israel's net defence costs, this aid reduces the profits of the Israeli defence industry and may, in the long term, hurt its sustainability and viability. Thus, the Israeli defence establishment should actively seek additional foreign markets via joint ventures, or mergers, with American and European defence firms.

Israel's strategic position and regional military balance

Since its establishment in 1948 Israel has been involved in a number of wars with its Arab neighbours: the 1948–49 War of Independence; the 1956 Suez War (the Sinai campaign, which marked the transformation of the IDF into a professional military force capable of large-scale operations); the 1967 Six-Day War; the 1973 Yom Kippur War; and the 1982–85 War in Lebanon against the Palestinian Liberation Organization (PLO) aided by Lebanese militia and the Syrian Army.[2] While there has been no major all-out war between Israel and the Arab countries since 1982, tensions between Israel and several of its neighbours have remained high throughout Israel's 60-year existence, during and between wars, and have frequently led to local skirmishes with neighbouring armies and militias and various forms of asymmetric warfare waged against Israel. Since 1967, Israel has been involved in military confrontations with the Palestinians in the West Bank and Gaza and Arab militias in Lebanon. In particular, since 1987, there have been two major Palestinian civil uprisings (*intifadas*) and many acts of terrorism aimed at Israeli civilians.

As result of the Camp David Peace Accord between Egypt and Israel, signed in 1977, Israel's southern border is no longer threatened by Egypt. The subsequent peace treaty with Jordan eliminated the Jordanian threat on Israel's eastern border and left Syria as Israel's potential major adversary in future.[3] Most of Syria's conventional weapons systems, however, are relatively old and not a match for the highly capable IDF. Without Soviet military and economic support and with no political and strategic partners among the Arab nations, Syria has opted for an asymmetric response to the continuing increase in Israeli military capabilities. That is, to counter Israel's superior air power, intelligence and precision guided munitions, Syria is said to have acquired terror weapons (TWP).[4] Saudi Arabia and the post-2003 Iraq are not seen as posing a direct threat to Israel. On the other hand, even though it has never been directly involved in a war against Israel, Iran is considered to be a major threat.[5] Iran boasts a large conventional army, a fairly large navy and, since the 1990s, has supported anti-Israel militias in Lebanon and has been suspected of developing weapons of mass destruction, including nuclear weapons.

Table 8.1 provides an overview of relative quantities of equipment and numbers of personnel deployed by Israel and its past, present and/or potential adversaries in the region. While Israel's Arab neighbours and Iran enjoy vast numerical superiority in manpower and equipment, the IDF benefits from the superior quality of its resource base, its capabilities based on modern US-made platforms and indigenous and US-made state-of-the-art weapons systems. The quality of its personnel is also vastly superior. Moreover, as Israel has never wanted to become totally dependent on US military support, it has developed its own state-of-the-art weapons systems. This high level of self-reliance is also intended to gain strategic leverage by forcing, if need be, America's hand.

Table 8.1 Military balance in the Middle East, 2003 (Volumes)

	Israel	Other countries combined [a]	Syria	Saudi Arabia	Egypt	Iraq	Jordan	Iran	Lebanon
Military personnel									
Army	141,000	1,241,000	215,000	75,000	320,000	133,000	88,000	350,000	60,000
Air Force	36,000	247,500	70,000	24,000	110,000	500	12,000	30,000	1,000
Navy	9,500	56,600	4,000	13,500	20,000	–	700	18,000	400
Total	186,500	1,726,100	289,000	171,500	450,000	133,500	100,700	520,000	61,400
Reserves	445,000	470,000	132,500	20,000	254,000	–	60,000	3,500	–
Army equipment									
Tanks	3,700	10,380	3,700	750	3,000	–	970	1,680	280
Armoured vehicles	7,710	17,990	5,060	4,630	3,680	–	1,815	1,570	1,235
Artillery	1,348	10,809	2,990	410	3,530	–	844	2,700	335
Helicopters	205	1,128	225	214	225	–	83	365	16
Navy equipment									
Combatants	15	133	16	27	62	–	–	28	–
Support Vessels	33	325	8	68	109	–	10	110	20
Submarines	5	7	–	–	4	–	–	3	–
Air Force equipment									
Tactical Aircraft	518	1,546	451	286	505	–	97	207	–
Support Aircraft	62	228	23	42	44	–	14	105	–

Source: Feldman and Shapir (2004).

Note: [a] Other countries combined: Syria, Saudi Arabia, Egypt, Iraq, Jordan, Iran and Lebanon.

Since the 1980s, Israel has been at the forefront of asymmetric warfare, an experience which has necessitated technological innovation and new product development on a scale that only much larger countries would normally contemplate. However, unlike most other countries, Israel had opportunities to test its new technologies and approaches in a war-fighting environment.

The perception of Israel's power by the Arab countries has been greatly affected by the unconditional support it has received from the USA. The US funding of the IDF has continued under a strategic umbrella, which the Arab world could have interpreted as a sign that the USA will intervene in Israel's favour, should it be involved in an all-out war with the coalition of Arab states. A large share of US military aid to Israel comprises high-technology American weapons, and Israel's growing technological advantage has also transformed into the development of unique advanced weapons systems, which Syria and other potential adversaries have not been able to match. Ben-Zvi (2003) estimates that, thanks to its investment in state-of-the-art military technologies, Israel has achieved effective deterrence capability to more than match the Arab countries' numerical superiority in conventional weapons. Ben-Zvi suggests, however, that Israel has done less to develop effective deterrence capabilities against TWP. This weakness explains Syria's determination to acquire TWP.

The perception of Israel as a power to be reckoned with was weakened by the Iraqi missile attack on Israel during the 1991 Gulf War, Israel's swift withdrawal from southern Lebanon in 2000, and the unwillingness of the Israeli public to tolerate high casualty levels. This perception of vulnerability has encouraged Israel's adversaries to test the endurance and response capabilities of Israeli society and the IDF by engaging Israel in a low-intensity, but continuous, conflict in the 1990s and 2000s. However, there are increasing signs (e.g., Israel's response to the second Palestinian *Intifada*) that the Israeli defence establishment, with its highly skilled human resources and state-of-the-art military technologies, is capable of effectively defending Israel against a variety of threats, and that the IDF is clearly the most powerful military force in the Middle East. Gordon (2003) estimates that Israel has a 33 per cent advantage in the face of any possible alignment of Arab countries' aerial capabilities, and a 6.5-fold advantage over Syria in the attack capabilities of its air force.

While its military capabilities have grown, Israel's defence expenditure (in constant prices) has remained stable during the closing years of the twentieth century and in the early 2000s. The burden of defence has also decreased as, given Israel's relatively fast GDP growth, the share of defence expenditure in GDP decreased from 14 per cent in 1982 to 6 per cent in 2002 (Blech and Davidson, 2002).

The Israeli defence establishment: size, structure, budget and procurement

Defence establishment

The Israeli defence establishment comprises three elements:

- *political* – the Minister of Defence in charge of the Ministry of Defence (MoD) and the IDF;
- *civilian* – the MoD and government-owned defence firms. The MoD's Director General is appointed by and reports to the Minister of Defence.
- *military*: the IDF.

The chief of staff of the IDF is appointed by and reports to the Israeli government (through the Minister of Defence). This ensures the dominance of the civilian government over the IDF. The MoD is responsible for the IDF's procurement and finances, and administers Israeli defence exports controls. Overseas procurement is carried out by the MoD missions in the USA and Europe.

Israeli Defence Force

Table 8.2 presents the IDF's order of battle during 1982–2003. Military personnel increased by about 10 per cent during this period while the overall population increased by 66 per cent.[6] The volume of Army equipment remained largely unchanged while the number of attack aircrafts and combat vessels decreased. However, the reduction in the number of the various types of equipment was offset by a dramatic improvement in the quality of Israeli aircraft, naval vessels and other types of weapons systems (for example, older A-4 Skyhawks and F-4 Phantoms were replaced by new F-15s Eagles and

Table 8.2 The IDF's order of battle, 1982–2003

Year	1982	1985	1990	1995	2000	2003
Military Personnel (numbers)						
Army	130,000	130,000	133,000	136,000	141,000	141,000
Air Force	30,000	30,000	31,000	32,500	36,000	36,000
Navy	10,000	10,000	10,000	9,000	9,500	9,500
Total	170,000	170,000	174,000	177,500	186,500	186,500
Reserves	370,000	370,000	430,000	427,000	445,000	445,000
Army Equipment (numbers)						
Tanks	3,600	3,800	3,860	3,845	3,930	3,700
Armored Vehicles	8,000	8,000	8,100	8,000	8,040	7,710
Artillery	900	1,000	1,300	1,300	1,348	1,348
Helicopters	175	190	218	269	287	205
Navy Equipment (numbers)						
Combatants	23	26	23	22	20	15
Support Vessels	47	47	47	36	32	33
Submarines	3	3	3	3	6	5
Air Force Equipment (numbers)						
Tactical Aircraft	630	645	638	677	628	518
Support Aircraft	75	90	91	83	77	62

Source: The Middle East Military Balance, various years.

F-16s Fighting Falcons, older M-60 tanks replaced by new Merkava IV tanks, aging TOW antitank missiles by the new Spike antitank missiles). Basically, almost all Israeli platforms and their equipment comprise state-of-the-art computerised systems, sensors and wireless communication systems. Israel also deploys various satellites, air defence and intelligence systems that are not available to its potential adversaries in the Middle East.[7] In view of the IDF's technological superiority, the volume figures shown in Tables 8.1 and 8.2 underestimate the qualitative superiority of Israeli weapons systems relative to those held by Israel's Arab neighbours.[8]

The IDF is responsible for all operational activity, and for defining its operational needs and the technical specifications of its weapon systems. It also provides the MoD with estimates of the budget required to fund its projected operations and to procure the required weapons systems. The MoD is responsible for choosing suppliers and contractors, managing the orders and contracts, broader economic aspects of military procurement, price and cost analysis, budgetary control, and finance and expenditure management. These activities are supported by computerised management and information systems, and are carried out on the basis of full cooperation and recognition of mutual dependence between relevant branches of the IDF and MoD. The structure of the IDF is shown in Figure 8.1.

The basic elements of the IDF's proclaimed doctrine are:

- purely defensive stance at the strategic level: Israel has no territorial ambitions;
- the use of political initiatives to avoid war and prevent conflict escalation;
- credible deterrence;
- quick and decisive determination of the outcome of a potential armed conflict: rapid transfer of battles to the enemy's territory and quick attainment of war objectives;
- commitment to combat terrorism;
- avoidance of high casualty rate;
- a small (core) standing army with an early warning capability, regular air force and navy;
- efficient mobilisation of reserves; and
- efficient coordination of the services.

The defence budget

Figure 8.2 presents Israel's military expenditure (total, including the US military aid, and domestic) as a percentage of GDP from 1950 until 2003. It shows a gradual increase during the late 1960s and early 1970s, a response to the Soviet Union's support of the military build-up in Egypt and Syria, and the more modest build-up of the Jordanian military. Israel's defence expenditure accelerated prior to the Six-Day War in 1967 and peaked in the aftermath of the Yom Kippur War in 1973. In the three years

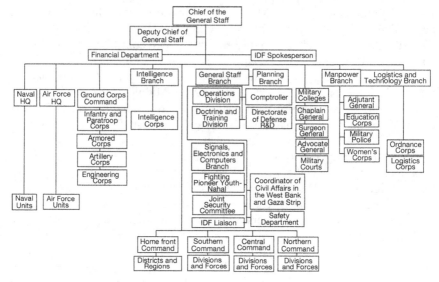

Figure 8.1 Structure of the Israeli Defence Force

Source: IMoD (2004a), IDF (2004)

following the Yom Kippur War, Israel re-built and re-equipped its defence forces, bringing the share of military expenditure in GDP to a record high of over 30 per cent. Since 1977, there has been a gradual decline in Israel's military expenditure, down to a level of about 10 per cent of GDP in 1994–2002 and a low of 6.4 per cent in 1999. This downward trend was halted in 2000 and reversed with the second Palestinian *intifada*, which started later that year.

In 2004, the Israeli defence budget amounted to US$7.9 billion, more than a quarter of which came as the US military aid. Most of the US aid budget is tied (by US regulations) to procurement in the USA. Some 26.3 per cent of the aid package (about 5.7 per cent of the total Israeli defence budget) can be exchanged into local currency and used to finance non-American procurement. Figure 8.3 presents the Israeli defence budget in real (2004) US$.[9] Table 8.3 shows Israel's defence budget, total government budget and GDP in 2004.

Table 8.3 Israel's defence budget, total government budget and GDP in 2004

US$ billion (2004 prices)	
7.92	Total defence budget
5.74	Local resources
2.18	US military aid to Israel
54.80	Israel's total government budget
113.20	Israel's GDP

Source: Ministry of Finance (2004).

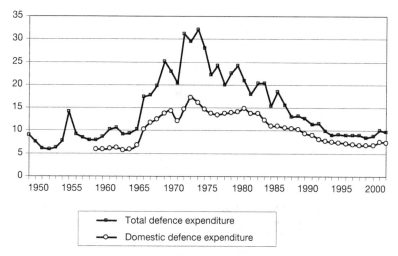

Figure 8.2 Israel's defence expenditure as a percentage of GDP, 1950–2003
Source: Ministry of Finance (various years)

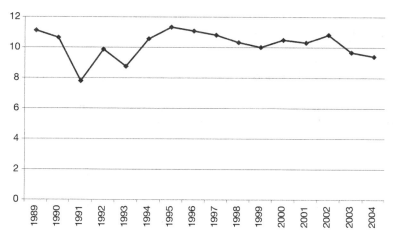

Figure 8.3 Israel's defence budget in US$ billion (2004 prices)
Source: Ministry of Finance (various years)

Figure 8.4 presents Israel's 2004 defence budget, divided into six major expenditure categories. About 42 per cent of the budget is appropriated to manpower expenses (regular military combatant and non-combatant personnel, mandatory service soldiers, reserve forces, MoD personnel).[10] About 28 per cent of budget outlays is allocated to R&D, weapons systems procurement, and other defence materiel, including replacement and upgrades of older equipment. About 54 per cent of the procurement and R&D budget originates in the USA and US military aid also funds part of the local procurement.

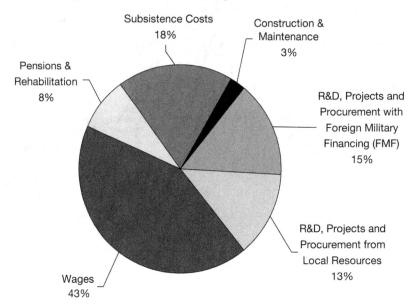

Figure 8.4 Israel's 2004 defence budget by type of expenditure

Source: Ministry of Finance (2004)

Most of the locally funded budget for procurement and R&D is used for local procurement while about US$130 million of local resources (1.5 per cent of the overall defence budget) is spent on procurement from abroad (mainly from Europe). The defence budget can, therefore, be divided into:

- local expenditure (about 80 per cent of the defence budget) comprising the local budget (denominated in NIS) funded from local resources, and the 26.3 per cent of the US military aid which Israel is allowed to exchange into local currency for procurement of defence goods and services, including research and development, in Israel;
- *imports or overseas expenditure* (about 20 per cent of the defence budget). Most of this expenditure is based on the US military aid to Israel and, as noted, is spent in the USA (see below). Israeli imports of defence goods and services from countries other than the USA are at a very low level, as the IDF seeks to ensure that its equipment is compatible with US standards, and prefers to purchase from local industry whenever possible.

The procurement process

Lavie (2000) lists the following characteristics of Israeli public procurement management:

1 Israeli public procurement management is very bureaucratic. While the term may have negative connotations, it also implies a stable system that draws a balance between the desire to quickly implement procurement programmemes and the need for tight control over public spending.

2 Israeli law requires that in public procurements all tenderers are treated equally, except when it specifically allows the government to apply 'buy local' policies. This principle forces the government, except when the procurement is paid for by US military aid to Israel, to provide the same information and negotiate equally with all potential participants in public tenders, and set internal guidelines to support the equitable treatment of tenderers. 'Buy local' policies are also necessitated by foreign currency restrictions as most of the locally allocated Israeli funds are in the local currency (NIS). Only 2 per cent of Israel's total defence budget is denominated in foreign currencies (except, of course, for the funds from the US military aid to Israel).

3 Under the 1992 Obligatory Tender Act, government offices and government-owned defence firms must take part in a public tender if they are to sell to the Israeli government.

4 The MoD is the largest single buyer of defence equipment and products in Israel, and as a result the Israeli government sets specific rules and regulations for military procurements.

5 The large scale of the MoD's public spending enables the Israeli government to support non-defence objectives (prevent or reduce unemployment, for example) in Israel by directing some of the MoD's procurements to designated local suppliers located close to the borders or in officially declared development zones. This policy often conflicts with the least cost sourcing of defence materiel and other MoD objectives and cost premia may have to be paid when supplies are sourced from these designated contractors.[11]

6 The government budget in Israel is determined for a single year, with limited latitude for long-term budgeting requirements. Practically, the Ministry of Finance determines the overall budget of the IDF, and the IDF is responsible for the budget allocation to its own branches and operations. Across-the-board budget cuts are common in Israel. Thus, publicly funded projects may be changed in mid-course and procurements may be cancelled due to budget cuts.

Israeli defence procurement is managed through two principal channels: the Directory for Procurement and Production, which is located in Israel, and the MoD's Mission to the USA. The Directory for Procurement and Production is mainly responsible for local procurements while the Mission to the USA is the implementation arm for procurements funded by US military aid to Israel.

The Israeli government's defence procurement in the USA is described in the US Department of Commerce, Bureau of Industry and Security (2004). The MoD Mission in New York employs about 200 persons to handle all purchases of US equipment, including direct commercial contracts paid by FMF (US Foreign Military Funded Programme) funds.[12] Potential Israeli procurements in the USA are advertised by the MoD in the US press and the Israeli New York Mission places and executes defence contracts directly. Many contracts financed by US aid to Israel include offset arrangements. Contracts advertised and executed in Israel are subject to Israeli law and are open to US, Israeli and European competitors.[13] Finally, the USA-Israel Free Trade Area agreement (implemented on January 1, 1995) eliminated all the duties on imports of US products to Israel. However, the Israeli MoD favours local industry or foreign defence firms which cooperate with local ones and/or produce some of their products locally.

In the early 2000s, a US$4.5 billion dollar purchase of 102 F-16I aircraft (from Lockheed Martin) became Israel's single largest military procurement deal. This purchase was financed by US-Israel military aid and a deferred payment installment package. The purchase of 25 F-15I aircraft (from Boeing) cost the MoD approximately US$84 million per aircraft and a total of US$2.5 billion. Other notable procurement deals have included 48 Multiple Launch Rocket Systems (MLRS), 12 AH-64 D Apache Longbow Radar-Enhanced Helicopters, several purchases of Electronic Intelligence Gathering Aircraft, the Merkava IV battle tanks (which are produced and purchased in Israel), TOW-2A long-range anti-tank missiles, and various precision guided munitions.

Defence R&D

Israel has throughout its history put major emphasis on maintaining an independent defence R&D capability. At an extreme quantitative disadvantage relative to its enemies, Israel's only long-standing option has been its decisive qualitative advantage, which it obtains through its superior personnel and indigenously developed weapon systems.

About 9 per cent of Israel's defence budget is spent on R&D activities (see Ben-Israel, 2001; Nevo and Shur-Shmueli, 2004). Ben-Israel (2001) estimates that about 2.5 per cent of the defence budget is invested in basic and applied research activities, which is slightly less than the US and French percentages. However, Israel is considered to be very efficient in its R&D, procurement and maintenance processes (Ben-Zvi, 2002).

Defence R&D is conducted in Israel by a 'triangle' whose vertices are: the branches and corps of the IDF (e.g., Army, Air Force, Navy, Intelligence, and C⁴I); the Directorate of Defence R&D in the MoD (DDR&D or, as it is known in Hebrew, *MAFAT*); and defence industry, which includes government-owned firms like Israeli Aircraft Industries (IAI), Israel Military Industries (IMI), Rafael, privately held companies like Elbit, and various research institutes (IMoD, 2004b).[14] The IDF branches and corps are responsible for defining military operational needs and requirements. These requirements are derived using a 'reference scenario', defined by the IDF general staff, which takes into account the entire spectrum of threats, challenges, emerging technologies, strategic opportunities and budget constraints (Yaalon, 2002).

Operational needs that are approved by the military general staff initiate the R&D process, which is managed by the DDR&D (IMoD, 2004b; IMoD, 2004c). The DDR&D is responsible for initiating weapon systems programmes (including feasibility studies), publishing the required Requests for Information (RFI) and Requests for Proposal (RFP), conducting negotiations, signing contracts and overseeing the programme implementation during its development phase (Tov, 1998). The DDR&D is also responsible for building and promoting the relevant scientific and technological infrastructure, directing the advancement of future technological concepts through the identification and exploitation of technological opportunities, and coordinating all the R&D-related processes in the IDF and MoD.

Surprisingly, given its modest resources, Israel's defence R&D community succeeds in developing state-of-the-art weapon systems, often the first of their kind in the world (for examples, see Box 8.1). There are several reasons for this. First, most of the Israeli R&D is carried out by the Israeli defence firms (with MoD funding) which, in most cases, employ engineers and technicians who have served in the IDF, are familiar with the IDF needs and, thus, have a thorough understanding of the important characteristics of the weapons and equipment under development. Second, most weapons and equipment development by Israeli defence firms is undertaken in close cooperation with the IDF, even when the IDF is not committed to purchase these items. This collaboration with the IDF and former IDF's soldiers is an aspect of 'concurrent' system development that is essential for the development of high quality products at a low development cost. Third, as suggested by Setter and Tishler (2005), it might be optimal for a country with a relatively small defence budget to invest in highly uncertain technologies. Although risky, this strategy allows a small country to develop highly advanced, radically innovative defence capabilities, which outperform the less risky but also less capable conventional systems. Box 8.1 provides examples.

The escalating share of personnel costs in the defence budget is driving a corresponding decline in resources available for defence R&D, and funding will have to be obtained from other sources if a reasonable level of defence R&D is to be maintained. Thus, in the future, it is likely that many R&D programmes will be arranged as international collaborative programmes. This may ease the budget constraint but will require changes in procurement mechanisms to streamline the relatively complex transactions that are associated with international collaborative R&D effort (e.g., the sharing and management of intellectual property).

The US defence aid to Israel

The Israeli and the US defence systems have an extensive and complex relationship that spans almost all facets of possible relations between two

---

Box 8.1 Innovative capability development programmes

Ofeq satellites

The *Ofeq* satellites are a family of low earth orbiting (LEO) observation satellites, providing high resolution imaging. The first *Ofeq-1* satellite was launched in 1988 (Israeli Weapons, 2004). Though the USA and other countries have long since been deploying observation satellites, they have always been heavy (over a ton) and required very big launchers. Not being able to afford such a programme, Israel opted for light-weight satellites (of about 300kg), which are easier to launch but require a very high level of sophistication to achieve comparable performance. This risky strategy proved to be very successful, and led to Israel's membership in the prestigious club of countries with space capability.

The Arrow missile system

The *Arrow* missile system is a joint US-Israeli programme that, in March 2000, became the *first* operational ballistic missile defence system in the world (IMoD, 2004c). The various parts of the system were developed and manufactured by several Israeli defence firms, including the IAI, Rafael, and IMI, under the leadership of the MLM division of the IAI. In the 1990s, the system underwent extensive system tests culminating in a live fire test against a real Scud B ballistic missile in July 2004.

Python 5 short-range air-to-air missile

The *Python* 5 short-range air-to-air missile, introduced by Rafael in June 2003 (Rafael, 2004) was considered by many to be the most advanced of its kind. Its unique aerodynamic capabilities allow it to hit any enemy fighter plane within range, regardless of its relative aspect angle to the carrying fighter plane.

---

sovereign countries. US military aid to Israel totalled more than US$45 billion (in 2003 prices) between 1948 and 2003. Figure 8.5 presents the development of the US (military and civilian) assistance to Israel from 1948 to 2004. In terms of its form, volume and political circumstances prevailing at the time the aid was provided, there were three distinct phases in the US military assistance:

- until the beginning of the 1970s, the total US aid to Israel was rather small, averaging about US$63 million per year;
- the volume of aid increased between the early 1970s and the early 1980s to about US$600 million per year;

- following the Israeli withdrawal from Sinai in 1982, it increased further to about US$2 billion annually.

Since the late 1970s, Israel has been the major US foreign aid recipient (Israel receives about 50 per cent of total American Foreign Military Funding and about 25 per cent of total American Economic Support Funding.

Since the late 1970s, there have been several special additions to the annual foreign military support given to Israel, most notably the support for the redeployment in Sinai (1979), special support for Israeli redeployment due to the Wye agreement (2000), and the emergency wartime supplemental assistance during the 2003 war in Iraq. Since 1998, when it run at US$1.2 billion per annum, there has been a year-by-year reduction in the American Civilian Economic Support Fund (ESF) partially offset by an annual increase in American Foreign Military Support, also known as the Foreign Military Funds (FMF). The increase in FMF was to offset half of the ESF reduction. The entire Civilian Economic Support to Israel was to end in 2008 while the aid provided under Foreign Military Funds was to stabilise at US$2.4 billion.

Most of the US foreign aid to Israel is provided under the FMF scheme and takes the form of monetary transfers deposited in a Federal Reserve Bank holding account from which Israel can draw funds to purchase US military systems up to the amount of the aid. These funds are used to purchase both major items (e.g., main defence platforms) and other defence materiel (e.g., jet fuel). Some 26.3 per cent of FMF has been converted into Israeli currency to supplement Israel's own military budget resources. Other forms of assistance include Special Military Support (e.g., special support for

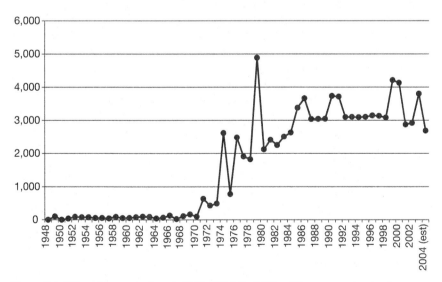

Figure 8.5 US assistance to Israel, 1948–2004 (in US$ million, current prices)

Source: Ministry of Finance (various years)

counter-terrorism activities), Special Military Gifts (which mainly include US military surplus items such as Apache helicopters and various munitions, and German-built submarines) and the interest that the FMF accumulates when it is pre-deposited in special US funds.

Israel's defence industry[15]

The main characteristics of Israel's defence industry and the position it seeks to occupy within the world's defence industry are the focal points of this section. The size of Israel's defence industry is disproportionate to the size of the economy; for example, in 2002, the share of the Israeli defence industry's exports in total Israeli exports was about 7.5 per cent compared to about 2 per cent in the UK. The Israeli defence industry was also the birthplace of Israel's highly developed high-tech industry (Ben-Israel, 2001).

The defence industries of the USA and Western Europe (mainly the UK, France, Germany, Italy, Sweden, and Spain) are led by a small number of very large firms (systems integrators) that employ state-of-the-art technologies and sell about 90 per cent of their production to their own governments (Golde and Tishler, 2004). Although these firms do not depend for their existence on sales in the global market, they nevertheless compete in it fiercely. Israeli defence firms also employ state-of-the-art technologies, albeit on a much smaller scale than their US and European counterparts, but are highly dependent on the sales of their products in the international markets. As Shefi and Tishler (2005) show, Israeli defence exports amount to about 70 per cent of production.

It appears that the technologies and the production processes used by US, European and Israeli firms are fairly similar, as are the prices of their competing products. It is thus interesting to ask why Israeli firms are 'small' while the US and Western European firms (main system integrators) are 'large'. Following Shefi and Tishler (2005), we assume that the weapons production cost functions of all firms are similar. Marketing costs, however, distinguish defence firms in a small country from those in a large country.[16] European and US defence firms benefit from the economic and political leverage of their governments in their marketing efforts.[17] The marketing of defence goods by Israeli firms is more difficult and their marketing costs increase as these firms strive to increase their sales, particularly to overseas customers. This is due to the small size of the Israeli economy (hence, the limited economic leverage of the Israeli government and Israeli defence firms) and the political constraints under which the Israeli government operates. Finally, US military aid to Israel, which affects the optimal behaviour of both the Israeli government and the Israeli and US defence industries, plays an integral part in our model.

Structure, production capabilities and performance

The Israeli defence industry was established during the early 1920s, but developed into a modern industry following the 1967 Six-Day War (for details, see Dvir and Tishler, 2000; Lifshitz, 2003). In the early 2000s, it consisted of about 150 firms, exporting about 70 per cent of their production. These exports comprise only a small fraction of world military trade but are significant for Israel's national economy. Figures 8.6 and 8.7 show the levels of defence procurement and defence exports, respectively, of the USA, Western Europe, and Israel during 1990–2002. Figure 8.8 shows trends in Israeli

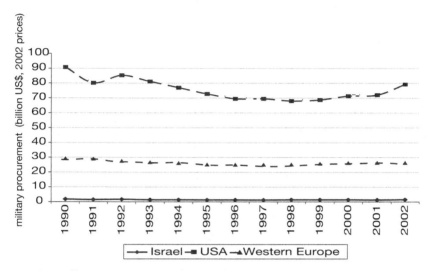

Figure 8.6 Military procurements of the USA, Western Europe and Israel, 1990–2002

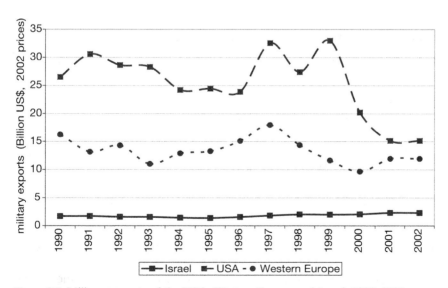

Figure 8.7 Military exports of the USA, Western Europe and Israel, 1990–2002

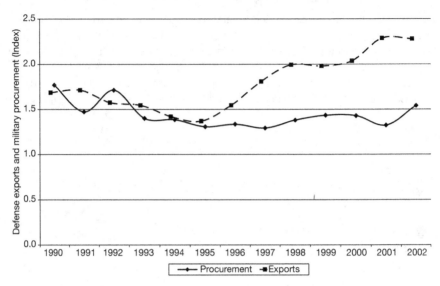

Figure 8.8 Military procurement of the Israeli government and Israeli defence exports, 1990–2002

Source: Shefi (2004)

defence procurement and defence exports during 1990–2002. Export performance was relatively strong in the late 1990s and early 2000s when domestic defence procurement reached a plateau.

The increase in Israeli defence exports in the second half of that period was due to three factors:

- the decline in Israel's local procurement was accompanied by a reduction in the prices of local Israeli defence products making Israeli exports more attractive for other countries;
- as Israel did not produce main weapons platforms, its exports were based on precision guided munitions, intelligence systems, command and control systems, upgrades of older platforms and home-security products. The demand for at least some of these products increased at the turn of the century;
- the Israeli industry, with the help of the Israeli MoD, developed several markets in the Third World (e.g., India) and was able to increase exports to these specific markets.

Israeli defence firms can be divided into three groups on the basis of size and ownership. The first group includes three large defence organizations, all government-owned – IAI, IMI and Rafael – which mainly develop and produce defence systems. The second group consists of one large and several medium-sized privately-owned firms, most notably Elbit Systems, which concentrates almost entirely on defence products. Other firms in this group – such as ECI, Motorola and Tadiran – produce mainly civilian products (communication equipment), but have small defence system divisions. The third group consists of relatively small, privately-owned firms, each specialising in a narrow line of defence products. In addition to these three groups, there are several large refurbishment and maintenance centers which are part of the Army's Division of Technology and Logistics.

In the early 2000s, Israeli domestic production included the development and production of radars, various other early warning systems, missile detection systems, ground surveillance, SAR radars, ELINT equipment, EW jammers, radio voice scramblers and encryption units, airborne ESM systems, navy equipment, satellite launchers (Shavit), the Ofeq series satellite, Amos/ MILCOM communications satellites, EROS imaging satellites, air force equipment, and more (JCSS, 2004). The Merkava IV tank was produced by the logistics branch of the IDF, which was also involved in the high priority development, jointly with the US, of theatre ballistic defence systems such as the Arrow. In addition, the Israeli defence sector was involved in upgrading combat aircraft and helicopters, in AEW aircraft conversion, in developing and producing TV- and laser-guided bombs, air-refuelling systems, UAVs and mini-UAVs. Table 8.4 shows the sales, workforce numbers and production capabilities of Israel's six largest defence firms at the beginning of the 2000s.

Israeli firms are disadvantaged by size in their global marketing efforts when compared with larger US and European counterparts. They must also compete fiercely against other Israeli firms with similar technologies in the same international market segments. Although, by the end of the 1990s, Israeli defence firms were increasingly determined to collaborate with each other to increase their combined share of export markets, the process of industry consolidation through mergers and acquisitions, so evident in US and European defence sectors in the 1990s, came late to Israel. It was only in the early 2000s that larger Israeli firms began to expand by acquiring smaller firms (e.g., the Elbit Corporation purchased El-op and a controlling share in Elisra). This process of slow consolidation continues.

The Israeli government is also heavily involved in the nation's defence industry as the owner of some of the main defence organisations (see Table 8.4) and as the industry's main customer. The Israeli MoD has been instrumental in helping Israeli defence firms to penetrate new markets, marketing weapon systems to various governments, testing and cooperating in the development of new weapon systems, and synchronising some of the defence firms' activities (see, for example, Coren, 2005). The government also controls defence exports through a special division of the MoD, which licenses exports of classified products. The relations between the military and the defence firms are very close. This is largely because Israel is a small country and almost all its citizens share a common background of military service. The number of engineering schools is also small. Over the years, these close relations have enabled the development of some unique weapon systems

Table 8.4 Sales, workforce numbers and production capabilities of Israel's six largest defence firms in 2001

	Workforce (numbers)	Sales (US$ billions)	Production capabilities
IAI Israel Aircraft Industries	12,000	1,760	Maintenance and refurbishment of military aircraft and helicopters; UAVs; intelligence systems; space systems; theatre ballistic missiles and defence systems; naval attack and defence systems; air-to-ground weapons; air defence systems.
Rafael	4,815	720	Air-to-air missiles; air-to-surface weapons; air defence; infantry weapons; anti-armour missile systems; combat vehicle systems; naval weapon systems; electronic warfare; targeting systems; naval combat suits; command and control systems; space propulsion; micro satellites; satellite launchers.
IMI (*TAAS*) Israeli Military Industries	3,747	386	Heavy ammunition; aircraft systems; rocket systems; smart weapon systems; electronic equipment; weapons and armoured fighting vehicles; small arms, small arms ammunition.
Elbit	5,000	718	Aircraft and helicopter upgrades and systems; helmet-mounted systems; combat vehicle upgrades and systems; UAVs; battlefield information systems; sensors and countermeasures; intelligence, surveillance and reconnaissance.
Elta (subsidiary of IAI)	2,498	378	Radars; sigint systems; airborne early warning systems.
Elisra (partially government owned)	1,530	288	Self-protection suits for fighter jets and helicopters; comint and elint systems; battlefield management and control systems, theatre missile defence systems; microwave sub-systems and components.

Source: Lifshitz (2003); Dvir and Tishler (2000); Shefi and Tishler (2005); www.iai.co.il; www.rafael.co.il. www.imi-israel.com; www.elbitsystems.com.

tailored to the particular conditions in the Middle East and to the special needs of the IDF.

However, despite their export successes, and contrary to common belief, several Israeli defence firms were struggling in the early 2000s. IMI had been losing money for many years (Barzilay, 2004; Korin-Liber, 2004) and was practically insolvent (Rapoport and Etinger, 2005). IAI's profits were positive but very low i.e., they were less than 4 per cent of sales revenue in 2000–2002 and below 1 per cent in 2003 and 2004 (Barzilay, 2005). The privately-owned Elbit was performing better at the turn of the century, but it was not clear whether Rafael, recently transformed from a government agency into a government-owned firm, was profitable. These financial difficulties were largely attributed to Israeli firms' small size and, thus, their inability to penetrate the US and European markets and compete against large US and European firms in Third World markets. More specifically, since Israel's technological strength lies in advanced weapons systems, these systems are hard to export to the US and European countries that produce similar equipment. In turn, the IDF and Third World countries do not generate enough demand to support several major system integrators in Israel (this point is further elaborated below).

Israel's defence industry model and predictions

To analyse the effects of changes in the number of defence firms in Israel and the size of the US military aid to Israel on the Israeli defence industry's exports and profits, Israel's procurement of arms and its net defence cost (Israel's net defence cost equals its procurement minus the profits of its defence industry), we use the formal model described in Box 8.2. The calibration of the model's parameters, using data for 1985–2002, is described in detail in Shefi and Tishler (2005). Here we discuss the inferences drawn from the model when the calibrated parameters are used to assess the effects of changes in several exogenous variables on the model's solution.

Generally, an increase in the number of Israeli defence firms has two conflicting effects. First, there is a *competition effect* that slightly reduces the price of the Israeli defence products since there are more Israeli (and overall) defence firms in the world market. Second, there is a *marketing cost effect* that increases the marginal costs (including marketing) of each Israeli firm and hence raises the price of Israeli defence products. In the mid-2000s, there were four major Israeli defence firms (systems integrators). Reducing this number to three or two results in a decrease of the price of the Israeli defence goods (that is, the effect of the reduction in marginal cost dominates the effect of the reduction in the number of defence firms in Israel and worldwide). As a result, Israeli exports increase. This conclusion is reversed when the number of defence firms in Israel is one, causing a reduction in Israel's exports (that is, the effect of the reduction in the number of defence firms in Israel dominates the reduction in marginal marketing cost). Increasing the number of defence firms in Israel from four to five or more results in an increase in the price of the Israeli defence goods (that is, the fast increase in the marginal marketing cost of each Israeli firm dominates the rather small effect of the increase in the number of defence firms in Israel). Overall, an increase in the number of Israeli defence firms reduces Israeli procurement since, on average, world

Box 8.2 The model

The formal model is adapted from Mantin and Tishler (2004) and Shefi
and Tishler (2005). It describes the optimal behaviour of the defence
industries in three developed countries: Israel, the USA and Western
Europe. The products of the defence firms are substitutes (they may be
similar, but they are not identical). The end product, the defence good, of
each firm is an aggregate of modern platforms (fighter planes, missiles,
integrated weapon and intelligence systems, and so on) and their peripherals,
as well as sophisticated munitions and other high-tech equipment.

The 'rest of the world' includes all the other countries in the world.
There is no production of defence goods in the rest of the world. The three
developed countries are not enemies, but they may have enemies or
potential enemies in the rest of the world. The rest of the world features
downward-sloping demand functions for the defence goods that are
produced by the defence firms in the developed countries.

The defence industries in the three developed countries must satisfy local
demand by their governments before they are allowed to export the
defence goods to the rest of the world. The governments of the three
developed countries purchase the defence goods only from the local
defence industry. In addition, we assume that the USA is committed to
provide military aid to Israel. The procurement of Israel includes the aid it
receives from the USA and the amount of this aid, which is given in the
form of defence goods produced in the USA, is exogenous to the model.

Security in each of the arms-producing countries is a function of the size
of the country's stock of weapon systems relative to the stock of weapons
of its potential enemies. The *target* security level of each developed country
is determined by military and political decision makers who assess the
country's potential enemies. The target security levels are exogenously
given in this model.

The technology of each firm in each of the developed countries is
represented by a cost function comprising two parts. The first part represents the cost of the production stage, and the second represents the cost of
the marketing stage. The cost functions of the production stage are linear.
As already noted, in practice, the marketing of weapon systems normally
involves the active help, as well as the economic and political leverage,
provided by the government of the arms-producing country. This implies,
as we argued before, that marketing is more costly for Israel. Thus, we
assume that the cost functions of the marketing stage of the USA and
Western Europe are linear, while the cost function of the marketing stage
of Israel is quadratic.

Following Mantin and Tishler (2004) and Shefi and Tishler (2005),
the decisions in this model are taken in two steps as follows. At step 1,
conditional on the values of the *target* security levels, the governments
of the arms-producing countries commit themselves, simultaneously and

non-cooperatively, to the amounts of the defence goods that they will purchase from their defence industries. At step 2, given the commitments of the arms-producing governments to purchase the defence goods from their own defence industries, and the rest of the world's demand functions for the defence goods, the defence firms in the arms-producing countries determine, via the Cournot conjecture, the exports of their defence goods in order to maximise their profits.

prices decline somewhat and Israeli procurement (and the procurement of the USA and Western Europe) is proportional to world exports.

Operating profits of the Israeli defence industry increase when the number of firms is reduced from four to three or less (the decline in the marginal cost of marketing of each Israeli defence firm dominates the impact of a decline in the number of Israeli firms). Industry operating profits (in contrast to profits per firm) of the Israeli defence industry increase when the number of Israeli firms is larger than four (the number of defence firms dominates the increase in marginal cost of each firm). However, industry operating profits are maximal when there is only one defence firm in Israel. (Overall profit is smaller when one takes into account fixed costs per firm, which are ignored in the present discussion). Israel's net defence cost (government expenditure on defence minus the defence industry profits) is also minimal when there is only one Israeli defence firm. In the model, Israel is better off having only one defence firm.

The model shows that changes in US aid to Israel have only a minimal effect on the USA and Western Europe. They have, however, a large impact on Israel. Israel's exports are almost unaffected by the size of the US aid to Israel, showing a slight increase as the aid increases. However, Israel's procurement from its own defence industry declines when US military aid increases, since goods and services provided as the US aid are close substitutes for local production. Consequently, the profits of Israel's defence industry also decline. Larger US military aid to Israel reduces government expenditure in Israel at a faster rate than the reduction in the Israeli defence industry's profits and, hence, reduces Israel's net defence cost (government expenditure on defence minus the defence industry profits).

The model shows that, overall, Israel is likely to gain from a consolidation of its defence industry similar to the consolidations that took place in the USA and Western Europe during the 1990s. However, with a single indigenous supplier, regulating a local defence monopoly would not be an easy task.[18] To ensure efficiency in the procurement process, the Israeli MoD should guarantee genuinely competitive bidding for its requirements with equal access for foreign defence firms. Net defence costs are higher for an Israeli defence industry with two defence firms, but not by much. Thus, if the Israeli MoD is not prepared to open almost all of its procurement to bidding by foreign defence firms, it will have to assess the costs and benefits of having two local defence firms (ensuring that the local bidding for some of its procurement is relatively competitive) or a local monopoly (with a difficult, possibly problematic, regulatory process). We believe that as long as the R&D process is carried out by local agencies, opening the bidding for Israeli procurement to foreign firms is the appropriate policy.[19]

Conclusion

The main conclusions of the chapter are as follows. First, the superiority of the Israeli military over its potential regional adversaries derives from its huge advantage in skilled human resources, technology and the military assistance that it receives from the USA. Second, Israel will continue to invest intensively in defence R&D in order to enhance its technological advantage. Third, Israel's superior technology requires a healthy defence industry. Since this industry exports most of its production, it must be able to successfully compete in the world market for defence goods and services. The competitive advantage of the Israeli defence industry depends, among other things, on the strategic interactions between the market structure of the world's defence industry and the security requirements of the USA, Western Europe and Israel, as well as on the third world's demand for weapons systems.

Our main results and the implied policy recommendations for Israel are as follows. First, the net defence costs of Israel (its expenditure on defence minus the profits of its defence industry) are minimal when there is only one major indigenous defence firm. Thus, Israel is likely to gain from a consolidation of its defence industry. Second, the US military aid to Israel is beneficial to the Israeli economy, since it reduces Israel's net defence cost and enhances technology transfer from the USA to Israel. However, the US aid also reduces the profits of the Israeli defence industry and may, in the long term, hurt the sustainability and viability of Israel's defence industry. On the other hand, a large share of the US military aid to Israel takes the form of platforms (aircrafts, for example) and other major items that cannot, and will not, be produced in Israel. Should the USA decide to cease its military aid to Israel, such platforms would have to be purchased from the USA or Europe and paid for with Israel's own resources. Thus, it seems that the benefits of the US military aid to Israel far exceed its costs (particularly since the Israeli civilian high-tech sector is always seeking high-quality engineers and other R&D personnel), and the Israeli defence establishment will be better off actively seeking additional foreign markets via joint ventures or mergers with American and European defence firms.

Notes

1 In 2004, its population was about 6.9 million and its gross domestic product (GDP) US$110 billion.

2 For most of the following 14 years Israel had maintained a narrow security zone in southern Lebanon, adjacent to its northern border, to safeguard its population in the Galilee against attacks by hostile elements of the Lebanese militia. It withdrew from the security zone in 1999.

3 The economic crisis that enveloped Syria in the late 1980s put an end to its effort to gain strategic parity with Israel (see Hilan, 1993, and Ma'oz, 1999). Apart from the cost of its accelerating arms race with Israel, it was a crisis brought about, among other things, by its support for Iran in the Iran–Iraq war (which led to its isolation in the Arab world), and the collapse of the USSR – its main economic and military supporter.

4 In this study we adopt Cordesman's (2004) definition of weapons of mass destruction (WMD) and terror weapons (TWP). WMD are divided into four major categories: chemical, biological, radiological, and nuclear (CBRN). TWP are WMD that can attack, contaminate and affect only a relatively small area (they do not include fully developed nuclear weapons). Terror weapons are cheaper and seem to lend significant deterrence capabilities. At the beginning of the 1990s, Syria started to develop its own production capabilities of chemical and biological weapon systems (CBW), and surface-to-surface missiles (SSMs) which can be deployed with CBW warheads, in order to achieve deterrence in its arms race with Israel. Indeed, Kagan *et al.* (2005) demonstrate that Syria coerced Israel into allocating enormous resources in order to effectively counter the threat of its TWP. In the 1990s, Syria shifted its procurement and its own defence production capabilities almost solely to TWP. Shoham (2002a, 2000b) describes how, with the assistance of China and North Korea, Syria had been building sheltered storage and launching facilities for stationary ground-to-ground Scud C missiles. Pine (2000) estimates the annual expenditure of Syria on TWP at about US$1–2 billion. Although this is likely to be an over-estimate, particularly when considering the relatively low cost of the technologically unsophisticated Scud ballistic missiles and the associated infrastructure, the expenditure on TWP is the largest and most important part of the Syrian defence budget. According to Kozyulin (2000), ballistic missiles armed with chemical and biological warheads are the most important component of Syria's TWP.

5 See Kam (2004) for an excellent analysis of the Iranian threat in general and to Israel in particular.

6 The IDF relies on a mandatory three-year service by all eligible men and a mandatory two-year service by all eligible women conscripted at the age of 18. These regular forces are the primary source of personnel for the IDF.

7 See, for example, the home pages of the Israeli defence firms, IAI, Rafael and Elbit, for descriptions of some of these intelligence and air-defence systems.

8 However, Egypt, which obtains some of its platforms from the USA, may be an exception and Syria and Iran are believed to have quantities of TWP.

9 The NIS was floated in the second half of the 1980s. Thus, presenting the Israeli defence budget in US$ is meaningful only from the end of the 1980s.

10 During the past few years there has been much public debate over the military budget allocation to wages and retirement pensions, which have risen due to public sector wage agreements that also apply to the military (which is a part of the public sector). Since 1995, the IDF and MoD have been implementing processes aimed at lowering the share of the budget allocation to manpower. Note that the combined effect of the increase in the wage rate (throughout the public sector) and the practically constant size of the overall defence budget during 1985 and 2003 are the main reasons for the continuous increase of the budget share allocated to wages (and the subsequent decline in the budget share allocated to procurement and R&D).

11 This policy could be carried out even if the MoD was not a monopsony in the defence market in Israel.

12 US FMF – US Foreign Military Funded Programs. The FMF are provided in the form of monetary transfers that enable Israel to purchase US military systems up to the amount of the aid. These funds are used to purchase both major items, such as main defence platforms, and non-major items, such as jet fuel.

13 The Israeli MoD has exclusive jurisdiction over defence trade.

14 The R&D activities are usually performed in research institutes (such as universities or other facilities) and in the defence firms. The IDF also operates some internal, specialist R&D units.

15 This section is based on Shefi and Tishler (2005) and Tishler and Shefi (2005).

16 As the only customers in the market for modern weapons systems, the governments of all arms-producing countries, including Israel, are actively involved in the marketing activities of their defence firms. This involvement may include direct political pressure, large subsidies to local defence firms, offsets, economic aid that is (at least indirectly) conditional on defence sales, restrictions on use (or exports) of locally produced weapons that include foreign-made (US or European) components, and so on.

17 See Shefi and Tishler (2005) for examples of the use of economic and political leverage by the US and European governments in support of their defence firms.

18 In the 1990s, the Israeli MoD and many industry leaders supported the existence of four indigenous system integrators. In the 2000s, after some years of debate within the Israeli MoD, there is a growing acceptance of industry consolidation around a smaller number of system integrators. Consolidation around one or two private companies was seen as a viable, and probably optimal, option (see Barzilay, 2005; Cohen, 2005). But the consolidation process has been impeded by local political ambitions and lack of efficient regulatory tradition and expert knowledge on how to decentralise and privatise complicated industries.

19 See Shefi and Tishler (2005) on the involvement of the Israeli MoD in Israeli defence exports.

References

Barzilay, A. (2004) 'Mofaz: the privatization of imi or a merger with rafael will be decided before 2005', *Haaretz* (20 September).

—— (2005) 'Huge losses for the Bedek division of IAI', *Haaretz*, 4 April.

Ben-Israel, I. (2001) 'Security, technology and the future battlefield', in H. Golan (ed.) *Israel's Security Web*, Tel Aviv: Ma'arachot (in Hebrew).

Ben-Zvi, S. (2002) 'Expenditure and total cost of security', in I. Tov (ed.) *National Security and the Israeli Economy*, Tel Aviv: Jaffe Center for Strategic Studies (JCSS), Tel Aviv University (in Hebrew).

—— (2003) 'Israeli defence expenditure allocation considerations and their impact on the Israeli economy', mimeo (in Hebrew).

Blech, A. and Davidson, A. (2002) 'Defence expenditure in Israel 1950–2001', Working Paper 23/2002, Jerusalem: Central Bureau of Statistics (in Hebrew).

Cohen, N. (2005) 'Mofaz ordered the MoD to take action to merge the Israeli defence firms within five years', *Haaretz*, 19 May.

Cordesman, A. H. (2004) *The Proliferation of Weapons of Mass Destruction in the Middle East*, Washington, DC: Center for Strategic and International Studies.

Coren, O. (2005) 'Smiles, ceremony, aerobatics hide tension at Paris Air Show', *Haaretz*, 15 June.

Dvir, D. and Tishler, A. (2000) 'The changing role of the defence industry in Israel's industrial and technological development', *Defence Analysis*, 16(1): 33–52.

Feldman, S. and Shapir, Y. S. (eds) (2004) *The Middle East Strategic Military Balance 2003–2004*, Tel Aviv: Jaffe Center for Strategic Studies (JCSS), Tel Aviv University.

Golde, S. and Tishler, A. (2004) 'Security needs and the performance of the defence industry: determining the security level', *Journal of Conflict Resolution*, 48: 672–98.

Gordon, L. S. (2003) *Dimensions of Quality: A New Approach to Net Assessment of Airpower*, Jaffe Center for Strategic Studies (JCSS), Tel Aviv University.

Hilan, R. (1993) 'The effects on economic development in Syria of a just and long-lasting peace', in S. Fischer, D. Rodrik and E. Tuma (eds) *The Economics of Middle East Peace*, Cambridge, MA: MIT Press.

IDF (2004) Official Internet Website of the Israeli Defence Forces, www1.idf.il/DOVER/site/homepage.asp.

IMoD (2004a) Official Internet Website of the Israeli Ministry of Defence. Online. Available at: www.mod.gov.il.

—— (2004b) Official Internet Website of the Israeli Ministry of Defence. Online. Available at: www.mod.gov.il/pages/mafat/mafat.asp.

—— (2004c) Official Arrow Weapon System Website. Online. Available at: www.mod.gov.il.

Israeli Weapons (2004) www.israeli-weapons.com/weapons/space/ofeq/OFEQ.html

James, A. D. (2000) 'The Place of the U.K. Industry in its National Innovation System: Co-evolution of National, Sectoral and Technological Systems', Occasional Papers #25: *The Place of the Defence Industry in National Systems of Innovation*, Ithaca, NY: Cornell University Press.

JCSS (various years) 'The Military Balance in the Middle East', Jaffe Center for Strategic Studies, Tel Aviv University.

Kagan K., Tishler, A. and Weiss, A. (2005) 'On the use of terror weapons vs. modern weapon systems in an arms race between developed and less developed countries', *Defence and Peace Economics*, 16(5): 331–46.

Kam, E. (2004) *From Terror to Nuclear Bombs: The Significance of the Iranian Threat*, Tel Aviv: Ministry of Defence.

Korin-Liber, S. (2004) 'What is the decision on IMI?', *Globs*, 7 September.

Kozyulin, V. (2000) 'Syria's missile deterrent: final breakthrough?', *PIR Arms Control Letters*, electronic version.

Lavie, Z. (2000) 'Procurement Management – From Theory to Practice', Tel Aviv: Ministry of Defence (in Hebrew).

Lifshitz, Y. (2003) *The Economics of Producing Defence: Illustrated by the Israeli Case*, Dordrecht: Kluwer Academic Publishers.

Mantin, B. and Tishler, A. (2004) 'The structure of the defence industry and the security needs of the country: a differentiated products model', *Defence and Peace Economics*, 15: 397–419.

Ma'oz, M. (1999) 'Changes in Syria's regional strategic position vis-à-vis Israel', in M. Ma'oz, J. Ginat and O. Winckler (eds) *Modern Syria: From Ottoman Rule to Pivotal Role in the Middle East*, Brighton: Sussex Academic Press, pp. 257–71.

Markusen, A. (2000) 'Should We Welcome a Transnational Defence Industry?', Occasional Papers #25: *The Place of the Defence Industry in National Systems of Innovation*, Ithaca, NY: Cornell University Press.

Ministry of Finance (various years) The Israeli State Fiscal Year Budget.

Nevo, B. and Shur-Shmueli, Y. (2004) *The Israel Defence Forces and the National Economy of Israel*, Jerusalem: The Israeli Democracy Institute (in Hebrew).

Pine, S. (2000) 'Preparing for Peace? Syrian Defence Expenditures and Its Drive for Regional Hegemony', Policy Paper 98, Ariel Center for Policy Research, Israel.

Rafael (2004) News release. Online. Available at: http://www.rafael.co.il/web/rafnew/news/news-120603.htm.

Rapoport, A and Etinger, A. (2005) 'IMI is falling apart', *Maariv*, 10 June.

Setter, O. and Tishler, A. (2005) 'Budget allocation to advanced technologies under technological uncertainty', presented at the 9th International Conference on Economics and Security, Bristol, June.

Shefi, Y. (2004) 'The effects of the world defence industry and the US military aid to Israel on Israel's defence industry', MSc thesis, Faculty of Management, Tel Aviv University.

Shefi, Y. and Tishler, A. (2005) 'The effects of the world defence industry and U.S. military aid to Israel on the Israeli defence industry: a differentiated products model'. *Defence and Peace Economics*, 16(6): 427–48.

Shoham, D. (2002a) 'Guile, gas, and germs: Syria's ultimate weapons', *Middle East Quarterly*, 9, Summer: 53–61.

—— (2002b) 'Poisoned missiles: Syria's doomsday deterrent', *Middle East Quarterly*, 9, Fall: 13–22.

SIPRI (2003) *SIPRI Yearbooks 1998–2003: Armament, Disarmament and International Security*, Oxford: Oxford University Press.

Taverna, M., Sparaco, P. and Nativ, A. (2005) 'Together, at last', *Aviation Week & Space Technology*, 7 February.

Tishler, A. and Shefi, Y. (2005) *The Optimal Structure of the Defense Industry in Israel: Significance and Implications*, Jaffe Center for Strategic Studies (JCSS), Tel Aviv University (in Hebrew).

Tov, I. (1998) *The Price of Defence Power*, Tel Aviv: Ministry of Defence Publishing.

US Department of Commerce, Bureau of Industry and Security (2004) 'Israel defence industry environment'. Online. Available at: www.bxa.doc.gov/DefenceIndustrialBase Programmes/OSIES/ExportMarketGuides/MidEast/israel.pdf.

Vlachos-Dengler, K. (2004) *Off Track? The Future of the European Defence Industry*, Santa Monica, CA: RAND International Defence Research Institute.

Yaalon, M. (2002) 'Force build-up under time and resource constraints', in I. Tov (ed.) *National Security and the Israeli Economy*, Jaffe Center for Strategic Studies (JCSS), Tel Aviv University (in Hebrew).

9   Small country 'Total Defence'

A case study of Singapore

Ron Matthews and Nellie Zhang Yan

Defence: tough for the small guys?

As in many countries, Singapore's defence procurement strategy has been shaped by a national response to the specific security challenges the country has seen itself confronting. When the British departed Singapore in 1965, they left behind a security vacuum. Thus, although independence had been gained, the challenge was then to defend it. This was not easy, given that the political tensions between the ruling united Malays National Organisation and the People's Action Party had become so serious that Singapore had to be separated from the Malaysian Federation to forestall racial conflict (Tan, 1999: 451).

Britain initially continued to maintain a large military presence in the city-state due to the ongoing Indonesian *Konfrontasi* crisis, but there was continued uncertainty over Singapore's defence relations with Malaysia now that the former country had left the Federation and the Anglo-Malaysian Defence Agreement no longer applied. Singapore was vulnerable, and one of the principal fears was that Kuala Lumpur might move to close the causeway and cut off the water supply. An added anxiety was that some of Singapore's key installations were guarded by Malaysian troops. Indeed, many of the troops that formed part of Singapore's two infantry battalions were Malay. The government managed these tensions, and the battalions were reconstituted to reflect the preponderance of Chinese in local society.

Creating a robust defence capability in the immediate post-independence period was a challenge. Resources for the local provision of military equipment were meagre and weapon systems remained those inherited from the British. By 1968, the British military had withdrawn from the island, leaving Singapore with no air force and navy, and just the rudiments of an army. Equally calamitous, was the closure of Britain's military base on the island, leading to the loss of 40,000 jobs and a fifth of Singapore's national income (Drysdale, 1984: 401–2). Defence planning thus required not only acknowledgement of the security challenges facing the country but also a procurement strategy to establish the military capabilities required to meet them. The shape of this strategy, detailed later in the chapter, marks Singapore out as a country focused on evolving indigenous, supply-side capability embedded in a larger industrial structure.

The sudden loss of Singapore's defence infrastructure in the 1960s created national uncertainty, not least because Singapore's predominantly Chinese population faced an axis of Islamic countries amounting to nearly 300 million people. This remains contentious, even to this day, reflecting long-standing tensions in South-East Asia. Anti-Chinese feelings regularly bubble to the surface, as they did in Malaysia in 1964. Five years later, in May 1969, 2,000 people died in the Malay-Chinese riots across Malaysia (Tan, 1999: 453). More recently in 1998, anti-Chinese disturbances broke out in Indonesia. A likely cause of this anti-Chinese rioting is the extraordinarily high proportion of Chinese private assets among the total assets of business communities in South-East Asia, as evidenced by the data shown in Table 9.1.

Among neighbouring countries, most observers view Malaysia as Singapore's principal threat. This is due to a series of troubling disputes between these two erstwhile 'federated' allies. First, the question of an unfettered supply of water from the Malaysian Peninsula to Singapore has always been a dangerous flashpoint. Since independence, Singapore has been obliged to purchase 50 per cent of its water from across the causeway, and this has bred tensions, particularly at the contract renewal stage.[1] Second, there has been an immigration control dispute that has festered since the late 1980s. This arose over Singapore's proposed relocation of customs and immigration facilities at the 'Malaysian-owned' Tanjong Pagar railway station in Central Singapore to the Woodlands, near Malaysia's border. An unrelated dispute occurred in 1998, when Malaysia closed its airspace to Singaporean Air Force planes. Coincidentally, Singapore was advised that clearance would be required before its naval ships could enter Malaysian waters. This and other maritime disputes over territorial claims and counter-claims have proved acrimonious. In 2002, for example, tensions over the sovereignty of Pedra Branca (a small island located in the waterway between the two countries) were heightened when Kuala Lumpar accused Singapore of blocking its fishing vessels from the seas around the island.[2] Moreover, all four of Singapore's main air bases are well within artillery range of Peninsular

Table 9.1 Chinese diaspora: shares of private assets and population in selected South-East Asian countries

	Chinese population (million)	Share of population (%)	Share of private assets held by Chinese (%)
Singapore	2.7	77	81
Malaysia	5.8	29	61
Thailand	5.8	10	81
Indonesia	7.2	3.5	73
The Philippines	0.9	2	50

Source: Backman (1995).

Malaysia, causing the island to fortify these bases with aircraft shelters and underground parking aprons; there are also at least three nearby highways that can quickly be converted into runways should the need arise (Chang, 2003: 116).

Such politico-strategic frictions, including the emerging and potential threats from the proliferation of piracy, the knock-on impact of military tensions over the Spratley Islands in the South China Sea, and the dangers of a possible return to Indonesia's aggressive *Konfrontasi* posture, all reinforce Singapore's view that a strong military capability is essential to protect its national interests. This, in turn, has sharpened its interest in sustaining indigenous defence industry supply capabilities – a key influence in defence acquisition decisions.

Singapore's success in having addressed the economic and military challenges it faces ranks as a major 'small country' success story in the contemporary era. There are several possible explanations. First, from a political perspective, there was strong, stable and decisive leadership under Prime Minister Lee Kuan Yew. The resulting political unity encouraged long-term planning, especially in the field of economic advancement. A constant theme was the development of dynamic comparative advantages in emerging industrial and technological fields. Investment in human capital was particularly emphasised, supporting the unending search for sustainable competitive advantage. In this regard, Singapore was fortunate to be located at an international trading crossroads. Shipping, insurance, banking, related services and tourism all prospered due to Singapore's beneficial geographical position. Success was also partially due to the government's deliberate strategy of enhancing technological development through the adoption of an open and welcoming approach to foreign investment.

Even today, more than 70 per cent of Singapore's investment is foreign-sourced. This dependence on foreign capital leaves Singapore exposed to the vagaries of the market, but after 40 years, it is a development 'model' that has worked well and is the envy of small (and large) countries the world over. The development model recognises that the fusion of political stability, social cohesion and economic development is mutually reinforcing. To that end, successful pursuit of economic objectives diminished the potential for internal unrest, a constant problem facing Singapore's neighbouring countries of Malaysia and Indonesia.

A second factor accounting for Singapore's success is that the government's management of the economy has proved both enlightened and visionary. The central economic authorities adopted an interventionist strategy, with government playing a paternal role: coaxing, guiding and supporting business to take a proactive approach in identifying and investing in the economic growth poles of the global economy. Singapore's institutionally planned and orchestrated development strategy has proved successful because policies and resources were introduced to support the achievement of 'sustainable' competitive advantages. This interventionist strategy was used to manage Singapore through the 1997 Asia-Pacific financial crisis and also the recent and

ongoing economic challenge posed by the rapid emergence of China's powerful economy. Singapore's response has been to move quickly to introduce
policies designed to secure higher value-added activities through the development of next-generation technological endeavour.[3] Singapore, of course,
cannot compete with China on scale and cost, but it can compete on technological innovation. This focus on technology has been a constant in the
island-state's development process, and is probably the key reason for its success.

A further, less tangible, contextual consideration accounting for Singapore's
developmental success is rooted in the social and cultural fabric of its people.
Observers with an understanding of Singapore will attest to the commitment
and hard-working values of its citizens. There is a cultural consensus that
transcends those of other communities in the region, and possibly even of
China itself. This has much to do with the proximity that comes from 'small
size', arguably strengthening social bonds and enhancing the socio-economic
benefits of *Mianzi* and *guanxi* within Chinese culture.[4]

For all these reasons, Singapore – a country with a land mass of just 699 sq
kms, a population of just 4.3 million people, and a strategic location bordered
on all sides by Islamic countries – has achieved a quality of life that is the
envy of the world and certainly its Asia-Pacific neighbours. At US$25,900,
Singapore's per capita income is higher than nearly all Asia-Pacific countries
(see Table 9.2). Singapore, moreover, is regularly ranked among the top
five of the world's most competitive economies,[5] its health and educational
sectors are benchmarked as among the world's best and, importantly, its
defence is in the hands of one of the world's most efficient Armed Forces.
Singapore's military prowess reflects not just the professionalism of its Armed
Forces, but also allied doctrinal, industrial and cultural considerations. In
every sense, the cornerstone of Singaporean national security is the adoption
of an all-embracing approach towards 'total' defence.

Singapore's force multiplier: Total Defence

Singapore's defence policy is constructed on the foundations of diplomacy
and deterrence. From the diplomacy perspective, the country views itself as
non-aligned, seeking friendly relations with all states. It actively participates
in international organisations, such as the World Trade Organisation and
ASEAN, and serves also as a rotational member of the UN Security Council
(2001–2). Deterrence, the other aspect of defence, is rationalised on the basis
that Singapore must possess the capacity to deter, in the event that diplomacy
fails. A deterrence posture must therefore be developed, not so much to
address particular external threats but to prevent them from arising in the first
place. The strength of Singapore's deterrent capability has led it to be characterised on occasions as a 'poisonous shrimp'. This metaphor was based on
the fact that predators would face the high probability of sustaining unacceptably high operational losses from an attack on Singapore. Although the

Table 9.2 Defence and economic data for selected countries

	Economic indicators						Armed forces		
	GDP (US$ bn) (2005)	MILEX (US$ bn) (2005)	Pop. (m) (2005)	GDP per capita (US$ '000) (2005)	MILEX/GDP (%) (2005)	MILEX per capita (US$) (2004)	Active ('000) (2006)	Reserves ('000) (2006)	Total ('000) (2006)
Brunei	5	0.36	0.37	14.2	5.7	805	7	0.7	7.7
China (PRC)	1570	29.5	1306.3	1.5	1.5	19	2255	800	3055
Indonesia	277	2.6	242	1.1	3.0	32	302	400	702
Japan	4700	44.7	127.4	36.8	1.0	355	260	44	304
Malaysia	128	2.47	24.0	5.3	2.3	117	110	52	162
Philippines	96	0.84	87.9	1.1	1.0	10	106	131	237
Singapore	**114**	**5.6**	**4.4**	**25.9**	**4.8**	**1172**	**73**	**313**	**386**
Thailand	178	1.95	64.2	2.8	1.2	30	307	200	507
Australia	665	13.2	20.0	33.1	2.4	719	53	21	74
France	2150	53.8	60.7	35.5	2.6	872	255	22	247
Germany	2850	38.5	82.4	34.7	1.4	458	285	355	640
UK	2230	51.7	60.4	36.8	2.3	832	217	242	459
US	12,500	495.0	295.7	42.2	3.9	1556	1546	956	2505

Source: ISSS (2007).

Note: Constant 2003 US$ prices.

military capability of the Singapore Armed Forces (SAF) is impressive, and without doubt the strongest in South-East Asia, the city-state takes care not to intimidate its neighbours with ostentatious deployment of modern weapon systems. The term 'defence creep' has been coined to describe how Singapore's initial acquisitions are small in number, building up gradually over time, with proportions of the inventory deployed abroad for training purposes (Huxley, 2000: 173).

Deterrence strategy is operationalised through 'Total Defence'. This concept was first enunciated in 1984, designed to unite all sectors of society – government, business and the people – in defence of Singapore. Total Defence subordinates the purely military aspect to just one of five elements in what is conceived to be a broader 'defence' effort. The five key elements of Total Defence are:

- *Psychological Defence* achieved through an array of educational campaigns aimed at creating the collective will and commitment among Singapore's citizens to defend the country.
- *Civil Defence* to protect and maintain civil resources and infrastructure during conflict. As an island state, Singapore is particularly vulnerable to external dislocation of trade, food, water and energy resources. Civil defence is aimed at instilling confidence and resilience during times of national crisis.
- *Social Defence* achieved through high levels of social cohesion and successful integration of all elements of the Singaporean society. Although Singapore's population is predominantly Chinese in origin, the government has long recognised the need for all ethnic groups to be assimilated into the community so that a meritocracy based on multicultural consensus is achieved.
- *Economic Defence*, which refers to more than just the husbanding of strategic resources and the conversion of civil industry for the provision of surge-capacity during times of international conflict, it also recognises that military power depends on economic strength, and possibly vice versa. Historically, the world's strong economies have also been major military powers. In the absence of a strong economy, the costs of creating and maintaining an effective twenty-first-century military capability would almost certainly be too high.
- *Military Defence*: the most direct symbol of defence, of course, is the military, and since 1965 Singapore has been highly successful in building up its military strength.

Although the lack of critical mass has acted as a constraint on some aspects of defence policy, Singapore's unique military 'model' demonstrates that the downside of small country size can be compensated by the crafting of an appropriate, efficient and most importantly, effective Total Defence paradigm.

Singapore armed forces: small but strong

Willingness to bear the burden

Singapore has continuously demonstrated its commitment to deterrence. The Ministry of Defence (MINDEF) is able to spend up to 6 per cent of GDP on defence every year although, in the early 2000s, the average defence expenditure has been capped at about 5 per cent per annum (FI, 2004: 45). This is not only one of the highest defence budgets in Asia-Pacific, but also one of the highest defence per capita spends in the world (see Table 9.2). Singapore's defence expenditure for the fiscal year to March 2006 was S$9.26 billion (US$5.46 billion) representing a 7.4 per cent increase over the previous year.[6] Defence spending represents over 31 per cent of the S$30 billion government budget, the biggest share of government spending among all of the Singapore government ministries. Together with the Home Affairs and Foreign Affairs Ministries, security and external relations accounts for over 40 per cent of the country's national budget.

Punching above its weight

Under the Total Defence concept, Singaporean security is leveraged on the commitment of its stakeholders, and the most important of these are its citizens. On this basis, Singapore determined in 1967 that due to the limitations of a small population, conscription was the only means of maintaining a standing military force of a size adequate for credible deterrence. Moreover, given the parallel emphasis on 'economic defence', a large standing military would be counterproductive in a benign regional strategic environment. The SAF therefore presently has a career military force of just 14,200.[7] This is supplemented by 40,800 conscripts on National Service; the latter being compulsory for able-bodied young men. However, Singapore has an additional trained 225,000 body of reservists available for operational duty. Under the *1970 Enlistment Act*, all Singapore citizens and permanent residents become liable for National Service on reaching the age of 16.5 years, and are required to serve two to two-and-a-half years of full-time service; this is then followed by up to 40 days of reservist service annually until the age of 40, or 50 in the case of officers (Huxley, 2000: 94). Despite Singapore's small population, the data in Table 9.2 show clearly that the SAF's total mobilised personnel strength exceeds that of many of the larger Asia-Pacific countries, including Australia, Malaysia and Japan. Singapore's military is exceedingly well trained; its professionalism allowing the SAF to militarily 'punch above its weight'. This force multiplier factor will be increasingly important in the years ahead as declining birth rates will reduce Singapore's National Service intake.[8]

In times of national emergency, Singapore's strong reservist force of operationally trained personnel can be rapidly mobilised, but during normal times they are able to continue to work in the civil economy. The SAF has been structured according to tiers of readiness, enabling those at the highest level of readiness to react speedily at very short notice to military or humanitarian emergencies. The system appears to work well: the mobilisation response rate is consistently at least 95 per cent, and units are normally operationally deployable within a few hours.[9] Operation Flying Eagle, Singapore's relief mission after the Boxing Day Tsunami disaster, aptly demonstrates this rapid reaction capability.[10]

Singapore's Armed Forces also have at their disposal some of the world's most modern weapon systems. The Air Force inventory includes squadrons of F5, Skyhawk and F16 fighters. There are Apache Longbow attack helicopters, Super Puma rotary wing aircraft, and other military aircraft covering the spectrum, from KC-130 transport aircraft, E-2C surveillance Hawkeyes, S-211 Aermacchi trainers and a squadron of unmanned Aerial Vehicles. The Republic of Singapore Navy (RSN) is similarly impressive, having transformed itself from a 1980s 'maritime guerrilla force' to a twenty-first-century navy with a balanced capability to achieve its primary mission of territorial defence and protection of the country's sea lines of communication (Karniol, 2004). The range of platforms illustrates the Navy's three-dimensional maritime strength. It has LaFayette stealthy frigates, missile corvettes, anti-submarine warfare patrol vessels, Landsort class mine-hunters and Endurance class landing ships. Above the water, there are Fokker 50 Enforcer Maritime Patrol Aircraft, with plans for the RSN's first ship-borne helicopters. Below the water, there are four Sjoormen class submarines. On land, the SAF's 40,000-strong force has around 350 AMX-13 SM1 tanks and 22 AMX-10 PAC 90s. Additionally, there are several Singapore Technology (ST) families of land systems, including: the Kinetics Bionix cluster of Infantry Fighting Vehicles, comprising the Bionix 25, Bionix 40/50, Bionix armoured vehicle-launched bridge and the Bionix recovery vehicle; the ST Kinetics Bronco family of articulated all-terrain tracked carriers, including the troop carrier as well as the engineer, re-supply and ambulance versions; and the ST Kinetics Primus 155mm lightweight self-propelled howitzer.

Dual-acquisition strategy: foreign 'off-the-shelf' with local niche specialisation

Procurement process

At the heart of MINDEF's acquisition strategy is the aim to develop a high technology, 'transformational' warfare capability. This makes sense for a small country with limited manpower resources, and is consistent with Singapore's ambitions to develop a smaller but technologically sophisticated military inspired by the Revolution in Military Affairs (RMA). Singapore has never sought to construct a comprehensive, self-reliant full systems capability across the armaments spectrum but rather one that exploits selectively its successes in high technology manufacturing and dual-use industrialisation. The resulting mix of foreign off-the-shelf systems with indigenous development of niche defence industrial expertise is well suited to Singapore's limited size. MINDEF's acquisition strategy also accommodates the transition from a 1980s second-generation SAF, characterised by 'force modernisation', to a third generation SAF, focused on expeditionary warfare and force projection. Driving this transition on the demand side, MINDEF has constructed a rigorous and layered procurement process for acquiring weapons systems (for a lucid explanation, see Huxley, 2000:176–7). The acquisition cycle has much in common with the general schema outlined earlier in the book but, following Huxley, may be viewed as having five stages:

1 *Master Plan*: To initiate the acquisition process, a Master Plan for the future five-year period is established. The Defence Technology Group drives the development of the Plan, following consultation with the principal stakeholders, including the Joint Staff, Planning Staff and representatives from the Treasury. The Plan reflects agreed future operational priorities, influenced by threat assessments and resource constraints.

2 *Requirements Definition*: This process defines details of the capability, and the acquisition choice is facilitated by an 'Analytical Hierarchy Process' methodology. Criterion variables, appropriately weighted, may include price, quality, compliance with the requirements specification, life-cycle support, technology transfer, and the tenderer's reputation and previous performance.

3 *Bid Evaluation*: This stage is concerned with evaluating the competing bids and determining the most cost-effective options. For MINDEF, value-for-money is the key driver of the acquisition decision. Cost reduction is achieved through open competition and this is the normal route for low-value component or service procurement. Dual-use software and IT systems will likely be sourced locally through again open competition, dependent on the degree of sophistication sought. MINDEF might consider collaborative ventures with appropriate off-shore vendors, such as Israel. The alternative option is to purchase a bespoke package 'off-the-shelf' from major defence-industrial players, such as American and British defence contractors. Acquisition of major weapons systems, such as the Apache helicopter project and the US F-15 or French Rafale replacement for the A4 SU Skyhawk fighter aircraft, are conducted by a closed tender process in which pre-selected contractors are invited to bid. Here, acquisition decisions are normally only reached after a lengthy evaluation process. Down selection of preferred bidders signals a period of intense negotiation to ensure that price, technical quality, and the through-life support costs of the preferred weapon system, are acceptable. If the proposed acquisition impacts on strategic and diplomatic concerns, senior civil servants and government ministers are also

consulted. For major acquisitions, strategies may be developed to manage the anxieties of neighbouring countries, particularly if the acquisition represents a step-change in Singapore's military capability.

4   *In-service Acceptance*: The acquisition contract is signed, deadlines are agreed, deliveries commenced and the weapon system accepted into service. The integrated logistics support package is then activated.

5   *Life-cycle Review*: As the weapons technology matures, the focus will be on whether the system should be considered for mid-life upgrade or replacement. From the supply perspective, Singapore's indigenous defence-industrial base has developed the capability to service the 'mixed' systems requirements of the SAF, ranging from retro-fitting to upgrade and even to the replacement or addition of complete weapon systems.

Local industry involvement

While the procurement process in Singapore has much in common with our general model, its overall acquisition strategy – extending to the supply side – is distinguished by a very long view of force development.[11] It is part of the strategy to integrate purchasing with the development of production capabilities in the nation's technologically sophisticated defence industry base. The dominant player on the supply side is the state-owned enterprise, Singapore Technologies (ST).

The origins of ST go back to 1967 with the creation of Chartered Industries. Throughout the next two decades specialised undertakings in sectors such as aerospace and shipbuilding began to emerge. In 1989, Singapore Technologies was created, incorporating both civil and military activities. By 1997, ST had grown into an international group, employing 21,000 people worldwide in over 200 wholly and partially owned subsidiaries, with an annual turnover of US$2.36 billion (Matthews, 1999: 23). In 2003, sales had increased to US$7.3 billion, with defence accounting for just 12 per cent of the total (SIPRI, 2005, Table 9A.1). The value of ST's defence sales gives it a global ranking of 45, higher than France's GIAT Industries (49), Israeli's Rafael (51), Germany's Kraus-Maffei Wegmann (53) and India's Hindustan Aeronautics (58) (ibid.). Some of ST's divisions are highly defence-specialised. ST Engineering, for instance, is 55 per cent state-owned, has 11,750 workers and is 49 per cent focused on defence output (ibid.). ST's success may be measured by its growing global reputation as a supplier of high technology upgrade solutions.

Notwithstanding ST's remarkable growth performance, Singapore's lack of scale, scope and critical mass has meant that it has never sought complete defence-industrial sovereignty. Instead, it has pursued a niche industrial strategy focused on the cost-effective development of 'add-on' engineering, upgrading and retro-fitting capabilities – maximising added value wherever possible. Retro-fitting has been a focal activity involving the integration of new sub-systems into existing weapons platforms to enhance operational capability (the 'secret technological edge' concept) and lengthen in-service life. Local upgrading connotes technological insertion into platforms of higher integrated capability. Development of such 'systems' expertise has been the first step towards designing, developing and integrating, indigenously, RMA-type networked enabled capability systems – a remarkable feat for a small country.

ST's record of achievement is impressive. For instance, the locally upgraded A4 Super Skyhawk Fighters boast improved engines, longer flight capability, and heavier payloads. Similarly, the upgraded Northrop F-5E Tiger II enjoys enhanced air combat and ground attack capability and improved weapons delivery and navigation systems. Land systems have also benefited from systems upgrades. Examples here include the modification of the AMX-13 SM1 tank to better suit the local operating environment and SAF requirements. The improved tank has faster acceleration, higher speeds, the capability to travel longer distances and the ability to engage the enemy with greater precision at higher speeds. Expression of ST's upgrade expertise can be evidenced by ST Aero's winning of international competitions, including a contract, with Israeli collaboration, to upgrade Turkey's F-5E aircraft and another to modify Brazil's F-5 aircraft (Sobie, 2004: 42–7). In 2005, for example, ST Aero was bidding to win an upgrade programme for New Zealand's C-130 aircraft (ibid.). Its export hopes in this sector are anchored to MINDEF's plans to upgrade Singapore's ten C130 E/H aircraft. ST Aero also harbours future intentions to expand into Lockheed Martin F-16 avionics upgrades (ibid.).

MINDEF's acquisition strategy, however, goes beyond upgrade projects, as it also seeks to contract ST to develop and completely manufacture weapon systems in country. Examples include the Bionix family of Infantry Fighting Vehicles, the FH-2000 155 mm howitzer and RSN missile corvettes. Singapore's future local content strategy envisages even more ambitious developments – achieved through the likely procurement of the Joint Strike Fighter/ F-35. Singapore joined the programme consortium in 2003 as a security cooperation participant (SCP). Alongside fellow 'small country' SCP, Israel, Singapore seeks access to technical JSF data (for a nominal payment) to support informed decision-making on the future acquisition of the JSF platform. Whilst SCP countries do not gain the benefits available to full members, they can explore the spectrum of JSF configurations to meet their unique operational requirements, access JSF production after 2012, and, importantly, be able to compete for SDD work.[12] Acquisition of the F-35 may hinge, however, on the extent of technology transfer, particularly access to source codes – typically, a sticking point with the USA.

Singapore's mini-RMA: the search for a secret technological edge

Singapore's powerful array of diverse high technology weapon systems reflects a major facet of its defence-industrial strategy, a reliance on technology multipliers to compensate for its inability to deploy a large military force. The policy focus is on developing a secretive technological edge, thus achieving technological superiority over potential aggressors. To ensure the technological edge acts as a deterrent, its possession is an 'open' secret, but, the nature of the edge remains unspecified. This approach is neatly captured in a quote from Singapore President, S.R. Nathan: 'we must develop indigenously ... *technological edge*. And this has to be developed secretly – in strict secrecy – so that nobody knows the kinds of defence – related technology and capability that we have developed' (Nathan, 2002: 17).

The importance that Singapore's MINDEF attaches to technological prowess suggests that it is essentially the unwritten sixth component of the Total Defence concept. MINDEF's determination to embrace many aspects of RMA has been a major policy thrust since the late 1990s. The scope of this 'mini-RMA' embraces not only acquisition strategy but also associated operational concepts and force structures.

Singapore's mini-RMA has its roots in the Defence Science Organisation (DSO). Established in 1977, it initially focused on electronic warfare. However, its portfolio of activities expanded over time to encompass artificial intelligence and expert systems, software engineering, guidance and control, communications and electro-optics. DSO has also sought in recent years to develop a dynamic comparative advantage in systems integration and associated software development. DSO makes an important contribution to MINDEF's goal of gaining a 'secret technological edge' by working closely with the SAF in identifying niche technologies that will enhance operational capability. These mostly lie in the 'dual-use' technology fields, having both civil and military application. DSO's integration with the commercial sector was assisted by two developments.

First, defence benefited from the government's commitment to promote and harness its formidable national science and technology reserves to build a powerful indigenous R&D capability. This interventionist policy approach was crystallised in the 1991 Strategic Economic Plan, focusing on eight strategic thrusts, including: enhancement of human resources (education and training); sharper international focus (greater outward investment); the fostering of innovation (greater investment into R&D); and support for the development of industrial and technological clusters, having the greatest potential for rapid economic growth (Matthews, 1999: 24). The early industrial clusters included biotechnology, electronics and manufacturing technology, and information technology. These have now expanded to include nanotechnology and robotic engineering. Complementing the Strategic Plan was the 1996 National Science and Technology Plan, providing a S$ 4bn (US$2.36) Five Year Programme for the enhancement of local R&D (NSTB, 1996). The aim was to develop Singapore as a regional R&D centre, employing 65 researchers per 10,000 workers. This, in turn, would help to achieve the government's overall vision of transforming the island-State into 'a world class science and technology base in fields that match Singapore's competitive strengths, spurring the growth of new high value-added industries'.[13]

The second factor assisting the defence R&D effort was the progressive commercialisation of DSO, moving it from a traditional cloistered government entity to a more networked, incentivised and innovative organisation. The corporatisation process began in 1997 when DSO became DSO National Laboratories. In 2000, the latter organisation was absorbed into the new Defence Science and Technology Agency (DSTA). The leaner, more flexible DSO, is now heavily engaged in collaborative research projects with local universities and government-owned enterprises, such as Singapore Technologies. Moreover, while DSO remains essentially focused on defence, it also seeks to exploit its dual use technology credentials by increasingly bidding for commercial sector projects.

Singapore's intense policy focus on civil-military R&D has led to the creation of an innovative, futuristic, RMA capability, supported by the efforts of over 2,000 highly skilled scientists and engineers.[14] This is evidenced by the nature of DSTA's R&D activities. For instance, in 2005, its biggest project was the computerisation of a stealth warship so that it runs on half the normal complement of crew (Seno, 2004: E24). Another high technology project is the development of an Advanced Combat Man System, producing a lightweight hand guard that controls an integrated laser range finder, digital compass and targeting camera (ibid.). The challenge for Singapore, as a small country, facing a spectrum of conventional and asymmetrical threats, is to achieve a balanced defence-related technology capability. Singapore has been successful in developing and exploiting its high technology resources and infrastructure to seize the opportunities offered by the contemporary RMA. This is particularly the case in the RMA-critical areas of precision weapons, command, control, and computer-processing (C^4I), and intelligence, surveillance and reconnaissance (ISR) (see Huxley, 2004). To ensure that momentum in these fields is maintained, MINDEF has formed a new Future Systems Directorate, tasked with developing and implementing future network centric warfare capabilities and enhancing future battlefield control.

These initiatives reflect changes in, and are a response to, Singapore's unpredictable strategic environment, and the operational priority of deterring conventional attack. Accordingly, continued development of RMA-type systems, such as airborne early warning and UAVs, will be critical to the SAF's maintenance of regional military supremacy.[15] However, Singapore faces broader security threats, including Indonesia's potential secessionist conflicts, as well as other regional 'complex emergencies', such as the prevalence of piracy, illegal immigration, disease, and environmental disasters (e. g., the Tsunami devastation of nearby Banda Aceh). Also, the emergence of international terrorism raises the spectre of asymmetrical conflict. Here, the range of threats includes cyber attacks, resource contamination, and nuclear, biological and chemical attacks to both military and civilian targets.

The growing threat of 'catastrophic terrorism' has added further complexity to the country's security framework. As has happened elsewhere, the emergence of international terrorism, particularly the radical Islamist group,

Jemaah Islamiyah, has led to shifts in MINDEF's policy focus but has done little to disrupt the focused development of SAF capability. Thus, efforts have intensified to protect installations and enhanced air-defences and expanded naval patrols are in train. Further capabilities will deal with chemical, biological, radiological and explosive threats while advancing doctrine and technology underpinning operations of the country's special forces will counter unfolding terrorist threats. Counter-terrorism resourcing is an additional layer of the SAF capability that integrates well into Singapore's changing defence posture. Thus, Singapore's policy-makers are seeking to ensure that investments in RMA-type capabilities are relevant to the potential of both high-intensity conventional warfare and the broad range of asymmetrical threats.

Cooperation: a trouble shared is a trouble halved

Small states invariably do not have the minimum critical mass to gain strategic and defence-industrial capability in all domains. A requisite of small country defence-development, therefore, is cooperation; the need to share the defence burden. There are two layers to Singapore's strategic cooperation model. The first has regard to the training of its military forces. With a heavily urbanised and densely populated territory, and only limited airspace, Singapore is clearly disadvantaged with respect to training opportunities. For example, the Army's training area has shrunk from 200 sq kms to 80 sq kms in the last 15 years.[16] In overcoming this limitation, the SAF has engineered training arrangements with other countries. The oldest is the 1971 Five Power Defence Arrangements with Australia, Malaysia, New Zealand and the United Kingdom. However, there are numerous other training relationships. For instance, the USA offers a broad array of training opportunities. Singaporean F-16C/D fighter pilots routinely train at two airbases in New Mexico and Arizona (Chang, 2003: 117). Singaporean personnel also train at an Army National Guard base in Texas to learn to operate and maintain CH-47D heavy-lift helicopters (ibid.). A similar training provision has been made for Singapore's AH-64D attack helicopters.

In 2003, the USA and Singapore jointly announced their intention to negotiate a Framework Agreement for the promotion of a Strategic Cooperation Partnership in Defence and Security. The aim of the Framework is to expand on the scope of current bilateral cooperation in areas of defence and security, such as counter-terrorism, counter-proliferation of weapons of mass destruction, joint military exercises and training, policy dialogues and defence technology.

Aside from the USA, SAF training takes place in Brunei, Indonesia, South Africa, Thailand and Taiwan. The Singaporean Air Force uses air and ground ranges in Sumatra; there are also squadrons operating from Oakley and Pearce Air Bases in Australia, where there is also a flying school and the basing of AS-532 helicopters and 27 S-211 jet trainers (ibid.). About 18 T/A A-4SU attack aircraft and 200 personnel are also assigned to Cazaux Air Base in

South Western France, offering bombing ranges and airspace over the Atlantic to practice combat (Tan, 1999: 461). Beijing offered military training facilities on Hainan Island in 2000, aimed perhaps at weaning Singapore off its long-standing use of Taiwanese training camps under an arrangement called Operation Hsing Kuang (Chang, 2003: 118). In 2004, the SAF conducted about 70 exercises with over 20 Armed Forces, an average of nearly 1.4 exercises per week with other countries.[17]

The second layer of cooperation is defence-industrial. In this regard, one of the most widely used mechanisms for forging cooperation with offshore defence contractors are offset requirements. Although Singapore has never published a formal set of offset guidelines, MINDEF has nurtured inward technology transfer to facilitate the development of an indigenous defence industry. Rather than employing the term, offsets, MINDEF prefers to euphemistically call them *Industrial Cooperation Programmes* (ICPs). Whatever the terminology, the process of absorbing, adapting and diffusing, particularly 'dual-use', technology has, by and large, worked well, not least because Singapore possesses the absorptive capacity to effectively digest and transform foreign technologies. The SAR 80 assault rifle (based on a design purchased from the British Sterling company) provides an early example of this successful transformation process. The gun went through several redesigns before the high-tech derivative, the SAR 21, was finally adopted as standard issue equipment (Huxley, 2000: 189). More generally, Singapore's ICPs have enabled its defence industry to develop the capacity, through licensed production, of converting and upgrading next generation weapon systems. Examples include the technological refurbishment of the RSAF's A-4s and F-5 fighters, the AMX-13 light tanks, the licensed production of Swedish Landsort-class mine-hunters, French LaFayette 3,000 tonne stealthy frigates, and, significantly, local design and production of the FH-88 (30km range) and FH-2000 (40km range) 155m howitzer guns, 'Fearless' class patrol vessels and 'Endurance' class 8,500-tonne landing ships.

Defence-related ICPs, negotiated on a case-by-case basis, have acted to develop the infrastructure and skills for creating and upgrading Singapore's defence-industrial base. As Singapore's defence capability has developed, the benefits from ICPs have become less clear as the costs of the offsets package have been incorporated into the product price. In some cases it was found that the cost of offset obligations had raised the price by as much as 7–8 per cent and, as contractors have exaggerated their costs, sometimes by a factor of ten, the 'real' value of the offset credits are seriously diminished.[18] Thus, although Singapore's policy approach is generally not in favour of offsets, licensed production is employed as a means of accessing foreign technology, but only after careful and cautious deliberation of the costs and benefits of this acquisition option. The important policy point is that for Singapore, judicious use of defence offsets has worked well over the years in promoting defence industrial capability. Significantly, Singapore is one of only a handful of countries, globally, where that claim could be made.

Conclusion

As a case study of 'small country' defence-development, Singapore has proved remarkably successful. Based on the island-state's Total Defence concept, scarce resources have been harnessed to construct a consensual society, a powerful economy, and a strong military, all committed to the defence of sovereignty. The constraints of 'small size' have been overcome by several factors: a sensible and visionary defence policy; a conscription and reservist manpower model; a 'dual-use' approach to defence industrialisation; a force multiplier policy aimed at exploiting Singapore's revealed technological comparative advantage; and a training and international diplomacy regime fostering friendly relations with some of the world's most powerful nations. Two caveats to this broad conclusion are highlighted, however. First, remembering that the overarching purpose of defence policy is the pursuit of effective military capability, it has to be noted that the SAF remains untested in anger, unlike, say, the Israeli Cahal. Second, while technology access through domestic licensed production appears to have produced positive social returns for the broader economy and specific returns for the SAF, there is a lack of evidence to unequivocally posit that offsets have proven to be the optimal 'development' option. Incontestable, however, is the fact that Singapore's national security strategy has led to this small country becoming the most militarily strong nation in South-East Asia. Perhaps an exception to the rule, but for the Lion-city, size appears unimportant.

Notes

1 In 2001, the island consumed roughly 1.2mn cubic metres of water daily, but Singapore's reservoirs provided only half that amount (Chang, 2003: 120).
2 The dispute has been referred to the International Court of Justice at The Hague for legal interpretation and adjudication.
3 This is reflected by the authorities' present pre-occupation with the development of local capabilities in the bio- and nanotechnology areas. In 2003, the Singapore government opened a US$300mn medical science park called Biopolis, housing five publicly-funded bio-medical research institutes, as part of the country's bid to become a global biotechnology hub.
4 Chinese culture is built around the important concepts of *mianzi* (losing and creating 'face') and *guanxi* (networking).
5 World Economic Forum (Davos, Switzerland) competitiveness rankings.
6 Online. Available at: http://www.mabico.com/en/news/20050218/foreign_exchange/article17782/.
7 See http://www.state.gov/r/pa/ei/bgn/2798.htm (accessed 26 April 2005).
8 The declining birth-rate will oblige the SAF to focus on smaller units, with enhanced firepower, better educated service personnel, adopt outsourcing strategies and accelerate computerisation and automation.
9 Statement by Minister Teo Chee Hean, Committee of Supply Debate 2005, Singapore: Singapore Government.
10 Within 24 hours, the SAF had stand-by teams ready for deployment; within 48 hours, a C-130 transport plane with relief and medical supplies had been despatched to Medan; within 72 hours, an advance medical team and two Chinook heavy lift

helicopters had also been deployed to Medan, followed later by two Super Puma helicopters despatched to Phuket Island; these were then followed by the despatch of three helicopter landing ships and the RSS *Endurance*, along with 470 specialised personnel, comprising medical, engineering, naval and communications experts (ibid.).

11 Statement by Singapore Chief of Defence Forces, Major General Ng Yat Chung reported in *Jane's Defence Weekly* (18 February, 2004).

12 See *Defense Daily International*, 3(24): 1 of 20 June 2003.

13 Ibid.: introductory page and vi.

14 Speech by Cedric Foo, Minister of State for Defence and National Development, Committee of Supply Debate 2005, Singapore.

15 Singapore is niching its expertise into future RMA technologies such as UAVs. For example, ST Aero is developing a vertical take-off and landing (VTOL) Fan Tail UAV. Work is also being conducted on a Long Enduring Endurance 'battle management' drone and collaborative work with Israel on advanced UAVs.

16 See http://www.austrade-gov.au/australia.

17 Statement by Minister Teo Chee Hean, Committee of Supply Debate 2005, Singapore.

18 Speech by Cedric Foo, Minister of State for Defence and National Development, Committee of Supply Debate 2005, Singapore.

References

Backman, M. (1995) *Overseas Chinese Business Networks in Asia*, East Asia Analytical Unit, Canberra: Department of Foreign Affairs and Trade.

Chang, F. K. (2003) 'In defense of Singapore', *Defense Daily International*, 3(24): 1. (20 June).

Drysdale, J. (1984) *Singapore: Struggle for Success*, North Sydney: George Allen & Unwin.

FI (2004) 'Singaporean spree continues', *Flight International*, 165/4922 (24 Feb – 1 March).

Huxley, T. (2004) *Defending the Lion City: The Armed Forces of Singapore*, London: Allen & Unwin.

—— 'Singapore and the revolution in military affairs: An outsider's perspective', *Journal of the Singapore Armed Forces*, 30(1): 33–44. Online. Available at: http://www.mindef.gov.sg/safti/pointer/back/journals/2004/vol30_1/4.htm (accessed 26 April 2005).

IISS (2007) *The Military Balance*, London: Routledge for the International Institute for Strategic Studies.

Karniol, R. (2004) 'Country briefing: Singapore-master plan', *Jane's Defence Weekly* 18 February.

Matthews, R. (1999) 'Singapore's defence-industrial "model"', *Asia-Pacific Defence Reporter*, April/May.

Nathan, S. R. (2002) 'Creating the technology edge', *Singapore 1972–2003*, Singapore: DSO National Laboratories.

NSTB (1996) *National Science and Technology Plan ... Towards 2000 and Beyond: Sensing Our Future*, Singapore: National Science and Technology Board.

Seno, A. A. (2004) 'Bond would love this', *Newsweek*, 144/16, 18 October.

SIPRI (2005) *SIPRI Yearbook, 2005*, Oxford: Oxford University Press for Stockholm International Peace Research Institute. Online. Available at: http://www.SIPRI.org/contents/MILAP/MILEX/apsod/SIPRIDATA.html.

Sobie, B. (2004) 'Building a future', *Flight International*, 165/4922, 24 Feb.–1 March.

Tan, A. H. (1999) 'Singapore's defence: capabilities, trends and implications', *Contemporary South-East Asia*, 21(3): 451–74.

10 Importing defence technologies

Why have Spanish policies changed?

Jordi Molas-Gallart

Introduction

Since the 1980s, Spain's defence industrial and procurement policies have undergone substantial transformation. In some areas of defence procurement change has been steady, often slow. Yet when it comes to importing weapons systems and defence technologies, Spain's approach has involved a number of shifts. This chapter explores the nature of these changes and discusses the reasons why policy in this has been so changeable. In so doing it illustrates a general theme of this book – that defence procurement decisions are forged in an overtly political context and within a process that itself evolves through learning from experience. In Spain, learning has focused importantly on the design and implementation of defence offsets and collaborative relationships with overseas suppliers. The Spanish experience offers potentially valuable lessons for other small- and medium-sized powers seeking to build domestic industrial and technological capability on defence procurement expenditures.

Throughout the last two to three decades, the main declared policy objective has remained the same: the pursuit of 'compensations' (countertrade and offsetting investments) from foreign suppliers to allow Spanish firms to upgrade their technological capabilities and thus strengthen the Spanish defence industrial base. But from an initial focus on offsets, the preferred approach for dealing with foreign suppliers changed in an attempt to extract better terms and adapt to changing circumstances. The policy shift explored here should thus be seen against a background of comparatively stable objectives, suggesting either that policy outcomes fell short of delivering the results initially expected, or that other political forces were at play, or both.

This chapter traces the factors that influenced the evolution of Spain's defence industry policy, and identifies three distinct phases in that process: (1) the early 1980s to the early 1990s – the era of offsets; (2) the early 1990s to the late 1990s – a period of programme-based international collaboration; and (3) the late 1990s to the mid-2000s – with its focus on foreign direct investment. In the light of changing political conditions locally and Spain's reactions to world events, the chapter concludes that such shifts look set to continue.

The 1980s: offset programmes

Shortly before the Spanish Socialist Workers' Party was elected to power in 1982, Spain agreed to buy 84 F-18s from the USA (the order was later reduced to 72). Accompanying the purchase was an offsets programme that was, by a substantial margin, the largest arrangement of its kind that Spain had ever put in place.

When Spain signed the offsets agreement, Spain's defence industry was mainly state-owned, fragmented into many small plants, in constant financial difficulties, and technologically backward by European standards. The purchase of the F-18 fighters was one of the largest acquisitions ever undertaken by the Spanish Armed Forces and came after a period in the mid to late 1970s when there had been no new large military procurement programmes. In the context of political and economic crisis of the early 1980s, the programme was highly unpopular: a planned expenditure of US$1.54 billion did not sit well with the double-digit inflation *and* unemployment besetting Spain at the time. That the programme would create jobs became one of the government's main arguments to win public support, a purely military rationale not being appreciated by a public opinion that regarded the military with suspicion. Central to the link between arms imports and job creation was the offsets programme, which became a key element in the political debate between 1981, when the decision to purchase the fighters was made public, and 1984, when the contract was signed.

Most of the negotiations and the eventual signing of the programme were carried out by the Socialist administration elected to power in 1982. The new government sought to modernise the Spanish Armed Forces, and developed a defence technology and industrial policy as a key component of a modernisation agenda.[1]

The F-18 offsets agreement was an early opportunity to implement fledgling policies to use defence procurement to support domestic 'high-technology' industries. Two main sets of objectives thus drove the early development of the offset programme. Politically, the initiative was an attempt to present in a positive light the contested acquisition of very expensive arms systems. From a procurement policy perspective, the goal was to leverage the import of weapons systems in support of domestic technological capabilities. The intertwining of political, economic and technology policy objectives would characterise the evolution of Spanish offsets policies throughout the following two decades.

The F-18 Offset Programme agreement was signed in July 1984. Under this agreement McDonnell Douglas (MDD) committed to offer offsets with a total value of US$1.8 billion over a period of ten years.[2] This was the largest and most complex contract of this type ever signed by Spain. It specified four different types of offset projects and established various targets, either ceilings or minimum levels, for different types of offsets. For instance, the contract limited the amount of indirect commercial offsets and established a minimum level of offsets involving technology transfer and work directly related to the F-18 project.[3]

The management of the offset programme proved a difficult and labour-intensive task. Although a dedicated office was set up in Spain to administer the programme (the '*Gerencia de compensaciones*', Offsets Management Office), its limited capabilities were soon overwhelmed with thousands of off-sets project applications. The procedure devised to run the project required the Office to approve proposals submitted by McDonnell Douglas. The Office had to satisfy itself that the proposals complied with a set of minimum requirements. For instance, indirect commercial offsets had to involve a net increase in Spanish exports: they could not substitute for trade flows already in place. It was up to the Office to determine, for every commercial offset proposal, whether the operation would represent new business for Spain as a whole, or merely substitute for already-existing commercial flows. In cases of technology transfer the Office had to assess the economic value assigned to the transaction.

McDonnell Douglas submitted thousands of offset project proposals, many of them very small. During the ten-year life of the offset programme 7,759 proposals were submitted, of which the Office rejected 1,190 (about 15 per cent). Of the more than 6,000 projects accepted, only a few were substantial in size or involved any form of technology transfer or learning. The result was a highly skewed distribution of projects: despite the large number of initiatives and over 400 firms involved in the scheme. Two companies alone (CASA and the electronics firm INDRA) accounted for almost 30 per cent of the value of all offsets received by Spain under the programme. Further, despite the very large number of proposals and projects, by the end of the ten-year period the targets set up in the contract had not been achieved. Under the initial arrangements for the programme, a three-year 'grace period' was to be negotiated. When the time arrived, the Spanish managers close to the pro-gramme felt that the large overhead costs of running it were not justified by the marginal benefits obtained. In the ensuing renegotiation and in other programmes launched during the 1990s, it was clear that hard lessons had been learned. A change was evident in the way Spain sought to derive industrial and other benefits from the acquisition of new weapons systems.

During the negotiations for the additional offsets that would have to be received during the three-year grace period for the F-18 programme, Spain sought to sharpen the focus of the offsets project by concentrating on a few selected objectives. In 1994, Spanish negotiators required offsets directly linked to maintenance and support tasks for the F-18 aircraft, and resisted suggestions to include indirect offsets in the programme extension. Spanish policy was evolving and Spain's adaptations to its weapons acquisition poli-cies showed the benefits of learning from experience.

Pursuing advanced technologies and direct offsets had already been an objective in the original F-18 offset programme, but the presence of a large component of commercial and other indirect offsets had diverted substantial management effort to other types of operation. By the end of the ten-year programme, the value of technology transfers and defence-related offsets was small when compared with the indirect commercial offsets.[4] This is not to say that the programme did not have any beneficial effects for Spanish technological capabilities. Although no systematic evaluation of the effects of this programme has been made public, there had been highly publicised cases of Spanish firms using the F-18 offset programme to build areas of expertise that they could subsequently incorporate in their technological portfolios and new investment programmes. One of the best-known examples is the work on simulators carried out by the Spanish electronics company CESELSA. The firm, now merged within the Spanish electronics conglomerate INDRA, continued to work in this field in subsequent years and has built a significant capacity that allows it now to participate in international programmes and/or develop its own systems.

It would also be unfair to assess the results of the F-18 offsets programme by standards applicable ten or twenty years later. When negotiating the F-18 acquisition in the early 1980s, Spain's ability to be directly involved in a programme of this kind was severely limited by its relatively backward and inexperienced industry. Thus, high proportion of commercial and indirect offsets arranged under the F-18 offsets deal has to be seen against the background of the limited domestic defence industry capabilities at the time.

During the late 1980s, Spain was determined to pursue a policy aimed at upgrading the technological capabilities of its struggling defence industry. Subsidies had traditionally been used to support the industry and, in practice, it was rare for the publicly-owned defence concerns to deliver profits in any single year. Yet, this support had usually been passive; defence firms, like the rest of the economy, conducted very little, if any, research, and concentrated on manufacturing tasks particularly within technologically mature sectors.[5] It was not until the 1980s that an attempt was made to energise the chronically under-resourced and lethargic Spanish science and technology system. The defence sector became a key field where a deliberate effort was made to support the development of 'high-technology industries'. Defence R&D rocketed. From the mid-1980s, Spanish defence R&D rose from negligible levels to almost 30 per cent of government *total* R&D expenditure in 1991. This was also part of an effort to bring the defence industrial base up to 'European level' and to involve it in European collaborative arms development and production programmes, which Spain was now able to access as a NATO and European Union member. Most of this new R&D investment was placed in European collaborative projects, and mainly in the then European Fighter Aircraft (EFA, later Eurofighter, and EF-2000), which in the early 1990s accounted for more than 60 per cent of all Spanish defence R&D investment.

The outcomes of these policies have been discussed in detail elsewhere (see Molas-Gallart, 1990, 1995). For the purposes of this chapter suffice to say that when the negotiations for the F-18 offsets 'grace period' took place in 1993, the structure of Spanish defence industry had already started to change.

Several firms were involved in international arms development and production programmes, and production experience and technological capacity was starting to grow. The 'grace period' negotiations turned out to be a tough affair and reflected a change in the relative strengths of the parties involved. It was no longer left to the US firms to present proposals for approval by the Spanish management: the composition of this last batch of offsets was to be specified and agreed *ex ante*. The Spanish negotiators now had a clear idea of what they wanted: direct offsets linked to the maintenance and support of the F-18 fighters. From the Spanish perspective, the monetary value of an offsets transaction was less important than its content and indirect offsets were, by and large, abandoned. In part, this change can be attributed to the cumulative experience of the 1980s offsets programme. In part, however, it represented a new commitment to international defence collaboration that Spain had made since the late 1980s.

The 1990s: From offsets to international collaboration

By 1993, the Spanish defence industrial and political landscape bore little similarity to that of ten years earlier. Spanish firms had gained experience in international collaboration, the domestic political situation had stabilised, and Spain was now an active member of NATO and the European Union. If anything, Spain was struggling to keep up with the raft of international arms development programmes which it had committed itself to in the late 1980s and early 1990s, when almost every European arms development programme that was launched had a Spanish partner. Spain was soon forced to cancel its participation in some programmes, but managed to keep its share of the most important (for Spain) European Fighter Aircraft programme.

Without any explicitly declared change in policy, Spanish arms acquisition programmes had quietly shifted their emphasis away from offsets and in favour of international collaborative arrangements. To a certain extent this shift had a political aspect. 'Buying American' meant buying military-off-the-shelf systems (MOTS), perhaps, but necessarily adapted to the needs of the Spanish Armed Forces. These purchases were accompanied by offsets. The collaborative projects were mainly European programmes and often invoked the principle of *juste retour*. Thus, 'Buying European' often meant contributing to the development of a new system within the framework of an international collaborative agreement where partners had an early say in the configuration of the system yet to be developed and could negotiate work-shares and areas of activity from a stronger position than that of a small buyer of MOTS systems.

Although work-shares could be negotiated prior to the launch of a project, international arms development programmes could, however, still generate problems. During the late 1980s and early 1990s Spain entered a myriad of collaborative projects, most of them European. Many of these projects were cancelled as partner countries proved unprepared to make the long-term and growing commitments necessary when projects evolved from their early development phases to the more costly stages of full-scale development, engineering and production. Often the remaining participants have to increase their commitments to salvage a project after other partners dropped out.

Exits, project failures and escalating participation costs were only three of the problems that international collaborative projects presented. In Spain, it was also feared that the role of Spanish firms in international projects could be marginal, given the low technological content involved. Through collaboration, some argued, Spanish industry risked losing capabilities painfully acquired over the years of protected programmes so that Spanish firms could end up as lower-tier subcontractors in a bigger, integrated European defence market. This type of argument was made with considerable vigour in the late 1980s when Spain was considering its degree of participation in the European Fighter Aircraft programme. Already in 1986 the '*Informe Castells*', a detailed study of Spanish science and technology commissioned by the prime minister's office, was arguing that international programmes could lead to the neglect of domestic initiatives. The report quoted an example widely debated during the following years: an embryonic domestic project for a light ground attack aircraft was in danger of being abandoned to allow domestic firms to contribute to the EFA programme (Melero, 1986). The defence of this domestic project (the AX aircraft) became commonplace among critics who believed Spain's level of commitment to international programmes to be excessive. This debate was, however, short-lived and today is all but forgotten. The AX did not get past the feasibility stage and Spain joined the EFA programme at a level of participation that stretched its limited industrial and technological capabilities.

Spain now moved towards specifying in more detail and up-front the 'compensations' that would accompany weapons systems purchases. The nature of the offsets agreements that Spain entered into during the 1990s changed in three main respects. First, in a clear departure from the F-18 model, in which the offsets were approved after the contract was signed, the compensations would now be negotiated together with the purchase of the system. The first example of such an approach took place as early as 1989 when the modernisation programme for Chinook helicopters negotiated with Boeing included detailed discussions of offsets tasks and projects that would accompany the programme. Second, the focus of offsets agreements shifted to undertakings that would cover the life-cycle of a project and offer support for systems maintenance and upgrade. There were different mechanisms to pursue this objective. In 1991, the acquisition of S-76 Sikorsky helicopters was accompanied by a life-cycle clause according to which the offset agreement would automatically extend to any other future acquisitions linked directly to the initial purchase (ISDEFE, 2004). The specific tasks covered by the agreement could also be targeted to cover work necessary for the maintenance and support of the systems, as had been the case with the extension period of the F-18 offset agreement discussed above. Third, indirect offsets were practically eliminated from Spanish offsets practice.

The distinction between collaborative projects and the new types of offset agreement became blurred. For instance, in the early 1990s the Spanish Armed Forces bought eight new Harriers and modernised 12 Harriers AV-8B already in service. The operation was structured as a joint programme between the USA, Italy and Spain for the development of a new Harrier variant. Tasks would include traditional 'local content' work and collaborative work related to the development of the Harrier variant to be operated by the Spanish and Italian air forces. Although the project was presented as 'collaboration', the extent to which the partners could affect the characteristics of the purchased system was constrained by the fact that the work was limited to relatively small changes in producing a variant of an existing aircraft. This was, in fact, closer to an offsets agreement than a collaborative weapons development agreement.

In the Harrier programme, as with most of the programmes that came to dominate Spanish arms acquisition policy during the 1990s, Spanish industry was involved from the early stages of the programme, following a division of tasks agreed to a large extent before the contract was signed. Theoretically, such 'collaborative' agreements allowed Spanish firms to interact more closely with their foreign senior partners and eliminated the need for micro-managing tasks that had absorbed so much effort in F-18 offsets programme.

In summary, during the 1990s the approach to the acquisition of foreign defence systems and technology changed markedly. International collaboration became the preferred procurement avenue, and the acquisition of foreign systems was accompanied by the up-front negotiation of direct defence offsets. The managerial effort needed to administer the complex system of indirect offsets in the F-18 programme drew Spanish managers and policymakers away from such an approach. With slowly improving technological capabilities opportunities to participate in collaborative programmes increased. This allowed Spanish buyers to concentrate on direct defence offsets when negotiating the acquisition of foreign arms systems. Life-cycle objectives featured prominently in Spain's negotiation strategies, which favoured offsets that were linked to the maintenance and operations of the imported systems.

Yet, for all these changes the policies did not shape up as a stable industrial strategy. The cancellation of many international collaborative projects in the early 1990s appeared a waste of scarce resources. Industrialists continued to complain about a lack of resources, and a gap emerged between ambitious policy declarations and poor implementation hampered by unreliable budgetary provisions. The concern persisted that Spanish participants in international programmes would be restricted to relatively 'low-tech' tasks.[6] All in all, participation in international programmes was seen by analysts close to Spanish defence industry as a fickle, often unreliable and mostly short-term response to the challenge of creating technological capabilities for Spanish industry.

In 1996, a new, right-wing government was elected to power. Under the Partido Popular administration, Spanish defence industrial policy witnessed yet another shift, and with it a new approach to international programmes. This third stage in Spain's evolving arms import policy focused on foreign direct investment (FDI) as a means of strengthening the domestic defence industrial base.

The 2000s: From programme-based collaboration to foreign direct investment

Procurement programmes had been used before to attract foreign capital to Spanish defence producers although on a modest scale. During the late 1960s and early 1970s, US and French firms took minority shares in state-owned Spanish defence companies in operations linked to specific procurement programmes. For instance, Northrop took a 20 per cent share in the Spanish aerospace firm CASA in 1965 when Spain bought 70 F-5 fighter aircraft to be assembled under licence by CASA.[7] This type of involvement proved to be short-lived. As the programmes that had led to their involvement were completed, the interest of the foreign shareholders faded and they progressively reduced their holdings.

In the late 1980s and early 1990s, a slightly different type of involvement emerged, this time connected to Spanish participation in the European Fighter Aircraft programme. Spanish aerospace subcontractors lacked the technological capability to be involved as independent subcontracts and, instead, set up joint ventures and new companies with European firms, thus becoming Spanish partners in joint entities supplying some of the fighter subsystems.[8] These joint operations, however, did not extend to the relatively larger Spanish prime contractors. ENSB, Izar (previously Bazán) and CASA continued to be 100 per cent state-owned. At the policy level, emphasis was given to the possibility of longer-term linkages with foreign partners to help develop the long-term technological capability of these firms. Foreign partners, it was hoped, would link Spanish defence industry to foreign state-of-the art industry capabilities and provide a more stable basis for its development. The policy also fitted well with the privatising philosophy of the new government. But attracting foreign investors to loss-making, state-owned defence companies was not easy.

The first large Spanish defence contractor to be privatised was the aerospace firm CASA. In June 1999, the Spanish Ministry of Industry and Daimler Chrysler Aerospace agreed a deal under which a new firm, DASA-CASA, was created and the public sector holding that had until then controlled CASA (SEPI) obtained a 12.5 per cent stake in the new international corporation. A few months later, in December 1999, DASA-CASA and Aerospatiale had agreed to form the European aerospace conglomerate EADS. The Spanish government thus relinquished ownership control over its most important military-related firm; CASA is now a junior partner in EADS.

This case shows how privatisation and internationalisation went hand in hand. Yet CASA's privatisation is different from other cases discussed here in at least two respects. First, it did not involve the acquisition of a Spanish company or part of it by a foreign corporation but rather was part of an international merger. Second, it was not linked to any specific defence acquisition programme.[9] The privatisation of ENSB, on the other hand, corresponds to the 'traditional' model involving the injection of foreign capital into Spanish firms linked to a procurement programme. Privatising ENSB was always going to be more difficult. ENSB had continually suffered losses since it was created as a result of a merger of pre-existing arsenals and other plants in the late 1950s. Its calamitous situation reached a low point in 1995 when it recorded losses three times its total annual sales. The government was eager to see the company's results improve and had long been involved in negotiations to attract private shareholders to the firm. The outcome is a telling example of the difficulties in linking procurement programmes to industrial policy measures.

In practice, ENSB's privatisation was linked to the programme to procure a new Main Battle Tank for the Spanish Army to replace the ageing AMX-30 built in Spain under French licence in the early 1970s. This procurement programme had been in the planning stages since the mid-1980s but had suffered several postponements due to political and budgetary problems. The ten-year, €1,800 million procurement contract was finally awarded in 1996, with the German Leopard 2 tank emerging as the winner. The acquisition involved the purchase of 225 tanks to be assembled under licence by ENSB over a period of ten years. In the meantime the Spanish Army would lease a fleet of Leopards.

Apart from the details of a local content package, the negotiations with the potential suppliers[10] included discussions on the future of ENSB and how the winning company would support it. There is little doubt that the intent was to link ENSB's (total or partial) privatisation with the tank procurement programme. Yet, the tank acquisition and the sale of the company were two distinct operations. And, while the German success in the tank competition had placed Krauss-Maffei as a clear frontrunner for the ENSB privatisation, a formal privatisation procedure had to be followed.

Eventually the publicly-held SEPI received three formal offers for the company: from Krauss Maffei, General Dynamics Land Systems, and the Spanish Unión Española de Explosivos. SEPI's CEO had hinted that a wholesale privatisation was not being considered: 'Talking about privatisation does not mean that the State will sell the firm, rather it means the entry of private shareholders bringing technology and commercial networks' (Ferreras, 1999).

Against this background, the decision to sell the whole company to General Dynamics, made in Spring 2000, came as a surprise. This was a full sale of the firm to a buyer who was the most direct global competitor of Krauss Maffei, the company that four years earlier had won the most important contract in which ENSB would be involved during the 2000s.

There were two reasons for this change in strategy. As a matter of politics, the previous Socialist administration that had backed the Leopard procurement programme had traditionally maintained close and friendly links with Germany.[11] The new Partido Popular leadership was more concerned with strengthening transatlantic links, and its relationship with its French and German allies was more distant and, at times, distinctively frosty. The pro-US shift in the political environment was reflected in defence procurement decisions. The sale of ENSB to General Dynamics was one among several other initiatives involving closer collaboration between Spanish and US firms.

The second reason for the sale of ENSB to General Dynamics pertained to the economic benefits offered by the American firm. Crucially, General Dynamics committed not to close any of ENSB's surviving plants for five years. Krauss Maffei, a smaller firm suffering financial difficulties, opted for a tougher position aiming to streamline ENSB into a profitable business as soon as possible. General Dynamics' willingness to make the financial effort to support the size of the loss-making firm clinched the deal. The Spanish government offered as its part of the deal the promise of future acquisitions that could help support ENSB's dispersed manufacturing facilities.

Initially there were doubts as to whether the Leopard contract would go ahead under the new ownership arrangements. But a system of 'Chinese walls' was set up separating all the work on Leopard from the rest of the company's operations. This strict separation of activities includes a set of detailed procedures, and is backed up by stiff penalties in favour of Krauss Maffei if these procedures are not followed. This system appears to be working. In addition, since the take-over, the US management has introduced new administrative, monitoring and auditing practices. Weekly reporting procedures are now in place across the company, and it is expected that these will result in efficiency improvements. However, the level of domestic orders appears to have fallen short of General Dynamic's expectations, triggering early, still private, tensions with the Spanish government.

The outcome of the process by which a procurement programme was informally linked to FDI raises a number of questions. First, in Spain, General Dynamics is producing the tank of its main competitor, Krauss Maffei. The extent to which the Spanish Leopard programme will achieve its objectives, and whether the system of Chinese walls will affect the development of ENSB's technological capabilities at a corporate level are yet to be seen. Second, there is clearly an attempt to attract foreign capital to the Spanish armaments industry and thus to create a more stable basis on which to build domestic defence industrial capability. Yet, the need to link this goal with specific procurement programmes is likely to generate difficulties. General Dynamics may find that the domestic Spanish defence market is not providing the opportunities it expected and tensions may emerge if, in the medium term, ENSB cannot yield a reasonable return for its new owners. The previous experience of procurement-linked FDI in Spanish defence firms during the 1960s and 1970s showed that, in the absence of a continuing stream of new programmes, and therefore orders, the involvement of foreign partners can be a fleeting affair.

Conclusions: policy drivers and policy instability

This chapter has traced the continuous shifts in Spain's strategies when import-ing defence systems or technologies. The way in which successive Spanish governments have tried to leverage arms procurement to support domestic industrial capabilities has evolved for both political and economic reasons. Policy learning derived from the implementation of previous programmes has interacted with political shifts that have changed the orientation of Spain's international policies and, consequently, its defence procurement decisions.

The lessons from policy implementation are probably the most important. With the benefit of hindsight, the F-18 offset programme proved to be an unwieldy programme to administer, dealing with too broad a portfolio of projects, lack-ing (from the Spanish point of view) a clear strategic vision. To make matters worse, it ultimately failed to deliver on its contractual commitments. The firms that benefited most from these investments were largely those that had received most of the F-18 direct offsets value: the main state-owned aerospace firm and public and private electronics companies. Throughout the 1980s, the Spanish government saw military demand as a source of incentives to technological development in key, 'high-tech' sectors of the economy. The implementation mechanisms, however, shifted away from the large offsets agreement that had dominated the mid-1980s towards more targeted direct offsets agreements and other collaborative approaches in which the local content of these programmes was discussed in detail *before* firm commitments were made.

In the 1990s, the *Offsets Management Office* changed its name to the *Industrial Co-operation Management Office*. The name-change was indicative of a shift in the approach to defence systems procurement in international markets. Yet continuity in the operations of the Office has been remarkable. As of mid-2000s, it was part of the state-owned defence systems engineering firm ISDEFE. It continues to advise on international defence industrial deals and negotiate industrial agreements on behalf of the Ministry of Defence. The same director had remained in post for 20 years and its offices (in the ground floor of an unassuming block of flats in the centre of Madrid) had remained in the same location. This continuity in the management of significant ele-ments of international procurement enabled the cumulative experience of many different projects to be translated into effective lessons for policy-makers. Spanish policies reflect learning and adaptation from each new set of procurement programmes. For example, the response to the heavy manage-ment overheads and dispersion of large offsets programmes was to increase the policy focus on direct offsets targeting maintenance and support and to move, whenever possible, to other forms of international acquisition.

International arms development programmes are, however, costly to run and often vulnerable to changes in the political and strategic priorities of the participating countries. International mergers and acquisitions can provide a structural link to foreign partners and integrate domestic industries into international production networks. However, if a national defence organisation wishes to retain and improve specific in-country technological capabilities, it may be compelled to provide a stream of domestic procurement projects to sustain targeted industry capabilities. As similar capabilities may already exist in other countries, the local content policy may ultimately support the involvement of foreign partners in Spanish defence production.[12] In addition to the large financial investments necessary, prior to privatisation, to return the ailing government-owned companies to the level of financial viability demanded by private investors, an ongoing flow of procurement programmes is needed to provide the orders needed for the firms' continuing profitable operation. It must be noted, however, that the situation in EADS-CASA, a firm now subsumed within a larger international corporation with interests in all areas of the aerospace industry, is likely to be different from that in ENSB. The latter is a specialised defence manufacturer with an overwhelming orientation towards the domestic military market that remains dependent on Ministry of Defence programmes to continue with production. Such dependence continued despite the new, now foreign, ownership of the firm.

Economic and managerial considerations have not been the only forces shaping the nature of Spanish international arms development and production policies. Political factors have also been important in defence procurement and have sometimes overridden decisions made by those involved in policy implementation. For instance, there had been several years of negotiations with Krauss Maffei to define the nature of their contribution to the future of ENSB and to determine how the Spanish Leopard manufacturing programme might strengthen ENSB. This work was rendered obsolete when the government decided to sell ENSB to General Dynamics.

The evidence presented in this chapter suggests that the relationship between political decision-makers and the offices and agencies in charge of policy implementation has been at times difficult. To explain the evolution of Spanish offset policies, it is necessary to acknowledge political factors as well as the pragmatic lessons learnt from policy implementation. The importance of such political factors was demonstrated again following the election of the Socialist administration in March 2004. The new administration explicitly sought to rekindle Spain's close links with Germany and France, while the country's relationship with the USA, to put it euphemistically, cooled. The withdrawal of Spanish troops from Iraq shortly after the election pointed clearly to Spanish-US differences and it appeared likely that such differences would affect the nature of Spain's approach to arms imports and defence industrial collaboration. These developments were, however, triggered by the political context, a context that, as we have seen in the recent past, is also unstable.

Notes

1 These policies are also analysed in some detail in Molas-Gallart (1990, 1992).
2 The amount was proportionally reduced to US$1.54 billion later when the number of planes to be acquired was reduced from 84 to 72. Officials stated that the value

of the offsets amounted to 100 per cent of the contract value, although this percentage was not contractually stated.
3 A more detailed analysis of this program can be found in Molas-Gallart (1996).
4 For instance, defence-related offsets (including direct offsets) accounted for only 28 per cent of total programme value.
5 For a comprehensive review of science and technology policy in Spain since 1939, see Sanz Menéndez (1997), and in particular its analysis of scarcity of resources available for research activities.
6 This is an enduring concern. A 2001 report from a research group with close links to the Partido Popular administration that ruled Spain between 1996 and 2004 states the concerns clearly when referring to the process of European defence industrial integration (my translation):

> The process of (European) integration also generates risks and uncertainties, especially for smaller and technologically weaker partners. Thus, the biggest risk for our (Spanish) industry is to be absorbed in this process of integration and be turned into a mere subordinate to the large industrial groups of the major partner countries.
>
> (GEES 2001: 2)

7 For an analysis of these deals and their impact on Spanish defence technology, see Ranninger (1987).
8 Rolls Royce's 49 per cent share in the newly created aero-engine components manufacturer ITP is the most important and best-known example.
9 On the contrary, the civilian turnover of the resulting entity, EADS, is larger than its military sales.
10 General Dynamics, for instance, had also been a competitor with a version of its M1 Abrams tank.
11 Some trace this 'special relationship' to the support that the German Social Democrats had given to their Spanish counterparts throughout the 1970s.
12 Probably, it is not a coincidence that the privatisation effort has been accompanied by large procurement programmes (Leopard for the Army; and EF-2000 for the Air Force) benefiting the privatised core defence systems manufacturers (ENSB and CASA).

References

Ferreras, P. (1999) *Entrevista. Pedro Ferreras. 'Queremos dar a nuestras empresas un proyecto ilusionante*, Ministry of Defence. Online. Available at: http://www.mde.es/mde/infoes/indus2/pen.htm (accessed 1 May 2000).
GEES (2001) 'La identidad española en la industria de defensa europea', *Análisis*, No. 11, Madrid: Grupo de Estudios Estratégicos.
ISDEFE (2004) *Evolución de la Gerencia de Cooperación Industrial*, ISDEFE. Online. Available at: http://www.isdefe.es/webisdefe.nsf/0/165211DE0F925633C1256B870054E235?OpenDocument (accessed 29 December 2004).
Melero, J. (1986) 'Las Nuevas Tecnologias y la Industria de Defensa', in M. Castells (ed.) *Nuevas Tecnologias, Economia y Sociedad en Espana*, Madrid: Alianza Editorial.
Molas-Gallart, J. (1990) 'Spanish participation in the international development and production of arms systems', *Defence Analysis*, 6(4): 351–65.
—— (1992) 'Military production and innovation in Spain', in K. Hartley and N. Hooper (eds) *Studies in Defence Economics*, London: Harwood Academic Publishers.

—— (1995) 'The Industrial strategies of military producers and the future of the defence firm in Spain', in A. Latham and N. Hooper (eds) *The Future of the Defence Firm: New Challenges, New Directions*, Dordrecht: Kluwer Academic Publishers.

—— (1996) 'From offsets to industrial cooperation: Spain's changing strategies as an arms importer', in S. Martin (ed.) *The Economics of Offsets: Defence Procurement and Countertrade*, Amsterdam: Harwood Academic Publishers.

Ranninger, H. (1987) 'La transferencia internacional de tecnología, teoría y evidencia. El caso de la industria militar española', doctoral dissertation, Facultad de Ciencias Económicas y Empresariales, Universidad Complutense de Madrid, Madrid.

Sanz Menéndez, L. (1997) *Estado, ciencia y tecnología en España: 1939–1977*, Madrid: Alianza Editorial.

11 From certainty to uncertainty

Sweden's armament policy in transition

Björn Hagelin

This chapter presents the case of a medium-sized country, Sweden, transitioning from a commitment to wide-ranging defence industry capabilities in support of 'armed neutrality' to a more selective subset of technological competences relevant to post-Cold War conditions. In the new environment, interdependence and international co-operation in acquisition are increasingly prominent features and although some medium-sized countries may differ from Sweden in their strategic posture, the challenges it now faces have a familiar flavour more generally. The Swedish dilemma is largely captured in the title of this chapter. After decades of apparent certainty, Sweden faces a number of rather confusing choices as to how to re-structure its defence-related industry and, in particular, how it is to be integrated into the international division of labour: what to make, what to import and what to export?

Historical context

Sweden's Cold War defence and security policy could, in summary, be defined as 'armed neutrality'. The policy developed during World War II in response to Sweden's experiences during the 1930s when, after a period of disarmament in the 1920s, it was unable to import the weapons it sought in the market. During World War II, the armed forces and industry engaged in advanced military research and development (R&D) in areas such as jet engines and other 'emerging' military technologies. Following an unsuccessful attempt to establish the Nordic Defence Union in 1949, Sweden chose to remain non-aligned and continue building an advanced military-industrial base over a broad range of military technologies. A post-war plan to become a nuclear power was, however, abandoned in 1968; the government believing such weapons could not be used in country against invading forces and might in themselves make Sweden a military target in a European war. (At the same time the Stockholm International Peace Research Institute (SIPRI) was established to celebrate Sweden's 150 years of non-participation in war.)

The rhetoric of Sweden's policy of armed neutrality was to prevail for about 40 years.[1] During that period, the electorate accepted the cost of a high level of military self-reliance because of what seemed like a convincing national security strategy. A sophisticated defence force with a 'Swedish pro-file' supported non-alignment and underpinned Sweden's military and poli-tical independence by: (1) deterring foreign attempts to influence its defence and foreign policies in peacetime; and (2) discouraging foreign powers from challenging its neutrality in wartime. Official military doctrine contained the implicit assumption that Sweden would only be attacked by the Soviet Bloc in the event of a major European war. Unless nuclear weapons were used, the Swedish Armed Forces would be effective against the limited Soviet forces available to invade Sweden.

For over 20 years, the policy of armed neutrality was beyond political question and the rhetoric of commitment to armed neutrality continued until the end of the Cold War. This allowed close relationships to develop between the Social Democratic government and the Armed Forces, the Defence Procurement Agency (FMV), defence-related industry, and research agencies such as the National Defence Research Institute (FOA) and the Aeronautical Research Institute (FFA). The country's defence industry was not only regarded as 'guarantor' of national security, it was also an important employer expected to contribute to regional development and national economic growth.

From the mid-1970s, however, the high cost of staying at the forefront of much of the spectrum of advanced military technologies was becoming apparent. Sweden's need for military and political independence and high defence expenditures all became the subject of national debate.[2] There were other social priorities and the superpowers were by now pursuing policies of limited accommodation (détente). Many Swedes thus concluded that military expenditures could be reduced. Military expenditures and arms exports also came under international scrutiny. A 1981 United Nations (UN) study suggested a positive correlation between disarmament and economic devel-opment. The terms 'military conversion' and 'peace dividend' entered common usage throughout the world (UN, 1981). And, in 1984, the Swedish Ministry for Foreign Affairs produced a national 'case study' of conversion that suggested that a peace dividend could be harvested locally (Swedish Government, 1984).

Although the concept of a peace dividend remained politically con-troversial, declining demand in any case caused the domestic military market to shrink and Sweden's military-industrial base embarked on a process of transformation through mergers and acquisitions.[3] By the 1980s, there were fewer major companies increasingly specialising in either military or civilian production (see Hagelin, 1997).

Defence companies now looked abroad for new business opportunities and export orders to sustain development, production and employment. This presented the government with a dilemma. Since the 1970s, politicians had unofficially recognised the benefits of international military co-operation and increased exports. But this would have been contrary to Sweden's formal policy of military self-reliance and its public commitment to arms export

restrictions. Political support for sustaining a technologically advanced military-industrial base in Sweden thus persisted and the scope for international
military cooperation was limited to R&D cooperation with the 'N-countries',
i.e., the European neutrals and the Nordic countries. Military exports continued to be viewed as exceptional and export guidelines remained restrictive.
But the dilemma had to be confronted during the 1990s as the relative stability of the Cold War years gave way to the uncertainties of a post-1990
'lukewarm' peace.

How Sweden has dealt with these challenges is explored in the remainder of
this chapter. The following section describes developments from the early
1990s – changes to the overall security policy environment, the military-
industrial base, military-technology policy, institutional relationships around
defence procurement and trade patterns in military products. This helps in
understanding why the traditional policy of armed neutrality was abandoned.
The next section discusses implications of these changes and lessons from the
Swedish experience are drawn in the final section.

Dimensions of change

The changing defence environment: policy objectives, budgets and organisation

In the 1990s, Sweden, together with France, Germany, Italy, Spain and the
UK, laid the foundations for Europe's military-industrial future through a
Letter of Intent (LoI) process aimed at restructuring European defence
industry and the development of Europe's security and defence policy
(ESDP).[4] This may suggest that Sweden should have been well positioned to
meet the new military-industrial and national security challenges but a
number of significant hurdles lay along the way.

Despite the impediments to change, Sweden's defence policy is now no
longer based on preparing for (Soviet) invasion in a European war but, rather,
to defend against armed attacks of any sort. It seeks to maintain Swedish
territorial integrity; contribute, jointly with other countries, to peace and
security in the world; and assist Swedish society in times of severe civil
emergencies (Swedish Government, 2004a: 5). To achieve such objectives, the
nation's armed forces need to be flexible, versatile and 'network-enabled'
(network-centric).

About the only certainty in the early 1990s was that the size of Sweden's
military organisation and its self-reliance ambitions were unsustainable.
Since 1992, Sweden has been transforming its military capabilities to fit new
but largely undefined military demands. It has been suggested that the associated reductions in manpower, number of units and training will eventually
turn out to be bigger than any undertaken since the 1920s.[5] But there have
also been major impediments to speeding up the decommissioning of old
systems as well as to restructuring politically sensitive elements of the

military-industrial base still fulfilling orders for platforms designed during the Cold War, and to creating an alternative, slimmed-down industrial structure. The military roles the industrial base will in future be expected to support remain unclear.

The uncertainty of the current environment has made Swedish defence and security policy a hotly contested political issue. The *Swedish Defence Review* (also referred to below as the *2004 Defence White Paper*) was withdrawn a month after its initial release in September 2004 in the face of strident parliamentary criticism. An ensuing political debate revolved around how to spend the defence budget and implement force restructuring, and a political majority allowing a way forward was achieved only when the Social Democrats and Greens made concessions to the left. When the government directed the Commander-in-Chief to assess the consequences of reductions additional to those specified in the Review, the CIC proposed cancelling of major domestic projects and replacing them with imports.[6]

The additional cuts followed reductions already partially implemented and the GDP share of Sweden's defence expenditure, below 3 per cent during the 1980s, continued its decline in the 1990s. In the years following 2001, it dropped below 2 per cent (see Table 11.1). Real defence expenditure, however, remained relatively stable, reflecting the difficulty of making cuts in key areas.

Since 1994, Sweden has participated in a number of international peace-keeping and peace-enforcement missions as part of its involvement in Partnership for Peace (PfP) and has also taken part 'in the spirit of PfP' exercises. The Swedish Armed Forces International Centre (SWEDINT) was established in 1997 and is recognised as a 'PfP regional training centre'.[7] In 2003, about 14 per cent of Sweden's military personnel served abroad.

Between 1995 and 2003, reduced demand halved the number of conscripts enlisted each year, and the employment of military and civilian personnel also decreased significantly (Table 11.1).[8] This mirrors a two-thirds reduction in the number of military units. By 2001, defence activities in 19 garrison towns had been closed and the land and installations mostly sold. Reductions continued in 2002–3 and in 2004 the closure of another seven locations was decided (Swedish Government, 2004a).[9]

Traditionally, Sweden's concept of 'total national defence' comprised four parts: military defence, civil defence, psychological defence and economic defence. With the disappearance of the Soviet military threat and increased focus on transnational crime and terrorism, this four-part structure of national defence effort has changed. In particular, since 2002, responsibility for economic defence, primarily concerned with the security of critical supplies (e.g., emergency stocks of oil) has been vested in a new agency: the Swedish Emergency Management Agency (SEMA). SEMA works with municipalities, county councils and central government authorities, the business community and other public and private organisations to reduce the vulnerability of the economy to external shocks.[10] Military units may also be tasked to assist in major civilian emergencies, including terrorist attacks.[11]

Table 11.1 Swedish defence characteristics

	1994/95	1995/96	1997	1998	1999	2000	2001	2002	2003
Defence expenditure									
Current (SEK million)	36,622	41,932	37,580	38,767	40,372	42,227	41,077	40,668	41,069
Constant (2000 US$ million)	4,564	3,001	4,392	4,515	4,689	4,861	4,610	4,486	4,363
Share of GNP (%)	2.6	2.3	2.1	2.0	2.1	2.1	< 2.0	< 2.0	< 2.0
Defence employment									
Military personnel (no.)	16,900	16,700	16,100	15,300	14,700	13,700	12,800	12,200	12,000
Civilian personnel (no.)	13,600	13,300	11500	10,800	10,600	10,500	10,120	10,600	10,400
New conscripts (no.)	33,600	50,100	23,900	19,200	18,800	17,000	13,700	14,500	15,500
Units									
Military units (no.)	145	144	139	113	111	71	69	61	58
International activities									
Peacekeeping ops. and tasks (no.)	14	16	16	19	28	20	15	18	16
Training exercises (no.)	–	12	16	18	16	16	12	25	

Sources: M. Johnsson, Military HQ, C GRO Plan, Nov. 2004; *Försvarsmaktensårsredovisningar* (Defence annual reports), Stockholm: Military HQ, annual; and SIPRI (2004: 355) (US$ figures).

Notes: Defence expenditure figures for 1995/96 cover 18 months. Military units include garrisons, schools, centres, staff units, and a few other units. The numbers for international participation are rough figures since the annual reporting format changed over time. The figures for international peace ops/tasks cover Swedish participation in planning and/or operations, while the international training figures cover Swedish participation in bi- and multi-lateral exercises (figures not available for 1994/95 and 1995/96).

The changing military-industrial base

Three overlapping phases characterise the recent restructuring of Sweden's military-industrial base. First, domestic mergers and acquisitions resulted in an increased concentration of military production in fewer companies. Second, privatisation and internationalisation increased during the 1990s and bilateral industrial cooperation increased. Also, the foreign ownership of military companies in Sweden was accepted. Third, industrial aspirations changed from 'strategic' to niche-focused, reflecting Sweden's increased willingness to participate in multilateral collaborative projects.

By 2003, about 14,000 people were directly involved in defence-related production compared with over 20,000 in 1991. Labour force shrinkage is likely to continue as major projects reach completion, technological ambitions become more limited and multinational cooperation increases.[12] From the relatively large number of Swedish companies active in 1990, four major military companies or groups have emerged: the Saab group (including Saab-Bofors Dynamics), BAE Systems Bofors, BAE Systems Hägglunds, and Kockums. One other major company, Volvo Aero is also involved in defence-related activities (aero engines). Nammo Sweden and EURENCO Bofors are Swedish subsidiaries of multinational manufacturers of munitions and explosives.[13] They illustrate the transnationalisation of the military-industrial base (see also Hagelin, 2000).

Since 1993, Swedish arms export policy has made international military-industrial cooperation in R&D and manufacture an official government objective.[14] Under the policy, the N-countries ceased to be Sweden's only officially designated military-industrial partners, state-owned military companies were privatised to compete in the global market, and foreign ownership of military companies was allowed. In consequence, the four major companies became partly or wholly foreign-owned (see Table 11.2). In 2004–5, BAE Systems reduced its ownership share in Saab but acquired the British vehicle producer Alvis and the US military vehicle and artillery producer United

Table 11.2 Foreign shareholders in military companies in Sweden[a]

Company name	Foreign shareholder (% share)	Product lines
BAE Systems Hägglunds	BAE Systems, UK (100)	Land vehicles
BAE Systems Bofors	BAE Systems, UK (100)	Artillery and ammunition
Kockums AB	Thyssen Krupp, Germany (75)	Surface ships and submarines
Saab AB	BAE Systems, UK (20), plus a mix of Swedish and foreign owners	Aircraft and a variety of other aerospace/advanced systems

Note: [a] For details, see *NATO's Nations and Partners for Peace*, 2004. No. 1: 174–6. See also *Jane's Defence Weekly*, 4 May 2005, pp. 23–6. Simon Surry, SIPRI research associate, assisted in compiling this and other defence industry-related information.

Defence. As a result, BAE Systems remained a shareholder in Saab but also became the owner of Hägglunds and Bofors Defence AB.[15] By the mid-2000s, among the major military producers, only Volvo Aero remained 100 per cent Swedish-owned.

The shift in Swedish defence industry policy has led to a Swedish military-industrial base that comprises military companies located in Sweden rather than Swedish military companies (ibid.: 125–38). The traditional goal of military-industrial independence has been replaced by dependence on foreign shareholder interests and an acceptance that Swedish military orders alone are insufficient to sustain major defence producers. While defence-related employment in Sweden has declined, the Saab group bought a majority share in a Finnish systems integration company in 2004 and declared that foreign acquisitions would be its major strategy.[16]

While some major Swedish military companies were already members of the European Defence Industry Group (EDIG) and/or the European Association of Aerospace Industries (AECMA), they and defence R&D agencies have more recently also joined other multilateral structures such as the European Research Establishments Association (EREA), the Western European Armaments Group (WEAG)[17] and the LoI framework (the latter two in 2000). Between 1993 and 2003, 38 new permissions were granted for bilateral military cooperation with the UK, Germany and France. Together with the USA, these countries accounted for 50 per cent of all new Swedish (bilateral) permissions during this period.[18] In 2004, AECMA, EDIG and the Association of the European Space Industry (EUROSPACE) strengthened their common base for influencing EU policy by merging into the AeroSpace and Defence Industries Association of Europe (ASD).[19]

The first Swedish agreement on multilateral military industrial cooperation was signed with France and Germany in 2002, and involved the manufacture of front fuselages for the NH90 helicopter acquired by Sweden jointly with other Nordic countries. It was followed by an agreement with France and Finland in 2003 to establish the Eurenco company.[20] In 2004, two multinational agreements were signed with France and Spain and with Germany and the USA. Military companies in Sweden now participate in private multilateral projects not formally involving government-to-government agreements or facilitation by the Swedish Defence Procurement Agency, FMV.

Table 11.3 shows the large number of bi- and multi-lateral industrial cooperation agreements signed by 2004. Sweden was by then party to several international agreements of military-industrial or defence policy relevance. In addition to the LoI, these agreements included the Thales memorandum in 1996, facilitating joint programmes between government research organisations, and the 'European Understandings for Research Organisation, Programmes and Activities' (EUROPA) signed in 2001 covering a wide variety of long-term research and technology (R&T) projects and programmes. Sweden joined the NATO Partnership for Peace (PfP) programme in 1994 and since 1995 has been a full member of the European Union (EU), participating in

Table 11.3 Swedish bi- and multi-lateral military-industrial cooperation agreements, 1995–2004

	1995	1996	1997	1998	1999	2000	2001	2002	2003	2004
Active licence agreements (no.)	90	85	84	85	76	82	95	104	115	109
New licence agreements (no.)	0	2	5	5	6	5	5	3	5	6
Active co-dev./co-prod. agreements (no.)	76	76	81	111	69	77	80	79	86	91
New bilateral co-dev./co-prod. agreements (no.)	6	8	11	14	9	12	16	9	9	13
New multinational co-dev./ co-prod. agreements (no.)								1	1	2

Source: *Regeringens skrivelse till riksdagen om vapenexporten* (2004) [Government report to Parliament on arms transfers], Stockholm: Swedish Government, annual.

joint European military planning and operations.[21] In 2004, Sweden became a member of the European Defence Agency (EDA) and secured the position of EDA Director for Industry and Markets.[22] Sweden, Finland and Norway also declared their intent to establish an EU Battle Group in accordance with EU defence policy.[23]

Changing military technology policy

Sweden's military technology ambitions remain high but, in contrast to the previous policy of broad military-industrial self-sufficiency, its strategy has come to emphasise selectivity – sustaining specific 'niche' competitive technological competences. It comprises three elements: (1) focusing on advanced but narrow military-technological niche competences; (2) seeking civil-military synergies from private, government and university R&D; and (3) international cooperation. The change in policy focus was apparent in the *2004 Defence Review* and can also be seen at work in policy implementation.

Long-term defence-related national *technological competences* (thus, technological niches) are defined by the Armed Forces' R&T programs (SAF, 1997, 2002).[24] It is hoped that these technological competences can generate and underpin competitive advantage for Swedish industry, drawing, however, on international cooperation when necessary. Among the roughly 20 S&T areas, the largest research projects by the Defence Research Establishment (FOI) and the National Defence College (NDC) concern weapons effect and protection (WEP), and electronic warfare. Joint developments by the FMV and industry mainly involve technology demonstrators, sensors and to some extent WEP. Sensors and WEP were the two largest R&T programmes in 2002, while technology demonstrators topped the list in 2003.[25] The *2004 Defence Review* specified the main areas for future R&T as command and network-centric solutions, aerial vehicles, ground vehicles, short-range systems and robust telecommunications. Sweden, through Saab, was to cooperate with France (via EADS) on developing aerial vehicle technology.[26]

Sweden also has a focus on developing *civil-military synergies,* i.e., military benefits derived from adopting civilian technologies in areas of military importance, a counterpoint to the older idea of creating spin-offs, which relates to the civilian diffusion of military technologies (see Hagelin, 2004). Civil-military synergies are being sought through national and international networks linking private and public sector organisations and universities. A general civil strategy for innovative synergies in support of economic development was presented in 2004,[27] as well as a blueprint for a Swedish R&D structure better suited for EU R&D programmes.[28] The National Aeronautical Research Programme (NFFP) was established in 1994 and extended to 2008, and a national strategy for security research to position Sweden in EU security research was promulgated in February 2005.[29]

The changing role and relationships of the FMV

The traditional Swedish acquisition process involved close and direct contacts between the Armed Forces, the FMV (the Defence Procurement Agency) and Swedish defence companies under arrangements forged by a partnership between the Social Democratic Party and big business. This structure came under pressure as a result of military-industrial cooperation in international projects generating outputs for which the Swedish government was not the final purchaser. In 2004, a report by Sweden's Audit Organisation (*Riksrevisionen*, RIR), analysed three international missile development projects, none of which was set up by the Swedish government but all of which involved the participation of Swedish companies.[30] The report suggested that when Sweden was a minor partner (e.g., a sub-contractor in an international project), FMV's influence when buying on behalf of the Swedish Armed Forces could be undermined (RIR, 2004).

The *2004 Defence Review* proposed: (1) strengthening the hand of 'Swedish' military companies in international projects by defining their role as 'partners' rather than sub-contractors; and (2) making Swedish companies working as technology integrators responsible for delivering specific weapons systems while FMV concentrated on the nation-wide 'system of systems'.

Exports and imports

A shrinking national market, coupled with a continuing emphasis on advanced military technologies, has made Sweden increasingly dependent on exports. The export share of Sweden's military production increased by nearly 50 per cent between 1998 and 2004 (see Figure 11.1). Most exports have involved war-fighting equipment as opposed to support services and dual use products. The trend is probably strongly influenced by Saab, the largest military producer, whose export share accounts for about 50 per cent of production.[31]

With increasing Swedish participation in international R&D and manufacture, the export share of production is likely to go on rising. The *2004 Defence Review* envisaged an increased export share underpinning the development and sustainability of defence-related industrial technologies and competences (Swedish Government, 2004a: 132–3). Exploiting export possibilities may be considered a part of the national acquisition strategy particularly in the light of a new emphasis on exporting technology and services within defined niches. Such exports are expected to result from technology demonstrators and collaborative development work on system concepts rather than from trade in individual weapons. Exports of services are also likely to increase as foreign nations make greater use of Swedish test and training facilities.[32]

Part of the new emphasis on exports includes leasing major weapons systems to foreign nations or companies (e.g., the leasing of a submarine, including crew, to the US Navy[33]). Although sales are preferable, leasing can bridge the gap between a signed order and delivery, as illustrated by the lease of Gripen combat aircraft to the Czech Republic in 2004.

A 2005 review of Sweden's arms export policy suggested that government arms imports be reported to better fulfil Sweden's commitments to the UN, the OSCE and under the Wassenaar Arrangement. An often-cited official figure for Sweden's self-sufficiency in arms procurement has been 70 per cent. In certain technologies and weapon categories, however, the import share was known to be 100 per cent and some indigenous manufacture took place under licence from foreign firms (e.g., jet engines, elements of electronics). None of Sweden's combat aircraft would have been in the air, or armed with advanced air-to-air missiles, had it not been for arms imports.

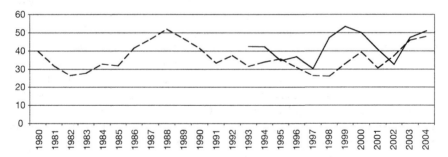

Figure 11.1 The share of Sweden's military exports in total military production and in war-fighting equipment, 1980–2004 (%)

Source: Regeringens skrivelse till riksdagen om vapenexporten (2004) [Government report to Parliament on arms transfers], Stockholm: Swedish Government, annual.

Note: The continuous line represents the percentage share of war-fighting equipment, while the dotted line shows the export share of all military products.

Implications of changing security policy

Two of the three components of Sweden's security policy were revised during the 1990s: independence became interdependence, and neutrality in wartime was no longer the only, or even most likely, option should there be a war in Europe. Only non-alignment to NATO remained as a formal policy although Sweden is a (NATO) Partner for Peace and EU member taking part in military planning and operations and, while not an 'ordinary' NATO member, Sweden has formed (with Norway and Finland) an EU Battle Group. Sweden's 2004 Defence Review argued that increasing European co-operation had increased confidence in the potential success of joint military action. It was thus unlikely Sweden would be completely alone should its basic security interests be threatened. That said, the new stance brought its own dilemmas. How should Sweden balance national aspirations to retain technological competences and minimise risk with new commitments to international cooperation in acquisition? And with which countries should Sweden seek to forge such international arrangements?

International cooperation, acquisition risks and supply chain dependability

Just as the limitations of Sweden's ambitions for self-sufficiency were not publicly acknowledged, there is also a reluctance to concede the potential national security risks from Swedish participation in international co-operative ventures – now the key element of Swedish political and industrial strategy. For example, while national projects are risky in that a domestic supplier may fail to deliver what is expected of it, within budget and on schedule, the Swedish government, through its procurement agency FMV, may have considerable leverage to influence the project outcome. At the very least, FMV is in a strong position to decide whether to continue with the project as is, re-contract or cancel it. In the case of an international collaborative project, Sweden is only one of potentially several partner nations. As more players are involved, pursuing potentially diverse national and commercial interests, there is a risk that the end product may not meet specific Swedish requirements or, for reasons unrelated to the Swedish involvement in the project, that it may not be completed as intended (or, indeed, at all). The possibility that an international participant may withdraw from a joint project is an example. On the other hand, the involvement of several nations in a project may also increase the likelihood of a successful outcome as governments keen on making the project a success put pressure on nations reluctant to keep going. As in all equity-sharing arrangements, the dynamics of the relationship between the parties can only be determined in a project-specific context. While international collaborative projects are not *inherently* more risky than uni-national ones, it is clearly harder for a government of a small country, that pays only a proportion of the total cost and is not a significant source of future demands, to wield more influence than its equity in the venture.

To address the challenges of procurement in an environment of international collaboration, there is a heightened awareness of the need to focus on success in achieving defined military specifications, cost targets and delivery times in military projects. While it is perceived that some aspects of projects are relatively susceptible to control, it has been recognised that others – often arising from external influences and risk factors – lie beyond the direct control of the project manager. The Swedish notion of 'acquisition security' bundles together all forms of threat and risk to the delivery of a system as specified, on time and within budget.[34] To deal with all aspects of 'acquisition security', the *2004 Defence Review* suggested that decisions should be made on a step-by-step basis as projects proceeded from one phase to another. Also, small batches should be ordered initially with an option for further acquisitions in future (incremental or evolutionary acquisition).

The term 'acquisition security' can also be interpreted more broadly to include, in contradistinction to risks specific to the initial acquisition of equipment (project-specific risks), risks associated with the provision of through-life logistic support for and future upgrades and modifications of the equipment. As discussed at length in Part I of this volume, risks associated with the sustainment of a military capability over time are normally different from those specific to the initial acquisition of capability elements. Thus, the *dependability of a supply chain* that sustains an asset in use, especially during military contingencies, is critical for a country that aspires to a degree of military independence. The availability of industry and technological support capabilities in-country normally reduces the vulnerability of the supply chain to external shocks, as spare parts, consumables and modifications can be made domestically rather than having to be imported from abroad. However, stationary industry facilities are also highly vulnerable during military emergencies.

Thus, the sourcing of equipment through international collaborative projects may impact on 'acquisition security' in a variety of ways. On the one hand, it may be more difficult to sustain equipment in use when IP and manufacturing capabilities are dispersed between a number of countries. On the other, supply lines may be less vulnerable during major conflicts as they are more dispersed and alternative sources of supply are easier to arrange. Small countries like Sweden will also have to decide whether strategic stock-holdings of spare parts and consumables acquired up-front improve 'acquisition security' by reducing the risk of potential supply chain disruption.

Defence industry partners

Sweden's major military-industrial partners are the Nordic countries, the LoI co-signatories and the USA. Non-Nordic suppliers have always been more important to Sweden than Nordic suppliers. For the period 1993–2003, for example, Germany led the USA as main source of supplies to Sweden. But the historic importance of the USA to Sweden is reflected in the fact that

Sweden's first bilateral defence-related government-to-government agreement was signed with the USA in 1952. And today, there exists a Swedish-US 'Declaration of Principles' for enhanced cooperation in matters of defence equipment and industry.[35]

The experience of collaborative Nordic acquisitions in the 1990s casts doubt over the real value of the 'Nordic arms market' (see Hagelin, 2005). Although cost savings have probably been achieved through intra-Nordic co-operation, they have probably been small. It has been difficult to pool national requirements to achieve scale economies through joint acquisitions and the scope for collaborative efforts in future is limited since major increases in national military expenditures are unlikely. Further, the establishment of the EDA in 2004 may limit the room for particular sub-regional defence equipment cooperation like the Nordic arms market in favor of broader coordinated solutions among the EU members.

Lessons from Sweden's experience

Sweden relatively quickly adjusted its defence and national security *policy* and its military-industrial *strategy* to the post-Cold War security environment. However, the *implementation* of the new approach has proved more challenging and has taken longer to achieve. The government has not been able to define and implement an effective process for achieving a smaller defence industry base and more flexible Armed Forces. On the other hand, the industrial transformation started when the Cold War ended and it might even be said that the speed and smoothness of the change suggest Sweden's self-sufficiency aspirations were unattainable in the first place. The unpublicised foreign military trade and technology transfers that developed during the Cold War have become apparent and provided the basis for a new policy. This history suggests that the rapidity and success of similar transformations in other countries may depend on the realities of their earlier experience too. History counts – whatever politicians may have said or admitted in earlier years to disguise politically unpalatable realities.

As this chapter notes, Sweden has retained military-technological ambitions, and the pursuit of niche competences and greater international cooperation offer the potential for increasing trade in defence-related goods and services. While the in-country design, development and manufacture of military platforms (and any associated employment) are likely to decline, Sweden could, like other countries, find new opportunities for non-military employment growth in civil-military synergies. And while Sweden's offsets policy is controversial, it is likely to remain in place as long as other trading and project partners impose offsets demands, presenting the potential for both benefits and cost for all involved.

Further EU-isation of military development and acquisition may be expected as Swedish procurement decisions are linked to EU and NATO standards and interoperability and the importance of 'Swedish identity' declines. Building links to larger economic and strategic groupings are common occurrences for smaller and medium-sized countries around the world and the implications of such developments for Sweden are thus likely to be relevant to similarly placed nations. Growing multinational co-operation may well re-fashion the traditionally close relationships between the government, the FMV, military companies and the Armed Forces and transform FMV's traditional role as buyer of major weapons for the Swedish Armed Forces. It is still not clear how the commercial interests of foreign shareholders and Swedish government demands are to be balanced.

Should the EU establish a common military R&D and procurement market seeking to make more efficient use of European industrial and technological skills in competition with the USA, the transatlantic debate about 'Fortress Europe' is likely to be re-opened. Should, however, the USA allow greater European participation and technology sharing in its military market and projects, this might create a 'British dilemma' for Sweden, i.e., how to balance its participation in European and US projects. This is especially so if the EDA and/or EU programmes show limited success. EU-US relations will be important to Sweden as there are strong Swedish political, military and military-industrial demands for sustaining close and good relations with the USA as well as with Europe. Medium-sized countries inside and outside the EU face the same issues.

The Swedish dilemmas over conflicting policy goals are common to most countries, large and medium-sized, and each country has to resolve such dilemmas for itself. To the extent, for example, that domestic defence-industry production was seen as valuable for achieving national job-growth targets, other countries too will have to think through the employment implications of their increasingly internationalised procurement programs. While the institutional relationships in other countries may not replicate the Swedish case, the bigger lesson is that moves towards multinational procurement arrangements are bound to re-shape the nature of domestic institutional links forged in a world focused more on maximising local content. Some may think this is for the best but, as the Swedish case suggests, medium-sized countries will need to be wary of the threats to their sovereignty in procurement decisions when powerful foreign government and commercial interests are involved.

Notes

1 Sweden's neutrality was an adopted national policy and not a guarantee of its sovereignty by international powers.
2 The Swedish Peace and Arbitration Society was the major NGO involved. Publications that contributed to the debate include Hagelin (1974, 1977, 1978, 1985, 1986).
3 The counter-disarmament argument that military expenditures support economic growth became a public and an academic issue, and several studies questioned such a positive correlation. For a review of econometric studies, see Gleditsch *et al.* (1999) and Brauer and Dunne (2004).

4   See SIPRI at http://projects.sipri.se/expcon/loi/indrest02.htm.
5   *Dagens Nyheter*, 18 Sep. 2004: 14.
6   *Svenska Dagbladet*, 11 Dec. 2004: 7.
7   *Svenska Dagbladet*, 20 Dec. 2004: 11.
8   Sweden retains a system of male conscription and voluntary enlistment for women.
9   *Årsredovisning 2001* [Annual report 2001], Eskilstuna: Fortifikationsverket, 2002: 20–1; *Årsfakta verksamhetsåret 2002* [Annual facts 2002], Eskilstuna: Fortifikationsverket, 2003: 45; *Årsfakta verksamhetsåret 2003*, Eskilstuna: Fortifikationsverket, 2004: 45.
10 Six 'co-ordination areas' define operations deemed to be of special importance: technical infrastructure; transport; spreading of toxic substances; economic security; co-ordination, interaction and information by area; and protection, rescue and care (see www.krisberedskapsmyndigheten.se).
11 Also, following the criticism of the government's response to the 2004 tsunami in South-East Asia and a severe storm in Sweden in January 2005, the Swedish Rescue Service has been tasked with operational responsibilities in major crises involving Swedish citizens abroad (see Foreign Minister Freivalds and Defence Minister Björklund, in *Dagens Nyheter*, 14 Jan. 2005) and *2004* http://www.dn.se/DNet/jsp/polopoly.jsp?d=572&a=365357&previousRenderType=2.
12 *Svenska Dagbladet*, 17 Dec. 2004: 16; *Svenska Dagbladet*, 18 Dec. 2004: 8; and *Svenska Dagbladet*, 20 Dec. 2004: 11.
13 For more information, see Swedish Defence Industry Association. Online. Available at: http://www.defind.se/.
14 'Lag om krigsmateriel 1992' [Law on military materiel 1992], Government proposition to Parliament 1991/92, Stockholm: Ministry for Foreign Affairs, 1992: 174.
15 Saab Press Release, 7 Dec. 2004.
16 *Svenska Dagbladet* (Näringsliv), 2 Oct. 2004: 7; and *Dagens Nyheter* (Ekonomi), 28 Sep. 2004: 2.
17 For information about the WEU, see http://www.weu.int/weag. The setting up in 1995 of a WEAO Research Cell (WRC) within the WEU structure extended and improved Panel II research activities.
18 'Regeringens skrivelse till riksdagen om vapenexporten' [Government report to Parliament on arms transfers], Stockholm: the Swedish Government (annual).
19 'European Aeronautics, Space and Defence Industries join forces in ASD', Press Release, ASD, 22 April 2004 (available at: http://www.asd-europe.org/pr0104_ASD_Launch.htm). EUROSPACE will continue to exist as a legal entity under French law, but deal with space matters within ASD.
20 'Regeringens skrivelse till riksdagen om vapenexporten 2004' – see note 16.
21 In March 1994, NATO (Danish) troops engaged for the first time in joint aircraft and battle tank peacekeeping training exercises with Swedish forces.
22 It was reported that Sweden achieved this position in unjust competition with the Finnish candidate; see S. Lundberg, in *Dagens Nyheter*, 21 Oct. 2004: 15.
23 'All set for Swedish led EU Battle Group', Press Release, Stockholm: the Swedish Government, 22 Nov. 2004; European Commission (2003).
24 The R&T focus in 2002 and 2003 was on surveillance, communications, operative and protective capabilities with an annual budget of roughly SEK950 million.
25 Annual report, HQ, 2002: 19–20, and Annual report, HQ, 2003: 20–2.
26 However, Sweden's participation in the so-called Neuron unmanned aerial vehicle (UAV) presented at Le Bourget in 2005 became controversial after the left-wing and the green parties questioned the need for UAVs in Sweden.
27 See the Swedish Government (2004b).
28 'Samspel och integration. Nationell organisation för ett integrerat deltagande i EU:s forsknings-och utvecklingsarbete' [Cooperation and integration: national organisation for integrated participation in EU R&D], SOU 2004: 60, Stockholm: the Swedish Government, 2004.

29 'Nationell strategi för säkerhetsforskning' [National strategy for security research]. Online. Available at: http://www.vinnova.se/main.aspx?ID=C89EDBAE-566F-4939-83B4-77DB07AD4C6F.

30 The IRIS-T air-to-air missile (InfraRed Imaging System Tail/thrust vector controlled) ordered by the German government and with a German main supplier; the Meteor air-to-air missile ordered by Britain with a British-French joint venture as main supplier; and the NLAW (New generation Light Anti-armour Weapon), a Saab-Bofors Dynamics developed missile for the British forces and with Britain as the sole manufacturer.

31 *Dagens Nyheter*, 28 Sep. 2004: 2.

32 'Snö, mörker och kyla – utländska militärövningar i Sverige' [Snow, darkness and cold – foreign military training in Sweden], SOU 2004:77, Stockholm: the Swedish Government. Online. Available at: http://www.regeringen.se/content/1/c6/02/67/87/ff6cc946.pdf.

33 'Sverige samövar med USA på ubåtsområdet' [Sweden to train with the USA in the area of submarines], Press Release 28 Oct. 2004, Stockholm: the Swedish Government. See also 'US to borrow Swedish sub for training', *Defense News*, 27 Sep. 2004: 1, 8.

34 The editors of this volume refer to this as the acquisition risk which, for complex acquisitions, is a complex product of risks specific to different elements of the acquisition.

35 Amendment 2 to the Memorandum of Understanding between the Government of the United States and the Government of the Kingdom of Sweden relating to the (1987) Principles Governing Mutual Cooperation in the Defence Procurement Area, Stockholm: the Swedish Government 2003.

References

Brauer, J. and Dunne, J. P. (eds) (2004) *Arms Trade and Economic Development*, London and New York: Routledge.

European Commision (2003) *A Secure Europe in a Better World: European Security Strategy*, Brussels: European Commission, 12 Dec.

Gleditsch, N. P., Lindgren, G., Mouhleb, N., Smith, S. and de Soysa, P. (eds) (1999) *Making Peace Pay: A Bibliography on Disarmament and Conversion*, Claremont, CA: Regina Books.

Hagelin, B. (1977) *Militärindustriellt samarbete i Västeuropa* [Military-industrial cooperation in Western Europe], Stockholm: Centralförbundet Folk och Försvar.

—— (1978) 'The margins of security: politics and economics in Sweden', *Policy Science*, 2.

—— (1974) 'Sverige i århundradets vapenaffär' [Sweden in the arms deal of the century], *Internationella Studier*, No. 6.

—— (1977) 'Militärindustriellt samarbete i Västeurope' [Military-industrial cooperation in Western Europe], *Centralförbundet Folk och Försvar*.

—— (1985) 'Kulorna rullar: Ekonomi och politik kring svensk militär export' [The bullets are rolling: economics and politics of Swedish military exports], *Ordfront*.

—— (1986) 'Nordic armaments and military dependencies', *Current Research on Peace and Violence*, Nos 1–2.

—— (1997) 'Sweden', in P. Gummet and J. A. Stein (eds) *European Defence Technology in Transition*, Amsterdam: Harwood Academic Publishers, Chap. 8.

—— (2000) 'Swedish for how long? The nation's defence industry in an international context', in A. Erikson and J. Hallenberg (eds) *The Changing European Defence Industry Sector: Consequences for Sweden?*, Stockholm: National Defence College

—— (2004) 'Science- and technology-based military innovation: the United States and Europe', in SIPRI *SIPRI Yearbook 2004: Armaments, Disarmament and International Security*, Oxford: Oxford University Press, pp. 285–304.

—— (2005) *Hardware Politics, Hard Politics or Where Politics? Nordic Defence Equipment Cooperation in the EU Context*, Stockholm: SIPRI.

RIR (2004) *Materiel för miljarder* [Equipment worth billions], *RIR*, 2004: 6, Chap. 4, Stockholm: Riskrevisionen,

SAF (1997) *Swedish Armed Forces Strategy for Research and Technology*, Stockholm: Swedish Armed Forces.

—— (2002) *Swedish Armed Forces Strategy for Research and Technology*, Stockholm: Swedish Armed Forces.

SIPRI (2004) *SIPRI Yearbook 2004: Armaments, Disarmament and International Security*, Oxford: Oxford University Press

Swedish Government (1984) *In Pursuit of Disarmament*, Stockholm: the Swedish Government.

——(2004a) *Vårt framtida försvar* [Our future defence], Defence White Paper, proposition 2004/05, Stockholm: the Swedish Government.

—— (2004b) *Innovativa Sverige* [Innovative Sweden], Ds 2004: 36, Stockholm: the Swedish Government.

—— (2004c) 'Samspel och integration. Nationell organisation för ett integrerat deltagande i EU:s forsknings-och utvecklingsarbete' [Cooperation and integration: national organisation for integrated participation in EU R&D], SOU 2004: 60, Stockholm: the Swedish Government.

UN (1981) *Study on the Relationship between Disarmament and Development*, New York: The United Nations.

12 National Defence Organisation and defence procurement in The Netherlands

Erik Dirksen

Introduction

This chapter provides an overview of the Dutch approach to defence procurement and industry policies. It begins with a brief overview of the Dutch armed forces, defence budget and recent military operations. The next two sections focus on the materiel procurement policy and process. This is followed by an overview of the Dutch defence-related industry. Next is a section entitled 'Defence industry policies and offsets', which considers different aspects of industry support in some detail. Two case studies conclude the chapter. The two cases contrast a relatively simple acquisition of an imported MOTS vehicle with that of a complex and protracted multinational collaborative procurement of another vehicle.

The main mission of the Dutch armed forces is to:

- protect the integrity of national and Alliance territories, including the Netherlands Antilles and Aruba;
- promote international law and contribute to the maintenance of international stability; and
- support civil authorities in national emergencies, including disaster relief and humanitarian assistance in-country and overseas.(MoD, 2007: 5)

The Netherlands is a member of NATO and a significant player in the emergent European Union defence arrangements. In the latter case, The Netherlands is a member of the European Defence Agency and participates actively in OCCAR-managed projects (see Chapter 4 in this volume). Within the NATO framework, the Dutch armed forces closely co-operate with The Netherlands' immediate neighbours, Belgium and Germany.

The Dutch armed forces

In 2007, the Dutch Ministry of Defence (MoD) employed over 49,000 military and about 20,000 civilian personnel. The MoD civilians were employed in the Defence Central Organisation (1,300), the Support Command (7,170), the Defence Materiel Organisation (4,890) and four main Services: the Royal Netherlands Navy (1,100 personnel), the Royal Netherlands Army (4,450), the Royal Netherlands Air Force (730) and the Royal Constabulary (500). On the military side, the RN Navy employed 10,400 personnel, the RN Army 22,500, the RN Air Force 10,140 and the Royal Constabulary 6,050 (ibid., Table 6: 62–3). Between 1991 and 2007, civilian personnel decreased from 23,450 to 20,170 persons while the military personnel nearly halved from 94,140 down to 49,090 (46 per cent) (ibid., Table 9: 64–5). Since 1996, the Dutch armed forces have been entirely made up of voluntary (professional) personnel. Conscription was abandoned in 1997.

In 2007, capital assets of the Dutch armed forces included the Navy's four air-warfare frigates, four Walrus class submarines, two conventional frigates, two landing platform docks and several smaller vessels and helicopters; the Army's 110 Leopard 2A6 tanks, 39 armoured howitzers, 765 YPR-765 armoured tracked infantry vehicles (see case studies below) and hundreds of other military fighting vehicles, artillery pieces and reconnaissance systems; and the Air Force's 105 F-16 fighters, 24 Apache attack helicopters, 11 Chinook heavy lift helicopters and several other helicopters and transport aircraft (ibid.: 41–50). Overall, it is a well-equipped modern defence force structured for deployments in Europe and overseas.

Defence budget

In 2007, the Dutch defence budget amounted to €7.9 billion, of which nearly 18 per cent was spent on the Army, over 8 per cent on the Air Force and nearly a similar amount on the Navy, less than 5 per cent on the Royal Constabulary, nearly 10 per cent on Support Command and 29 per cent on the Defence Materiel Organisation. Other expenditures and 'crisis-response operations' accounted for the balance. In terms of expenditure categories, salaries and other personnel expenditure accounted for 39 per cent of the budget, military materiel for 21 per cent, and investments in 'major materiel' (major capital items), infrastructure and information management for nearly 22 per cent. Between 1991 and 2007, the share of defence expenditure in GDP decreased from 3.5 per cent to 1.5 per cent (ibid.: 67–8).

Since the end of the Cold War, the resourcing of the Dutch Defence Organisation has changed significantly:

- defence budgets have steadily decreased;
- defence personnel numbers have decreased;
- the unit cost of defence has increased with growing capital and knowledge intensity of defence capabilities;
- budgetary and operational pressures (see below) have increased the importance of value-for-money considerations in defence procurement decisions.

To slow down cost escalation, the Dutch government has encouraged the use of commercial components and dual technologies in procurement of military systems. The Dutch government's involvement in the procurement of military materiel, R&D support and export licensing means it still exerts considerable influence in the Dutch defence market.

Peace-keeping and peace-enforcement operations

Since the end of the Cold War, the Dutch armed forces have adopted an expeditionary posture. The deployment of military personnel for international humanitarian and 'peace operations' is an important feature of Dutch national security policy. Peace-keeping and peace-enforcement operations are now as important as the traditional task of national territorial defence.[1] In Dutch usage, the term 'peace operations' describes observatory missions; peace-keeping and peace-enforcement operations and missions with a strongly humanitarian focus.

In 1992–93, The Netherlands supplied a battalion of marines which successfully participated in the United Nations Transitional Authority – Cambodia (UNTAC). *Dutchbat*, the infantry battalion stationed in Srebrenica (United Nations Protection Force Bosnia – UNPROFOR) from early 1994, was less successful.[2] Later Dutch contributions to the Peace Implementation Force (IFOR) and Peace Stabilisation Force (SFOR) in Bosnia went better thanks to clear lines of command. From 1999 to 2000, The Netherlands made a substantial contribution to the Kosovo Force (KFOR) whose mission was to drive the Serbian military out of Kosovo. The main Dutch contribution comprised air-force units, an artillery battalion, a battalion of engineers and some infantry units. The Kosovo mission was followed by participation in the UN Mission in Ethiopia and Eritrea (UNMEE), 2000–01, a battalion of Marines accounting for the bulk of the Dutch contribution. From August 2003–March 2005, Dutch Marines and infantry contributed to keeping public order in Iraq. In 2004, 1,400 Dutch servicemen and women were active in Iraq. In 2006, over 10,500 military personnel were deployed in 'crisis-response' operations (MoD, 2007: 8). These operations included NATO Response Forces in stand-by mode; European Military Force (EUFOR) deployments in Bosnia; the EU Monitoring Mission (EUMM) in Serbia-Kosovo-Albania and Kosovo Force (KFOR) in Kosovo; a NATO training mission in Baghdad; work by the United Nations Truce Supervision Organisation (UNTSO) and EU Border Assistance Mission (EU BAM) in the Middle East; International Security Assistance Force (ISAF) and Operation Enduring Freedom (OEF) operations in Afghanistan; EU Police Mission (EUPOL), EU Security Sector Reform Mission (EUSEC) and EUFOR in Congo; the International Military Advisory Team (IMAT) and the United Nations Mission in Sudan (UNMIS); and other humanitarian missions in different parts of the world (ibid.: 8–15).

Materiel procurement policy

In line with the country's stated national security objectives, the aim of defence materiel procurement policy is to equip the Dutch armed forces in support of their three main tasks. In general, MoD's preferred policy is to buy military materiel 'off-the-shelf'. The Defence Memorandum 2000 of the Dutch MoD states the following:

> The leading principle of the procurement policy of the MoD is that the equipment of the armed forces is tailored to the three main tasks. When choosing defence materiel, the safety of the personnel and military effectiveness come first. This approach does not leave room for dogmatic 'pro-American' or 'pro-European' views, the more so because the size and the composition of the Dutch defence industry is of such a nature that our country only plays a limited role in developments at the international level. Naturally, the MoD recognises the interests of the Dutch defence-related industries but these industries must be internationally competitive in the USA and in Europe.
>
> To provide the armed forces, given the budgetary constraints, with modern, effective and safe equipment, it is important that the choice of equipment and contractors is guided by a transparent procurement policy ... (A key aspect of this policy is) ... 'smart procurement', which requires – among other things – innovative ways of outsourcing. Where appropriate, procurement strategies should include the use of competition to limit the technical and financial risks.
>
> (Muller *et al.*, 2004: 486)

The Defence Materiel Organisation is responsible for the administration of materiel procurement, the development of internal procurement guidelines and the provision of through-life support for systems in service (DMO, 2007: 3).

Defence materiel process

The *Defence Materiel Process* (DMP) provides the decision-making framework for all defence equipment acquisition projects. Under the DMP, approved processes vary with projects value.

- Projects worth €5–25 million: after approval by the Chief of Defence Staff (CDS), projects are listed as planned acquisitions subject to approval by the lower chamber of the Dutch Parliament;
- Projects worth €25–100 million: initially put before the lower chamber of the Dutch Parliament by the Deputy Minister for Defence and, when approved, referred to the relevant Service branch for further, in-detail development (see below);

- Projects worth over €100 million: require the support of the Deputy Minister for Defence subject to approval by the lower chamber of the Dutch Parliament; and
- Projects over €250 million must be first discussed by the Dutch Cabinet, the lower chamber of the Dutch Parliament is informed afterwards.

The approval processes ensure that the Dutch Parliament is informed about all important defence procurement decisions at an early stage. Equally important, the procedure helps ensure that the introduction of new equipment is approached holistically, recognising that a new capability element requires complementary investments in infrastructure, facilities and other equipment, the recruitment and training of personnel, and changes in doctrine, procedures and regulations.

The decision-making process for all projects of over €25 million involves four stages:

1 *Stage A* – given the strategic guidance provided by government, operational military needs are determined and equipment (functional) requirements developed.
2 *Stage B* – further scoping of requirements is undertaken to determine technical specifications for the equipment. If product specifications are satisfactory and the acquisition is to proceed, this stage also incorporates a market scoping study to produce a 'long-list' of potential suppliers and expected lead times.
3 *Stage C* – a shortlist of suppliers is drawn up for existing MOTS/COTS product designs or a decision is made to proceed with a developmental project.
4 *Stage D* – solicitation and evaluation of supply offers, with further evaluation and acceptance tests if necessary. The preferred supplier is then selected by the MoD, while financial experts from its Control Service assess the offer's compliance with broader administrative, financial and legal requirements. The Ministry of Economic Affairs (MEA) also becomes involved at this stage to ensure that Dutch industry is sufficiently engaged in the project. Contracts are only signed when the lower chamber of the Parliament agrees to proceed with the acquisition at this stage. (Stages A through D do not have to be completed by small projects under €25 million.)

The DMP cycle may often take several years to complete and during that time political priorities may change, technologies may evolve and the budgetary situation may also change. Thus, to verify the continuing relevance of the acquisition, the original requirements are reconsidered at each phase of the DMP cycle.

For large 'mega-projects' (so-called), annual progress reports and accompanying audit reports are required by the lower chamber. For example, at the end of 2004, four mega-projects were under way:

1   the construction of four air-warfare frigates (LCFs) for the Royal Netherlands Navy;
2   the procurement of Naval NH-90 helicopters;
3   the development and construction of a new generation of armoured infantry vehicles for the Royal Netherlands Army (CV-90; Fennek and the OCCAR-managed Boxer vehicle families, see the case studies below); and
4   participation in the development and construction of the *Joint Strike Fighter* (JSF – see Chapter 2, Box 2.1).

In 2004, the total value of these four projects is expected to exceed €10 billion (Muller *et al.*, 2004: 486–8).

Defence-related industry

Sectoral structure

In 2004, defence-related industries in The Netherlands included some 245 companies that were *active* suppliers of goods and services to military customers. Table 12.1 shows the sectoral distribution of defence-related firms. A number of firms are active in two or more industry sectors with aerospace, maritime, C3 and IT showing the highest participation rates (hence the total number of firms in Table 12.1 exceeds 245). About 90 per cent of firms in defence-related industry were also engaged in civil production activities. The significance of civil sales has led to use of the term 'defence-related industries', as opposed to 'defence industry', in The Netherlands.

Table 12.1 Sectoral distribution of defence-related firms in 2004

Industry sector	Number of firms
Aerospace	87
Maritime industry	78
Command, control and communications ('C3')	66
Information technology (IT)	64
Electronics	38
Automotive	36
Optics and optronics	35
Metalworking	25
Infrastructure	25
Munitions	23
Research institutes	13
Synthetics and synthetic fibres	9
Firing range/Simulation	4
Textiles and clothing	3
Other sectors	15

Source: SDI (2004): 19

The Netherlands' defence-related industry is not expanding and is becoming increasingly concentrated. As a result, only a handful of firms are able to develop and produce a large weapons system. There is also an ever-increasing penetration of the industry by foreign firms while firms resident in The Netherlands are becoming increasingly export-oriented and involved in foreign direct investment.

Employment

Table 12.2 shows the distribution of employment (by size) in defence-related industry in 2004. Some 57 per cent of defence-related firms are small, employing less than 100 people. Only about a quarter of these companies employ more than 500 people.

In 2004, about 7 per cent of jobs in the 245 defence-related companies were defence-specific with some 12,000 people filling about 11,000 full-time-equivalent positions. Some 3,500 of full-time positions involved R&D activities. Thus, about one in three defence-specific jobs was an R&D-related position and some 3,000 of these jobs were located in the various research establishments of the National Defence Group of the Netherlands Organisation for Applied Scientific Research (TNO – see Box 12.1).

Box 12.1 The TNO National Defence Group

TNO, founded in 1932, is a statutory agency engaged in contract research and specialist advisory services for government and other public agencies, including the military, and the private sector. It tests and certifies products and services and provides independent quality appraisals. As an independent statutory body, it is expected to be the bi-partisan source of the state-of-the-art advice and expertise. It also issues licences the use of patents and specialist software. It employs over 5,000 people in new knowledge development and dissemination tasks in five core areas: quality of life; defence and national security; manufacturing industry and technology; construction, and ICT. Apart from the statutory TNO organisation, there is also the holding TNO Bedrijven BV (TNO Enterprises Ltd), which sets up new firms to market innovations that would otherwise remain unused.

TNO is internationally recognised research agency and much of its work involves co-operation with leading universities and technological institutions. TNO also participates in a large number of projects funded under the European Union's R&D programme. TNO co-operates with private sector companies, in particular those involved in the TNO Co-financing Scheme. Its *modus operandi*, involves the use of project teams comprising experts from different disciplines such as, *inter alia*, materials technology, product development, behavioural science, design engineering, and software development.

The core area of Defence and (national) Security (D&S) supplies innovative solutions to enhance national security. In this area, TNO is a strategic partner of the Dutch MoD and supports R&D requirements of the MoD across the range of activities: military operations, military resources, command and operational decision-making, threat evaluation and protection, education and training. In the field of civil security, it focuses on combating crime, national disasters, and terrorism. TNO D&S is also active in aviation security and in the maritime sector (shipbuilding) as these are areas where TNO's expert knowledge can easily find commercial applications. Among TNO's D&S customers are the Dutch MoD and the ministries of Internal Affairs, Foreign Affairs, and Transport & Public Works. Furthermore, TNO caters to regional and national police forces and fire brigades, and to national and international (defence-related) industries.

Sales

The most recent 'reliable' data on defence-related industry sales refer to 1997, when they stood at about €1.5 billion. Based on company surveys, defence-related sales in 2001 and 2002 were *estimated* at €1.62 billion and €1.72 billion, respectively. (This gives an average defence-related turnover of €7 million per company in 2002.)

Table 12.3 shows the percentage distribution of Dutch defence contractors by their defence-related sales in 2004. Table 12.3 shows that defence-related

Table 12.2 Employment by firm size in 2004

Number of employees	Number of firms	Percentage of all firms
< 10	28	11
10–99	114	46
100–500	45	18
> 500	58	24
Total	245	100

Source: SDI (2004): 13

Table 12.3 Distribution of defence contractors by their defence-related sales in 2004

Defence-related sales	Firms (%)
< €1 million	57
€1 million – €9.99 million	31
€10 million – €100 million	11
> €100 million	1
Total	100

Source: SDI (2004): 21

sales were relatively small for the majority of firms. Only 12 per cent of firms reported sales in excess of €10 million.

Ownership and external orientation

In 2004, of the 245 defence-related companies, 46 per cent were fully Dutch-owned and had no foreign subsidiaries. Another 25 per cent were Dutch-owned multinationals in that they had at least one foreign subsidiary. A further 29 per cent were subsidiaries or branches of foreign companies, some of which had more than one subsidiary in The Netherlands.

Almost half of the companies (48 per cent) were either direct exporters or involved in some form of international co-production with exports accounting for 72 per cent of their defence-related sales. The three largest markets for Dutch exports of military products were Germany, the USA and the UK. In 2002, about €770 million of the total sales revenue of €1.72 billion (about 45 per cent) was derived from exports.

Defence industry policy and offsets

Intra-EU trade in defence goods

Currently, under Article 296 of the EU Treaty, each EU member state is allowed to protect its defence-related industries and pursue local content preferences and other import-substitution policies. Only dual-technology (civil-military) products come within the scope of the liberalised EU market. In particular, defence offsets are used by several European countries, including The Netherlands, as a means of providing work for domestic suppliers.

Despite its reliance on offsets, The Netherlands actively supports all initiatives aimed at the liberalisation of the intra-EU market for defence-specific goods even though this would spell the end of the Dutch offset policy. As a small economy, The Netherlands has relatively little influence on the pace and scope of market liberalisation. (In the period leading up to the Maastricht Treaty, it unsuccessfully tried to have Article 296 struck off the Treaty.)

Defence industry and offsets policies

Dutch defence industry policy aims at maintaining a small but technologically advanced and internationally competitive defence-related industry specialising in the development and production of subsystems and components. The policy tries to ensure that if in future the European defence market is liberalised, Dutch companies will be well positioned as internationally competitive sub-contractors and specialised component and equipment manufacturers.

The Netherlands applies offsets requirements to all defence materiel imports with a value in excess of €5 million (MEA, 2007).[3] Offsets demands are administered by the Ministry of Economic Affairs (MEA) as expressly directed by the Dutch Parliament (for an illustrative example of offsets application see the case study of the CV-90 acquisition below). Offset demands are justified on the grounds that domestic military spending is very important for the Dutch economy and because of the lack of opportunities for Dutch companies to compete in international defence markets.[4] In the case of international collaborative acquisitions, suppliers of the co-operating countries are allocated work on the basis of 'cost share equals work-share' (*juste retour*). Work-share agreements are negotiated by collaborating states ahead of the contract and normally cover both product development and production stages in the materiel acquisition cycle.

Under the offsets scheme, the foreign supplier undertakes to place orders with Dutch manufacturing industry, within an agreed period of time (not exceeding ten years) and for an amount at least equal the value of the Dutch import order. When Dutch industry is involved in the production or main-tenance of imported defence systems, this comes under the heading of *direct offsets*. *Indirect offsets*, on the other hand, involve orders placed with Dutch industry that are not directly related to the offset-liable acquisition. In the second half of the 1990s, 10 per cent of the total annual value of orders placed by the Dutch MoD, or 30 per cent of orders places abroad, involved offsets obligations (Muller *et al.*, 2004: 489). Offset orders placed with Dutch firms should involve knowledge-intensive and high value-added activities. For indirect offsets, these activities must involve firms operating within designated 'high-tech' civil sectors such as aerospace, IT and maritime tech-nology. In some cases, it may be possible to 'offset' Dutch import orders against equal-valued orders from a foreign MoD placed with firms resident in The Netherlands – the 'quid-pro-quo principle'.

Also, under the Dutch offsets policy, foreign suppliers themselves can determine how to discharge their offsets obligations. In 2000, for example, about €160 million worth of new offsets obligations (40 per cent) were (defence-related) direct offsets and €240 million were indirect offsets (60 per cent). Nearly 10 per cent of total defence-related local industry sales of €1.7 billion were generated through the offset policy. Direct offsets obligations represent 20 per cent of export sales currently running at about €0.8 billion per year. Indirect offsets involve civil export orders, technology transfers, etc., and are closely monitored by the MEA.

Traditionally, the offsets-related trade diversion from foreign to domestic contractors aimed to create jobs in The Netherlands. Since the late 1990s, though, the main objective of Dutch offsets policy has changed and employ-ment creation has given way to ensuring the economic viability and sustain-ment of offsets-assisted firms. The MEA's preferred approach is to use offsets to facilitate participation in international development projects and to provide incentives for offset beneficiaries to be innovative and export-oriented. As a result, Dutch defence-related industries now participate in some significant international co-operative programmes, e.g., the Joint Strike Fighter (JSF), the Boxer armoured vehicle, and the NH-90 helicopter.

Efforts have also been made to encourage defence-related offsets and the outsourcing of work to Dutch defence companies through the application of differentiated offsets *multipliers*. For example, when a Dutch company is selected during the (system) development phase as 'sole source' or 'preferred supplier' of high-value components, the maximum multiplier of five applies instead of the 'standard' multiplier of three. That is, the value of an offset credit needed to discharge an offset obligation is five times the value of the eligible outsourcing contract. To encourage R&D activities, the maximum multiplier for R&D-related offsets is set at ten. The relevant multiplier is determined on a case-by-case basis.

Firms can also have their remaining offset obligations cancelled when they achieve a previously agreed percentage of their offset obligation by placing military rather than civil orders with Dutch companies. These incentives apply only to off-the-shelf purchases from foreign suppliers. Despite these incentives to promote direct offsets, it is expected that, on average, the 50 per cent share of direct offsets in all offset obligations is the maximum that can be achieved. Hence civil (indirect) offsets are as important as (and most likely more important than) direct offsets. To maximise offsets-related benefits for the Dutch economy, preference is given to indirect offsets that encourage knowledge/technology transfers to Dutch civil firms and foreign direct investment in The Netherlands. Again, high value multipliers have been used to encourage such activities.

It has also been shown that the use of offsets to divert business to Dutch firms has resulted in small cost premia, on average of about 2.6 per cent (or €10 million per year), relative to the cost of fully imported products.[5] If accurate, this is a rather modest figure, which reflects the high international competitiveness of Dutch companies. In the opinion of the MEA, other forms of support or protection for Dutch defence-related industry (like, for instance, national development orders or subsidies) would be more costly to apply than offsets. They could also limit the Dutch MoD's freedom to procure the equipment it needs as it could fall hostage to vested local industrial interests. The application of offset requirements offers the opportunity to take advantage of market forces while pursuing trade diversion objectives in the national interest (see note 5).

Multilateral collaborative projects

Dutch offsets policy has primarily been in response to import barriers and other trade impediments imposed by larger countries. However, the Dutch government has also tried to influence other nations to adopt a common approach to offsets demands. This was to prevent the fragmentation of European defence industry when large defence contractors respond to offset requirements imposed by individual buyer nations by fragmenting their production capacities between different countries and duplicating their production facilities. This fragmented national industry capabilities have been hard to sustain over time, especially at sub-contractor levels, once offsets-related orders have been completed and firms in other countries selected to discharge the prime contractor's offset obligations imposed by other governments.

One option, favoured by the Dutch government, has been to encourage multinational work-share arrangements. There, a number of countries coordinate their purchases and offsets requirements with the aim of preventing industry fragmentation and improving long-term sustainability of their defence-related industries. This appears a cost-effective and least market-disruptive policy if work-share arrangements are aimed at balancing the allocation of work between participants in multinational projects over a number of projects rather than for each individual project.

Case studies

In 1997, the Dutch MoD initiated the programme *Vervanging Pantservoertuigen YPR765 en M577* (Replacement for Armoured Vehicles YPR765 and M577), involving the procurement of three new families of armoured vehicles for the Royal Netherlands Army. The three vehicle types involved were the Fennek (a light-wheeled armoured vehicle), the CV-90 (a tracked infantry combat vehicle), and PWV/Boxer (a large-wheeled armoured vehicle). The following two cases focus on the CV-90 and Boxer acquisitions.

CV-90 tracked infantry combat vehicle[6]

The CV-90 tracked infantry combat vehicle was to replace the YPR 765, a substantially improved and upgraded version of the M113 'battle taxi' that was first introduced in 1979 and due for replacement between 2007 and 2012. The YPR 765 vehicle had reached the end of its useful life and had become obsolete, given the demands of the modern battlefield and the likely deployment scenarios. The Dutch Army's requirement was for 200 new vehicles, including training and reserve fleets: 150 'pantser-rups infanterievoertuigen' (PRI – a tracked armoured infantry combat vehicle), 34 'pantser-rups commandovoertuigen' (PRCO – a tracked armoured command vehicle), and 16 'pantser-rups bergingsvoertuigen' (PRB – a tracked armoured recovery vehicle).

After initial screening, three candidate vehicles were considered: the Ulan (produced by Steyr Daimler Puch), the CV-90 (produced by Alvis-Hägglunds), and the Puma (produced by the PSM-consortium, a 50/50 joint venture of Krauss-Maffei Wegmann and Rheinmetall Land Systems). In February 2004, the three shortlisted suppliers were invited to tender for the provision of both an evaluation vehicle and the entire requirement. Following evaluation of the tenders and field trials of test vehicles, the CV-90 emerged as the preferred option. The CV-90 offer met all the requirements, was least risky, had the shortest delivery schedule and was the least costly. Also, the CV-90 had already been introduced in Finland, Norway, Sweden and Switzerland. There were therefore opportunities for international collaboration in procuring spare parts and maintenance.

The other two candidate vehicles offered less value for money. The Ulan needed substantial modification to meet the Dutch requirements. This involved high developmental risks and, even after successful modifications, it had little growth potential as its weight reserve was already used up to meet present-day protection requirements. If extra armour were to be applied, this would reduce the vehicle's driving power and, thus, its operational mobility. The price of the Ulan was also considerably higher than that of the CV-90 and batch deliveries could only begin in 2010. The Puma, on the other hand, was completely new and, at the time, it was still under development. The vehicle had yet to be tested and, at the time the Dutch MoD had to commit itself, the German MoD had not yet decided on further development of the vehicle. Thus, the risks inherent in the acquisition were deemed to be excessive. The Puma model under consideration was also too small to transport a Dutch infantry group with its essential equipment and much more expensive than the CV-90.

The differences between the three offers were clear enough to enable the Dutch MoD to select the CV-90 in late 2004. This allowed an earlier delivery than had previously been anticipated with the first batch expected to be supplied in 2007 to replace the aging and increasingly obsolete YPR combat vehicles. The delivery was to be completed in 2011. The chosen vehicle variant was the CV-9035 Mk III with a 35 mm Bushmaster cannon. In 2005, the total sum budgeted for the project was €988 million (in 2004 prices), of which the Alvis-Hägglunds contract represented €891 million and the balance of €97 million included the testing expenditure, a simulator, supplies of ammunition, and a management reserve for unforeseen expenditures.

All three shortlisted suppliers were willing to *offset* the total tender value through orders in The Netherlands. Again, the CV-90 was viewed as representing a better deal since at least 36 per cent in offset orders were guaranteed, against 22 per cent for the Ulan, and an as yet unspecified amount for the Puma (for which, given its early stage of development, no meaningful guarantees could be given). A separate offset agreement had been concluded between the Dutch MEA and Alvis-Hägglunds before the order to supply the CV-90 was placed with the Swedish supplier. The offset arrangement included, among other things, the sourcing in The Netherlands of thermal-image field glasses developed in The Netherlands, a combined air-conditioning and NBC protection system, and the production of road wheels and complete road-wheel systems. In February 2005, Hägglunds announced that it had selected a relatively small Dutch firm, Van Halteren Metaal, as its main local production partner. It would assume responsibility for the complete turret assembly. The selection of Van Halteren Metaal was a major blow to Thales Nederland, the largest defence contractor in The Netherlands and the only competing contender for the turret contract.[7]

In sum, this case illustrates a successful procurement project, with the tendering and evaluation stages concluded promptly and the deliveries planned ahead of previously anticipated schedule. The case also shows how offsets requirements are applied.

The Boxer project: challenges of multinational work-share arrangements

This case study focuses on the early history of the German-Dutch Boxer project which was ultimately placed under OCCAR management (see Chapter 4).[8] This case highlights the challenges involved in the arranging international collaborative procurement with a number of participating governments and national industry 'champions'.

French, German and British collaboration

In 1990, the German Army developed a tactical concept for a new wheeled armoured transport vehicle the GTK (*Gepanzertes Transport Kraftfahrzeug*) to replace the tracked M113 'battle taxi' and the wheeled Fuchs vehicle. Shortly afterwards, the DGA (the French Délégation Générale pour l'Armement) sought proposals to meet the requirements for a *Véhicule Blindé de Combat d'Infanterie* (VBCI, an armoured infantry combat vehicle). In 1993, Germany and France agreed to develop a joint military requirement for a GTK/VBCI and, in 1996, were joined by Britain, which sought a Multi-role Armoured Vehicle (MRAV). The joint GTK-VBCI-MRAV programme was to develop a new armoured vehicle capable of meeting individual requirements of every country. The tender was to be managed by the German procurement agency BWB in Koblenz on behalf of the three participating nations. France, however, withdrew from the programme two years later and Britain in July 2003.

Industry cooperation

In the early 1990s, transnational industry teams were formed to respond to the then uni-national French and German requirements for armoured vehicles. Panhard and Mercedes-Benz expressed interest in the proposed vehicle to the French Ministry of Defence and GIAT and Krauss-Maffei approached the German Ministry of Defence. In 1993, the CEOs of Krauss-Maffei, Rheinmetall and Wegmann agreed to collaborate on the detailed GTK proposal and formed the Arbeitsgemeinschaft GTK (ARGE GTK). Later, ARGE GTK teamed up with the British GKN (supported by Alvis). In 1996, the French GIAT signed a Letter of Intent to collaborate with ARGE GTK and GKN on the GTK proposal with an aim of forming a multinational supplier consortium. In 1997, a competing tri-national consortium was formed by the German Henschel (supported by Kuka), the British Vickers Defence Systems and the French Panhard & Levassor (PSA Group). This second consortium was called TEAM International.

Both consortia submitted their offers to the German procurement agency BWB in April 1997. All three national MoDs favoured the ARGE GTK (the so-called Eurokonsortium) proposal and their choice was announced in April 1998. Management of the project was subsequently transferred to the newly formed OCCAR (see below).

In 1997, Krauss-Maffei and Wegmann merged their defence activities to form a new entity, Krauss-Maffei-Wegmann Wehrtechnik GmbH, in which Krauss-Maffei held a 49 per cent share and Wegmann 51 per cent. The new entity also included the Dutch Stork PWV of Eindhoven (NL), in which Wegmann held a 51 per cent share.

In 2003, the British partner Alvis withdrew from the Eurokonsortium (effective from late 2004). In 2004, to continue the project, the remaining ARTEC GmbH (successor to the Eurokonsortium) partners (Krauss-Maffei-Wegmann, Germany; Rheinmetall Landsysteme, Germany; and the Dutch Rheinmetall Nederland, the former Stork PWV) submitted a revised project proposal which included, among other things, new work-share arrangements, the associated division of liabilities and the provision of supplier guarantees.

OCCAR: the German-Dutch Boxer project

OCCAR took on management of the multinational GTK/MRAV/PWV procurement programme (in which PWV represents the Dutch involvement) and, in 2003, saw it renamed as the Boxer project. The formal Dutch contract for the delivery of 200 Boxer vehicles was signed in 2006. With the withdrawal of Britain, the project became a joint German-Dutch venture and extension of the development phase included transferring the former British workload to German and Dutch suppliers.[9] A considerable amount of work was to be undertaken by the Dutch industry, including production of an ambulance version of the Boxer to be made by Rheinmetall Nederland, the former Stork PWV. However, following the British withdrawal, the remaining partners were no longer able to confirm previous price guarantees for unit vehicle costs. Nevertheless, the now bilateral contract was not expected to increase significantly the Dutch share of the total cost.[10]

In December 2006, OCCAR placed the contract with ARTEC GmbH for the batch production of 279 vehicles, in four versions, for Germany and 200 vehicles (in five different versions) for The Netherlands. ARTEC GmbH was also contracted to continue the development of the vehicle.[11] Batch deliveries are expected to start in 2009 and the vehicle is to remain in service with the German and Dutch forces for about 30 years. By early 2006, 16 years after the German operational concept was first developed, the Boxer project was still in the late-development-early-production phase.

Conclusion

The deployment of the Dutch armed forces in international humanitarian and peace operations is an important feature of the Dutch national security policy. As noted, peace-keeping and peace-enforcement operations are now as important as the traditional task of national territorial defence. This means that the Dutch armed forces have to be equipped for a wide range of missions at home and abroad. The role of the MEA in the Dutch procurement model illustrates how democratic governments use defence procurement to advance non-defence procurement objectives. In doing so, the Dutch government appears to satisfy the diverse spectrum of Dutch community interests represented in the Dutch Parliament at relatively modest cost to the MoD's capability development objectives. Finally, the two case studies discussed in this chapter also provide an interesting contrast between an uni- and multi-national acquisitions of equipment and the challenges posed by multinational procurement projects.

Acknowledgements

The author wishes to thank Rini Goos, MSc, of the Dutch MEA, and Coen Hoenkamp, MSc, consultant, for their very useful additional information and for their comments on an earlier draft of this chapter.

Notes

1 Considerable peace-enforcement experience was gained, still during the Cold War, through the Dutch participation in the UNIFIL mission in Lebanon. This mission, which lasted from March 1979 till the end of October 1985, cost the lives of nine servicemen. The Dutch contribution consisted of supplying a full armoured-infantry battalion, which ultimately proved to be rather a large burden for the Dutch armed forces.

2 In July 1995, it was not able to prevent the mass murder of about 7,000 male Muslims in Srebrenica.

3 In 2004, the threshold value was increased from €2.5 million to €5 million. This is because the application of offset requirements to small orders has been rather counter-productive as most of these offsets are too small to produce economically viable and sustainable outcomes, in particular new investments in The Netherlands by foreign firms and knowledge transfers to Dutch offset recipients.

4 The above is based on p. 3 of the letter from the Dutch Deputy Minister of Defence to the Dutch Lower Chamber, dated 2 June 2004.

5 Letter from the Dutch Deputy Minister of Defence to the Dutch Lower Chamber of Parliament (16 July 2004).

6 A large part of this case study is based on the letter from the Dutch Deputy Minister of Defence to the Dutch Lower Chamber (29 October 2004).

7 *Jane's Defence Weekly*, 16 February 2005, p. 20.

8 Most information on the Boxer project was supplied by Coen Hoenkamp, MSc, consultant, formerly of the Dutch Ministry of Foreign Affairs.

9 The cost of re-design of the British prototypes was absorbed by the United Kingdom so the British withdrawal did not result in the overrun of the €113 million budget earmarked for the development phase.

10 Letter from the Dutch Deputy Minister of Defence to the Dutch Lower Chamber of Parliament (8 April 2004).

11 See http://www.occar-ea.org/view.php?nid=76 (accessed July 2008).

References

DMO (2007) *Defence Materiel Organisation*, The Hague: Defence Materiel Organisation.

MEA (2007) 'Guidelines to an industrial benefits and offsets program in the Netherlands', Guidelines Brochure Version 1.5, The Hague: Ministry of Economic Affairs.

MoD (2007) *Facts and Figures about the Armed Forces*, The Hague: Ministry of Defence of the Netherlands.

Muller, E. R., Starink, D., Bosch, J. M. J., and de Jong, I. M. (eds) (2004) *Krijgsmacht – Studies over de organisatie en het optreden* [The Dutch Armed Forces: studies of their organisation and operations], trans. E. Dirksen, Alphen aan den Rijn: Kluwer, p. 486.

SDI (2004) *Sectoranalyse defensiegerelateerde industrie* [Sectoral analysis of defence-related industries], trans. E. Dirksen, The Hague: Ministry of Economic Affairs of the Netherlands.

Part III

Industry case studies

13 Industry case study

Australian naval shipbuilding

Stefan Markowski and Robert Wylie

Introduction

Defence procurement links together government demand for new military capabilities and industry supply of the equipment and materiel inputs that help form those capabilities. The relationship between the procurement agency and industry is crucial to determining the success (or otherwise) of the capabilities Defence acquires. Particularly in smaller countries, defence procurement agencies face a difficult challenge when seeking to acquire new capability that is either intrinsically complex or idiosyncratically tailored to local needs. If they seek to rely on production in-country, they are obliged to draw on domestic infrastructure almost certainly too limited in its technological breadth and depth for the task of efficiently producing a wide range of sophisticated military products, and likely to be economically uncompetitive into the bargain. If they look to overseas suppliers, they often lack the market power to negotiate favourable terms and sometimes to have their requirements met at all. When they seek their supplies from government-owned arsenals and shipyards, they may find it difficult to resist political pressures to preserve legacy sectors and products. And, if they 'leave it to the market', award contracts on the basis of a competitive process and set up arm's-length relationships to pursue compliance, they may find themselves hostage to suppliers that cannot be replaced once the contract is under way. These issues, and the related matter of using procurement to support domestic industry, have been discussed earlier in this book.

In this chapter we examine the particular case of defence procurement for naval vessels and support services in a specific smaller country, Australia, which has long had domestic warship building facilities and maintenance capabilities. This enables us to trace how such a country has grappled with the challenges noted above and how the government has been driven to increase its responsibility for managing shipbuilding projects after a period of seeking to rely more heavily on the forces of competitive industrial supply. As in some other smaller countries, naval procurement and shipbuilding have a special significance in Australia, where the sector 'is the jewel in the defence industry crown. Naval vessels are the only major platforms built in Australia, and firms that build them are the highest profile and most prestigious element of defence industry' (ASPI, 2002: 8). But lessons apparent in this sector are also relevant to other parts of defence industry and its relationship with defence procurement agencies. More than any other area of defence procurement, however, naval shipbuilding has consistently captured the attention of the nation – from the troubled government shipyards of the 1950s and 1960s through to the Collins submarine project of the 1990s (ibid.). This is partly because the procurement of naval assets and the disposition of industry facilities have long been highly politicised, with the federal government balancing the competing interests of different states, services and industries. As a result, the Australian naval shipbuilding and repair sector has consistently presented governments of the day 'with a series of interwoven challenges' (ibid.: 1). The response to such challenges has been embedded for 20 years or more in economic and institutional reforms applying to Australian defence industry overall and the sector has benefited particularly from reforms to the defence supply chain (see Chapter 6 and below). However, while considerable improvements have been achieved, accounts of project delays and cost overruns still attract media attention and embarrass successive governments.

By the standards of older maritime nations, the industry may not have a long history but it has had its share of both failure and success. Among the former, arguably the most publicised has been the procurement of the Collins Class submarines in the 1980s and 1990s. No other Australian defence acquisition in recent years has had a more profound impact on how the government goes about the acquisition of major strategic capabilities and on the mechanics of the defence acquisition process. As the subsequent cycle of naval acquisitions started to unfold, the key question was what lessons had been learned, and with what implications for new process.

This would become clear as the Australian government sought to handle two forms of competition. On the one hand, prime contractors, main systems integrators and some OEMs competed *for* a market, the market in new capability formation, by offering alternative specifications of capabilities sought by Defence (i.e., different platform designs and combat systems). On the other hand, lower tier contractors competed *in* a market, the market for work subcontracted by primes and higher tier contractors. In each case, local content requirements and defence procurement policy had a role to play.

This case study is structured as follows. First, we review the history of naval shipbuilding and repair in Australia. This complements the historic perspective on Australian defence procurement presented in Chapter 6. We discuss the three post-World War II ship acquisition cycles, which are critical to the understanding of how successive Australian governments have approached naval acquisitions and defence procurement in general. Second, we consider the in-country maritime industry, i.e., shipbuilders and maintainers, facilities and industry disposition, the changing division of labour and the associated supply chains. Finally, we draw some lessons from the Australian naval shipbuilding experience.

Naval shipbuilding in Australia

Post-war shipbuilding cycles

During World War II, Australia became a significant builder and repairer of naval vessels. In total, 113 naval ships were built for the Royal Australian Navy (RAN) at ten Australian dockyards. Also, 4,000 ship repairs were completed for the RAN, 500 for the US Navy (USN) and nearly 400 for the Royal Navy (Parliament of Australia, 2006: 41). The scale of activity declined significantly during the post-war period. Since 1945, Australia has experienced two major naval building cycles separated by a 15-year period of low activity and a third was under way by 2008.

In the 1950s and 1960s, the first cycle saw nine Daring and River Class destroyers built at the government-owned Williamstown and Cockatoo Island dockyards. The cycle also included an afloat support ship, hydro vessels and Attack Class patrol boats. In the 1970s and early 1980s, no surface combatants were built in Australia although four large naval support and hydrographic vessels were completed as well as eight heavy landing craft (LCH) and 14 Fremantle Class patrol boats.

The second naval combatant building cycle began in 1984 with an order for two guided missile frigates (FFGs). This was followed by orders for six Collins Class submarines, ten ANZAC Class frigates (involving work-share arrangements with New Zealand), six mine-hunters and other ships (e.g., Pacific Class patrol boats and two hydrographic ships). The second cycle will end with the commissioning into service of the last Armidale Class patrol boats in the late 2000s.

The third cycle (much smaller by volume) began in the late 2000s with tenders for the construction of three air warfare destroyers (AWD), two large landing helicopter dock (LHD) ships, afloat support ships and the watercraft element of the amphibious deployment and sustainment (ADAS) project. This cycle of naval shipbuilding is expected to end around 2016–17 with the next cycle expected to start around 2018.

The first cycle: the troubled years

The construction of Daring and River Class destroyers was notorious for its cost overruns, schedule slippages and industrial disputes. As noted by the Australian Senate inquiry into naval shipbuilding, 'Australia's increasing resort over the 1960s and 1970s to purchasing foreign naval vessels for the RAN reflected the poor performance of domestic naval shipbuilding projects' (Parliament of Australia, 2006: 41). Apart from two oceanographic ships, the Williamstown dockyard did not commission a naval vessel between 1971 and 1991 (ibid.: 42). And, after launching *HMAS Torrens* in 1968, the Cockatoo Island dockyard did not commission another naval vessel until 1986. Thus, no warships were launched in Australia for over 20 years. This preference for imports left Australian naval shipyards with mostly repair and (limited) refit work (ibid.: 42).

An example of local construction problems in the 1970s was the ill-fated DDL (light) destroyer project approved in 1972. Starting in 1975, three locally designed ships were to be built at the Williamstown dockyard. While it was accepted that cost premia for local build were to be incurred, they were justified on the grounds that local shipyards would later be best positioned to provide logistic through-life support and battle damage repairs. Also, investments needed to pump-prime local shipbuilding capabilities were aimed at enhancing the in-country skill base and technological know-how. The project was cancelled in 1973 as the Navy and the Department of Defence found the initial cost estimates to be grossly over-optimistic and a Joint Parliamentary Committee took the position that risks inherent in a local design were excessive (ibid.: 43). A lesson drawn from this experience was 'the need for tighter controls on Navy's design requirements. Part of the problem was that those involved with the specifications for the project were without responsibility for cost and schedule' (ibid.).

Following the cancellation of the DDL project, the government turned to overseas shipyards to initiate the acquisition of guided missile frigates. In 1974, the purchase of two imported FFGs was approved by the government. The vessels were to be built in the USA and acquired under foreign military sales (FMS) arrangements managed by USN. The purchase of a third FFG was approved in 1977 and a fourth in 1980. The ships were delivered between 1980 and 1984, mostly on schedule, but the cost of acquisition ballooned (ibid.: 43–4). In part, the cost overrun was due to higher than anticipated inflation and exchange rate re-alignment. But the purchase also revealed systemic problems in Australian defence procurement. As new technologies emerged, the first three frigates had to be retrofitted with long-range sonar systems and more capable helicopters. The design of the fourth FFG was altered to incorporate several modifications requested by the RAN. It was argued that some cost overruns might have been avoided 'had the RAN seized opportunities to incorporate modifications during the construction phase' (ibid.: 44). The procurement process was thus, apparently, neither sufficiently flexible nor agile to cope with changes in the technical specification of the deliverables.

There were also problems with the use of FMS arrangements. A 1974 Memorandum of Agreement with the US allowed Australia to withdraw from the project if the ships failed to meet the RAN's requirements or turned out to be 'unacceptably costly'. However, the USN and the US Department of Defense resisted changes requested by Australia (ibid.: 44). The Agreement also included a limited 'offset-type' provision providing for Australian industry manufacture and supply of components for both the RAN and the USN FFGs. The actual FMS arrangement, as opposed to what was initially envisaged, frustrated all such local content initiatives and restricted the scope for Australian industry participation. A lesson drawn from this experience was that 'in future, it was necessary to sign deeds of agreement with the prime contractors before negotiating a Letter of Offer and Acceptance with the U.S. government' (ibid.: 44). Another lesson drawn was that Australian industry was not competitive enough to win work on its own merit and that earlier participation of potential suppliers was needed at the project planning stages if any in-project import substitution was to be achieved (ibid.: 45).

By the end of the 1970s, it was apparent that the naval shipbuilding sector in Australia was suffering from deeply ingrained systemic problems (see Box 13.1 for an example of a high profile failure). Industrial relations were particularly bad as naval shipyards were seen by both the unions and the shipyard management as Defence-funded sheltered workshops (ibid.). The Department of Defence lacked the ability to specify its needs precisely enough to prevent

---

Box 13.1 *HMAS Success*: A triumph of hope over experience

By the mid-1970s, the government had reverted to its earlier preference for sourcing warships from Australian shipyards. However, the government also recognised that local industry capabilities had to be significantly enhanced if increased local content was to be achieved without massive cost penalties, schedule slippages and quality degradation. The decision to acquire a large naval replenishment ship *HMAS Success*, in 1977, was intended to initiate a new era of local industry support. To avoid problems associated with indigenous ship design, thus, to avoid turning the RAN into the sole parent of a unique design, the modified Endurance Class ship design was imported from France while the vessel was to be constructed locally by Vickers Cockatoo Dockyard Pty Ltd with the delivery date set for 1983. Nevertheless, the contract had to be renegotiated in 1983 and the ship was finally commissioned three years late at a cost (in current prices) nearly three times that approved at the outset of the project (Parliament of Australia, 2006: 45).

An acrimonious dispute between the shipbuilder and the Department of Defence followed. It concerned the ship blueprints and technical specifications contained in the French-supplied 'production package' (PP). 'There is evidence that the Department of Defence significantly underestimated the extent of the differences between the original building specifications and the French PP ... and ... Defence argued that the builder had deliberately underestimated the value of its original contract price in order to recover the costs from a significantly more expensive design package' (ibid.: 45). The project was also plagued by industrial disputes (resulting in a loss of 171 working days) and skill shortages. Inadequate project management and quality assurance also contributed to this poor outcome (ibid.: 46). As a harbinger of a new era of local industry involvement, *HMAS Success* was anything but a success story.

endemic requirements creep. It also lacked effective contracting skills. This was an important limitation as changing technologies, especially the growing use of electronics and information technology, made naval vessels increasingl complex and knowledge-intensive. Project management skills were also lacking in Defence and there were shortages of critical shipbuilding skills at naval yards.

Fresh start

The *1976 Defence White Paper* called for the development of local defence industry capabilities to enhance Australia's defence self-reliance. In line with this aim, the Australian Frigate Project (AFP) was initiated in 1978. The FFG-7 Class frigate was to be constructed locally to an imported design that was seen as flexible enough to accommodate high local content requirements. In 1980, the government decided to build two FFG-7 frigates at the Williamstown dockyard providing that the shipyard 'demonstrated its capacity to build the ships to the RAN's requirements' (ibid.: 46–7).

The new Labor government elected in 1983 not only re-affirmed self-reliance but also committed to microeconomic reform aimed at increasing the competitiveness of Australian manufacturing industry. The government was keen to build warships in-country providing that significant improvements in shipyard productivity could be negotiated and delivered. Preferably, this was to be achieved through transferring ownership to the private sector. Privatisation of government factories and shipyards, including naval shipbuilding facilities, was seen by the government as an essential part of its broader package of microeconomic reform (see Chapter 6). The new government was also ready to confront unions by resisting their demands to build a tanker at Cockatoo Island 'ultimately condemning the yard to extinction' (ibid.: 47).

The two FFGs were to be built at the Williamstown dockyard providing that its productivity could be lifted, cost and schedule discipline imposed and a series of enforceable agreements concluded to tighten work practices and restrict the drift of product specifications. A contract between the Department of Defence (customer) and the Department of Defence Support (contractor) was signed in 1983 for the two ships to be delivered between 1992 and 1994. The contract was to facilitate extensive local industry involvement to enhance national defence self-reliance and navy preparedness. As revealed by the 1986 review of the project by the Joint Committee of Public Accounts, the project budget included a cost premium for the local build of about 30 per cent (ibid.: 48). In 1987, the government sold the Williamstown naval dockyard, with the FFG arrangement, to the Australian Marine Engineering Corporation (AMEC). The privatisation of the yard turned out to be a very successful initiative. Both ships were launched by AMEC ahead of their initially agreed schedule and within the original cost estimates (in real terms). The only real cost increase was attributed to the privatisation process *per se*. Further, local industry content accounted for 90 per cent of the AMEC-borne cost and 75 per cent of the total project cost (ibid.).

The second cycle: back on track

While the beginning of the second shipbuilding cycle may be associated with the FFG project, it really unfolded in the late 1980s. The *1987 Defence White Paper* reaffirmed the Labor government's commitment to the development of competitive local defence industry capabilities, particularly in the shipbuilding sector, and to the policy of defence self-reliance. The second cycle got under way following the government's decision to build six Collins Class submarines, awarding the contract to the Australian Submarine Corporation in 1987; and ten ANZAC (Meko 200 Class) frigates, the contract going to the AMEC-Blohm+Voss consortium in 1989. In 1994, another major contract was awarded to the then Australian Defence Industries (ADI), now Thales, this time to build, to an Italian design, six Huon Class coastal minehunters. The final contract in the second cycle was signed in 2003 with Defence Maritime Services Pty (DMS), a joint venture between P&O Maritime Services and Serco Australia for the delivery of 14 Armidale Class patrol boats. The fleet was built by Austal Ships Ltd, Australia's largest commercial shipbuilder, and is to be fully supported by DMS throughout its service life (Kerr, 2008a). The second cycle also included some minor naval construction (e.g., Freedom Class patrol boats and hydrographic ships). In contrast to previous periods, nearly all ships required by the RAN during the second cycle were built in country. The main shipbuilders and projects are discussed below.

ASC and the Collins submarine project

To facilitate building submarines in Australia, the Australian Submarine Corporation (ASC) was established in 1985 as a joint venture between Sweden's Kockums (as shipbuilder and designer holding 49 per cent of the company's shares), the Australian government-owned Australian Industry Development Corporation (49 per cent) and Wormalds International and Chicago Bridge and Iron (holding the two per cent balance of shares). In 1987, ASC was chosen as the prime contractor for the fixed cost Aus$3.9 billion (1986 prices) project to deliver and support, through-life, six submarines. With over 73 per cent local content for the six platforms, at least 3,500 suppliers, and 1,600 individual contracts (Parliament of Australia, op. cit.: 56), the project was 'Australia's most ambitious and technically advanced defence project ever' (McIntosh and Prescott, 1999: 5).

The submarines experienced much publicised teething problems but were eventually acclaimed as 'world class' (Parliament of Australia, 2006). The main early problem was attributed to a decision to acquire a sophisticated combat data system (CDS) independently of the platform design when the most straightforward approach would have been to select a design with the CDS fitted as standard (Woolner, 2006: 72). This was compounded by Navy's preference for the CDS to be developed to order to meet its unique requirements rather than purchased as a military-off-the-shelf (MOTS) system

(Woolner, 2001: 9). 'By including the combat system with the platform in the single prime contract, with a unique military specification, Defence left itself widen open to ... technological problems' (McIntosh and Prescott, 1999). By 1993, it had become apparent that Rockwell, the CDS sub-contractor and designer, was not able to meet the Navy's specifications and Defence did not authorise a replacement MOTS system. The first submarine was provisionally accepted into service in 1996 with the combat system incomplete and by the late 1990s, the Collins Class project had become a major embarrassment for Defence and the government.

In 1999, the government terminated the failed CDS sub-contract and sought another CDS contractor through open competition. In 2001, however, the government decided to scrap the tender process and awarded the contract to the US firm Raytheon. Later that year, the RAN and the USN signed an agreement to cooperate in equipment-sourcing and logistic support and to enhance Collins Class interoperability with US ships. The German STN Atlas was also awarded a contract for sonar and navigation equipment (Parliament of Australia, 2006: 59–60).

The sequence in which the six hulls were constructed allowed for little learning by doing. As a former high-ranking naval officer argued during a 2006 parliamentary inquiry, 'There is a need to have an increased gap between the lead ship of a class and its successor. The lead ship needs to be evaluated and give the all clear before the successor is completed' (ibid.: 59, n 31). Instead, the ships were largely manufactured and constructed in batches. While economies of scale and scope are unavoidably lost through fragmenting the sequence of ship construction, there is more opportunity to alter the specifications of successor ships by learning from the in-service performance of their predecessors. This principle of 'spiral' or incremental new capability formation was well understood and practised in Sweden where the Collins Class design originated.[1]

Criticism has also been directed towards how the project was commissioned and managed by Defence. A fixed price contract was used to avoid cost overruns associated with traditional cost-plus contracts, and to shift most product-related and (construction) process-related risks from the Commonwealth to the contractor. However, the use of a fixed price contract for that reason was flawed on three accounts:

1   For a country lacking experience as the builder of modern, sophisticated weapons systems, the magnitude of the technological challenge inherent in this project was grossly underestimated both by the ASC as a contractor and by Defence as a customer. There was too much reliance on Kockums' expertise as a builder of submarine platforms and a rather poor understanding of technological challenges posed by the development of the bespoke CDS. In such circumstances, the Commonwealth (Defence) might have realised the limitations of risk-shifting between the parties and, instead, relied on risk-sharing mechanisms such as

those provided by incentive contracts, and risk mitigation through more collaborative management of the project.

2 Given the developmental nature of the project, the use of a fixed price contract provides little effective protection for the buyer (Defence) since contract variations are inevitable. An *ex-ante* fixed-price contract may in reality, become an *ex-post* cost-plus arrangement. If contract variations are regularly approved, there is no incentive for the contractor to seek cost efficiencies. It would have been preferable to use a flexible form of contract to allow for learning, to provide incentives to improve and share risks rather than to end up with the *de facto* cost-plus arrangement dressed up as a fixed price contract.

3 A belief that project risk could be shifted to the contractor to reduce the Commonwealth's exposure was naïve, given the ASC equity structure. With its 49 per cent share of equity, the Commonwealth was both the sole buyer of the ships and a key shareholder on the supply side. In 2000, when Kockums was acquired by the German submarine builder HDW, the Australian government stepped in to buy the Kockums' share of ASC equity.

This contractual debacle was summarised by an Australian parliamentary researcher thus:

> The most compelling lesson that can be learnt from the Collins submarine program is the importance of selecting the procurement strategy to suit the nature of the project. In hindsight, the point where it was decided to develop a unique design for the new submarines was the time to change the procurement strategy.
>
> (Woolner, 2001: 47)

The nationalisation of ASC was an embarrassment for a government overtly committed to the privatisation process: 'There was more than a touch of irony in the fact that after decades of effort to transfer all defence production capability to commercial industry, the Government finds itself the owner of ASC' (ASPI, 2002: 24). But, the nationalisation of ASC also exposed a more serious flaw in the procurement philosophy that was inherent in the Collins Class acquisition. Under the original contract, Kockums retained much intellectual property (IP) rights in the vessel's design. The ASC shareholding arrangement made it difficult to determine the ownership of various IP changes to the original design, new IP elements and the associated body of design data that were critical to access if ASC was to carry on as the ship's maintainer and modifier. The resultant legal dispute took until 2004 to resolve. Under the new arrangement, Kockums owns the legacy IP but ASC has full access to it (Parliament of Australia, 2006: 55).

The introduction of sensitive US technology into the vessels and the involvement of the US firm Electric Boat as a capability partner with ASC added another degree of complexity to the IP dispute. The inadequacies of the Collins Class technology management highlight the critical importance of access to proprietary technological know-how and IP in all knowledge-intensive projects. This is often poorly understood in large, technologically complex, developmental projects where a detailed design does not exist at the time a contract to proceed with the project is signed. Thus, a classic 'hold-up' relationship may emerge between the parties as the buyer belatedly realises that its ownership of an asset is incomplete without the transfer of all IP. The incompleteness of ownership rights imposes severe limitations on who is allowed to maintain the asset and who has the right to modify it. By the time the buyer becomes aware of such problems, the cost of contract renegotiation may be prohibitive and opportunities for switching suppliers very limited. This problem is compounded when the product design incorporates 'black boxes', which can only be accessed by the original supplier or its agent and which are subject to technology restrictions imposed by the supplier's home government.

In sum, the Collins Class project 'exposed serious flaws in defence's procurement processes' (ibid.: 57). Its well-publicised difficulties were not only embarrassing for the government but also made the government determined to change the nature of its principal–agent relationship with Defence. Following yet another review of new capability formation and procurement management by Defence (Kinnaird Report), the government decided to establish the Defence Materiel Organisation (DMO) as a 'prescribed agency' (partially detached from Defence and reporting directly to the government) to handle defence procurement and through-life capability support (see Chapter 6). In particular, DMO was to foster the kind of professional project management expertise required to bring greater rigour and experience into the procurement process.

The Tenix and ANZAC frigate project

At Aus$7 billion (2006 prices), the ANZAC Frigate project, was the largest *single* defence design and construction contract awarded in Australia in the closing decades of the twentieth century. It was also the only European-style naval 'work-share' contract. There were two customers, the navies of Australia (eight ships) and New Zealand (two ships) and the industry workload was shared between the two countries. It was expected that neither navy would cross-subsidise the shipbuilding costs of the other; sub-contractors were to be selected competitively; and the achieved work-share between the two countries was to reflect the overall cost shares.

Two consortia competed for the work and in 1989 AMEC-Blohm+Voss was declared the winning group for the 15-year design–construct–test project. The frigates were to be assembled at the newly acquired AMEC shipyard at Williamstown with modules to be built at Newcastle and Williamstown and at Whangarei in New Zealand. This was the first large naval surface ship constructed in Australia in this manner. During the contract life the ship-builder assumed prime responsibility for the project and changed its name twice to finally become Tenix Marine Division of Tenix Defence Pty Ltd. (Parliament of Australia, 2006). By the early 2000s, Tenix Defence, incorporating the marine division, had become one of Australia's largest defence contractors.

Despite its initially limited experience as a shipbuilder, Tenix completed the project on schedule and on budget. This outcome was helped by the modular ship construction and by a collaborative and highly synergistic arrangement with SAAB, the combat system supplier, to test the combat system prior to installation (Tasman Asia Pacific, 2000: 9). A requirement for the project was to achieve high levels of local content (the then government policy of Australian Industry Involvement, AII – see Chapter 6). This was in part accomplished through effective sub-contracting with the help of the Industrial Supplies Office (ISO), an agency set up to assist small and medium-sized enterprises (SME) in broadening their customer base. The search for sub-contractors to meet the AII target sometimes involved what a Tenix manager described[2] as 'reverse garage sales', i.e., components were put on display and SMEs were invited to decide which of these products could be made locally. This approach to sub-contracting has been acclaimed as a factor contributing to the project's cost and schedule discipline and copied by other projects (ibid.).

In 2001, Tenix, SAAB and the DMO (Defence) signed a tripartite long-term alliance agreement (the first of its kind) to provide in-service support for the ANZACs and to collaborate in future modifications and capability enhancements of the class (Parliament of Australia, 2006). This agreement concluded Tenix's involvement in the second shipbuilding cycle and positioned the company favourably as a bidder for construction work in the third cycle (see below).

ADI-Thales Australia and the minehunter project

In 1989, Australian Defence Industries (ADI) was formed as a corporatised, government-owned entity set up to consolidate major defence industry facilities still in government ownership. This included naval engineering at the Garden Island dockyard. ADI was awarded the prime contract for the Huon Class minehunters, based on an Italian design but with ADI as the designated design authority to modify and Australianise the design. The Aus\$ 917 million (1994 prices) project was the first Australian-sourced naval project in which the local prime contractor was given design authority (Parliament of Australia, 2006: 67). The six ships were built on schedule at a greenfield site facility in Newcastle employing new, 'greenfield' labour force (ibid.). The first composite hull was made in Italy and the remaining five at the Newcastle facility. The key to tight schedule success was an onshore facility that integrated and tested the combat system prior to its installation (Tasman

Economics, 2002: 9). As with ANZAC frigates, the Huon Class had also to comply with a high local content target of nearly 70 per cent.

In 1999, the French Thales company and the Australian company Transfield bought ADI from the Federal Government as a 50–50 venture (Parliament of Australia, 2006: 71). In 2006, Thales Australia was granted government permission to acquire the Transfield's share and consolidate it with its other Australian assets. This acquisition has turned Thales into one of Australia's largest defence contractors and a key naval repair, maintenance and upgrade contractor.

ADI-Thales Australia and the FFG upgrade project

In contrast to the very successful minehunter project, ADI's Aus$1 billion upgrade of four FFGs has been plagued with problems. This project, commissioned in 1999, involves the upgrade of ships' combat systems. Initially, it was to cover six ships but as the first ship was delivered three years late (in 2006) and over budget, the project scope was reduced to four vessels. The upgrade is very extensive and has required advanced design and engineering work, including the ADI-designed and developed Australian Distributed Architecture Combat System (Parliament of Australia, 2006: 69). However, 'the Department of Defence noted that while ADI is viable in the ship repair and upgrade activity, it is having problems in meeting schedule and performance specifications' (ibid.: 69). Comments such as this cast doubt on Thales' chances of success in the next shipbuilding cycle, even though, in 2007, it was Australia's largest defence contractor (Hinz and Ziesing, 2007–8).

Patrol boats and multi-hull builders

In Australia, there are two relatively small but internationally competitive commercial builders of aluminium multi-hulls: Austal Ships Ltd (Austal) and Incat. While they have no experience of building large steel vessels, both companies have established market niches in wave-piercing multi-hulls, fast multi-hull ferries and luxury motor yachts. Both companies have also been successful exporters and are well regarded internationally for their innovative designs.

In 2003, Austal won an Aus$553 million project to build 14 Armidale Class patrol boats – the last major contract of the second shipbuilding cycle. This contract was innovative in that Defence's requirements were framed in terms of operational performance specifications (e.g., operational availability) rather than set as detailed technical guidelines for ship designers.

In 2001, Austal also opened a US shipbuilding facility at Mobile in Alabama. From this foothold in the US shipbuilding market Austal operates as part of the General Dynamics team building prototype littoral combat ships (LCS) for the US Navy. Austal's role is to design and build the LCS platform for USN. If the LCS programme proceeds, the US LCS trimaran project may involve the building of 60 vessels at a cost of US$15 billion (Parliament of Australia, 2006: 72). Austal is the only Australian naval shipbuilder to be involved in foreign direct investment in offshore construction facility while retaining its core design team in Australia.

In the early 2000s, Incat sold and leased out high-speed catamarans to naval users, including the Australian Defence and the US Department of Defense. However, while the adaptability of these civil ship designs to military uses provides an example of dual-technology opportunities inherent in civilian designs, the company has no intention of expanding its operations into naval shipbuilding (ibid.: 74). Other small shipbuilders and repairers include: Forgacs with its facilities in Newcastle (NSW) and Brisbane (QLD), and NQEA based in Cairns (QLD).

Third post-war cycle

Based on the 2006 *Defence Capability Plan* (DCP) and anticipated upgrades and maintenance, Defence intends to spend about Aus$30.5 billion (2006 prices) on naval construction and sustainment programmes between 2006 and 2025 (ADO, 2006b: para. 3.4). While the proportion of local content differs from project to project, about Aus$19 billion (63 per cent) could be spent in Australia.

At the start of the third construction cycle in 2007, much Defence demand for naval construction and through-life support work over the subsequent period was committed under supply arrangements already in place or soon to be finalised. They included:

- the sustainment contracts for ANZAC frigates (Tenix Marine with SAAB as the combat systems integrator), Collins Class submarines (ASC with Raytheon as the combat systems integrator), and Armidale Class patrol boats (Defence Maritime Services);
- a construction contract for three air warfare destroyers (AWD) awarded to ASC and a contract with Raytheon for the AWD combat system, which is likely to be followed by a future contract for through-life support with the two companies;
- a contract for two landing helicopter dock (LHD) ships awarded to Tenix Marine, which is also well positioned to win a future contract for the LHD sustainment support.

The early commitment of such a large proportion of the 2006–18 spend limits the scope available to Defence to attract new competition into the domestically located market before the onset of the fourth shipbuilding cycle around 2018. Although the support arrangements for the AWDs and LHDs are yet to be decided when their construction phase draws to a close (the first ships are expected to be delivered in 2012–13), the logic of Defence sustainment requirements favours the existing supplier consortia.

Also, with the resource export boom in the late 2000s and, thus, tight labour markets, Defence has an incentive to build non-combatant vessels overseas. At an international level, competition is already strong and the competitiveness of the market could be reinforced by the availability of second-hand civil ships that could be adapted locally or overseas for Australian use.

Defence continues to source overseas designs for its major platforms (e.g., AWDs and LHDs). However, past schedule slippages and cost overruns have reduced its appetite for extensive Australianisation. As the success of the Spanish Navantia in winning the AWD and LHD contracts has demonstrated, overseas shipbuilders with successful designs adopted by a foreign parent navy will be able to compete for work in Australia by teaming with Australian prime contractors. Over the past 20 years, this preference for imported designs has produced competition between design-based consortia of shipbuilders, integrators and OEMs, fronted by domestic prime contractors but also including overseas designers and suppliers. This form of competition, and the increased market contestability resulting from the threat of foreign entry, have benefited Defence in that it has produced greater market rivalry and increased scope for benchmarking alternative delivery arrangements.

Naval maritime industry

Shipbuilders and ship repairers

The traditional concept of a 'naval maritime industry' focuses essentially on shipyard-based shipbuilding and ship repair/maintenance activities. In this narrowly focused approach to defining the industry, ship assembly and module manufacturing are included as long as module building and component manufacture are undertaken by specialised shipbuilders. Second-tier suppliers of major maritime equipment such as power plants or navionics, normally OEMs, and maritime service providers such as naval architects and surveyors are also included. However, jobbing firms supplying components made to order are likely to be excluded as are most third tier subcontractors.

Another distinction has traditionally been drawn between *shipbuilding*, including capability upgrades, and *ship sustainment* (maintenance and repair, including battle damage rectification). These two sub-sectors are essentially shipyard-based, using specialised infrastructure such as dry docks and sea lifts. In Australia, these two sectors have tended to operate in parallel, with the yards involved in ship repair and maintenance separated from those used in shipbuilding (e.g., the Garden Island dockyard specialising in ship repair while the Williamstown dockyard is used to integrate new vessels). This division of labour has evolved to allow platforms, once constructed by specialised and often overseas-based shipbuilders, to be maintained and repaired by 'jobbing' repair yards with on-board equipment supported by OEMs and jobbing contractors. This division of labour often required long supply chains linking OEMs to maintenance shipyards and led to delays in the availability of parts and long repair turnaround times.

Changes to the traditional division of labour between shipbuilding and ship repair/maintenance were driven by the growing complexity of platforms: ships were becoming increasingly automated, requiring the integration of on-board equipment into larger, network-based and knowledge-intensive systems. Sophisticated ships such as modern submarines and AWDs are increasingly maintained by their builders, companies that retain the IP they have created in platform design and/or work closely with the design authority to protect and support the integrity of ship design. The retention of or access to design IP, the use of dedicated facilities and the tacitness of ship-specific knowledge gained during the construction phase underpin the shipbuilders' competitive advantage in through-life upgrade and maintenance work. Thus, strong synergies (economies of scope) arise between the construction and sustainment phases of naval capability. Also, when ships are built in small batches with long gaps between shipbuilding cycles, resources used in construction (e.g., specialised labour, docking facilities) may subsequently be redeployed in fleet sustainment.

In Australia, this synergistic relationship between ship construction and sustainment phases was first exploited in the Collins Class submarine project: the Osborne construction facility is dedicated to the production and deep maintenance (full docking) cycles of the class. However, routine maintenance work is undertaken in Western Australia, where the ships are home-ported. This model of 'construction-enabled' ship maintenance has now been adopted in the sustainment of other vessels (e.g., the ANZACs) and is also likely to be used in support of future additions to the fleet (e.g., AWDs and LHDs).[3]

Australia's naval shipbuilding activity is largely confined to four main shipbuilders: ASC, Tenix Marine, Thales (ADI) and Austal. Of these, ASC and Austal are currently Australian-owned while Thales is a fully-owned subsidiary of the French parent company and BAE Systems has announced its intention to purchase Tenix Marine.[4] As the third post-war building cycle began to unfold, three of these companies were involved in the construction of the AWDs, LHDs, and afloat support ships; the progressive upgrades of ANZAC and FFG frigates, the Collins Class submarines, minehunters and other minor war vessels; and maintenance of the fleet-in-being. Defence Maritime Services (DMS) are responsible for the maintenance of Armidale Class patrol boats built by Austal. (Some module building and consolidation work and maintenance activity has been undertaken by smaller maritime suppliers such as Forgacs, with facilities in Newcastle and Brisbane, and NQEA in Cairns.) The three shipbuilders and DMS are also the main providers of naval sustainment support: the submarine deep and intermediate maintenance cycles, ANZAC and FFG frigate sustainment, support for minehunters, patrol boats and other minor war vessels.

Facility disposition and ownership

In the 2000s, Defence's preferred industry disposition reflects the RAN's fleet basing strategy, which envisages the maintenance and home-porting of major surface ships on the east coast of Australia (Sydney) at Fleet Base East (FBE) and on the west coast (near Perth) at Fleet Base West (FBW). The submarines are home ported and maintained at FBW but all full cycle dockings (deep maintenance) are carried out at Osborne in South Australia. Minor war vessels are mostly home-ported and supported in Darwin and Cairns.

The home-porting of naval vessels at FBW has spawned the development of navy-preparedness-related industries in close proximity to the ships they support. Thus, in addition to major shipbuilders and repairers (e.g., Tenix Marine, ASC, Austal), other designers and builders of aluminium boats and ships, and engineering firms supporting resource projects have clustered in Western Australia, in particular at the Australian Marine Complex (AMC) in Henderson. There appear to be strong *agglomeration economies* that naval firms can gain by locating at AMC. There is also more scope for forging direct business links between firms that operate in close proximity.

In the previous naval shipbuilding cycle, ownership of capital-intensive facilities (e.g., shiplifts and dry docks) was a key characteristic of naval ship-builders. This is still largely the case. However, the high cost of establishing and maintaining such facilities constitutes a formidable barrier to entry into the Australian market for naval shipbuilding and repair. The provision of these facilities involves high fixed costs which can only be recouped over the long term and which even the largest marine companies have difficulty absorbing in the relatively small Australian market. An example of such a facility is the shiplift/transfer system operated by Tenix Marine's facility also located at Henderson, WA. This facility, initially funded by Defence and the WA State Government and subsequently sold to Tenix Marine, comprises a ship lift capable of handling ships of over 8,000 tonnes, a rail transfer system and an innovative turntable arrangement connecting four work stations to the ship lift, thereby eliminating the need for ships to queue for dry docking.[5] Subsequently, the West Australian (state) government developed adjacent to the Tenix facility a protected deepwater harbour, a 15,000-tonne service and heavy lift wharf, a 3,000-tonne load-out wharf, a 4,800 sq m mobile assembly hall with a 200-tonne mobile portal crane, 39 hectares of paved laydown area, and offices, workshops and other amenities. This investment, completed in mid-2003, is owned by the State Government and operated by AMC Management (WA) Pty Ltd as a common user facility (CUF).

While Tenix's Henderson facility is maintained by the company for its own use, the CUF is deliberately designed for multiple users including the oil and gas, resources, marine and defence industries and is sufficiently large to accommodate several projects simultaneously. Parties using the facility pro-vide their own management and workforce and accept normal project accountabilities. They use the CUF only when their projects require it and are charged only for the specific facilities they use for a particular period. This arrangement greatly reduces project set-up costs and company overheads, thereby enhancing CUF-users' potential ability to win contracts.

Initial infrastructural investments in the Henderson CUF attracted complementary private investment on land adjacent to the marine complex (e.g., ASC is establishing its submarine maintenance facility there). In response to these developments, the West Australian government invested a further Aus $81.5 million in a floating dock to launch and dock large ships and a rail transfer system to allow construction and repair within the CUF's undercover facilities; an extension and upgrade of the existing wharves to accommodate all types of naval and commercial vessels; and the installation of marine services such as power, seawater fire main, wharf communications and sewerage off-take.

The South Australian government followed suit with plans to invest Aus$300 million in Techport Australia, including a CUF adjacent to ASC in Osborne (Kerr, 2008b: 2). The SA CUF is scheduled for completion in 2010 and, like its WA counterpart, is intended to support multiple projects concurrently. The nearest equivalents to such infrastructure on the east coast are the Captain Cook Dock (leased by the Commonwealth to Thales at Garden Island, Sydney).

The introduction of CUFs funded by state governments and, subject to leasing arrangements, on-going Commonwealth ownership of the Captain Cook Dock combine to reduce the significance of facilities ownership as a barrier to entry, particularly in the market for naval ship repair. As an indicator of policy trends, they also suggest a reappraisal of the value of public ownership of assets which governments were so determined to privatise in the late 1980s and 1990s.

Changing division of labour

The impact of defence procurement on industry was traditionally viewed in terms of the relationship between an agency responsible for defence procurement and the prime contractors with which it negotiated. These days, however, it is recognised that effective procurement depends on the activities and performance of a much wider range of industry players, domestically and overseas.

Defence considers the naval maritime industry in broad terms which embrace not only shipbuilders and maintainers but also a myriad of second- and third-tier SME suppliers (ADO, 2006a: paras 1.18–1.20). The latter reportedly account for some 70 per cent of the total cost of a shipbuilding project.[6] As noted in the Defence submission to the 2006 Senate Inquiry, a 'typical' frigate comprises some 170,000 parts and components provided by 600 suppliers and sub-contractors and takes 1.2 million person-hours, spread over 22 months, to construct. A large conventional submarine may consist of some 500,000 parts provided by 1,600 suppliers and takes 2.5 million person-hours and 60 months to construct (ibid.: Figure 1).

Table 13.1 shows the stylised breakdown of typical warship production costs that includes all on-board combat systems but excludes capability elements that are shore-rather than ship-based. In the table, the platform element of capability accounts for 33 per cent of the total production cost for a more technologically complex naval combatant, say, a 3,500-tonne frigate costing about Aus$600 million to build, while on-board combat systems account for 42 per cent of the cost. The other two cost items are largely platform-related and represent the cost of logistic support acquired during the construction phase and the cost of project (delivery process) management. By way of comparison, for a large naval support ship constructed closer to commercial standards, on-board combat systems account for only 15 per cent of all costs and the platform for 47 per cent of the total. For a naval combatant capability, therefore, the combat systems component of the overall system is the most important element, both in cost and functional terms. This is reversed in the case of the naval support capability. For a typical combatant ship, imported combat systems and other major equipment account for 50 per cent of the construction cost (ibid.: para 2.5). For technologically complex vessels such as the submarines and the AWDs, the proportion is likely to be much higher.

In Australia, combat systems integrators (e.g., Raytheon, Thales, BAE Systems) and OEMs (e.g., STN Atlas) are either subsidiaries or agents of major overseas companies (with the notable exception of CEA Technologies). In the early 2000s, the Australian industrial footprint of these multinational companies varied from significant (Raytheon, Thales) to small (Lockheed Martin). The footprint could in most cases be flexibly expanded or shrunk, depending on the quantity of in-country work in hand. Much has been claimed by these subsidiaries for their direct access to the parent company's global network and technology. However, Defence has at times observed, 'experience indicates that they have difficulty obtaining suitable licensing and intellectual property rights which in turn may have time and cost implications particularly in providing sustainment' (ibid.: para. 2.9). For this reason the Commonwealth sometimes facilitates technology transfers using

Table 13.1 Percentage cost breakdown in warship production

Production cost element	Surface combatant ship (%)	Support ship (%)
Platform design, hull, machinery and equipment	3	47
Combat systems	41	15
Logistics support and training (mostly platform-related)	17	25
Project management	9	13
Total	100	100

government-to-government arrangements (e.g., the US FMS framework) to secure access to sensitive foreign equipment, military technologies and IP (e.g., the direct purchase of the US Aegis combat system for the AWDs by Defence from the US Navy under the FMS arrangement). Such Commonwealth action has direct implications for the role of prime contractors, an issue we address below.

Critical to the provision of through-life support is access to the IP behind the *ship design*. At the smaller-vessel end of the naval market, Austal is, arguably, the only Australian shipbuilder offering world competitive naval design expertise for multi-hull aluminium vessels.[7] For larger and/or more complex ships, Australia has been an importer of ship design, usually from parent navy ship designers such as the German Blohm+Voss for Meko 200 Class frigates (ANZAC ships) and the Swedish Kockums for the Collins Class submarines. However, design adaptation to meet the Australian Navy's unique requirements and political pressures to increase local content have resulted in considerable Australianisation of original designs. In the Collins Class case, this was further complicated by the transfer of ASC ownership to the Commonwealth. It was only when the Commonwealth negotiated the full access to the Kockums-owned IP that ASC became the *de facto* design authority for the class of which the RAN is the parent navy. Similarly, Tenix Defence is the *de facto* design authority for ANZAC ships. The Huon Class minehunter was 'the first Australian-sourced naval defence project in which the prime contractor (ADI now Thales) *was given* design authority' (ibid.: para. 4.39 – our italics). This is in marked contrast to the ANZAC ship and Collins Class projects, where Tenix and ASC effectively became design authorities by default.

Defence appears to be determined to avoid excessive Australianisation in ship design in the next generation of vessels to be constructed in Australia: the AWDs, LHDs and afloat support ships. For example, in the case of AWDs, the government overruled Navy's reported preference for the unproven Gibbs & Cox adaptation of the Arleigh Burke destroyer in favour of the already operational Spanish design based on the Navantia-built F100 destroyer (*The Australian*, 1 March 2007: 8).

Marine industry supply chains

Defence's broader approach to what constitutes the naval marine industry has also shifted the emphasis from functionally-based naval industry sectors, such as shipbuilders, OEMs and ship repairers, to capability-centred supply chains that include combat systems integrators and the plethora of second- and third-tier suppliers, many straddling sectoral divisions and serving different customers in different industries. While the functional representation is helpful in identifying firms largely dedicated to shipbuilding and fleet sustainment, the supply chain framework sheds more light on the competitive dynamics of defence capability supply.

Two types of prime contractor arrangements and, thus, supply chain structures, have dominated the interface between Defence and Australian naval shipbuilders:

- a *conventional single channel model* under which a single prime contractor is engaged by Defence to lead and manage the supply chain and to orchestrate all the back-to-back contracts with upstream suppliers of systems, equipment, components and services;
- a *complex multi-channel model*, where two or more prime contractors are engaged by Defence to lead and manage parallel supply channels that jointly produce the required capability element.

These two models are used both in shipbuilding and through-life fleet sustainment. To illustrate, consider Figure 13.1, where two stylised traditional supply chain management (SCM) models are shown, one for the construction of a support ship and another for a major weapons upgrade.[8] In the shipbuilding case, the shipbuilder is also a prime contractor who engages a system integrator and OEMs as well as a large number of small second and third tier subcontractors to produce the end product: a platform with all systems and equipment integrated into it or on it. Although the ship design is likely to be imported and Australianised, it is a relatively simple design. Given its role in the process, the prime contractor, as the project's manager, accounts for about 13 per cent of the total project cost. In the weapons upgrade case, much greater weight (and cost share) are assigned to combat system integration but project management by the prime contractor accounts for about 12 per cent of the total project cost.

The conventional prime contracting model has traditionally been used by Defence as a risk management arrangement under which the prime contractor is expected to manage and mitigate risks associated with the operation

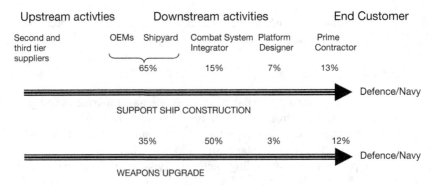

Figure 13.1 Conventional value chains for support ship and weapons upgrade: total project cost breakdown by supplier category

Source: Based on ADO (2006a, Table 1: 8)

of the supply chain. This model was used by Defence during the second building cycle in all major shipbuilding projects, including, initially, the Collins Class submarines. But the conventional model failed the test when the Collins Class project ran into problems with combat system integration. By 1993, Rockwell, the combat systems integrator, was not able to comply with Navy's specifications and 'ASC effectively lost control of the Rockwell sub-contract' (Parliament of Australia, 2006: para. 4.18). As noted earlier, the solution involved replacing the original combat system integrator and Defence awarding the contract to Raytheon in 2001 (ibid.). Under this arrangement, Raytheon became a parallel prime contractor for system integration. To complicate the model further, '*Defence itself has essentially primed*' the subsequent Aus$500 million combat data system replacement programme by purchasing the FMS-mediated software and working *with* ASC, Raytheon, Atlas Electronics and Thales Underwater Systems to integrate all combat systems (ibid.: para. 4.20 – our italics).

The resulting structure is represented in Figure 13.2, which shows a complex, multi-channel supply chain (say, for a frigate-type naval combatant). In Figure 13.2, the stylised supply chain involves two *parallel channels* of progressive value-adding activity: platform construction and systems integration. Figure 13.2 highlights downstream activities (close to the end customer) such as project management, design, and platform integration along the platform construction supply channel and combat system integration along the systems integration channel. Further upstream are OEMs that provide equipment and subsystems for downstream platform and systems integrators and other second and third tier subcontractors who provide inputs for OEMs and downstream integration activities. Some of these smaller second/third tier contractors are specialised naval suppliers but most tend to be broadly based manufacturers and service providers. Also, some apparently small subcontractors (in terms of quantities and dollar value of supplies) are subsidiaries or agents of large producers of generic products. As we move from right to left along each supply channel, from downstream to

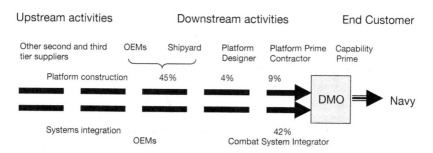

Figure 13.2 Complex supply chain for a naval combatant: total project cost breakdown by supplier category

Source: Based on ADO (2006a, Table 1: 8)

upstream activities, suppliers are less likely to be dedicated to the production of naval systems. The reduced role of the prime contractor for the platform is indicated by the smaller proportion of the total project cost (9 per cent).

This representation of the naval construction supply chain for complex projects emphasises the changing concept of the prime contractor. In this case, there are two prime contractors operating *in parallel*, the shipbuilder (prime contractor for the platforms) and the systems integrator (prime contractor for the combat system). Shipbuilding activity accounts for nearly 60 per cent of the total project cost and systems acquisition and integration for over 40 per cent. Figure 13.2 highlights an important aspect of complex naval ship construction: the *management of the supply chain is distributed between two or more prime contractors*, each responsible for the orchestration/management of construction/integration activities along its particular supply *channel*. This at once raises a higher-level coordination problem: Defence, through its procurement agency DMO (shown in Figure 13.2 as a 'capability prime'), is now responsible for coordinating the activities of the two prime contractors. This necessarily implies that Defence cannot (as it has often sought to) adopt and maintain an arm's-length relationship with its suppliers. The new model has already been applied in the acquisition of the AWDs via an alliance-based contracting strategy.[9] This strategy is given practical effect through an Alliance Based Target Incentive Agreement signed in October 2007 by the Defence Materiel Organisation, ASC as the designated builder and prime contractor for the Navantia-designed AWD platform and Raytheon Australia as the combat system integrator.[10] Defence is also directly involved in the supply chain management as it purchased directly from the US Navy the Aus$1 billion US Lockheed Martin Aegis combat system, which Raytheon is to integrate with the platform and other on-board systems.

Competition for large, complex projects

During the second shipbuilding cycle, the competitive conduct of defence naval suppliers was assigned a pivotal role in achieving 'value for money' for the Commonwealth and became a mantra of Defence procurement (see also Chapter 6). Competition to take on the role of prime contractor for larger, complex naval projects took the form of rivalry among consortia formed between Australian shipbuilders, overseas designers, and Australian subsidiaries of overseas systems houses. The competitive process led to the award of contracts to successful consortia (e.g., AMEC-Blohm+Voss for the ANZAC Ships) using the conventional model of engagement between the prime contractor and Defence. This mode of engagement had worked reasonably well for projects involving less complex deliverables, e.g., the ANZAC ships. However, as the experience of the Collins project demonstrated, the conventional model based on the arm's-length relationship between Defence and prime was not suitable for procuring complex capabilities such as submarines or technologically challenging systems upgrade (re: the troubled FFG upgrade). A key reason for the difficulty lies in elements of hold-up present in the relationship between the incumbent prime contractor and Defence.

While competition is normally used to engage prime contractors fronting competing overseas designs, competitive pressure on prime contractors, combat systems integrators and often key OEMs tends to fall away once the prime contract is signed. If the prime contractor fails to deliver contracted performance, slips behind schedule or runs over the budget, Defence is heavily constrained in its option for remedial action. Switching prime contractors and/or main sub-contractors is often technologically infeasible, financially prohibitive or politically too embarrassing. Even for a medium-sized naval project, such as the FFG upgrade, the prime contractor was allowed to continue with the project, despite public expressions of dissatisfaction from the client and an adverse national audit report. Despite tough rhetoric in public, Defence in reality has only limited scope to bring a contractor into line. A financial penalty for contractual default, for example, may be no more than a slap with the business equivalent of a feather. And, when the worst comes to the worst, as in the case of Rockwell's failure to deliver the CDS system for the Collins Class submarines, Defence decided against re-competing the requirement and, instead, *appointed* a substitute, Raytheon, to take over as system integrator.

In the third naval procurement cycle, much of the competitive process for major naval projects was completed early on, with winning consortia announced for AWDs and LHDs and large, long-term support contracts for ANZACs and Collins submarines given to Tenix and ASC. It seemed unlikely that any prime contractor would subsequently be dumped and replaced by another contractor. However, there was a key difference between the second and the third shipbuilding cycles. Defence had become aware that lack of effective competitive pressure, following contract award had deprived it of effective market power vis-à-vis its larger prime contractors. The complex, multi-channel procurement model described above can be viewed as an evolutionary adaptation responding to Defence's recognition that, to maximise the likelihood of success for its projects, it would have to embrace fully its ultimate responsibility as 'prime contractor of the last resort'. It had been obliged to accept that the prospects for shifting project risk to primes in large, strategically important projects were at best limited and, realistically, often unachievable. For successful outcomes, Defence would have to manage projects more proactively and build close, synergistic relationships with primes rather than relying on contract specifications, impracticable penalties for non-performance and arm's-length dealings with contractors.

Conclusion

The purpose of this industry case study has been twofold. First, it illustrates a range of problems typical of many Defence-Industry relationships in small countries. These include, *inter alia*: local production vs. imports, political and economic vs. strategic aspects of in-country sourcing of materiel, the role of competition, the management of procurement risks, and business models used to engage suppliers and mitigate the risks of inadequate supplier performance. Second, this case complements the 'Australian' chapter in this volume (Chapter 6). It shows in greater detail how various industry policies and procurement initiatives have worked over the past thirty years. By focusing on naval shipbuilding and repair, we have not only selected a sector that is seen in Australia as the jewel in the defence industry crown but also one that comprises a wide variety of business entities – from diversified large contractors to highly specialised small firms, including new forms of 'government shipyards' such CUF – and technologies: mechanical (platforms), IT (combat systems, specialised equipment). We conclude this case study by highlighting what we regard are key lessons to be drawn from Australian naval shipbuilding experience.

Demand

Lumpiness of demand

For reasons associated with durability, cost and the usually gradual advance of military technological knowledge, most defence equipment, including that embedded in naval systems, tends to be replaced at relatively widely spaced intervals rather than continuously. This applies to simple weapons systems, such as small arms, but particularly to large and 'chunky' elements of capability such as naval ships that tend to be replaced as fleets. This batching of demands can be smoothed by Defence to the extent that fleet replacements can be staggered, but some lumpiness of demand seems unavoidable. Long-term forward plans, such as the Australian DCP, make it easier for industry to anticipate forthcoming demand and ramp up for future tenders. But Defence has to be flexible enough in its forward commitments to meet changes in strategic and economic circumstances, sometimes at very short notice.

Asset ownership

The complete control of 'use rights' is necessary for key combat assets such as naval combatants. This can be achieved through the conventional full ownership of ships, or leases, particularly the leasing of vessels from foreign governments. However, more flexible arrangements can be used to procure the services of secondary assets such as patrol boats, which tend to operate in peacetime in more stable roles and predictable circumstances. As demonstrated by the Armidale patrol boat arrangement, the procurement of ship services from a private consortium of maritime service providers rather than the full ownership of vessels can be feasible and attractive. And, in the event of war, the nature of the relationship can be changed by placing the vessels under complete naval control.

Local content requirements

The history of Australian naval shipbuilding and repair highlights often-encountered trade-offs between local and overseas sources of supply and naval preparedness (see Chapter 6). In Australia, as in other small countries, it is increasingly accepted that building ships in country is politically as much as strategically driven. In modern warfare, there is no time to replace combat assets such as ships and nations are unlikely to engage in wars of equipment attrition. It is thus perceived as more important to have domestic industry capability on hand to undertake ship repair and modification, including battle damage rectification. The LHDs project, incorporating hull construction at Navantia's Ferrol shipyard in Spain and superstructure by Tenix in Australia, departs from the recent tradition of building ships in-country to an imported design. However, the procurement of the AWDs follows the conventional path, with expectations that substantial premia will be paid for the political decision to construct them in South Australia (Dodd, 2008).

Australia continues to import naval ship designs and the recent tendency is to minimise design Australianisation (Kerr, 2008a, 2008b). To reduce risks of 'design parentage', the approach is to incorporate MOTS components in imported systems and make considerable use of the design authority's established supply chain (e.g., the AWD and LHD arrangements with Navantia). Political pressures are likely to support ongoing high levels of local content in platform construction but strategic issues may be more important in influencing levels of local content in combat systems maintenance and modification. Defence may be worried about the risk of relying on local supply for developmental components. For example, the locally-developed CEAFAR active phased array radar for the AWDs has not been included in the baseline specification as it is still under development by its maker, a small but high profile Australian firm CEA. But, the new technology is likely to be incorporated as it matures (Kerr, 2008b).

Business models

A range of new business models has evolved in Defence to engage suppliers in the most effective way. These models tend to be tailored to the nature of the product and the characteristics of the supplier. Where mature products are supplied by established contractors, the inherent risks of performance degradation and schedule slippages are low and traditional fixed/firm price models can be used. An evolved model of this kind has been used to acquire the services of the Armidale Class patrol boats. When the developmental content of the product increases and if the supplier's track record also inspires less confidence, various forms of incentive and incremental contracting are more likely to be used (e.g., the acquisition of the electronic warfare system for the AWDs, ibid.: 6). And for technologically sophisticated, complex and politically high-profile acquisitions, such as the AWDs, it is now accepted that the

Commonwealth cannot divest itself of its ultimate responsibility for strategic capability formation. In the emergence of the multi-prime contractor model (where DMO has entered a 'prime alliance' with shipbuilder and systems supplier), it has been recognised that the buyer's procurement agency must engage in relationship management and that even a very detailed contract cannot take all risks away from the Commonwealth to commercial prime contractors.

Supply

Facility ownership

It was widely claimed in the 1980s and 1990s that privatising government shipyards and factories was a necessary precondition for their improved productivity and reliability (see Chapter 6). In 2000s, however, it became increasingly apparent that the private sector would not invest in capital-intensive assets such as shipyards unless it could reasonably expect an adequate return on its investment. Commercial owners would only invest in new shipbuilding facilities if their order books justified the heavy capital commitment. This in turn depended on owners' confidence in a continuing flow of potentially profitable orders – hard to create in the face of a history of long intermissions in demand and the competitive processes for allocating work. It has, thus, been recognised that competitive sourcing might have to be abandoned in favour of sole or dual sourcing if local platform builders and maintainers are to be encouraged to invest in capital-intensive facilities. It also seems increasingly accepted that lack of competition and not the public ownership was the main cause of poor performance of government shipyards and factories. The designation of a private contractor as sole source provider to Defence is likely to lead to many problems previously experienced with government-owned enterprise.

As the third post-war building cycle unfolded, the competition between the States for defence orders has resulted in renewed public investment in capital infrastructure in shipbuilding and repair. The CUF model was pioneered by Western Australia and adopted by South Australia. And, the Commonwealth has retained its ownership of the Garden Island dock leased to Thales. Under CUF arrangements, governments attract and sustain private naval investment by investing in complementary infrastructure and engage in a form of quasi-vertical integration under which the publicly-owned asset is then leased to a private contractor for the period it requires to supply goods and services to Defence.

The 1990s and 2000s have also witnessed increased penetration of the Australian shipbuilding sector by overseas capital. Of the three largest naval shipbuilders, two (ADI and Tenix) have become subsidiaries of foreign companies (Thales and, subject to satisfactory negotiations, BAE Systems, respectively). The third, ASC, was to be sold in the late 2000s, and may yet end up in overseas ownership. All systems integrators and nearly all major OEMs (except CEA) are subsidiaries of overseas companies. And P&O Maritime Services and Serco Australia have pioneered the provision of fully supported services for minor naval vessels (the Armidale Class). This trend is very much in keeping with global developments in defence industry. Few small countries can support indigenous systems integrators and OEMs while exporting of defence-related products from small countries poses well-known difficulties (see Chapter 3).

Structure

The 1990s and 2000s have also seen the increased consolidation of ship assembly in fewer hands and, in a clear break with the past, a growing integration between shipbuilding and repair. In part, the latter trend reflects the changing global division of labour as systems houses and OEMs become increasingly involved in the provision of through-life support for their products. In part, it also reflects the shift of emphasis in Australian industry policy from a focus on platform construction to through-life capability support. The three large projects of the second shipbuilding cycle have also had implications for the size distribution of firms in the sector. The building of the ANZACs, Collins submarines and Huon minehunters attracted a large number of firms to third tier naval subcontracting. As a result, the size distribution takes a Pareto form with a small number of large naval firms operating in the first and second tiers, downstream in the supply chain, and a large number of third-tier sub-contractors are engaged in the upstream segments of the chain.

Conduct

In the 1990s and 2000s, firms have increasingly made efforts to collaborate along the supply chain rather than to do business with each other at arm's length. On the other hand, firms also appear to have been competing with increasing frequency and intensity for markets opening up for all segments of the naval supply chain. Firms' awareness of their mutual dependence in the network of supply arrangements appears to be driving a tendency to greater collaboration once the principal contract has been awarded.

Performance

The second shipbuilding cycle saw a marked increase in shipyard productivity, and less severe budget overruns and schedule slippages. The Collins Class project was the most troublesome acquisition of the period, but by no means because of problems restricted to the supply side. The FFG upgrade project appears to have suffered from the classic syndrome of supplier overconfidence: ADI seems to have lacked awareness of its capability limitations and underestimated the importance of technical challenges that were likely to arise in a project of such complexity. As the third shipbuilding cycle unfolded, Defence (and indirectly the government) appeared reluctant to risk quality-budget-schedule outcomes by trying to over-Australianise designs and aiming at high local content targets. 'Buying MOTS' and minimising the local developmental content characterised its strategy to head off poor performance.

Demand-supply interface: Competition for and in the market

Arguably the most striking development since the end of the second ship-building cycle, particularly in the aftermath of the Collins project, has been much better understanding by Defence of competitive processes, especially the difference between for- and in-the market competition. This reflects the growing maturity of Defence as an investor in new capability elements and buyer of military materiel. It is increasingly accepted that different competitive processes operate for different segments of the naval supply chain. Creating a competitive environment in downstream segments of the chain calls for opening the market to overseas participants. When this is done, the range of competing designs and combat systems is broadened as overseas consortia of platform builders, system integrators and OEMs (sometimes combining with local firms) come to contest the market. Once a preferred package has been selected, competition in the market follows, sub-contractors vying for various elements of the package. Domestic subcontractors can be assured a major role in this part of the process if local content requirements are in force.

Finally, it appears that Defence has become more aware of the difference between the pre- and post-contract opportunities open to it in sourcing supplies. It now appears to be better understood that, once the contract is signed, switching suppliers and supplies may be impossible for technological, budgetary or political reasons. As a project progresses through the tendering process, the scope for product and supplier substitution decreases and, for major projects, there may be no way, realistically, of returning to *status quo ante*. It now also seems to be accepted that applying a 'one-size-fits-all' business model can often be a recipe for failure in defence procurement. But, to tailor different models to different acquisitions, it is necessary to acquire good understanding of supply conditions and commercial business processes. Following its designation as a prescribed agency, the DMO has become increasingly professionalised as a procurement agency and as a hands-on equity partner in major acquisition projects.

To sum up. Faced with the challenge of efficiently procuring naval vessels of increasing technological sophistication, the Australian government has learned over recent decades that contract arrangements alone are often insufficient to allow it to address and remedy problems, especially where developmental issues are at stake. While fixed-cost contracts, for example, apparently offer the Defence customer the prospect of shifting all risk to its industry suppliers, the experience of the Collins Class submarine clearly showed that when the success of the project was seriously threatened, the government felt it had little option but to intervene directly to re-organise supply side production arrangements. As the nature of the naval warship has changed with technological innovation, it has also become clear that government must take on an overarching prime responsibility if the production tasks involved are to be effectively coordinated. A warship is a sea-borne platform carrying weapons. But the business of designing and building seaworthy and battle-ready vessels is altogether different from the enterprise of designing and producing the highly sophisticated, often network-integrated weapons systems that the warship must support. We have shown that the Australian government has recognised the force of this reality by creating different industry primes for platform-building and weapons production and adopting the coordinating role for itself. Despite past rhetoric to the contrary, innovation and complexity in design and production thus appear to create conditions in which governments find themselves obliged to form close and durable relationships with suppliers if they wish to maximise the likelihood of project success. It may neither be realistic, given the industry structure, nor wise, given the alternatives available to suppliers, for governments to threaten competitive recontracting as their sole, or even principal, means of discipline and performance control.

For political reasons familiar in most countries (smaller ones being no exception), governments routinely find themselves under pressure to favour domestically-located supply. If the depth and breadth of expertise and capabilities in local defence industry are limited, there is the potential of conflict with the goals of successfully procuring increasingly sophisticated systems, especially if tailored idiosyncratically to national requirements. As this chapter has shown, Australia has at times focused heavily on local content requirements in naval shipbuilding and, whatever the benefits, has sometimes paid a high price for doing so. The issues around such requirements are not likely to disappear in Australia or in other countries in the foreseeable future. In relation to naval ships, it may appear eminently sensible and potentially efficient to provide sustainment, repair and maintenance for warships domestically but more problematic to justify actually building the vessels in country. On the other hand, it can be argued that such a large fraction of through-life costs relate to post-delivery support that any cost premium on domestic construction can be discounted as relatively unimportant. If local through-life support is more efficient when ships are also built locally in the first place, the argument is reinforced. Analogous arguments may also be applied to other sorts of platform and weapons system. No simple generic solution indicates when 'make' domestically should be preferred to 'buy' overseas in such cases. But the historic experience of substantial cost premia on local content in small country environments suggests that a critical eye should always be applied to *ex ante* predictions of large expected net benefits from locally producing the more innovative and idiosyncratic weapons systems.

Acknowledgements

The authors wish to acknowledge the generous assistance provided by Dr Mark Thomson of the Australian Strategic Policy Institute, Australia's foremost expert on Defence finance and a leading commentator on naval shipbuilding. However, all opinions expressed in this chapters are theirs not his.

Notes

1 Sweden has traditionally ordered its submarines in very small batches to allow for benefits of learning-by-doing and technological change to be continuously absorbed into subsequent designs even though it has been well understood that cost premia would be incurred as a result of fragmented production.
2 During one of the authors' visit to the Williamstown shipyard in the mid-1990s.
3 Under this model of construction-enabled ship maintenance, two major contracts were let. In 2001, Defence signed a long-term alliance agreement, underpinned by a through-life support contract, with Tenix Marine (shipbuilder) and SAAB (system integrator) covering the development of all future capability change packages for the ANZAC ships, and, in 2003, it signed another long-term contract with ASC for the 25 year through-life support for the *Collins* Class submarines.
4 However, in 2007, Tenix Defence, including its Tenix Marine Division, was offered for sale and BAE Systems Australia was rumored to be the most probable buyer of. Also, as ASC is likely to be offered for sale in the late 2000s, Australian subsidiaries of major foreign companies may be invited to bid for it.
5 See http://www.tenix.com/Main.asp?ID=426&ListID=21.
6 These suppliers are said to contribute '70% by value of a project' (ADO, 2006a: 1.18). However, the third-tier contractors as well as other tiers of suppliers should not be seen as a reflection of a hierarchical industry structure. These relationships are project-specific. Thus, a large firm that is engaged as a prime contractor in one project may be a third tier sub-contractor in another.
7 This is reflected in its aforementioned involvement as a ship designer and potential builder in the General Dynamics-led bid for the US Navy Littoral Combat Ship.
8 The figure has been stylised using total project cost breakdown by project elements shown in ADO (2006a), Table 1: 8. Thus, the cost of 'platform design' is imputed to Platform Designer; the cost of 'combat systems' is imputed to Combat System Integrator; and the cost of 'project management' to Prime Contractor. The cost of 'hull, machinery, equipment' and 'logistics support, including training' is attributed to Shipyard (operator) and OEMs. Other second- and third-tier suppliers are included in OEM, Shipyard and Combat Integration cost elements.
9 See http://www.defence.gov.au/dmo/awd/sea4000/sea4000.cfm (accessed 28 February 2008).
10 The arrangement takes the form of Alliance-based Target Incentive Agreement (ABTIA) between the Commonwealth, represented by the Defence Materiel Organisation, ASC as the shipbuilder and Raytheon Australia as the mission systems integrator. 'The broad AWD procurement principles articulated by the Alliance comprise value for money, efficient and effective process, ethics and probity, accountability and transparency, good faith and fair dealing and *competition*' (Kerr, 2008b: 2–3; our italics). Under this arrangement, major equipment is

already specified by Navantia SA, the Spanish designer, and the Alliance is to utilise Navantia's established supply chain. Navantia will perform all the required design modifications and will maintain design configuration control. Raytheon will undertake the Australianisation of the combat system around the fully imported Aegis core sourced by the Commonwealth via the US FMS (ibid.).

References

ADO (2006a) 'Defence Submission to the Senate Inquiry into Naval Shipbuilding', Canberra: Australian Defence Organisation. Online. Available at: http://www.aph.gov.au/Senate/committee/fadt_ctte/shipping/submissions/sub20.pdf (accessed 10 Dec 2007).

—— (2006b) 'Defence demand for Naval Shipbuilding and In-service Support', Defence Submission to the Senate Inquiry into Naval Shipbuilding, Section 3 update, Canberra: Australian Defence Organisation, 18 Aug 2006.

ASPI (2002) *Setting a Course for Australia's Naval Shipbuilding and Repair Industry*, An ASPI Policy Report, Canberra: Australian Strategic Policy Institute.

Dodd, M. (2008) 'Downsized fleet 'the way to go': Navy cost sinking budget', *The Australian*, 7 January.

Hinz, J. and Ziesing, K. (2007–8) 'ADM's Top 40: Thales takes top spot in growing Australian defence business sector', *Australian Defence Magazine*, 16(1): 34–5.

Kerr, J. (2008a) 'Armidales back at work', *Australian Defence Magazine*, Pacific 2008 Insert, 16(1): 30–1.

—— (2008b) 'Mobilising the naval industry', *Australian Defence Magazine*, Pacific 2008 Insert, 16(1): 2–6.

McIntosh, M. and Prescott, J. (1999) *Report to the Minister for Defence on the Collins Class Submarine and Related Matters*, Canberra: Commonwealth of Australia. Online. Available at: http://www.minister.defence.gov.au/1999/collins.html (accessed 10 Dec 2007).

Parliament of Australia (2006) 'Blue water ships: consolidating past achievements', Senate Inquiry into Naval Shipbuilding in Australia, Senate Foreign Affairs, Defence and Trade Committee, Canberra: Commonwealth of Australia.

Tasman Asia Pacific (2000) *Impact of Major Defence Projects: A Case Study of the ANZAC Ship Project*, Final Report, Canberra: Tasman Asia Pacific, Economic, Management and Policy Consultants.

Tasman Economics (2002) *Impact of Major Defence Projects: A Case Study of the Minehunter Coastal Project*, Final Report, Canberra: Tasman Economics.

Woolner, D. (2001) 'Getting in Early: Lessons of the Collins Submarine Program for Improved Oversight of Defence Procurement', Research Paper No. 3, 2001–2, Canberra: Parliamentary Library.

—— (2006) 'The air-warfare destroyer: managing defence procurement', in CEDA *The Business of Defence: Sustaining Capability*, CEDA Growth No. 57, Melbourne: Committee for Economic Development of Australia.

14 Managing the defence value-adding chain

Australian procurement of over-the-horizon radar

Robert Wylie and Stefan Markowski

Chapter 1 of this volume envisaged the production of national security in terms of a *defence value-adding chain* which converts intermediate inputs (including goods and services produced by industry) into military capability outputs and, ultimately, national security outcomes. This chapter uses the development, procurement and deployment of over-the-horizon radar by the Australian Defence Organisation to illustrate how the defence value-adding chain works in the kind of smaller but economically developed parliamentary democracies covered in this volume. In doing so, the chapter amplifies the reference to the Jindalee Operational Radar Network (JORN) in Box 6.1 in Chapter 6.

The defence procurement process is a key institutional feature of the defence value-adding chain in smaller democratic states. This chapter analyses the part played by different defence procurement actors (including defence scientists, defence capability planners, defence procurement managers, military users and elected Ministers) in the development, procurement and deployment of over-the-horizon radar to meet Australia's requirement for effective surveillance of the continent's vast northern maritime approaches. The chapter explores the over-the-horizon radar's halting progress through the various elements of Australia's defence value-adding chain. The chapter concludes with a discussion of what other, comparable countries can learn from the structure and operation of Australia's defence value-adding chain in this case.

Maritime surveillance and the Australian defence value-adding chain

The chapter's underlying premise is that, as the final product of the defence value-adding chain, national security provision should drive that chain in the sense that, ultimately, defence decision-makers should justify allocating resources to one capability input rather than to another on the basis of the relative value of their respective contribution to national security. In what follows we use Australia's requirement for maritime surveillance to explore the meaning of 'value' in the present context.

Priority for effective surveillance of Australian northern maritime approaches has pervaded Australian strategic guidance for at least four decades. For example, the Australian government's extant strategic guidance states:

> The key to defending Australia is to control the sea and air approaches to our continent, so as to deny them to hostile ships and aircraft, and provide the maximum freedom of action for our forces. That means we need a fundamentally maritime strategy. Our strategic geography, our relatively small population and our comparative advantage in a range of technologies all dictate that our defence should focus on our sea and air approaches.
>
> (DoD, 2000: 47)

In Australia's circumstances, therefore, a primary measure of the value of military capability for maritime surveillance is therefore simply the extent to which it enables Australian governments to control the sea and air approaches to the Australian continent.

Australia's maritime surveillance capability is based on an evolving portfolio of maritime surveillance assets, the defence element of which currently includes patrol boats, P-3 Orion long-range maritime patrol aircraft; airborne early warning and control aircraft; and JORN. This portfolio of maritime surveillance assets is managed as a comprehensive surveillance system providing continuous coverage of the nation's extended air and sea approaches.

JORN, the focus of this chapter, comprises three over-the-horizon radars (located in Queensland, Northern Territory and Western Australia) operated as a network via a control centre located in South Australia. JORN, like any other radar, works by transmitting a radio signal which illuminates a target and by then receiving and analysing the return signal reflected by that target. Over-the-horizon radar (OTHR), however, transmits high frequency radio signals that do not travel along 'line of sight' but are refracted through the various layers of the Earth's ionosphere. This refraction enables OTHR to illuminate a target area on the Earth's surface thousands of kilometres from the transmitter. Objects – ships or aircraft – so illuminated reflect the radio signal, scattering it in all directions. A minute amount of this reflected radar energy is refracted back through the ionosphere to a receiver. High-powered computers, sophisticated antennas and other technologies enable operators to capture this relatively weak return signal, distinguish it from background clutter and analyse it to locate and characterise ships or aircraft moving in the target area. The radar signal's actual path through the ionosphere and, hence, the target area it illuminates depend importantly on the signal's frequency. Operators adjust the signal's frequency to 'steer the beam' in searching for and tracking targets in real time.

But over-the-horizon radar does not, and cannot, provide a complete solution to Australia's surveillance requirements. As the Australian National Audit Office (ANAO) has observed, current OTHR technology generally does not give the accurate resolution necessary to guide fighter aircraft precisely to air and naval targets. Ionospheric disruptions (particularly at night, dawn and dusk) also degrade OTHR performance (ANAO, 1996: 3). JORN's value therefore needs to be gauged in terms of its contribution to a portfolio of maritime surveillance assets which the government operates as an increasingly cohesive maritime surveillance system by progressively integrating data distribution and command and control networks. Hence, for example, the broad area surveillance provided by the JORN network in real time enables more efficient and effective use of maritime patrol aircraft which can, in turn, reduce the number of patrol boats required for effective response to incursions.

The balance of this chapter uses the history of JORN to illustrate the roles played by different actors in the Australian defence value-adding chain and how they interacted in the development, production and procurement of the system.

Organisational perspective

JORN would not have eventuated without the reorganisation of the Defence Group of Departments in 1974 (see the discussion of the Tange reforms in Chapter 6). The reorganisation removed the then Australian Defence Scientific Service from the Department of Supply and re-established it in the new Defence Department as the Defence Science and Technology Organisation (DSTO). Tange envisaged DSTO adding value by exercising strict policy control over defence-oriented research and by providing the 'clear sighted administration' required to concentrate resources on defence research priorities (Tange, 1973: 119–20).

Australian defence scientists had been interested in exploiting ionospheric refraction of radar signals for defence purposes since the 1950s (Sinnott, 2005). In 1970, the then Australian Defence Scientific Service reorganised previous opportunity-based research into an organised, funded, goal-driven research programme. An early research task was to determine whether ionospheric propagation from Australia towards the equator was sufficiently stable to permit the detection of targets with the computing and other technology then available to Australia. This research underpinned the *1976 Defence White Paper*'s express recognition of the JORN programme's strategic and operational significance and led DSTO to commission a pilot over-the-horizon radar system near Alice Springs in central Australia. Over the next two years, the JORN pilot system demonstrated its capacity to track civil aircraft, surface ships and eventually manoeuvring military aircraft.

Thus encouraged, the government in 1978 authorised DSTO to undertake the system's full-scale engineering development. By 1984–85, the defence scientists were working with the Air Force to test the radar's capacity in different ionospheric conditions, to detect and track single and multiple targets manoeuvring at various speeds and ranges and to generate the data required to pre-position an aircraft to intercept a target.

8

Research by dedicated DSTO scientists dominated this relatively early stage of JORN's development. Viewed from a defence value-adding chain perspective, Industry's contribution to JORN research was subordinate to, and supportive of, publicly funded research and development. For example, Amalgamated Wireless Australasia Ltd (AWA) supplied and supported much of the hardware used by DSTO scientists at the JORN test bed near Alice Springs. The transition from publicly funded R&D to commercially based production of JORN – a key test of the defence value-adding chain – was to come later (see below).

Sinnott and others emphasise the benefit early Australian OTHR research gained from the liaison between Australian defence scientists and their US counterparts involved in comparable OTHR research. This liaison had begun in 1970 as a by-product of exchanges of radar-related research by Australian, US and British scientists under the auspices of The Technical Cooperation Program (TTCP – see below).

The institutional arrangements underpinning these discussions were then, and are now, a critical part of Australia's defence value-adding chain. Australia's alliance with the USA fosters institutions by which Australian government officials (both civilian and military) gain access to, among other things, US military and technological innovations. This access, while not unrestricted, is sufficiently important to prompt the Australian government to acknowledge that 'The kind of ADF that we need is not achievable without the technology access provided by the US alliance' (DoD, 2000: 35). These alliance-based institutions include, for example, the 1968 US-Australia Memorandum of Understanding on Cooperative Research and Development which in turn provided an umbrella for conclusion of an OTHR-specific agreement between the two governments in 1975. These trusted institutional arrangements enabled the DSTO scientists to trade the results of their OTHR research for access to prior US experience in development of OTHR until the USA abandoned its programme at the end of the Cold War. Importantly, Australian research was not simply duplicating that in the USA. Access to US innovation expedited, but did not supplant, indigenous research and development.

Australian research aimed to understand the unique features of the Australian ionosphere and equatorially-oriented radar signal propagation. It took advantage of the relatively low-powered radar signals required to generate worthwhile radar returns in the relatively benign Australian ionospheric environment. (US researchers, in contrast, relied on immensely powerful radar signals to generate useful returns in the polar ionospheric environment relevant to their programme.) But to exploit this feature of the Australian environment, contractors would be required to develop radar receivers characterised by unprecedented low internally generated electrical noise. Similarly, to meet Australia's requirement for 'steerable' radar beams, contractors would be required to develop extremely flexible transmitters, able to transmit a variety of waveforms over a wide range of frequencies at will.[1] These requirements caused US and Australian OTHR developments to diverge and exacerbated the technical risk inherent in procurement of JORN.

JORN's protracted development combined with perennial defence resource constraints to render the programme acutely vulnerable to wider political criticism and to Defence organisational and management perturbations (see Chapter 6). DSTO's ability to continue depended critically on sustained support by the centralised strategic planning, force structure development and financial programming elements of the new Defence Department. In particular, such support from Defence central elements was essential to DSTO's ability to win adequate funding for the project in the annual budget cycle despite intense internal Defence competition for limited resources. A particular focus of this competition was the perception, articulated by advocates of airborne early warning aircraft for the Royal Australian Air Force,[2] that procurement of a network of over-the-horizon radars[3] would pre-empt funding for these aircraft.

By the mid-1980s, the government and its advisors were satisfied that DSTO understood enough about OTHR technology to enable procurement of the system at acceptable technical risk. For the government of the day the issue was whether to endorse an Air Force proposal for a low risk – and relatively minor – upgrade of the single OTHR system operated by DSTO for research purposes or whether to incur the much greater risk required to establish an integrated OTHR network that promised 80–90 per cent probability of detection of ships and aircraft in Australia's northern maritime approaches.[4]

To inform this choice the Secretary of the Defence Department and the Chief of the Defence Force jointly commissioned a study in 1985 of options for future development of OTHR.[5] The resulting report recommended setting aside the limited upgrade option (the estimated cost of which was Aus$46 million) in favour of developing an integrated OTHR network (tentatively estimated at over Aus$500 million). In so recommending, the authors envisaged that Defence would take full advantage of US experience in order to mitigate the cost, schedule and technical risk involved. The then Minister for Defence announced the government's decision to procure an integrated OTHR system in 1986.

At this point in the JORN story the locus of the value-adding chain shifts away from DSTO (which continued to undertake OTHR research and development) to the Defence Acquisition Organisation (DAO). The interface between the DAO (another product of the 1973 Tange reorganisation – see Chapter 6) and Industry in the acquisition of JORN is the subject of the next section of this case study.

Procurement perspective

As indicated in Chapter 1, defence procurement entails fundamental choices about:

- the range of eligible suppliers or sources;
- the mechanism of source selection;
- the purchaser–provider relationship.

In JORN's case, the DAO had prime carriage of these choices. DAO was linked organisationally and procedurally to those elements of the Department responsible for force structure development, programming and financial management but administered separately from them within the Department of Defence. As such, the DAO was responsible for converting the technology developed by DSTO into specifications, for synthesising those specifications and other policy objectives including local industry involvement, for translating the resulting synthesis into requests for tender (RFT), for managing the release of those RFT to industry, for evaluating tenders received and for negotiating the ensuing contracts with the preferred tenderer.

Choice of eligible JORN suppliers

The DAO had a menu of both domestic and overseas candidate suppliers for JORN which was a product of both prior economic development and government policy choices.

The government's policy for Australian Industry Participation (AIP) in defence purchases of major defence capital equipment stopped well short of mandating complete self-sufficiency in the supply of and support for defence equipment. But the policy did recognise that:

> The capacity to maintain, repair, modify and adapt defence equipment to the Australian environment, independently of overseas sources, is of fundamental importance for our combat effectiveness in all levels of conflict. This requires Australian involvement in design, development and production to acquire the necessary detailed knowledge, skills and facilities. Through such work, local industry can make an important contribution to the sustained operational effectiveness of our forces in combat.
>
> (DoD, 1987: 76)

Defence industry policy was formulated and administered by the DAO as part of its responsibility for procuring major capital equipment. In the early 1980s, the US government denied Australia access to, among other things, the software Australia required to program the radar warning technology embedded in the Air Force's F/A-18 aircraft.[6] This denial added an edge to the DAO's parameters for Australian industry participation in the JORN program and culminated in the government and its advisers insisting on an Australian prime contractor for JORN, primarily to ensure Australian access to key JORN operating software.

The DAO implemented the policy through provision for Australian industry involvement in defence capital equipment procurement contracts.

Implementation in turn depended on the growth of indigenous electronic companies and the establishment of local subsidiaries of overseas electronic suppliers. The commercial viability of this element of the defence value-adding chain was reinforced by preference accorded local suppliers in government purchasing and a vigorous Government offsets policy (see Chapter 6). Telecom, the Australian government's monopoly supplier and operator of telecommunications equipment also supported the local electronics industry.[7]

In May 1989, the DAO restricted the Request for Tender for supply of the integrated JORN system to three Australian companies: Amalgamated Wireless Australasia Ltd (AWA), Broken Hill Propriety Ltd (BHP) and Telecom Australia (Telecom). As the inaugural JORN project director was to explain later:

> The prime contract bidders for the JORN contract were restricted to Australian companies although it was expected that they would need to import technology through overseas subcontractors. Because of the strategic nature of the JORN capability, it was considered critical that an Australian company have the carriage of JORN to maximize the technology transfer to Australia to ensure an indigenous base for its support and continuing enhancement. By restricting the prime contractor to an Australian company, it was recognized that the experience level in dealing with a large complex development project would be low and, indeed, one of the objectives of the JORN project was to grow in an Australian company the ongoing capability to undertake such projects.
>
> (Brennan, 1996)[8]

Hence AWA (which had previous experience with JORN via DSTO) teamed with US company General Electric (GE), which had experience with the US Air Force over-the-horizon radar program. BHP teamed with another US company, Raytheon, which had constructed the US Navy over-the-horizon radar. Telecom teamed with the UK company: GEC Marconi. The latter lacked experience in OTHR technology but had built a high frequency digital receiver potentially suited to JORN.

The mechanism of JORN source selection[9]

AWA/GE, BHP/Raytheon and Telecom/GEC Marconi were invited to tender for a JORN system, the performance of which far exceeded that of the DSTO pilot radar. In addition, the two new sites were to be networked while incorporating data generated by the existing DSTO radar and the whole system was to be operated remotely (Brennan, 1996: 2).

In order to reduce project risk and to help the DAO identify the capabilities of the three tenderers, Defence awarded them contracts for preliminary design studies. The DAO eliminated the BHP team via this process and in May 1990 released a supplementary request for tender (RFT) to the two remaining bidders. AWA offered a lower price than Telecom but capped its liability for cost, schedule and technical risk. Telecom, on the other hand, effectively accepted open-ended liability and undertook to pay any cost overruns. In addition, AWA encountered substantial financial difficulties during the tender evaluation period. A perception that AWA posed greater commercial risk than Telecom (a Commonwealth-owned utility), the latter's willingness to accept all project risk and a perception that GEC Marconi's digitised hardware was better suited to future development of JORN led the DAO to award the contract to the Telecom/GEC Marconi team, despite the AWA/GE team's demonstrably superior experience and lower price.

As the Australian National Audit Office (ANAO) reported six years later, the contract between DAO and Telecom merely marked the end of the beginning of Australia's efforts to deploy a viable broad area surveillance system based on OTHR (ANAO, 1996). By 1996, according to the ANAO, 80 per cent of the JORN budget had been spent and 80 per cent of the project schedule had elapsed, yet the consortium had finalised less than 20 per cent of the JORN deliverables (ibid.: 21).

The ANAO attributed many of JORN's difficulties and slippages to Defence's failure to appoint an experienced project management team ready and able to deal firmly and proactively with the consortium when slippages and management problems became apparent (ibid.: xi). For its part, Telecom seemed to ignore its uncritical approach to risk during the 1990 contract negotiations and insisted to the ANAO that

> [T]he flawed attempt to establish a fixed schedule for a large scale research and development project coupled with the associated lack of a technical baseline has produced the perception that the project is running late when in fact it was not possible, from the outset, to establish a true project duration.
>
> (ibid.: 9)

These divergent perspectives constitute a vivid demonstration of the unavoidable problems inherent in writing contracts for the supply of complex, developmental projects. Such problems are not confined to the interaction between prime contractor and defence customer. They also occur between prime contractor and sub-contractor. Many of JORN's early difficulties can be attributed to the flawed contracting arrangements between Telecom, the JORN prime contractor and GEC Marconi, its key sub-contractor responsible for supply of the radar and the associated frequency management system, transmit and receive sub-systems and command and control systems. GEC Marconi was required to deliver these items to Telecom after verification that they met the relevant specifications. As a parliamentary committee was to observe later, 'GEC Marconi was not responsible, however, for the installation, integration, and testing of these items as sub-systems or systems' (ibid.: 56). In effect, the sub-contractor was obliged to deliver equipment as specified, not equipment that worked.

These growing difficulties with the 1990 JORN procurement contract rendered the DAO – and the Australian government – receptive to an unsolicited proposal by Lockheed Martin that, subject to due diligence processes, it take over management of JORN, re-baseline the project and then assume full contract responsibility for delivery of a reconfigured JORN project. Importantly, the DAO was not required to incur the additional transaction costs of testing the market again and was able to confine negotiations to Lockheed Martin.

In formulating the above unsolicited proposal, Lockheed Martin sought, and received, confirmation by Defence that it should form an alliance with an Australian-owned, Australian-controlled partner to help ensure that key JORN technology and know-how remained in Australia. Accordingly, Lockheed Martin then formed a joint venture with Tenix, at that time a highly successful Australian naval shipbuilder but not, at that stage of the company's development, a systems house. The Lockheed Martin–Tenix joint venture – called RLM – assumed progressive control of the JORN programme. In 1999, the DAO offered the actual JORN production contract to RLM and Telecom withdrew from the defence market.

Under these arrangements, RLM was accountable to the DAO for the fundamental tasks of systems engineering; computer software development; and system integration, test and set-to-work. To deliver a reconfigured JORN project on a commercially viable basis within Defence policy constraints, RLM did the following:

- established an experienced management team drawing heavily on staff with experience in construction of US nuclear submarines;
- established a close collaborative working relationship with DSTO in order to facilitate uptake of the locally developed JORN technology;
- formed a team based on hand-picked software engineers, other technical personnel and sub-contractors (including many engaged under the previous JORN contract);
- co-located software development and system integration teams in a purpose-built software development and integration facility dedicated to completion of the reconfigured project;
- stopped all software development pending a review of requirements, associated interfaces and validation/rectification of all existing software components;
- used proven methodologies, tools and techniques to design/re-design software components around new middleware so as to achieve required system performance and system interoperability, including new embedded diagnostics to assist system integration and test;
- revised project management arrangements based on earned value management principles; clarified risk and introduced a formal, stringent risk management process; aligned commercial incentives and project outputs.[10]

The Royal Australian Air Force (the actual JORN operators) accepted JORN into service in April 2003. For all its manifest difficulties, the process by which JORN had been developed and acquired meant that all the lessons learnt and the skills and capabilities required to further develop and support the JORN system in its 20–30 years of life were resident largely in Australia. In particular, the key software-related intellectual property is Australian-owned and fully supportable locally.[11]

The relationship between the DAO and the JORN joint venture

As we point out in Chapter 1, a defence procurement agency and its supplier (s) must choose how they will consummate their agreement for the provision of defence goods and services. One pivotal choice for the parties to a defence supply contract is how to allocate the financial risk involved.

The DAO had recognised that, as a developmental project, JORN entailed substantial financial risk. In an attempt to manage this risk, the DAO had sought competitive target price and price ceiling incentive bids from respondents to its 1990 request for tender. According to the ANAO, the price ceiling/cost incentive contract eventually concluded between the Telecom consortium and Defence provided for:

- a target price;
- a ceiling price payable by Defence equal to the target price plus 60 per cent of any cost overruns up to a maximum of 10 per cent above the target price;
- arrangements for sharing financial risk under which the consortium was responsible for 40 per cent of any cost overruns up to the ceiling price and for 100 per cent of all costs that exceeded the ceiling price;
- the sharing of any savings, with Telecom entitled to 40 per cent of the savings if JORN was completed for less than the target price (ANAO, 1996: 42).

This price ceiling/incentive contract model for a developmental contract contrasts sharply with the kind of partnering between government and commercial supplier that characterises comparable development programs in, for example, the United States.

There, for example, the US Defense Department and Lockheed Martin are engaged in the seventh phase of development of the 30-year-old Aegis combat system under a so-called spiral development process which aims to mitigate the risk inherent in development projects. Spiral development is based on long-term contracts and a close relationship between all stakeholders which enables both the defence customer and the commercial supplier to learn from experience with the initial capability and its subsequent increments.

By contrast, the 1999 JORN production contract between the DAO and RLM was based on a transactional relationship that effectively terminated when the system was handed over to the Air Force in 2003. The 1999 production contract was replaced by a four-year contract for JORN Operational Maintenance and Support.[12] The levels of expertise required for JORN maintenance and support were orders of magnitude lower than those involved in the JORN acquisition programme. The completion of the JORN acquisition contract and the hiatus in Australian defence system business caused by preparation of the *2000 Defence White Paper* (DoD, 2000: 29–31), and certain other developments caused the joint venture to sack 60 per cent of its JORN acquisition workforce, reduce its software engineers to the cadre needed for JORN maintenance and close/dispose of its Aus$45 million software development/integration facility.[13]

Subsequent developments in the JORN project suggest that Defence is moving closer to the spiral development model pioneered in the United States. In 2004, the government approved a new phase of the JORN programme designed to exploit (at a cost of some Aus$62 million, 2006 prices/exchange rates) on-going DSTO research and development and JORN operational experience – particularly that accumulated by the RAAF. In order to husband DSTO expertise, operational experience, and industry knowledge gained since JORN's acceptance into service in 2003, Defence has created an OTHR centre of excellence. The centre is based in South Australia and includes, in addition to Defence's OTHR Systems Project Office and DSTO's Intelligence, Surveillance and Radar Division, such key companies as RLM Management (JORN Prime Contractor) and BAE Systems (who supports DSTO OTHR research at Alice Springs). Defence intends to place contracts for the above JORN upgrade with RLM and BAE Systems.[14]

Defence technology innovation in democracies

After 40 years in gestation, some 1100 scientist-years' worth of effort and the expenditure of some Aus$1.24 billion, JORN is now a key element of Australia's northern maritime surveillance system. After encountering widely publicised difficulties, Australian industry now has the capacity to support and manage on-going development of the system in response to technological developments and operator experience. This local industry capacity reinforces Australian governments' sovereign control over performance of the strategically vital surveillance task. Looking back on the JORN experience from this favourable vantage point, the following elements seem more generally applicable to defence technological innovation by the small open democracies addressed in this book:

- the nation-specific nature of defence technological innovation by small countries;
- the implications of an adversarial political culture for publicly funded innovation;

- the importance of understanding the system sustaining defence technological innovation to efficient and effective capture of prospective value;
- the nature of the business model, including the allocation of risk between government customer and commercial supplier, required for successful prosecution of developmental projects in small countries.

Nation-specific innovation

The JORN experience suggests that strategically significant innovation by small countries is not only expensive in absolute terms but also entails major opportunity costs in terms of other developments and procurements foregone. To sustain such innovation from initial research to successful deployment, small states need, first, a compelling requirement for the capability that cannot be met from overseas sources – in Australia's case, effective surveillance of its northern maritime approaches. Second, strategically significant innovation seems easiest to sustain when it is based on some distinctive national circumstance. Over-the-horizon radar, for example, is peculiarly suited to Australia's relatively benign, equatorially oriented ionospheric environment and continental distances.

The impact of political culture

All of the small democratic nations analysed in this book seek to exploit the benefits of advanced technology in the competition for military advantage. To obtain the benefits of such advanced technology, whether domestically produced or imported, all small states must experiment. Failure and learning are integral parts of any such experimentation.

However. all the small democratic nations analysed in this book have adversarial political cultures. In Australia, the politicisation of the JORN project's difficulties led to widespread questioning of the benefits of indigenous innovation and, in turn, to pervasive risk aversion. A political culture fundamentally intolerant of the 'failure' inherent in experimentation has encouraged capability managers to look abroad for advanced technological solutions to capability requirements. For small democracies, access to overseas innovation may indeed reduce the political and financial cost of military innovation. But unless small democracies manage their access to overseas innovation carefully, they may well reduce project cost but at the price of reduced sovereign control over the use of the platforms and systems incorporating that innovation.

A defence innovation system

The difficulty Australia encountered in transitioning JORN from a successful – if protracted – public research and development programme to procurement from commercial suppliers highlights a critical weakness of the

Australian defence innovation system at that stage of its development. Sub-sequent investigation by the Auditor General and the Parliament of JORN's difficulties indicates that these derived not from the technological challenges involved but from management deficiencies on both customer and supplier sides of the transaction.

This dichotomy between widely acknowledged technological challenges and belated recognition of widespread managerial deficiencies suggests that, in Australia at least, innovation was seen as a matter for scientists and no attempt was made to prepare industry for taking over from where the scien-tists left off. The quarantining of defence science from defence industry and the latter's lack of appreciation of what was required of it is a striking feature of the early JORN program. In hindsight, it seems likely that a more holistic approach, involving greater industry exposure to, and involvement in, the project at an earlier stage would have eased the transition from DSTO to industry.

More generally, the JORN experience certainly corroborates the emphasis in the innovation literature about the importance of prior investment in independent technological and managerial expertise to a country's capacity to absorb overseas innovation. But JORN also demonstrates how small coun-tries must walk a fine line in seeking to take advantage of access to overseas technological and managerial developments to reduce the cost of domestic innovation without, at the same time, stifling the incentive to pursue it. The policy and management failures that characterised the early phases of the JORN programme highlight the importance of rigorous policies and finely tuned administrative skills to small states' ability to pursue indigenous inno-vation while at the same time taking advantage of the international division of labour.

Even where the strategic priority of a requirement for a given military capability (say, maritime surveillance) is widely agreed, there is rarely a single, universally agreed solution to that requirement. The JORN experience sug-gests that if one candidate solution involves major innovation, that candidate is unlikely to have a natural constituency in the user community. In small states, where the allocation of resources to and within the defence function is perennially contested, advocates of more conventional solutions are likely to view the innovation with at best indifference and at worst hostility. In these circumstances the innovation must not only demonstrate overriding value but will also need effective advocates and a robust system of adjudicating priorities to capture that value.

Most states will seek to enhance sovereign control over the operation of military equipment – whether imported or locally made – by insisting on a local capacity to repair, maintain and adapt that equipment. In small demo-cratic states, local industry is often a natural advocate for high levels of local content in defence procurement. But the state's strategic interest in indigenous capacity to support equipment and local industry's interest in the commercial opportunities offered by that state's defence procurement are two separate matters which, typically, require careful and astute policy management to align. The JORN experience demonstrates how conflation of local content policies and strategic requirements can cause a substantial loss of value – in Telecom's case some Aus$500 million, to say nothing of damage to its reputation. In the early stages of the JORN project, pursuit of Australian industry participation equivalent to 80 per cent of the contract value seems to have displaced the need to devise ways for local industry to gain a detailed understanding of JORN software at more acceptable risk in cost, schedule and technical terms.

Governments in small states will often encounter considerable pressure to recoup the cost of publicly funded innovation by selling rights to use the intellectual property so generated to commercial interests. In doing so governments may be inclined to restrict the sale of such licences to locally owned and controlled companies in an effort to protect and advance the national interest. The JORN experience illustrates how value can be dissipated when policy-makers use blunt policy instruments – in this case, local ownership and control of defence suppliers in an effort to advance more subtle interests – in JORN's case, ensuring that valuable intellectual property generated through public funding is exploited in the national interest. Thus, DAO's well-intentioned efforts to ensure local companies exploited JORN intellectual property generated by the DSTO scientists initially stifled access to critical overseas – particularly US – expertise. As the author of the seminal 1986 report on Australia's options for deployment of OTHR later observed 'Everything we wrote in our report was predicated upon technology flow and assistance coming from the US.'[15]

Choosing the right business model

In small states, the nature and scale of value generated by upstream elements of the defence value-adding chain, and the ability of downstream elements of the chain to capture that value, seem to depend particularly heavily on what risks are taken, by whom and how they are managed. One striking feature of the early phases of the JORN programme is how, on the customer side of the transaction, Defence preoccupation with the technical risk inherent in the project deflected attention from the managerial risk inherent in converting what the scientists had developed into an operating system.

The JORN price cap/incentive contracting arrangement between Defence and Telecom was designed to apportion most cost and schedule risk to the contractor – a normal arrangement where the technologies and products involved are well understood by both parties. JORN, however, was a developmental project in which the technology required to meet functional – as distinct from technical – requirements was not fully understood by either party. In the early years of the project, Defence refused to engage the prime contractor in substantive discussion of technical problems for fear of diluting the contractor's responsibility for technical risk. This 'risk aversion' eroded the contractor's incentive to progress the development task for fear of getting it wrong and then being required to fix the development at the contractor's expense should it subsequently not work in the manner Defence specified.[16]

Analogous managerial difficulties occurred on the supplier side of the transaction. As JORN prime contractor, Telecom was responsible for translating the customer's functional requirements into technical specifications and then to engage sub-contractors to supply hardware and software in accordance with those specifications. Telecom engaged GEC Marconi to develop and manufacture JORN transmitters and receivers on this basis, even though, in a developmental project, neither party could be sure that the equipment so supplied would actually work in accordance with the requirements of the JORN system as whole. When GEC Marconi's equipment proved inconsistent with the requirements of the overall system, the managerial arrangements between Telecom as JORN prime contractor and GEC Marconi as a key sub-contractor lacked the capacity to adjust production in response to the evolving requirements of a developmental project.

Conclusion

JORN's primary contribution to Australian defence capability lies in enhancing the efficiency and effectiveness of more precise but more circumscribed maritime surveillance assets such as airborne early warning and control aircraft. In the short term, JORN also broadens the military options available to Australian governments by enabling them to re-assign other elements of the maritime surveillance portfolio to other military tasks without prejudicing the security of the northern maritime approaches. In the longer term, the more effective JORN is, the less Defence needs to spend on, for example, upgrading the capability of its existing maritime patrol aircraft or, looking to the future, the longer it can defer major investments in new assets like unattended aerial vehicles and space-based surveillance systems.

JORN fostered an indigenous capacity to supply and support JORN software, thereby providing limited insurance against the risk that overseas supply and support of other elements of Australia's maritime surveillance portfolio may not be forthcoming in a time frame, on a scale or of a nature best suited to Australian national interest. Australia still needs such insurance: As the ANAO has noted, local industry capacity to provide in-service support of Air Force airborne early warning aircraft has been compromised by failure to gain US government export licences and precluded Australian industry involvement in areas such as design and development of sensors, mission systems, communication systems, electronic warfare systems, electronic support systems and tactical intelligence sub-systems (ANAO, 2004: 44).

As indicated in Chapter 6, Australia relies heavily on access to US innovation in an effort to retain, at acceptable cost and risk, a 'knowledge edge' in an economically dynamic and strategically fluid region. In these circumstances, a key task for future Australian policy-makers will be to provide the guidance that procurement managers need in deciding when to allocate scarce resources to risky, protracted and expensive indigenous innovation and when to take advantage of overseas investment by importing solutions to requirements for advanced military capability.

Notes

1 Dr William Bardo, testimony to the Joint Parliamentary Committee of Public Accounts and Audit, *Hansard*, Canberra: Parliament of Australia, 29 November 1996: 4.
2 See, for example, 'RAAF in war with Navy on spending', in *Sydney Morning Herald*, 11 March 1987: 7; and 'Libs call for stricter watch on North', in *Sydney Morning Herald*, 26 January 1988: 4; and statement by A. Ayers at Hearings by the Joint Parliamentary Committee of Public Accounts and Audit, *Hansard*, Canberra: Parliament of Australia, 6 December 1996: 86.
3 See Beazley (1986).
4 Dr Mike Gilligan's testimony to the Joint Parliamentary Committee of Public Accounts and Audit, *Hansard*, Canberra: Parliament of Australia, 5 December 1996: 24.
5 See extracts from *Report of Options for Over the Horizon Radar prepared for the Secretary and Chief of the Defence Force* by the Department of Defence, cited in JCPAA (1996): Exhibit 12, 126.
6 See, for example, comments by M. Brennan at Public Hearing into JORN by the Joint Parliamentary Committee of Public Accounts and Audit, *Hansard*, Canberra: Parliament of Australia, 6 December 1996: 42; and by A. Ayers (ibid.: 82).
7 Telecom later changed its name to Telstra.
8 See Brennan (1996): 4. [0]
9 The following discussion draws heavily on CoA (1988): 35–40.
10 Online. Available at: http://www.rlmsystems.com.au/proj_jorn.aspx (accessed 25 July 2005).
11 Paul Johnson, CEO RLM, private communication, July 2005.
12 Online. Available at: http://www.rlmsystems.com.au/cap_jornmands.aspx (accessed 25 July 2005).
13 Paul Johnson, CEO RLM, private communication, July 2005.
14 See http://www.defence.gov.au/dmo/esd/jp2025/jp2025.cfm (accessed 25 February 2008).
15 Dr Mike Gilligan's testimony to the Joint Parliamentary Committee of Public Accounts and Audit, *Hansard*, Canberra: Parliament of Australia, 5 December 1996: 27.
16 See L. Yelland, testimony to the Joint Parliamentary Committee of Public Accounts and Audit, *Hansard*, Canberra: Parliament of Australia, 6 December 1996: 66.

References

ANAO (1996) *Jindalee Operational Radar Network*, Audit Report No. 28, Australian National Audit Office, Canberra: Australian Government Publishing Service.
—— (2004) *Wedgetail Airborne Early Warning and Control Aircraft: Project Management*, Australian National Audit Office, Canberra. Online. Available at: http://www.anao.gov.au/WebSite.nsf/Publications (accessed 15 June 2005).
Beazley, K. (1986) 'Australia to have a network of over-the-horizon radar', Minister for Defence News Release, 149/86, 14 October.

Brennan, M. (1996) 'Submission to Public Hearing into JORN by the Joint Parliamentary Committee of Public Accounts and Audit', *Hansard*, Canberra: Parliament of Australia, 6 December. [0]

CoA (1988) *The Jindalee Operational Radar Network*, Joint Committee of Public Accounts and Audit Report 357, March, Canberra: Commonwealth of Australia.

DoD (1987) *Australian Defence*, Canberra: Australian Government Publishing Service.

—— (2000) *Defence 2000: Our Future Defence Force*, Canberra: Commonwealth of Australia.

JCPAA (1996) *The Jindalee Operational Radar Network*, Report No. 357, Joint Committee of Public Accounts and Audit, Canberra: Commonwealth of Australia.

Sinnott, D. H. (2005) 'The Development of Over-the-horizon radar in Australia'. Online. Available at: http://www.dsto.defence.gov.au/corporate/history/othr (accessed 13 June 2005).

Tange, A. (1973) Australian Defence: Report on the Reorganisation of the Defence Group of Departments, Canberra: Department of Defence.

15 Conclusion

Stefan Markowski, Peter Hall and Robert Wylie

The tensions inherent in the defence procurement process are unlikely ever to disappear in countries of any size. Defence expenditures are, very often, a source of controversy and arms purchases tend to stir conflicting emotions – from those who admire military weapons for their power and technological sophistication to those who view them with abhorrence as killing machines to those who just see them as necessary tools for the job of conducting war and keeping peace. Such emotions will continue to underlie arguments about defence procurement, even though they may surface only in disguise. And they will persist as potent sources of inspiration for what might appear as otherwise dry debates about efficiency and local content policies. In this book, we have confined ourselves as much as possible to issues surrounding the difficulties of identifying coolly and dispassionately how best to spend public money on defence capability inputs. In this brief conclusion, we take it for granted that defence procurement will remain a focus for controversy but try to identify what developments are likely to shape the debate.

Our first point relates to the shift from *national to multi-national* frame of reference. Most traditional analysis of defence procurement was framed in terms of decisions taken at the level of the nation state. This was because, historically, defence was always considered the responsibility of Government – the government of a nation. Defence has usually been represented as a national public good, the primary beneficiaries viewed in state terms, and the level of provision considered as the outcome of choices among competing claims for a national budget. Much of the theoretical economic analysis of defence procurement, moreover, has implicitly been shaped by the experience of a superpower, the USA, in connection with which a single-nation frame of reference is not grossly misleading. Particularly in relation to the defence procurement experience of smaller countries, however, discussion in this book has pointed to the emergence of a multi-national context for decision-making and analysis.

At one level, individual nations now acknowledge that, at least in principle, they can both import and export the final product 'security'. They must therefore decide not just how much to spend from the national budget on defence as against, say, health and education. They must also decide, at the same time, how much they want to rely on overseas governments to assist in supplying security and whether and to what extent they wish to provide security services to others. To some extent, these decisions are driven by strategic considerations, reflecting the pursuit of a strategic commonality of interest through, for example, security alliances. But opportunity cost is also a key driver. Depending upon their treaty obligations and the dependability of their allies, countries can, by joining alliances, cut defence outlays without any perceived reduction in the level of national security they enjoy. As the costs of building and maintaining defence capabilities continue to rise, the economic argument for the multi-national supply of security is likely to become increasingly compelling. But the trend towards multinational supply will not proceed without controversy. The extent to which alliance arrangements threaten sovereignty will, for each country, be a matter for judgement – on which disagreement is inevitable. And the degree to which alliances can, in fact, promise to ameliorate costs will also remain a question open to debate.

We have also noted, however, the emerging significance of multinational supply at the level of inputs into defence capability. Largely for reasons of cost, supply chains have become increasingly globalised. This leads back to traditional questions about security of supply but also much sharpens the debate about the costs and benefits of local content policy, whatever its objectives. Particularly given the exemption of defence-related trade and industry from international restrictions on government support, policymakers will be confronted with a dilemma. A focus on local content could lead to cost premia if globalised supply chains have opened the gap between domestic and cheaper imported supplies. On the other hand, investing in and supporting local industry, at least in the early stages of a new development, could be the only way of generating the scale economies and learning necessary to allow domestic firms to bid for entry into global supply chains themselves. It is apparent, however, that as weapons systems become more complex and costly, the 'small country' perspective that we have adopted in this volume is becoming increasingly relevant for larger countries. Even superpowers, although mostly self-sufficient in their weapons sourcing, must decide on the extent to which the convenience of in-country procurement of military materiel outweighs the benefits of the international division of labour and trade. The issues confronting all countries are very similar; it is only that the bigger spenders have more resources to throw at them. We expect to see much more debate on this issue.

Our second point looks back to our repeated references to the sometimes *irresolvable uncertainty* that pervades defence procurement – and forward to ongoing and future responses to it. We have been at pains to say how difficult we believe it is for those involved in defence procurement to identify, develop and express what it is that they require. What they require is the capability to deal successfully with whatever challenge they may face. In the strategic dimension, uncertainty springs from the fact that the specifics of future challenges cannot be known with certainty. (Potential adversaries are continually, deliberately and *secretly* redefining the nature of military operations by investing in weapons technology and changing their doctrine and organisation. More generally, Government may ask Defence to perform entirely new types of task or to operate in arenas for which existing capabilities were not designed.) But even when future challenges are thought to be well-defined, uncertainty is inevitable in the technological dimension – in the process of seeking to convert a capability concept into a functional and then a technical specification for a system which will meet the need. In generic terms, the constant is that these sources of uncertainty will never go away. On the other hand, the specifics of the uncertainty are in constant flux. Technological knowledge inaccessible or unknowable in the past becomes available and, in principle, knowable as research leads to discovery and learning embeds it in human agents. Knowledge that would have had little value in the past becomes crucial if circumstances change (while technological knowledge, for example, vital in the past becomes worthless in future if innovation renders it obsolete).

For defence procurement agencies, there are deep issues here. Historic acquisitions are a poor and possibly misleading guide to current purchases if future challenges differ significantly from those of the past. Further, since weaponry can only become operational in the context of a defence organisation, procurement must also aim to take account not only of changing external challenges but also of the changing doctrinal and organisational environment in which the systems will be put to work. (While, in the past, this could be viewed as a difficult issue within a national defence organisation, it has become an even more difficult problem as nations enter multi-national alliances. See above.) Coming to terms with the implications of such developments calls upon defence procurement agencies to use strategies based on more broadly-based information. This information may relate to strategic issues that are politically sensitive or controversial and technological trends that may be crucial but largely invisible. Such strategies relate both to how decisions are made and who is involved in taking them.

On the question of how decisions are made, a current trend noted in earlier chapters is to employ evolutionary or 'relational' procurement methods. This general approach concedes that decision-makers cannot know all they would wish at the outset but seek to capitalise on learning that might take place as the procurement proceeds. This seems to meet some of the logical conundrums posed by irresolvable uncertainty – but at the price of introducing a new problem. Since the requirement itself evolves with the project, it becomes a moving target that offers only a shifting, and potentially unreliable, basis for assessing performance. An alternative approach is to make decisions that embrace not just procurement of the weapons system up to point of delivery but also contracts for through-life maintenance and support. One way of arguing for this approach is to say that it allows risk-associated product availability for use to be shifted back from procurement agency to contractor. Since the contractor's long-term profits now reflect maintenance as well as initial production costs, it is in the interests of the contractor to build a high-quality product at the outset in order to minimise subsequent outlays on support. Alternatively, one might say that, given the inevitable uncertainties associated with producing (and procuring) a new weapons system, through-life contracting offers an opportunity to 'pick up the pieces' after delivery if and when problems arise. The coming years will reveal whether these approaches to dealing with uncertainty yield better outcomes.

The question of who is and should be involved in the procurement process leads to our third point: the *relative strengths of the demand side and supply* in determining outcomes and development paths in the production of defence capability inputs. We have taken the position in this book that the demand for inputs into defence capability is derived from the demand for capability itself which in turn is determined by demand for the final output, national security. The logical implication is that production of those inputs and Industry's investments in its own physical, human and intellectual capital are also derived from the demand for defence capabilities and outputs. As we ourselves have discussed, however, not all suppliers rely wholly, or even to a large extent, on Defence orders for their business and so may have capabilities that are only coincidentally relevant to the needs of a Defence customer. Some contributions to the defence procurement literature have modelled the procurement process as a game in which players might include any or all of Government, the Armed Services, Defence Procurement Agency, and Industry. We agree that it is relevant and important to acknowledge that the procurement process incorporates the interactive roles of a constellation of players. But we take the view that uncertainty enters the problem in ways that can be addressed fully only by thinking in terms of re-casting relationships among the players rather than relying wholly on the design of contracts and their implied incentives. The sort of uncertainties we have described suggest that more will have to be done on relational contracting and how it can be used by the parties to facilitate the progressive adaptation of complex procurement deals to previously unanticipated circumstances and the associated behavioural hazards.

Finally, this volume has focused on defence procurement as the acquisition of complex, costly and long-lived weapons systems presents particular challenges for governments. For smaller countries, these procurement challenges are arguably the most difficult of all equipment-sourcing decisions faced by their governments as providers of public goods. However, procurement challenges discussed in this volume are by no means limited to the provision of national security. In future, the provision of non-defence public goods such as health, environmental services and education will grow in complexity and, thus, lessons learned from defence procurement should be of interest to all those involved in physical investment decisions in large public organisations.

Index of authors

Alchian, A. 104
Alic, J.A. *et al.* 175
Alton, S. 214, 215
Arndt, S.W. and Kierzkowski, H. 107
Arrow, K.J. and Lind, R.C. 70
Arrowsmith, S. and Hartley, K. 1
Arseneault, J.W. 220
Augustine, Norman 79n8
Ayers, A. 369n2, 369n6

Backman, M. 256
Baldwin, J. and Lin, Z. 217, 218
Bardo, Dr William 369n1
Baron, D.P. and Besanko, D.E. 128
Baron, D.P. and Myerson, R.B. 128
Barzilay, A. 246, 247, 252n18
Beazley, K. 369n3
Becker, J. 218, 224
Ben-Israel, I. 238, 242
Ben-Zvi, S. 231, 238
Berkok, Urughan 75, 141, 209–25, x
Betts, R.K. 187
Bland, D.L. 27
Blech, A. and Davidson, A. 231
Bower, A.G. and Dertouzos, J.N. 31
Boyd, Jr., F.L. 219
Brabin-Smith, R. 188
Braddon, D. 103, 107
Brauer, J. and Dunne, J.P. 85, 139, 141,
    149n23, 299n3
Brauer, Jürgen 149n23
Brennan, M. 360, 369n6, 369n8
Brito, D.L. and Intriligator, M.D. 52
Buchanan, J.M. 158, 159, 181n1
Byers, R.B. 218

Chang, F.K. 257, 268–69, 270n1
Cohen, N. 252n18
Cohen, W.M. and Levinthal, D.A. 175

Cordesman, A.H. 251n4
Coren, O. 245
Coulthard-Clark, C. 198
Cowan, R. *et al.* 104

Davies, A. 79n8
De Fraja, G. and Hartley, K. 128
DeMille, D. and Priestley, S. 209
Dibb, Paul 189, 190, 191, 202
Dirksen, Erik 141, 303–18, x
Dixit, A.K. 89
Dodd, M. 347
Domberger, S. 35
Dowdall, P. 91, 106, 107
Dowdall, P. *et al.* 93, 100, 102, 104
Drysdale, J. 255
Dunne, J.P. 99
Dunne, J.P. and Surry, E. 90, 96, 98–99,
    100, 101, 109, 111n7
Dunne, Paul 149n23
Dupont, A. 190, 191
Dvir, D. and Tishler, A. 243, 246

Ergas, H. and Menezes, F. 49–50, 64

Feldman, S. and Shapir, Y.S. 230
Ferguson, G. 76
Fergusson, J. 213, 215, 218, 219
Ferreras, P. 280
Flamm, K. 174
Foo, Cedric 271n14
Fredland, J.E. 110
Furlotti, M. 32, 67, 79n14, 133–34,
    149n19

Gansler, J.S. 52
Gilligan, Dr Mike 369n4, 369n15
Gleditsch, N.P. *et al.* 299n3
Golde, S. and Tishler, A. 242

Goos, Rini 318
Gordon, H. *et al.* 145
Gordon, L.S. 228, 231
Granatstein, J.L. 220
Grover, B. 214
Gubler, A.S. 78–79n6

Hagelin, Björn 141, 286–301, x
Hall, P. and Markowski, S. 139, 140
Hall, Peter 1–8, 11–43, 45–79, 82–111,
    115–50, 153–82, 371–74, x
Hardstone, G.A.P. 51
Hart, O. *et al.* 132
Hartley, K. 31, 35, 85, 178, 179
Hartley, K. and Sandler, T. 1, 32, 111n8,
    118
Hartley, K. *et al.* 91
Hay, D. and Morris, D. 87
Hendrikse, G. 43n26, 134
Hilan, R. 251n3
Hildebrandt, G.G. and Sze, Man-bing
    53
Hinz, J. and Ziesing, K. 334
Hoenkamp, Coen 318
Holmqvist, C. 109
Howells, J. 104
Huxley, T. 260, 261, 263, 267, 269

Jackson, I. 101
Jaggi, U. 223
Johnson, Paul 369n13
Johnsson, M. 290
Jubb, C.D. and Markowski, S. 61, 93

Kagan, K. *et al.* 251n4
Kagan, Kobi 228–52, x
Kam, E. 251n5
Karniol, R. 262
Kausal, B.A. and Markowski, S. 59
Kerr, J. 339, 347
King, S. and Pitchford, R. 167
Kinnaird, M. *et al.* 193–94, 332
Kirkpatrick, D.L.I. 79n8
Kirkpatrick, D.L.I. and Pugh, P.G. 79n8
Korin-Liber, S. 246
Kozyulin, V. 251n4

Labs, E.J. 63
Laffont, J.-J. and Tirole, J. 128
Langlois, R.N. and Steinmueller, W.E.
    174
Lavie, Z. 236–37
Leahy, P. 191
Lee Kwan Yew 257

Lifshitz, Y. 243, 246
Loeb, M. and Magat, W. 128
Lundberg, S. 300n22

McAfee, R.P. and McMillan, J. 128
McIntosh, M. and Prescott, J. 329, 330
McIntosh, M.K. and Prescott, J.B. 206
McNamara, Robert 193
Manson, P. 211
Mantin, B. and Tishler, A. 248–49
Ma'oz, M. 251n3
Markowski, S. and Hall, P. 27, 101,
    139–40, 141, 149n23, 170, 224
Markowski, S. and Jubb, C.D. 61, 93
Markowski, S. and Wylie, R. 71,
    150n24, 150n28, 179, 180
Markowski, Stefan 1–8, 11–43, 45–79,
    82–111, 115–50, 153–82, 187–207,
    323–53, 354–69, 371–74, x–xi
Markusen, A. 95, 110
Martimort, D. 211
Martin, S. and Hartley, K. 145
Matthews, Ron 255–71, xi
Mattoo, A. 145
Melero, J. 277
Michael, E.J. 155
Middlemiss, D. 216, 224
Mirus, R. and Yeung, B. 79n12
Molas-Gallart, Jordi 141, 272–84, xi
Monczka, R. *et al.* 71, 72, 74, 79n16,
    148n5
Mowery, D. and Nelson, R. 174
Muller, A.R. *et al.* 306, 308, 312

Nathan, S.R. 266
Nevo, B. and Shur-Shmueli, Y. 238
Newsome, B. 26
Ng Yat Chung, Major General 271n11
Niskanen, W.A. 28, 212
Nixon, President Richard M. 181n2, 188
Nordhaus, W. and Tobin, J. 41n11

Oden, M. 84, 101

Pages, E. 84
Parker, D. and Hartley, K. 31
Pepall, L.M. and Shapiro, D.M. 214
Pine, S. 251n4
Priestley, S. 222
Pugh, P.G. 79n8

Ranninger, H. 284n7
Rapoport, A. and Etinger, A. 247
Regehr, E. 214

Richardson, J. and Roumasset, J. 32, 121–23
Rizk, Sabrina 224
Rogerson, W.P. 128–32, 148n3
Rossignol, M. 223
Ruttan, V.W. 174

Salanié, B. 212
Sandler, T. and Hartley, K. 1, 28, 83, 93, 96
Sanz Menéndez, L. 284n5
Scherer, F. 87
Searle, A.D. and Goody, C.S. 104
Seno, A.A. 267
Setter, O. and Tishler, A. 239
Setter, Oren 228–52, xi
Shefi, Y. and Tishler, A. 242, 246, 247, 248–49, 252n15, 252n17, 252n19
Shefi, Yoad 228–52, xi
Shoham, D. 251n4
Shy, O. 99
Singer, P.W. 100, 165
Sinnott, D.H. 356
Sköns, E. and Surry, E. 84
Sobie, B. 265
Solomon, B. 214, 215, 217
Spence, M.A. 89
Spulber, D.F. 16
Stowsky, J. 67, 175

Surry, E. 84, 100
Surry, Simon 291
Susman, G. and O'Keefe, S. 107

Tan, A.H. 255, 256, 269
Tange, Sir Arthur 192, 356
Teece, D. 106
Teo Chee Hean 270n9, 271n17
Throsby, D. and Withers, G.A. 23, 26
Tishler, A. and Shefi, Y. 252n15
Tishler, Asher 228–52, xi–xii
Tov, I. 239
Trajtenberg, M. 42n17, 97
Trope, R.L. and Witt, M. 70

Utz, J. *et al.* 193

Wang Ping 145
Williams, Alan S. 74, 211, 212, 213, 215, 219, 224, 225n5
Williamson, O.E. 31
Woolner, D. 329–30, 331
Wrigley, Alan K. 200
Wylie, Robert 1–8, 11–43, 45–79, 82–111, 115–50, 153–82, 187–207, 323–53, 354–69, 371–74, xii

Yaalon, M. 239
Yan, Nellie Zhang 255–71, xii
Yelland, L. 369n16

Index of subjects

ABTIA (Alliance-based Target Incentive Agreement) 352–53n10
accountability 75–77; external governance in Australia and 195–96
ACOA (Atlantic Canada Opportunities Agency) 213, 225n2
ADI (Australian Defence Industries) 111n9, 198, 329, 333, 334, 337, 341, 348, 349–50; ADI-Thales and FFG upgrade project 334; ADI-Thales and minehunter project 333–34
ADM (Mat), Assistant Deputy Minister (Materiel), Canada 211, 213
Advanced Combat Man System, Singapore 267
AECMA (European Association of Aerospace Industries) 292
A4 Super Skyhawk fighter 265
AFP (Australian Frigate Project) 328
agglomeration, economies of 93–95
AGP (Agreements on Government Procurement) 117, 145–46
Agusta-Westland 223
AII (Australian Industry Involvement) 202–3
AIP (Australian Industry Participation) policy 359
Alvis-Hägglunds 315
AMEC (Australian Marine Engineering Corporation) 328, 329, 332, 344
ANAO (Australian National Audit Office) 355–56, 361
ANZUS Alliance 20
approval processes 74
ARGE GTK 316–17
armed neutrality, policy of 286, 287
Armidale Class patrol boats, procurement of 201

arms production of: Australia 84; Canada 84; Israel 84; Singapore 84; Spain 84; Sweden 84
Arrow missile system, Israel 240
ARTEC GmbH 317
ASC (Australian Submarine Corporation) and Collins submarine project 329–32
ASD (Aerospace and Defence Industries Association of Europe) 292
Asia-Pacific financial crisis 257–58
asset ownership in Australia 346
asymmetric uncertainty 129–31
Atlas Electronics 343
atomistic competition: buyer-seller interaction 120; supply chain 33
Audit Organisation (*Riksrevisionen, RIR*), Sweden 294
Australia 7–8n1, 52, 159; ABTIA (Alliance-based Target Incentive Agreement) 352–53n10; ADF (Australian Defence Force), restructuring of 188–89, 191; ADI (Australian Defence Industries) 111n9, 198, 329, 333, 334, 337, 341, 348, 349–50; ADI-Thales Australia and FFG upgrade project 334; ADI-Thales Australia and minehunter project 333–34; AFP (Australian Frigate Project) 328; AII (Australian Industry Defence Involvement) 202–3; AMEC (Australian Marine Engineering Corporation) 328, 329, 332, 344; Armidale Class patrol boats, procurement of 201; arms production of 84; ASC (Australian Submarine Corporation) and Collins submarine project 329–32; asset ownership 346; business models in defence 347–48;

business models in defence procurement 203–4; capability development processes, experimentation with 193–95; capacity, duplication of 200; Cockatoo Island Dockyard 198, 325, 328; Cold War end, response to 189–90; Collins Class submarines, acquisition of 206, 324, 329–32; competition, for and in market 350–52; conduct of defence firms 349; contracting out 109; CSP (Commercial Support Programme) 200–201; DCP (Defence Capability Plan, 2006) 335–36; DDL Destroyer project 326; defence industry policy 202–3; defence policy objectives 188–91; Defence White Paper (1976), fresh start 328; demand issues 346–48; demand lumpiness 346; demand-supply interface 350–52; democratic technology innovation 364–68; development processes, experimentation with 193–95; division of labour, change in 339–41; DMO (Defence Materiel Organisation) 43n25, 194, 332; DMO (Defence Materiel Organisation), materiel acquisition and sustainment agreements 196–97; DMS (Defence Maritime Services) 329; dockyards, reform in 198; export assistance 198–99; external governance and accountability 195–96; facility disposition and ownership 338–39; facility ownership 348–49; FDA (Force Development and Analysis) 193; fixed price contract flaws 330–31; fixed price contracts, preference for 204; Garden Island Dockyard 198, 333, 336, 339, 348; government factories, reform in 198; Guam Doctrine, response to 188–89; HMAS Success, triumph of hope over experience 327; import substitution 199; industry in value-adding chain, role of 197–203; institutional experiments 191–97; internal governance and conformance 196–97; ionosphere and equitorially-oriented radar signal propagation 357–58; ISO (Industrial Supplies Office) 333; JORN, acquisition of 205, 354–69; JSF (Joint Strike Fighter) – F-35 199;

'knowledge edge,' procurement for 368–69; local capabilities, prioritisation of 202; local content requirements 347, 351–52; maritime surveillance and defence value-adding chain 354–56; market competition 350–52; measurement of defence performance 40n4; military capabilities 187–88, 207n1; military-off-the-shelf (MOTS) 329–30; nationalisation of ASC (Australian Submarine Corporation) 331–32; naval maritime industry 336–41; naval shipbuilding 323–53; organisational reform 191–93; over-the-horizon radar procurement 254–69; overseas supply options 202; patrol boats and multi-hull builders 334–35; PBS (Portfolio Budget Statements) 195–96; performance of defence firms 349–50; performance targets 196; project completion (large, complex projects) 344–45; reform of defence organisation 191–93; shipbuilding and ship repairers 336–37; sourcing supplies, pre- and post-contract opportunities 350; strategic objectives 188–91; structure of marine industry 349; supply chains, marine industry 341–44; supply issues 348–50; systemic problems in naval shipbuilding 325–28; technological innovation, contract management for 350–51; Techport Australia 339; Tenex Defence and ANZAC frigate project 199, 325, 329, 332–33; terrorist attacks, response to 190–91; US technological innovation, access to 202; value-adding chain 187–207; value-adding chain, role of industry in 197–203; Williamstown Naval Dockyard 198, 325, 326, 328, 332, 336, 352n2; *see also* JORN

Austria 7–8n1
AVRO Arrow CF-105 215, 216, 218
AWA (Amalgamated Wireless Australasia) 357, 360, 361
AX Aircraft project in Spain 277

BAE Systems 84, 100, 106, 109, 201, 291, 292, 340
balance of payments 172, 175–76
bargaining power 147
barriers to entry 89, 98–100

Battle Tank programme in Spain 280–81
battlefield effectiveness 53–54
bilateral monopoly: buyer-seller
  interaction 119, 120; supply chain 33
Blohm+Voss 329, 332, 341, 344
Boeing 84, 100, 109, 238
Bofors Defence AB 291, 292
Brazil: arms production of 84; Embraer
  100
break even 126–27
bundling of requirements 61–63, 65,
  116, 140, 143
business models: choice for JORN
  367–68; in defence procurement
  203–4; evolution of new models
  347–48
buyback 79n12, 116, 140
buyer-seller interaction 115–50; AGP
  (Agreements on Government
  Procurement) 117, 145; agreements on
  government procurement 145–46;
  asymmetric uncertainty 129–31;
  atomistic competition 120;
  authorisation of suppliers 137;
  bargaining power 147; bilateral
  monopoly 119, 120; break even
  126–27; bundling requirements 116,
  140, 143; buyback 79n12, 116, 140;
  CoBPSC (Code of Best Practice in the
  Supply Chain) 145; collaborative
  procurement 142–43; competition
  118–19; competition for and in the
  market 118, 119; contract design
  128–32; contract management and
  enforcement 133–34; contract
  variations 133; contracting and
  contract management 125–39;
  contracting arrangements 126–28,
  148n5; contractual incompleteness
  133–34; coordination costs 122; cost
  plus contracts 126, 127; cost
  reimbursement contracts 126, 127,
  131, 135, 137; cost-sharing contracts
  128; costs of management of suppliers
  122; countertrade 116, 139; defence
  offsets 139–41; defence procurement,
  implications for 136–39; domestic
  supply sources 118; DPAs (Defence
  Procurement Agencies) 115–16, 117,
  119; DPAs (Defence Procurement
  Agencies), contract management
  125–26; DPAs (Defence Procurement
  Agencies), source selection strategy
  124–25; 'early bird' incentives 119;

EDA (European Defence Agency)
  144–45, 147; enforcement of contracts
  133–34; Eurofighter Typhoon 142;
  fixed price contracts 126, 127–28,
  137–38; free trade facilitation and
  regulation 145–47; government
  procurement agreements 145–46; ICPs
  (Industrial Cooperation Programmes)
  141; import dependence, sovereignty
  and 119; incentive costs 122;
  incentives and contract design
  128–32; inter-temporal work-share
  facilitation 143–45; international
  collaborative procurement 116–17,
  142–43; IRB (Industrial and Regional
  Benefits) 141; ITAR (International
  Traffic in Arms Regulations), US 117,
  146–47; JSF (Joint Strike Fighter) –
  F-35 143; local content requirements
  116, 139–40; market competition
  118–19; market power 121; market
  structures, alternative 119–21;
  monitoring costs 122; monopolistic
  competition 120; monopoly 119–20;
  monopsony 119; multinational DPAs
  143–45, 147, 148n4, 149n22; multiple
  supply sources 121; NDOs (National
  Defence Organisations) 115–16;
  OCCAR (Organisation Conjoint pour
  la Coopération en matière
  d'Armement) 143–44, 147; offsets
  116; offsets, restrictive trade and 140;
  offsets, social usefulness of 141;
  oligopoly 120; one-to-one
  arrangements 117; parallel supply
  sources 121–22; performance
  assurance 122; principal-agent
  framework 116; principal-agent
  theory framework 117–18;
  procurement contracting
  arrangements, evolution of 136–37;
  publicness of defence-related products
  115; qualifications and caveats
  132–33; relational contracts 134,
  138–39; residual authority 135–36;
  residual rights 134–36; sharing costs
  128, 130; sole supply sources 122;
  source selection 118–25; source
  selection, strategies for 121–25; source
  selection model (Richardson and
  Roumasset) 122–24; specific and
  residual rights 134–36, 149n20; sunk
  costs 118; symmetric uncertainty
  129–31; Tenex Defence and ANZAC

frigate project 142–43; uncertainty 147; uncertainty, symmetric and asymmetric 129–31; under-performance costs 122; work-share arrangements 142–43, 143–45
buyers of defence production 86–87

Camp David Peace Accord 229
Canada 7–8n1, 52, 158, 199; ACOA (Atlantic Canada Opportunities Agency) 213, 225n2; ADM (Mat), Assistant Deputy Minister (Materiel) 211, 213; arms production of 84; AVRO Arrow CF-105, development of 215, 216, 218; capability demand analysis 218; CDC (Computing Devices Canada) 214; CITT (Canadian International Trade Tribunal) 216; Commercial Corporation 214; CPFs (Canadian Patrol Frigates) 214–15; DDH-280 frigates-destroyers, acquisition of 220–22; defence expenditure 209; defence organization 210–11; DFAIT (Department for Foreign Affairs and International Trade) 214; DND (Department of National Defence) 74–75, 209–10, 211–12, 213, 215, 216, 219, 220, 223, 224; DPDSA (Defence Production and Development Sharing Arrangements) 216–17; future of procurement in 224; GMDD (General Motors Diesel Division) 214; HRC (Human Resources Canada) 213; industrial base, technology policy and 217–18; industrial base, trade and 213–17; international citizenship, tradition of 209; International Trade Tribunal 215–16; investment analysis 218; IRBs (Industrial and Regional Benefits) 211, 212, 213, 215, 217–18, 219–20, 221, 223–24, 225n3; Long Term Capital Equipment Plan 211; maritime helicopters, procurement of 222–24; NAFTA (North American Free Trade Agreement) 215, 216, 225n5; national defence organization 210–11; national security policy 210; NDHQ (national Defence Headquarters) 210–11; offsets 220; PCO (Privy Council Office) 213; phases of procurement policies 218–20; PMO (Project Management Office) 213; procurement 209–25;

procurement, organizational framework for 211–13; procurement, policy and conflicting objectives 218–20; public choice analysis 218; PWGSC (Public Works and Government Services Canada) 74–75, 156, 211–12, 213, 222, 224, 225n8; rapidly deployable forces 209; Rolls Royce 216, 225n5; SPAC (Senior Project Advisory Committee) 213; Standard Aero 216; technology policy 217–18; TPC (Technology Partnerships Canada) 217–18; trade issues and International Trade Tribunal 215–16; trade-offs 219; transparency in 155–56; US defence industry, links with 216–17; WTO-AGP (Agreement of Government Procurement) 215, 216, 225n5
capability: capability effectiveness 197; choices among defence capabilities 153; contingent capability 17; demand analysis 218; development processes, experimentation with 193–95; development programmes in Israel 240; dynamic capabilities 106–7; increments 17; requirements analysis 27–28; 'surge' capabilities 109–10
capacity, duplication of 200
capital-intensive combat systems 51–52
CASA, Spain 274, 279, 283, 284n12
causality, derived demand and direction of 20, 37
CDC (Computing Devices Canada) 214
CESELSA, Spain 275
China 7–8n1, 55, 251n4, 258, 259; anti-Chinese feelings in Singapore 256
CITT (Canadian International Trade Tribunal) 216; trade issues and 215–16
civil defence in Singapore 260
civil-military synergies in Sweden 294
CoBPSC (Code of Best Practice in the Supply Chain) 145
Cockatoo Island Dockyard 198, 325, 328
Cold War, Australian response to end of 189–90
collaboration: collaborative Nordic acquisitions 298; collaborative procurement 142–43; multilateral collaborative projects in Netherlands 313–14; offsets and collaborative projects in Spain 278

Collins Class submarines 206, 324, 329–32
collusion, danger of 88–89
combat-related performance 22–23
Commercial Corporation of Canada 214
commercial-off-the-shelf (COTS) 48, 53, 55, 76, 78, 137, 224
comparative advantage, principle of 178
'compensations,' Spanish pursuit of 272, 277
competition: buyer-seller interaction 118–19; competing defence bids, evaluation of 263–64; effect in Israel 247; for and in market 118, 119, 350–52; market competition 33–34
competitiveness 53, 54, 88–89, 91, 96, 107, 175, 214, 313, 328, 336
conscript enlistment in Sweden 289
consolidation: of defence industry, gains from 249–50; of demand 47; strategy of 107
consumables 19
contestability 32–35; contested processes, management of 159–60
contingent outputs 15, 22–23
contracts: buyer-seller interaction and contracting arrangements 126–28, 148n5; contract-governed relationships 30–31; contracting and contract management 125–39; contracting out in Australia 109; contractual incompleteness 67–68, 133–34; cost plus contracts 126, 127; cost reimbursement contracts 126, 127, 131, 135, 137; cost-sharing contracts 128; design of 128–32; government policy and contracting arrangements 162, 169–70; JORN contracting arrangement 367–68; legal redress for contract failure 70; limits of contractability 68; management and enforcement of 133–34; variations in 133
CoPS (Complex Product Systems) 51
costs: coordination costs 122; cost plus contracts 126, 127; cost reimbursement contracts 126, 127, 131, 135, 137; cost-sharing contracts 128; defence costs Israel 228, 250; innovation costs, pressure to recoup 367; of large projects 76; of management of suppliers 122; monitoring costs 122; of negotiation 31; sharing costs 128, 130; of

transactions 47; under-performance costs 122
countertrade: buyer-seller interaction 116, 139; Spain 272
CPFs (Canadian Patrol Frigates) 214–15
CSP (Commercial Support Programme), Australia 200–201
CV-90 tracked infantry combat vehicle 314–16

DAO (Defence Acquisition Organisation), Australia 358, 359, 363–64
DASA-CASA, Spain 279
DCP (Defence Capability Plan, 2006), Australia 335–36
DDH-280 frigates-destroyers 220–22
DDL Destroyer project in Australia 326
decision-makers: defence decision-making process in Netherlands 307; framework for 154–56; supply chain and 24–30
defence: budget in Israel 233–36; budget in Netherlands 304–5; budget in Sweden 289; capability enhancement through JORN 368; challenge in Singapore 255–58; characteristics in Sweden 290; costs Israel 228, 250; decision-making process in Netherlands 307; defence-industrial cooperation in Singapore 269; defence-industry relationships 32–35; demands of supply chain 35–37; environment in Sweden, change in 288–89; establishment in Israel 231–38; establishment in Israel, structure of 232–33, 234; expenditure, constraints on 38; expenditure in Canada 209; expenditure in Israel 231, 233–36; innovation system, problems of 365–67; military defence of Singapore 260; military expenditure Israel 233–36; and military materiels 46–47; military organisation in Sweden 288–89; military response options 15; mission, organisation and structure of 26–27; offsets 139–41; organisation and structure of 26–27, 42n19; organization in Canada 210–11; planning in Singapore 255–56; policy constraints, reconfiguration for JORN 362; policy in Sweden 288; policy objectives in Australia 188–91;

posture, historical context in Sweden 286–88; procurement agency 27–28; production chain 11, 14–15; products and supply chain 13–21; requirements in Singapore, definition of 263; structure, procurement and industry in Israel 228–52; structure of 26–27; supply chain 12, 24; systems procurement, Spanish shift in approach to 282; value creation 154–60

defence industry: capabilities, supply chain and 39; concentration of 90–91; defence-related industry in Netherlands 308–11; definition of 82–83; evolution of defence industry policy in Spain 272; external orientation of defence firms in Netherlands 311; firms 83, 101–8; global industry 83–85; heterogeneousness of 83; industrial base in Canada, technology policy and 217–18; industrial base in Canada, trade and 213–17; industry-related procurement strategies 176–80; Israel 242–50; marine industry in Australia, structure of 349; military goods and services 49–56; military-industrial base, change in Sweden of 291–93; model in Israel 247–50; multi-dimensionality of demand on 77–78; multi-national supply 371–72; multiple supply sources 121; national industry 85–86; operating profits in Israel 249; partners in Sweden 297–98; performance in Israel 242–47; policy and offsets in Netherlands 311–14; policy in Australia 202–3; production capabilities 19–20; R&D (Research and Development) in 88, 97, 98, 105–6; sales in Netherlands 310–11; structure and operations of 87–101; structure in Netherlands 308–9; supplier relations management 162, 170; in Sweden 100; systemic problems in Australian naval shipbuilding 325–28; value-adding chain, role of 197–203; willingness to participate in 87; *see also* supply, defence industry and

Defence Review (2004), in Sweden 289, 293–94, 295, 296, 297

Defence White Paper (1976), in Australia 328

demand: accountability 75–77; approval processes 74; battlefield effectiveness 53–54; bundled acquisition 61, 65; bundling of requirements 61–63; capital-intensive combat systems 51–52; centralisation of procurement function 72–75; commercial-off-the-shelf (COTS) 48, 53, 55, 76, 78, 137, 224; consolidation of 47; contractability limits 68; contractual incompleteness 67–68; CoPS (Complex Product Systems) 51; costs of large projects 76; defence and military materiels 46–47; defence procurement accounts 45; demand stretching 171–72; demand-supply interface in Australia 350–52; derived or dependent 2, 20; developmental systems 55; DMO (Defence Materiel Organisation) 75–76; DPAs (Defence Procurement Agencies) 48, 72, 75, 76; DPAs (Defence Procurement Agencies), responsibilities of 73–74; durability 48–49; EDA (European Defence Agency) 45–46; effectiveness 75–77; Eurofighter Typhoon 71; fragmentation of 47, 53; generic technological information 51; import substitution 53; in-country production, case for 56; inter-operative weapons systems 50; international collaborative procurement 71; issues in Australia 346–48; ITAR (International Traffic in Arms Regulations), US 70; JSF (Joint Strike Fighter) – F-35 71; knowledge-intensive combat systems 51–52; learning experience, in-country production and 56; legal redress for contract failure 70; lethality 49; life spans of military materiels 47; lumpiness in Australia 346; military goods and services 49–56; military-off-the-shelf (MOTS) 48, 53, 55, 76, 78, 137, 303; multi-dimensionality 77–78; NDOs (National Defence Organisations) 45, 46–47, 48, 49, 70; off-the-shelf 55, 78; organisational design theory 71–72; ownership rights and obligations 66–67; platforms 54–55; preparedness 55–56; procurement 45; procurement cycles, viability between 65–66; procurement function 68–71; procurement

function, challenge for 69–71;
procurement organisation 71–77;
product range 56–57; production
function 48; products and
procurement organisation 45–79;
property rights 47–48, 66–68, 78;
property rights, obligations and
66–67; quantity discounts, scale and
47, 57–59, 61, 73, 111n5; relational
contracts 77; requirements, scale and
scope of 56–63; requirements creep
64, 69–70; residual rights 78; risk
absorption 76–77; scale 56, 57–59;
scale and scope of requirements
56–63; scope 56, 59–60; socio-
economic objectives, procurement
function and 70–71; specialised
procurement, grouping of 71–72; and
supply, relative strengths of 374;
supply and, relative strengths of 374;
support in-service 78; sustainment
55–56; systems of systems 50;
technical complexity 49–54, 78, 78n4;
technical complexity, relative nature
of 52, 53; technological sophistication
50–53; technology imperative 53;
technology transfer 74–75; Tenex
Defence and ANZAC frigate project
71; timeframe 63–66; trade-offs 65;
transaction costs 47; uncertainty 48;
US defence spending 46
democracy: democratic technology
innovation 364–68; leadership and
155
deployment: deployment-related outputs
14–15; flexibility in 17–18
deterrence 14, 15, 16, 20, 22–23, 158,
231, 233, 251n4; strategy of 'total
defence' in Singapore 258–60
DFAIT (Department for Foreign Affairs
and International Trade), Canada 214
DIB (Defence Industry Base) 82–87
discovery process 18
diversification 100–101
division of labour, change in 339–41
DMO (Defence Materiel Organisation):
in Australia 43n25, 194, 196–97, 332;
demand and 75–76; materiel
acquisition and sustainment
agreements 196–97
DMP (Defence Materiel Process) in
Netherlands 306–8
DMS (Defence Maritime Services) in
Australia 329

DND (Department of National
Defence) in Canada 74–75, 209–10,
211–12, 213, 215, 216, 219, 220,
223, 224
DPAs (Defence Procurement Agencies):
buyer-seller interaction 115–16, 117,
119; contract management 125–26;
demand 48, 72, 75, 76; multinational
DPAs 143–45, 147, 148n4, 149n22;
responsibilities of 73–74; source
selection strategy 124–25; supply
chain 24–25, 34, 36
DPDSA (Defence Production and
Development Sharing Arrangements),
Canada 216–17
DSO (Defence Science Organisation),
Singapore 266–67
DSTA (Defence Science and Technology
Agency), Singapore 267
DSTO (Defence Science and
Technology Organisation), Australia
356–58
dual-acquisition strategy in Singapore
262–65
durability: demand 48–49; supply chain
18
dynamic capabilities 106–7

EADS-CASA, Spain 279, 283
'early bird' incentives 119
East Timor 21
economics: agglomeration, economies
of 93–95; constraints on small
countries 6; economic defence in
Singapore 260, 261; economic
management in Singapore 257–58;
ESF (Economic Support Fund) for
Israel 241; government economic
objectives 172; MEA (Ministry of
Economic Affairs), involvement in
Netherlands 307, 311–12, 313, 315,
318; scale and scope, economies of
91–96, 102–3; socio-economic
objectives, procurement function and
70–71; Spanish economic
considerations 283
The Economist 212–13, 218, 220, 221
EDA (European Defence Agency):
buyer-seller interaction 144–45, 147;
demand 45–46; government policy
180; Netherlands 303; Sweden 293,
299
EDIG (European Defence Industry
Group) 292

effectiveness 51, 71, 159, 203; battlefield effectiveness 53, 359; capability effectiveness 197; cost-effectiveness 56, 123, 163; demand 75–77; efficiency of industry and 13, 368; military effectiveness 306; of offset policies 141; of procurement process 136; technical effectiveness 63; of weapons systems 63

Egypt and Israel 229, 233

Elbit Systems 100, 238, 244–45, 246, 247, 251n7

Embraer 100

employment: government policy and 172–73; in Netherlands defence industry 309

enforcement: of contracts 133–34; costs of 31

ENSB, Spain 279, 280, 281, 283

EREA (European Research Establishments Association) 292

ESF (Economic Support Fund), US for Israel 241

EURENCO 291, 292

Eurofighter Typhoon: buyer-seller interaction 142; demand 71; for Spain 275, 277

EUROPA (European Understandings for Research Organisation, Programmes and Activities) 292

European Union (EU) 199, 276, 292–93, 298–99; BAM (Border Assistance Mission) 305; ESDP (European Security and Defence Policy) 288; EUFOR (European Military Force) 305; EUMM (European Monitoring Mission) 305; EUPOL (EU Police Mission) 305; intra-EU trade in defence goods 311; Nordic Battle Group 296; OSCE (Organisation for Security and Cooperation in Europe) 295; SEC (Security Sector Reform Mission) 305

EUROSPACE 292

exports: Australian export assistance 198–99; and imports from and to Sweden 294–95; from Israel 244; policy in Sweden on 291; supply chain and 20–21, 43n28

F-18 Offset Programme in Spain 273–75, 278, 282

FDA (Force Development and Analysis) in Australia 193

FFA (Aeronautical Research Institute) in Sweden 287

Finland 292, 296; arms production of 84

fixed price contracts: Australian preference for 204; buyer-seller interaction 126, 127–28, 137–38; flaws of 330–31

FMF (Foreign Military Funds) in Israel 241–42

FMV (Defence Procurement Agency) in Sweden 287, 292, 293, 294, 296, 299

FOA (Defence Research Institute) in Sweden 287

foreign direct investment (FDI): in Singapore 257; in Spain 279–81, 283

fragmentation of demand 47, 53

France 7–8n1, 288, 292, 294, 316

free trade facilitation and regulation 145–47

functional specification 35

Garden Island Dockyard, Australia 198, 333, 336, 339, 348

GEC Marconi 360, 361, 368

General Dynamics 219, 280, 281, 283

General Electric 216

Germany 7–8n1, 288, 292, 297, 316; arms production of 85

GKN 316

GMDD (General Motors Diesel Division), Canada 214

government policy 153–82; balance of payments 175–76; choices among defence capabilities 153; comparative advantage, principle of 178; contested processes, management of 159–60; contracting arrangements 162, 169–70; decision-making framework 154–56; defence value creation 154–60; defence value creation, challenges of 156–58; demand stretching 171–72; democracy, leadership and 155; domestic preference 177; domestic preference margins 177; economic objectives 172; EDA (European Defence Agency) 180; employment 172–73; external governance and accountability in Australia 195–96; government factories, reform in Australia 198; government role in defence value chain 153–54; import substitution 177–78; industry policy challenges 170–76; industry policy framework, procurement and 160–64; industry-related procurement strategies 176–80; informational asymmetries 157; innovation 174–75; institutions and public policy process 158–60; interest groups 155; internal governance and conformance in Australia 196–97; key role of 89–90; knowledge spillover 173; leadership and democracy 155; local content 164–67; local content, requirement for 162, 177; local industry capabilities, sustainment of 171–72; make-or-buy 162, 167–68; 'market failure,' rationale of 157–58; military alliances 178–79; multinational purchases, work-share agreements and 178–80; national security provision 25–26; NATO (North Atlantic Treaty Organisation) 179; NDIB (National Defence Industry Base) 164, 165, 166, 170–75, 176–80, 182n9; NDOs (National Defence Organisations), defence procurement policy 162; OCCAR (Organisation Conjoint pour la Coopération en matière d'Armement) 180; offsets 178; opportunity cost 156; peacetime, social worth of defence in 153; precautionary orders 172; principal-agent framework 155; procedural transparency 159–60; procurement agreements 145–46; procurement and industry policy framework 160–64; procurement policy, industry policy as subset of 163–64; procurement policy, objectives of 162–63; procurement policy challenges 164–70; procurement strategies, industry-related 176–80; public choice, issues of 154; public choice, theory of 159; public policy framework 154–60; public policy process, institutions and 158–60; public value, assessment of 157; resource allocation 153; social value added 157; source selection 168–69; source selection requirements 162; 'state,' public value and 155; strategic dimension of procurement policy 162–63; supplier relations management 162, 170; and supply chain relationships 38–39; supply dependability 162, 164, 170–71; transparency 155–56, 159–60; value,

variable perceptions of 158; value-for-money objective 162; work-share agreements and multinational purchases 178–80
Guam Doctrine, Australian response to 188–89
Gulf Wars 21, 109

Hägglunds 291, 292
Harrier programme in Spain 278
Henschel 316
HMAS Success, triumph of hope over experience 327
Honeywell 216
HRC (Human Resources Canada) 213
hypothecation 17–18

IAI (Israeli Aircraft Industries) 84, 238, 240, 244, 246, 247, 251n7
ICPs (Industrial Cooperation Programmes) 141, 269
IDF (Israeli Defence Force) 232–33
IFOR (Implementation Force, Bosnia) 305
IISS (International Institute for Strategic Studies) 7–8n1
IMAT (International Military Advisory Team) 305
IMI (Israeli Military Industries) 238, 240, 244, 246
import substitution: in Australia 199; demand and 53; government policy on 177–78; supply chain and 34
imports: import dependence, sovereignty and 119; for Israel 236; supply chain and 20–21; Swedish exports and 294–95; of technologies into Spain 272–84
incentives: and contract design 128–32; incentive costs 122
Indonesian *Konfrontasi* crisis 255, 257
INDRA Electronics, Spain 274, 275
industry investment 374
industry policy 3–4; challenges for 170–76; framework for, procurement and 160–64; performance in production 3–4; structure of industry 3; as subset of procurement policy 4; *see also* government policy; supply
industry structure 13
industry studies 7
informational asymmetries 23, 157
innovation: costs of, pressure to recoup 367; defence innovation system,

problems of 365–67; in democracies
364–68; government policy 174–75;
nation-specific innovation 365; supply,
defence industry and 97–98, 103–4;
technological innovation, issues for
364–65
institutions: institutional experiments in
Australia 191–97; and public policy
process 158–60
interest groups, government policy and
155
international citizenship, tradition in
Canada of 209
international collaborative procurement:
buyer-seller interaction 116–17,
142–43; demand and 71; by Spain
276–79, 282–83
international component sourcing 107–8
international cooperation by Sweden
296–97
International Trade Tribunal in Canada
215–16
investment analysis 218
ionosphere 357–58
IP (intellectual property) 18, 46, 66, 67,
297, 331–32, 337, 341
Iran and Israel 229
IRBs (Industrial and Regional Benefits)
141; in Canada 211, 212, 213, 215,
217–18, 219–20, 221, 223–24, 225n3
Ireland 7–8n1
IRIS-T air-to-air missile in Sweden
301n30
ISAF (International Security Assistance
Force) 305
ISDEFE, Spain 282
ISO (Industrial Supplies Office),
Australia 333
Israel 7–8n1, 52, 158; arms production
of 84; Arrow missile system 240;
budget for defence 233–36; Camp
David Peace Accord 229; capability
development programmes 240;
competition effect 247; consolidation
of defence industry, gains from
249–50; defence costs 228, 250;
defence establishment 231–38; defence
expenditure 231, 233–36; defence
industry 242–50; defence industry
model 247–50; defence industry
performance 242–47; defence
structure, procurement and industry
228–52; doctrine of IDF, elements of
233; Egypt and 229, 233; Elbit

Systems 100, 238, 244–45, 246, 247,
251n7; ESF (Economic Support
Fund), US 241; exports 244; FMF
(Foreign Military Funds) 241–42; IAI
(Israeli Aircraft Industries) 84, 238,
240, 244, 246, 247, 251n7; IDF
(Israeli Defence Force) 232–33; IMI
(Israeli Military Industries) 238, 240,
244, 246; imports 236; Iran and 229;
local procurement 236; marketing cost
effect 247; military expenditure
233–36; Ofeq satellites 240; operating
profits in defence industry 249;
operational activity, IDF and 233;
Palestinian *Intifada,* response to 231,
234; PLO (Palestine Liberation
Organisation) and 229; policy
recommendations implied for 250;
power of, Arab perception of 231;
procurement process 236–38; public
procurement management 236–37;
Python 5 short-range air-to-air missile
240; Rafael 100, 106, 238, 240, 244,
246, 247, 251n7; R&D for defence
238–39, 250; regional military balance
229–31, 250; Saudi Arabia and 229;
Six Day War (1967) 229, 233, 242–43;
sovereignty, contestation of 228;
strategic position 228, 229–31;
structure of defence establishment
232–33; structure of IDF 234; Suez
War (1956) 229; Syria and 229, 231,
233; target security level 248–49;
TWP (Terror Weapons) 229, 231,
251n4; US defence aid to 239–42, 250;
US procurement 237–38; War in
Lebanon (1982–85) 229, 231; WMD
(Weapons of Mass Destruction)
251n4; Yom Kippur War (1973) 229,
233–34
Italy 7–8n1, 288
ITAR (International Traffic in Arms
Regulations), US 70, 117, 146–47
Izar, Spain 279

Japan 7–8n1; arms production of 85
Jemaah Islamiyah 268
JORN (Jindalee Operational Radar
Network) 205, 354–69; acceptance
into service 363; AIP (Australian
Industry Participation) policy 359;
ANAO (National Audit Office)
355–56, 361; AWA (Amalgamated
Wireless Australasia) 357, 360, 361;

business model, choice of 367–68; choice of eligible suppliers 359–60; contracting arrangement 367–68; contribution to maritime surveillance 355–56; cost of innovation, pressure to recoup 367; DAO (Defence Acquisition Organisation) 358, 359, 363–64; defence capability enhancement through 368; defence innovation system, problems of 365–67; defence policy constraints, reconfiguration for 362; DSTO (Defence Science and Technology Organisation) 356–58; GEC Marconi 360, 361, 368; indigenous capacity, insurance of 368; local content policies, value loss and 366–67; managerial difficulties 368; nation-specific innovation 365; organisational perspective 356–58; OTHR (over-the-horizon-radar) 355, 357, 358; political culture, impact of 365; procurement perspective 358–64; project management failures 361; relationship between DAO and JORN joint venture 363–64; resource constraints and protracted development 358; RLM (Lockheed Martin-Tenex joint venture) 362, 363, 364; software 359, 362–63, 364, 367, 368; source selection, mechanism of 360–63; technological innovation, issues for 364–65; technology innovation in democracies 364–68; Telecom Australia 360, 361, 362, 363, 367, 368, 369n7
JSF (Joint Strike Fighter)/F-35 62–63, 71, 143, 199, 265

KFOR (Kosovo Force) 305
knowledge: inputs and supply chain 19; knowledge base, learning and 103–4; 'knowledge edge,' procurement for 368–69; knowledge-intensive combat systems 51–52; spillover of 173
Kockums, Sweden 111n9, 206, 291, 329, 330, 331, 341
Korea Aerospace Industries 100
Krauss Maffei 280, 281, 283, 317

Land Systems Hagglunds 100
leadership: democracy and 155; strength in Singapore of 257
learning: in-country production and experience 56; learning-by-doing

104–5; production costs and learning curve 93
leasing 35, 110, 295, 339, 346
legal contracts 31
legal redress for contract failure 70
lethality 49
local content: Australian requirements 347, 351–52; government policy 164–67; policies for, value loss and 366–67; prioritisation of local capabilities in Australia 202; procurement in Israel 236; requirement for 116, 139–40, 162, 177; Singapore local industry involvement 264–65; sustainment of local industry capabilities 171–72
Lockheed Martin 84, 238, 340, 344
Long Term Capital Equipment Plan, Canada 211

McDonnell-Douglas 219, 273–74
make-or-buy policy 162, 167–68
Malaysia 255, 256
maritime helicopters, procurement of 222–24
maritime surveillance and defence value-adding chain 354–56
markets: alternative structures 119–21; market barriers to entry 99; market competition 118–19, 350–52; 'market failure,' rationale of 157–58; marketing cost effect 247; power of 121; structure of 32–35
MEA (Ministry of Economic Affairs), Netherlands 307, 311–12, 313, 315, 318
mega-projects 307–8
Mercedes-Benz 316
Middle East, regional military balance in 229–31, 250
military alliances 178–79
military capabilities: Australia 187–88, 207n1; contingent outputs and 16–18; counter-terrorist capability 42n17; defence products and 13–21; supply chain 12, 16–17, 22, 23–24
military contingencies 15
military-off-the-shelf (MOTS): Australia 329–30; demand 48, 53, 55, 76, 78, 137, 303; Spain 276
MINDEF (Ministry of Defence), Singapore 261, 262–65, 266, 267–68, 269
monopolistic competition: buyer-seller interaction 120; supply chain 33

monopoly: buyer-seller interaction 119–20; supply chain 33

monopsony: buyer-seller interaction 119; supply chain 32–33, 86–87

MRAV (Multi-role Armoured Vehicle) 316, 317

NAFTA (North American Free Trade Agreement) 215, 216, 225n5

Nammo Sweden 291

National Science and Technology Plan (1996), Singapore 266

national security: contingent good 14–16; defence organisation and procurement in Netherlands 303–18; defence organization in Canada 210–11; government and provision of 25–26; policy in Canada 210; provision, supply chain and 25; public good 16, 38, 43n27

National Service in Singapore 261

national sovereignty 21

NATO (North Atlantic Treaty Organisation) 20, 199, 221, 224, 276, 296, 298, 303; government policy and 179; supply, defence industry and 84

naval shipbuilding in Australia 323–53

Navantia, Spain 84, 344

NDC (National Defence College), Sweden 293

NDHQ (National Defence Headquarters), Canada 210–11

NDIB (National Defence Industry Base) 164, 165, 166, 170–75, 176–80, 182n9

NDOs (National Defence Organisations) 2, 3, 4; buyer-seller interaction 115–16; decision-making by 37, 38; defence procurement policy 162; demand and 45, 46–47, 48, 49, 70; supply, defence industry and 82; supply chain 15–16, 17, 18, 20, 21, 26, 36

negotiation, costs of 31

Netherlands 7–8n1; CV-90 tracked infantry combat vehicle 314–16; defence budget 304–5; defence decision-making process 307; defence industry policy and offsets 311–14; defence industry structure 308–9; defence-related firms, sectoral distribution 308–9; defence-related industry 308–11; DMP (Defence Materiel Process) 306–8; Dutch armed forces 303–4; Dutch armed

forces, main mission 303; Dutch Defence Organisation 303–4, 304–5; EDA (European Defence Agency) 303; employment in defence industry 309; external orientation of defence firms 311; indirect offsets 312; intra-EU trade in defence goods 311; materiels procurement policy 306; MEA (Ministry of Economic Affairs), involvement of 307, 311–12, 313, 315, 318; mega-projects, progress reports on 307–8; multilateral collaborative projects 313–14; multinational work-share arrangements 316–17; national defence organisation, procurement and 303–18; OCCAR (German-Dutch Boxer project) 316, 317; offsets multipliers 313; offsets policy 311–13; offsets scheme 312–13; ownership of defence firms 311; peace-keeping and enforcement operations 305, 317–18; sales of defence industry 310–11; TNO National Defence Group 309–10; transnational industry cooperation 316–17

NFFP (National Aeronautical Research Programme), Sweden 294

NH Industries 223

Northrop Grumman 84, 100

Norway 296; arms production of 84

OCCAR (Organisation Conjoint pour la Coopération en matière d'Armement) 143–44, 147, 316, 317; government policy 180

OEF (Operation Enduring Freedom) 305

Ofeq satellites 240

off-the-shelf demand 55, 78

offsets: buyer-seller interaction 116; Canada 220; focus in Spain on 272, 273; government policy 178; indirect offsets 312; multipliers in Netherlands 313; offset programmes in Spain 273–76; Offsets Management Office in Spain 282; policy in Netherlands 311–13; restrictive trade and 140; scheme in Netherlands 312–13; social usefulness of 141

oligopoly: buyer-seller interaction 120; supply chain 33

opportunity cost 156

organisational design theory 71–72

organisational perspective on JORN 356–58
organisational reform in Australia 191–93
OSCE (Organisation for Security and Cooperation in Europe) 295
OTHR (over-the-horizon-radar) 254–69, 355, 357, 358
ownership: of defence firms in Netherlands 311; facility disposition and ownership in Australia 338–39; private ownership 34–35; rights and obligations of 66–67; supply, defence industry and 108–11

Palestinian *Intifada* 231, 234
Panhard 316
parallel supply sources 121–22
patrol boats and multi-hull builders in Australia 334–35
PBS (Portfolio Budget Statements), Australia 195–96
PCO (Privy Council Office), Canada 213
peace dividend, controversy of 287–88
peace-keeping and enforcement operations: Netherlands 305, 317–18; Sweden 289
peacetime: operations, supply chain and 26–27; social worth of defence in 153
Pedra Branca 256
performance: assurance of 122; of defence firms in Australia 349–50; measurement of defence performance 40n4; targets in Australia 196
PFIs (Private Finance Initiatives) 110
PfP (Partnership for Peace) 289, 292, 296
platforms 47, 50, 54–55, 248, 262; *see also* weapons systems
PLO (Palestine Liberation Organisation) 229
PMO (Project Management Office), Canada 213
politico-strategic frictions in Singapore 256–57
Pratt & Whitney 216
precautionary orders 172
preparedness 55–56
principal-agent framework: buyer-seller interaction 116; government policy 155; supply chain 25; theory of 117–18
private ownership 34–35
procedural barriers to entry 99
procedural transparency 159–60

procurement 1–2; acquisition cycle 263–64; acquisition security 297; budget decision-making 371–72, 373; Canada 209–25; centralisation of procurement function 72–75; challenge of 371–74; complexity in acquisition 18; contracting arrangements 3; contracting arrangements, evolution of 136–37; cycles, viability between 65–66; demand 45; future in Canada for 224; and industry policy framework 160–64; insurance, comparison with 42n15; local content 3; make-or-buy 3; master plan for acquisition, establishment in Singapore of 263; materiels procurement policy, Netherlands 306; military operations, secret redefinition of 373; multi-national supply 371–72; opportunity cost 372; organizational framework for Canada 211–13; phases of Canadian procurement policies 218–20; policy and conflicting objectives in Canada 218–20; policy for, challenges in 164–70; policy for, industry policy as subset of 163–64; policy for, objectives of 162–63; process 371–74; process in Israel 236–38; procurement agencies, issues for 373; procurement organisation 71–77; procurement perspective on JORN 358–64; procurement policy 3; procurement process 1–2; products and procurement organisation 45–79; public procurement management in Israel 236–37; relational procurement methods 373–74; security, product of 371–72; shift from national to multi-national reference 371–72; source selection 3; specialised procurement, grouping of 71–72; strategic dimension of procurement policy 162–63; strategies for, industry-related 176–80; supplier relations 3; technological knowledge, accessibility of 373; tensions of process 371; transactions for, components of 30; uncertainty, irresolvable, in 372–73; value-adding context 2; *see also* government policy; buyer-seller interaction
procurement function: challenge for 69–71; demand and 68–71

product differentiation 96–97
product range 56–57
production: minimum efficient scale of (MES) 91; production chain framework 23–24; production function 48
property rights: demand and 47–48, 66–68, 78; obligations and 66–67; specific and residual rights 134–36, 149n20
PSA Group (Panhard & Levassor) 316
psychological defence 260
public choice: analysis of 218; issues of 154; theory of 159
public policy: framework for 154–60; process of, institutions and 158–60
public value, assessment of 157
'publicness' of defence-related products 29, 115
PWGSC (Public Works and Government Services Canada) 74–75, 156, 211–12, 213, 222, 224, 225n8
Python 5 short-range air-to-air missile 240

qualifications, caveats and 132–33
quantity discounts, scale and 47, 57–59, 61, 73, 111n5

Rafael, Israel 100, 106, 238, 240, 244, 246, 247, 251n7
Raytheon 84, 330, 340, 343, 345
R&D (Research and Development): capability in Singapore 266–67; for defence in Israel 238–39, 250; defence industry and 88, 97, 98, 105–6; in Spain 275; supply chain and 18
relational contracts: buyer-seller interaction 134, 138–39; demand 77
relationships: between DAO and JORN joint venture 363–64; defence-industry and supply chain 32–35; government policy and 38–39; links in supply chain and 13, 30–39; transactions and 30–32
requirements: requirements creep 64, 69–70; scale and scope of 56–63; specification of 36–37
residual authority 135–36
residual rights: buyer-seller interaction 134–36; demand and 78
resource allocation: constraints and protracted development of JORN 358; government policy 153; limits in Singapore 255; supply chain 23

Rheinmetall Landsysteme 317
risk absorption 76–77
RLM (Lockheed Martin-Tenex joint venture) 362, 363, 364
RMA (Revolution in Military Affairs) 262–63
Rockwell 343, 345
Rolls Royce 216, 225n5

SAAB 84, 106, 291, 294, 333
SAF (Singapore Armed Forces) 260, 261–62, 263, 264, 265, 266–68, 268–69, 270–71n10
salesmanship and supply chain 37
Samsung 100
Saudi Arabia and Israel 229
scale: demand and 56, 57–59; economies of 91–92; and scope, economies of 91–96, 102–3; and scope of requirements 56–63
scope: demand and 56, 59–60; economies of 93–95
search costs 31
security: policy on, change in Sweden 288–94, 296–98; target security level in Israel 248–49; *see also* national security
self-reliance: sourcing on basis of 37; in supply chain 21; in Sweden 287–88
self-sufficiency 39
SEMA (Swedish Emergency Management Agency) 289
SEPI, Spain 280
Serco Sodexho Defence Services 109
SFOR (Stabilisation Force, Bosnia) 305
shipbuilding and ship repairers in Australia 336–37
Sikorsky 223
Singapore 7–8n1, 52; A4 Super Skyhawk fighters, local upgrading of 265; acquisition cycle 263–64; Advanced Combat Man System 267; anti-Chinese feelings 256; armed forces strength 261–62; arms production of 84; Asia-Pacific financial crisis 257–58; Britain, withdrawal of 255–56; civil defence 260; commitment to deterrence 261; competing defence bids, evaluation of 263–64; cooperation 268–69; defence, challenge of 255–58; defence-industrial cooperation 269; defence planning, challenge of 255–56; defence requirements, definition of

263; deterrence strategy of 'total defence' 258–60; developmental success 257–58; DSO (Defence Science Organisation) 266–67; DSTA (Defence Science and Technology Agency) 267; dual-acquisition strategy 262–65; economic defence 260, 261; economic management 257–58; foreign investment in 257; ICPs (Industrial Cooperation Programmes) 269; in-service acceptance of weapons systems 264; Indonesian *Konfrontasi* crisis 255, 257; *Jemaah Islamiyah* 268; JSF/F-35 programme consortium 265; leadership, strength of 257; life-cycle review of weapons systems 264; local industry involvement 264–65; Malaysia, defence relations with 255, 256; Malaysia, tensions with 256; master plan for acquisition, establishment of 263; military defence 260; MINDEF (Ministry of Defence) and acquisition strategy 261, 262–65, 266, 267–68, 269; mini-RMA, technological edge and 265–68; National Science and Technology Plan (1996) 266; National Service 261; Pedra Branca, sovereignty of 256; politico-strategic frictions 256–57; psychological defence 260; R&D capability 266–67; resources, limits on 255; RMA (Revolution in Military Affairs), inspiration from 262–63; SAF (Singapore Armed Forces) 260, 261–62, 263, 264, 265, 266–68, 268–69, 270–71n10; social and cultural fabric 258; social defence 260; ST (Singapore Technologies) 264–65; strategic environment, unpredictability in 267; strategic location 258; terrorism, threat of 'catastrophic terrorism' 267–68; 'total defence' 255–71; training of armed forces, cooperation in 268–69; value-for-money of weapons systems 263; weapons systems, modernity of 262
SIPRI (Stockholm International Peace Research Institute) 7, 84, 90, 100–101, 286
Six Day War (1967) 229, 233, 242–43
small country perspective 4–7, 7–8n1, 372; alliances 6; bargaining power 5; cost penalties 5; economic constraints 6; joint ventures 5; neutrality 6; price

negotiation 5; procurement differences from larger countries 4–5, 6; retention of advanced producers 5; self-reliance 6; 'smart' procurement 6–7; strategic implications 5–6; subsidiaries 5; vulnerability 6; *see also* Australia; Canada; Israel; Singapore; Spain; Sweden; Netherlands
social and cultural fabric in Singapore 258
social costs and benefits 22
social defence in Singapore 260
social value added 157
social value of in-country capability 39–40
socio-economic objectives, procurement function and 70–71
software for JORN 359, 362–63, 364, 367, 368
sole supply sources 122
source selection: buyer-seller interaction 118–25; government policy 168–69; mechanism for JORN 360–63; model for (Richardson and Roumasset) 122–24; pre- and post-contract opportunities 350; requirements of 162; sourcing decisions, 'legacy' and 37; strategies for 121–25
South Africa, arms production of 84
South Korea 7–8n1; arms production of 84; Korea Aerospace Industries 100; Samsung 100
sovereignty, contestation of 228
SPAC (Senior Project Advisory Committee), Canada 213
Spain 7–8n1, 288, 292; arms production of 84; AX Aircraft project 277; Battle Tank programme 280–81; CASA 274, 279, 283, 284n12; CESELSA 275; collaborative projects, offsets and 278; 'compensations,' pursuit of 272, 277; countertrade 272; DASA-CASA 279; defence systems procurement, shift in approach to 282; EADS-CASA 279, 283; economic considerations 283; ENSB 279, 280, 281, 283; Eurofighter Typhoon 275, 277; evolution of defence industry policy 272; F-18 Offset Programme 273–75, 278, 282; foreign direct investment (2000s) 279–81, 283; Harrier programme 278; importing technologies 272–84; INDRA Electronics 274, 275; international collaboration (1990s)

276–79, 282–83; ISDEFE 282; Izar 279; management considerations 283; military-off-the-shelf (MOTS) 276; offset programmes (1980s) 273–76; offsets, focus on 272, 273; Offsets Management Office 282; policy drivers 282–83; policy implementation, lessons from 282; R&D (Research and Development) 275; SEPI 280; Unión Española de Explosivos 280

Spotless Group 109

Spratley Islands 257

ST (Singapore Technologies) 264–65

Standard Aero, Canada 216

STN Atlas 330

Stork PWV, Eindhoven 317

strategic location of Singapore 258, 267

strategic objectives of Australia 188–91

strategic position of Israel 228, 229–31

submarine procurement in Sweden 352n1

Suez War (1956) 229

sunk costs: buyer-seller interaction 118; supply, defence industry and 88–89

supply, defence industry and 82–111; agglomeration, economies of 93–95; barriers to entry 89, 98–100; buyers 86–87; collusion, danger of 88–89; competitiveness 88; concentration of industry 90–91; consolidation, strategy of 107; defence industry, definition of 82–83; defence industry, willingness to participate in 87; demand and, relative strengths of 374; DIB (Defence Industry Base) 82–87; diversification 100–101; dynamic capabilities 106–7; economies of scale and scope 91–96, 102–3; firms 83, 101–8; global industry 83–85; governments, key role of 89–90; heterogeneousness of defence industry 83; innovation 97–98, 103–4; international component sourcing 107–8; knowledge base, learning and 103–4; learning-by-doing 104–5; learning curve, production costs and 93; market barriers to entry 99; multi-national supply 371–72; national industry 85–86; NATO (North Atlantic Treaty Organisation) 84; NDOs (National Defence Organisations) 82; ownership 108–11; PFIs (Private Finance Initiatives) 110;

procedural barriers to entry 99; product differentiation 96–97; production, minimum efficient scale of (MES) 91; R&D (Research and Development) 88, 97, 98, 105–6; scale, economies of 91–92; scale and scope, economies of 91–96, 102–3; scope, economies of 93–95; SIPRI (Stockholm International Peace Research Institute) 84, 90, 100–101; structure and operations of industry 87–101; sunk costs 88–89; supply and demand, relative strengths of 374; supply chain management 107–8; 'surge' capabilities 109–10; technological barriers to entry 99; uncertainties, management of 106–7; vertical integration 101; Warrior Armoured Fighting Vehicle 91; world arms production 84; *see also* supply chain

supply chain 2, 11–43; ANZUS Alliance 20; atomistic competition 33; authorisation of suppliers 137; bilateral monopoly 33; capability increments 17; capability requirements analysis 27–28; causality, derived demand and direction of 20, 37; combat-related performance 22–23; competition in the market 33–34; complementarity of production chain framework 23–24; complexity in acquisition 19; consumables 19; contestability of 32–35; contingent capability 17; contingent outputs 15, 22–23; contract-governed relationships 30–31; decision-makers 24–30; defence demands 35–37; defence expenditure, constraints on 38; defence industry capabilities 39; defence-industry relationships 32–35; defence procurement agency 27–28; defence production chain 11, 14–15; defence products 13–21; defence supply chain 12, 24; defence value 22; demand, derived or dependent 20; dependability in Sweden 297; deployment flexibility 17–18; deployment-related outputs 14–15; discovery process 18; domestic defence-related production 39; DPAs (Defence Procurement Agencies) 24–25, 34, 36; durability 18; enforcement costs 31; exports 20–21,

43n28; framework 24–25; functional specification 35; government and provision of national security 25–26; government policy and relationships 38–39; hypothecation 17–18; import substitution 34; imports 20–21; industry production capabilities 19–20; industry structure 13; industry suppliers 28–30; informational asymmetries 23; insurance, comparison with 42n15; IP (intellectual property) 18; knowledge inputs 19; leasing 35; legal contracts 31; links, relationships and 13, 30–39; management of 107–8; of marine industry in Australia 341–44; market structure 32–35; military capabilities 12, 16–17, 22, 23–24; military capabilities, contingent outputs and 16–18; military capabilities, defence products and 13–21; military contingencies 15; military response options 15; mission, organisation and structure of defence 26–27; monopolistic competition 33; monopoly 33; monopsony 32–33, 86–87; national security, contingent good 14–16; national security, government and provision of 25–26; national security, public good 16, 38, 43n27; national security provision 25; national sovereignty 21; NATO 20; NDOs (National Defence Organisations) 15–16, 17, 18, 20, 21, 26, 36; NDOs (National Defence Organisations), decision-making by 37, 38; negotiation, costs of 31; oligopoly 33; organisation and structure of defence 26–27, 42n19; peacetime operations 26–27; policy-generated relationships 39; principal-agent framework 25; private ownership 34–35; procurement transactions, components of 30; products procured 18–19; 'publicness' of defence-related products 29; R&D (Research and Development) 18; relationships, defence-industry 32–35; relationships, government policy and 38–39; relationships, links and 13, 30–39; relationships, transactions and 30–32; requirement specification 36–37; resource allocation 23; salesmanship 37; search costs 31;

self-reliance 21; self-reliance, sourcing on basis of 37; self-sufficiency 39; social costs and benefits 22; social value of in-country capability 39–40; sourcing decisions, 'legacy' and 37; structure of defence 26–27; technical complexity 18, 19; technical specification 35–36; trade-offs, resource related 26; transaction-like exchanges 16; transactions, nature of 13; transactions, relationships and 30–32; trust, importance of 31–32; unknowable response options 23; value-adding chain 22; value creation 21–24; vertical integration 34; volume 18; wartime operations 26–27; *see also* supply, defence industry and
supply dependability 162, 164, 170–71
'surge' capabilities 109–10
sustainment 55–56, 171–72, 196–97
Sweden 7–8n1, 52; acquisition security 297; aramament policy in transition 286–301; armed neutrality, policy of 286, 287; arms production of 84; Audit Organisation (*Riksrevisionen, RIR*) 294; change in security policy, dimensions of 288–94; change in security policy, implications of 296–98; civil-military synergies, focus on 294; collaborative Nordic acquisitions 298; conscript enlistment 289; conscription 289; defence budget 289; defence characteristics 290; defence environment, change in 288–89; defence industry in 100; defence industry partners 297–98; defence policy 288; defence posture, historical context 286–88; *Defence Review* (2004) 289, 293–94, 295, 296, 297; EDA (European Defence Agency) 293, 299; EU Nordic Battle Group 296; experience of, lessons of 298–99; export policy 291; exports and imports 294–95; FFA (Aeronautical Research Institute) 287; FMV (Defence Procurement Agency) 287, 292, 293, 294, 296, 299; FOA (Defence Research Institute) 287; implementation of change, challenge of 298–99; imports, exports and 294–95; international cooperation 296–97; IRIS-T air-to-air missile 301n30; Land Systems Hagglunds 100; military-industrial base, change

in 291–93; military organisation 288–89; Nammo Sweden 291; NDC (National Defence College) 293; NFFP (National Aeronautical Research Programme) 294; OSCE (Organisation for Security and Cooperation in Europe) 295; peace dividend, controversy of 287–88; peace-keeping and enforcement operations 289; PfP (Partnership for Peace) 289, 292, 296; SAAB 291, 294; self-reliance 287–88; SEMA (Swedish Emergency Management Agency) 289; submarine procurement 352n1; supply chain dependability 297; SWEDINT (Swedish Armed Forces International Centre) 289; technology policy, change in 293–94; total national defence, concept of 289; uncertainty, post-Cold War 288–89; Wassenaar Agreement 295

SWEDINT (Swedish Armed Forces International Centre) 289

Switzerland, arms production of 84

symmetric uncertainty 129–31

Syria and Israel 229, 231, 233

systems of systems 50

TEAM International 316

technical complexity: demand and 49–54, 78, 78n4; relative nature of 52, 53; supply chain and 18, 19

technical specification 35–36

technology: generic technological information 51; imperative of 53; innovation in democracies 364–68; policy, change in Sweden 293–94; policy in Canada 217–18; sophistication in 50–53; technological barriers to entry 99; technological innovation, contract management for 350–51; technological innovation, issues for 364–65; transfer of 74–75

Techport Australia 339

Telecom Australia 360, 361, 362, 363, 367, 368, 369n7

Tenex Defence and ANZAC frigate project 71, 142–43, 199, 325, 329, 332–33

Tenex Toll 109

terrorism: Australian response to terrorist attacks 190–91; threat of

'catastrophic terrorism' in Singapore 267–68

Thales (formerly ADI) 106, 109, 333–34, 340, 343

timeframe, demand and 63–66

TNO National Defence Group, Netherlands 309–10

Toronto Globe and Mail 223

'total defence': policy in Singapore 255–71; total national defence, concept in Sweden of 289

TPC (Technology Partnerships Canada) 217–18

trade-offs: in Canada 219; demand and 65; resource related 26

transactions: costs of 47; nature of 13; relationships and 30–32; transaction-like exchanges 16

transnational industry cooperation 316–17

transparency: in Canada 155–56; in government policy 155–56, 159–60; procedural transparency 159–60

trust, importance of 31–32

TWP (Terror Weapons) 229, 231, 251n4

uncertainty: asymmetric uncertainty 129–31; buyer-seller interaction 147; demand 48; management of 106–7; in post-Cold War Sweden 288–89; symmetric uncertainty 129–31

Unión Española de Explosivos 280

United Kingdom 7–8n1, 288, 316; arms production of 84; withdrawal from Singapore 255–56

United Nations (UN) 287, 295; UNMEE (Mission in Ethiopia and Eritrea) 305; UNPROFOR (Protection Force, Bosnia) 305; UNTAC (Transitional Authority – Cambodia) 305; UNTSO (Truce Supervision Organisation) 305

United States 7–8n1, 158, 292, 297–98, 299, 371; Aegis combat system 341, 344; arms production of 84; defence aid to Israel 239–42, 250; defence industry, links with Canada 216–17; defence procurement function in 73; defence spending 46; military self-sufficiency 41n10; procurement for Israel 237–38; technological innovation, access for Australia 202; technological sophistication 50–51; uncertainties, management of 106–7

value: creation of 21–24; value chain 2; variable perceptions of 158
value-adding chain: Australia 187–207; role of industry in 197–203; supply chain 22
value-for-money: objective of 162; of weapons systems 263
Van Halteren Metall 315
vertical integration: defence industry and 101; supply chain 34
Vickers Defence Systems 316
Volvo Aero 291, 292

War in Lebanon (1982–85) 229, 231
Warrior Armoured Fighting Vehicle 91
wartime operations, supply chain for 26–27
Wassenaar Agreement 295
WEAG (Western European Armaments Group) 292
weapons systems: in-service acceptance of 264; inter-operative weapons systems 50; knowledge-intensive combat systems 51–52; lethality 49; life-cycle review of 264; modernity of, in Singapore 262; value-for-money of 263
Wegmann 316, 317
Williamstown Naval Dockyard, Australia 198, 325, 326, 328, 332, 336, 352n2
WMD (Weapons of Mass Destruction) 49; Israel and 251n4
work-sharing: agreements and multinational purchases 178–80; arrangements for 142–43, 143–45; inter-temporal work-share facilitation 143–45; multinational purchases, work-share agreements and 178–80; multinational work-share arrangements in Netherlands 316–17
World Bank 7–8n1
WTO-AGP (Agreement of Government Procurement) 215, 216, 225n5

Yom Kippur War (1973) 229, 233–34